Mr. Jefferson's
UNIVERSITY
A HISTORY

Mr. Jefferson's
UNIVERSITY

A HISTORY

Virginius Dabney

UNIVERSITY PRESS OF VIRGINIA

Charlottesville

THE UNIVERSITY PRESS OF VIRGINIA
Copyright © 1981 by the Rector and Visitors
of the University of Virginia

First published 1981
First paperback printing 1988

Frontispiece: Thomas Jefferson, painted by Rembrandt Peale in 1800

Library of Congress Cataloging in Publication Data

Dabney, Virginius, 1901–
  Mr. Jefferson's University.

  Bibliography: p.
  Includes index.
  1. University of Virginia—History. 2. Jefferson,
Thomas, 1743–1826. I. Title.
LD5678.D3   378.755'481   81–3392

ISBN 0-8139-0904-X (cloth)   0-8139-1213-X (paper)   AACR2

Printed in the United States of America

This volume is dedicated to my great-great-grandfather

JOHN ANDREW GARDINER DAVIS

who lost his life on the Lawn in the service of the university

and to my father

RICHARD HEATH DABNEY

a member of the university faculty for forty-nine years

Contents

Illustrations

Preface

I WAS BORN AT THE UNIVERSITY OF VIRGINIA, THE SON OF A professor, and attended the institution for four years, so my biases in its favor may be taken for granted. Yet I have striven to be objective in the present work and to record both the good and the bad in the story of my alma mater. There is, in truth, some of both, although the good predominates.

Tremendous progress has been made in recent decades in elevating the university's intellectual level, raising its standards for entrance and graduation, and bringing in faculty of great distinction. In these respects the University of Virginia has been virtually transformed.

Alumni of the institution have incurred a certain amount of raillery because of their penchant, especially in past years, for referring to "the university." Graduates of rival centers of learning have been wont to show their amusement by writing pointedly of "THE university," or "*the* university." The inference has been drawn that those who spend their student days at Charlottesville are a supercilious lot, looking down their noses at lesser breeds.

This is hardly fair. The expression "the university" seems to have had its origin in the fact that when the institution was founded by Thomas Jefferson in the early nineteenth century, it was, in fact, the only center of higher education in the country worthy to be called a university. Timothy Dwight, president of Yale College, observed in 1816 that America had no universities, only colleges and seminaries. Thus it will be seen that early references to "the university" were made in recognition of the fact that it was then in a class by itself. The phrase caught on, and unfortunately is still used occasionally when it is no longer appropriate, except in the immediate vicinity of the University of Virginia. The expression is heard less and less nowadays.

The institution's reputation for excessive carousing is undoubtedly widespread. An effort has been made in these pages to show that impressions as to the supposed bacchanalian revels at Charlottesville are based on highly colored and often inaccurate reports. Intemperate and uncouth behavior occurs there from time to time, and with too great frequency, but where is one to find a large university of which this cannot be said?

One of the unusual aspects of life at the University of Virginia is the prevailing practice of addressing professors as "Mr." rather than "Dr."—except those who hold medical degrees. The origins of this custom are obscure. It could conceivably have some relation to the frequent references around the university over the years to "Mr. Jefferson," a mode of address consistent with the master of Monticello's much-stressed belief in democracy and his democratic ways, in contrast to the more aristocratically inclined Hamiltonians. A group of prominent University of Virginia professors signed a petition in the 1920s, or perhaps somewhat earlier, requesting that they be addressed as "Mr.," although they were all Ph.D.'s. The use of "Mr." is not uncommon today at Harvard. The custom there goes back to the seventeenth century, when the laws of the colony reserved the title of "Mr." to the "upper classes." As more and more faculty arrive in Charlottesville from institutions where "Dr." is the almost universal mode of address, "Mr." becomes less and less in vogue.

Although I have quoted many times in the following pages from the *Cavalier Daily*, it should be said that this student publication has frequently been held in low esteem by both faculty and undergraduates. Its statements cannot be accepted unreservedly as representative of student opinion. The paper has had able and responsible editors, but too often it has been erratic and even pernicious and reprehensible in its viewpoint.

My indebtedness to Philip Alexander Bruce and his monumental five-volume centennial history of the university is great. In writing my chapter on the institution's first century, I have relied heavily on Bruce. The rest of my history deals with the period 1919–74—the years that followed the era addressed by him. It should be emphasized that my account ends with 1974, the year of Edgar Shannon's retirement from the presidency. Hence any events that took place thereafter, or any trends that developed, could not be mentioned.

I am grateful for the cooperation and assistance of many persons. First among them is President Frank L. Hereford, Jr., whose invitation to prepare this work was eagerly accepted and whose aid has been readily forthcoming at all times. He has read and criticized the entire manuscript. Others who have done likewise are Charles E. Moran, Jr., whose vast knowledge as the university's History Officer was invaluable, and Francis L. Berkeley, Jr., whose encyclopedic grasp of the institution's story and traditions was extremely helpful. Alexander G. Gilliam, Jr., assistant to President Hereford, and William H. Fishback, Jr., director of university relations, have given me the benefit of their valuable insights. Mr. Fishback also has aided me greatly with the illustrations. An incomplete list of others who have read portions of the manuscript includes Edgar F. Shannon, Jr., John L. Snook, Jr., J. Harvie Wilkinson, Jr., Shearer D. Bowman, Gilbert J. Sullivan, Eugene F. Corrigan, William L. Zimmer III, the Reverend Gordon Peerman, Raymond C. Bice, O. Allan Gianniny, Jr., Joseph L. Vaughan, Vincent Shea, Edward R. Slaughter, and Evan J. Male.

The staff of the University of Virginia Library, notably that of the Manuscripts and Archives Reading Room, has been especially helpful and cooperative, particularly Edmund Berkeley, Jr., Gregory A. Johnson, Michael F. Plunkett, Douglas W. Tanner, and Helen Troy. Director of Libraries Ray W. Frantz, Jr., has placed me greatly in his debt, as have Carolyn M. Beckham, Margaret M. O'Bryant, and Lucille B. Richards.

Among those to whom I owe thanks for assistance beyond the call of duty are B. F. D. Runk, Dr. Byrd S. Leavell, Dr. Harry J. Warthen, Jr., J. Harvie Wilkinson III, Edgar F. Shannon, Jr., Donald Macdonald, Dr. G. Slaughter Fitz-Hugh, Robert L. Baxter, John H. Barringer, Clifton McCleskey, Frank Talbott, Jr., C. Waller Barrett, and James W. Kinard.

I also am most grateful to Frank W. Rogers, Dr. Russell V. Bowers, John M. Bowers, Dr. duPont Guerry III, Dr. Beverly C. Smith, Dr. Wilhelm Moll, Dr. Kenneth R. Crispell, Joseph H. McConnell, Jack R. Hunter, Robert I. Boswell, William B. O'Neal, Staige D. Blackford, Jr., Edwin L. Dooley, Jr., William A. Booth, Bernard P. Chamberlain, Hardy C. Dillard, Eleanor Shannon, James H. Bash, Richard M. Brandt, Evelyn D. Wyllie, William M. E. Rachal, Irby B. Cauthen, Jr., Colgate W. Darden, Jr., F. Palmer Weber, Eunice Davis, Frances Farmer, John J. Owen, W. Bedford Moore, Lucille Reynolds, James I. Robertson, Jr., Langbourne M. Williams, Jr., David Carliner, Weldon Cooper, Emerson G. Spies, Thomas M. Carruthers, Tipton R. Snavely, Lewis M. Hammond, John M. Jennings, Frank W. Finger, Henry L. Kinnier, Jean Holliday, Francis G. Lankford, Jr., Robert J. Harris, Robert T. Canevari, D. Alan Williams, William A. Forrest, Jr., Lawrence Lewis, Jr., D. French Slaughter, Jr., Dr. Hunter H. McGuire, Jr., T. Munford Boyd, Edward Younger, Patrick Partridge, Doyle Smith, John N. Richardson, Jr., Jeanette Ern, and William T. Thomas.

It goes without saying that none of the abovementioned individuals shares any responsibility for the book's shortcomings.

The photographs for the jacket and endpapers were kindly supplied by Mr. Joseph C. Farber.

I am greatly indebted in writing chapter 10 to Shearer Davis Bowman, '71, a member of the Honor Committee and a brilliant student, who wrote two highly significant and informative papers: "The University of Virginia Honor System since September of 1955—A Critical Study," senior thesis in the university's Department of History (1971), and "Honor and Consensus in the 1960s: The University of Virginia Honor System," graduate study seminar paper, Department of History, University of California at Berkeley (1975), which concludes with the 1970–71 academic year. Bowman is the only person to write a history of the system who had been a member of the Honor Committee and hence had access to the committee's files and records. Another useful study is that of Thomas Taylor, done for a university liberal arts seminar at the 1962–63 session and entitled "The History of the Honor System of the University of Virginia from 1900–1956." It will be seen that Taylor carries the account down to the middle fifties; Bowman picks up the story at that point and brings it through the year 1971. Students of the Honor System will find these papers invaluable.

Walker Cowen, director of the University Press of Virginia, has been totally cooperative, understanding, and helpful at all times. Gerald Trett, my editor at the Press, has been a sure guide, and has placed me everlastingly in his debt. Joan Baxter did a professional job of typing the manuscript. My wife, Douglas, has been my "best friend and severest critic" in reading the manuscript and pointing out factual and stylistic errors.

Richmond, Virginia   VIRGINIUS DABNEY

Mr. Jefferson's
UNIVERSITY

A HISTORY

ONE

The
University's First Century

THOMAS JEFFERSON'S VISION of a great university founded on educational principles never before applied on this continent became a reality when the University of Virginia opened its doors in 1825. He had struggled toward this end for almost half a century and had surmounted tremendous personal, political, and financial obstacles.

With his many-sided genius, Jefferson had not only created an institution that was unique but had also provided it with a classical group of buildings that has evoked the admiration of the world. The Rotunda, modeled after the Roman Pantheon, stands majestically at the head of the rectangular Lawn, a lovely stretch of green bordered by towering trees. Greco-Roman pavilions and colonnades, with variances inspired by the great Italian architect Palladio, furnish an enchanting ensemble. If Jefferson were to return to earth, he would find his stunning "academical village" almost exactly as it was in his day.

Massachusetts-born historian Herbert Baxter Adams has termed the founding of this center of learning "the noblest work of Jefferson's life." Jefferson himself chose it as one of only three achievements that he wanted cited on his tomb, the others being his authorship of the Declaration of Independence and of the Virginia statute for religious freedom.

The University of Virginia quickly became the most admired institution of higher education in the southern states, and so remained throughout the nineteenth century. Innovations included a faculty composed mainly of professors brought over from Europe, complete rejection of any organized religion or theological dogma, a curriculum divided into separate schools and offering courses in mathematics, sciences, and modern languages, and a novel elective system. The first degree was conferred in 1828. A successful student who was not seeking a degree received a certificate of graduation in the school or schools whose requirements he had completed. No honorary degrees have ever been conferred.

The staggering problems that the founder confronted in establishing the institution were compounded, soon after it opened, by the riotous behavior of the students. These scions of the southern aristocracy behaved like hooligans and almost tore the place down, a fact that grieved and disappointed Jefferson profoundly and actually reduced him to tears.

The situation that Jefferson encountered as he strove to bring the university into existence was graphically described by C. Waller Barrett in his Founder's Day address at the university in 1973. Barrett pointed to the founder's "personal woes, his desperate financial problems, physical disabilities and heartbreaking family circumstances," and added that the "Father of the University of Virginia," as he referred to himself in the epitaph he composed, "had to purchase the land, to plan the grounds and buildings, to supervise the construction, to direct the engagement of professors, to devise the curriculum, and finally to act as chief executive officer and also as secretary, taking notes, writing the minutes, and compiling voluminous reports for the authorities in Richmond." In the words of an early historian of the University: "The thousand and one matters that college presidents and boards of trustees usually leave to professional architects and skilled labor, were thought out and carefully specified" by the master of Monticello.

The university had its beginnings in the Albemarle Academy, a classical school that had existed on paper since just after the turn of the nineteenth century but never got into actual operation. In 1814 Jefferson was chosen a trustee, and he suggested that the school be expanded into an institution of higher learning to be called Central College. The General Assembly gave its approval. A Board of Visitors for Central College was named; it included not only Jefferson but President James Monroe and former President James Madison. Also on the board were Joseph Carrington Cabell and John Hartwell Cocke, two of the remarkable men of that era without whose aid the University of Virginia might never have come into being. Cabell had entered the General Assembly at the instigation of Jefferson and proved indefatigable in his support of the latter's educational program. Like Jefferson, he suffered at times from poor health, but he refused to lessen his efforts. Cocke was the owner of Bremo, his family's ancestral estate on the James River. His work in supervising the building of the Rotunda, Lawn, and Ranges during Jefferson's lifetime and after his death was vitally important. Cocke was one of the most independent-minded men of his generation, a staunch and outspoken foe of slavery and of dueling as well as a pioneer advocate of abolishing alcoholic beverages. Pilgrims along the James in the county of Fluvanna have long noted his "temperance fountain" at Bremo near the river bank.

Central College was carefully planned by Jefferson, its curriculum outlined, its buildings designed. The cornerstone of the first structure, Pavilion VII on the Lawn, today's Colonnade Club, was laid in 1817, with Jefferson, Madison, and Monroe in attendance.

Next came a bitter fight in the General Assembly by Cabell and other spokesmen for Jefferson to establish a state university, a move that was opposed by William and Mary alumni. The college at Williamsburg had retrogressed markedly since the pre-Revolutionary era and was described as "a decaying institution." The bill to establish the university was finally passed in 1818, but without specific designation of a site. A board of twenty-four commissioners was to decide this question. Lexington, Staunton, and Charlottesville contended for the honor.

Jefferson and Madison were among the commissioners, and Jefferson, who was chosen chairman, was anxious to have the university located at Charlottesville. The group met in August at Rockfish Gap in the Blue Ridge, with instructions not only to choose a site but to plan the buildings and recommend the courses to be taught, the number and kind of professorships, and the administrative structure.

Since Central College buildings were already being constructed at Charlottesville, its claims carried particular weight. Elaborate plans for the college had been drawn by Jefferson, and, as noted, the cornerstone for the first building had been laid. Washington College at Lexington made a determined effort to win the contest, but its advocates could not quite counter the arguments on behalf of Central College, especially that it was obviously nearer the population center of the commonwealth.

The commissioners accordingly voted in favor of Charlottesville, and their findings were conveyed to the state legislature. Elements of that body continued to battle for another location or to fight the whole idea of establishing a university. But the University of Virginia's partisans finally won out, and the institution was officially chartered Jan. 25, 1819. Jefferson's great dream was on the way to realization.

A Literary Fund had been created by the General Assembly in 1810, and more than a million dollars had accumulated. The income was set aside for educational purposes, with $45,000 designated annually for the schooling of poor children and $15,000 for the establishment and support of a state university. This $15,000 was now available. Such a sum was, of course, far greater in purchasing power at that time, although completely inadequate for the founding of a university. In addition, over $40,000 had been raised toward the establishment of Central College, which was prepared to dedicate this sum to the new institution.

Plans for Central College were modified and expanded to take account of the needs of a comprehensive university. Jefferson was named rector, and he set about outlining the various departments and courses and designing the additional buildings. For the last-named task he obtained the advice of two eminent architects, Benjamin H. Latrobe and Dr. William Thornton, but in most respects the entire enterprise was virtually a one-man operation. Here was exemplified once more the versatility of Thomas Jefferson, who was able almost singlehandedly to bring into being this institution embodying novel and far-reaching educational and architectural concepts.

He spent countless hours on the grounds of the fledgling university, and when he was not there in person he often watched construction of the buildings from Monticello through

1. *William Wertenbaker, fellow student of Edgar Allan Poe and university librarian for over half a century.*

a spyglass. Special attention was given to the raising of the serpentine walls, which he had doubtless seen in English gardens and which Charles Fenton Mercer had on his estate near Middleburg.

A loan of $180,000 from the Literary Fund made possible the erection of the pavilions, hotels, and student rooms along the Lawn and Ranges. Completion of the Rotunda was financed by a $50,000 appropriation of the General Assembly, which also forgave the abovementioned loan. The Rotunda was only partially finished in 1824, when the Revolutionary hero the marquis de Lafayette was entertained there at an elaborate dinner. It was completed not long thereafter.

The ensemble that then greeted the eye was termed by Boston-born George Ticknor, a Harvard professor renowned as a scholar and author on both sides of the Atlantic, as "a mass of buildings more beautiful than anything architectural in New England, and more appropriate to a university than are to be found, perhaps in the world." Stanford White, the noted New York architect who restored the Rotunda after the fire of 1895, called the university's original structures the "most perfect and exquisite group of collegiate buildings in the world." And Dr. Ernst Beutler, director of the Goethe Museum in Frankfurt, Germany, wrote, following a visit to this country around the middle of the twentieth century: "Of the university towns, those that fascinated me the most were the ones which combine an atmosphere of learning with a natural setting: Princeton, Ithaca, Madison, Bloomington, Ann Arbor, and most beautiful of all, Charlottesville."

The university finally opened its doors in March 1825 after various delays. The entering class numbered only about 40 students, a figure that would rise to 116 by the end of the year—far fewer than had been expected. Efforts to obtain several distinguished Americans for the faculty had failed, and Francis Walker Gilmer, a young native of Albemarle whom Jefferson termed "the best-educated subject we have raised since the Revolution," had been sent to England and Scotland to round up a teaching staff. He managed to engage five talented young men and to get them across the ocean in time for classes to begin.

They were George Long, who would occupy the chair of ancient languages, and Thomas H. Key, mathematics, both from Cambridge University; Robley Dunglison, with a wide reputation as a writer on medical subjects, who would instruct in medicine; Charles Bonnycastle, son of a noted mathematician, to occupy the chair of natural philosophy; and George Blaettermann, a German living in England, modern languages. John P. Emmet, a native of Ireland and nephew of the famous Irish patriot Robert Emmet, was brought from Charleston, S.C., to give courses in natural philosophy.

Dr. Robley Dunglison was "the first full-time professor of medicine in an American university," and a novel feature of his contract, unheard of at the time in America, was the restriction of his practice outside the university to consultation, Dr. Wilhelm Moll, director of the university's health sciences laboratory, wrote in the *Virginia Medical Monthly*. Another innovation under Dunglison was his decision to issue medical diplomas in English rather than Latin so that they "may be intelligible to everyone."

Seven of the eight chairs had been filled when the university opened in 1825, only that of law being vacant. It was felt that law and moral philosophy, or ethics, ought to be taught by Americans. The brilliant and versatile William Wirt, then attorney general of the United States and chief prosecutor of Aaron Burr at his trial for treason in 1807, was offered the professorship of law, along with the presidency of the university. Jefferson had not contemplated electing anyone president of the institution, since he preferred a chairman of the faculty, but in order to get Wirt it was felt necessary to offer him the two positions. He declined, and the university continued to operate for the rest of the century with a rotating chairman of the faculty. During that period it was the only college or university of stature in the United States that functioned under this system.

When Wirt was found to be unavailable, John T. Lomax, a well-known Fredericksburg attorney, was chosen professor of law. The chair of moral philosophy was tendered to George Tucker, member of Congress and distinguished author in the field of both fiction and finance. Tucker, decidedly the eldest, was named the first chairman.

It has frequently been stated that Jefferson was unwilling to allow the law students even to study the doctrines of the hated Federalists and that no textbooks setting forth those doctrines were allowed. Such was, indeed, Jefferson's desire, but at the instigation of Madison the plan was modified for the better. The *Federalist Papers* were accordingly included. Also there was no restriction on the use of additional books.

Jefferson invited all the students in the university to dine with him in small groups on his mountaintop. One who entered about a year after the institution opened, and remained only about ten months, was Edgar Allan Poe, who is presumed to have sat at Jefferson's table. Poe's record as a student was by no means as lurid as is commonly supposed. Although he incurred heavy gambling debts, in part because his foster father, John Allan, refused to furnish him with enough funds to meet his minimum expenses, the amount of his drinking, then and later, is authoritatively stated to have been exaggerated. He made an excellent scholastic record at the university and was not in trouble at any time with the authorities, in contrast to the riotous behavior of many others enrolled there.

Jefferson had worked out a plan for student self-government for he believed that young men from the best families could be counted on to govern themselves and remain reasonably well-behaved. He was promptly disillusioned. It was an age when youth was in rebellion against authority, in both North and South. Riots on college campuses were frequent, and the institution at Charlottesville was no exception.

Many of the young men there apparently had been accustomed at home to carrying firearms and to drinking and gambling. Given almost complete freedom at the university, they soon became disorderly. Several times during that first summer there were "vicious irregularities," as Jefferson phrased it, and then in the early autumn almost unbelievable rowdyism erupted.

"Down with the European professors!" was the cry of a crowd of masked students gathered on the Lawn after dark. Professors Emmet and Tucker went to investigate the uproar. Emmet seized hold of a counterpane in which one student had wrapped himself, whereupon another student threw a brick at him. Tucker was attacked with a cane, and vulgar abuse was hurled at the two professors amid loud and derisive howls. As if this were not enough, sixty-five students signed a resolution next day sharply assailing Emmet and Tucker for daring to lay hands on the bedraped student! Not surprisingly, the faculty announced that if effective policing were not put into effect at once, they would all resign.

On Jefferson's recommendation, the Board of Visitors accordingly adopted extremely strict regulations, and the students most seriously involved in the riot were expelled. The visitors ordered every student to retire to his room at 9 o'clock each night and to rise with the dawn and eat breakfast by candlelight. All had to wear an officially prescribed dull gray uniform. Gambling, smoking, and drinking were forbidden, and students were required to deposit all their funds with the proctor, who could dole out small sums according to his whims.

These draconian rules were deeply resented, but things remained relatively quiet until 1831, when another riot occurred. Then in 1836 still worse disorder broke out. Many windows in the pavilions were smashed with stones and sticks, there was much firing of muskets under the arcades, and the uneasy professors armed themselves and fled with their families to the upper floors. Two years later, in another outburst, the pavilion of Prof. William Barton Rogers was attacked, many windows were broken, and the door was battered down. The following year Prof. Gessner Harrison, chairman of the faculty, was assaulted by two students and horsewhipped while at least one hundred other students looked on and did nothing to stop the outrage.

But the climactic atrocity occurred in 1840. Two students were firing shots and making an uproar on the Lawn, and John A. G. Davis, chairman of the faculty and professor of law, came out of his residence in Pavilion X to investigate. One of the youths was masked; Davis approached him and tried to remove the mask in order to identify him. The youth, Joseph E. Semmes of Georgia, drew a pistol and shot Davis, wounding him fatally. Semmes was apprehended, and while awaiting trial was released on $25,000 bail. He disappeared and is said to have committed suicide.

The murder of the faculty's admired chairman sent shock waves throughout the state and beyond. It had the effect of bringing the university students at least temporarily to their senses, and while there were other disorders, the number of such episodes tended to diminish with the years. Moreover, the Honor System was introduced in 1842, and its success was in part due to the new and more serious mood.

Henry St. George Tucker, a distinguished judge, was appointed professor of law to succeed the slain Davis. Judge Tucker soon became aware of the rankling resentment engendered by the uniform and early rising regulations, which were still in effect. He took a leading role in obtaining revocation of the obnoxious rules. He also noted the atmosphere of suspicion surrounding examinations, during which faculty members watched the young men closely to prevent cheating. Tucker accordingly recommended that each student be required to sign a statement that he had received no assistance. This was done, and the declaration was expanded later to include a pledge that no assistance had been given to anyone else. Members of the faculty continued to keep watch in the examination room, but this surveillance was lifted gradually. After the Civil War the Honor System as it is known today came into being, with the students in full control and without faculty supervision or participation.

At both ends of the two Ranges, and in the middle of each, was a structure called a "hotel," larger than the adjacent rooms for students. In these buildings, which are used today for other purposes, the students had their meals. During the first half-dozen years after the university opened, the food is said to have been satisfactory, but then came fervent complaints that the menus were lacking in variety and the cooking execrable. The boys vented their ire by throwing rolls at each other in the dining room and engaging in other forms of disorder. The hotelkeepers, for their part, stated that their charge for the meals, fixed by the university, was so low that they could not afford any better fare. In 1849 the General Assembly decreed that meals for students should be free of charge and paid for by the state, but this legislation was repealed seven years later.

Until 1857, when a small infirmary was built, there were no facilities for caring for ill students, and the ailing undergraduate had to "tough it out" in his room, with only an occasional visit from a physician and such care as a black servant could give. A typhoid epidemic broke out in 1829, and a score of students came down with the malady and several died. The

2. Gen. John Hartwell Cocke, one of Jefferson's coadjutors in launching the university. From an 1850 daguerreotype.

lor of Arts. However, the B.A. was not a prerequisite to the M.A., which was widely regarded as among the nation's top academic awards until the end of the nineteenth century.

An examination in English grammar and spelling had to be passed before graduation could take place in any of the schools. However, no courses in English composition or English literature were provided until shortly before the Civil War, in accordance with the prevailing practice in many preparatory schools and colleges. There was great concentration on Latin and Greek literature, as well as on the literatures of France, Germany, Spain, and Italy. But the works of such English writers as Chaucer, Shakespeare, and Milton seem to have been completely ignored in the classes at the university, along with those of all American writers. The works of some of them were available in the library. Many of the students were deeply devoted to the poetry of Lord Byron, while the poems of Thomas Campbell and Thomas Moore also had loyal partisans. Although Sir Walter Scott enjoyed great popularity at the period, he appears not to have had a comparable group of admirers at the university.

Recognizing the dearth of instruction in English composition, a group of students launched a magazine in 1838 called *The Collegian*. It lasted for only four years, but in 1849 the *University Magazine* performed a similar function. It would continue to appear down the years to the present, under a variety of names.

A professor, in the beginning, received a free residence in one of the Lawn pavilions and a salary of $1,500, plus a $25 fee for each of his students. Some classes were large, and those teachers enjoyed substantial incomes from fees, while others with smaller classes were not so well situated. This caused unhappiness, and in 1850 the fee system was finally abandoned in favor of a flat annual salary of $3,000 for all.

There were other problems with the professors, in addition to those involving compensation. For example, the German-born Blaettermann was arbitrary, temperamental, and apparently endowed with a Prussian personality. He engaged in heated altercations with his students, and his lectures were interrupted by loud noises emanating from various parts of the classroom. On one occasion, Blaettermann knocked a student's hat off, and the latter punched the professor repeatedly.

Blaettermann's relations with his wife were equally hectic and unconventional, for he was given to cowhiding her both in private and in public. Blaettermann was finally dismissed by unanimous vote of the Visitors.

His place was filled by Charles Kraitsir, a Hungarian, who, like Blaettermann, was a wizard with modern languages. But Kraitsir's lectures were unpopular, his fees fell off in consequence, and he was unhappy; at the same time, his colleagues on the faculty were disappointed with his performance as a teacher. On top of all else, his wife, a powerful woman, was in the habit of beating him and turning him out of the house in the middle of the night. Kraitsir was dropped from the faculty. He complained: "The Board of Visitors . . . was hard to please. They kicked Dr. Blaettermann out because he had whipped his wife, and they have kicked me out because I have been whipped by my wife. What did they really want?"

A more fortunate acquisition for the teaching staff was that of the brilliant Basil L. Gildersleeve, who joined the faculty as professor of Greek in 1856 and became one of the great scholars in that language. He was also widely recognized as the author of Latin grammars and readers. The swarthy, heavily bearded Gildersleeve served in the Confederate army, was severely wounded, and limped for the rest of his life. Although he returned to the university after the war, he joined the faculty of the newly formed John Hopkins University in 1876, where he made an international reputation.

Gildersleeve had succeeded Gessner Harrison as professor of Greek at the university. Harrison, who joined the teaching staff at age twenty-one as professor of both Latin and Greek, taught only Latin after the coming of Gildersleeve. He, too, was a noted classical scholar and was chosen chairman of the faculty five times. Upon his retirement, the faculty in a formal resolution said that he had "done more than any other man for the cause of education and sound learning in his native state." Harrison was extremely devout, and he and his brother, as students, declined Thomas Jefferson's invitation to Sunday dinner at Monticello on the ground that it would be a desecration of the Sabbath.

A picturesque addition to the university faculty was Maximilian Rudolph Schele de Vere, who succeeded Kraitsir as professor of modern languages and remained for more than fifty years. He was born in a castle in Sweden and moved to south Germany, where his father commanded a fortress near the Polish border. "Old Schele" was in the diplomatic service before coming to America. His knowledge of half a dozen languages was astonishing and his capacity as an instructor exceptional. As he strolled the Lawn with his silk hat in winter and his expensive straw in summer, he set the fashion for students and faculty alike.

Thomas Jonathan (Stonewall) Jackson, with a spectacular record in the Mexican war, was an applicant for the chair of mathematics at the university in the mid-nineteenth century. The chair had become vacant with the retirement of Prof. Edward H. Courtenay, who had served as faculty chairman and was a much admired teacher. Albert Taylor Bledsoe, whose record as a mathematician was much more impressive than Jackson's, received the appointment. Bledsoe was said to have found the answer to a mathematical problem of Archimedes that nobody else had been able to solve. After seven years on the university faculty he entered the Confederate service and was appointed assistant secretary of war. Following the surrender at Appomattox he devoted his undoubtedly great talents to fighting again the cause of the South in a weary round of books and magazine articles in which he took the ultrareactionary position on every issue.

One of the most distinguished of all the faculty members at the university was James Lawrence Cabell, who joined the staff in 1837 as professor of anatomy and surgery, to remain until his death in 1889. A nephew of Joseph C. Cabell, who rendered such indispensable aid to Jefferson as a member of the General Assembly, he revealed a great capacity for original inquiry. Cabell was ahead of Charles Darwin in publishing a work that recognized the theory of evolution, for his *Testimony to the Unity of Mankind* appeared several months before Darwin's *Origin of Species*. He also anticipated by many years Hugo de Vries's theory of mutations. Far-reaching as were these discoveries, Cabell is honored even more for his pioneering work in the field of public health. He was the organizer and first president of the National Board of Health and also president of the American Public Health Association.

The Davis family has had an almost continuous connection with the university since 1830. In that year John A. G. Davis

3. *Edgar Allan Poe's room as it looks today, with furniture of the period.*

was named professor of law. His son, John Staige Davis, was extremely precocious and became a University of Virginia Master of Arts at fifteen and a Doctor of Medicine at sixteen. In 1847 young Davis joined the medical staff as a demonstrator of anatomy under Dr. Cabell and remained there as a beloved faculty member until his death in 1885. He was succeeded on the medical faculty a few years later by his son, another much admired John Staige Davis. The next of that name, grandson of the original bearer, was graduated from the medical school in the 1920s and became a prominent private practitioner in New York. His son, John Staige Davis IV, is now an able member of the medical faculty.

Another important teacher in the medical school before, during, and after the Civil War was Socrates Maupin, whose chair was chemistry and pharmacy. Highly respected, Maupin served as chairman of the faculty from 1854 until the end of the Civil War. He had great administrative ability, and the faculty credited him with doing more than anyone else to keep the university functioning during the war and immediately thereafter. He was fatally injured in Lynchburg in 1871, when a horse ran away and threw him out of the carriage in which he was riding.

One of the extraordinary members of the university's teaching staff was George Frederick Holmes, a British citizen throughout his life, and an encyclopedic scholar. Holmes joined the faculty in 1857, after serving as professor at Richmond College and the College of William and Mary and as the first president of the University of Mississippi, all before he was thirty years old. Resigning from the last-named post, he lived for nine years in southwest Virginia, farming and contributing learned articles to leading periodicals. He was called to occupy a new chair of history and literature at the University of Virginia. For the first time, thanks to Holmes, students at the University of Virginia were drilled in composition and introduced to the beauties of English literature. "Daddy" Holmes, as he was known in his latter years, remained on the faculty until the 1890s, recognized as a prodigy of knowledge in many fields.

In the early days of the university's history, about two-thirds of the students were dropped at the end of their first year for failure to meet scholastic requirements or for flagrant violation of the regulations. Approximately as many were usually eliminated after the first session in the years immediately following the Civil War.

The boys rightly resented the early-rising rules, which remained in effect for nearly two decades, but disregard of these requirements was less frequent than might be imagined. And it is hardly surprising that the students' rooms along the Lawn and Ranges were often in a disordered state, that the simple furniture was knocked about, or that tobacco juice stained the walls at times.

A black slave, hired by the hotelkeeper responsible for each group of rooms, entered the apartment at about 6 A.M. daily, bearing a pitcher of water, often at near-freezing temperatures. He started the fire in the grate and cleaned the shoes. After the student had dressed in great haste and hurried to breakfast by candlelight in the nearby hotel, the slave made up the beds, swept the floor, and carried out the ashes. In winter he brought wood for the fireplace and in summer ice. Candles were the only form of illumination in the rooms and elsewhere until about 1838, when oil lamps came into vogue.

The dress of the students in those far off days was astonishing by modern standards. Frock or swallowtail coats were the prevailing mode, while "the more daring wore their calico study gowns to lecture as well as to meals," said Frederick W. Page, writing concerning the sartorial situation as of 1843.

Diversions were bucolic and uninspiring by today's criteria. Classes lasted from 7:30 A.M. to 4:30 P.M., which left little time for much else, especially since early rising and in-the-room-by-9 P.M. requirements continued until the mid-1840s. An athletic instructor, with primitive facilities, taught boxing, fencing, and quarter-staff, or single stick. Instruction was given in two low structures with flat roofs adjoining the basement of the Rotunda on the east and west. Intercollegiate sports were, of course, unknown.

In the 1850s a Pole named J. E. D'Alfonce operated a gymnasium for the students in which he put them through various exercises on parallel bars, ladders, and ropes. Authority for construction of a new gymnasium, at the modest cost of $1,500, was granted in 1857 by the Board of Visitors. The edifice thus erected was termed by the student magazine "a mere apology for a gymnasium."

Walks in the country on Sunday, the only free day, provided one form of relaxation for the young men. Playing of musical instruments was indulged in, but this was forbidden during class hours and on Sunday. By special dispensation, the boys were allowed to go to Charlottesville on the Sabbath, where they could even attend parties. Neither horses nor dogs could be kept by the students, nor were cockfights allowed, but the last-named form of divertissement was sometimes engaged in surreptitiously. Pitching quoits and the game of marbles had numerous adherents, but quoits too was forbidden on Sunday. Skating in winter on the pond near the site of the present university chapel was enjoyed when the ice was sufficiently thick.

It should be emphasized that bacchanalian revels were not the regular order of the day or night and that these occurred mainly on special occasions and at fairly wide intervals. In the 1850s those who were found to be transgressing heinously were given the alternative of signing the pledge with the Temperance Society or being expelled. Many chose the former option.

In the decade before the Civil War students were often caught up in such religious activities as the Bible classes taught by Professor McGuffey, and they also did missionary work in the Ragged Mountains.

During the same period eleven Greek letter fraternities established themselves at the university. Delta Kappa Epsilon, founded in 1852, was the first; it had originated at Yale some years before. The others were Phi Kappa Psi, Phi Kappa Sigma, Beta Theta Pi, Chi Phi, Sigma Alpha Epsilon, Phi Gamma Delta, Delta Psi, Theta Delta Chi, Delta Kappa, and Kappa Alpha. The fraternities existed primarily for social purposes and promotion of close ties between the members. Various others established chapters in later years.

Dancing classes were provided by private instructors almost throughout the university's antebellum existence, but no student could take lessons more than three times a week lest they interfere with his studies. Cotillions were held in the hall of the Jefferson Society and also at the Eagle Tavern in town. As relations with the professors improved, they gave balls for the students. Furthermore, each professor, as a gesture of good will, provided an annual supper for the members of his classes.

During the years when the obnoxious uniform and early-rising rules held sway, the boys couldn't even have "a little chicken supper" in their rooms without permission from the chairman of the faculty. But with the elimination of these restrictions, it became possible for the students to have meals in their quarters, provided there was no liquor.

An amusing extracurricular feature was the annual ceremony on the Lawn held by what was named the "Ugly Club." It involved selection of the "ugliest man" in the student body, as well as the "prettiest man" and the "vainest man." The "ugliest man" had to accept his prize of a $15 pair of boots with an appropriately humorous speech.

"Laughing-Gas Day" was another yearly event on the Lawn. The professor of chemistry provided the gas and administered it to a previously selected victim. The latter thereupon went into a series of extraordinary antics, laughing hysterically and otherwise making a spectacle of himself. In fact, one student was so overcome that he engaged in what was termed improper behavior, and Laughing-Gas Day was discontinued.

The "dyke" and the "calathump" were forms of student diversion during these years which continued into the era immediately following the war. The dyke was a concerted effort on the part of students to embarrass any fellow collegian who was found to be en route to a rendezvous with his fair one. On such occasions, all the noisemaking apparatus that could be assembled, such as drums, horns, whistles, and coal scuttles belabored with pokers, was brought into action. The shouting and screeching crowd surrounded the young man and accompanied him as far as his ladylove's door. If it was at night, the participants in the dyke carried improvised torches. Often the youth was required to make a few brief remarks to the assembled multitude before he was permitted to enter the home of his inamorata. At times the mob lay in wait until he emerged, whereupon it greeted him again with raucous din and ear-splitting cacophony.

A calathump was another form of frolic in the mid-nineteenth century and after. It began innocently enough with the formation of a college band known as the Calathumpians, who serenaded the professors on the Lawn. But a disorderly element got control, and there was not only a great deal of noise but in 1845 the Calathumpians launched a prolonged disturbance during which they smashed blinds and windows on the professors' pavilions and even damaged the Rotunda. This particular riot was so violent that the university authorities called out the militia, which calmed the situation, at least temporarily.

The university's prestige was so impaired throughout Virginia and beyond by these disorders, and the earlier murder of Professor Davis, that a group of prominent alumni issued a statement designed to put the situation at the institution in perspective. They pointed to the training of innumerable young men by the university, men who had taken positions of leadership, and emphasized that it was not a place for educating just the sons of the rich since many students were having to work their way through. The alumni also protested the small size of the annual state appropriation to the institution, still only $15,000, and the low scale of professors' salaries. They noted that one of their group, while a student at Harvard, had witnessed an assault by his fellow collegians on a regiment of militia. Evidently such behavior was by no means limited to students at the University of Virginia.

By the session of 1846–47 things were more serene along the Lawn and Ranges, and relations between the faculty and the undergraduates were harmonious. Then in 1848–49 not a single student was dismissed or suspended, and the conduct of the young men was regarded as exceptionally good. Enrollment was increasing rapidly and behavior of the undergraduates seemed to improve in proportion. A few pranksters climbed to the dome of the Rotunda in 1859 and remained there for an hour, but no serious damage was done.

A notable event of this period was the jailing in 1852 of John S. Mosby, a second-year student at the university, afterward the famous Confederate partisan. Mosby shot a fellow student in an altercation and was given a year in jail and a $500 fine. He served some eight months, but there was doubt that he had provoked the fight, and the wound he inflicted was a slight one. Gov. Joseph Johnson accordingly pardoned

4. Gessner Harrison, chairman of the faculty, who was horse-whipped by students in 1839.

him and the General Assembly rescinded the fine. Mosby did not return to the university but took up the practice of law.

The university's highest enrollment of the antebellum era, and for many years thereafter, was 645, a figure reached during the session of 1856–57. Practically all of these students were from Virginia or other southern states. For various reasons enrollment had more than quadrupled in ten years. Improved behavior of the students gave the institution a better reputation. The prosperity of the South during these years enabled more parents to send their sons to college, and growing animosity between the sections caused them to choose a school below Mason and Dixon's line. Also, Charlottesville was now accessible by rail. The extraordinary increase in enrollment took place despite the fact that the university was one of the country's most expensive centers of higher learning, even more so than Harvard, Yale, or Princeton. The overall annual cost of sending a student to Charlottesville in 1845 was estimated at $332.

The increased matriculation at the university greatly overburdened classrooms and other facilities. A committee accordingly was appointed in 1850 to make recommendations. The celebrated architect Robert Mills was retained, and he designed an annex on the north side of the Rotunda, to include lecture rooms, a large area for storage of apparatus, and a public hall seating twelve hundred persons. It was conceded by the architect that this structure would be out of harmony with Jefferson's symmetrical design, but it was felt to be the best solution for pressing problems. At the rear of the Rotunda in 1850 was a portico, approached from the two sides by long flights of stone steps. The steep bank below was covered with Scotch broom. The portico was pulled down to make way for the annex. Building operations were virtually complete by 1853. Paul Balze's copy of Raphael's *School of Athens* was purchased by alumni to adorn the wall behind the platform in the public hall.

Erection of Dawson's Row just before the Civil War was made possible by a bequest from Martin Dawson, a citizen of Albemarle County, who left his farm to the university. Sale of the property brought over $19,000, and this was used to construct six modest boxlike structures for use as student dormitories. They were known as Houses A, B, C, D, E, and F. Many years later the university found the money to add two columns to the face of each, thus improving the row's appearance, and to terrace the land in front and place a sidewalk there. Dawson's Row was gradually torn down in the twentieth century to make way for more essential facilities, including Clark Hall, home for a time of the Law School. But it served a necessary purpose over a long period.

Hostility between the North and the South was mounting in the late 1850s, and the university faculty and students were caught up in the rising tension. On the eve of the election of 1860, both the Washington and Jefferson societies voted overwhelmingly that the southern states should secede if Lincoln were elected. The students preferred Bell and Everett, the Union Party candidates, in that election. A majority of the faculty opposed secession at that time.

South Carolina withdrew from the Union in December, and the students immediately formed two companies, the Sons of Liberty and the Southern Guard, commanded by William Tabb and Edward S. Hutter, respectively. They wore picturesque uniforms and drilled on the Lawn and Carr's Hill. In February a Confederate flag was put together and somehow gotten to the roof of the Rotunda in the middle of the night and lashed to the lightning rod. It caused a sensation next morning as it floated in the breeze. This was said to have been the first Confederate flag flown publicly in Virginia.

Events were moving with great rapidity, and many students were leaving to offer their services to the Confederacy. On Founder's Day, Apr. 13, a military parade was held on the Lawn. While it was in progress, the fall of Fort Sumter was announced. Four days later Virginia seceded, and the two student companies joined two others from Charlottesville and proceeded under orders to Harpers Ferry. The federal arsenal there was the objective, but the Federals burned it before their arrival. The students accordingly returned to their classes. At Finals, 138 were graduated. Fifty graduates and others then organized a company and left at once for Clifton Forge to serve under Col. Henry A. Wise. Their service in the mountains of what is now West Virginia was strenuous and uncomfortable, and they were under fire at times, but they suffered few casualties and were mustered out on their return

in January 1862. It was felt that too much good officer material was being wasted by being concentrated in the ranks of
this unit, and it was therefore decided that the young men
would disband and join military organizations from their
home communities.

No other units represented the university in the Confederate forces thereafter, but some twenty-five hundred alumni
served in all branches, about 27 percent of the total body of
alumni. Approximately five hundred lost their lives. One faculty member, Lewis Minor Coleman, professor of Latin, was
mortally wounded at the Battle of Fredericksburg. Charles S.
Venable served on the staff of Gen. Robert E. Lee and joined
the faculty immediately after the war. As noted, Prof. Albert
Taylor Bledsoe was assistant secretary of war, and Prof. Basil
L. Gildersleeve served on Gen. John B. Gordon's staff. Prof.
John W. Mallet, an internationally famous chemist, devised the
method whereby the Confederacy's shrinking niter supply for
manufacturing explosives was replenished. It was done by collecting urine daily in scores of communities and shipping it
to boiling vats, where the urea was extracted. This last was
sent posthaste to Augusta, Ga., where it was turned into gun-
powder.

During the war the university managed to remain open, but
the only students were youths too young to serve or veterans
who had been severely wounded. Typical of the latter were
George L. Christian of Richmond, later a much respected
judge, who lost one entire foot and the heel of another at the
Bloody Angle, and W. C. Holmes of Mississippi, who was
badly crippled in his right arm. Holmes helped Christian to
walk and Christian helped Holmes to take notes in class. They
slept together on the floor of their almost bare room on one
of the blankets they had salvaged from the army, covering
themselves with the other.

Extreme austerity was also the rule with the members of the
faculty who were not in the field. They numbered no more
than eight at any one time, while the students totaled between
forty-six and sixty-six during the four years. All suffered together the shortages of food and fuel. With the rapid decline
in the value of Confederate currency, the professors in
1864–65 were receiving an annual wage equivalent to $31.95

5. John A. G. Davis, chairman of the faculty, who was fatally shot by a student in 1840.

in gold. On top of all else, the university authorities made the dormitories and the Rotunda available as temporary hospitals for hundreds of Confederate wounded.

Arrival at the university of Sheridan's cavalry in March 1865 aroused fears that the buildings would be burned, a fate suffered by the Virginia Military Institute the year before. Prof. John B. Minor, with a white handkerchief tied to a walking cane, headed a group of faculty members who stood near the site of the present chapel to meet the Union troops. There was intense relief when Gen. George A. Custer, commanding the advance guard, courteously ordered that the property be given every protection. No serious damage was done.

The surrender at Appomattox came the following month, and the university authorities viewed prospects for the session of 1865–66 with much concern. Scarcely any funds were available and the physical plant was in dismal condition. But enrollment in the fall was a surprising 258, and since the professors were able once more to collect fees from their students, they soon were in better fiscal shape than they had anticipated. The following year enrollment leaped to 490.

But with the South impoverished, its economic system a shambles and the slaves freed, it faced the formidable task of rebuilding. Young men found the problem of earning a living quite different from that which had confronted them before the war. There was a greater demand for practical training in such areas as the sciences and engineering. To meet this need, civil engineering was added to the university curriculum in 1866, chemistry in 1867, and agriculture two years later. Courses in geology were made available in 1879.

The high enrollment was short-lived, for it fell steadily until 1883, when it was only 298. The drop may be attributed, in part, to the fact that many of the veterans who had returned to college from the war had completed their education. Also, there was a serious nationwide depression beginning in 1873. Then, too, Dean William M. Thornton charged many years later in his history of the Engineering School that "the sloth of the executive officials" of the university was mainly responsible for the skidding enrollment. "So indolent were they," he wrote, "that they had not even circulated the printed catalogues put into their hands, or made effectual use of the advertising pages of the newspapers." After a change of administration the enrollment rose sharply. Also, the depression had ended.

During the latter third of the nineteenth century no distinction was made between first-year men and upperclassmen. In the early 1900s just-matriculated students would be admonished to wear hats and not frequent the Corner, but all were on a plane of complete equality during the postbellum years. They were also, for the most part, equal in poverty. The Phi Kappa Psi fraternity, for example, tried in the late 1870s and early 1880s to have a soirée, but the brothers could never find a time during the three-year period "when everybody had a dollar."

There were notable orators at Finals during the era that followed the war. Ralph Waldo Emerson was the speaker in 1876, Grover Cleveland in 1888, Henry W. Grady in 1889, Henry Watterson in 1891, and Chauncey M. Depew in 1894.

Erection of the Brooks Museum in 1876 brought to the Grounds a structure that has been controversial ever since. The usual outraged observation has been that, as an example of Victorian design, it is totally out of keeping architecturally with Jefferson's classical concepts. But the Brooks Museum won a prize for architectural excellence when it was built, and modern architects have referred to it as an "expression appropriate to its time and place," an example of the Second Empire style then coming into vogue.

Among the new additions to the faculty immediately after the close of hostilities was Col. William E. Peters, of Confederate fame. When ordered to take part in the burning of Chambersburg, Pa., in retaliation for burnings perpetrated by the Union army in Virginia, he refused, on the ground that he had not enlisted "to fight women and children." "You may take my sword," he told his commanding officer—but he was not disciplined. As professor of Latin, "Old Pete" concentrated on grammar and syntax and was concerned scarcely at all with the literary quality of the great Latin writers.

Prof. Thomas R. Price, another Confederate veteran, was first given the chair of Greek, but he took over the teaching of English when it was decided that instruction in the mother tongue was being sadly neglected. Loved for his affectionate and outgoing personality, Price was one of the nation's pioneers in elucidating the beauties of the language. His reputation was such that he was called to a prestigious chair at Columbia University.

After serving with distinction on Robert E. Lee's staff, Lt. Col. Charles S. Venable joined the faculty in 1865 as professor of mathematics and continued in that post until his retirement in 1896. He had graduated from Hampden-Sydney College at age fifteen, served as an instructor at the college, and had studied in Germany. At the university after the war he was chairman of the faculty in 1870–73 and 1886–88. Highly respected by all, "Old Ven" is regarded as chiefly responsible for persuading the General Assembly to increase the university's annual appropriation from $15,000 to $40,000. He also had much to do with the establishment of new schools in astronomy, biology and agriculture, applied chemistry, engineering, and natural history and geology. His daughter Natalie married Prof. Raleigh C. Minor.

Credit for the high position occupied by the University of Virginia Law School today is due Raleigh Minor's father, John B. Minor, more than any other man. He became the only professor of law in 1845 at age thirty-two and continued there as a teacher and writer on the law for half a century. Minor raised the requirements for entrance and graduation soon after joining the faculty. With a handful of other professors, he continued to teach underage youths and wounded veterans during the Civil War, and at the end of hostilities joined with Prof. Socrates Maupin in borrowing, on their personal credit, enough money to keep the struggling institution operating. Minor was an authoritative writer on legal subjects, and his *Institutes of Common and Statute Law* (1875–95) has long been recognized as a standard work. "Old John B." was greatly venerated by his students, and Minor Hall, the home of the Law School erected in 1911, was named in his honor.

Prof. Noah K. Davis was another notable postbellum addition to the faculty. He succeeded McGuffey in the chair of moral philosophy and was a conspicuous and impressive figure as he strolled the Lawn in his long, black frock coat and high silk hat, his full beard flowing, his body bent forward, his brow furrowed in deep thought.

Prof. Francis H. Smith, who had been appointed in 1853 to succeed the eminent William Barton Rogers in the chair of natural philosophy, occupied that chair until the early years of the twentieth century. "Frank" Smith was noted for the eloquence, lucidity, and polish of his lectures and for the consideration that he showed his students. Not for him the occasionally sarcastic remarks of professorial colleagues in their comments to floundering undergraduates. Voted several times the most popular member of the faculty, Professor Smith remained active as a teacher until 1908; he then lived on for twenty more years on the Lawn until age ninety-eight, the last lingering survivor of the ancien régime.

Although the war wiped out nearly all of Virginia's private academies, others were established after Appomattox, and they furnished the university with many of the foremost students of that era. This was especially significant for the Honor System, since these institutions introduced the youths to the system as schoolboys. Hence when they came to Charlottesville they were admirably trained to carry on the tradition. The Episcopal High School at Alexandria had survived through the war, while other important private schools, such as McGuire's in Richmond, McCabe's in Petersburg, and Woodberry Forest near Orange, were established after the conflict. Graduates of these schools and of similar ones in Virginia and other southern states furnished much of the student leadership in the late nineteenth and early twentieth centuries. The university had only a few hundred matriculates in those days, and the alumni of the private academies were influential in setting the prevailing tone. It was not until the session of 1899–1900 that the university enrollment of 645 in 1856–57 was surpassed, and then only barely.

During the first two decades after the Civil War, the B.A. degree was not highly regarded, but the M.A. retained its prestige. Requirements for the B.A. were so rigid that many became discouraged, while the extremely difficult M.A. also frightened away large numbers. In the seventies, the "length of examinations" was fourteen hours, Dr. David M. R. Culbreth wrote in his book of reminiscences concerning his student days. For these and other reasons, three-fifths of the students did not return after their first year. Numerous changes were made in the requirements for the B.A. in the hope that it would be more attractive to students but without noticeable effect. The Ph.D. was offered for the first time in 1880, with specialization in two related fields required, and in 1885 the first Ph.D. was awarded to Samuel M. Barton, in mathematics and related subjects.

There were modifications in degree requirements during the nineties. The old M.A., with perhaps the toughest work schedule in the United States, was made less difficult in 1892. It would now be necessary to take only four M.A. courses in order to get the degree, whereas previously half a dozen, the highest in each discipline, had been called for. Four years later requirements for the Ph.D. were modified, and three years' residence, a major and two minor subjects, plus a dissertation were stipulated. Ph.D.'s were being awarded in greater numbers, with eight conferred at the 1901 finals.

Grievously inadequate knowledge of the English language on the part of undergraduates led the Board of Visitors in 1882 to establish a separate School of English Language and Literature, with directives for thorough courses in the subject. Prof. James M. Garnett was named to this chair, and the versatile Professor Holmes was switched to teaching historical science. Instruction in English received further emphasis when another chair in this discipline was added in 1893, with Prof. Charles W. Kent appointed to fill it. He edited texts of several important American and English writers and was the first literary editor of the *Library of Southern Literature*. "Chucky" Kent, as he was affectionately known, married Eleanor Smith, the daughter of Prof. Francis H. Smith.

The Schools of English, Romanic Languages, and Teutonic Languages were reorganized in 1896 as the School of Modern Languages. Prof. James A. Harrison headed the School of Teutonic Languages, which offered courses in Anglo-Saxon, Middle English, the history and philology of English, and the language and literature of Germany. An able and creative student of the writings of Edgar Allan Poe, Harrison edited a seventeen-volume edition of Poe's works, published in 1902, and known as both the Virginia Edition and the Monticello Edition. It is to this day the best and most complete edition of Poe.

William M. Thornton's appointment in 1875 to the engineering faculty as adjunct professor of applied mathematics

6. *Medal belonging to Gen. John H. Cocke, who led in building*
Temperance Hall at the university in the 1850s.

was a significant event. Thornton was teaching Greek at Davidson College when he was prevailed upon to come to Charlottesville—another example of the versatility of that generation of scholars. He was instrumental in adding mechanical engineering to the curriculum in 1891, under William H. Echols; electrical engineering in 1897, under Lewis H. Holladay; and chemical engineering in 1908, under Robert M. Bird. Civil engineering had been taught at the university as early as 1836. A brilliant man, Thornton served as chairman of the faculty from 1888 to 1896, succeeding Charles S. Venable, and was appointed the first dean of engineering in 1904, at which time Richard H. Whitehead was named dean of medicine and James M. Page dean of the college.

Two brothers, William C. and Walter D. Dabney, served briefly on the medical and law faculties, respectively, in the late eighties and nineties. William joined the medical faculty in 1886, and Dr. Byrd S. Leavell, of the School of Medicine, writes that "his intelligence, character, personality, energy, enthusiasm and dedication marked him as a remarkable individual of many talents." Dabney was the organizer and first president of the State Medical Examining Board. He wrote some fifty "highly important contributions to medical journals," according to Philip A. Bruce, and translated twice that many articles from the German and French. He would travel great distances to attend a patient even when certain that he would receive no fee. Dabney died of typhoid fever at age forty-five. His brother, Walter, was a leading member of the Virginia House of Delegates, being chairman of two of its most important committees. He served as solicitor to the State Department under President Grover Cleveland before joining the university's law faculty. Walter Dabney also died at the height of his career.

Another addition to the faculty in the late nineteenth century was Richard Heath Dabney, appointed adjunct professor of history in 1889. Like several other members of the university teaching staff who took the M.A. at the university, Dabney had then studied in Germany, where he won his Ph.D. at Heidelberg, multa cum laude. He remained on the University of Virginia faculty for forty-nine years. In addition to teaching all of the history for thirty-four years, he also provided the only courses in economics for nine of those years and served as dean of the graduate school for eighteen years. Such a load seems incredible today, but the university was so poverty-stricken that various professors had to carry these heavy burdens of work. This was a major factor in explaining their failure to be more productive as scholars.

The university's poverty also caused Dr. Paul B. Barringer, chairman of the faculty from 1896 to 1903, to urge the abolition of the School of Engineering and its transfer to Blacksburg where, he said, "excellent work [is] being done." The suggestion was not adopted, but it generated considerable antagonism toward the man who made it.

Barringer was a member of a prominent North Carolina family whose father was a Confederate general and his grandfather a general in the War of 1812. He was recommended for a position on the university medical faculty by the famous Dr. James L. Cabell, who asked that Barringer succeed him. The young Tar Heel had established a course in premedical training at Davidson College from which such well-equipped men came to the university's Medical School that Cabell regarded him as an excellent selection. He joined the faculty in 1888 and was chiefly responsible for construction of the University Hospital in the face of opposition from those who objected to a "pesthouse" on the Grounds. Work was begun, nevertheless, but the foundation stood for more than a year full of water and was derisively termed "Barringer's frog pond." The first unit was finally finished in 1901 and the hospital was able to accommodate twenty-five patients the following year. Long afterward, when the hospital was much larger, a new wing was named for Dr. Barringer.

Known as "Oom Paul," after Paul Kruger, president of the Transvaal in the Boer War, Dr. Barringer resigned from the faculty in 1907 to accept the presidency of Virginia Polytechnic Institute. He remained in Blacksburg for six years but gave up the presidency there when harassed from various directions by politicians and subjected to petty criticism by alumni. (See "The Rise and Fall of 'Oom Paul,'" by Jenkins M. Robertson, *Virginia Tech Magazine*, April-May 1979.) A favorite at university alumni gatherings, where his jovial spirit and ability as a raconteur made him a center of attention, Dr. Barringer spent his remaining years in retirement, the last fifteen on Oakhurst Circle, Charlottesville.

With the defeat of the South in the Civil War and destruction of its mode of life, careers in public office seemed less attractive than previously. Hence the emphasis on oratory at the university declined after the war, especially for members of the Washington and Jefferson societies. But the main reason why the societies languished, according to the university annual, was "the craze for athletics."

A rudimentary game of baseball had been played informally on the Grounds in the seventies, but it was not until 1889 that the baseball field was fenced in and admission charged. An early variety of football also had been introduced in the seventies, and Virginia's first intercollegiate game was played in 1888. Six years later football had become the most popular sport at the institution, although baseball had its ardent following. In view of the 280-pound behemoths who grace our gridirons today, it is interesting to reflect that the heaviest man in the university in 1888 weighed 184 pounds, according to *Corks and Curls* for that year. Running, jumping, and wrestling had been introduced, as well as boat races on the Rivanna River. Tennis was played as early as 1881. A General Athletic Association was organized in 1892 to take charge of all athletics. Land was purchased and a five-acre athletic field was constructed behind the site of subsequently erected Madison Hall. Then came the building of Fayerweather Gymnasium in 1893 at a cost of $30,000, largest and most complete gymnasium in the South.

The *Virginia University Magazine* was the sole postbellum publication of the students until they brought out their first annual in 1888 and gave it the unique name *Corks and Curls*—widely misinterpreted as signifying "wine and women." In that era, to "cork" in class was to flunk, while to "curl" was to make a high grade. The name *Corks and Curls* is said to have been suggested either by Ernest M. Stires, a student who later became Episcopal bishop of Long Island, or by J. H. C. Bagby, the annual's first editor, later a distinguished member of the Hampden-Sydney College faculty. *College Topics*, the school newspaper, was founded in 1890.

Since the end of the Civil War the university colors had been silver gray and cardinal red, symbolizing the Confederate uniform dyed in blood. With the intensification of the "athletic craze," the view was expressed by student leaders that these colors were inappropriate for athletic events and that the gray was lacking in durability, especially on the football field. A mass meeting of students was accordingly held in 1888 to consider the adoption of a new set of colors. There was great difference of opinion, and nobody seemed to have a clear idea concerning the proper substitute. Suddenly an undergraduate spied an orange and blue scarf around the neck of Allen Potts, one of the university's star athletes, who had gotten it on a boating expedition at Oxford University the previous summer. The student pulled the scarf from Potts's neck and, waving it to the assembled group called out, "How will this do?" Orange and blue were promptly adopted as the university colors and have so remained.

Next came the composition of the "The Good Old Song." Edward H. Craighill, Jr., of Lynchburg is usually credited with having composed it, but he wrote in the *University of Virginia Magazine* for October 1922 that "no one man should be credited with the authorship" of the first stanza. He said it appeared in 1893 as the by-product of a bibulous welcome to a victorious football team and was the joint production of several students. A "wah-hoo-wah" yell, said to have been "borrowed from Dartmouth College," was already in vogue at the university, and this was incorporated into the song. The second and third stanzas were written later—almost certainly by Craighill.

Relations between students and faculty in these years were deferential, a far cry from the brick-throwing, cowhiding, and shooting that characterized the institution's early days. True, the boys had surreptitious nicknames for some of the professors, such as "Dismal Jimmy" in the case of one such mentor— "Gummy" was the sobriquet of another some forty years later—but on the whole relations were altogether cordial.

The first of the ribbon societies came into being in 1878 when Eli Banana was organized. The society took its name from the Japanese Order of Eli Banana, to which only citizens of the highest rank were admitted. Eleven years later T.I.L.K.A.

made its appearance, the name reportedly an acronym for five mystical words, probably Hindu. These two societies, purely social in nature, held soirées and sponsored dances.

Eli Banana was ordered disbanded in the nineties when its soirées got completely out of hand. The organization was denounced by the faculty as "a disgrace to the University," and mention was made of "outrageous annoyance of ladies and sick persons by drunken orgies prolonged far into the morning of each recurring Easter Sunday, followed by annual disturbance of the congregations of the Charlottesville churches in the midst of Easter services." The Elis were allowed to begin functioning again in 1897, on promises of better behavior. Meanwhile the Tilkas had been capturing most of the student offices. Then the Elis staged a comeback and regained much of their lost prestige. The two societies managed in several subsequent years to elect their members to nearly all of the prestigious student positions.

The coming of *Uncle Tom's Cabin* to Charlottesville's theater on Main Street near the turn of the century was a decidedly provocative event. This dramatization of Harriet Beecher Stowe's novel, with its highly critical picture of the antebellum South, led some of the university students to concoct a plan of retaliation. A group of them attended the opening performance and contented themselves with booing. But they "cased" the play and discovered that when Eliza crossed the ice, she was pursued by live bloodhounds. This gave them their opening. The next night several of them came to the show with pieces of meat to which strong strings were tied. When the hounds bayed onto the stage, the boys, who were on the first row, threw the meat in front of them. The dogs forgot all about Eliza and made for the beef. Once they had gotten their teeth into it they refused to let go, and the students yanked them over the footlights. It was an easy matter to convey them thence out into the street, where they were released and allowed to chew to their hearts' content. They thereupon disappeared and could not be found. It just about broke up the show. The management protested to the university authorities, but the latter were so amused at the ingenuity of the boys, and so annoyed that such a play had been brought into the South, that little if any punishment seems to have been meted out.

Lith. of P. S. Duval, Philad.

7. John B. Minor as a young man soon after joining the law faculty.

The Rotunda fire of 1895 was a catastrophe of the first magnitude. It not only gutted the Rotunda itself and completely destroyed the Annex, but it threatened to spread to adjacent structures on the Lawn.

The fire was discovered burning fiercely in the Annex on Sunday morning, Oct. 27, and the alarm was broadcast by "Uncle Henry" Martin, the university bellringer. He sounded the tocsin more loudly and frantically than he had ever sounded it before, and faculty and students came running. At their head was Prof. William H. Echols, who had supervision of buildings and grounds. "Reddy" Echols, a magnificently masculine, broad-shouldered, red-haired man of about six feet four, was utterly fearless. At considerable risk he tried, without result, to check the flames raging through the Annex. He then put together a hundred pounds of dynamite and attempted to blast away the link between the Annex and the Rotunda, to keep the fire from spreading. The effort failed, and the only remaining hope lay in throwing dynamite from the roof of the Rotunda onto the connecting link. Echols mounted to the dome, carrying the explosives in a sack, and hurled it down upon the connecting structure. The terrific detonation was heard fifteen miles away, but it did not check the leaping flames. The Rotunda was engulfed in a roaring inferno. Much of its contents, including the Galt statue of Jefferson, was removed by the faculty and students, but then the roof fell in, and the building was left an empty shell. A fortunate shift in the direction of the wind may have saved some of the Lawn pavilions and dormitories from destruction.

The ruins were still smoldering when the faculty met that afternoon and resolved, despite the disaster, to carry on the work of the university. They praised the students unstintingly for their courageous rescue of books and portraits, the Galt statue, and other valuables. Classes would be held next day, as usual, although many would be moved to new locations, since the Rotunda's classrooms had been destroyed. Efforts were got underway to raise funds for the restoration and for needed new structures. Stanford White of New York was retained as the architect.

White's plan called for closing the lower end of the Lawn with three buildings—Cabell Hall, facing the Rotunda; a physics building on the east, and a mechanical building across from it on the west. White also designed the president's house on Carr's Hill and the Commons, or Refectory.

The pediment over the entrance to Cabell Hall presented a problem. George Julian Zolnay, the Hungarian sculptor who was executing it, needed some nude female models. No local talent could be found until, as Anna Barringer relates it in her delightful reminiscences in the *Magazine of Albemarle County History*: "An official telephone call was made to 'Aunt Mat,' the Negro proprietress of the most respectable bordello in town (occupants and clientele white). . . . Where and when they posed is shrouded in mystery. . . . The Pediment was finished in classic style."

In rebuilding the Rotunda, the architect decided not to restore the great area under the dome exactly as it was before the fire. Stanford White spoke of "the unquestionable fact that it was only practical necessity [to obtain space for laboratories and lecture halls] which forced Jefferson . . . to cut the Rotunda into two stories, and that he would have planned the interior as a simple, single and noble room had he been able to do so." White persuaded the Board of Visitors that the "single, domed room" was not only the "most practical but the proper treatment of the interior." However, there appears to be no documentary evidence that Jefferson ever wanted to build the Rotunda with only one floor between the basement and the dome. The faculty and alumni wanted to restore the structure just as it had been before the fire, but White convinced the Visitors that his plan was better and more authentic. Three-quarters of a century later, when a more exacting adaptive restoration of the Rotunda was carried out, the interior was reconstructed as Jefferson built it originally.

The rebuilding also called for wings on the north front corresponding to those on the south front and linked to them by colonnades on both the western and eastern sides.

The Rotunda clock had been destroyed in the fire, and the new one was given a bullet-resistant face, since its predecessor had often been shot at by celebrating students.

The university's Gothic chapel was built in 1890, with the entire cost of $30,000 raised by private subscription. Episcopalians were more numerous in the student body at this period than members of any other denomination, and this situation continued for many years, but the chapel services were nondenominational. For a time, the university chaplain held morning prayers daily in the chapel and prayer meetings there on Friday and Sunday afternoons. In 1896 the chaplaincy was discontinued, and guest clergymen were invited to conduct services on Sunday.

The beginning of work in 1901 on twenty-one-acre Lambeth Field, named for Dr. William A. Lambeth, often called "the father of athletics at the University of Virginia," greatly accelerated the development of football, baseball, and track. And four years later Mrs. William E. Dodge of New York donated funds for the construction of Madison Hall, thus providing a suitable home for the YMCA.

The question whether proper management of the university's affairs required the election of a president was much debated in the nineties. Every other leading institution of higher learning in the country was operating under this form of governance, and more and more friends of the university were coming to feel that it should follow suit and abandon the chairman-of-the-faculty system. As early as 1845 the Society of Alumni had advocated such a step, and similar sentiment was rising half a century later. Most of the university faculty were against the idea, but the Board of Visitors and the alumni were backing the move, and *College Topics* endorsed it.

All this culminated in 1902 in the offer of the presidency of the university to Woodrow Wilson, then a professor at Princeton, but he declined. Two years later it was tendered to forty-three-year-old Edwin Anderson Alderman, and he accepted. Alderman was president of Tulane at the time and had held the same office previously at the University of North Carolina. A native of that state and a Ph.B. of the university at Chapel Hill, Alderman had been a zealous and dedicated promoter of the public schools throughout the South. While at Tulane he wrote that he had stood for "the public schools as no other university president had ever done in this region" and added that "my reputation, whatever it is, comes out of this effort." The New York *Tribune* aptly commented that his election as president of the University of Virginia linked the university "with the democratization of education."

Within a few years Alderman had won over the faculty, im-

8. *Basil L. Gildersleeve, famous classics professor.*

pressed the alumni, obtained larger appropriations from the General Assembly, increased the endowment, reorganized the college, and laid the foundation for future development of the professional schools. He was not without mannerisms, as Dumas Malone, his biographer, has pointed out, but he was endowed with personal charm and superlative gifts as an orator. After accomplishing all this, he was found in 1912 to have contracted tuberculosis, and from that time until his death in 1931 he was gravely handicapped.

The university entered a new era under Alderman. With steadily increasing enrollment—it was 662 the year Alderman took over—the number of students passed the 1,000 mark for the first time in 1915–16, and of that number a growing percentage came from the public schools. Ninety-one graduates of Virginia's public high schools, one-third of all their male graduates for the previous session, entered the university in the fall of 1916. In the following year the number entering from public schools exceeded that from private schools for the first time. As had been the case from the beginning, the vast majority of matriculates came from Virginia and other southern states. This would begin changing in a few years, with the Northeast contributing a greatly increased percentage, and the proportion from the South falling drastically, as the colleges and universities in that region expanded and improved.

A Department of Education was established by President Alderman to further the cause of the public schools, and Peabody Hall was built to serve as its headquarters. Also, as a part of this process a summer school was instituted. On a different level the Department of Graduate Studies was established.

The University of Virginia was elected to the Association of American Universities soon after Alderman took over, the first southern institution to achieve that distinction. In 1907 the university was awarded a chapter of Phi Beta Kappa. The Raven Society had been organized three years before in the absence of such a chapter. In 1913–14 the university's library totaled 80,000 volumes and was claimed to be the largest in the South, although the Rotunda, where it was housed, was ill-suited to the demands of a modern library. In the same year the Law Department began publishing the *Virginia Law Review*, the first periodical of its kind to appear below Mason and

Dixon's Line. It ranked from the first with the top law journals in the country.

As noted above, state appropriations to the university went up under Alderman. He was able to announce in 1906 that the General Assembly had raised the annual allotment to the institution from $50,000 to $75,000, the first increase since 1880. By 1915 the figure had risen to about $100,000. During Alderman's first decade, entrance requirements were tightened in all departments, and the law course was extended from two to three years. The university faculty numbered approximately forty in 1904 and had doubled in size a decade later.

Enrolled students were falling by the wayside in astonishing numbers. In the first ten years of the Alderman regime, only 1,145 of the 2,241 first-year men returned for the second year. While this can be attributed, in part, to lack of scholastic accomplishment, another factor was what President Henry Louis Smith of Washington and Lee University called "the icebound frigidity of the University of Virginia." It was the custom for students to speak to students or others whom they knew, but to no one else. Thus first-year men who came to the institution with few acquaintances felt snubbed and unhappy. Many did not return. Since at various other colleges and universities it was the practice to greet all passersby, the lack of similar civility at the university caused it to be termed snobbish. Its defenders contended, in a controversy extending over many years, that it was not snobbishness but simply a long-established custom not to speak to persons with whom one was not personally acquainted.

The year 1911 witnessed the demise of the Hot Feet, a student organization whose annual public coronation of its "king" was a piquant ceremonial. The coronation at the southern end of East Range was preceded by a procession around the Grounds, with the king at the head followed by the queen, court poet, wizards, chancellor, archbishop, pages, musicians, cupbearers, guards, jesters, and chamberlains. Ambassadors from the Kingdoms of Dawson's Row and West Range, the principality of Monroe Hill, and the independent republic of Carr's Hill were present. After the formal induction of the king into office, the public was invited to partake of royal viands in the somewhat unkingly precincts of Randall

Hall. All this came to an abrupt end when the Hot Feet behaved in such cantankerous fashion as to draw down upon themselves the wrath of the administration. One of their more raucous nighttime performances consisted of removing the stuffed animals, snakes, and other varmints from the Cabell Hall basement, where they were stored, and stationing them behind the professors' classroom desks and in front of their residences on the Lawn. This assemblage, which included a kangaroo, a tiger, an ostrich, a moose, boa constrictor, three-toed emu, and other animals, fowls, and reptiles, greeted the dumbfounded citizenry on Easter Sunday morning. On top of this, some well-lubricated Hot Feet bulled their way into a student's room, roughed him up, and carried off a beer stein. He complained to President Alderman. Four of the miscreants were expelled, four more were suspended for a year, and the university administration proclaimed: "The Hot Feet Society has been, on the whole, very detrimental to the University's welfare, and it is, therefore, unanimously resolved that the existence of the Hot Feet Society, and of all other organizations which promote disorder in the University, shall be forbidden."

The Hot Feet had been disbanded for only a short time when the IMP Society made its appearance. It had many of the same members, but its carryings-on were more discreet, and while it too crowned a king, the coronation was less of a public spectacle. The IMPs are still in business at the university.

The Corner, rendezvous of students from time immemorial, was undergoing an upgrading at this time. As an article appearing in the *Alumni News* in 1913 had it, "The Corner, in all the majesty of its unsightliness, is doomed." Temperance Hall, erected before the Civil War as a symbol of the antebellum drive for greater abstemiousness, was being pulled down. Fraternity initiations had been held on its second floor after the war, in the days before there were any fraternity houses. Woodrow Wilson had been initiated there into Phi Kappa Psi.

In his book *The Natural Bent* Dr. Paul Barringer makes the rather startling statement that the Temperance Union—formerly the Temperance Society—with headquarters in the building, "was one of the most popular institutions at the University" in the latter part of the nineteenth century. "A young

fellow who found himself drinking too much," writes Dr. Barringer, "sent in his name, and in the presence of his fellow
reprobates, took the pledge for the rest of the session."

Drab Temperance Hall was being replaced in 1913 by a
more pleasing brick structure containing a post office, stores,
and rooms for various agencies. The hope was expressed in
the *Alumni News* that the other side of the street, which was
not under university control, would be improved by the own-
ers of the property there. The entire area was greatly upgraded by the erection of the Senff Memorial Gateway at the
lower end of the "Long Walk," the gift of Mrs. Charles H.
Senff of New York in memory of her husband and as a tribute
to the Honor System. The "South Gate" at the other end of
Hospital Drive was also given by Mrs. Senff. Another improvement on the Grounds at about this time was the planting of
formal gardens within the serpentine walls linking East Lawn
and East Range, where thickets of brambles had taken over.
And the area between West Lawn and West Range, in large
part a dumping ground for miscellaneous refuse, with dilapidated small buildings and piles of loose bricks, was cleaned
up, leveled, and graded.

The term "campus," subsequently exorcised in favor of "the
Grounds," was used rather widely during the early 1900s.
Later it would be taboo.

At the turn of the century discussions by members of the
medical faculty with the students of what was termed "the social evil" would have been unthinkable, but by 1913 annual
explorations of the subject were inaugurated. "The Cyprian
evil," the term used by Bruce in his history, could now be
brought halfway into the open. "The fight against venereal
disease [now] is regarded in the same light as the organized
fight against tuberculosis," *College Topics* observed.

The death of "Uncle Henry" Martin, the university's black
bellringer, was a sad event of the year 1915. The student
newspaper expressed the view that "he was known personally
to more alumni than any living man" and "is said to have
known by name . . . every student who resided here during
his long service as bell-ringer." Uncle Henry had been janitor
and bellringer from 1868 to 1909 and had been employed
around the University since 1847. He said he was born at
Monticello in 1826, the year Jefferson died, and that his par-

ents were slaves there; his mother was "married to Mr. Jefferson's body servant." Always nattily dressed, wearing a cravat and stiff collar and a clean white apron, Uncle Henry was extremely faithful and reliable in ringing the Rotunda bell. He rang it until the fire of 1895, and thereafter tolled the chapel bell with equal dedication.

Prof. C. Alphonso Smith interviewed Uncle Henry for *Corks and Curls* when the latter retired in his nineties (he lived to be about ninety-nine). The delightful result is published in the annual for 1914.

Yes sir, I was bell ringer at the University for fifty-three years, and P'fessor, I been as true to that bell as to my God. . . . They don't seem to pay much 'tention to the bell now, but I had to wake up the cooks and the dormitory students. . . .

I can't read but I had fifteen children and I made 'em all learn to read and write; not any more. Politeness beats learnin'. Politeness ain't never sent a man to the penitentiary, but I know plenty o' colored folks that went there 'cause they knowed too much . . .

This bell they got now, it sound just the same for a funeral as for a game of football; but when I rang it everybody knew what I was ringin' it for. There's that bell now. It don't seem to me to say nothin'. It just hollers.

Uncle Henry had some recollections of the Civil War. "Durin' the war," said he, "I nursed hundreds right there in that Rotunda, and when I go in it now, I ain't studyin' 'bout the books I see. No sir, I'm thinkin' on the soldiers that I seen layin' on the floor. It didn't make no difference how much they was sufferin', they didn't make no noise. No sir, they lay right still, a-lookin' straight up at the ceilin'."

After Uncle Henry's retirement in 1909 his regular pay was continued for the rest of his life. His death brought genuine sorrow to the university community and to alumni everywhere.

A less dignified figure was "Uncle Peter" Briggs, born a slave in 1828, and somewhat clownish in his behavior. Uncle Peter died in 1912 after serving for many years as janitor and gardener around the university. As *Topics* put it, "Two generations of students remember the slight, under-sized figure with its bowed legs, the cheerful laugh and Rebel yell, and buzzard dance. . . . When the students heard that he was to be given a

9. *Dr. John Staige Davis of the medical faculty, the first of that name.*

pauper's burial, they raised the money necessary to bear all the expenses of interment."

English Prof. C. Alphonso Smith, who interviewed Uncle Henry Martin, was one of the ablest lecturers in the university's history. This fact undoubtedly explains, at least in part, the invitation that he received to lecture at the University of Berlin in 1910–11, where his courses were well received. He had been dean of the Graduate School at the University of North Carolina before coming to Charlottesville and was the author of several important works in the field of American literature. After seven years on the University of Virginia faculty, where his English classes were among the most popular in the institution, Dr. Smith accepted a call in 1917 to the United States Naval Academy. Many who attended the academy and the university still recall his enthralling and witty lectures.

The question whether to admit women to the university under any conditions was raised in 1892 by the application of Miss Caroline Preston Davis of University, Va., for permission to take the examinations required during the ensuing session of candidates for the B.A. degree in the School of Mathematics. Miss Davis, apparently self-taught, was granted permission, but it was on condition that she stand the tests elsewhere than with the male students; if she passed, she would receive a certificate of proficiency, not a degree. Her performance was excellent, and she was awarded the certificate.

Miss Addis M. Meade of Boyce, Va., also applied in 1892 for permission to register for the course in mathematics, but she was only seventeen, and the faculty stated that "the law precludes the registration of women under eighteen." No "law" was cited. Miss Meade was allowed to register after her eighteenth birthday. Her name is listed with those completing the "M.A. course for mathematics in the Graduate School," 1894.

All this precipitated a debate as to whether the foregoing was the proper method of handling applications from women desirous of matriculating in the university. Both the faculty and the Board of Visitors ended by voting in 1894 against admitting women under any conditions, even those prescribed for Miss Davis two years before. The faculty vote was twelve to four and the visitors were all but unanimous, only one member dissenting.

Reasons given by the faculty majority for their stand, as paraphrased by Bruce, included the contention that admission of women to the university "would only serve to draw them away from those excellencies which made that sex such a power in the home." Furthermore, "under the arcades they would be certain to grow boisterous, familiar and bold in manners, and perhaps even rudely aggressive, under the influence of an ambitious rivalry with the male collegians." And to quote the report verbatim: "According to medical authority, the strain on young women in severe competitive work (in the higher schools of learning) does often physically unsex them, and they afterwards fail in the demands of motherhood." The faculty added: "Let us not be bullied into a false position by the clamor of a noisy minority of the public, thereby breaking irrevocably with and condemning the University's past. . . . It would require supervision inconsistent with the Honor System and the system of discipline."

The controversy was renewed in 1910 with the introduction into the General Assembly of legislation looking to the establishment of a coordinate college for women near the university. The bill was defeated, but the following year it was endorsed by forty-two of the forty-seven members of the university faculty. Similar legislation was introduced at each biennial session of the General Assembly until 1918, with President Alderman and Armistead C. Gordon, rector, supporting it as the only means of avoiding coeducation throughout the institution. Alderman expressed his support of a coordinate college, arguing that it "would assure economy of force, unity of effort and a better understanding between the men leaders and the women leaders in social effort." Mrs. Mary Cooke Branch Munford appeared at many hearings down the years as the principal woman advocate of admitting women to the university to the maximum degree possible. Murray M. McGuire was the spokesman for opposing alumni. The Board of Visitors endorsed the plan for a coordinate college, and in 1916 the Senate passed it; it lost in the House by only two votes. The Reverend James Cannon, Jr., the prohibitionist crusader who at that time was a dominant political force in Virginia and was principal of the Blackstone Female Institute at Blackstone, Va., was credited with a large share in the defeat of the measure. Cannon circularized every member of the General Assembly against the bill, and spoke against it. Finally the General Assembly decided to admit women to the university's graduate and professional schools at the session of 1920–21, and to the College of William and Mary on the same basis as men. The foregoing action would have been taken somewhat sooner, had it not been for complications caused by entry of the United States into World War I.

Male University of Virginia alumni have always occupied prominent and influential positions in public life. For the period 1842–61 the institution produced thirteen U.S. senators from various states, as well as two Speakers of the House of Representatives and sixty-two other members of that body. At the congressional session of 1903–4, chosen at random, the university had six members of the Senate as against seven for Yale, three for Harvard, and nine for Princeton, although Virginia's enrollment was only 600 compared to 2,700 for Yale, 5,100 for Harvard, and 1,350 for Princeton. Virginia had twenty-one members of the House in 1906 as against nineteen for Yale and eleven for Harvard. Four years later the proportions were approximately the same.

With the rapid rise in the popularity of athletics at the university in the 1890s, several famous athletes emerged. Archibald R. Hoxton, weighing only 137 pounds, was a bright star in both football and baseball, Murray M. McGuire in baseball, and Addison Greenway in football.

In contrast to these men, who were bona fide amateurs, the 1890s and early 1900s were marked, according to Bruce, by the arrival at the university of "professional athletes in disguise" who had "registered from every section of the country." This was highly disturbing to President Alderman when he took office in 1904, and he appointed an investigative committee, headed by Professor Echols. It recommended a series of stringent regulations that put a stop to the professionalism, and a code governing athletics was adopted by the faculty in 1906. Control of athletics was vested in a faculty committee on which Professors Lambeth and Lefevre were the dominating factors for many years.

10. Dr. Walter Reed, conqueror of yellow fever.

Professional football and baseball coaches were employed in the nineties, but at the end of the decade it was decided to adopt an alumni coaching system. This lasted for only two years, after which professionals were again employed. In 1906–7 the alumni system was brought back, and under it the Virginia teams were remarkably successful. One reason was that intercollegiate athletics was in its infancy, and high pressure, grossly commercialized athletic systems had not been developed. Virginia has never gone in wholeheartedly for the latter type of competition, with the result that, in recent decades, university teams have been far less successful.

James A. Rector, the university's scintillating dash man in the early 1900s, had done the hundred yards in 9.1 and 9.2 seconds—although neither time was officially recognized—and was the fastest runner in the United States at short distances, with an official clocking of 9.3. He was expected to win the 100 meters at the 1908 Olympics in London. The night before the race, the coach of the South African team asked Rector to show H. Walker, South Africa's entry in the 100 meters, how to make a "crouching start"—standard at the time in America but unknown in South Africa. It was a strange request from the coach of a rival athlete, but Rector, with consummate sportsmanship, gave Walker careful instructions. Next day Walker beat him by six inches for the Olympic gold medal.

In football, Robert K. Gooch, afterward a longtime distinguished member of the faculty, was one of the most brilliant quarterbacks in the university's history, while halfback Eugene N. (Buck) Mayer is the only University of Virginia player to be chosen to Walter Camp's all-American team. In baseball Eppa Rixey went straight from Virginia to the Philadelphia Phillies and then to the Cincinnati Reds. Recognized as one of the top left-handed pitchers in the history of the National League, he was elected to the Baseball Hall of Fame.

The university community was shaken to its foundations in 1909 when Archer Christian, a greatly admired student, was fatally injured in a football game at Georgetown University. His body was brought from Washington to his Richmond home, and services in St. Paul's Episcopal Church were attended by delegations from the Virginia and Georgetown student bodies. There was much agitation for abolition of football, but it all ended with mere changes in the rules to make the game somewhat safer.

A memorable athletic event of the era took place in 1915, when Virginia defeated Yale 10–0 in football, the first time that a southern team had accomplished this feat. The same University of Virginia eleven held Harvard to three field goals with All-American Eddie Mahan in the Harvard backfield. Norborne Berkeley, the 150-pound Virginia quarterback, called these two masterful games. Eugene N. (Buck) Mayer was a backfield star. The Boston press was high in praise of the Virginia players who helped the Harvard men up from the sod after tackling them.

Completion of the stadium on Lambeth Field in 1913 provided a facility seating 8,000 persons, and baseball, football, and track were thus accommodated for several decades. The stadium cost $35,000.

The coming of Henry H. (Pop) Lannigan to the university's athletic staff in 1905 was a milestone. As coach and trainer in a number of sports for several decades Pop Lannigan was to make a lasting contribution to athletics at Virginia. As *College Topics* expressed it in 1911: "With the exception of Dr. Lambeth, Lannigan has done more for athletics at the University of Virginia than any man ever connected with the department. It was he who introduced basketball, not before practiced here. He put track work on a different footing. He is the life and spirit in every branch of athletics."

Alumni activities in the late nineteenth and early twentieth centuries were limited in character. Without a class system, it was difficult to bring the "old grads" together for any purpose, and most reunions were desultory and sparsely attended affairs. The Alumni Board of Trustees of the University of Virginia Endowment Fund was organized for the purpose of receiving, holding, investing, and disbursing the income from gifts made by alumni and friends.

Dean James M. Page, general secretary of the Alumni Association, sent invitations to alumni of the classes of 1905, 1895, 1890, and on back to 1840, to hold reunions at the 1910 finals. Some two hundred fifty attended, and it was the most successful such gathering up to that time.

Then came the election of Lewis D. Crenshaw as alumni

secretary on a full-time basis, and things began to happen. Crenshaw, a man of superb ingenuity, complete dedication, and driving energy, organized the alumni office more thoroughly than it had ever been organized before. The *Alumni News* was founded. Crenshaw's class of 1908 held its fifth reunion in 1913, and novel plans of the most varied sort were devised to create interest. The Big Tent, a place of rendezvous and good fellowship for Virginia men of all ages, made its appearance between Minor Hall and Dawson's Row. Nearly four hundred alumni attended the reunion, and it was pronounced a complete success. Conduct of those in attendance was said to have been exemplary. The following year nearly four hundred alumni were again on hand.

But despite repeated appeals from Lewis Crenshaw for at least a minimum of cooperation from alumni in carrying on the routine business of the association, it was not forthcoming. They were derelict in paying their dues and unwilling to answer correspondence. In order to prepare food and other entertainment for the various reunions, Crenshaw had to have some sort of idea of the number to be expected, but fewer than 15 percent of those who came let him know in advance, despite countless requests that they do so. His office was operating on the barest shoestring, and his own modest salary was sometimes far in arrears.

In the absence of a class system, a Class Officers' Association was formed, with Crenshaw as president, in order to promote "class organization and class reunions in every possible way." All this was largely in vain, given the lackadaisical attitude of the average alumnus.

With the entry of the United States into World War I, all alumni and other university activities were curtailed or drastically altered. Crenshaw was rejected for military duty because of physical disability and could have had a well-paying government job, but he announced that he would open a bureau in Paris for University of Virginia men in the service. Funds were raised for the enterprise, and he sailed for France.

Again his imagination and ingenuity were manifest as he fitted out the bureau in a manner to bring Virginia men on leave from the trenches a maximum of comfort in a homelike atmosphere. Pictures of the Lawn and Ranges adorned the walls, and files of *College Topics* and *Corks and Curls* were available. University servicemen were able to get in touch with one another through the bureau and to meet there for later relaxation along the boulevards.

Crenshaw even translated "The Good Old Song" into French. The opening line of this unique rendition was "La belle chanson de 'wah-hoo-wah.'"

Back at the University, the *Alumni News* noted that "the alumni office has done its share of war work . . . by raising two U.Va. Ambulance Sections for the U.S. Army, and by cooperating with Dr. [William H.] Goodwin in the organization of the U.Va. Base Hospital." Crenshaw had been the sparkplug in the foregoing activities. Base Hospital 41, with Dr. Goodwin commanding, reached Paris in July 1918 and went into operation at nearby St. Denis. It made a splendid record.

A member of the university faculty was dismissed for making a militantly pacifist speech at Sweet Briar College in November 1917. He was Leon R. Whipple, adjunct professor of journalism, who was widely denounced in the press and assailed without a dissenting voice by the faculty. President Alderman recommended that his appointment be rescinded. (French prof. Richard H. Wilson was absent from the city when the faculty voted, and on his return he publicly defended Whipple's right to hold and express unpopular views, even though he himself disagreed with those views.) The Board of Visitors, holding Whipple's pacifist utterances to be "a gross abuse of freedom of speech," agreed unanimously with Alderman, and the professor's appointment was terminated. As a rule, Dumas Malone writes in his biography of Alderman, the spiritual climate at the university "was one of generous tolerance," but Whipple was deemed to have exceeded all proper bounds. The American Association of University Professors went on record officially during the war as advocating dismissal of any professor guilty of such conduct as Whipple's.

Enrollment at the university fell from 1,064 for the session of 1916–17 to 761 and then to 536, despite the exhortation from Gen. Leonard Wood, speaking for the Wilson administration, that all college students stay in college until called. A Reserve Officers' Training Corps (ROTC) was organized as soon as we entered the war, and it was replaced later by the

Students Army Training Corps (SATC). Physically fit students eighteen years of age were automatically enrolled. The curriculum was modified to include courses needed in wartime. During the dreadful influenza epidemic in the fall of 1918 all students wore white masks, in the hope of avoiding the deadly pestilence. Many fell ill and some died, including able Prof. William Harry Heck, who was lecturing on how to avoid the flu. A truck drivers' school was organized and constructed at the university on directions from the War Department and at the university's expense.

With the arrival of the armistice, Nov. 11, 1918, there was fervent rejoicing on both sides of the Atlantic. Robert P. Hamilton, Jr., a university student who was serving in one of the institution's ambulance units and was later a Rhodes Scholar, was in Paris on that memorable day. He wrote his mother at once, expressing his deep emotional involvement: "Paris on November the eleventh, 1918, was the stage of such scenes as occur once in the history of the world. They had no rehearsal and they can have no repetition. Ten years out of the ordinary life would have been a modest price of admission. For my part I had rather die tomorrow with the precious memories of yesterday thrilling my soul than live to seventy with that golden date erased from my mind."

The most unforgettable scene of all, he said, was that night, when Madame Chénal sang the "Marseillaise" from the balcony of the Opera to a crowd that packed the huge square and all adjacent streets. "Suddenly, dramatically," he wrote, "in the very center of the balcony there stood forth the heroic figure of France personified—a superb woman draped in the colors of the nation's flag and crowned with the revolutionary cockade. . . . Tears flowed unabashed and unashamed. . . . The magnificent woman flung out her beautiful arms in a splendid gesture, and not one but thirty thousand voices took up the refrain, *Aux armes, citoyens! Formez vos battaillons!* . . . It was irresistible—that great, spontaneous, unforeseen roar and surge of song."

On New Year's Eve Lewis Crenshaw was on the job with arrangements for a "fumoir" (smoker) for Virginia men in a Paris café. He announced it for 8 P.M., to continue "jusqu'au moment où les vaches rentrent chez elles" ('til the cows come home). On the menu was "de l'egg nogg véritable."

11. *Ruins of the Rotunda after the fire of 1895.*

The year 1919 marked the centennial of the university's chartering. Hundreds of university servicemen were still overseas that spring, and Crenshaw arranged a Founder's Day observance for Apr. 12 and 13 in Paris. The program included ceremonies on the site of the residence Thomas Jefferson occupied as minister to France, a banquet that evening, and a frolicsome boat trip on the Seine to St. Germain on Jefferson's birthday. Nearly three hundred university alumni attended the various events, "the largest reunion of the former students of an American university ever held in Europe." A tablet marking the site of Jefferson's dwelling, corner Rue de Berri and the Champs-Elysées, was put in place later.

The American Expeditionary Force was being rapidly demobilized. By the fall of 1919 large numbers of former students were returning to the Lawn and Ranges to complete their education. Some twenty-seven hundred University of Virginia alumni and students had served in the armed forces, and eighty had given their lives. Among the latter was James Rogers McConnell, in his student days king of the Hot Feet and editor of *Corks and Curls*. He enlisted in France's Lafayette Escadrille before our entry into the war and was shot down by the Germans over the battle lines in France. "Jim" McConnell would have had it no other way. His mother, broken in health, urged him to obtain his release from the French army, but he replied, "If I knew I was to be killed within a minute, and I was absolutely free to leave untouched, I would not do so." Among his effects a letter written in anticipation of his fate, was found. "Good luck to the rest of you," it read, "Vive la France! My death is of no importance." His statue, by Gutzon Borglum is one of the most notable monuments on the Grounds. On it are the words "Soaring like an Eagle into New Heavens of Valor and Devotion."

The University of Virginia's first hundred years was at an end. The institution had survived its early throes when student riots threatened to close the place down, and then had passed successfully through two major wars. It was stronger than ever as its second century dawned.

TWO

The Alderman Years

DEMOBILIZED SERVICEMEN, many of whom had not had time to shed their uniforms, were flooding back to the arcades in the autumn of 1919. No fewer than fourteen hundred students had registered by the end of September, much the largest enrollment in University of Virginia history to that time.

There were glad handshakes at the Corner as men greeted one another and prepared to resume their academic pursuits; and there was sorrow for those who would never return. The faculty had not yet been expanded to take care of the increased enrollment, and many of the same professors the students had known before the war were on hand to greet them. Deans James M. Page of the College, William M. Lile of the Law School, Theodore Hough of the Medical School, William M. Thornton of the Engineering School, and Richard Heath Dabney of the Graduate School welcomed the older matriculates and the first-year men.

At the Corner, Johnny LaRowe was operating his pool room; he would later become famous as the admired coach of Virginia's championship boxing teams. Also among those present were several other personalities familiar to at least a generation of Virginia men—R. M. Balthis and T. Jameson, operators of Anderson Brothers' Bookstore; "Captain" Schneider, the one-armed news vendor; Charlie Hopkins, the black baggageman; and Charlie and Willie Brown, the dapper black barbers with their handsome collection of shaving mugs bearing the names, in gilt lettering, of such patrons as President Alderman and Professors Albert Lefevre and Armistead Dobie.

Things were almost back to normal with classes getting under way, football practice starting up, fraternities rushing prospective "goats," the Washington and Jefferson societies beginning to function, and other peacetime activities being resumed. Special courses instituted for the war had been abandoned, and the prewar curriculum was once more in effect.

President Alderman had been at the university throughout the conflict, after seventeen months at Saranac Lake, N.Y., battling tuberculosis. He had been permitted by his physicians to resume his duties, but was warned that he would have to be careful for the rest of his life and work at only half the normal tempo. His morale had been greatly lifted on his return to the university in the fall of 1914 when some nine hundred students, practically the entire student body, met him at the station with a tumultuous welcome and escorted him, in the glow of torchlights, to his home on Carr's Hill.

Varsity football had been discontinued the previous year because of the war but was resumed in the fall of 1919. Basketball, baseball, and track had functioned in the winter and spring of the 1918–19 session, following the termination of the world conflict in November 1918. The athletic record in 1919–20 was a ragged one, although the basketball team under the coaching of the returned Pop Lannigan made an excellent showing.

In football Virginia began the season with only two lettermen and won only two games. One of the losses was to the sensational and previously obscure team from little Centre College of Danville, Ky. The morning before the game, a man named McMillan showed up at LaRowe's pool room, said he was the Centre quarterback, and offered to bet even money to all comers that he would personally score more points than the entire Virginia team. Loyal Virginia rooters hastened to cover his bets. The man was "Bo" McMillan—who turned out later to be an all-American—and he led the "Praying Colonels" of Centre College to a 49 to 7 walloping of the Orange and Blue. McMillan scored several touchdowns and returned to Danville with a large wad of currency.

Observance of the university's centennial, originally planned for 1919, was postponed until 1921 "because of disturbed world conditions following the Great War." John Stewart Bryan, rector of the university, and Frederic W. Scott, a member of the board, were "joint and alternate chairmen" of the Centennial Endowment Fund drive for $3,000,000, launched in the fall of 1920. Prof. Armistead M. Dobie was given a year's leave of absence from the law school to serve as executive director. John L. Newcomb, then a professor in the School of Engineering, was chosen general chairman of the centennial celebration, which was set for May 31–June 3, 1921.

Publication of Philip Alexander Bruce's monumental five-volume history of the university's first hundred years was a feature of the observance, as was the appearance of a book of poems, *The Enchanted Years*, contributed by American and British poets in honor of the occasion. There was also a motion picture.

No effort had been made since the 1916 Finals to attract the alumni back to alma mater. This policy was continued in 1920 in order that all energies might be devoted to achieving a record-breaking turnout for the centennial observance the following year. Lewis Crenshaw, back from Paris, said his alumni office would "start work in earnest . . . to see that every human critter that can walk or hop or crawl or fly or swim, or even float down the Rivanna on his back, gets within calling distance of the old Rotunda." He was searching for the "oldest living specimen of the genus *alumnus Virginiensis*, who we will have seated on the throne of extinct beer kegs [prohibition being in full force], and crowned with a chaplet of fragrant mint leaves."

The celebration brought many alumni back to the Grounds, as well as internationally known speakers from both sides of the Atlantic—French Ambassador Jules Jusserand, President Abbott Lawrence Lowell of Harvard, Prof. Henry van Dyke of Princeton, and British Ambassador Sir Auckland Geddes. There were greetings from President Woodrow Wilson and from leading European universities. The Distinguished Service Cross of Serbia was presented to Dr. Alderman.

Dedication of the McIntire Theater, incorrectly called the McIntire Amphitheater—an amphitheater is circular or oval in shape—was an important event. The theater was made possible by a $120,000 gift from Paul Goodloe McIntire, one of the university's greatest benefactors, who had donated

$155,000 for the School of Fine Arts in 1919 and whose contribution of an additional $200,000 to establish a Department of Commerce and Finance was announced during the centennial.

The Shadow of the Builder, a centennial pageant by Frances O. J. Gaither, was a significant event. *Corks and Curls* was especially complimentary to "the dancing girls from Mississippi" and "the torchlight procession of the Athenian youths after the footrace." It also found "admirable" the acting of "Dr. W. M. Forrest as Jefferson, Dr. R. H. Dabney as Socrates, Dr. J. J. Luck as an American citizen, and Prof. Francis H. Abbot as an Italian stonecutter." An augmented symphony orchestra rendered musical interludes composed by John Powell, internationally known pianist and university alumnus, and there was a choral number composed by George Harris of Richmond.

A tablet to the eighty University of Virginia men who lost their lives in World War I, the gift of the classes of 1918, 1919, 1920 and the Seven Society, was unveiled on the south front of the Rotunda. The dedicatory address was delivered by Capt. A. D. Barksdale, a much-decorated alumnus. On the tablet were these lines by Laurence Binyon:

> They shall not grow old as we that are left grow old,
> Age shall not weary them, nor the years condemn.
> At the going down of the sun and in the morning
> We will remember them.

The centennial celebration ended with a pyrotechnic display on the Lawn showing the head of the founder, and in letters of fire the words "Jefferson Still Lives."

A somewhat somber note had been injected when Dr. Alderman announced that only $1,300,000 of the $3,000,000 sought for the Centennial Endowment Fund had been raised or pledged. Actually the amount was found later to be only $1,200,000; furthermore, a considerable part of this sum would never be collected. Unfavorable business conditions were a major factor in this outcome.

Failure of many former students to honor their commitments was the most distressing aspect of the drive's lack of success. C. Venable Minor, attorney for the Alumni Board of Trustees, reported in 1928 that approximately fifteen hundred

MASS-MEETING

Of All the Student Body

PUBLIC HALL

TONIGHT, NOV. 11, AT 7.15

to take action on the recent

OUTRAGE !

of the illegal arrest of certain
students by the Charlottesville Police,
Saturday night.

Dr. Barringer will preside. Speeches by Professors Lile, Dabney, Dr. Lambeth, and others.

Every Man in College Must Come

W. C. Benet, Jr., Pres. Law Class.   H. B. Taylor, Pres. Medical Class.
A. M Doble, Pres. Academic Class.   B. C. Willis, Pres. G. A. A.
L. P. Chamberlayne, Ed tor-In-Chief Topics.

*12. Professors joined students at the turn of the century in
protesting an "outrage" by Charlottesville police.*

students enrolled in the university in 1920–21 subscribed a total of $142,000. This money was to go toward the building of the new gymnasium, as a memorial to the men from the university who had died in the war, and was to be paid by Jan. 1, 1926. Only $57,000 had been collected by that date, and 654 of the delinquent subscribers refused to answer any correspondence on the subject. At the end of the drive, total collections from all sources were only $1,037,851.54. Yet, as Robert B. Tunstall, treasurer of the Alumni Board of Trustees of the Endowment Fund, reported in 1931, the fund "rendered possible the erection of the gymnasium, of the orthopedic and obstetrical wing of the hospital, and the completion of the new medical group of buildings; and the income from it has been, and is being, of help to the University in a variety of important ways."

A contribution of $1,000 to the fund was promised by "the Knights of the Ku Klux Klan" in a letter published in 1921 in *College Topics*. Payment was pledged by Jan. 1, 1926. Nothing further was heard, and no effort seems to have been made to collect the money.

The Klan was undergoing a revival at the time in various parts of the country. It was much less vigorous in Virginia than in most areas, but for the next few years there would be occasional parades in Charlottesville, at least one speech by a Klansman at the courthouse, and a couple of meetings in downtown churches. A University of Virginia Klan was formed by a few students, but they soon withdrew from the organization in a letter to Imperial Wizard William J. Simmons in Atlanta, citing "misconduct, misrepresentation, broken promises, financial ambitions contrary to the principles of the order."

A branch of an organization called the Anglo-Saxon Clubs of America was then formed at the university, under the leadership of John Powell, the pianist, with Dr. Paul B. Barringer as president. Its purposes were described as "to preserve the purity of the white race and to maintain the qualities and purposes of the Anglo-Saxon race." With Powell spearheading the effort, it successfully sponsored legislation at the 1924 session of the General Assembly forbidding any intermarriage between whites and those with a single drop of Negro blood. Nothing further was heard of the organization.

Although the Ku Klux Klan managed to participate in a few church gatherings in Charlottesville, it had no role in such services at the university. The usual weekly worship in the chapel was abandoned in 1920, and one well-attended service each term was substituted. Prominent speakers were obtained, and the chapel was often crowded to capacity. Most of the university's religious life revolved around the student YMCA, which worked with the various churches of the community in promoting student attendance. Prof. John C. Metcalf's Sunday Bible Class was also a major religious event.

In the previous chapter we noted the controversy over admission of women to the university. It began in the 1890s and ended, temporarily, in their admission, over the strong objections of professors, students, and alumni, to the graduate and professional schools at the session of 1920–21.

Arrival of the first group of females, numbering seventeen, in September 1920 was greeted with a distinct lack of enthusiasm by the male contingent. In fact, their entry into classes was signalized at times by loud stamping of feet—so much so, that in at least one instance the professor felt it necessary to lecture the group concerning their lack of courtesy. Various student organizations commented that they didn't like having the ladies either but that stamping was unmannerly, that the coeds were "here to stay," and the men should make the best of it. Most professors were decidedly unhappy over the entry of the women, but only one went as far as French Prof. Richard H. Wilson. He ordered a coed out of his class.

By 1922 Dean of Women Adelaide Douglas Simpson reported that "the furore attending the admission of women to the university has had two years in which to die away, and . . . it no longer causes a sensation for a woman to appear in a classroom or laboratory."

Shortly after the admission of the ladies in 1920–21, they organized an association known as the Women's Self-Government Association. Among their chief desires was a women's dormitory or women's building that would make possible some sort of social life. They were living in widely separated places throughout the community. A series of informal teas was held each Friday afternoon in Peabody Hall.

By the opening of the 1924–25 session, sixty-one coeds were enrolled, distributed as follows: law, two; medicine, seven; graduate, fourteen; education, thirty-six; college, two. Three years later the first sorority, Chi Omega, established a chapter at the university, and Kappa Delta followed in 1932.

A suite of three rooms on West Range was made available in 1929 for coed rest and recreation, with President and Mrs. Alderman as hosts for the opening. The rooms, formerly used by art and architecture students, had been completely redecorated. The largest room was equipped with a piano and orthophonic victrola, comfortable chairs, and an open fireplace. The second room had kitchen equipment, and the third was a rest room. A maid was in attendance part of each day to serve tea.

Mrs. Mary Jeffcoat Hamblin, who had been named dean of women to succeed Dean Simpson, resigned in 1934, and in the following year Miss Roberta Hollingsworth was appointed to the position. Miss Hollingsworth would serve until 1967, nearly a third of a century, almost until the entry of women on the same basis as men. She was an A.B. of Goucher College and a Ph.D. of the University of Virginia. After four years as instructor in Spanish at Agnes Scott College, she joined the university's Spanish faculty. A woman of considerable good looks, charm, and executive ability, she was active in various aspects of university affairs. In 1953 she married Prof. Allan T. Gwathmey of the chemistry faculty. Her last years were shadowed by her husband's premature death and her own serious illnesses.

In the early 1930s the vast majority of students were still unalterably opposed to coeducation under any circumstances. *College Topics*, edited by Murat Williams, said in 1934: "If Virginia draws more coeds, and the lure and lilt of the Lawn gives way to the love-making atmosphere of the mid-Western campus, we advocate a second Rotunda fire and the deletion of the last phrase, 'founder [*sic*] of the University of Virginia,' from Jefferson's epitaph."

And Prof. Herman Patrick Johnson, a bachelor, opined, "Women are lovely creatures, but they should not be educated."

President Alderman assumed that the commonwealth would eventually establish a college for women, but he opposed creation of an entirely separate institution. His original preference had been for a coordinate college similar to those at

Harvard, Columbia, Oxford, and Cambridge, at or near the university. Subsequently he came to the view that one of Virginia's normal schools should be converted for the purpose.

A hearing on establishment of a coordinate college was held at the Capitol in Richmond in late 1929 before a state commission headed by Judge Don P. Halsey of Lynchburg. Representatives of various organizations, with Mrs. Mary Cooke Branch Munford as spokeswoman, said that the college should be at Charlottesville, and if this was refused, "the General Assembly will make the university coeducational."

Dr. Alderman and five of the seven members of the Board of Visitors present preferred placing the college away from Charlottesville, with Alderman specifically favoring either the Fredericksburg or Harrisonburg State Teachers' College. The Halsey Commission, in its report, recommended that the institution be located at or near Roanoke, Lynchburg, Harrisonburg, or Fredericksburg. Legislation was passed by the General Assembly in 1930 stipulating that any college coordinate with the university be located at least thirty miles from Charlottesville. Nothing further was done about the matter for a good many years.

Another controversy engulfed the university over a long period. It involved the effort to move the Medical School to Richmond on the ground that Charlottesville was so small that the school lacked adequate clinical facilities. This contention was advanced by two members of the university's faculty as early as the mid-1830s, before any medical institution had been established in Richmond and was revived on various occasions after the Medical College of Virginia (MCV) began operations there.

As chairman of a Virginia Education Commission in 1912, Dr. Alderman advocated a merger of the two schools in Richmond, in accordance with the findings of the commission. He was to change his mind later as to the desirability of this move, but at that time he doubted whether an adequate medical school could be developed in a small town.

Dean Theodore Hough conceded when the controversy over the proposed merger was at its height that from about 1905 to 1915 "we could not honestly say that we were sure that ultimate success could be attained" by the university's

Medical School. It was his view that "if adequate funds were offered to place the school on its proper basis, either at the University or in Richmond, it was our duty to seize the opportunity, provided University ideals and control were assured."

Gov. Westmoreland Davis recommended in his message to the 1920 General Assembly creation of a Commission on Medical Education charged with the duty of studying the desirability of establishing a single state-supported medical school, with suggestions as to how this might be achieved. After the report of the commission, the UVA and MCV Boards of Visitors would meet and try to agree upon a plan of consolidation. Delegate Wilbur C. Hall of Loudoun was named commission chairman with Dean Hough as secretary.

It seemed probable as the hearings got under way that there was general agreement among commission members that the two medical schools should be consolidated, since there was the strong feeling that two state-supported medical schools were too many. There remained the problems of where the consolidated institution would be located and how it would be financed.

Advocates of placing the projected school at Charlottesville argued that adequate clinical material could be provided there. They pointed to the fact that highly successful medical schools had been developed in small towns by the state universities of Michigan, Iowa, and Wisconsin.

However, following the commission hearings, that body voted five to four that there should be a merger of the two institutions at Richmond. A bill carrying out this recommendation was introduced in the General Assembly at the 1922 session. It provided that the University of Virginia should "establish the Medical Department of the university, including the School of Pharmacy and Dentistry, at the city of Richmond, upon the unconditional transfer to them of the property of the Medical College of Virginia, subject only to its existing liabilities." But those liabilities were great; the college at Richmond was, in fact, on the verge of bankruptcy. No provision was made in the legislation for additional financing or facilities, and this whole vital aspect of the matter was left vaguely to the future. A group of Richmond bankers and businessmen did agree to pay off a $207,000 indebtedness of MCV if the merger should be effected.

13. *"Uncle Henry" Martin, the university's bellringer for decades.*

The university's partisans determined to fight the bill. President Alderman testified at length, as did Dean Hough, and both risked serious illness with their strenuous exertions. With tongue in cheek Prof. John L. Newcomb told the committee: "Yes, we agree that the Medical School ought to be in Richmond where there are fine clinical facilities; and we also want the Engineering School at Pittsburgh, where there are more factories, and the Modern Language Department in Switzerland, the linguistic capital of the world."

Garland M. McNutt, '10, headed the university's lobby against the bill and was credited with doing extremely effective work. State Sen. N. B. Early, '94, of Greene County led the opposition on the floor of the Senate. The bill was soundly defeated there by a vote of 24 to 16. That ended efforts to move the university's medical school to Richmond. (There was brief discussion in the late 1940s of a "partial merger" of the two schools, but the subject was soon dropped.)

Alderman came home in triumph from the 1922 hearing. As in 1914, the students went to the railroad station to greet him; with them was a band and an ancient tallyho. They pulled the vehicle, bearing him and Dean Hough, to the Corner and called upon them to speak. In a letter to a friend Alderman wrote: "The boys had gotten a cow, covered it with white sheeting, and in large letters had written: 'THE VICTORY IS OURS—AND THIS AIN'T NO BULL.' I caught sight of myself in a store window as the tallyho went by and, believe me, I was a helluva-looking hero."

Since the Medical School was now free from the threat of being moved to Richmond, Dean Hough and his associates could address themselves to the effective development of its needs. Some of these were met by a gift of $50,000 from Paul Goodloe McIntire toward the erection of a new $118,000 building for obstetrics, orthopedics, and pediatrics and additional private rooms. It opened in 1924. Also, recent consolidation of the public health work of the university, the city of Charlottesville, and the county of Albemarle "places on our very doorsteps one of the strongest health units in the South," said Hough. He saw it as an exceptional opportunity to train men for public health service, especially in the rural areas.

The faculty of the School of Medicine made a significant decision in 1926 when they agreed to accept income "ceilings."

Fees over and above the ceiling formed the basis for a departmental fund in each clinical department. Later the money thus collected was distributed through the university bursar's office, after certain amounts had been deducted for departmental purposes.

The Ennion G. Williams Preventorium was constructed in 1927 with $40,000 contributed by the Virginia State Teachers' Association. Paul G. McIntire made a $75,000 gift in 1932 for the study of psychiatry. This sum, plus a grant from the federal Works Progress Administration, made possible the addition in 1936 of two floors atop the preventorium. Completion of the new Medical Building at a cost of $1,400,000, was a significant event of 1929. This was made possible by an $800,000 grant from the General Education Board, a $250,000 appropriation from the Virginia legislature, and a number of smaller gifts from alumni and friends totaling $350,000. A nurses' home was constructed in 1931, thanks to a bequest from Dr. Randolph McKim, and it was appropriately named McKim Hall. The $200,000 Barringer Wing of the hospital, named for Dr. Paul Barringer, was opened in 1936, to provide special accommodations and service to private patients. An interns' building in the rear of McKim Hall was completed in 1941, and in that same year the West Wing of the hospital was added thanks to a $325,000 appropriation from the General Assembly. This wing provided improved facilities for ward patients.

The School of Nursing received an important impetus in 1926 when $50,000 was made available by the Graduate Nurses' Association for the establishment of the Sadie Heath Cabaness School of Nursing; it became a subdivision of the School of Education in 1928. At that time there were just two faculty members and three students. Adequate library, laboratory, and other facilities were lacking, as were well-prepared nurse instructors and graduate nurse supervisors, but it was a beginning.

Two years in high school had been required in 1920 as a prerequisite to nursing, with college work on degrees preferred. Before that time the requirement consisted of a practical nursing class weekly and night classes at varying times. One hundred nurses had been recruited for Base Hospital 41 in World War I, and distinguished service was rendered. The

School of Nursing's new modern classroom building, completed in 1972, was named for Josephine McLeod, who made an exceptional record as superintendent from 1924 to 1937.

It was difficult in the early years of the century to persuade women to go into nursing. The profession was looked down on, and one mother told her daughter who planned to begin training as a nurse, "I'd rather see you dead and buried." This was a fairly common attitude.

Effective supplementary service was provided the nurses at the hospital by the Women's Auxiliary, Circle of King's Daughters. It was composed of wives of professors in all departments. "Outsiders and divorcees, as well as the newer doctors' wives, were taboo" and could not be members, according to Sarah S. Matthews, author of a highly readable history of the hospital's first fifty years. The taboo was lifted subsequently.

Dr. Stephen H. Watts, nationally known head of the Department of Surgery, was the most prominent member of the medical faculty in these years. Known as "Burly" to the students, when he wasn't listening, Dr. Watts achieved celebrity by reconstructing the nose of a man whose proboscis had been shot away while turkey hunting in the early 1900s. One of the man's friends apparently "mistook his nose for a turkey," and it was shot almost entirely off. A substitute nose was fashioned from the patient's little finger, and was covered with a flap of skin from another part of his anatomy. The result was said to be of such quality that the man's physiognomy seemed virtually normal.

Watts had been trained at Johns Hopkins under the famous Dr. William S. Halsted. The surgical department at the University of Virginia, as it is known today, dates from 1907, when Watts was appointed its head. He introduced the residence system for surgeons, the first in the South, and excelled both as a teacher and a clinician. Many were dismayed when he announced in 1928 that he was retiring, after twenty-one years as head of the department. He was then at the height of his powers and lived until 1953, aged seventy-five. He left $500,000 to the Medical School.

Dr. William H. Goodwin worked with Dr. Watts, and for a quarter of a century he and Watts were, in effect, the Department of Surgery and Gynecology. Goodwin organized Base

14. Dr. Paul B. Barringer, chairman of the faculty, 1896–1903.

Hospital 41 in World War I and was chief surgeon with the rank of colonel. He became a full professor in 1926 and retired ten years later. It was said that teaching was not his forte and he disliked administration, but he was a dedicated surgeon and popular with both faculty and students.

Dr. Edwin P. Lehman succeeded Watts as chief surgeon in 1928 and served until he retired in 1953. An honor graduate of Harvard Medical School and a leader in cancer control and research, he was elected president of the American Cancer Society in 1947. He was also president of the Southern Surgical Association. Lehman was an especially skillful teacher.

Dr. John Staige Davis, who taught the practice of medicine for more than thirty years, was the second of that name to serve on the medical faculty. He was noted for the charm of his lectures. Jokes, anecdotes, and witticisms made them memorable, and as Dr. Harry J. Warthen, Jr., expressed it in 1935 in presenting the university a portrait of Davis, the gift of the class of 1925, "His classical references and apt quotations enlivened the most prosaic subject, and what was still more important, they enabled us to remember it." Davis's personality and character left a lasting impress on many of his students. A small, wiry, high-strung man who moved quickly and seemed always to be in a hurry, he was a pioneer in neurology and psychiatry. That department was accordingly named for him, as were the wards for patients suffering from those disabilities. His end was a sad one, for he lay paralyzed from a stroke for nearly six years. He died in 1933.

Dean Theodore Hough's death occurred in 1924, partly, perhaps, as a result of his unremitting exertions in the Medical School fight. An able administrator with a somewhat forbidding personality, he was succeeded as dean by Dr. James C. Flippin, a member of the faculty since 1902, who served as dean until 1939. Under his firm leadership the Medical School made further progress and acquired new buildings costing over $2,000,000. Flippin was an excellent teacher and was famous for his sense of humor and contagious chuckle.

Another notable member of the faculty was Dr. Halstead S. Hedges, a specialist in diseases of the eye, ear, nose, and throat, who served from 1905 to 1938. Hedges lived to be nearly 102 and was a well-known archer and angler.

No account of medical affairs in the 1920s would be complete without reference to Dr. John A. Hornsby, superintendent of the hospital from 1923 to 1931. A former U.S. Army medical man and obvious martinet, he "inspired fear and loved it, gleefully bullying the timid," Sarah S. Matthews writes. "I haven't time to say good morning," Hornsby barked in his parade ground voice. Unaccustomed to dealing with blacks, he discharged the entire kitchen and dining room force and installed white mountaineers. It soon developed that they couldn't cook anything but the simplest dishes, and those in a style unappetizing to lowlanders. Furthermore, they got drunk on pay day and engaged in a free-for-all in the kitchen. The bellicose Dr. Hornsby waded into the melee, disarmed the ringleader and fired the entire lot. The black help were reinstated.

On a trip to Washington, D.C., Hornsby was knocked down by an automobile and promptly taken to Walter Reed Hospital. When he asked how they happened to take him to Walter Reed instead of some other hospital, the reply was, "We knew you were an army man; you were giving orders before you hit the ground." Despite, or perhaps because of, his modus operandi, the hospital made considerable progress during his regime. It was a period of "tremendous growth and change," with much hiring and firing. The hospital was placed on the accredited list of the American College of Surgeons. Hornsby retired in 1931 but "refused with scorn the customary farewell honors," says Sarah Matthews.

A notable personality around the hospital for more than half a century was Stewart R. Fuller, a black major domo known with admiration and affection to generations of teachers, patients, and students. Endowed with polished manners, innate dignity, and fabulous ability to remember names, Fuller was hardly less than an institution. "There are two perfect gentlemen in the university," Dr. Paul Barringer remarked, "Dr. Alderman in the president's office and Stewart Fuller in the hospital." Fuller was honored in 1953 by the Medical Alumni Association on his completion of half a century of service. He was made an honorary member of the association, given the "class designation" of the medical class of 1903, and a loving cup and watch and chain. He remained in his position for several more years until failing health forced his retirement.

University enrollment was beginning to tilt in the late 1920s toward the Northeast and away from the Southeast and South. In former days New York, New Jersey, and Pennsylvania had been represented only to a minor extent in the student body, but that picture was changing. The number of Jewish students, especially from New York, was growing. Aware that there was a minimum of anti-Semitism at Virginia, Jews were applying in greater numbers, until for the session of 1926–27 they constituted about 8.5 percent of the student body, as compared with 5 percent three or four years before. They were usually among the ablest scholars in the institution.

Entrance requirements at the university in the 1920s were extremely low and had been the subject of debate for years. However, former Dean B. F. D. Runk, long a distinguished member of the faculty, stated in 1969 that the curriculum in the 1920s "was as tough as, if not tougher, than it is today. Required courses were rigid. . . . Requirements for remaining in the university were very liberal, but it was difficult to get that degree." Of course "Dee" Runk deplored the ease with which students were admitted during those years.

College Topics said editorially in 1927 that the institution had "practically no entrance requirements" and "everyone who can write an English sentence of three words is admitted." This was an obvious exaggeration, but the time had come to do something about the situation. At the session of 1927–28 requirements were substantially tightened, and about two hundred students who had been allowed to stay in school despite dismal academic performance were dropped. The university had been plagued for many years by the presence of mediocre undergraduates, with too little ambition and too much money. Frequently they were flunk-outs from Ivy League colleges or they had been rejected by one or more of those institutions. The university was strapped for funds and needed their tuition fees; but things had gotten out of hand.

In the Law School, too, requirements were being raised. Law had been a two-year course before 1909; at that time it was expanded to three years. However, there was no requirement for prelaw college work, and one year of such work was added in 1920–21. In 1922–23 another year of prelaw was stipulated. Dean Lile called attention to the fact that he and his colleagues were carrying an excessive burden. He stated that "six hours a week is the normal schedule in other law schools of our class. . . . Our schedule calls for nine hours a week (six periods of 1–½ hours. . . . This was the schedule in 1881–82 when I was a student)." Dean Lile and Professors Charles A. Graves, Raleigh C. Minor, Armistead M. Dobie, and George B. Eager constituted the faculty, and in addition to the lectures each of them corrected from 500 to 700 examination papers during the session. Graves had passed the age of retirement, Minor's health was failing rapidly, and Lile was within three years of retiring.

Other complaints as to the inadequacy of staff were being made throughout the university. For example, biology Prof. Ivey F. Lewis said, apropos of his department, that he did not believe "there exists anywhere in this university or in any other institution of coordinate rank . . . so grave and pressing a condition of understaffed instruction." He and Prof. William A. Kepner were carrying the entire load, with only $1,500 for "a subsidiary instructional budget." He requested the extraordinarily modest sum of $500 for research. Such was the shoestring on which the university was being operated in those days.

The Department of Engineering also was suffering from an insufficient number of teachers, but, like the Law School, it was broadening and raising its requirements. Effective in 1919–20, all candidates for engineering degrees were required to take courses in English literature, economics, and business administration. This approach was developed further in 1926–27, when in order to provide a broader culture for the students, other liberal arts courses were incorporated into the curriculum. And to answer the demand for research, a fifth year was provided, "at the end of which the successful student will receive the titled degree in civil, mechanical, electrical, chemical and mining engineering."

In the Department of Graduate Studies, requirements were raised in 1921–22 for the M.A. and M.S. degrees; a thesis was required for the first time as a prerequisite for those diplomas. Graduate work had received little emphasis or encouragement from President Alderman until the early 1920s. Dumas

Malone observed in his biography of Alderman: "He never valued minute research as some of his colleagues thought he should have; and even if he had, obviously he was convinced that the time to emphasize it in the South and in this institution had not yet come. It is not surprising, therefore, that the enrollment in the Department of Graduate Studies in this decade [Alderman's first as president] hovered in the thirties. He placed far greater emphasis on the professional departments."

As Graduate Dean Richard Heath Dabney put it in a letter to Alderman during the 1920–21 session, the department "can never become a flourishing one until we have a larger teaching force." He expressed the hope that the endowment fund sought in connection with the centennial would make this possible. And during the next session Dabney wrote Alderman concerning the office of the graduate department, which he described as a "wretched hole with a rotten floor, with a ceiling and walls that are constantly dropping scales of plaster upon the table and floor, and with unworthy, dilapidated furniture." These accommodations had been occupied by the department for some years. Dabney resigned as dean in 1923 "to devote more time to teaching and writing." He had served in the position since 1905.

In addition to the foregoing obstacles affecting the development of an adequate graduate school, there was what Prof. L. G. Hoxton, long head of the Physics Department, termed "a certain attitude of indifference amounting to hostility toward research, particularly on the part of older and influential members of the faculty." Hoxton joined the faculty in 1906, and he said that "it did not take long" to sense the foregoing attitude. "Remarks were made such as 'Thomas Jefferson founded the University of Virginia for the imparting of knowledge, not its discovery'(!!)," Hoxton wrote in 1948, on his retirement. "Scorn was expressed for 'these Hopkins specialists.' 'Our business is to teach these boys and not to rush into print,' and so on. . . . An alumnus, a physicist, once said to me: 'About 1872 a crust of self-satisfaction began to form.' . . . This picture, on the whole, is correct."

Prof. John C. Metcalf, a greatly admired teacher of English, was named dean of the Department of Graduate Studies succeeding Dabney, and in Malone's words, the "hitherto neglected" department was assigned the entire pavilion on the

15. Eppa Rixey, star university pitcher who went to the major leagues and was elected to the Baseball Hall of Fame in 1963.

Lawn formerly occupied by the late Prof. Raleigh C. Minor and family. This immediately made possible a more effective operation. Also, in the next few years it was financially feasible for the university to employ additional teaching staff.

Writing to a member of the university faculty, Prof. Edgar F. Shannon of Washington and Lee, father of the future president of the University of Virginia, stated that the latter institution was the "natural place" for development of a first-rate graduate school for the South and that he hoped to see such a school there. The low state of graduate studies at Charlottesville as of 1925 was seen in a poll of hundreds of professors in American colleges and universities, ranking the nation's graduate schools in twenty fields of study. The University of Virginia was not even mentioned. Yet in 1925 the university awarded more than twice as many Ph.D.s as any other southern institution, as follows: Virginia, nine; North Carolina, four; Texas, Tulane, Rice, and South Carolina, two each.

A significant pioneering effort was initiated two years later by the Richmond alumni chapter, with Dr. Carrington Williams and Andrew D. Christian as the leaders. The chapter pledged to provide $20,000, payable $4,000 a year for five years, for the establishment of a research fellowship in history. The following year Raphael Semmes of Trinity College was named to the position, but he lasted through only one session. Dumas Malone, who had joined the faculty several years before, was then chosen the research fellow. He made a distinguished record, as did Thomas P. Abernethy, who succeeded him.

The primary impetus to research during these years was provided by establishment of the Institute for Research in the Social Sciences, with Wilson Gee as director. The institute was to give particular attention to problems of the state of Virginia. A gift from the Laura Spelman Rockefeller Foundation provided $27,500 annually for research over a five-year period. Banking and currency, labor, industrialization, criminal justice, local finances, and taxes were among the subjects to be addressed. By the end of 1929 Wilson Gee was able to announce that ten of the eighteen studies projected by the institute had been completed, with three more approaching completion.

President Alderman was now enthusiastically behind the development of more and better graduate work. He wrote that the Graduate School, "carrying forward work on the highest level, is the supreme contribution of the university to society." He also declared that "in the great fields of mathematics, history, astronomy, political science, economics and sociology eight research professorships or associates exist, the incumbents of which devote practically their entire time to research and publication." Comprehensive examinations for all M.A. candidates were introduced in 1926–27. Dean Metcalf asserted in 1928 that, "taken as a whole, the University of Virginia is ahead of all other Southern universities in research" and that "this has been confirmed by an expert who has investigated graduate study and research in Southern institutions." The important role of the Institute for Research in the Social Sciences was stressed by Prof. Stringfellow Barr, who had been aided by the institute in writing his life of Mazzini. "It would be difficult to exaggerate the value of the institute in developing historical research at the university," he wrote, "and it would be difficult to exaggerate the sympathetic intelligence with which its director and council have met requests for aid from members of the history faculty." On the institute's tenth anniversary in 1936, it was announced that the various faculties in the social sciences had published forty-four volumes, of which twenty-six were prepared under institute auspices. Furthermore, the General Assembly, for the first time in its history, appropriated "a significant lump sum specifically for research at the university," an appropriation that was increased two years later.

There were many complaints from faculty members during the 1920s that their salary scale was too low. A 25 percent increase across the board had been put into effect for the session of 1919–20, but inflation following World War I more than wiped this out, and the teaching staff was extremely unhappy. Eighty-four of them signed resolutions in 1928 requesting a minimum increase of 40 percent, since this would "restore the actual value of the salaries paid to the economic level of the salaries paid in the year 1913." One of their grievances was that the university had embarked on a costly building program while failing to give due attention to the professorial pay scale. Furthermore, at the time of the centennial President Alderman had led them to believe, no doubt in entire good faith, that the centennial endowment fund would make higher salaries possible. The fund failed by a wide margin to reach its goal, and salaries were among the casualties.

Suddenly it was made known that Philip Francis du Pont, a recently deceased alumnus, member of the wealthy du Pont family of Wilmington, Del., and author of several volumes of verse, had bequeathed to the university a trust fund of $6,000,000—half of it for fellowships and scholarships and the rest unrestricted. The bequest was made despite the fact that du Pont was dismissed from the university in 1900 for "persistent neglect of duty," apparently for inattention to his classwork. His handsome gift not only raised the institution's endowment to $10,000,000, a figure exceeded by only two or three state universities, but it made possible substantial salary increases for the administrative and teaching staffs, effective with the session of 1930–31. Full professors in the college and graduate departments were getting $4,500 and now would be raised to $6,000; associate professors might receive as much as $4,250, and assistant professors $3,400. Still larger raises were provided in some of the professional departments, and deans and assistant deans shared in the good fortune. But with the Great Depression underway and getting steadily worse, the euphoria was short lived.

In the student body the customs and traditions of earlier days were being maintained in the 1920s, and coats and ties were worn at all times, but alarm was expressed in the collegiate organs of opinion lest the enrollment get out of hand; if it went beyond two thousand, they said, the old university would be no more. (By the end of the decade the figure was approaching twenty-five hundred.) Among the long-established customs was the tipping of hats by students to professors and by professors to students, with the latter showing complete deference on all occasions. There was never any thought of making "demands" on the administration or the faculty; a polite request was the maximum that anybody considered. If you passed a group of students you knew, there was no hat tipping, of course, but you usually said "Good morning, gentlemen" or just "Gentlemen." In an article in the *Outlook* George

16. Robert K. (Bobby) Gooch, brilliant university quarterback.

Marvin wrote: "At the University of Virginia the word 'gentleman' means something very definite. In some localities in these hurrying times it has lost its definition."

On the other hand, there was the very real danger that gentlemanliness at Virginia was degenerating into supercilious indifference. A well-nigh pathological fear of "sticking one's neck out" seemed to cause near-paralysis when an effort was made to get the students to act affirmatively for the good of the university or even to answer questions in class. Anyone who replied to a question addressed by the professor to the class as a whole was widely regarded as a show-off. In the early 1920s it was also taboo to wear a preparatory or high school athletic letter on Lambeth Field; the proper thing was to turn the sweater wrong-side-out, lest one's "neck" protrude unduly. During one whole session it was considered bad form to wear anything but a white shirt and solid black tie; if anybody had had the gall to appear in a striped cravat, he would have been blackballed from one end of the Grounds to the other. Also, it was always called the "Grounds," never the "campus." "Campus" was considered too "collegiate," as was excessive cheering at games. In the same vein it was "first-year men," never "freshmen"; and the first-year men did not wear beanies in the manner of those at the despised "rah-rah" institutions; their instructions were to wear hats and not hang around the Corner. *College Topics* protested that "every worthwhile thing that has been accomplished has simply been the work of some individual sticking out his neck," but the prevailing attitude was to the contrary.

Director of Athletics James G. Driver, an alumnus who had attended or been affiliated with several other institutions, remarked in 1930: "There is less effort on the part of clubs and fraternities and other organizations to do some constructive work for the university than I have found at any other college or university with which I have ever been connected."

University of Virginia students in the 1920s also were overwhelmingly lacking in anything remotely resembling a social conscience. Concern for the poor or the disadvantaged was almost unknown among them, and the race problem for them was virtually nonexistent. It was much the same at other institutions in that era. "College life was just a continuation of prep school," an alumnus of another university observed in later years.

Weekends on the Grounds were quiet and uneventful. Classes met six days a week, and hardly anybody had an automobile; hence the temptation to take off for Hollins or Sweet Briar, Washington or New York was at a minimum. Nearly everybody stayed at the university; it was an opportunity to see more of one's fellow students, to do a little sociable drinking, or even to catch up on neglected class assignments. There were tennis courts behind Madison Hall, but Madison Hall outraged the young men by issuing a ukase that nobody could use them on Sunday. Impromptu games of baseball or touch football could be arranged on Lambeth Field, or basketball in the gymnasium. Since the enrollment was smaller and the student body more homogeneous than it later became, close relations existed betwen students in the college and those in the professional or graduate schools, and this situation was enhanced on weekends. Students also intermingled with the faculty at such times and were entertained by the professors and their families.

Greater understanding between faculty and students likewise was promoted by what was called "College Hour" or "University Hour." This was a monthly rite in Cabell Hall from 1908 to 1922, was then abandoned because of little student interest, but was revived three years later. It had previously involved only speakers from the college, but on being reinstituted embraced the entire university. Students, alumni, and even outsiders were invited to be on the program.

Fraternities did their rushing in the early fall as the decade opened, but in 1924 the Interfraternity Council proposed that pledging of "goats" be delayed until February, a proposal heartily endorsed by President Alderman and Dean Page. Early rushing was one of the main causes for the poor scholastic showing of many first-year men, about one-third of whom were being dropped annually at the end of their freshman year. Thirteen of the thirty fraternities endorsed the plan for postponed rushing and put it into effect, but the plan was abandoned soon thereafter. Fraternity pledging and the problems surrounding it would be a subject of controversy over a long period.

Only about half of the students belonged to the relatively expensive fraternities, and the university was never a "rich man's school," reports to the contrary notwithstanding. The charge that a poor boy had "no chance of getting an education" at Charlottesville, made during the medical school fight, was answered by Dr. Alderman with the statement that 47 percent of the student body were working their way through, in whole or in part. Seventy percent of the medical class "are partially self-supporting," he declared.

The leap in enrollment after World War I caused serious crowding around the Grounds. Living quarters were hard to find, and students were having to reside as far away as High Street downtown and at Fry's Spring. Classrooms and laboratories were badly overloaded. Yet construction of the first new dormitories in over a century was viewed with alarm because of a rule that first-year men would have to live in them. Compulsory living in the dorms, it was argued, might well mean undermining university traditions of individual liberty and lead to the class system—another of those greatly feared characteristics of "rah-rah" institutions. On the other hand, the class system was endorsed on more than one occasion by university publications. However, Dean Page expressed his opposition, a factor weighty in the scales. He said that the faculty had never favored it, and added: "The university was organized as an institution for men and not for boys, and it is for this reason that we have never had anything like hazing at the university. The fear has been expressed by some that if we introduced freshmen, sophomores, and other classes, the college would lose something of its ancient dignity on account of class rushes, etc."

The first dormitories, situated west of Monroe Hill overlooking the old golf links, were completed and occupied in 1929, and the twelve units were named for that number of professors who served during the nineteenth century—George Tucker, George Long, Gessner Harrison, William B. Rogers, William H. McGuffey, Basil L. Gildersleeve, George F. Holmes, Charles S. Venable, William E. Peters, John W. Mallet, Noah K. Davis, and Francis H. Smith.

While the first-year men were being required to live in the dormitories, the older ones were finding rooms with the fraternities or in rooming houses. Among the latter, Miss Betty

Cocke's and Miss Betty Booker's, on University Avenue between Madison Lane and Chancellor Street, were the most popular. They housed students for generations; Miss Cocke and Miss Booker were viewed with affection by their roomers and were personalities in their own right. Miss Virginia Mason and Mrs. Robert P. Hamilton, who had highly-regarded rooming houses on Madison Lane and Chancellor Street, respectively, also were ladies of charm. The top-ranking place for meals in this era was Mrs. E. M. Page's, on University Avenue just west of the Corner. For a quick snack many patronized Johnson's on Main Street at the crest of the hill beyond the C&O bridge, where a motion picture house was built later. This eatery was established in 1895, and a special service was the delivery of letters to the night trains. Amorous swains trudged down to Johnson's in the late hours so that their missives would reach their inamoratas next day. The establishment boasted in 1930 that it had handled "over six million letters in the past 34 years."

Many of the boys who wrote these letters invited their fair ones to the university for Easter Week, observed annually during the week following Easter Sunday. Easter Week was the social highlight of the year over a long period. For nearly all of the nineteenth century, however, Finals was the time for merriment and wassail, for terpsichorean diversions in the Rotunda and Chinese lanterns on the Lawn. But just before the turn of the century Easter Week, or "Easters," as it came to be called, began taking the spotlight. Fayerweather Gymnasium was the scene of the Easter dances, with a dance each night from Monday through Saturday; they were moved to the new Memorial Gym in the mid-1920s. "Openings" in the fall and "Midwinters" were less strenuous and prolonged. The participating young people at all of these events were dressed in their best, the girls in evening dresses, perfumed and powdered, the boys in white tie and tails. These formal dances were in glaring contrast to the carryings-on at Easters in the 1970s, when many students and their dates wallowed about in mudholes, swilling grain alcohol drinks from large fruit juice cans.

A "name" orchestra, usually Meyer Davis, furnished the music in the 1920s for the Easter dances, which continued until 3 A.M. on weeknights, occasionally to 5 A.M. These dances were variously sponsored by the Elis, Tilkas, PK Society, German Club, Beta Theta Pi fraternity, *Corks and Curls*, and the IMPs. All dances were "pledged," that is, no student could attend who had had a drink of alcohol since noon of that day, and were chaperoned by faculty wives. Students who took part in these nocturnal revels found difficulty in getting to their classes, and class-cutting was frequent.

No fraternity house dances were permitted, and girls did not so much as enter those houses except on very special occasions, and then with adequate chaperonage. Several fraternities had carefully controlled house parties. A petition in 1929 from seventeen fraternities for permission to have dances after those in the gymnasium had ended was denied by the university's Administrative Council. There were loud lamentations that this was "about the last thing in prep school rules." *College Topics* issued a comprehensive blast not only against the ban on late fraternity dances but also against "compulsory attendance at classes, drinking and parking rules." It went on to say that "requests made upon gentlemen are far more effective" than regulations of this kind.

Fayerweather Gymnasium had been taken over by the art and architecture students and was the scene of the annual Beaux Arts Ball in the late 1920s and for some years thereafter. Sponsored by Alpha Rho Chi, the architecture fraternity, each ball had a theme, and the hall was tastefully decorated, with costumes of the dancers to match. For example, the Beaux Arts Ball of 1930 had as its theme the lost city of Atlantis; the former gym was transformed into a temple in the sunken city, with the orchestra at one end of the balcony and a huge green idol at the other.

Important contrasts in the mores of that day and this may be mentioned. One of them is seen in the poll taken in 1916 of 230 Princeton University seniors, forty-three of whom said they had never kissed a girl; forty said they thought it would be wrong to do so. Things were changing a bit a few years later, as evidenced by an editorial observation in 1922 by the *Virginia Reel*, the university's humorous monthly: "Holding hands has given way to the experiment of the so unsavory named 'petting party.'" Such parties gravitated to what were known as the "petting pits," two former ice pits behind Pop Lannigan's house that had been converted into "rustic bowers

17. *The 1915 football team that defeated Yale and made athletic history. Front row, left to right: George Wayne Anderson, Claude Moore, Eugene N. Mayer; Captain Harris W. Coleman, Edward C. Anderson, Harold A. Sparr, and James C. Ward. Second row: William A. Stuart, Richard E. Tippett, John C. Calhoun, Richard N. Stillwell, John D. Brown, and Norborne Berkeley. Third row: James L. White, Thomas G. Coleman, and Allen G. Thurman. Back row: John K. Gunby, assistant manager; Walter A. Williams, Jr., manager; Dr. Harry H. Varner, coach; and Henry H. (Pop) Lannigan, trainer.*

connected by a subterranean walk." Dr. W. A. Lambeth, who was responsible for the university grounds, explained that the pits had not been rehabilitated for the purpose of providing a secluded spot for "spooning"; their roofs had caved in and they had become dangerous, he said; there was a hole in one of them into which a cow had fallen. However, it was stated that "gallant young men and their frail charges sought the old ice pits for the place of their heart-throbbing romances." This petter's paradise fell into disuse with the coming of the automobile.

For many years the University of Virginia has had a reputation for excessive drinking, a reputation that informed persons believe to be undeserved. At most institutions bacchanalian carouses are held behind closed doors, and the public is unaware of them, but at Virginia drinking is more open. For example, since the late nineteenth century the Eli Banana ribbon society has paraded from time to time on Saturday nights with drums beating and the members proclaiming to all the sundry in the words of their alcoholic anthem, "We are drunk boys, yes every one." While it could hardly be maintained that these youths are all cold sober, neither are they all drunk. Yet the amount of noise they make in public contributes to the legend that Jefferson's university is soaked in rum.

The coming of state and national prohibition had little effect on the drinking habits of students at this university or at most others. Nineteen saloons had been operating night and day on Charlottesville's Main Street, according to Charlie Brown, the respected university barber, and when these were closed, Dean Page rejoiced. But ere long the moonshiners and bootleggers were in action, and almost the only difference was that an inferior brand of whiskey was being sold. It came from the fastnesses of the not distant Blue Ridge foothills, with Shifflett's Hollow reputedly the principal source; emissaries would canvass the fraternity houses, calling from the front door to those within, "Yawl want any cawn likker today?" Their project was raw and loaded with fusel oil, it might contain dead bugs or other similar ingredients, and its potency was such that, when swallowed, it seemed likely to remove the top of one's cranium. But this "white lightning" was somehow consumed without lethal effects; the hangovers were awesome but the sufferers survived.

The manufacture of home brew was not widely pursued in the years immediately following the enactment of prohibition, but the technique was soon acquired and perfected. By the mid-1920s the boys were brewing and bottling beer in substantial quantities. The 1928 diary of Harrison (Tiz) Williams, Jr., a popular senior engineering student who lived on the lawn and was tragically killed in a motorcycle accident almost immediately following his graduation, affords abundant evidence of this. As for the price of moonshine at that time, Williams records that he bought five gallons of raw corn whiskey for $30. Rye was $8 a gallon.

Another important statement in the diary is that a representative of something calling itself the Intercollegiate Prohibition Association asked Dean Page to allow three of its stooges to register as students and spy on the boys in order to get evidence of dry law violations. It was said to have been one of the rare occasions when the dean allowed himself to indulge in unrestrained profanity.

Despite wild charges of drunken orgies at the university, consumption of alcohol there seems to have been no greater than at the average institution of higher learning. Stern regulations, spelled out in the university catalogue, provided for dismissal of any student convicted of public drunkenness, and there were expulsions. The Charlottesville police said they would enforce the prohibition law strictly against the students, and President Alderman, a believer in prohibition, said he thought such enforcement was proper. The student body passed resolutions condemning drunkenness in public.

There were stringent rules also against violation of the dry laws by the faculty, and this led to the suspension for a year of Prof. Albert Lefevre. He was driving to Richmond with friends when the car was involved in a slight accident. A flask partially filled with liquor was discovered by a local sheriff in Lefevre's possession, and he was convicted of violating the Volstead Law. Although Lefevre said he was returning the flask as a favor from a friend to a friend by whom it had been inadvertently left behind and that he did not know it contained liquor, he offered to resign from the faculty. The Board of Visitors would not permit him to do so but suspended him from all teaching for a year.

One of the perennial outbursts against the university's supposed iniquities came in 1926 at a meeting of the Law Enforcement and Observance League. A federal dry officer, addressing the organization's Richmond convention, said that the university's fraternity houses were distributing pints of liquor and that "when a new member is first taken in . . . he is handed a cigarette and a cocktail, and given to understand that he is not a good sport unless he smokes and drinks." The Interfraternity Council replied: "Instead of encouraging drinking on the part of first-year men, the fraternities have consistently opposed it. Many have rules prohibiting liquor in their houses under any circumstances. All exercise careful supervision over their first-year men in the matter of drinking. Many require that all new men pledge themselves not to drink during their first year at the university. The others seriously censure drinking by the new men and require a 'liquor pledge' from any man who shows a tendency to drink to excess."

The *Alumni News*, edited by McLane Tilton, a prominent Charlottesville businessman, entered the controversy with this statement: "We do not hesitate to declare that there is less drinking at the University of Virginia than at any other institution of like size in the country. . . . [Recently] there visited here the distinguished dean of one of America's oldest and greatest universities. He was here for four days. He made it his business to get about the community, alone and with others, both day and night. In conversation just before his departure he volunteered the tribute that ours was the quietest, most orderly and studious and dignified institution he had ever visited."

Yet in the autumn of 1928 there was another salvo of criticism against the university, this time from the Reverend R. V. Lancaster of Fredericksburg, a Presbyterian clergyman. He attended the Virginia–North Carolina football game, and in a letter to a Fredericksburg newspaper estimated that three out of four students and their dates were intoxicated. This manifest absurdity was seized upon by the Reverend David Hepburn, superintendent of the Virginia Anti-Saloon League, who pronounced drinking at the University of Virginia "a statewide scandal." The *Alumni News* denied the truth of the charge and added the pungent thought that Dr. Alderman "is as unable to control his flock as to sporadic cases as the Rev. Hepburn or any other preacher is to control his congrega-

18. James Rogers McConnell in the uniform of the French air force.

tional drinking." Alderman sent a long and detailed reply to Hepburn, saying that "in every case . . . in which proof of public drunkenness is clear, the student has been immediately dismissed." He added that drinking at the university was "on a par with similar institutions throughout the country."

Intrigued by these repeated charges of excessive drinking at the university, the *Flat Hat*, published by the students at William and Mary, sent a reporter to Charlottesville to appraise the situation. He reported the following findings in that paper, as summarized by the *Virginia Spectator*, temporary successor to the *University of Virginia Magazine*: "He had not seen a single drop of liquor, a single student who showed the slightest sign of having been partaking of liquor, or a single exhibition of conduct indicative of the probability or actuality of liquor in the near future."

Use or possession of intoxicating liquor by students in any of the dormitories or other university buildings, or otherwise within the precincts of the university, was forbidden, under heavy penalties, in a regulation adopted by the president and Administrative Council of the university in 1929.

Yet charges of open violations of the prohibition law at the Virginia–Washington and Lee football game in 1930 were made against the university by the Reverend H. C. Marsh, a Methodist pastor of Waynesboro. Persons who attended the VMI-VPI game at Roanoke shortly before said there was just as much drinking there as at the Charlottesville contest, but nobody made any public outcry. Eleven persons were arrested at the Virginia game, but none was a student. The press of the state came vigorously to the defense of the university, and the Lynchburg *Advance*'s comment was typical: "Any football fan who attends the gridiron contests knows that there is no more drinking on Lambeth Field than on any other athletic field in Virginia."

A staunch defender of conditions at the university was James Anderson Hawes, for a quarter of a century national secretary of the Delta Kappa Epsilon fraternity, in which capacity he visited institutions in many parts of the country. As early as 1914 Hawes issued a strong defense of the state of things at Virginia, based on his personal observations, and he reiterated these views in his autobiographical work *Twenty Years among the Twenty Year Olds*, published in 1929. "The idea that there is more drinking at Virginia than at other colleges is, to my own knowledge, absolutely unfounded," he wrote. "Everything is done in the open, and the students have never been trained along lines of fear and hypocrisy, so general elsewhere. . . . I can state absolutely that there is less sex and other immorality at Virginia than at any other college of its size in the country."

The foregoing conjecture as to the amount of sexual activity among students at the university is probably more or less correct. While no one can make an accurate comparison between institutions of higher learning in such an area, it seems unlikely that many University of Virginia men patronized the Charlottesville red light district. In the late nineteenth and early twentieth centuries "Aunt Mat" Thomas, to whom reference was made in the preceding chapter, was the best-known operator of a bawdy house in the town. Her establishment was one of several "near the C&O station," according to Tim Wheeler, writing in the *Cavalier Daily* in 1972. Marguiretta Crescioli, variously described as a Creole, part Indian or black, opened what is said to have been a high-class establishment on Fifth Street in 1922, just after houses of prostitution had been outlawed by the Virginia legislature. "Aunt Mat" also continued to operate until late in the 1920s, if not longer.

One day she called on Dr. Barringer, chairman of the faculty, and told him that she understood a certain university student would be unable to return the following session for lack of funds. She wished to provide the money, on condition that the student not be told whence it came. Dr. Barringer asked "Aunt Mat" why she was so interested in the young man, and she explained that she and her parents had been slaves of the student's father and mother, and they had been so extremely kind and considerate to her and the other members of her family that she wished to show her appreciation. Dr. Barringer agreed to the arrangement, and she pulled out a huge roll of bills and paid the university fees for the following session. The young man returned and got his degree, never knowing that his benefactor was "Aunt Mat."

Marguiretta's fancy establishment was finally closed by the police in 1946 or 1949—there are conflicting accounts—and came spectacularly to public notice in 1972, when the building was torn down and substantial sums of money were found mysteriously buried on the premises. Marguiretta, like Aunt Mat, was "charitable to those in need, including any number of starving children," according to a rather incredible newspaper account.

If Virginia students in the 1920s were largely uninterested in the downtown brothels, they exhibited the same attitude, as already noted, toward much else in the community and on the Grounds. For example, *College Topics* suspended operations temporarily in 1926, since only a small minority of matriculates were subscribing. Until *Topics* could be got back into operation, the General Athletic Association published a special bulletin informing the students of upcoming athletic events.

The *University of Virginia Magazine*, normally the most sedate of publications, ran into heavy weather when its October 1926 number was denounced by both President Alderman and *College Topics*, chiefly for its story "Mulatto Flair." Reviewing the issue, Prof. Stringfellow Barr remarked sardonically: "The suggestion that local flappers have Negro blood, while not very interesting, was one of the few suggestions not yet advanced about them." The editor of the magazine was discharged from that post by his own staff and left the university. Soon thereafter the magazine was superseded for six years by the *Virginia Spectator*. Then a charge of "vulgar obscenity which bursts violently into the recent issue" was made against the humor magazine, the *Virginia Reel*, by *College Topics*. A new publication called the *Cavalier* replaced the *Reel*, announcing that it would give its readers "a minimum of filth" and avoid "the course of moronic collegiatism." But the *Cavalier* got into hot water when it published a "Scott's Issue" in October 1931 simultaneously with the dedication of the Scott Stadium, presented to the university by Frederic W. Scott. On the cover were two rolls of prominently displayed "Scot Issue" toilet paper. The *Cavalier* was permanently suppressed by order of the university's Administrative Council. Such occasional flagrant violations of the canons of good taste apparently occur at virtually all colleges and universities.

An anonymous sheet called the *Yellow Journal* made its appearance once annually during most of the years from 1920 through 1934. It had burst upon the scene for the first time in 1912, under the auspices of Sigma Delta Chi journalistic fraternity and was published for several successive years thereafter. Publication was resumed in 1920, with no sponsorship by Sigma Delta Chi and no indication concerning the authorship of the various items, most of which contained sly digs at prominent members of the university community.

The anonymous character of the publication brought a statement from fifty-one students in 1923 denouncing the *Journal* as "inconsistent with the ideals and traditions of the University of Virginia." *College Topics* carried the statement with an editorial captioned "'Vale' Yellow Journal," and over the students' attack it placed the words "Hic Jacet." The anonymous executive committee of the *Journal's* board retorted that it had no intention of discontinuing and signed off "Hic Jacet Hell."

By 1928 the university administration and faculty had become greatly annoyed by the *Yellow Journal's* shafts aimed at tender portions of professors' and students' anatomies. The faculty senate adopted a resolution viewing "with profound disapprobation anonymous publications," and "earnestly requesting the students responsible" to abandon the enterprise. The *Journal's* unidentified editors replied that they would continue publication, but would make no further references to the faculty. Professors Albert Lefevre, William H. Faulkner, and Robert H. Webb retorted that what they objected to was the paper's anonymous character. And Lefevre was so agitated that he delivered a long speech in Cabell Hall excoriating the *Yellow Journal* as "unworthy of the student body and gravely injurious to the spirit of this place and its good name." However, on a show of hands, about three-fourths of the students present favored the *Journal's* continuance. A compromise was reached to the effect that the sheet would be sponsored by the OWL journalistic fraternity, the members of which were known. For the next three years this sponsorship was noted on the masthead, with the following variation in 1929 and 1930: "Sponsored by the OWLS (the damned fools)." The *Journal* seems to have appeared for the last time in 1934, at which time the OWLS were not mentioned. The university's Administrative Council issued an order in that year forbidding "the publication or sale of any anonymous paper, and

[we] desire to record our unanimous condemnation of the recent number of the *Yellow Journal* as scurrilous and indecent in the extreme."

On a quite different level the *Virginia Quarterly Review* made its debut in 1925, to great acclaim. This highly intellectual journal was ably edited by James Southall Wilson, who abandoned his cherished plan to write a biography of Poe in order to accept President Alderman's urgent invitation that he launch the quarterly. From the first, the magazine was a succès d'estime—by no means a financial bonanza since it has always had to be subsidized, but able to publish leading writers from both sides of the Atlantic. Part of the money needed to get the *VQR* off the ground came from funds allotted to the *Alumni Bulletin*, which was discontinued after being published since 1894.

Perhaps the only sour note greeting the first number of the quarterly issued from the sanctum of the Baltimore *Evening Sun*, which said: "The *VQR* is quite as correct as a white tie with a dress suit or a mint julep without a maraschino cherry. What matters it, therefore, if it fails to shake the dear old commonwealth from that delightful Bourbon trait of neither forgetting anything nor learning anything?" The Norfolk *Virginian-Pilot* replied that the *Evening Sun* was belittling the magazine because it was not like the University of North Carolina's *Journal of Social Forces*, and added: "The university at Chapel Hill has broken out with a vigorous journal of social research. . . . Its editors were galluses and overalls. The university at Charlottesville has given birth to . . . a magazine . . . with its chief emphasis on literary and political criticism or belles lettres as distinguished from better homes and babies. Its editors wear spectacles and white collars. To compare the two journals is like comparing the American Federation of Labor and the American Academy of Arts and Letters." Two years later the elegant Boston *Transcript*, organ of the New England Brahmins, called the *Virginia Quarterly* and the *Yale Review* "the only two worthwhile quarterlies in this country." On its fifth anniversary the *VQR* was solidly established, with subscribers in every state in the Union and a score of foreign lands. "It has probably created more good will for the university among intelligent people everywhere than any other agency that has been created by the university during the last

19. Edwin Anderson Alderman, president of the university, 1904–31.

quarter of a century," said the *Alumni News*. Contributors included Thomas Mann, André Gide, Walter de la Mare, Gerald W. Johnson, Howard Mumford Jones, and many others of like distinction. Offices of the magazine were moved from the basement of the Graduate House on West Lawn to One West Range, previously occupied by the physiology laboratory, where it remains today. James Southall Wilson retired as editor in 1930, after a highly successful six years, and was succeeded by Stringfellow Barr, who held the post for three years, and then turned it over to Lambert Davis. The publication's quality was maintained under these editors.

The university's literary prestige also was enhanced, albeit in later decades, by the spectacular success of two students, Julien Green and Erskine Caldwell, who became internationally recognized writers. Green, born in France of American parents, attended the university for nearly three years, beginning in 1919. An introvert and homosexual, he was not well known on the Grounds and left without graduating. In 1971 he was elected to the French Academy, the only non-Frenchman ever to achieve this rare honor. In at least two of his books, *Moira* and *Terre lointaine*, he has dealt with his life at the university. Caldwell was desperately poor at times during his years at Charlottesville (1922, 1925–26). He swept the floor at LaRowe's pool room and cleaned up the place working his way through, and held other odd jobs. Helen Lannigan, Pop Lannigan's daughter, was his first wife. In later years Caldwell's books sold in the millions of copies, and the play *Tobacco Road*, based on one of his novels, had a tremendous run on Broadway.

Establishment of the Institute of Public Affairs in 1927 further enhanced the university's standing. Dean Charles G. Maphis, the director, was credited with suggesting the ambitious enterprise, and various alumni and friends provided the necessary start-up funds. Among those most active in supporting and contributing to the institute was C. Bascom Slemp, a university alumnus and Republican leader from southwest Virginia who had been private secretary to President Calvin Coolidge. Yet the institute was completely nonpartisan politically; Gov. Harry F. Byrd, the state's foremost Democrat, was chairman of the advisory committee, and Norman Thomas, the perennial Socialist candidate for the presidency, was a leading speaker for a number of years. The institute differed from others in the United States, notably the Williamstown Institute of Politics, in that it emphasized domestic rather than foreign affairs. Held for two weeks in the summer, it included round table discussions as well as numerous formal addresses both during the day and in the evening. Such subjects as unionization of southern industry, public versus private ownership of public utilities, and prohibition versus repeal were freely and frankly debated by prominent speakers. The 1928 session was especially exciting since the Herbert Hoover–Alfred E. Smith presidential campaign was in full swing. This provoked lively, if not heated, discussions, particularly concerning the religious issue. The Reverend A. C. Dieffenbach, Boston Unitarian and editor of the *Christian Observer*, stirred up a storm by pronouncing "Al" Smith unfit for the presidency because of his membership in the Roman Catholic Church. And the 1931 institute was widely credited with having been the jumping-off place for the presidential candidacy of Franklin D. Roosevelt; he spoke there on states' rights, and his address was heralded as the opening gun in his successful quest for the Democratic nomination in 1932.

The Institute of Public Affairs was the most conspicuous feature of the summer program at the university, but the Summer School, which had been in operation on a limited scale since the early 1900s, also was developing steadily. When the University of Virginia established the school in 1919 as an integral part of the university year, with courses in the College of Arts and Sciences of equal credit value with those offered during the rest of the session, it was the first university in the South to do so. In former years the Summer School had been maintained for the benefit of public school administrators and for teachers desirous of meeting certification requirements, as well as for students who had failed one or more courses during the regular session and wished to make them up. But by 1920 Dean Maphis, head of the Summer School, announced that "college courses in practically every subject taught in the college in the regular session will be offered young men and women to shorten the time required to secure academic degrees." In 1923 the total enrollment for both summer terms, with duplications eliminated, was 2,523, of whom one-fourth were men, an overall enrollment considerably larger than that for the regular session.

A series of rather elaborate Rural Life Conferences was held annually at the university as part of the Summer School, beginning in the early 1900s. These were terminated in the early 1920s.

Charles G. Maphis, then professor of secondary education, was appointed in 1915–16 as the university's first director of extension services. Those services had been formally introduced in 1912, when several professors agreed to lecture anywhere in Virginia if requested to do so. The first extension course for college credit was given in 1919, but, like so many other department and division heads at the university during these years, Maphis was operating on a wholly inadequate budget. He pointed in 1922–23 to the fact that the University of North Carolina Extension Division's budget was nearly five times his and that it had a full-time director and a much larger staff. He had only one full-time employee but managed an enrollment of between 600 and 700 as compared with 200 in North Carolina. Courses in a dozen subjects were being given at ten locations in Virginia, and the same degree credits were awarded as were available to full-time students. Special bulletins and handbooks containing information on pertinent subjects suitable for public discussion were distributed through the Virginia High School Literary and Athletic League to any school, club, or other organization requesting them.

George B. Zehmer, professor of education, was appointed in 1925 as the first full-time director of the Extension Division. He stated later that the "great majority" of the faculty "were either indifferent or openly hostile to the idea of university extension" and that they "called a meeting to express through deliberate and joint action their objection not only to specific forms of extension education but to the concept of University Extension education." By contrast, President Alderman termed the extension concept "the most daring and beautiful and moving movement of advance in the whole history of the university," and the Extension Division became well established. In subsequent years the faculty reversed its position, and Zehmer wrote: "I question whether any extension director in any

other university can report as good a record of faculty cooperation."

The School of Education, established by President Alderman soon after he took office, was operated on the sound
theory that administrators and teachers in the public schools
need to be professionally trained. The theory was unassail-
able, but for many years its working out left much to be desired. Excessive emphasis on methodology and too little on
subjects to be taught caused the School of Education to be
regarded during its early decades with decided skepticism by
most of the faculty members in other disciplines. Some of this
prejudice was unfair; in fact, some professors at the university
apparently believed that it was a mistake ever to have established a School of Education at the institution. Worthwhile
contributions were made by such faculty members as William
R. Smithey, Richard A. Meade, George O. Ferguson, George
B. Zehmer, and Francis G. Lankford, Jr. Yet some of the subjects assigned for theses and dissertations were hardly less
than ludicrous. This situation might well have been changed
for the better if Prof. Bruce R. Payne had not left in 1911 to
accept the presidency of Peabody Teachers' College in Nash-
ville, Tenn., and William Harry Heck, the school's first professor of education, had not died in the great influenza epidemic
of 1918–19. Dean John L. Manahan announced in 1922 that
the school's library in Peabody Hall had been named for Professor Heck, whose well-selected private library of two thousand volumes had been given to the school by his widow, Anna
Tuttle Heck. Mrs. Heck, the university's assistant librarian before her husband's death, was chosen the institution's registrar, succeeding the courtly Howard Winston, who retired
after serving in the post for fifteen years.

Appropriations to the university by the General Assembly
were still extremely low, as Dr. Alderman was wont to point
out at periodic intervals. Hence he took particular pleasure in
announcing the receipt of substantial sums from private
sources. On Founder's Day 1930, for example, he called attention to gifts and bequests totaling more than one million dollars, among them $350,000 from William A. Clark, Jr., for a
new law building, $300,000 from Frederic W. Scott for a new
athletic stadium, and a $140,000 bequest from Alderman's old

friend John B. Cobb, which was used for an addition to the chemistry laboratory. The university's greatest need was for an adequate library, but as yet no one had come forward with the necessary funds. In 1924 Alderman had heavily stressed the lack of support from the state legislature; in addition to other statistical shockers he declared that "the University of Virginia is receiving from the state a smaller portion of its maintenance than any other state university in the world." The various schools—they were not called departments until after World War II—were having to get along somehow on these meager allotments from the coffers of the commonwealth.

One of the university's intangible assets that could not be computed in dollars but was nonetheless of incalculable value was the influence and personality of Dean James M. Page, who had been the last chairman of the faculty before Alderman's coming. He seemed to have an uncanny ability to understand young men, to discipline them, and at the same time retain their affection. Students summoned to his sanctum on the Lawn were greeted with "a half chuckle and half growl," as one of them aptly expressed it, but the growl was distinctly pianissimo, and any young man called on the carpet knew that the dean would deal with him fairly. Given the small enrollment in the College by comparison with later years, Dean Page was personally acquainted with practically every undergraduate and was well-informed as to whether any one of them was behaving himself and doing a reasonable amount of studying or was "wasting his substance in riotous living." Compulsive drinkers and gamblers were likely to be haled before him, given a friendly but stern lecture, and told that he would like their pledged word to cease their misdeeds until further notice. The oral pledge was forthcoming and was observed. If a miscreant later felt an uncontrollable urge to drink or gamble, he might ask the dean to release him for a weekend, and the dean might or might not grant the request. Thanks to Dean Page's wisdom, kindness, and understanding this informal system worked remarkably well. Few, if any, deans in American education have rivaled James Morris Page in his ability to maintain a moderate degree of discipline and at the same time seldom provoke even so much as a murmur of criticism from those whom he called to account. James Anderson Hawes said that during his travels to many colleges and universities he

20. *Carl Zeisberg, whose cartoons appeared in* Corks and Curls *over a twenty-year period, comments on the dire prospect that a limited number of women will be admitted to the university in 1920.*

had known only two truly great deans of men, Page of Virginia and Gauss of Princeton.

Dean Page possessed a unique asset in his secretary, Miss Mary Proffitt, who was a virtually ideal occupant of her position. She, too, knew personally nearly all the students in the College and was familiar with their records, scholastic and otherwise. The dean was relieved of certain disciplinary problems by Miss Proffitt who, acting unilaterally and with his approval, called in any student she knew to be guilty of neglecting his studies or consuming excessive amounts of alcohol and demanded an explanation. Like "Jim" Page, Mary Proffitt was regarded with a combination of affection and awe, and her reprimands carried genuine weight. She once told a young man that he was wasting his time at the university and to go home; he went the next day. On the other hand, Miss Proffitt would take the side of any student up for suspension if she thought he could be persuaded to mend his ways. "She probably kept more students from being thrown out, and got more suspensions changed to reprimands than anyone else in the university," said B. F. D. Runk, who later occupied the deanship with great distinction. "They worshipped her for it." In the semifacetious words of an alumnus, "Miss Proffitt ran a darned good university." She continued as secretary to Ivey F. Lewis when he succeeded to the position of dean after the death of Dean Page—an overall total for Miss Proffitt in that position of some forty years. It was revealed after her death that she had been elected to the exclusive and secret Seven Society.

Dean Page, as well as everybody else connected with the university, was anxious to obtain a new library, but it was nowhere in sight in the 1920s. However, the appointment of Harry Clemons in 1927 as librarian was a long step forward. A Princeton graduate, he had served as that university's reference librarian for four years and then as librarian at the University of Nanking, China, from 1914 to 1927—a position from which he was driven by Chinese bandits. At the University of Virginia, Clemons succeeded John S. Patton, who had been in charge of the library since 1904, and made the best of a bad situation. A significant acquisition in 1922 had been the eight-thousand-volume collection of W. Gordon McCabe, the schoolmaster, poet, and essayist, given to the university in his memory by his son, W. Gordon McCabe, Jr. It contained many personally inscribed works of Browning, Arnold, Tennyson, and other nineteenth century English writers who were friends of the elder McCabe.

In his report for 1928 Harry Clemons stated that there were 151,333 volumes in the university library, but that only 88,881 could be accommodated in the Rotunda, with most of the remainder housed in a variety of unsuitable places around the Grounds. He went on to say that the University of North Carolina last year "added six times as many books as we did, and already surpasses us by 30,000." A more dedicated advocate of a new library than Harry Clemons could not have been found, and he spent his waking hours working toward that end.

Another baffling problem involved the decades-long struggle of students in Prof. Thomas Fitzhugh's Latin classes to understand what he called "the sacred tripudium." Fitzhugh felt that he had discovered a rhythmic element in the Latin language, but his oft-reiterated "tum te tum te tum," in class and out, failed to elucidate the matter for the frustrated and bewildered young men under his tutelage. His book on the subject *The Sacred Tripudium and the Evolution of Latin Rhythmic Art* left everybody as much in the dark as ever. What, then, was the astonishment of Colgate Darden, when president of the university, to learn, in calling on the retired Professor Fitzhugh with Prof. Arthur Kyle Davis, Jr., that the discoverer of the sacred tripudium had found that it was nonsense. "Oh it was all a bunch of rubbish, nothing to it; I found that out years ago," he told his startled callers. Darden had introduced the subject by saying "Uncle Tom, we have often thought of the sacred tripudium." Leaving the house, Darden remarked to Davis, "A. K., he's a talented person, but he found out years later what everybody in the class knew at the time. . . . It didn't make any sense to any of us, but we had to fall in line with it or we didn't get any degree."

The decade of the 1920s marked the centennial of various university events, and in 1925 the Jefferson Society observed the hundredth anniversary of its founding. Sen. Oscar W. Underwood of Alabama, who had been president of the society in his student days, was the speaker of the occasion in Cabell Hall. A banquet was held that evening in the Dolly Madison

Inn. The "Jeff" claims to be "the oldest functioning collegiate literary society in the nation."

The Honor System had not yet celebrated its centennial. It was functioning well, but as long ago as 1914 Prof. William H. Echols had said concerning the system during the preceding twenty years, "Eternal vigilance has been absolutely necessary for its preservation." Librarian John S. Patton reported that in 1920–21 a total of 52,000 volumes had been checked out of the library and that only about 2 volumes had been lost—in glaring contrast to the huge number of books that would be disappearing from the library some fifty years later. Yet failure of students to pay their subscriptions to publications or their pledges to various causes was noted indignantly in 1928 by the student newspaper; it said these bad debts totaled from 20 to 50 percent, in many instances, as against 10 to 12 percent in other colleges and universities. "All the university publications and more especially Madison Hall are the heaviest suffers from this frivolous and patently dishonorable attitude," said *College Topics*.

Professors William A. Lambeth and Albert Lefevre, who had dominated the athletic scene at Virginia since just after the turn of the century, resigned in 1921 from the General Athletic Association's executive committee. Differences between that committee and the students and alumni concerning athletic policy and the university's lack of success in football caused the two professors to take this action. Lambeth and Lefevre had always stressed clean athletics, and their unremitting efforts to maintain this policy were appreciated by everyone connected with the university, but it was felt that a more effective type of organization would bring better results in the "win" column. The other faculty members of the G.A.A.'s executive committee also resigned, and what was called the 3–3–3 Athletic Council was created in its stead. This body was composed of three faculty members, three students, and three alumni. General control of all intercollegiate sport at Virginia, insofar as scheduling, selection of coaches, and eligibility and related problems were concerned, was placed in the hands of the 3–3–3. The G.A.A. board retained virtually the same authority it had before with respect to financial management, appointment of team managers, super-

21. Dean James M. Page, last chairman of the faculty and the
first dean of the university, 1904–34, a legend in his time.

vision of schedules, and award of varsity letters. A major aim of the new system was to encourage every student to take part in some form of athletics.

David Ellis Brown, an alumnus, was chosen graduate manager of athletics, and G. J. Campbell of Harvard was appointed head football coach, succeeding Rice Warren. Warren, an alumnus, had been chosen head coach in 1920, following a decision to have only professional mentors for football. Coaching by unpaid alumni had been highly successful for a few years, but then the results had been disappointing. Warren also achieved dismaying results and resigned. Campbell was accordingly employed, and the football season of 1922 was termed "highly successful," with four wins, four defeats, and one tie. In the previous disastrous year the Virginia eleven had scored a grand total of three points in its last four games. In 1923 Earl (Greasy) Neale was hired as head coach of both football and baseball, with the understanding that he would be on the Grounds the year 'round. Neale had made an excellent record in both sports, as a participant and as coach.

On another sector of the athletic front Pop Lannigan's ability to turn inexperienced runners into track stars was strikingly evident when the university's mile relay team won that event at the Penn Relays in 1924, against the fastest teams in America, and won the South Atlantic mile relay four years in a row. The runners who achieved these feats, several of whom had never donned a track shoe until they came to the university, were Benjamin M. Baker, Jr., and Eldridge H. Campbell, both future Rhodes Scholars; E. Lee Douglas, Frank Talbott, Jr., Charles Castleman, M. T. Bohannon, and Jed H. Irvine. The last four listed won at the Penn Relays in 1924.

Intercollegiate boxing had its inception at Virginia in 1922. Beginning on a small scale, it soon became extremely popular and took the center of the stage as teams wearing the orange and blue became extraordinarily successful and nationally famous. As with track, success was due in large measure to the coach—Johnny LaRowe. After serving in the U.S. Marine Corps, LaRowe opened his billiard parlor at the university in 1904. When boxing was inaugurated, he coached the Virginia team for several years without pay. His conception of sportsmanship was unusually high, and he often said that he was "more interested in making men than boxers." Matches were first held in Cabell Hall, and the 1923 team had an undefeated season, while in 1924 only one match was lost. Similar results were achieved in succeeding years, and boxing was made a major sport in 1927–28. With completion of Memorial Gymnasium the matches were moved there, and its 5,000 seats were often packed for the bouts. Adolph Leftwich, the conspicuous star of the mid-1920s, won every bout over a four-year period except his first and was captain in 1924 and 1925. Leftwich won a place on the U.S. Olympic boxing team at the 1924 games, held in Paris, but was defeated by Black, a Canadian.

By 1927–28 the overall athletic situation at the university appeared much improved. In football, baseball, basketball, boxing, and track a total of "47 opponents were conquered while only 23 defeats were sustained." Inside the state the university won 27 contests and lost only 2. Henry H. Cumming, twice captain of track, was undefeated during the year in the 100 and 220. Harrison F. Flippin, national pentathlon champion in 1927, lost only one hurdle race and was chosen team captain, succeeding Cumming. He set world records in the 50- and 60-yard hurdles, although the first of the two marks was not recognized since official timers were not present. Flippin, a great all-around athlete, who later became as eminent in medicine as he was in athletics did not make the 1928 Olympic team but Cumming did; he sailed for Amsterdam with Marcus W. Dinwiddie, a university student and member of the U.S. rifle team. Neither placed at Amsterdam.

The University Band made its appearance in the mid-1920s and was a factor in arousing enthusiasm at pregame rallies and at the games. Attitudes of the students toward the teams ranged from high enthusiasm to bland indifference, depending to some extent on whether that particular team was having a successful season. Even when successful, the baseball nine began drawing only a few hundred students to its games, and little enthusiasm was shown. Interest in tennis took an upturn with the completion in 1930 of the Lady Astor Courts near the gymnasium with funds contributed by Nancy, Lady Astor, Virginia-born member of the British Parliament, on condition that an additional sum was raised. Tennis had been recognized as a minor sport a decade previously and golf received that recognition in 1929. Lacrosse and swimming had their beginnings shortly before.

Sportsmanship between contesting institutions in the 1920s was generally of a high order. *College Topics* often congratulated visiting teams when they defeated Virginia and sharply criticized university students when they occasionally went beyond proper limits in razzing opposing players. In 1924 the Virginia football team eked out a 13 to 9 victory in the last quarter over Hampden-Sydney; Captain Sam Maphis of the Virginia eleven walked across the field and gave the football to Captain Blankinship of the Tigers, saying "You deserve it." The gesture brought unstinted praise from the *Tiger*, Hampden-Sydney's student newspaper. At the basketball game with the University of North Carolina at Chapel Hill the following year lights were turned out at the half, and the entire Carolina cheering section joined in singing "The Good Old Song." *Topics* thanked the Carolinians in its next issue and congratulated them on their team's victory over Virginia. It should be noted that rooters at basketball games in that era were careful to maintain complete silence while a player from either team was shooting from the foul line, in glaring contrast to the manufactured racket that often erupts today under such circumstances in an effort to disconcert any player from the opposing team who is trying to put the ball into the basket.

"The Good Old Song" is generally considered to have been the university's official alma mater song since about 1900, but it has never been formally adopted as such. In fact, student contests were held in 1923 for the best "alma mater song" and the best "fight song." John Albert Morrow won the alma mater contest with "Virginia, Hail All Hail" while Lawrence Lee and Fulton Lewis, Jr., were judged to have produced the best fight tune with "The Cavalier Song." Neither production made much impact; "Virginia, Hail All Hail" was forgotten almost at once and "The Cavalier Song" was heard thereafter at only rare intervals, despite periodic protests that the students should learn it and sing it at games, and the band should play it. "The Good Old Song," to the sedate rhythms of "Old Lang Syne," is far from being a fight song, but nothing else has caught the fancy of the average student of alumnus. "The

Cavalier Song" did have one immediate result: It caused Virginia teams to be called the Cavaliers. Before 1923 that term was not in use, but by 1924 it was an oft-heard expression and has so remained.

Whereas the university's athletic fortunes had appeared definitely improved in 1927–28, they skidded within two years to what was described by the *Alumni News* as probably an all-time low. There had been three losing football seasons in succession, the usually invincible boxing team was fifth in the conference, and showings in most other sports were equally dismal. The student body exhibited vast indifference, and on two afternoons in early November only twenty-seven men were out for football; three tackles had been injured and only one remained. Greasy Neale resigned as football coach to become assistant manager of the St. Louis Cardinals baseball club, and Earl Abell, former Colgate all-American, was chosen to succeed him. Ellis Brown resigned as graduate manager to enter the coal business. The scope of athletics had been greatly broadened during Brown's seven-year incumbency, with nineteen teams in intercollegiate competition during the session of 1928–29, about twice the number when he took over. Brown also was credited with having been an important factor in the development of boxing at Virginia. But in view of the general decline in the performance of Virginia's teams, there was little consolation for students and alumni in the Carnegie Foundation's 1929 report that the University of Virginia was one of the small minority, among 130 institutions studied, that were given a clean bill of health, athletically speaking.

The collapsing situation at Virginia, insofar as winning games was concerned, led to another reorganization of the athletic department. The position of director of athletics was created, replacing that of graduate manager, and James G. Driver, a three-letter man at Virginia and before that captain of football, baseball, basketball, and track at William and Mary, was named to fill it. He was given the rank of full professor and was provided with a capable assistant, Thomas M. Carruthers, and an office staff. Driver had coached four major sports at William and Mary and then had joined the athletic staff at the University of South Carolina, whence he was lured to Charlottesville.

In his first report to President Alderman in 1930, "Jim" Driver said he had "found a total lack of organization in the business affairs of the General Athletic Association and a lack of coordination in the coaching department." He added that he had remedied the G.A.A.'s abovementioned shortcomings and that the coaching staff was now "entirely harmonious." Great disappointment at the "lack of aggressiveness in our athletes, particularly football," was expressed by Driver, who said "they haven't the . . . will to win and the . . . will to give and take punishment." Most University of Virginia athletes "are not as tough and rugged as the boy who comes from a family of comparatively little means, and who has manual labor to do from childhood," he went on. Many Virginia men spend too much time at dances and parties when not in training, he added, and during the summer they go to a "resort and have a good time, whereas most of the athletes from other colleges work on the highways, in the steel mills or at some other sort of hard labor." The university "needs more of the better class of Virginia high school athletes," Driver declared. In speeches to alumni throughout the state and beyond he stressed the thought that "a well-rounded system of athletics, and not a world-beating team in any one sport, is what we want to develop." The new stadium was not being built with a view to placing undue emphasis on football, he said, but rather to provide larger gate receipts with which to equip more teams in various sports and greater recreational facilities for the whole student body. In his financial report for 1929–30 Assistant Athletic Director Carruthers pointed out that all sports at Virginia except football were being operated at a loss, including the popular boxing. Profits from football which for that year totaled only $49,000 were used to pay part of the cost of all other sports. But football obviously was yielding only meager returns after a succession of poor seasons, and the merry-go-round of changing coaches continued. Earl Abell resigned late in 1930 and Fred Dawson, for four years head football coach at the University of Nebraska, was chosen to succeed him.

A bright spot in the gloom was the play of William T. Thomas in the Virginia backfield in 1929, 1930, and 1931. Bill Thomas had captained all four sports at McGuire's School in Richmond and was a three-letter man at the university. In

22. Prof. Albert (Little Doc) Lefevre.

football he averaged over five yards per carry and had a punting average of forty-five yards. He was all-southern in football in 1930, received a certificate of "exceptional merit" from the All-America Board of Football, and was all-state in basketball in 1932. Thomas turned down a professional football contract to enter the Law School.

An important university landmark was lost when Pop Lannigan, trainer and coach in many sports for a quarter of a century, died at the end of 1930 after a lingering illness. Born in Wales, he emigrated to the United States in his early teens. A member of the athletic staff at Cornell University, Lannigan came to Virginia in 1905 and was a central figure in university sports thereafter. Noted as an athlete, he had an uncanny ability to coach and train others, especially track men and to a lesser degree basketball players. During his first year at Virginia he organized the first basketball team in the South, and for some time the university quint was dominant in the region.

Lannigan was an admired and beloved figure on the university scene. He could be gruff, but he was a person of sensitivity. His humorous stories when traveling with his teams were famous, and his laugh contagious. Since he was modest concerning his early athletic prowess, it was difficult to tell just what feats he had accomplished. It was said that he had excelled in track and field events, held the world record in the shotput for some years, "trained the great Fitzsimmons for the ring," and defeated the Swedish fencing champion. Whether all this was true remained something of a mystery. But Pop was certainly a topflight trainer and coach. Admiring Virginia students gave him an automobile in the 1920s. When he resigned in 1929 because of failing health, there were tributes from many directions. The 3–3–3 Athletic Council, which retired him on a "substantial pension," passed resolutions that said: "The affection in which Pop Lannigan is held by his old boys gives irrefutable evidence of those qualities of fairness, sportsmanship, patience and ability which have ever characterized his dealings with the students." Lynchburg alumni presented him with a gold watch and chain, and the 1930 *Corks and Curls* was dedicated to him. His passing at age sixty-five caused widespread sorrow.

Archie Hahn, head trainer and assistant track coach at Princeton, was chosen track coach at Virginia and trainer for varsity and freshman football. A former member of the U.S. Olympic Team, he was holder of two Olympic dash records.

Lewis Crenshaw returned to the university from Paris following World War I after closing his University of Virginia European Bureau, but he found it impossible to continue as alumni secretary. He had struggled before the war to get the alumni association on a firm financial basis but had received only minimum cooperation from alumni. With his salary in arrears much of the time and the whole operation barely solvent, Crenshaw felt that he could not resume his prewar duties unless guarantees of adequate financial support were forthcoming. None could be had, so he went back to Paris and opened an office with the words "International Contacts" on his letterhead. In 1920 William Matthews, '17, took over the job of assistant alumni secretary and editor of the *Alumni News* on a temporary basis. In response to a demand for more and better news concerning the university, Dr. Alderman authorized establishment of the University News Bureau, with Matthews in charge. Two years later McLane Tilton, '97, was named part-time alumni secretary, and William H. Wranek, '19, was made full-time head of the news bureau. Wranek was soon able to increase markedly the amount of material published in the press relative to the university. By 1925 he was getting many more inches of news into the leading Virginia newspapers than appeared concerning any other institution of higher learning in the state, news predominantly unrelated to sports.

The tendency of alumni to sigh for "the good old days" and to resent any changes, even when those changes are obviously for the better, was noted by the *Alumni News*. An alumnus complained of macadamized roads being built throughout the university. When asked why he objected to them, he replied that they were not here in his day. "O visions of blessed Albemarle mud!" exclaimed the *News*. "When shown the new law building another alumnus at once lost himself in a fog of memory and spoke tremulously of the austerities of the two rooms under the Rotunda that once housed our School of Law; and he never did enter the new building, but hurried away to look at the old. . . . It seems characteristic of every man who attends a university to want that university to remain exactly as it was when he graduated."

Beginning in 1924, pursuant to legislation passed by the General Assembly, at least three of the ten members of the university's Board of Visitors were to be chosen from a list of nominations submitted by the alumni association.

No alumnus was more illustrious in his profession than Dr. Hugh H. Young, '94, the Baltimore surgeon. A bust of him by Clare Sheridan was presented to the university's Medical School in 1926 by Robert Worth Bingham, '91, onetime ambassador to the Court of St. James's. After the unveiling ceremony a handsome lady rushed up to Dr. Young and said, "Dr. Young, I want you to know that I drove a hundred miles just to see your bust unveiled." "Madam," replied the gallant surgeon, "I'd travel twice as far to see yours."

Considerable momentum for adoption of a class system at the university was generated in 1926 and 1927 when *College Topics* endorsed the idea, and an alumni conference voiced approval. The question was debated at College Hour, with one student taking each side. President Alderman advocated the step, as did "the older men in college, the leaders," according to the *Alumni News.* But that publication disgustedly declared that "the first-year men . . . have remained unanimously and enthusiastically inert and silent. . . . The reason is the dread fear of 'sticking your neck out.'" That was the end of the effort.

The *Virginia Spectator* remarked that "the term *individualism* has been buried in a welter of sentimentalism only to appear in the garb of indolence. Rather than profit by this comparative freedom as expressed in a vaunted spirit of individualism and, acting on personal initiative, develop independent characteristics, the university student has complacently lain down on the job."

Establishment of an Alumni Fund was approved by the Board of Managers of the alumni association in 1928. Similar funds had been created in many universities. Gordon M. Buck, president of the association, pointed out that "friends and alumni would be enabled to contribute to a fund controlled by the alumni, rather than contribute to the commonwealth through donations to the university." He added the hope that "contributions to the fund would supplant the various appeals made from time to time on the alumni," who would not be solicited further during the year.

23. *Adolph Leftwich, who lost only one bout at Virginia in four years and went to the 1924 Olympics.*

McLane Tilton rendered his part-time service as alumni secretary while giving attention to his private business interests, but he devoted much conscientious effort and thought to his alumni post. During his eight-year stint he was instrumental in bringing about increased efficiency, wider service, improved finances, and new offices at the Corner. Near the end of his incumbency there were about fifteen hundred members of the association out of twelve thousand alumni, which he said was a better percentage than in any other southern university. Despite his ability, Tilton's aggressive manner antagonized some of those with whom he was associated, and a few of his editorials in the *News* raised hackles in the Alumni Board of Managers. In particular there was one editorial in 1930 suggesting a "compromise" with respect to the controversy over location of the proposed coordinate college for women. At a special meeting of the board this pronouncement was unanimously disapproved as "grossly inaccurate." Tilton's name was summarily removed as editor of the *News*, an editorial committee was substituted, and responsibility for all material in the publication was vested in that body. Taken aback, Tilton remained temporarily as treasurer of the association and was nominated for reelection to the Board of Managers but he declined. This terminated his official connection with the alumni association. His service to that organization had been unselfish and productive, although he did overstep proper bounds with a unilateral suggestion as to the coordinate college at a tense moment in the controversy concerning its location. One or two other editorials also irritated the board. His contributions to the development of the association were praised in letters from Dr. Alderman, Howard Turner, president of the Varsity Club, and others.

J. Malcolm Luck, '16, operator of an automobile business in Roanoke, was chosen alumni secretary in 1930. "Mac" Luck, an all-southern guard on the undefeated basketball team of 1915 and member of Delta Kappa Epsilon social fraternity and the Raven Society, took over at once. There were no more editorials in the *Alumni News* until the 1940s.

Benefactions of Paul Goodloe McIntire were a notable feature of the 1920s. Reference has been made to his gifts for strengthening various departments of the Medical School, for the creation of a School of Fine Arts, including music, and a School of Commerce, and construction of the McIntire Theater. In addition he gave $100,000 for cancer research and $47,500 for Pantops Farm, to be used for the study of psychiatry and nervous diseases. He also financed a series of concerts in Cabell Hall by internationally famous artists beginning in 1919. On top of all else, he donated a collection of rare books to the Alderman Library and nearly 500 art objects to the University of Virginia Art Museum in the Bayly Building. McIntire's benefactions to the university totaled overall in the vicinity of $750,000. All this was in addition to the handsome statues that he gave to the city of Charlottesville, together with four parks and the McIntire Public Library, as well as $174,000 provided the county of Albemarle to bolster its schools. Other quiet largesse was never publicized.

McIntire was a strange type of self-made millionaire. Shy, withdrawn, and without a sense of humor, giving the impression of being unhappy most of the time, he seemed ill at ease and had little to say in any group. Yet his generosity was extraordinary, and his alma mater, as well as his city and county, are much the better for his philanthropy. He attended the university for only one session, 1878–79, since he "had to make a living." In this he succeeded admirably, for he accumulated a fortune in Wall Street. McIntire moved back to his native Charlottesville from New York after World War I. He remained there for a couple of decades and then returned to Gotham. By that time he had given away almost his entire estate, for he told Prof. Tipton R. Snavely in 1942 that he had been struggling to keep his expenses within his life annuity of $6,000. He died ten years later.

Deaths of several eminent professors during the 1920s brought grief to the university community. Raleigh C. Minor died in 1923 at his home on the Lawn following a lingering illness. He had served thirty years on the law faculty and had endeared himself to more than a generation of students. A calm and placid personality in contrast to the ebullient and voluble Armistead Dobie, Professor Minor was a profound scholar. His *Conflict of Laws* was termed "a lasting contribution to legal scholarship," while his *A Republic of Nations* antedated Woodrow Wilson's proposal of a League of Nations. In his student days Raleigh Minor had been president of the Jefferson Society and a founder of T.I.L.K.A., and as a young professor he was active in establishing the Raven Society. His death was called "an irreparable loss" by the New York alumni.

Another serious loss was sustained in 1924 with the death of Prof. Thomas L. Watson, head of the geology department and state geologist. Only fifty-three years old when he died, Watson was the author of *Mineral Resources of Virginia*, which the Richmond *News Leader* termed "historic." The paper added that "no man since [Matthew Fontaine] Maury has done as much to open the eyes of Virginians to the riches of their hills and fields." Engineering Dean William M. Thornton wrote that Watson "left more than 150 important published books and papers as testimonials to his gift for investigation and research," and added: "A lucid and enthusiastic teacher, he stamped upon his students the fine impress of a gracious nature, a loyal soul and a scientific spirit."

Four years later Prof. Albert Lefevre, aged fifty-five, succumbed to a cerebral hemorrhage. "Little Doc" Lefevre's classes in philosophy were favorites of the students, and his famous annual lecture on the death of Socrates was frequently attended by outsiders. On the faculty for nearly a quarter of a century and head of the School of Philosophy, the diminutive professor was a collaborator with Dr. William A. Lambeth in founding the Southern Conference and promoting high standards of athletic eligibility. He was the author of several books and associate editor of the *Philosophical Review*. President Alderman termed him "among the great humanists and teachers of youth."

Charles A. Graves died in 1928, aged seventy-eight. He was one of the quartet of law professors who were the backbone of the law school for a generation, the others being William M. Lile, Raleigh Minor, and Armistead Dobie. A student at Washington College under the presidency of Robert E. Lee, Graves had won the Robinson medal in 1868 for the highest attainments in Latin, Greek, and mathematics, and in 1869 he won it again for similar attainments in history, English literature, moral philosophy, and modern languages. Following graduation he served as assistant professor of English and modern languages, and while teaching began the study of law, in which he graduated in 1873 with great distinction. After serving on the Washington and Lee law faculty until 1899, Graves joined the University of Virginia teaching staff. At that institution he won a secure place in the hearts of the students; his high-pitched voice together with his too small derby hat and other mannerisms were lovingly burlesqued in the annual Phi Delta Phi shows. University of Virginia and Washington and Lee alumni joined in tendering "Charlie" Graves a dinner in New York the year before his retirement at the end of the 1926–27 session.

Another student at Washington College under Robert E. Lee was Milton W. Humphreys, professor of Greek at Virginia for twenty-five years, who died in 1928. Having served as a Confederate artilleryman, Humphreys continued the study of ballistics and was recognized as a leading authority. His versatility is further attested by the fact that he refused university professorships in English, modern languages, and physics, gave courses in Hebrew, botany, and mathematics, and twice declined the presidency of a state university. Humphreys retired from the university faculty in 1912 but continued to live in the community until his death.

Dr. Harry T. Marshall of the medical faculty died of pneumonia in 1929 at the American Hospital in Paris, following an operation. He was described by Medical Dean Harvey E. Jordan as "the greatly beloved and widely honored professor of pathology and bacteriology." A man of compassion and high sensitivity, he was also notably absentminded. After a score of years on the faculty, Dr. Marshall's health began to fail, and he went to Europe in hope of recovery. He was buried in Brussels. During his active years he served as president of the Association of Pathologists and Bacteriologists and as a member of the State Board of Health.

Another loss to the university was the departure in 1930 of the Reverend Noble C. Powell, for ten years rector of St. Paul's Episcopal Church, to accept a call from Emmanuel Church, Baltimore. "Parson" Powell, as he was known to the undergraduates, had entered into the life of the student body in many ways and was greatly admired and highly popular. *College Topics* commented that "he has set a standard for future college rectors that will be either a severe handicap or a powerful inspiration to his successors. . . . It will be hard to think of the university without him."

Formal tribute to the memory of Woodrow Wilson was paid on Founder's Day 1929 when a bronze tablet, the gift of the classes of 1925 and 1928, was unveiled on the south front of the Rotunda. S. D. Blackford, '25, made the presentation and Dr. Alderman responded. The room at 31 West Range, occupied by Wilson as a student, was restored and equipped with late nineteenth-century furniture, thanks to the generosity of Cary N. Weisiger and Bernard M. Baruch. The refurbished room was officially opened on the day the memorial tablet was unveiled; Mrs. Wilson visited it and expressed herself as pleased.

Another addition to the Grounds in these years was an ancient fourteen-foot limestone pinnacle that had adorned the chapel at Merton College, Oxford University, and was a gift to the University of Virginia. Four such pinnacles had been erected on the chapel in 1451, and when they were declared unsafe in recent times, it was decided to distribute them. The university's arrived in 1927 and was placed in the garden of Pavilion VI between East Lawn and East Range.

The Raven Society completed an important project in 1928 that had been on its agenda for nearly a decade and a half, namely, marking the grave of Elizabeth Arnold Poe in St. John's churchyard, Richmond. The plan to place a stone at the unmarked resting place of Edgar Allan Poe's beautiful and talented mother was suggested in 1912 by Henry A. Cowardin, Jr., a member of the society, and was enthusiastically approved by the membership. Entertainment consisting of music, readings, and speeches was given in Cabell Hall the following month to raise funds for the project, and in the succeeding year Miss Betty Booker gave a concert in Madison Hall for the same purpose. Finally in 1928 the actual marking took place in Richmond, with James Southall Wilson as the speaker. The precise location of the grave had to be guessed at, for Elizabeth Poe had been buried near the wall in one corner of the churchyard since actresses were looked down on in the early nineteenth century. Samuel P. Cowardin, Jr., a Raven, deserves much credit for bringing about the ultimate success of the effort.

Poe's room at 13 West Range was completely refurnished by the Ravens in 1930, thanks to "gracious and invaluable feminine assistance." Then in 1941 a more elaborate restoration

24. William Minor Lile in 1911, dean of the Law School, 1904–32.

was carried out under the direction of Edmund S. Campbell, head of the School of Architecture, who did considerable research to make the project authentic. Alterations recreated the room as it was in Poe's day. For example, the relatively modern door was replaced by an original door from 49 West Range, while iron latches for the shutters were taken from No. 51. Brick for the hearth came from the anatomical building, an original Jeffersonian structure destroyed to make way for Alderman Library. Twin closets, one on each side of the fireplace, were put back, while panes of original glass were collected here and there and placed in the window. Poe had spent $24 for second-hand furniture when he moved into the room in 1826, and Campbell went to great pains to obtain furniture appropriate to the period that would, according to his calculations, have sold in that year for about $24.

Edwin A. Alderman had come to the university as president under several handicaps, but these were surmounted. Chief among them was the opposition of most faculty members to abandoning the old chairman of the faculty system and serving under a president. The fact that Alderman was not a graduate of the university or a Virginian also was regarded by some as a liability. But it took him only a few years to win over faculty, students, and alumni. At the end of his sixth year in office, 1910, the teaching staff unanimously presented him with a loving cup which bore this inscription: "To Edwin A. Alderman in grateful recognition of his devoted and efficient services to the University of Virginia, in the increase of its resources, in the expansion of its work, in the enhancement of its usefulness without sacrifice of its standards and traditions, and also of his just and sympathetic attitude toward his colleagues." Dumas Malone regarded the presentation of this cup as "in some sense the most signal triumph of his [Alderman's] life."

As time went on, faculty support for the president's policies was no longer unanimous, although the attitude was predominantly favorable. For example, there were those who deplored his desire to increase the university's enrollment and his democratization of the institution by appealing for a larger contingent from the public schools. History Prof. Thomas Cary Johnson spoke with high admiration of Alderman's personal charm and excellent training for a university presidency, but added that he "was the man who first started the deterioration of the university; that is, turning it into a great democratic institution. . . . His first serious [mis]step was restricting the dormitories to first year students." Dean B. F. D. Runk also had "great respect for Alderman. . . . He was a gentleman and friendly with all the students . . . but I didn't like some of his ideas of trying to increase the university's size."

It was generally agreed that he was a man of great suavity and impressive presence in any company, but there was also criticism of his mannerisms and his undue awareness of his prestigious position. As he strolled over the Grounds with dignity he bowed ceremoniously to ladies as he passed, but frequently did not remove his hat. As Malone puts it, "At times he wore his honors with swagger," but "his humor was disarming." Well-liked by most professors, students, and alumni, he represented the university before foundations and the public with golden words and complete aplomb. His oratory was widely admired; indeed he was one of the most flawless public speakers of his era, and recognized, too, as the most prominent spokesman for the South. Some leading undergraduates were not among his admirers; Prof. Robert K. Gooch said concerning Alderman's early years at the university, when he himself was an undergraduate, "the kind of students that I respected were not very keen on President Alderman." Nicknamed "Tony" by the University of North Carolina students soon after he became president there because of his fondness for dressing well, the sobriquet followed him to Virginia. The word *tony* was in common usage in the late nineteenth and early twentieth centuries as signifying "high toned" or "genteel." As time passed, Alderman became increasingly fastidious as to his clothes, and his collection of thirty canes was almost awe-inspiring.

President Alderman was not a scholar in the ordinary sense of the term. His only earned degree was the Ph.B. that he received at Chapel Hill in 1882, and he made no effort to obtain a graduate diploma. From the University of North Carolina he went to the public schools, where his three-year statewide crusade in their behalf, with Charles McIver, was of well nigh legendary renown. Much later, of course, he was the recipient of honorary degrees from about a dozen institutions, including Harvard, Yale, Columbia, and Johns Hopkins. But he was not a profound student in any one discipline; rather he was a widely read, cultivated academician with a deep understanding of the meaning of education and exceptional capacity for elucidating his educational ideas.

But if Alderman was hardly a profound scholar, he was endowed with great literary skill, as is evidenced in his classic memorial address on the career of Woodrow Wilson, who had died Feb. 3, 1924, delivered to a joint session of the U.S. Congress on Dec. 15 of that year. Wilson had told Adm. Cary T. Grayson that he regarded Alderman as the most eloquent man he had known, and Mrs. Wilson suggested that the University of Virginia president be invited to make the memorial deliverance. At first he declined, as he was loaded with work at the time, but the date was postponed in the hope that he would accept, and he finally did so. Several months of reading and meditation went into the preparation of the address, and it is difficult to see how it could have been improved upon. Those who heard it were enthusiastic, but it is perhaps even more striking when read, and the rolling rhythms of the speaker's elegant prose can be thoughtfully savored. It would be difficult to find a single cliché in its thirty-eight printed pages, its tone is statesmanlike, and there is an inspirational quality from beginning to end. Wilson's faults are conceded; yet the man's greatness comes through with abundant clarity. As an example of Alderman's balanced judgments consider the following as a summing up of the rights and wrongs in the tragic fight over the League of Nations: "I may be permitted the reflection that something less of malice in the hearts of his enemies, and something more of compromise in his own heart, and something more of political genius and firm purpose in the hearts of those who held the faith, and there might have been another world!"

Alderman's platform technique was not the old-fashioned, stem-winding, table-pounding type for which the South had long been famous. "I deliberately refrained from a display of forensic oratory," he said later of his address on Wilson. "I wanted to show the North and West that a southerner could talk straight and clear without making a windmill of his arms or a megaphone of his voice." It was nothing new for him to rely upon freshness of diction and smoothness of delivery rather than histrionic effects. But in earlier years he had had to refrain entirely from public speaking, since the tuberculosis from which he suffered had settled in his larynx as well as his lungs. The cure was finally sufficiently complete for him to use his voice to great effect on public occasions.

Alderman was overwhelmed with congratulations on his address in commemoration of Wilson. Hundreds of letters poured in from all over the country, and the full text was published in numerous newspapers. Charles W. Eliot, the retired president of Harvard, said he was moved to tears several times as he read it, and Bernard M. Baruch, chairman of the War Industries Board under Wilson, wrote, "You lifted once more the torch that he lighted." Alderman was promptly elected to the American Academy of Arts and Letters. He also was mentioned in various quarters as a well-qualified candidate for the Democratic nomination for president of the United States. He was not at all interested and commented in writing to a friend: "Well, I am a cool-headed man getting well along in years, and free from all insensate ambitions. I once told Walter Page, and he howled like Gargantua when I said it, that I would rather catch a ten-pound land-locked salmon than to be the whole of Taft's administration." His one ambition, he declared to Sen. Claude Swanson, was to "see the University of Virginia retain its place as the foremost institution in the southern states," and he added: "Its preeminence is seriously threatened, and will be destroyed in a period of five years unless something is done."

Soon thereafter he declined the chancellorship of the University of Georgia. The University of Virginia Alumni Association's Board of Managers expressed its thanks in the following terms: "The 21 years during which you have directed the policies and energized the activities of our alma mater have been years of stirring achievement. Her gain in endowments, in student attendance, in academic authority, in scientific equipment, in teaching power, in public usefulness and in popular esteem have been magnificent and in large measure your personal work. They have won for you the sympathy, the support, the admiration, the confidence and the loyalty of our alumni."

Engineering Dean John L. Newcomb was formally appointed assistant to the president in 1926, before Alderman left on one of his numerous summer trips to Europe, some of which were paid for by wealthy friends. Newcomb's administrative ability had been demonstrated in his chairmanship of the centennial observance in 1921, and he had shown marked capacity for dealing with the General Assembly in helping to defeat the attempted removal of the Medical School to Richmond. As a matter of actual practice, Newcomb had been Alderman's assistant since the centennial, and this was now being made official. For all his merits, Alderman was not primarily an administrator; rather he was a planner, a dreamer, and an impressive personality who lent prestige to the university.

When Herbert Hoover was pitted against Alfred E. Smith for the presidency in the bitterly fought campaign of 1928, Alderman openly backed Smith, despite his own belief in national prohibition and Smith's well-known opposition to it. Alderman denounced the religious prejudice that was rampant because of Smith's Roman Catholicism, and spoke of the New York governor's "amazing and inspiring career . . . an executive of rare gifts. . . . I do not care to what church he belongs." Smith, of course, was badly defeated and even lost Virginia, until then a rock-ribbed Democratic stronghold. One of Jefferson's statues on the Grounds was promptly draped in black by unknown parties, and on it was a card with the following: "To the memory of Jeffersonian Democracy and Religious Freedom in Virginia—Died November 6, 1928."

In his 1929 Founder's Day address Alderman deplored what he called the students' "chiefest defect . . . a too intense individualism." This fault had been noted by others, and the president elaborated by saying that the attitude "tends to overemphasize one's rights and to minimize one's duties; and danger lies that way, and the great philosophy needs to be looked into, lest it become a vice instead of a virtue."

Alderman was completing twenty-five years as president of the university, and the progress achieved under his leadership was remarkable. The *Alumni News* published the following in its December 1928 issue:

	1904	1929
Officers of Instruction	48	290
University Departments	5	9
Academic Schools	15	28
Students, Regular Session	500	2,200

25. Lady Astor, donor of university tennis courts, greets Captain
Bill Luke of the university football team at a game with the
University of South Carolina in 1928. South Carolina Captain
Cooper holds the ball.

Students, Summer Quarter	0	2,700
Students, Extension Service	0	1,528
Students, Nurses' Training School	0	125
Total Annual Income	$160,000	$1,741,352
Productive Endowment	$350,000	$10,000,000
Annual State Appropriation	$50,000	$400,000
Value Bldgs. and Equipment	$1,500,000	$9,000,000

"Dr. Alderman's administration is as much an honor to himself as it is a glory and a power to the state," the Richmond *News Leader*, edited by Douglas S. Freeman, commented. "It is given to few men to achieve in a quarter of a century such amazing and solid advances." And the New York *Times* said: "The University of Virginia . . . during these 25 years has come to be more than a 'secluded nursery for the production of scholars and gentlemen.' It still performs that function, but it has come to be an institution to which all the people of the state may look for instruction and guidance. Democracy in these years has had no voice more eloquent and appealing than [Alderman's]. . . . He has done more than enlarge and improve Jefferson's institution; he has often spoken for America in shining and stately sentences that will be permanently preserved in American literature."

Another accolade came from the university's alumni during a luncheon at Finals, when they presented the president with a silver platter "in commemoration of the completion of 25 years of unselfish, abundant and inspired service enriched by rare eloquence, wise leadership and high vision of a future of dignity, beauty, power and renown for our alma mater." The Edwin Anderson Alderman Alumni Fund was established under a permanent board of fifteen, as a testimonial to "the distinguished services of the first president of the university." A year later a bust of Alderman by the Russian sculptor Sergei Konenkov, the gift of Charles Steele, '78, was presented to the university and placed in the Rotunda.

Surprisingly little seems to have been said in most published accounts of the grave health problems under which Alderman labored after 1912. His bout with tuberculosis made it necessary for him, throughout the remainder of his life, to spend only the latter half of the morning in his office, with rest in the early afternoon. He seldom went out in the evening, except for faculty or committee meetings. And there were several other illnesses while he was at the university, in addition to tuberculosis and its side effects. He was operated on for an abdominal hernia in 1919 and developed a gastric ulcer two years later, necessitating rigid diet. In the mid-1920s he broke his arm and suffered with a carbuncle. The following year he began having eye trouble and bad headaches. Alderman was fortunate in having so able an assistant as John L. Newcomb, who could keep the administrative machine operating while he was ill or recuperating or on vacation. His vacations were often prolonged. When he wasn't spending the summer in Europe he was likely to be fishing in Canada. Often he was invited by affluent friends to elaborate fishing camps, in one of which he pursued the elusive salmon and the other trout and bass. Alderman was never happier than when casting his lure into a lake or stream.

While his health had always been more or less precarious, the public was shocked to read in the press on the morning of Apr. 30, 1931, that he had suffered a fatal apoplectic stroke the previous night on board a Baltimore and Ohio railroad train, en route to the inauguration of Harry Woodburn Chase as president of the University of Illinois. Removed from the train at Connellsville, Pa., he died soon afterward in the hospital there, two weeks short of his seventieth birthday. He was buried in the university cemetery after services in the university chapel. Clergymen taking part were the Reverend Dwight M. Chalmers, pastor of the Charlottesville Presbyterian Church, of which Alderman was a member; the Reverend William Kyle Smith, secretary of Madison Hall; the Reverend Beverley D. Tucker, Jr., of St. Paul's Episcopal Church, Richmond, who had been a much-beloved rector of St. Paul's Church at the university; the Reverend Noble C. Powell of Emmanuel Episcopal Church, Baltimore, and the Reverend Walter L. Lingle, president of Davidson College. Eight students served as pallbearers.

Tributes to Alderman poured in from throughout the country. Scores of newspapers were high in praise of his achievements, and hundreds of letters and telegrams were received. Among those sending messages were President Herbert Hoover, John D. Rockefeller, Jr., and Mrs. Woodrow

Wilson. President Wilson had contemplated naming Alderman ambassador to the Court of St. James's, according to one published report, and many believed the appointment would have been made but for his health. A resolution of the Alumni Board of Managers termed Alderman "an orator without rival; a statesman without artifice; a philosopher without fanaticism; a scholar without pedantry; an administrator without pride; an instructor without bias; a wit without vinegar; a Christian without cant; a friend without hesitancy."

John L. Newcomb, dean of the Engineering School since 1925 and assistant to the president since 1926, was named acting president of the university, pending choice of a permanent successor.

Dumas Malone summed up the meaning of Alderman's life and career in his excellent biography: "Everywhere it was remarked that he had been the most conspicuous spokesman of the South in his day and the noblest interpreter of the section to itself and the outside world. . . . The ideas which he implemented and the faith which he kindled . . . will survive long after the echoes of his voice have died away. . . . This wearer of the mantle of Jefferson will continue to be regarded as one of the torchbearers of his time."

THREE

John Lloyd Newcomb
Takes Over

THE TASK OF finding a successor to Edwin Alderman as
president of the university was undertaken by the Board
of Visitors. A committee of the board, headed by the rector,
Frederic W. Scott, determined to search the country for the
best-qualified man. All kinds of public celebrities were being
talked of as potential choices. Judge T. Munford Boyd of the
Charlottesville Juvenile and Domestic Relations Court wrote
in *College Topics* that pretty much everybody whose name was
seen in headlines, "with the possible exception of Bishop
[James] Cannon and Mussolini," was being mentioned as a
possibility. The steady worsening of the Great Depression
seemed to call for an early decision.

There were two schools of thought as to the type of individual who should be selected. On the one hand there were
those who wanted a "big name," someone from politics, business, or the professions who would automatically cause the
institution to be known and would be useful in raising additional endowment. On the other there were those who
preferred a man from academic life who understood the management of a university and its special problems. Acting President Newcomb was thoroughly capable of carrying on routine
operations until the choice could be made; in fact he had been
virtually running the university for a decade while President
Alderman, working only part-time, served as "front man,"
making the speeches and appearing before the foundations.

The Board of Visitors began by approaching several prominent personalities from the nonacademic world. Harry F.
Byrd, who had just served out his term as governor of Virginia
and made a national reputation in the process, was the first to
be approached; he declined on the ground that he was "not
qualified by training or temperament." Byrd had refused
shortly before to be considered for the presidency of Washington and Lee. Newton D. Baker, secretary of war in Woodrow Wilson's cabinet, was the next celebrity to be approached.
He too declined. Baker was interviewed again after the Democratic National Convention of 1932, in which he had been an
unsuccessful candidate for the presidential nomination against
Franklin D. Roosevelt, and once more the answer was negative. The committee then journeyed to New York and called
on John W. Davis, eminent Wall Street lawyer and Democratic
nominee for the presidency in 1924. Like Baker, Davis was
gracious in his refusal, but he felt that he was "first and last a
lawyer" and that he ought not to stray into "other paths." In
late 1932 the visitors went back to Davis, hoping that he would
change his mind, but to no avail. (The foregoing facts appear
in an article by Brent Tarter, published in the *Virginia Magazine of History and Biography* for October 1979.)

Some nineteen months had passed since Alderman's death,
and the presidency had not been filled. Distinct annoyance
was being expressed by many faculty members as well as students. The latter evidenced their admiration for Acting President Newcomb in the spring by 1933 by voting him the first
Raven Award ever given by the Raven Society to a faculty
member. The citation read: "His extraordinary handling of
the university's problems, so that it has suffered in this crisis
[the depression] far less in proportion to other established institutions, have [*sic*] shown his preeminence and leadership
beyond question."

Finally, at a board meeting in June 1933, Rector Scott
moved Newcomb's election, but the board voted the motion
down. It desired additional names from the world of academe. Several more months went by, and faculty, students,
and alumni began openly expressing support of Newcomb. In
August sixteen professors, led by William H. Echols, urged his
election. The following month the entire faculty voted 110 to
3 for Newcomb, since he "has clearly demonstrated under cir-

26. Philip F. duPont, who left $6,000,000 to the university.

cumstances as difficult as any officer is likely to encounter, his extraordinary capacity as a university executive." Two days later the Student Senate adopted a resolution urging Newcomb's appointment, and heads of eighteen student organizations signed it. The resolution recommended the acting president as a man who would not "wish to foist on Virginia any experimental schemes or ultramodern theories of education."

This last was one of the undoubted secrets of Newcomb's strength with the university's faculty, students, and alumni. He was a man who could be counted on not to "rock the boat"; his views were well known. Most members of the faculty in that era were conservative, in contrast to many professors in later years, and they preferred a man who would move ahead in the old grooves to one who might go "wenching after strange gods." There was no telling what somebody brought in from outside might do. Most students and alumni agreed with the faculty on this. In addition, Newcomb had demonstrated marked ability in managing the university's affairs, especially under the stress of the mounting depression, and that too counted heavily in his favor. With so many university groups calling for his election and several alumni chapters following suit, the Board of Visitors capitulated. A minority were still reluctant to choose him, but they were won over, and on Oct. 6, 1933, John Lloyd Newcomb was elected unanimously to the presidency of the University of Virginia. He was fifty-one years old and had been born in Gloucester County, Va. A B.A. of William and Mary (1900), he took his Civil Engineering degree at the university in 1905. Four years later he joined the university's engineering faculty and the following session (1910) was made a full professor. After a decade and a half he was chosen dean of engineering, and the following year assistant to the president, a position that he held along with the deanship. He was married in 1924 to Mrs. Grace Shields Russell, a native of Richmond who had grown up there in what had been the girlhood home of Poe's first "Helen." The Newcombs had no children.

John L. Newcomb was as different from Edwin A. Alderman as anybody could be. Whereas Alderman was a spectacular personality, sometimes pompous and too conscious of his exalted state, Newcomb was an able administrator but modest and shy. Alderman was a superlative public speaker, aware of his wizardry with words; Newcomb was obviously embarrassed in making public appearances. He had a mild form of palsy, which added to his embarrassment. Alderman was nationally known; Newcomb was almost unheard of, except in certain educational circles.

It would not be fair to say, however, that Newcomb was a wholly unimaginative educational executive, concerned solely with day to day operations. He was interested in the philosophical side of education; almost as soon as he joined the university faculty in the early years of the century he published an article urging a broader training for engineering students, extending to disciplines outside the customary professional regimen, somewhat similar to the expanded curriculum adopted much later in the better engineering schools.

The catastrophic drop in state revenues that followed the worldwide business panic of 1929–32 had caused the General Assembly to decree a 10 percent across-the-board cut in appropriations to the university for 1932–33, before Newcomb took office as the full-fledged president of the institution. He had hardly gotten his seat warm in that position when another 10 percent slash was decreed. All members of the administrative and teaching staffs were accordingly hit with this 20 percent reduction in pay, and some of the allowances for fellowships and assistantships were cut much more heavily. Austerity was the rule throughout the university. Newcomb's great administrative ability, his intimate knowledge of the university's financial structure and the ramifications thereof, made it possible for the institution to weather the storm with less disruption than most. Throughout the period no faculty member failed to receive his pay check.

Student discipline was a perennial problem at Virginia, as at nearly all centers of the higher learning, but Acting Dean Ivey F. Lewis reported to the Staunton alumni in late 1932 that the young men were "working harder and behaving better than at any time in the seventeen years I have been connected with the university." Failures for the first term in that year were only about 20 percent. Hard times may have caused the students to take greater advantage of their opportunities. In former years, said the dean, the professors used to tell new students that there was one rule and one request. The rule was "Be a gentleman" and the request was "Don't shoot out the lights." He said he was seeking larger responsibilities for student government, specifically for the Student Senate, and a greater degree of cooperation between it and university officials. The Student Senate had been chosen by the Student Assembly, composed of representatives of fifty student organizations.

The Senate called a meeting of the Assembly in 1932 when *College Topics* suspended publication for lack of funds. The Assembly recommended that the Board of Visitors establish a compulsory student activity fee of $4.25 for each student, of which $1.50 would go to *Topics* and $2.75 to *Corks and Curls*. Furthermore, 500 additional subscriptions were obtained for the newspaper, sufficient to keep it alive. In 1934 the board approved a $1.50 student fee for *Topics* but nothing for *Corks and Curls*.

The enlarged role of the student Senate was spoken of at Finals by Acting President Newcomb. The Senate would become "increasingly representative of all student groups," he declared, and he added: "I would that there were time for me to speak of the formation of student committees on the Lawn, the Ranges and in some of the new dormitories, who have voluntarily undertaken to bring home to all students . . . a deeper sense of individual responsibility for the maintenance of proper student conduct."

The administration had been caught up in a real furor over the new dormitories, opened for the supposed benefit of first-year men. They were luxurious by comparison with the other accommodations for students, but the fact did not impress the average undergraduate, and the uproar was tremendous. Even before they were built west of Monroe Hill, many older students had objected to them in the belief that they would tend to undermine university traditions. After the dormitories were got into operation, they were "as far removed from the life of Virginia as if they had been built on Boston Common," as one critic put it. "They are laughed at by some," he said, "sneered at by others, and affectionately termed 'hell's half-acre' by those who live within hearing distance."

The Reverend Beverley D. Tucker, Jr., of Richmond, one of the university's first Rhodes Scholars, who served as rector of

St. Paul's church at the university from 1911 to 1920, attempted to calm the troubled waters. "The root of the problem is not the dormitories," he said in a letter to the college newspaper. "It is the expansion of the university from a small student body of 500 to 600 into a student body of 2,500. Some provision for housing was no longer a debatable question but a necessity. The dormitories no doubt present immediate questions of adjustment which it will probably take several years to solve. I can remember when Dawson's Row was the promised land of social prestige and rooms on the Lawn and Ranges were rated rather low in the scale. I understand that today there is a long waiting list for Lawn rooms and that Dawson's Row is hunting for lodgers."

These observations were without appreciable effect. T. K. Tindale, a student writing in the *University of Virginia Magazine* in 1932, declared that the dormitories were "hotbeds of sophomoric iniquity, and bedlam where no man can study" and that "wild tales of clandestine escapades fill the ears of the townspeople."

Finally in 1935 it was decreed that one suite in each of the twelve halls would be set aside for two older students who would serve as counselors. After their installation, Dean Lewis explained that "only the necessary minimum of supervision is given." The new arrangement was greeted with violent opposition from one element of students and with support from another. The former group saw in it the threat that "house mothers" would be employed in the future and that all phases of university life would be strictly supervised. Also it was seen as a plot of the fraternities to install their members as counselors, and through them to recruit choice "goats." Those undergraduates favoring the new arrangement viewed it as tending to remove a stain from the university's good name and as beneficial to the first-year men.

This controversy is typical of many that took place over the years at the university. Decade after decade students were protesting additional regulations as contrary to the traditions of individual liberty on which, they said, the institution had been founded. Virginia men, they contended, were supposed to be free "to go to hell in their own way," if such was their fancy. For example, Ben Dulany, one of the ablest students of that era, an extremely literate writer whose column "The Bedlam-

ite" in *College Topics* was original and refreshing, expressed this
view. Writing in the *Alumni News* in 1935, he declared that we
now have "proctors" in the dormitories, and he added: "First-
year men . . . will instinctively feel that these older students
are there to regulate their personal doings. 'Well, I'll try to get
away with it' will more and more replace 'I can't do it because
I'm a student at Virginia.'" (For a gracefully written, insight-
ful, and amusing analysis of what makes the University of
Virginia tick, see Dulany's "Enter by This Gateway" in the *University of Virginia Magazine*, Feb. 1932.)

In an effort to meet criticism, the administration devised
and put into effect a "modified form of self-government" for
the twelve halls. Under this plan each hall had a self-government committee of five, consisting of two counselors and three
elected first-year men. These committees were given responsibility for administering regulations adopted by the counselors and approved by members of the halls. "It is the desire of
the administration to have the first-year students living in the
dormitories assume the responsibilities of self-government as
rapidly as they show the development of a capacity to provide
effective control of disturbing elements in dormitory life," said
Dean Lewis.

Rooms in the dorms were solely for males, of course, and
the few coeds in the university were without such facilities.
Supposedly all women matriculates were enrolled in the
graduate or professional schools, but four girl graduates of
Lane High School in Charlottesville and one from St. Anne's
near the university were quietly admitted to the College in
September 1932. The university administration apparently
decided that since the parents of the young ladies were taxpayers, it would be the part of wisdom to let their daughters
in without any fuss. The first to apply was Eloise Virginia
Bishop; she informed two of her friends in the Lane High
graduating class, Virginia Snyder and Irene Rose Mann, of
her acceptance, and they too applied and were enrolled. All
were topflight students. The fourth alumna from Lane was
Carolyn Maddox, and the St. Anne's applicant was Mary Scott
Parker of the university. The presence of this quintet in the
College was obvious to the male students who had classes with
them, but it was not generally realized that they had been admitted straight from high school. Miss Bishop was instructed

27. Harrison F. Flippin, world record holder in high hurdles and national pentathlon champion in 1927.

to transfer to the School of Education for her senior year if she wished to take part in the 1936 graduation exercises, and she did so. Misses Snyder and Mann got their diplomas by waiting to graduate in that year's summer school; Miss Mann went on to take an M.A. and Ph.D. Misses Parker and Maddox were not candidates for degrees. A few wives and daughters of faculty members also were admitted to the College during these years, under a special dispensation.

Mrs. Mary Cooke Branch Munford (Mrs. Beverley B. Munford), who led the fight for many years to obtain the admission of women to the university on the same basis as men, was memorialized in 1941 with a handsome marble tablet in Alderman Library. She had died in 1938 after serving for twelve years on the university's Board of Visitors. Jackson Davis of the General Education Board made the presentation at the unveiling and praised Mrs. Munford for her work in educational and humanitarian fields. The tablet, which hangs on the wall of the library's reference reading room, was accepted by R. Gray Williams, rector of the university. It says: "She carried the devotion of a great mind and flaming spirit into unselfish service to public education throughout Virginia. . . . Her memorial is in numberless young lives set free."

The issue of Negro enrollment also arose during these years. Alice Jackson, daughter of a black Richmond druggist, applied in 1935 for admission to the graduate school, but the Board of Visitors instructed Dean Metcalf to reject her application on the ground that "education of white and colored persons in the same schools is contrary to long-established and fixed policy of the commonwealth of Virginia," and "for other good and sufficient reasons." The National Association for the Advancement of Colored People evidently decided that the time was not ripe for filing suit. Legal action would not be instituted by the NAACP until some years later and in connection with another application.

Disillusionment over conditions in the world as the aftermath of the 1914–18 war gave rise to a wave of pacifism in this country and Europe. The Oxford oath, under which young Englishmen pledged themselves "never to fight for king and country," was one extreme manifestation. The question whether to establish a Reserve Officers Training Corps at the University of Virginia arose in 1935 as part of this wide-ranging discussion. Federal funds totaling $35,000 were available for the purpose, but the Board of Visitors decided not to establish the ROTC unit at that time.

As war clouds loomed on the horizon, an organization called the Anti-War Committee of the University of Virginia, which included representatives of the Jefferson Society, Madison Hall, and the National Students' League, issued an appeal to all students to join in an antiwar rally on Apr. 12 in Cabell Hall. *College Topics* had published an editorial the month before headed "Pro Patria Mori Is Bunk." President Newcomb said classes would be suspended from 11:30 to 12:30 o'clock to permit the students to attend the meeting. President Franklin D. Roosevelt had said that the United States must avoid war at all costs, and various publications, including the Richmond *Times-Dispatch*, endorsed the rally. Murat Williams, outgoing editor of *College Topics* who would be a Rhodes Scholar, presided, and the principal speaker was J. B. Matthews, secretary of the Fellowship of Reconciliation. Brief antiwar talks were made by Dean Ivey Lewis and Professors Robert K. Gooch and Scott Buchanan. The hall was packed with about one thousand students, and "chaotic demonstrations" followed the declaration by Francis Franklin, representing the National Students' League, that tens of thousands of students would "take the Oxford oath never to support the government of the United States in any war it may undertake." No such action was suggested at the meeting, which ended without the adoption of any formal resolutions.

The National Students' League at the university—which was counterbalanced by the student chapter of the conservative American Liberty League—was headed by F. Palmer Weber, a native of Smithfield, who had triumphed over poverty and tuberculosis to become perhaps the most brilliant student in the institution. Regarded by his fellows as "the university's resident Communist," Weber described himself as a Christian Socialist. He was not a Communist, of course, but was the spokesman for left-wing radicalism on the Grounds and was active in antiwar rallies. In later years he became extremely successful in New York as an investment counselor and was generous in his financial support of the university.

Clarence Hathaway, editor of the Communist *Daily Worker*, spoke in Cabell Hall on May 21 to the accompaniment of boos, applause, and fights in the audience. Hathaway, representing the National Students' League, discussed the Communist program, and such pandemonium reigned during most of his address that he decided to adjourn the meeting and resume in Jeff Hall, where he finished his discourse and remained for three hours answering questions. Stern admonitions from the university's Administrative Council termed the disorder "ill-mannered and contrary to the habits and practice of the students at this university." "More drastic action" was promised if it occurred again.

Another antiwar rally was held on Nov. 8 at the request of the Jefferson Society and sixteen student organizations, including the Student Senate. Classes were again suspended for an hour, but only 450 attended. Francis P. Miller, chairman of the World Christian Student Federation, who would be a candidate for governor of Virginia in 1949, was the chief speaker. He called on the United States to develop a "positive foreign policy" since it now has "no foreign policy at all," and lead in forming an international police force to keep the peace. Engineering Dean W. S. Rodman also spoke, as did student leaders, one of whom asked, "Are we men enough to stay out of war?" All speeches were fairly mild. It was the last of the major antiwar rallies.

While the Jefferson Society had been prominent in arranging these affairs, the society at this time was only a pale reflection of its earlier self. A former president stated that "a membership of 200 is now but two score, an overflowing treasury is now an income-expense account." Another member said during the previous year that he was one of only eight members who were still attending meetings. The organization seemed almost ready to follow the example of the Washington Society, which had become extinct in the 1920s, but the "Jeff" would revive markedly in subsequent years. The "Wash" came back to life in 1939, although on an entirely different basis, with four prominent professors and sixteen student leaders as members. A spokesman stated that it would not compete in any way with the Jeff and "does not have any of the aims and purposes of the Jefferson Society." Its own aims and purposes were "to encourage intellectual curiosity, gentlemanliness, congeniality and the idealization of the Virginia gentleman," and to stress patriotism.

The Student Union, which had begun operations before World War I and then faded out, was revived in 1933 and opened for business on the redecorated lower floor of Madison Hall. Offices for *College Topics, Corks and Curls,* the university magazine, and the self-help bureau were there along with rooms for games, meetings, and reading. Three years later it was explained that the Student Union had "four separate and distinct divisions of activity": operating the Dulany Library for the nonprofitable exchange of second-hand books, a memorial to Thomas Carter Dulany, who died at the university in the 1920s while a student; assisting visitors to see the university through the cooperation of the information and guide division; arranging such activities as ping-pong and badminton tournaments; and providing entertainment for "the Sweet Briar contingent" and similar visitors, as well as for participants in the Virginia Literary and Athletic League.

A flurry of excitement was aroused in January 1934 by the appearance of a weekly student newspaper, the *University Forum.* While its primary object was explained as "not to damn *Topics,*" it published two anonymous blasts from members of that paper's staff, one of which termed *Topics* "deplorable." The other said, it "is so poor, so dull, so childish and at times illiterate, that I can see but one excuse for its continued existence—there must be some record of events at the University of Virginia. . . . The last five editors of *College Topics,* with one exception, have been members of the same fraternity."

The *University Forum* said it would "bring to light the true state of affairs, whether the truth be pleasing or otherwise," and would present both sides of local controversy, "provoke a little thought, and perhaps above all maintain a healthy sense of humor among the students." It presented arguments for and against abolishing intercollegiate athletics, with Allan T. Gwathmey taking the affirmative and Hunsdon Cary, Jr., the negative. Other live topics also were addressed. The last issue of the session appeared Apr. 6, and while the *Forum* expressed the intention of resuming publication in the fall, it did not do so. Hence it had a life of only about two and a half months.

Drinking at the university was an almost continuous subject of discussion, and a student poll, with fewer than half of the students voting, showed that 713 drank and 207 did not, 452 had gotten drunk and 436 had not, 547 favored modification of the dry law, 265 preferred outright repeal, 90 urged strict enforcement, and 18 liked the existing situation.

A prominent emissary from Shifflett's Hollow, perhaps the premier center of manufacture supplying moonshine to thirsty Virginia men, fell into the hands of the police. Described as "well known among Virginia students who often buy his farm produce," he was arrested in 1931 on University Circle "when engaged in making business calls." Bootleggers and moonshiners continued their regular traffic around the Grounds for a time after prohibition's repeal at the end of 1933. The depression was at its worst, and the dubious elixir known as "white mule" was cheaper than the wares vended in the state's newly established A.B.C. stores. By 1935 Ben Dulany was writing that "mason jars have gone to the limbo of spinning wheels and bustles," but the proclaimed demise of this receptacle was premature, since mason jars would be used around the Grounds for alcoholic potations of one sort of another over a period of several decades.

Beer was widely consumed in the local beer parlors after repeal. When the long drought ended and authentic Budweiser, Schlitz, and Pabst came on the market, the boys were quick to make the best of the opportunity. Hard liquor also was drunk in the fraternity houses and dormitories, mainly on weekends and in the form of highballs. The point was made in a *Topics* editorial that Virginia men "drink in the open, serving from our own bars, without any of the hypocritical sneakings to 'catch a short one' in the back room or lavatory . . . as students in other institutions are accustomed to do." The paper expressed the conviction that there is no more drinking, overall, at Virginia than at other schools and that "all respect that man who conducts himself as if he were in his own home."

Drunkenness at football games in the middle 1930s was "negligible," in the opinion of Capt. Norton Pritchett, director of athletics, who said in 1937 that in the previous three years "drinking has not been one of our problems." Several officials at other Virginia institutions agreed that there had been great improvement in this regard and attributed it to the repeal of prohibition. A University of Virginia student was expelled in 1939 for getting drunk and lying across the railroad tracks. Friends pulled him to safety, but he was removed from the

*28. Novelist Julien Green, an alum-
nus who became the only non-Frenchman ever elected to the French
Academy.*

university's rolls for "violating the laws of the commonwealth," in accord with the rule published in the catalogue.

Pledging of dances in the gym had been ended—that is, students who danced were no longer on their honor to have drunk no alcohol since noon of that day. The pledge had been in effect for most of the 1920s, although it had been abandoned temporarily in the early years of the decade, probably because an intoxicated student who apparently didn't fully realize what he was doing, danced a few steps and was expelled by the Honor Committee. This impressed some as an excessive penalty, under the circumstances, and soon thereafter the dances were "unpledged." But the floor committee charged with keeping order found the task beyond its capabilities, and the previous system was instituted once more. In 1933 it was decided to take off the pledge and put control into the hands of the dance societies. It apparently worked reasonably well in that year, and there was no more pledging.

The holding of dances in the fraternity houses was becoming more and more popular, and the university administration announced a set of rules governing all such affairs sponsored by student organizations in the university community: Permission to hold any such dance must be obtained from the dean's office; "applicants . . . must communicate with Mrs. R. H. Dabney, chairman of the committee on chaperones, who will provide the necessary chaperones; . . . a floor committee shall be appointed and the names listed in the dean's office," and the university "will hold the floor committee responsible for good behavior at all times."

The "excessive individualism" noted and criticized by Dr. Alderman and others continued into the 1930s under the heading "don't give a damnness." Combined with the often deplored aversion to "sticking out one's neck," the prevailing atmosphere around the Grounds was still hostile to any sort of group action designed to improve conditions. There was a flurry of hope that the old ways were being abandoned when Professors Robert K. Gooch and Stringfellow Barr reported that they had actually managed to get members of their classes to engage in open discussion, but this triumphant accomplishment was short-lived. A few years later teachers were bemoaning once more their inability to get students to speak out in class. There were mass departures of students on weekends, from Friday to Monday, or even longer. "The week-end is more of a Virginia tradition than stomping the neck-sticker," said an editorial in the *University of Virginia Magazine*. "It is the only local activity participated in by more than fifty of the student body."

True, hope was expressed during the session of 1931–32 that something in the nature of a renaissance had occurred. A growing number of students were said to be awakening to the fact that "don't give a damnness" was highly detrimental to the institution and that countervailing action should be taken. There was to be a reorganization of the Student Assembly, created two years before, so that it might "serve the university and become a powerful and concrete representative of student thought." This campaign for greater interest in literary, scholastic, and athletic activities achieved only a limited degree of success. An odd note was sounded by Prof. Albert G. A. Balz in a talk to the Jefferson Society. Jeremiads to the effect that the university is going to pot "lack perspective," he declared, since such lamentations had been sounded for twenty-five years, and the renaissance had taken place a quarter of a century ago.

As part of the individualist tradition, support for the athletic teams was spasmodic and uncertain, with the average student apparently taking the view that anything more aggressive would be contrary to the Virginia way of doing things. *College Topics* declared editorially that the atmosphere around the fraternities was "detrimental to interest in activities," and it added: "We are told that each week-end various 'brothers' try to persuade football men to go off pledge because football is no longer worth the work it requires," and "fraternity men bet against the team in open defiance to the feelings of any players who happen to be present." The players themselves refused, as in former years, to wear their "V" sweaters around the Grounds lest this be considered ostentatious.

The University of Virginia, Princeton, and Williams are "generally recognized as the 'country club' colleges of America," *College Topics* declared editorially. "And well may it be said," the paper went on, "for the students of these three take more pains in dress, and the etiquette of play than the students of any other colleges in the country. But does this detract from the specifications of a gentleman? It definitely does not." The editor went on to declare that "there is the other side of college life to consider—studies," and in this category the University of Virginia "stands neither highest nor lowest." The average Virginia student "is not a bookworm," but this does not "detract from the specifications of a gentleman." *Topics* concluded that Virginia men "lead the students of American colleges in the maintenance of a balance in college life."

There appears to be no evidence that the collegiate fads of the 1930s and 1940s—goldfish gulping and stuffing students into telephone booths to the maximum degree possible—had any followers at the university.

A typical Easter Week in the years just before this country entered World War II was that of 1941. It opened on Thursday evening with a dance in Memorial Gymnasium from 10 P.M. to 3 A.M. On Friday afternoon there was a golf match and baseball game with VPI; the annual Sigma Phi Epsilon "Purple Passion Party" followed at the S.P.E. house on Madison Lane from 4 to 6 P.M.; the Delta Tau Delta mint julep party at the D.T.D. house from 5 to 7 P.M.; the Phi Delta Phi Libel Show in Cabell Hall at 8 P.M.; and the dance in the gymnasium from 10 P.M. to 3 A.M. Saturday was inaugurated with a "baseball game" at 5 A.M. (yes, 5 A.M.) in Mad Bowl "between students and their dates"; there followed another baseball game at 3:30 P.M. on Lambeth Field with the University of Michigan; the Sigma Nu party at the Sigma Nu house from 4 to 6 P.M., and the Tommy Dorsey Concert in Cabell Hall from 5 to 6 P.M. The formal Easter Week festivities closed with a dance in the gym from 8 to 12 o'clock. The *Spectator* observed helpfully that "a Mason jar is a receptacle which makes its appearance every Easter Week filled with mint, sugar, ice and bourbon. Easy to hold (literally, not internally) when wrapped in a towel." The S.P.E. Purple Passion Party was not as lurid as it sounded, for the name was taken from the punch of grain alcohol and fruit juice, dubbed "Purple Passion Punch," served at the affair. The entire party took place on the first floor of the house. This S.P.E. bash was a regular feature of Easter Week for a number of years, both before and after the war.

A national magazine declared in 1937 that the University of Virginia is not a place for serious work but rather a place

29. *John S. LaRowe, Virginia's boxing coach, 1922–40.*

where a young man can spend a few years getting "the finest training for convivial intercourse to be found anywhere in the world." Paul B. Barringer, Jr., a prominent alumnus and New York attorney, denounced this "absolute libel" in an address to the alumni-graduate luncheon at Finals. "Every man who has graduated from the university knows that it is a libel," he declared, "but I regret that it expresses a reputation which is widespread in the outside world, which our rivals do not discourage and which . . . some members of our alumni appear in glory in." Barringer went on to comment on the individualism of the average Virginia man, and stated that "Virginia men simply do not take to organization." He added that time after time he had seen the officers of "a rich and numerous alumni association, such as New York, have to go down in their pockets to pay the postage bills and deficits on entertainments given by the association." Terming this "nothing short of a disgrace," he went on to say that "it is a wonder that men can be found to perform the sort of drudgery which maintaining these organizations entails."

Efforts were often made to explain the custom at Virginia of not speaking to persons with whom one had not become acquainted. Prof. Stringfellow Barr's analysis, published in the university *Handbook* for several years, beginning in 1932–33, seemed to be the most widely accepted. Entitled "Comments on a Social System," it pointed out that many men did not return after their first year because "nobody spoke to them," and went on to provide a defense and explanation. Barr's statement is too long to be quoted in full, but he says that "the reason so few Americans ever mature or find themselves is that they are too busy, back-slapping, hand-shaking, 'contacting,' making acquaintances," and he adds: "John Butler Yeats once remarked that Americans had a genius for acquaintance and no capacity for friendship." And he goes on:

I believe he was right, and I further believe that a university is a place in which growing minds can find friendship, in books, in ideas, in other minds. The atmosphere of a business convention is not favorable to the slow incubation of such friendships, any more than a billiard table is a good place for the incubation of an egg. . . . The man who resents not having people speak to him may always profitably ask himself what such people could get out of it if they did speak to him. A more worthwhile goal than achieving easy familiarity with his fellows is to make himself worth knowing. . . . An easy familiarity that denies all distinctions of merit or talent is mediocrity, vulgarity and death.

There is no doubt that the most "rah-rah" college in America is better organized, not necessarily to cure snobbery, but to punish any exhibition of snobbery than the University of Virginia. For that reason snobs flourish here more than in most places. But that the habit of dignity, the custom of restraint, and the determination not to bore other people with an intrusive personality or exuberant vulgarity should in itself be branded as snobbery is sheer nonsense.

There can be no question that the tradition of not speaking at Virginia alienated many of those not spoken to. A letter in the student newspaper in 1931, typical of numerous such expressions, said that the newcomer to the university "feels an iron wall of reserve about him." Five years later John C. Wyllie wrote in the *Alumni News* that students were no longer tipping their hats to every professor, "whether or not an acquaintance." The custom had been universally observed by both professors and students in the 1920s and early 1930s.

Eight fraternities had been virtually controlling elections and editorships for forty years or more, W. Brown Morton, Jr., declared in an article entitled "Virginia Tammany" in the *University of Virginia Magazine* for December 1934. Fraternity men constituted only about half of the student body, but the disproportionate influence wielded by them had been noted as long ago as 1895 by the editor of *Corks and Curls*. Nominations of candidates for officers of the college are "clandestine, so mystery-controlled that not one in ten students can possibly tell who has selected the three names," Morton wrote. "Lambda Pi and Skull & Keys name the slates, but where did these societies acquire this great privilege?" The president of the college was (and is) automatically chairman of the Honor Committee, and in the past ten years all ten presidents had been fraternity men, he pointed out. Nine of the ten editors in chief of *College Topics* were fraternity men, although more nonfraternity men were on the dean's list. Members of fraternities had completely dominated the G.A.A. elections.

In part, at least, as a result of the Morton article the students voted early in 1935 to change the method of nominating candidates for college offices. The new system was drawn up by the Honor Committee sitting in emergency session with several *Topics* editors. Nominations were to be made by the Student Assembly, composed of representatives of the active social and medical fraternities, the twelve halls or dormitories, plus Dawson's Row and Randall Hall, while any group of twenty students not otherwise represented could elect a spokesman. A referendum was held to ratify the foregoing, but the presence on the ballot of two proposals, one that the plan would be effective at once and the other next session, caused confusion. Another election was held and the decision was for immediate change. The result was that the slate of nominees in the spring of 1935 was much more representative of the student body as a whole. The old method of handpicking the slates was discarded for good.

Issuance of bad checks by students was a problem for many years. In most instances such issuance was due to carelessness in the keeping of bank balances or in the writing of checks on the wrong bank. But since the early 1920s stern warnings had emanated from the Honor Committee to the effect that any man who deliberately cashed a check, knowing that there was no money on deposit to cover it, was guilty of violating the honor code. A student Bad Check Committee was created, and in 1923–24 it succeeded in reducing the average number of checks that "bounced" from forty or fifty per week to eight. The Faculty Committee on Admissions announced in 1927 that no student with outstanding worthless checks would be allowed to reenter the university the following session without a satisfactory explanation. The Bad Check Committee reminded the students again in 1936 that drawing a check when the drawer knew he hadn't sufficient funds to cover it was an honor violation. The committee stated the following year that "several students have recently been dismissed from the university for such breaches of the honor code." Downtown Charlottesville merchants were more willing to cooperate with the committee by turning in bad checks than the Corner merchants. The latter were so completely dependent on student patronage that they were reluctant to do so.

Some of the burden was lifted from the Bad Check Committee by creation of a Board of Arbitration, composed of three students and two alternates who had been at the university for at least three years. This agency was not under the Honor Committee and sat in judgment on disputes between students and Charlottesville merchants involving unpaid debts. The board was empowered to decide such matters, with enforcement in the hands of the university administration. Excellent results were obtained. Some undergraduates contracted extremely large bills with merchants and left school. The Board of Arbitration was useful in bringing about settlements. It was not a debt-collection agency but an agency for arbitrating disagreements and arriving at solutions reasonably satisfactory to all concerned.

A Judicial Committee of students to take jurisdiction over all routine cases of student discipline was established in 1941 by the Student Senate. Such cases had previously been handled by the dean of the university. Explaining the function of the newly created agency, the *Alumni News* declared that "it has been established in an effort to control student discipline in the same traditional spirit of freedom and self-government which has been shown by the Honor Committee in its regulation of the ethical conduct of University of Virginia students for a hundred years." Dean Ivey Lewis, who had been handling all cases involving disciplinary action, "will in the future limit his control to special cases or to cases involving student groups," said the *News*.

Disorder in fraternity houses during the Summer Quarter led Dean George B. Zehmer to close the fraternities to students during the 1940 summer session and relegate the students to the Lawn and Ranges. In order to do this, the girls had to be transferred from those rooms to the dormitories. The disorder that had occurred in the fraternities accordingly shifted to the Lawn and Ranges, where the chief offenders were students who had failed most of their work during the regular session and failed most of it again in the summer. "They were nuisances in the classes they attended as well as in other respects during the summer," said Zehmer, who suggested more rigid requirements for admission to the Summer Quarter. In 1941–42 he arranged for an older student to serve as "a sort of night watchman" on the Lawn and Ranges from 4 P.M. to 4 A.M., with "satisfactory results" during the latter part of the summer session.

Announcements of dismissals under the Honor System were made in various ways over the years. In earlier days the entire student body was called into session, the name was made known, and the case discussed. This procedure was abandoned as too burdensome. Later, identities of those expelled were communicated to the students at University Hour, held once each term. This practice also was discarded but was revived in 1931, when the names were again announced at University Hour. Within a few years, however, the publicizing of individuals was stopped, and the publicity was limited to making known the types of offenses involved. In 1939–40, for example, the facts were published in *College Topics* at the end of the session, as follows: violating athletic eligibility pledge, one; cheating on quizzes, four; cheating on pledged papers, four; signing roll after nonattendance, one; total for the session, ten.

First-year men were being admonished at periodic intervals to wear their hats in accordance with long established custom, although there was no specific penalty for failure to do so. Lapses on the part of freshmen who went around bareheaded were noted from time to time in the collegiate press, and they were told that this custom and the rule against their hanging about the Corner added up to an extremely mild form of discrimination, especially when compared to the hazing at many colleges and universities. All students were supposed to wear coats and ties, and while this was rather universally observed until recent years, there were occasions, notably in the 1950s and 1960s, when the first-year men had to be warned that they were undermining the sacred traditions.

Footstamping in class was a phenomenon of the late 1920s and 1930s. It seemed to mean different things at different times—applause, a polite form of booing, or an expression of strong disapproval. Prof. George W. Spicer related that one of his students made himself a dreadful nuisance in class by repeatedly asking "irrelevant and even inane questions." He was effectively silenced by his fellow students, who stamped so loudly that it "sounded like the cavalry galloping down McCormick Road."

Undergraduates who had an average grade of 87 were termed Distinguished Students and given the privilege of cutting half of their classes. *Topics* stated that these students felt that they were "being 'eager'—deadliest of sins at Virginia"— if they did not take all of their cuts. The result was that "for at

30. *Zeisberg views the changing scene at the university.*

least half of the class periods, class membership was made up of those barely passing their work, the instructors were letting down in the quality of their lectures, and the students who could contribute most . . . were conspicuous by their absence."

A poll of several student leaders and faculty members by the *Spectator* returned a unanimous vote of opposition to unrestricted coeducation. One student expressed himself with great fervor: "Coeds—the very word makes me quiver!" Pleasanton L. Conquest III, whose column in *Topics* entitled "The Reflection Pool" was one of the most delightfully written productions of the era at the university, with notably clever verse, unbosomed himself as follows: "Why, oh why can't we get rid of the women in this college? Women are fine in their place, but their place is definitely elsewhere. . . . Take 'em out coach, beautiful or not (mostly not). A pox on the coed room and its beleaguered group of enraged lionesses." This was such strong stuff that the *Topics* editorial board announced that it was disassociating itself from the "recent diatribe against coeds," since "we believe that girls have a definite place here." About a year later Conquest relented; he said his criticisms of coeds had been "ungentlemanly" and were to be "taken in fun." It would not happen again, he added.

New rules for fraternity rushing, requiring the attainment of certain grades, were announced by President Newcomb in 1934. The two-week rushing period in the fall would be continued, but actual initiation would be postponed until January and "will be made conditioned upon the successful completion of at least nine term hours of work during the fall term." Newcomb added that under the old system "a few matriculates—I hesitate to call them students—somehow seemed to be of the opinion that they had reached the climax of their college careers when they had been initiated into a fraternity, and that nothing further was to be expected of them."

The Glee Club's fiftieth anniversary in 1936 was celebrated in Cabell Hall with a program of university melodies, southern songs, and other compositions, under the leadership of Prof. Harry Rogers Pratt. This program was broadcast over a Virginia radio network, and the following week the club made a joint appearance in New York with the Barnard College Glee Club. A concert was given by the Virginia vocalists the next night at the Plaza Hotel, sponsored by the Virginians of New

York in cooperation with the Southern Society. Other appearances in various cities followed. Some sixty singers, trained by Professor Pratt, participated.

The university's Student Band, under Prof. Robert E. Lutz, also was winning praise. Founded in 1934, it had gotten off to a somewhat shaky start, but was now playing at athletic contests with greater success.

"Punch and Julep," designed as a Virginia version of Princeton's "Triangle Club" and Harvard's "Hasty Pudding," was organized in 1939, with Harry Pratt again as adviser. It was revamped the following year and provided well-received musical comedies.

Omicron Delta Kappa, the national honorary leadership fraternity, had a chapter at the university from 1925 to 1929, but then, for some unexplained reason, it went out of existence. Ten years later the Student Senate appointed a committee to consider its revival. O.D.K. was reconstituted a short time thereafter, and twenty-seven students were elected to membership. It has been functioning on the Grounds ever since.

The "Spectator Award," to be given annually to the university's foremost scholar-athlete, was announced by the *Virginia Spectator*. A permanent trophy was provided on which each year the winner's name would be engraved. The G.A.A. banquet every spring was to be the scene of the award, with the recipient chosen by a committee composed of administration, faculty, and students.

The Virginia Literary and Athletic League met each year at the university throughout the 1930s with hundreds of high school students from all over the state in attendance. Literary and dramatic contests, public speaking and debating, a track meet, tennis matches, and other contests were on the agenda, as well as trips to McCormick Observatory and Monticello, a tea dance, and so on. Charles H. Kauffmann, executive secretary, who also was director of the university's Personnel and Placement Bureau, was in charge. Every effort was made to impress the visiting youths with the thought that the University of Virginia was the place where they should enroll for their collegiate training. The university students were besought by the authorities to be on their good behavior during the program. The Interfraternity Council sent a letter to all fraternities reminding them of their responsibilities. In 1940 the program was in its twenty-seventh year.

Enrollment in the university dropped to 2,435 at the bottom of the depression, but by 1937–38 it had risen to 2,741 and was still going up. Episcopalians were the largest religious denomination during the 1930s, as had been the case since the institution's founding. A poll in 1936 showed 730 members of that denomination, 330 Presbyterians, 325 Methodists, 252 Baptists, 216 Jews, 135 Roman Catholics, and the rest scattered.

President Roosevelt's New Deal evidently had its impact on the university, for in 1939 the *Spectator* carried an article by Harris H. Williams, the paper's assistant editor, entitled " 'One Third of a Nation'; the Back Door to Mr. Jefferson's University." It included photographs of Negro slums in Charlottesville and a black woman collecting food from garbage cans. The article said, among other things: "It will take much money and a long time to right these conditions; particularly it requires a progressive civic outlook, which as yet seems to have little voice in the City Council or even the civic leadership."

Graduate Dean John C. Metcalf reiterated in 1932 what he had said in 1928, namely, that the university was leading all other southern institutions in "scholarly investigation." By 1933 he had modified this statement to read "No other Southern institution is accomplishing more in the way of scholarly research." Subjects in which he said particularly good advanced work was being done were chemistry, biology, physics, astronomy, philosophy and psychology, social sciences, economics, romance languages, history, English, education, and medicine. Despite the depression, all twenty students awarded Ph.D.s in 1930 "have good positions," said the dean, the majority in "some of the best universities." Every applicant for the M.A. and M.S. degrees had been required since 1921–22 to present a thesis; it usually took two years in the 1930s to get this diploma.

In his annual report for the year 1932–33, Prof. Albert G. A. Balz stated that "the University of Virginia, alone in the South, is in a position to command respect as a source for men trained in professorships in philosophy." He referred to a re-

31. Henry H. (Pop) Lannigan, coach and trainer of many
Virginia teams, 1905–29. From a portrait by William Steene.

cent questionnaire which disclosed that "only one [southern] institution remotely approaches our facilities [library resources for teaching and research], and with respect to that institution (Texas) there is some ambiguity in the report."

Some months later Balz contributed an article to the *University of Virginia Magazine* in which he argued that the university was not "slipping scholastically," as some were claiming, and cited the undoubted advances made in the preceding decade. Algernon Bysshe replied in the subsequent issue of the magazine that this argument was largely meaningless, since other institutions also had made much progress during the same period.

However, Balz was very nearly correct with respect to the high rank he assigned to his own philosophy department, for its graduate facilities were rated ahead of all others in the South, except those at Texas, by the Committee on Graduate Instruction of the American Council on Education in a report announced in 1934.

Professor Metcalf's high rating of Virginia's graduate instruction had been somewhat oversanguine, since graduate study in only four disciplines at Virginia, including philosophy, was deemed "adequate," whereas there were ten such departments at Texas, including one that was "starred"; eight at North Carolina, one of them starred, and seven at Duke. The other three "adequate" graduate departments at Virginia were astronomy, the only one thus ranked in the South; economics, with Texas the only other southern institution listed; physics, with only Rice Institute as a competitor; and chemistry, with other "adequate" departments at North Carolina, Rice, and Duke.

There was perhaps consolation in the fact, pointed out by Professor Metcalf, that "from 30 to 50 percent of the 'jurors' either did not vote or sent in their votes too late to be recorded." He also termed the report "often inaccurate."

The Institute for Research in the Social Sciences continued to provide valuable assistance to professors engaged upon scholarly projects. "Practically every professor in economics, government, history, sociology and rural social economics has either recently completed a book or is actively engaged in preparing one on some topic of significant and vital interest," the *Alumni News* reported in 1935. "Many now have several titles to their credit." Assistance given by the institute took a variety of forms; usually it paid the salary of a substitute teacher while the regular member of the staff went on leave for the summer or a full year, in order to work on his project. Another form of assistance was payment for aid in research, for necessary supplies, or for stenographic help. Many different subjects were covered in the scholarly inquiries. One list mentioned taxation in Virginia, Swedish agriculture, behavior of infants, income in the South, Franco-British diplomacy in the Near East, American business cycles, French constitutional history, and the economics of cotton.

Wilson Gee, the person behind all this, was a somewhat complex man. The organization he founded and headed made a vitally important contribution to graduate work by the students and advanced research by the faculty and thereby enhanced the standing of the university in the educational world. Gee supervised the research of his students carefully and encouraged them to do good work, according to apparently reliable authority; yet it was widely reported that he graded so liberally on examinations that nobody failed. One able but unimpressed former student declares that "his lectures were dull and he passed everybody." Yet other competent members of his classes voted him one of their favorite professors and complimented him on his willingness to work with them on their problems. A faculty associate, on the other hand, said Gee was "quite egotistical" and difficult to work with. Gee persuaded President Alderman to let him leave the Department of Economics and establish his own separate Department of Rural Economics and Sociology, in which, it was said, he exercised "absolute control over those who worked under him." There is no question that he was avid for publicity. His department was allowed to go out of existence when he retired in 1959, but the institute continued to function, and was named for him—a deserved tribute.

There was a loud explosion of indignation in the early 1930s from individual students and from *College Topics* over the physical education course that was mandatory for first- and second-year men. One student called it "an ideal unworthy of a junior college," reminiscent of "Yankee mass-production methods." Another protested that during the autumn he was "forced to play namby-pamby games out in the open

where anyone can see him, and in general everything possible
is done to make him feel like a perfect idiot." *Topics* chimed in
with an editorial blast against "gym classes conducted as animal trainers perfect their dogs in sideshows . . . an absurdity
and a disgrace that a man to obtain a degree from Thomas
Jefferson's university should have to become proficient in
rope-climbing and tap dancing." The paper circulated a petition among the students calling for "abolition of compulsory
Physical Education classes as required for an academic degree. . . . Their existence is foreign to the principle of personal liberty inherent in the university." Over one thousand
students signed. But Dean Page's faculty committee ruled that
the Physical Education curriculum would stand, except that
tap dancing would become an elective. "Sublime Indifference"
was the caption over the irate comment by *Topics*. On the other
hand, John D. Martin, Jr., chairman of the Student Senate,
declared that he felt the "Phys Ed" requirements had been
"greatly liberalized or, better, humanized," and that the faculty
committee "listened most attentively to student arguments."
He did not elaborate.

Professor Metcalf took occasion in 1934, on the tenth anniversary of his incumbency as dean of the Graduate School, to
point out that "from an enrollment of fewer than 100 graduate students 10 years ago the number has grown to 280 in the
. . . regular session, while the Summer Quarter shows almost
as many." Hence the office "now has charge each year of about
500 graduate students, most of whom are candidates for Master's degrees." Dean Metcalf went on to stress the importance
of the library, saying: "The growth and the admirable administration of the University Library have greatly strengthened
graduate study and research. Ten years ago the libraries of
the university, general and departmental, had 125,000 books;
today they have 230,000. . . . Because of very limited space in
the general library, rooms in various other buildings have
been utilized for library purposes. The greatest need of the
university is an adequate general library building." Only about
half of the 230,000 volumes could be housed in the Rotunda.
Dean Metcalf resigned as head of the Graduate School at the
close of the 1936–37 session and was succeeded by James
Southall Wilson, his colleague in the English Department.

Both men were nationally known teachers, scholars, and lecturers.

One of the important events of this period took place in 1935 when the National Academy of Sciences held its annual meeting at the university, the first time the academy had ever met in the South. Nobel Prize Winners Robert A. Millikan and Harold C. Urey were on the program. Eleven of the fifty papers presented during the three-day session dealt with the work of University of Virginia faculty members and research associates. These papers were deemed to be of high quality, and they brought prestige to the university for its work in the natural sciences.

The superior training given in the Medical School during these years was stressed decades later by the eminent Dr. William B. Bean, son of Dr. Robert B. Bean of the medical faculty. Dr. William Bean had been graduated from the school in 1935 and had gone on to become nationally known, not only as a teacher of medicine but as an exceptionally talented writer on medical subjects. "When I went away from here to intern at Johns Hopkins," said he, "I was certainly as well-trained in general medicine, in internal medicine, as colleagues who were met there from Johns Hopkins and from Harvard and from many of the other medical schools. Part of this I am sure was related to the excellence of the faculty and part because the school was still of manageably small size. There was more individual attention, I believe, than there was in the earlier days. Maybe I should say in other schools."

New requirements for the B.A. and B.S. degrees were announced, effective for the session of 1936–37. The new curriculum, in the words of Dean George O. Ferguson, was designed to bring "a more comprehensive and permanent mastery of subjects as wholes." It was complained that under the existing system the choice of subjects resulted in a sort of pot pourri, often "from the 'crippiest' courses available," without definite aim or focus, whereas the new curriculum stipulated that two years before graduation the student must select a field in a major subject. In that field he would have to take at least five and not more than seven courses approved by his official adviser. A minimum of three courses in the major subject was required, and two in related subjects. Electives made

up the remainder. Comprehensive examinations in the field
of concentration, part written and part oral, were to be introduced for the first time. A writer in the *University of Virginia
Magazine* was enthusiastic over the innovations and said that
they would "undoubtedly raise the standard of the college degrees" and "result in a healthier and more abundant scholarship among students."

Further improvement was achieved when academic degrees
with honors were introduced at the session of 1937–38. President Newcomb explained that the "more favored students,
during the latter half of their four-year course, shall be enabled to pursue their studies in their chosen field of concentration on a firmer basis and a higher plane than the less
gifted." He added that these honor students would be afforded "unlimited opportunity, under proper guidance, to
master thoroughly their specially chosen subjects," and they
would be "at liberty . . . to claim exemption from course requirements." Final comprehensive examinations for a degree
with honors "will demand a rigid compliance with particularly
exacting standards of scholarship." Newcomb stated that half
a dozen of the university's schools had offered to plan honor
programs for the coming session.

Standards should be raised all along the line in both high
school and college, Prof. Richard Heath Dabney declared in a
letter to *College Topics*. He urged adoption of Jefferson's idea
that only the ablest students should be given a college education. "Jefferson was right," he said. "The unfit should be
weeded out, for their own good as well as that of the
public. . . . The best brains in the state should have the best
training available, but mediocre and stupid persons should be
positively discouraged from entering college and positively
prevented from getting degrees." Dabney appealed to Gov.
James H. Price to "lead Virginia in the footsteps of that su-
premely great man, Thomas Jefferson." Economics Prof. E. A.
Kincaid then wrote a letter expressing the view that the new
curriculum and honors system would make it easier to provide
"educated leadership." He urged that means be found to
bring to the university "men of intellectual promise who are
too poor to avail themselves of what we have to offer. . . .
Leadership must be sought out and developed." *College Topics*

32. *John Lloyd Newcomb, president of the university, 1933–46.*

published an open letter to Governor Price suggesting that he adopt the program of the two professors and make the university "a retreat for the intellectual aristocracy," as envisioned by Jefferson. There was widespread support in the Virginia press for the proposal; newspapers in Richmond, Petersburg, Danville, Bristol, and Roanoke endorsed it. There was, however, no audible response from Governor Price and no action.

The Law School was having its problems. Greatly admired Dean William Minor Lile had retired in 1932, and Armistead Dobie had been named to succeed him. The faculty had not been built up sufficiently to compensate for the loss of such revered figures as Lile, Minor, and Graves, and there were other shortcomings. The salary scale in the Law School was low. Except for Professors Garrard Glenn and Armistead M. Dobie, "the position of professor of law is financially less desirable than a similar position in the College," Prof. F. D. G. Ribble declared. "A professor of law gets and can get but $4,500 a year from the university," said he, whereas a professor of education—along with many other College faculty members—could frequently supplement his $4,500 salary by teaching in the Summer Quarter. Ribble expressed the hope that all full professors in the Law School would have their compensation raised to a minimum of $5,000, effective at once. The inferiority of the library also was emphasized. With 390 students, the Law School had only 30,000 books on its shelves, whereas the schools at Duke and Chapel Hill with less than half as many matriculates had much larger libraries. Three years of prelaw were made a prerequisite for entry to the University of Virginia school, and a resolution was passed denying any student the right to enter who was ineligible to return to any other law school previously attended. This latter stipulation was "directed at the problem of the 'bustee,' usually from Harvard," Ribble wrote. More than two-thirds of the entering law class during this period came from outside Virginia.

Of vital concern to the law faculty was President Roosevelt's "court-packing plan," under which he sought to appoint additional justices to the Supreme Court in order to outvote the conservative majority on that tribunal. The law faculty was unanimous in opposition, since the plan was felt to "undermine the judicial process." By contrast, the political science faculty was in favor of the scheme. Prof. James Hart argued for it in a series of addresses, and his colleagues Professors Robert K. Gooch, Rowland Egger, Raymond Uhl, and George W. Spicer backed it. Bob Gooch debated the issue with Dean Ribble in Cabell Hall.

President Newcomb seemed unconvinced for several years that the Law School was suffering seriously from lack of financial support. When he realized the true state of affairs he moved to strengthen the faculty and raise salaries, while the alumni of the school acted to bolster the sadly inadequate library. By 1935–36 F. D. G. Ribble, Leslie Buckler, Charles P. Nash, and Hardy C. Dillard had joined Armistead Dobie, George B. Eager, and Garrard Glenn on the law faculty. By 1941–42 John Ritchie, William H. White, Jr., Oscar W. Underwood, Jr., William J. Barron, and E. O. Belsheim had been added. The pay of full professors of law was raised to $5,000 in 1940–41, and in 1943–44 further raises were made effective for all departments in the university. Full professors in the academic school were paid as much as $8,000 in some instances, and the usual compensation for professors of that rank once again reached $6,000, the predepression level of a decade before. In the Medical School $6,000 had been the top figure paid by the state in 1941–42, but various professors were allowed to retain part of the funds they earned in private practice; and the Medical School was included, of course, in the university-wide increases of 1943–44.

Work of the university's Extension Division, directed by George B. Zehmer, was expanding to every section of Virginia during the 1930s and 1940s. Extension class work, discussion courses, cooperation with the secondary schools, sponsorship of extracurricular programs, extension publications, extension library service, and home study courses were included. The division functioned in both rural and urban areas. Extension courses were the equivalent of courses in residence and were offered away from the university for the benefit of those who could not attend the institution at Charlottesville. Emphasis was placed on courses in the humanities, the social sciences, and certain professional subjects. Since it was impossible for full-time members of the university faculty to journey to many of the points where classes were held, teachers from thirteen colleges and universities made themselves available. Bulletins, pamphlets, leaflets, magazine articles, and newspaper releases were used in promoting the program. Those attending the classes were mostly mature adults, with average age in the middle thirties. In time, said Zehmer, "the program attracted not only national but international attention, and over a 17-year period brought many visitors from other states and countries to observe the program in action." Members of the staff were invited to visit other areas of the globe in order "to advise and help in introducing somewhat similar programs abroad." Zehmer was elected president of the National University Extension Association for 1942–43, and was one of the founders and first president of the Adult Education Association of Virginia.

Interest at the university in the study of biology had been greatly stimulated by the trial in Tennessee of John T. Scopes for teaching the doctrine of evolution in a high school; applicants to take the course at Virginia were being turned away in the 1930s for lack of space. Prof. William A. Kepner of the department had testified for Scopes. Graduate studies in botany and zoology were strengthened by the opening of a biological station at Mountain Lake, Giles County, for summer instruction. Prof. Bruce D. Reynolds was in charge of the Mountain Lake Biological Station, with Prof. Ivey Lewis as associate director. This was the first such station established in the southern mountains. Construction of a laboratory, dining hall, and dormitories was made possible by a grant from the General Education Board, and these facilities were subsequently enlarged. An abundance of plant and animal specimens on the surrounding mountains, which rise to elevations of four thousand feet or more, afforded material comparable to that found in the Canadian zone and similar to much that was characteristic of the South. Instructors from institutions throughout Virginia and beyond were on the staff, with thirty to forty graduate students in attendance. Professor Lewis, who succeeded Reynolds as director of the station, was accorded a ceremonial tribute in 1940 upon his completion of twenty-five years on the university faculty. Friends and former students gathered on the Rotunda portico, where Lewis C. Williams, '98, spoke and presented him with a silver service and two books of letters from former pupils and other admirers.

It was an era of expansion for the Engineering School, although the course in mining engineering had been dropped after the session of 1931–32 on the recommendation of Acting Dean W. S. Rodman. He could find "no demand" for such instruction. Rodman had succeeded Dean William M. Thornton, following the latter's retirement in 1925. Construction of Thornton Hall, named for the dean, was begun in 1933 and completed two years later. It would be greatly enlarged in future years and represented a vast improvement over the inadequate quarters previously occupied. The humanities program which Deans Thornton and Newcomb had sought over a long period was made a reality in 1936, thus broadening greatly the engineering curriculum.

Failing health caused the resignation of James M. Page as dean of the university in 1934. He was succeeded by Ivey F. Lewis, who had been serving as acting dean. George O. Ferguson of the School of Education was appointed dean of the college.

Various faculty members recorded extraordinary achievements during these years.

Dr. Carl C. Speidel of the Medical School won the $1,000 prize of the American Association for the Advancement of Science in 1932 for being first, in the words of the New York *Times*, to learn "all the secrets of nerve growth by studying nerves inside animal organisms, thus settling a controversy lasting for 70 years." The paper went on to say that "by the use of entirely novel methods, Dr. Speidel has proved once and for all that the nerves do not grow as a result of cells forming a chain, but that each nerve grows out of a single cell in a central nervous system." Thus Speidel established "the 'outgrowth theory' as opposed to the 'chain theory.'"

An even more significant discovery, in the opinion of some authorities, who regarded it as perhaps the most important single contribution to medical science made down to that time by the university's Medical School, was that of Dr. duPont Guerry III, '36, then a young intern at the University Hospital, later the internationally known ophthalmologist. Dr. Guerry found that Vitamin K was of extreme importance in safeguarding the health of newborn infants, primarily as a means of preventing bleeding. Every newborn baby today is automatically given Vitamin K. Dr. William W. Waddell, '18, of the university's pediatrics staff, shared in the accolade.

Dr. Charles Bruce Morton II was entering upon a highly impressive career in surgery that would last until his retirement in 1970. He had won a fellowship at the Mayo Clinic, where he worked in Dr. Frank Mann's Institute of Experimental Medicine. The research Morton did there on the etiology of the peptic ulcer won for him the John Horsley Memorial Prize and the Sigma Xi Award, and forty years later the research was termed "still a classic."

Dr. Samuel A. Mitchell, professor of astronomy and best known as an authority on eclipses of the sun, nine of which he had observed, and for his study of parallaxes, was chosen president of the American Association of University Professors. He also was named a foreign associate of the Royal Astronomical Society of Great Britain and was elected to the National Academy of Sciences, the American Philosophical Society, and the American Academy of Arts and Sciences. Regarded by some as the foremost scientist of the South, Mitchell was one of only three scientists from the region south of Washington and east of the Mississippi who had been chosen a member of the three abovementioned American organizations of scholars.

Prof. Garrard Glenn of the Law School was elected to the Council of the American Law Institute. Only thirty-three jurists, attorneys, and teachers of law made up the council, which included Supreme Court Justices Benjamin Cardozo and Owen J. Roberts. Glenn had joined the university law faculty in 1929 after practicing in New York and teaching at the Columbia University Law School. He had won national fame as the successful defender of James Branch Cabell from charges of obscenity in the novel *Jurgen*.

The university's noted professor of mathematics Gordon T. Whyburn was winning the first of his long series of awards and other distinctions. Whyburn won the Chauvenet Prize of the Mathematical Association of America for the best expository article on mathematics published during the previous three years by a member of the association. The award, the fifth ever given to a mathematician, was for his article "On the Structure of Continua," which dealt with the subject of topology.

33. *John Calvin Metcalf, professor of English and dean of the
Graduate School of Arts and Sciences, 1924–37.*

Economics Prof. Tipton R. Snavely was chosen president of the Southern Economics Association and of Beta Gamma Sigma, national fraternity in economics and commerce. In the 1940s he would serve as chairman of a committee to examine the United States Mint, of the Virginia State Milk Commission, and of a legislative commission to study a sales and use tax for Virginia. As head of the James Wilson Department of Economics, Snavely reported to the president of the university for that department and the McIntire School of Commerce, headed by Prof. M. A. J. Barlow, since the two faculties worked as a unit. The School of Commerce was a division of the College of Arts and Sciences from 1920 to 1952, but in the latter year was established as an autonomous and coordinate school, similar to law or medicine.

Harvey E. Jordan, professor of histology and embryology at the university since 1911, was named dean of the Medical School in 1939, succeeding the late Dr. James C. Flippin. Dean Jordan was not an M.D., but a B.A. and M.A. of Lehigh University and a Ph.D. of Princeton. He rendered highly satisfactory service, nevertheless, as dean of the school. Hardly a charismatic figure, he knew the Medical School's problems and needs and achieved important results.

A contrasting individual was aggressive and voluble Armistead M. Dobie, who resigned as dean of the Law School in 1939 to accept appointment as judge of the U.S. District Court for Western Virginia; he was named soon thereafter to the U.S. Circuit Court of Appeals, Fourth Circuit. From his student days Dobie was a fast-talking, quick-thinking extrovert and exhibitionist. Once in Prof. Noah K. Davis's class he answered a question brilliantly but in a manner that Davis considered smart-alecky. The irritated professor walked to the blackboard, drew a curving line, and remarked, "I suppose, Mr. Dobie, that you can make a clever comment about that?" Dobie replied at once, "Sir, I should say that that is Noah's arc."

"Ten thousand words a minute are just his daily feed," was the phrase frequently used by Dobie to describe his own loquacity. His speaking style was like the firing of a machine gun. Words poured forth in a torrent, and his colorful phrases were quoted. Referring to participants in three sports, he termed them "mittmen, mattmen, and mermen." Haranguing the student body the night before the annual football game with Georgetown, he would shout the following each year: "I want you Virginia men to make the welkin ring for the Orange and Blue tomorrow afternoon during that gridiron classic with Georgetown, and in such stentorian tones as to make a broadside from the Atlantic Squadron sound like the dying groan of a consumptive gnat!" Dobie's lectures were never dull.

He was well-equipped for the federal bench, since he was nationally known as an authority on federal procedure and the author of a textbook and casebook on the subject. He had also written similar volumes on bailments and carriers and was coauthor of *Criminal Justice in Virginia*. As a federal judge, Dobie was no shrinking violet. Joseph Bryan III, writing in the *Saturday Evening Post*, stated that the jurist "had established a professional reputation as a judge who does not underestimate his own ability," and Bryan added this piquant note: "At the annual banquet of the Fourth Judicial Circuit, the speaker of the evening said: 'I recently tried a case in which Dobie had passed on a motion. When I read the opinion I found that he had cited two authorities—St. Paul's Epistle to the Ephesians and Dobie on Federal Procedure. They seemed to conflict, so he repudiated St. Paul and adhered to Dobie!'"

This flamboyant character was succeeded as dean of the Law School by F. D. G. Ribble, a highly respected, scholarly professor who exhibited none of the garrulity and cockiness of his predecessor. Ribble was an able administrator, and the Law School made important advances under his deanship.

A course in journalism, the first at the university since 1917, was instituted in 1937 by William H. Wranek, Jr., head of the University News Bureau. Wranek stated that various guest lecturers from the field of journalism would speak to the class. Instruction in journalism had been urged repeatedly by *College Topics*.

A significant addition to the academic faculty occurred the following year when John W. Wheeler-Bennett, a widely known British historian and biographer, was named lecturer in international law and relations. Wheeler-Bennett was already the author of a dozen books, including a biography of General von Hindenburg, and he had just completed an incisive study of the Brest-Litovsk treaty between Germany and

Russia. A resident of Albemarle County for several years, with intermittent trips to Europe, Wheeler-Bennett would soon marry Miss Ruth Risher, a charming resident of the university community and for some years the registrar and secretary of the Summer Quarter. He would continue as a popular and admired lecturer at the university for several decades. Author of the official biography of King George VI, he was knighted and became Sir John Wheeler-Bennett.

The *Virginia Quarterly Review* celebrated its tenth anniversary in 1935 with accolades from various directions. The Baltimore *Evening Sun*, which had greeted the publication's debut a decade before with down-the-nose observations, reversed its position and pronounced the magazine "a minor miracle." The New York *Times* declared that "it has won a high and honorable position among American periodicals." Lawrence Lee, assistant professor of romance languages, was named editor in 1939, succeeding Lambert Davis, who left to accept a position with a New York publishing house. Lee said he could hold the post for only one year, and Archibald Bolling Shepperson, associate professor of English, succeeded him in 1940.

Another anniversary was observed in 1938 when the *Virginia Law Review* passed its twenty-fifth milestone. Clarence O. Ammonette, '14, the first editor, contributed an article to the anniversary issue in which he explained the circumstances of the *Review*'s founding and listed the members of the first editorial staff. Prof. Leslie H. Buckler of the law faculty wrote congratulating the publication on its high standards.

There was a third anniversary in 1940, when *College Topics* took note of its founding half a century before. Judge A. C. Carson of Riverton, Va. one of five students who got out the initial issue in 1890, was present for the anniversary dinner at the Farmington Country Club. All living former editors and business managers were invited and many accepted. Dr. M. Estes Cocke, assistant president of Hollins College, a former editor, was the principal speaker. Suggestions that the name of the publication be changed had been made for several years. The *University of Virginia Magazine* called *College Topics* "a monstrous misnomer," and added: "No longer do a few college students gather once or twice a week to publish merely a bulletin of the topics of the *College*. Now a staff of approximately 60 covers the *University*, all six departments, and co-operates to publish almost every day, news of the university." *Topics* commented, "The sooner the change is effected, the better." The change did not take place until 1948, when the paper became the *Cavalier Daily*.

The *University of Virginia Magazine*, in the early 1920s an ultrasedate and intellectual journal, had metamorphosed by the 1930s into a much better-looking and livelier publication. Formerly printed on "butcher paper" with no drawings or other illustrations and hardly any advertising, the magazine was transformed a decade later into a slick-paper publication with prose, poetry, fiction, nonfiction, drawings, a colorful cover, and some color advertising. An editor in chief during this period was Ben Belitt, later a poet of national if not international stature, winner of the National Institute of Arts and Letters Award and various other important accolades and professor of English at Bennington College for decades.

A column in the magazine of more or less humor, entitled "Wahooria," was notable for what appears to have been the first published use of a term derived from "Wahoo," to denote Virginia students or events relating to them. Evidently stemming from "Wah-hoo-Wah" in "The Good Old Song," Virginia men would soon be using "Wahoo" along with "Cavalier" in speaking of themselves or their athletic teams. By 1940 "Wahoos" was in general use around the Grounds. Some decades later it would occasionally be abbreviated to "'Hoos" in student publications. The *University of Virginia Magazine* became the *Virginia Spectator* early in the session of 1935–36, with largely unchanged content and makeup. Both were sponsored by the Jefferson Society.

Although nearly all of the 1930s were depression years, some important construction was going on at the university. On the other hand, existing buildings were often in need of paint, repairs, or general tidying up. But this condition was not all bad, in the opinion of Stark Young, who wrote in the much-discussed manifesto of the southern agrarians *I'll Take My Stand*: "I shall never forget the encouragement with which I saw for the first time that some of the dormitory doors at the University of Virginia needed paint, so sick was I at the bang-up varnishing, rebuilding, plumbing, endowing, in some of the large Northern institutions. If they learn little at these Virginia halls, it is doubtless as much as they would learn at the others, and they at least escape the poison of the success idea that every building is almost sure to show, the belief that mechanical surface and the outer powers of money are the prime things in living."

New buildings, nevertheless, are essential at times, as even Stark Young would doubtless have conceded. One of these was Clark Hall, new home of the Law School. Minor Hall had been outgrown, and William Andrews Clark, Jr., gave $350,000 for the new structure, a memorial to his late wife. House D and House E on Dawson's Row had to be pulled down to make way for Clark Hall, which was dedicated in 1932. Murals by Allyn Cox adorned Memorial Hall in the center of the building.

Excavation was begun the following year for the Thomas H. Bayly Art Museum behind Fayerweather Hall. A $100,000 bequest from Mrs. Louis May McLane Tiffany of Baltimore plus a federal grant of $38,000 made the project possible. The museum would be a valuable adjunct to the School of the Fine Arts. A Peale portrait of George Washington was included in Mrs. Tiffany's bequest along with other art treasures. Paul G. McIntire also contributed a number of valuable objets d'art. The home of Dr. William A. Lambeth had to be demolished to make way for the museum.

Construction of Thornton Hall, new home of the School of Engineering, was begun in 1933, as noted in the previous chapter. This was made possible by a grant of $379,000 from the Public Works Administration (PWA), the federal agency that provided funds for many worthwhile structures during these years. Situated just across Highway 29 from Clark Hall, Thornton Hall consisted of three buildings surrounding a central court and facing McCormick Road. It would be greatly enlarged in later years. Like various other university buildings, Thornton Hall was designed by the university's Commission of Architects—Walter D. Blair of New York, R. E. Lee Taylor of Baltimore, John K. Peebles of Norfolk, and Prof. Edmund S. Campbell, head of the university's School of Art and Architecture.

A new $200,000 wing of the hospital was made feasible in 1934 by a PWA grant of that amount. It was exclusively for private patients and added 40 beds, bringing the overall total

34. F. Stringfellow Barr, history professor.

to about 250 beds. The wing, named for Dr. Paul B. Barringer, was opened in 1936.

The John Staige Davis Neuro-Psychiatric addition to the hospital, named for Dr. Davis, who taught courses in mental diseases there for many years, was opened in 1939. The addition cost $150,000, of which $82,000 was contributed by Paul G. McIntire and the remainder by PWA.

Two years later the five-story West Wing was added to the hospital, thanks to a $325,000 appropriation from the state. It included 171 additional ward beds as well as new administrative offices and quarters for several departments. The three above-mentioned additions to the hospital were referred to briefly in the previous chapter.

In 1938 Fayerweather Hall underwent its third remodeling within a period of fifteen years. No longer used as a gymnasium after 1923, it was taken over by the School of Art and Architecture. This provided the school with quarters claimed to be superior to those of any similar school in the South. In the 1920s it had occupied cramped rooms on West Range, after which it moved to the main floor of Fayerweather Hall, the basement of which was occupied by a pathology laboratory. When new quarters were provided for the laboratory, the School of Art and Architecture expanded into that area. Situated next door to the Bayly Museum, the school enjoyed excellent facilities for instruction.

An epoch-making event occurred in 1938 when running hot water suddenly became available in the students' rooms on East Range. It was the first time in more than a hundred years that students living in the quarters provided by Mr. Jefferson had been furnished with this amenity. The boon had not yet been vouchsafed to students on West Range or the Lawn, a fact that brought rumblings of discontent from those ill-used undergraduates. There had been no advance announcement of the coming of hot water to East Range, when suddenly it gushed from the spigots, to the accompaniment of loud cheers from the astonished beneficiaries.

Important as were these construction projects in the 1930s, the most important of all was that of the new university library, greatly desired by Dr. Alderman and earnestly sought over a period of a decade and a half before the necessary funds finally were obtained.

The unsuitability of the Rotunda for use as a modern library has been referred to. It had long since been outgrown, and the lack of an adequate repository for the institution's collections was recognized as a grave handicap to its standing in the educational world. In the early 1920s a faculty library committee, headed by Dr. John C. Metcalf, was appointed, and ways and means of acquiring the sorely needed facility were explored.

The coming of Harry Clemons as librarian in 1927 provided marked impetus for the effort to acquire the desired building. The need was great, as shown by statistics compiled the following year by the librarian at Princeton University. The University of Virginia stood anywhere from thirty-second to thirty-seventh among thirty-eight university libraries in this country with respect to number of volumes on shelves, expenditures for books, and appropriations for salaries.

Clemons declined an offer from Wesleyan University in 1928 to remain at the University of Virginia despite its library's dismal ranking. He did so on assurances from President Alderman that the latter would make every effort to obtain a new library and adequate funds for endowment, equipment, and books.

Dr. Alderman was much upset in 1930 or 1931 when Herbert Keller of the University of Chicago told him that he had just shipped several hundred thousand Virginia manuscripts to that institution's library. "He laughed in my face," Alderman told Clemons. "We must do something about this." It was high time. J. G. deRoulhac Hamilton had been touring Virginia, gathering up manuscripts by the bale for the University of North Carolina, and representatives of Duke University were doing the same thing. As a result of all this the Virginia Room was opened in the east wing of the Rotunda, and an effort was made to bring together there the university's rarest and most important books on Virginia history, together with such manuscripts as the university possessed. A more significant step was the bringing in of Lester Cappon to teach history and serve as the institution's first archivist. He would be invaluable.

R. E. Lee Taylor, '01, the Baltimore architect, was asked in

1935 to provide plans for a college and research library, with principal emphasis on adequate facilities for research, a number of small studios for researchers, ready availability to the files and stack rooms, and several rooms for "general browsing." Stacks for five hundred thousand volumes would be made available initially, with arrangements for easy expansion to accommodate 2 million. A large memorial entrance hall was contemplated. By the time these plans were prepared, the university had 232,000 volumes scattered among eighteen different buildings.

A carefully mapped campaign for funds lasting more than a year was launched by President Newcomb, Librarian Clemons, and Dr. Metcalf's faculty committee. A PWA grant of around $450,000 was sought, and Senators Carter Glass and Harry F. Byrd assisted actively. Finally on Sept. 12, 1936, a telegram came from Secretary of the Interior Harold Ickes officially confirming a PWA grant of $427,909, thus making possible the erection of a $950,000 library. The remaining cost would be covered by a bond issue.

Joy around the Grounds was spontaneous and uninhibited. President Newcomb held an impromptu celebration with the library staff under the colonnade east of the Rotunda, at which dignified, urbane Professor Metcalf made history by breaking into a clog dance. The extraordinary event was embalmed for posterity in Clemons's annual report on the library, as follows: "The clog dance executed that morning by Dean Metcalf has not only become a tradition of the Rotunda, but it is also symbolical; for he had, as chairman of the library committee, been present at and presided over every meeting of the committee during these 14 years of patient planning."

Construction got under way, and the new building, embodying many up-to-date features in library construction, was named for Dr. Alderman by unanimous agreement. Dedication took place on June 13, 1938, with Dumas Malone, then director of the Harvard University Press, as the speaker.

The architect R. E. Lee Taylor, an alumnus and native of Norfolk, was also the architect for Clark, Thornton, Monroe, and Peabody halls and the Lambeth Field and Scott stadiums. In each case he collaborated with the university's architectural commission, but he was recognized as the principal architect

35. *Miss Mary Proffitt, extraordinarily influential secretary to Deans James M. Page and Ivey F. Lewis. In the words of an alumnus, "She ran a darned good university." From a portrait by Clyde Carter.*

for each of the abovementioned structures. Taylor also had a leading role in designing various additions to the hospital. He and Prof. Edmund S. Campbell handled the design for the Bayly Museum of Art.

The only other architect who had a comparable role at the university was John K. Peebles, '90, of Norfolk, who died in 1934. He was credited with having been principal architect for Fayerweather Gymnasium, Minor Hall, the Monroe Hill dormitories, McKim Hall, and the addition to the Cobb Chemical Laboratory. Like Lee Taylor, Peebles collaborated with the other members of the architectural commission in designing the various structures.

John Powell, '01, the noted pianist, gave a concert in 1938 in Carnegie Hall, New York, celebrating his musical debut of 25 years before, and donated the proceeds to Alderman Library. The money was used for the purchase of letters between Thomas Jefferson and Joseph C. Cabell, some of which dealt with the university's founding. Powell's example led other alumni to purchase Jeffersonian correspondence for the library, with the result that ninety-seven original letters were acquired. He repeated the Carnegie Hall program at Cabell Hall a month later and gave the proceeds to aid in establishing a fund for bringing other musical attractions to the university.

Completion of Alderman Library resulted in highly significant acquisitions, particularly that of the McGregor Collection. Tracy W. McGregor of Detroit had assembled this treasure trove of books, pamphlets, and manuscripts having to do with U.S. history, and he provided in his will that the trustees of the McGregor Fund were to decide which college or university should get it. Their decision to present it to the University of Virginia brought to that institution a library now appraised at over $10,000,000. It is considered the most valuable assemblage of material on the history of the southeastern United States, and it also includes an extremely significant collection on the history of early New England as well as another in the field of English literature.

Almost simultaneously with the bequest of the McGregor Library the university received the professional collection of the late Algernon Coleman, '01, distinguished professor of French at the University of Chicago and internationally recognized scholar in the field of French literature. It consisted of more than one thousand volumes on the language and literature of France.

One of the few portraits from life of the poet Shelley was donated to the library by Nellie P. Dunn of Richmond, widow of Dr. John Dunn, in memory of her husband. The work of William E. West, an American artist who knew Shelley and Byron, the portrait was brought to the United States by West and bequeathed to his niece. It was purchased by Dr. Dunn in 1904.

Still another acquisition in the late 1930s was the antebellum library of Muscoe Garnett of Elmwood, Essex County, Va., the gift of Mrs. J. Clayton Mitchell of North Wales, Pa. It was transferred to the university intact and placed in a special room built to simulate a Virginia gentleman's library of the pre–Civil War era. There is a fireplace with shelves extending to the ceiling on both sides and to the ceiling on the opposite wall. Count Carlo Sforza, the Italian statesman who was exiled by Mussolini and gave a series of lectures at the university, was "visibly and deeply moved" at seeing the Garnett Room, Harry Clemons reported. "I feel more at home in this room than I have in any place since I left Italy," said the count. "My family had a library like this in our home. . . . The books had been much read. . . . We must not forget this. It gives comfort and courage." Later he brought his son to the university for a visit, and made a special point of showing him the library of the Garnett family.

Harry Clemons's dedication to Alderman Library's advancement was such that he frequently worked there into the early morning hours, as late as 2 A.M. True, he did not arrive at his office until around 10 A.M., but his zeal was such that he usually returned at night. On one such night he was leaving the building by the rear door when, in closing it, he slammed it shut on his trouser cuff. Try as he might, he could not disengage his pants from the viselike grip, and the only key he had was to the front entrance. In this crisis, he adopted what seemed the only available solution. He wriggled out of his trousers, went around to the front door minus his pantaloons, let himself in, and retrieved his breeches.

Following removal of the books from the Rotunda, portions

of the building's exterior were given something of a face-lifting. The crumbling concrete steps were replaced and the marble balustrades repaired. The work was paid for with a PWA grant of about $61,000, supplemented by a state appropriation of $75,000. All repairs were completed in time for the opening of the 1939–40 session.

The rehabilitated Rotunda was formally opened with a dance on the stormy night of Jan. 26, 1940. No such event had occurred there since the Gay Nineties, and the affair was a highlight of the university's social season. A nationally known band played for the dancing, and the ball was broadcast over station WRVA from 10:35 to 11 P.M. Despite the fact that the heaviest snowfall in decades blanketed the state that night, the affair was pronounced a roaring success.

The only unfortunate aspect of the university's acquisition of an adequate library lay in the fact that a building designed and constructed by Thomas Jefferson had to be demolished to make way for the new structure. This was the Anatomical Theater, a square brick building opposite the north end of West Range, with a cupola and railing on the roof. Burned in 1886, it was restored the following year, but the cupola and railing were omitted "for reasons of economy." A portico, designed by Prof. Fiske Kimball, was added in 1920. Condemned in 1924, the building was vacated by the departments housed there but was subsequently reconditioned and assigned to the School of Rural Social Economics. Upon its demolition in 1939, after completion of the library, most of its bricks were carefully preserved for use in repairing the serpentine walls and other original Jeffersonian structures. A widespread misconception is that the anatomical hall was the "stiff hall" where, in modern times, the medical school's pickled cadavers were kept. The "stiff hall," or anatomical laboratory, was behind Peabody Hall, on the site of today's Newcomb Hall. A letter to the newspaper in 1924 complained of an "offensive stench from the anatomical laboratory which daily infests the Peabody Hall lecture room," and the writer added: "Only last week I saw a large flock of great dark birds circling over the university. . . . No doubt every preventive measure possible is being taken . . . but this does not help matters for those who of necessity spend a large part of their time in Peabody Hall." The "stiff hall," demolished in the 1950s to make way for Newcomb Hall, was carefully avoided by small boys and others who gave its gruesome contents a wide berth. It was used at times in fraternity initiations. A fraternity "goat" in about the year 1918 was instructed to visit the "stiff hall" at midnight, pull one of the corpses out of its vat, and recite "The Raven." He survived.

The aroma from the anatomical laboratory was not the only cause of complaints from professors with quarters in Peabody Hall. In the mid-1920s the romance languages faculty was housed in the basement, and their ululations were both loud and heart-rending. For example, Prof. Francis H. Abbot, an unusually interesting lecturer, reported: "Three hours a week I teach in P.H.B. 2 [Peabody Hall basement], not a classroom at all, but a cellar, of which the ceiling is supported by pillars that shut off the students' view of the blackboard (*one* blackboard). . . . Part of this room has been enclosed to make somebody an office (a beaverboard office), and this professor has the privilege of passing in and out during my class. You enter this room through a dark limbo, stacked with old desks and chairs and lumber piled in confusion. . . . I can neither leave a book, nor hang a map nor send a student to the board in this room. Why they learn what they do is a mystery." Other professors of French and Spanish expressed themselves similarly. In 1928, however, the Romance Pavilion on the Lawn opened, with ten lecture rooms and an office, and in 1929 handsome murals executed by noted French artists were added. French Ambassador Claudel was present for the dedication in 1929. Simple exercises were held, and Dr. Alderman and Paul G. McIntire were given the French Legion of Honor, the latter because he had donated a hospital for the tuberculous in France.

The condition of Peabody Hall came in for further caustic criticism in the late 1930s from Dean John L. Manahan of the School of Education. Referring to the upper floors, he complained that "most of those rooms have never been painted since the building was constructed," and they were "sadly in need of reconditioning." "This building is entitled to at least one coat of good fresh paint," said the dean. Two years later he thanked President Newcomb for greatly improving the general appearance "of many of the classrooms, offices and auditoriums."

With the increase in the university's enrollment and the proliferation of various sports, Lambeth Field had been completely
outgrown by 1930. Varsity and first-year teams in track, baseball, lacrosse, and football were trying to work out on the field
in the spring of that year, and the situation became not only
chaotic but dangerous. Javelin and discus throwers imperiled
the other athletes, and spring football practice had to be discontinued, along with all forms of interfraternity athletics. Individual students who wished to get some outdoor exercise
were without facilities. Negotiations were begun for obtaining
a vacant lot somewhere in Charlottesville. Plans had been
completed for Scott Stadium, to be built "in a little valley at
the foot of Mt. Jefferson," but it would not be ready until October 1931.

By the spring of that year the pressure on Lambeth Field
had been greatly relieved through the acquisition of two large
practice fields between Ivy Road and the C&O Railroad
tracks. They would have excellent turf by September, thus
providing adequate facilities for various sports. Twenty-two
new tennis courts were in use, thanks to the generosity of
Lady Astor. Even so, there were not enough to supply the demand.

The university's record in athletics was spotty; in boxing it
was outstanding, and in track and various other sports good,
but in football it had been wretched since the late 1920s.
School spirit was sadly lacking, and many students appeared
indifferent as to whether the teams won or lost. The coming
of Fred Dawson as football coach in 1931 introduced a new
and dynamic personality, and under Dawson's prodding student indifference became considerably less marked. As explained by the 1932 *Corks and Curls*: "The lead was taken by
Coach Dawson and the Varsity Club. . . . The latter body decided that the most efficient way to cure the trouble was to
begin work on the first-year men before they too fell into the
lackadaisical attitudes then prevalent. . . . The initial response
was most encouraging. . . . Further talks and appeals were
made at mass meetings. The result was quite successful. At the
VPI game, for the first time in years, Virginia had a creditable
cheering section. The team put up a fight that no one
dreamed it could."

36. *Zeisberg contemplates the agony and ecstasy of exams.*

A year later *Corks and Curls* was again deploring the lack of desire in the average student to take part in athletics, an attitude that extended to dramatics, literary endeavors, and publications. Less than 10 percent of the more than twenty-five hundred students came out for any athletic team. Dawson's campaign had helped, but much remained to be done.

Various sports were doing well, but not football. The swimming team had had four successive winning seasons, and in 1932 Virginia teams won nearly two-thirds of their games in nine different fields of sport. The boxers banged their way to the Southern Conference championship for the third time in six years, and the baseball team had its best winning percentage in forty years.

But Fred Dawson was frustrated by his inability to produce football victories, and he asked in 1934 to be relieved of the remaining year of his contract. He had tried for three years to get results on the gridiron, but to little effect. "I am convinced," he said, "that at Virginia where there are no athletic scholarships or other equivalents that bring in football players, the football coach is under a great handicap; so great, in fact, that I am content to step aside and see what someone else can do with the situation." Dawson had been popular with both faculty and students, but he could not surmount the obstacles that confronted him.

Gus Tebell, who had come to the university in 1930 as assistant coach of football, basketball, and baseball and soon had become coach of basketball and baseball, was named to succeed Dawson. His football contract was for only one year, and he remained in charge of the other two sports.

So much dissatisfaction was being expressed with the athletic situation, especially the failure to record notable football victories over the years, that President Newcomb appointed a committee of faculty and alumni to study the problem and make recommendations. William H. White, Jr., of the law faculty was named chairman. After a careful examination of the pertinent factors, the committee came up with the following proposals:

(1) Abolish the present Athletic Council and the faculty position of director of athletics and eliminate the G.A.A. from all participation in athletic affairs. (2) Create a School of Athletics and Physical Education, with three division—intercolle-

giate, physical education, and intramural sports. (3) Head of the school to have the rank of dean, with three assistants responsible for the three divisions, the dean to report to the president of the university. (4) An Advisory Council of Nine (3–3–3 system) to act in a purely advisory capacity. (5) All full-time coaches, instructors, and assistants to be members of the faculty. (6) The university will conform to the rules of any intercollegiate conference to which it belongs, but there should be a faculty committee to pass on eligibility of all members of the university's intercollegiate teams and represent faculty opinion in arranging schedules and athletic policies. If the university should cease to be a member of any athletic conference, this committee would make rules and regulations for participation in intercollegiate contests. Every effort should be made to encourage the growth of intramural sports. The greatest need of the Athletic Department is for "an adequate field house," with Memorial Gymnasium set aside for the Division of Physical Education and intramurals.

The foregoing recommendations were adopted almost in toto in late 1934 by the Board of Visitors, who directed that the plan be put into effect at the opening of the session of 1935–36. The board stipulated, however, that the head of the proposed department should have the title of director, rather than dean, and that persons employed solely as coaches would not be members of the faculty.

The president and visitors opposed offering athletic scholarships in any form, directly or indirectly. Under the Southern Conference's rules, every player had to sign a statement that he or she had not been paid to play. It was felt that if Virginia athletes participated in any such scholarship scheme, they could not sign the required statement without violating the university's honor code. Scholarships would still be offered to athletes and nonathletes on the basis of financial need, scholarly performance, and qualities of leadership.

The students lost no time in expressing a contrary view. In a poll a few weeks later, they voted more than 6 to 1 for athletic scholarships and rejected plans for leaving the Southern Conference by slightly less than 2 to 1. About 60 percent of the entire student body participated. A faculty poll in which about half of the professors took part showed some two-thirds favoring either "an easier schedule with strictly amateur teams" or "absolute abandonment of intercollegiate football." Only a small minority voted for athletic scholarships, while a somewhat larger number advocated retaining the existing system.

Evidencing the sharp disagreement among the various groups, the Alumni Advisory Council promptly advocated athletic scholarships and resignation from the conference, but the Board of Visitors on the following day declared that "no compromise will be made with professionalism. . . . Games will not be won at the cost of the ideals of this university." The visitors asserted their firm opposition to "any plan of athletic scholarships."

At this juncture, with university opinion almost hopelessly divided, Capt. Norton Pritchett of Davidson College was employed as the new director of athletics, effective in September 1935. Pritchett was a man of fine personality and great integrity. "He found conditions almost at their worst," said *Corks and Curls*; "everyone, including alumni, laughed when the thought of Virginia's winning a [football] game came up. Everyone was discouraged but Captain Pritchett."

One of the early major developments was a proposal by the Richmond alumni of a plan for athletic scholarships patterned on the Rhodes Scholarships. Devised by three prominent Richmonders—the Reverend Beverley D. Tucker, Jr., Dr. Carrington Williams, and Stuart G. Christian—it was promptly endorsed by a number of other alumni chapters. The three highly respected men who had worked out the scheme said they were "resolved that some of the scholarships shall go to non-athletes, just as some of the Rhodes Scholarships are awarded to non-athletes." This latter feature of the scholarship plan did not materialize; few, if any, nonathletes were recipients of scholarships. It was evidently too utopian a concept for the average alumnus to grasp.

But before any such awards could be made to athletes, Virginia had to get out of the Southern Conference, lest the Honor System be badly weakened if not virtually destroyed. Scholarship recipients at institutions belonging to the conference had to sign a statement that they had never "been paid for athletic skill or knowledge," and hundreds of scholarship recipients at membership institutions were signing these declarations—this despite the fact that they were obviously being paid for their athletic skill. The Richmond *Times-Dispatch* asked campus newspapers at six Virginia conference institutions whether the existing system was undermining honor systems, and five replied that it was.

Captain Pritchett was instructed by the Board of Visitors to submit the university's resignation at the Southern Conference's annual meeting in December 1936. He did so and read a statement quoting Forrest Fletcher of Washington and Lee, president of the conference, wherein Fletcher said that "practically all member institutions have violated the spirit of our regulations."

Bernard P. Chamberlain, president of the University of Virginia Alumni Association, explained that the university had withdrawn "in the interest of open honesty in athletic policy, and in fairness to the students." As a result of the withdrawal, the Southern Conference boxing tournament, held regularly at Charlottesville, was transferred to the University of Maryland. It was announced that Virginia would take part in no more conference tournaments but would continue to meet individual teams in competition. James G. Driver, director of athletics since 1929, resigned to enter business.

With Virginia athletes no longer required to sign statements that they were not being rewarded for athletic ability, the university was free to make its own rules. The Richmond plan, based on the principles governing Rhodes Scholarships, was announced as having been adopted by various alumni chapters. The Reverend Beverley Tucker explained that these are "not merely athletic scholarships," since they also "demand scholastic ability and above all, the sort of character and personality that will make the award a coveted distinction." Lee McLaughlin, the first winner of an athletic scholarship from the Richmond chapter, did indeed meet these requirements, but it was not possible to maintain such lofty standards indefinitely.

Having gotten the university squared away insofar as athletic scholarships were concerned, Captain Pritchett proceeded to employ Frank J. Murray, for fifteen years head football coach at Marquette University, to take charge of football at Virginia. Murray, a professor of political science at Marquette, had compiled an extraordinary record on the gridiron, with ninety-three wins, twenty-nine losses and six ties—

and this against some of the strongest teams in the nation. He came to the university in February 1939, in time for spring practice. Art Guepe soon joined him as assistant coach.

Athletic morale at Charlottesville was improving but still was at a low ebb. It remained to be seen whether salutary results would flow from Virginia's resignation from the Southern Conference, after fifteen years in that body, and whether Frank Murray, with the aid of scholarships, could turn things around. Thomas Lomax Hunter, a Richmond *Times-Dispatch* columnist, injected a humorous note by observing concerning next steps at the university: "What we want, what we need, is a hairy-chested fellow whose name ends in *inski* who can grind opposing tacklers under foot and leave a wide swath of cripples in his wake."

A fifty-piece band had been organized and put into uniform a year or two previously, under the direction of Prof. Robert E. Lutz and was a factor in providing improved morale at athletic contests. Lutz appealed to the students to learn "The Cavalier Song" and "Hike Virginia!" and explained that "there is no adequate leadership or effort in getting the songs across." Two years later *College Topics* urged that "The Cavalier Song" be played and sung at games, since it was an air with "more pep and vigor" than "The Good Old Song." The latter should be reserved for "more serious occasions," said *Topics*, which added that it was "inappropriate" after a touchdown, for example. The paper remarked on the numerous efforts that had been made to popularize "The Cavalier Song," but "unfortunately too many students have not familiarized themselves with either the words or the tune."

An attempt to persuade winners of the "V" to wear their sweaters around the Grounds was launched by the "V" Club. That organization issued a statement: "Virginia is the only institution in the country . . . where a monogram winner cannot go from his home or fraternity house to his boarding house or gymnasium with his sweater on without a feeling of abashment or being out of place. . . . Has not Virginia been a little too different along athletic lines?" The exhortation had little effect.

By the time Frank Murray reached his second football season in the fall of 1938, things were definitely looking up. The 1937 season had been a losing one, but by early October 1938

37. *The Corner in the early thirties.*

near hysteria gripped the student body, and the rally in Cabell Hall before the Washington and Lee game was unlike anything seen there in a long time. It was preceded by a torchlight parade from the Corner, after which Armistead Dobie spouted in typical fashion from the platform. The atmosphere was described by *College Topics* in what seems to have been excessively purple prose: "In a burst of noise, song, cheers and poetry far in excess of anything seen at the university in many years, an overflow crowd of 1,500 mad, jubilant students, dates, faculty members and townspeople crowded Cabell Hall to the rafters." After the rally, "with savage shrieks the frenzied mob ran up the Lawn to the steps of the Rotunda," thence to the Corner, and into town, where traffic on Main Street was held up for over an hour, "as the merrymakers danced and howled their way." Next day the team defeated W&L 13 to 0 for Virginia's first significant victory in several seasons.

Other similar rallies were held that fall, with enthusiasm at the highest pitch, and the team carried off the state championship, winning four, losing four, and tying one. Murray said the rallies were a major factor in achieving this drastic reversal of form.

Murray's coaching and recruiting continued to bring excellent results, and by 1940 his Virginia team was winning national fame. In that year it journeyed to the Yale Bowl and defeated Old Eli 19 to 14. A bright star of that game was an eighteen-year-old from Bluefield, Va., named William M. Dudley, weighing only 165 to 170 pounds but able to "do it all." He could run, pass, kick, block, and tackle, and soon was recognized as the most magnificent football player ever to wear a Virginia uniform. By the 1941 season Bill Dudley was captain of the Virginia team—at nineteen the youngest captain of a major college eleven in the country—and despite his small size the sensation of the football world. Virginia won all its games that year except one, a 21–19 loss to Yale. Dudley was chosen to every important all-American team—Associated Press, United Press, International News Service, and Grantland Rice's selection for *Collier's Magazine*. Rice wrote of him later: "There may have been a few better, smarter football players than Bill Dudley, but for the moment we can't recall their names. This even includes Jim Thorpe, Red Grange,

Bronco Nagurski, Dutch Clarke and Ernie Nevers. . . . Dudley comes close to being the best all-around back we've ever seen . . . a fine ball carrier, a magnificent kicker, a first-class pass receiver and the best defensive back, especially against passes, that anyone knows." Dudley won so many awards that it is impossible to list them all.

At the close of the 1941–42 session he enlisted in the Army Air Corps and was commissioned a lieutenant. After World War II he turned professional and joined the Pittsburgh Steelers, where he led the National Football League in yards gained and in returning punts and intercepting passes. With the Steelers he played about fifty minutes of every game, on defense as well as offense. He was named the outstanding player in the league and presented with the Carr Award. He then signed a three-year contract with the Detroit Lions at the highest figure paid up to that time in professional football. Dudley was elected in 1956 to the College Football Hall of Fame and in 1966 to the Professional Football Hall of Fame. Twenty-five years after his graduation from Virginia, *Sports Illustrated* chose him along with other athletes for its "Silver Anniversary All-American Award," by virtue of "extraordinary achievement in life." He had been elected to the General Assembly from Lynchburg and was a successful businessman there. Despite his almost unprecedented athletic accomplishments and honors, Bill Dudley's head never became enlarged. He was the same modest fellow who had come to Virginia out of Bluefield High School many years before. After the war he returned to the university several times to help with the coaching.

When the university band was returning from the Yale game in Dudley's final year at Virginia, the bus on which it was traveling caught fire about sixteen miles north of Charlottesville. Eighty percent of the band's instruments and all of its uniforms were a total loss. None of the passengers was injured. Despite this catastrophe the organization, without uniforms and with borrowed instruments, put on a superlative performance at the University of Richmond game the following Saturday. The leader of the band, which served both for athletic contests and concerts, was James E. Berdahl.

In his report to the president for the session, Randall

Thompson, head of the music department, referred to the loss of the instruments and uniforms and said that "every branch of equipment for music owned by the university or by the division was in a grievous state of disrepair, neglect, dilapidation and sometimes total unusability at the beginning of this year." He requested larger appropriations and a full-time band director. Fortunately, two grants from the Carnegie Corporation "enabled us to realize many of the hopes expressed a year ago," Thompson reported for 1942–43. Great improvement in equipment resulted.

Virginia maintained the boxing supremacy it had acquired in the 1920s. Lawrence Perry, sports columnist for the New York *Sun*, wrote in 1934 that the university "probably has the best set of amateur boxers in the world," and "they really are amateurs, all students in good standing." From 1932 to 1936 the Cavalier ringmen were undefeated, winning twenty-four bouts in succession and six Southern Conference titles. Bobby Goldstein won the intercollegiate and Southern Conference lightweight titles, the latter championship three times in a row. Other Southern Conference titleholders included Harold Stuart, Gordon and Robert Rainey, Archie Hahn, Jr., and Maynard Womer. Ray Schmidt won the 175-pound intercollegiate title in 1937. Mortimer Caplin, later a member of the law faculty and U.S. Commissioner of Internal Revenue, was also a star member of the team.

Good seats for important matches in Memorial Gymnasium were gone by 6 P.M. on the night of the bouts, and every available inch of space was filled. Black ties were usually worn at ringside. Spectators were forbidden to cheer during the fights, but when a round ended or Virginia scored a victory, pandemonium reigned. Despite frequent warnings from officials and from *College Topics*, booing and hissing sometimes erupted over a referee's decisions deemed unfair or otherwise objectionable. Some of this was attributable to what was termed a "jerkwater element" from downtown, but students were partly responsible.

Periodic suggestions were made that intercollegiate boxing should be abolished at Virginia, since frequent blows to the head might cause permanent brain injury. These criticisms became louder and more insistent when a VMI cadet, William J.

Eastham, died in 1937 from a broken neck sustained in a bout with Maryland. But for the time being the sport was continued. On the other hand, intramural boxing was done away with in 1941, since supervision was deemed inadequate.

Coach Johnny LaRowe had a serious illness in 1936 and was confined thereafter to a wheel chair, but he reported daily for practice. In 1940 he died. There were many tributes to his high character and fine sportsmanship, especially from the young men who had boxed on his teams. The unanimity of their admiration and affection was indeed remarkable.

One of Johnny's closest friends was "Spike" Webb, boxing coach at the U.S. Naval Academy, whose teams Virginia defeated four times in succession; no other boxers had beaten Navy in twenty-one years. On one occasion Webb and LaRowe were in the same hotel, and Webb slipped LaRowe a loaded cigar, which exploded. Next morning Johnny stole into Spike's room and switched his shaving lotion and throat gargle. Webb took a mouthful of the lotion and thought his mouth was on fire. He hopped around the room in acute discomfort, while his friend, watching from the door, doubled up with mirth.

Fenton Gentry, one of LaRowe's boxing stars, a Southern Conference champion and Rhodes Scholar, said of his former coach: "He had a magic way of encouraging his boys to keep on fighting, although defeat stared them plumb in the eyes. . . . He was a one hundred per cent, 24-karat real man." Gentry was sure the other Virginia boys who had fought for LaRowe felt the same way. Scores of them returned in 1947, on the twenty-fifth anniversary of boxing at Virginia, when a bust of LaRowe by Francis Wadsworth was unveiled in the gym—scene of Johnny's greatest triumphs.

"Al" York, one of LaRowe's finest boxers, succeeded him as coach. As time went on, however, there was a mounting feeling that intercollegiate boxing was too dangerous. One college after another dropped the sport until there was hardly anybody left for Virginia to fight. Dr. Hugh Trout led the effort in the Board of Visitors for its abolition, at first without success. He stated in 1949 that parents of nine university boxers had written him urging that the sport be abolished. Five past presidents of the Medical Society of Virginia expressed the same view. But the Board of Visitors voted to continue the sport, with Trout the only dissenter. Colgate Darden, president of the university, recommended two years later that it be dropped, but the visitors disagreed. Finally in 1955 the Athletic Council decided that intercollegiate boxing should be eliminated, and the visitors concurred. They directed that boxing be purely intramural thereafter, a decision exactly the reverse of that reached in 1941.

In basketball Virginia's record over the years down to World War II was exceptionally good. The team had only one losing season during Pop Lannigan's twenty-five-year tenure ending in 1929, and Gus Tebell's quints also were successful. From 1939 to 1941 they won forty-six of sixty games, and the 1941 team won eighteen of twenty-two, one of the best records in the university's history. The cocaptains were Bill Harman and Billy McCann, with Dick Wiltshire also a star.

The track team was making a superlative record. By 1941 it had won twelve state championships in thirteen years under Coach Archie Hahn. As in the 1920s, the relay team was winning at the Penn Relays. It won the 480-yard shuttle hurdle relay in 1938 against the best teams in America and repeated the win the following year. In 1938 the team consisted of Duncan Hawley, Armistead Peyton, Lang Dayton, and Frank L. Fuller III, and it bested Harvard's 1936 Penn Relay record by four-tenths of a second. The victorious Virginia hurdlers in 1939 were Harvey Poe (later a Rhodes Scholar), Harry Stokes, Peyton, and Fuller. In 1940 at Chapel Hill, N.C., Captain Fuller set a new world record in the 70-yard high hurdles with a time of 8.4 seconds.

C. Alphonso Smith, Jr., a superb tennis player, matriculated at Virginia in the late 1920s. By 1930 he was captain of the tennis team, and again in 1931. Under his leadership Virginia netmen did well against tough competition. "Smithy" had won the National Boys Singles and Doubles Championships in 1924, and three years later the National Junior Doubles Championship. In 1974, exactly half a century after winning the national boys' titles, Smith and his partner Frank M. Goeltz made a grand slam of all national doubles championships for men sixty-five and over, winning on grass, clay, hard surface, and indoor. As a result of all this, Smith is listed in the Guiness Book of World Records. In 1975 the U.S. Tennis

38. *President Franklin D. Roosevelt spoke at the 1940 commencement exercises in Memorial Gymnasium. He made history by denouncing Mussolini for plunging his dagger into the back of his neighbor, France.*

Association presented him with a plaque inscribed "First man in the history of American athletics to win national titles 50 years apart." Alphonso Smith served as the nonplaying captain of the U.S. Davis Cup Team in 1963.

Records of a different kind were made in 1938 by J. Smith Ferebee, '27, whose demoniac energy as a golf player was well nigh incredible. To begin with, to settle a bet he played 144 holes in one day without benefit of golf carts. Then, on another bet, he proceeded to play 600 holes in four days, walking over each course and covering at least 72 holes each day in two different cities. To win this bet, Ferebee traveled 3,000 miles by plane from Los Angeles to Phoenix to Kansas City to St. Louis to Milwaukee to Chicago to Philadelphia to New York. He played the 600 holes in 2,860 strokes, averaging an hour and 15 minutes per 18 holes, and playing the 601st hole at midnight on the New York World's Fair Grounds. If this alumnus isn't in the Guiness Book of World Records, he ought to be. Ripley featured him in his "Believe It or Not" syndicated strip.

Intramural sports had their inception at Virginia during the session of 1933–34. Seven years previously an attempt had been made to launch an intramural program, but no funds could be found. However, by the fall of 1933 it became possible to inaugurate intramurals by charging a fee to each participating team. The teams represented the various fraternities, and the sports were touch football, volleyball, horseshoe pitching, basketball, boxing, swimming, handball, baseball, track and field, and tennis. There were 452 contests during the 1933–34 session, with sixteen hundred students taking part. The nonfraternity men had only a basketball league. A few years later it became possible to include them when the Division of Intramural Sports was organized under the capable direction of Robert N. Hoskins. By the late 1930s the program was operating effectively for both fraternity and nonfraternity men, and the games brought the two groups together, thus creating better relations.

Director of Athletics Pritchett reiterated in 1939 that the university's greatest material need was a field house. Pointing to the inadequacy of the Memorial Gymnasium, in view of the growing enrollment, he said: "The matter boils down to one of two possibilities—either a field house or a 'nut house.'" In the following year Pritchett wrote that the university seeks to realize its athletic objectives

by refusing to rationalize dishonesty in requiring students to disclaim "outside aid in any way related to athletic interest or ability"; by refusing to divert funds of the Athletic Association into any forms of scholarship or "aid"; by refusing to offer courses of study designed for easy maintenance of athletic eligibility; by refusing to make any subtle distinction between standards for eligibility and requirements for graduation (whereby the "athlete" competes for four years without hope of graduation); by refusing to encourage any athlete in the delusion that athletic fame is a guarantee of later success in life; in short, by refusing to recognize any distinction between "athletes" and other students.

Alumni affairs in the 1930s were looking up, despite the depression. Almost every member of the first three graduating classes in the decade affiliated with the Alumni Association, in contrast to what had occurred in some earlier years. Hundreds of alumni returned for the 1933 reunion at Finals, and the usual barbecue was held in the little green valley below the cemetery, near the second green on the university golf course and known at times as the Dell. The Big Tent was brought back in 1934, after an absence of a couple of decades, and erected just west of Peabody and Monroe halls. The inauguration of President Newcomb was the principal event of that year's Finals. Extremely simple ceremonies ushered in the new president. Rector Frederic W. Scott welcomed Newcomb to his responsibilities, and Gov. George C. Peery addressed the graduates.

The Edwin Anderson Alderman Alumni Fund, created in connection with the twenty-fifth anniversary of Alderman's coming to the university but subsequently neglected, was brought forcefully to the alumni's attention at the 1935 Finals. A campaign for contributions to the fund was launched in order that needed services and causes at the university might be underwritten. The intensive effort got under way in the fall, and after nearly six months of work about $32,000 were raised from over 2,000 alumni, for an average of $15 each. This result "surpasses last year's record of the alumni fund of any Southern college or university, some of which have been carrying on this for years," said the *Alumni News*. "It is better than the majority of the university alumni funds throughout the country. . . . Contributions have been received from 14 percent of the living alumni." Cary N. Weisiger, Jr., '05, chairman of the Alumni Council, was given the major share of the credit for the drive's success. He devoted "months of his personal time," as well as his money, to bring about this result.

Acquisition of a permanent home for the Alumni Association to replace the rented quarters at the Corner was the big event of 1936. The former home of Zeta Beta Tau and Phi Sigma Kappa fraternities, on Emmet Street (U.S. Highway 29) across from Memorial Gymnasium, was purchased for the association by the university. It was hoped that alumni would furnish sufficient money to put the building in proper condition, and the opinion was expressed that part of the just-raised Alderman Fund could be used for this purpose. The alumni reunion at the 1936 Finals was held in the Big Tent on the front lawn, since the building itself was not ready. But the Big Tent continued to be a frequent feature of alumni reunions after the association moved into its new quarters. In 1939 a loan was made to the association from the centennial fund of 1921 toward the cost of financing Alumni Hall.

The first of several annual trips through the South to meet with old grads in various cities was taken in 1937, pursuant to arrangements made by the Alumni Association. Dean Ivey F. Lewis, Director of Athletics Norton Pritchett, Alumni Association President Bernard P. Chamberlain, and Alumni Secretary J. Malcolm Luck made the three thousand-mile journey. It extended as far south as Miami and as far west as Memphis, with a half dozen other stops. Dean Lewis pointed out at the gatherings that over six hundred automobiles were owned by university students, and that four young men had been killed in accidents during the session. Captain Pritchett explained Virginia's withdrawal from the Southern Conference and said that it had been widely misinterpreted. "Virginia is not going in for 'big league' football and never will, so long as I can prevent it," he declared. "Our new rules are precisely those that have prevailed at Davidson College. . . . Dartmouth, Amherst and Williams . . . have exactly the regulations we have."

Partly as a result of these trips through the South, the

39. *William M. (Bill) Dudley, all-American, 1941, and all-pro, greatest football player in the university's history, despite his relatively small size.*

Alumni Association had become "a vigorous, forward-looking organization," C. Harrison Mann, '31, wrote in the *Alumni News*. Mann, chairman of the university's scholarship committee for the Washington, D.C., chapter, and later a prominent member of the General Assembly, discussed the upsurge in alumni interest in an article covering more than five pages of the *News*. "During the past several years," he wrote, "more spontaneous interest has been manifested by Virginia's alumni than ever before in the history of the university. The combustion has been energized by a curious mixture of loyalty, love and determination that a great university shall maintain its greatness, teach its principles of integrity of the individual in a world where individualism is fast becoming a heresy."

Activities of the medical alumni became better organized and more effective when the Medical Alumni Association was established at the university in 1940, with leading medical graduates in attendance. Such an association had been formed in 1914, with Dr. Hugh Young as the first president, and a meeting was held at Finals in 1916. But the organization became inactive and was not revived for nearly a quarter of a century. In 1938 Dr. Beverly C. Smith, '19, of New York, wrote Dr. David L. Lyman, 1900, of Wallingford, Conn., asking him to come to Gotham for a conference on the subject of forming a Medical Alumni Association. He accepted, and it was agreed when they met that an effort would be made to assemble a group of medical alumni at the university on April 20–21, 1940. Lyman and Smith wrote medical graduates in various parts of the country inviting them to the meeting, and a score accepted. The gathering was successful, and another was held a year later. Dr. Smith was elected chairman at that time, and the association grew into a powerful organization that has raised substantial funds and influenced the growth and importance of the Medical School in many ways.

The association was almost purely social for a good many years, and there was opposition to suggestions that it serve as an agency for raising funds for the Medical School. But in the early 1960s it was decided to change this policy, and William A. Booth was placed in charge of the fund raising, with notable success. At that time the Medical Alumni Advisory Committee was initiated under the direction of Beverly C. Smith and Jed Irvine. Mrs. Eunice Davis, who had served as executive director of the association, continued to edit the *Medical Alumni News Letter* until her retirement in 1974, and Booth became the organization's full-time director. The Medical School Foundation was established in 1972, adding greatly to the association's potency as a raiser of funds. The usefulness of the alumni to the Medical School has been vastly increased through the operations of the association. And the association is one of the reasons why the University of Virginia Medical School continues to rank as one of the foremost such schools in the South.

The alumni of the Law School have been similarly supportive of that school and have strengthened it in various ways. The University of Virginia Law School Association was organized in 1921 under the leadership of Prof. Raleigh C. Minor and Dean William M. Lile "to advance the cause of legal education, promote the interests and increase the usefulness of the . . . Law School and to promote mutual acquaintance and good fellowship among all members of the association." With the death of Professor Minor, the prime mover in establishing the association, it became inactive until 1934, when Dean Armistead M. Dobie called a meeting at which new officers were elected. Pressing needs of the school were brought forcefully to the attention of President Newcomb, President Darden, and others in authority over the years. Important results were achieved, especially in increasing the number of professors and raising their salary scales, greatly strengthening the law library, and fostering the establishment of the Law School Foundation. Annual drives for gifts to the foundation have produced substantial results.

The law library expanded spectacularly as a result of the devoted work of the alumni, combined with the dedication of Frances Farmer, who became law librarian in 1942 and was secretary-treasurer of the Law School Association for sixteen years. The library had only 30,000 volumes in 1942, but a decade later the total had reached 100,000, a milestone marked by an enthusiastic celebration. In that ten-year period the state of Virginia provided $150,000, while the alumni raised $165,000 in cash and books. By the early 1970s the library had 300,000 volumes and was the largest in the South. Frances Farmer received the distinguished service award of the Law School Foundation in 1957, and the following year was elected president of the American Association of Law Libraries. Among the prominent alumni who took leading roles in developing the library were Paul B. Barringer, Jr., '13, and W. Catesby Jones, '92, of New York, and Thomas B. Gay, '06, of Richmond. Executive directors of the foundation have been William H. White, Jr., 1952–62; Knox Turnbull, 1962–64, and Marion K. Kellogg, 1964–73.

An annual Law Alumni Day was introduced in 1958 and has become a great source of support for the Law School, bringing alumni back to see the school in action. A Law Alumni Directory is another feature of the association's program; it has been helpful in promoting fund raising for the foundation.

The association is headed by an elected nine-member council, plus officers and former association presidents, with a large number of committees which provide information and assistance for programs of the school, such as scholarships, library, curriculum, and so on.

A statement by Dean F. D. G. Ribble in 1952 put the work of the association in perspective: "The law alumni continue to be of vital help. . . . This is notable in the placement of graduates, and in advice and recommendations on the admission of new students. The law alumni have also been active in other phases of the Law School work, notably in advice on the area of curriculum and in advice and support in connection with the law library. The Law School Council is composed of a fine group of successful and effective lawyers, devoted to the school and willing to help in every way possible."

On another sector of the alumni front, the twentieth anniversary of William H. Wranek, Jr., as managing editor of the *Alumni News* was noted in the Sept.-Oct. 1941 number of that publication. Wranek succeeded Frank R. Reade, '23, in the summer of 1922, when McLane Tilton was editor and business manager. Tilton retired in 1930, and the Alumni Board of Managers did not elect another editor, but Wranek discharged the editor's duties. More recently he was given the post of business manager, which he combined with his other responsibilities.

A two-week Institute on Local Government was held at the university in the summer of 1936. It had the object of strengthening the university's offerings in political science and preparing the way for establishment at the following session of a Bureau of Public Administration, operating on a different basis from the bureau founded some years before. The summer institute brought nationally known figures to the Grounds, as well as persons distinguished in the field of local government.

A Bureau of Public Administration had been set up at the university in 1931 as a cooperative venture for research, with Rowland Egger as director. A grant from the Rockefeller Foundation in 1936 made possible the establishment of the bureau as an independent coordinate university agency, with Egger as director, Raymond Uhl as assistant director, and Vincent Shea as statistician and economist. Its functions would be threefold: (1) to serve as a clearing house for the planning and advisory agencies, institutions of higher learning, and individual researchers in public administration in Virginia; (2) to develop its own research program, and (3) to provide assistance in the instruction of students at the university in public administration. It would not be a policy-forming or policy-influencing agency.

Rowland Egger was appointed by Gov. James H. Price in 1939 as director of the state's reorganized Division of the Budget, and Raymond Uhl was named acting director of the bureau. It was the first of numerous extracurricular assignments of Professor Egger, not only in this country but in other parts of the world.

The bureau staff undertook research projects in Petersburg, Staunton, Roanoke, Williamsburg, and Albemarle County, while other similar projects were planned for the future. Pilot studies on the centralized executive were made in the above-mentioned political subdivisions.

The Virginia Council on Public Administration was created in 1938 with Governor Price as chairman and numerous state and university officials as members. Its secretariat was the Bureau of Public Administration. During its first two and a half years the bureau published seven studies and investigated more than a dozen additional problems in the institutions of higher learning.

A plan for the development of a research program in business, industry, and banking, under which the U.S. Bureau of

Foreign and Domestic Commerce would cooperate with social science research organizations and schools of business in the colleges and universities of the nation, was launched in 1939 at the university. Dr. Nathaniel H. Engle of the bureau said he was holding the first conference at the University of Virginia because Wilson Gee had been first to suggest the plan. A part of the scheme was for the university to cooperate with Virginia bankers in stimulating business throughout the state by developing small, local industries that would make use of surplus agricultural and natural products. A conference of bankers in Richmond endorsed the program.

Such plans as those of the bureaus mentioned above brought important personalities to the university. Other celebrities came when a different type of gathering took place in 1931. About two dozen leading southern authors were invited to the Grounds by James Southall Wilson after the idea had been suggested by Ellen Glasgow, the Richmond novelist. "The Relation of the Southern Author to His Public" was the general theme, but there was no formal program. Several New York critics attended. Miss Glasgow presided at the informal discussions on Friday, and DuBose Heyward on Saturday. Participants included James Boyd, William Faulkner, Allen Tate, Josephine Pinckney, Ulrich B. Phillips, Cale Young Rice, Archibald Henderson, Paul Green, Sherwood Anderson, and James Branch Cabell. A tea at the Colonnade Club, a reception at Farmington, a visit to Monticello, and tea at Castle Hill with Amelie Rives Troubetzkoy as hostess were on the agenda. The authors agreed that book pages outside of New York were inferior and in need of attention. Emily Clark, former editor of *The Reviewer*, wrote of the gathering in the New York *Herald Tribune*'s book section and said the meeting accomplished what several years of correspondence and conscientious reading of one another's books might never have achieved. She stated that various authors who were known to dislike each other's writings became the best of friends. Josephine Pinckney also wrote of the conference for the *Saturday Review of Literature*.

Other important personalities were brought to the university by the Institute of Public Affairs, which took place each summer until interrupted by World War II. The institute became increasingly successful, with audiences of five thousand

40. Prof. William H. (Reddy) Echols, hero of the 1895 Rotunda fire and longtime Grand Banana of the Elis.

packing the McIntire Theater for the evening addresses. The first attendance of that magnitude turned out in 1935 to hear Gen. Hugh S. (Ironpants) Johnson, czar of the National Recovery Administration (NRA), and Cong. James W. Wadsworth of New York. The following summer the institute was even more successful. Among those on the program were Secretary of the Interior Harold L. Ickes; Winthrop W. Aldrich; William L. Chenery, editor of *Collier's Magazine*; Earl Browder, Communist nominee for president; Norman Thomas, Socialist nominee for president; Walter Hampden, the actor; Charles W. Gay, president of the New York Stock Exchange; and Edward L. Bernays, noted public relations counsel.

Prof. Charles G. Maphis, who had presided ably over the institute from the beginning and had been active in other university affairs, died suddenly, and Prof. Robert K. Gooch took charge of the 1938 institute. He was assisted by Prof. Hardy C. Dillard '27. The following year Dillard was in complete charge and remained so until the institute was interrupted by the outbreak of World War II.

Hardy Dillard's leadership of the institute brought high praise. But Gordon M. Buck, former president of the University of Virginia Alumni Association, wrote the *Alumni News* protesting Dillard's action in inviting Earl Browder, general secretary of the Communist party, U.S.A., and Ambassador Oumansky of Russia to be on the program. Buck contended that Dillard "goes beyond freedom of speech when . . . he offers at the University of Virginia a rostrum from which [Browder and Oumansky] may spread subversive doctrines." He added that "search will be made in vain . . . for any instance in which Jefferson offered the university as a forum, or furnished any other facility for promulgating the principles of the Federalist Party, and that party sought merely an elastic construction, not the complete destruction, of our constitution." Dillard replied that "Mr. Buck has not only completely misunderstood the function of the institute, but more specifically he has misunderstood the reasons for the inclusion of Mr. Browder and Mr. Oumansky. . . . The general topic for the meetings was 'New Problems of Government: National and International.' Some 70 speakers participated in the two weeks' sessions. . . . Having selected topics which are important and timely, effort is directed at getting the best available speakers. . . . where controversial topics are selected both sides should be fairly heard." A spokesman for Nazi Germany also was on the program by invitation. Dillard pointed out that "the positions of both Russia and Germany were under heavy fire by a great number of other speakers. . . . It is certain that the institute, by pursuing its basic policy and inviting a hearing by both sides, did much to stimulate interest and thought." He added that "this has been the consistent policy of the institute [as] is amply demonstrated by its past programs."

Also in the area of public affairs was the "Little Congress," organized by the students in 1937, with Bolling Lambeth as chairman of the organizing committee. A unicameral student legislature for the discussion of national issues, it was modeled on the Oxford Union and the George Washington University Union. The previously referred-to debate between Professors Robert K. Gooch and F. D. G. Ribble on President Roosevelt's "court-packing plan" was held under the auspices of the congress and launched its activities auspiciously. More than one thousand students filled Cabell Hall.

The little Congress was established on the basis of a three-party system. Conservatives, liberals, and middle-of-the-roaders held conventions early in the school year and drafted their platforms on such public questions as farm tenancy, lynching, un-American activities, and the "court-packing plan." Public debates were an important part of the program, and these were followed by legislative sessions. "The object of the Little Congress is to provide a training ground for all those who are interested in how a legislative body works," G. C. Halsted III, chairman of the executive council, wrote. At its first legislative session in 1939 the Congress passed a bill favoring a military alliance between the United States and the other democracies. The organization functioned through the 1939–40 session, but, as with so many other activities, World War II put an end to its program.

A number of leading figures in the life of the university, men who represented the institution's finest ideals and who had served it for long periods, died during the decade that ended in 1941: Dr. John Staige Davis, William H. Echols, Dean William M. Thornton, Dean William Minor Lile, Dean James M. Page, John J. Luck, Dr. John H. Neff, Dean James C. Flippin,

Dr. Paul B. Barringer, and John S. Patton. It is to be doubted if any decade in the university's history has seen the loss of so many of the institution's memorable personalities.

Librarian John S. Patton, who died in 1932, had retired in the middle 1920s after serving for nearly a quarter of a century, during which he assumed the tremendous task of reorganizing the library after the Rotunda fire of 1895. He had previously been editor of the Roanoke *Times* and editor and part owner of the Charlottesville *Progress*.

The death of Dr. John Staige Davis in 1933, after an illness of nearly six years, following a paralytic stroke, was noted in the previous chapter. His witty and informative lectures were long remembered by his students. A grandson of John A. G. Davis, the chairman of the faculty who was fatally wounded by a rioting student in 1840, he had been on the teaching staff at the medical school since 1894.

William H. Echols, professor of mathematics, hero of the Rotunda fire in 1895, and longtime Grand Banana of the Elis, was next to go. He died of a heart attack in 1934 at his home on East Lawn after forty-four years on the faculty. "Reddy" Echols, so called because of his red hair, was a gripping lecturer and was venerated by the students. His annual address to the first-year men on the honor system was a classic. "Thousands of alumni are feeling a sense of personal loss," said the *Alumni News* concerning his passing. "Many came from a distance to attend the funeral." And the Richmond *News Leader* commented: "Sometimes a man emerges that incarnates the spirit of the whole body of which he is a member. Such a man was 'Reddy' Echols, for though he would have been the last to claim or realize it, yet in him was a burning and shining light which was the vital spirit of the university." The class of 1935 presented his portrait as its class gift.

William M. Thornton, chairman of the faculty for eight years and dean of engineering for twenty, died in 1935. His was a personality that impressed itself upon the institution whose faculty he had joined in 1875. A blood clot made necessary the amputation of his right leg in 1930. James Southall Wilson wrote of "Billy" Thornton: "Dean Thornton's distinction was threefold: as teacher and administrator in the Department of Engineering, and chairman of the faculty . . . and leader in the general affairs of the university, and as a gentleman and scholar unafraid, a speaker of force, a virile writer and rich personality." Prof. B. F. D. Runk stated that "Thornton was a genius; he could teach any subject, and they said that if they gave him six months, he could teach medicine . . . a wonderful person, a great scholar and a great friend of the students."

A few months later came the death of Dean William Minor Lile of the law school. He had joined the faculty in 1893, as John B. Minor was rounding out his half century of distinguished service. "Billy" Lile, as he was affectionately known to the students, was one of a great triumvirate. Raleigh Minor and "Charlie" Graves also had joined the law faculty in the 1890s, and with Lile were the mainstays of that teaching staff for decades. The position of dean was created in 1904, and Lile was appointed to the post. He occupied it with distinction until his retirement in 1932. In that position he led in reorganizing and strengthening the curriculum, thus maintaining the great prestige of the school. Armistead Dobie, who succeeded him as dean, wrote after his death: "No student who ever sat under him can forget his flashing wit, his keen power of legal analysis, his ability to arouse and sustain legal curiosity, and his almost uncanny power of clear, incisive statement in crisp and picturesque language."

Dean James M. Page died in 1936, and his death brought genuine grief to thousands. He had retired in 1934 because of ill health. Reference was made in the preceding chapter to "Jim" Page's genius for handling wayward students in a manner that was effective, while at the same time retaining their affection. As President Newcomb expressed it, "He possessed those rare qualities of heart and mind which enabled him to administer discipline to students in such a manner as to cause them to love him." Ben Dulany spoke for the students when he wrote: "Long before he left the colonnades he was a legend. That rarest of men he was who was true to his youth by staying young despite years. Somewhere he preserved the faculty of remembering what the eternal student is like, how he thinks and why he does what he does. We join in mourning. For while there are and will be many deans, Dr. Page will ever be The Dean." Nils Hammerstrand, a Scandinavian member of the faculty, wrote: "Of all the men I have known in different parts of the world none was equal to Dean Page." Four years before Dean Page's death, while he was still active, the Class of 1932 presented his portrait to the university.

John Jennings (Pot) Luck, chairman of the mathematics faculty for several years and a member of that faculty since 1916, died of a heart attack in 1938. Jovial and approachable, weighing in the vicinity of three hundred pounds, Professor Luck was an effective teacher who showed exceptional concern for his students. As an undergraduate he had won high scholastic honors and been elected to the Hot Feet and the IMPs, as well as to the presidency of the Academic School and the Jefferson Society. *Corks and Curls* was dedicated to him in 1931.

The community and state were shocked in November 1938 at the disappearance of Dr. John H. Neff, an admired and respected member of the medical faculty. His body was found floating in Payne's Pond fourteen miles east of Charlottesville, with his automobile parked at the pond's edge. A verdict of suicide was rendered by the coroner, but no conceivable motive or explanation was ever uncovered. "Johnny" Neff had been an extremely popular student at the university, president of the graduating class of 1910, captain of the football team, and member of the leading social organizations. During his years on the medical faculty he had achieved a wide reputation as a urologist. Dr. Neff left a wife and three children. His brother, Douglas W. Neff, had been captain of the baseball team and student leader in his day, and later entered the ministry of the Episcopal Church. He drowned himself in 1932.

Another shock to the Medical School came in 1939 when Dean James C. Flippin, aged sixty-one, was stricken at his home on West Lawn and died the next day without regaining consciousness. Born in Lunenburg County, he had been graduated in medicine in 1901. He joined the faculty the following year. On the death of Dean Theodore Hough in 1934 he was named to the deanship. The school expanded physically in significant ways during his incumbency, and its standards and reputation were maintained. Dean Flippin was highly regarded by his faculty colleagues as well as by the students and was esteemed for his human qualities no less than for his capacity as an administrator.

Dr. Paul B. Barringer, whose many contributions to the life of the university have been previously discussed, died at his home in 1941, after an illness of more than a year. He severed

41. *Armistead M. Dobie, dean of the Law School, addressing students in Cabell Hall.*

his connection with the university in 1907 to become president of VPI, but he resigned that position after six years for reasons outlined in an earlier chapter. Dr. Barringer spent his remaining years at or near the university. In 1938 he was elected the second honorary president of the University of Virginia Alumni Association, Armistead C. Gordon having been the first. In that year Dr. Barringer delivered the centennial address before the association.

Mrs. John L. Newcomb, wife of the university's president, also died in 1941, after an illness of several months. Then Japan attacked Pearl Harbor, and President Newcomb's burdens were greatly intensified, as wartime problems were added to those occasioned by the death of his wife. She had been a mainstay on the social side of his administration, serving as a gracious hostess at many functions. Mrs. Newcomb also was active in community welfare organizations. Her passing left her devoted husband greatly bereft and frightfully lonely in the big president's residence on Carr's Hill. He asked the Board of Visitors for permission to move to the Colonnade Club or an apartment, but the board refused.

Another well-known figure whose death caused genuine sorrow during these years was "Charlie" Brown, the affable, handsome, carefully groomed black barber, with his shop at the Corner. He had trimmed the hair and shaved the beards of generations of professors and students. Charlie and his father before him had been "tonsorial assistants to students and alumni since 1865," as they stated in their advertisement published in the *Alumni News* over a long period.

The retirement or resignation of several faculty members occurred during these years.

Prof. Charles W. Paul resigned in 1936 on account of ill health, after nearly thirty years of teaching the students the art of debating and speaking. He joined the teaching staff in 1908 and was for many years a member of the law faculty. He also taught students in the college, and was active in developing student debaters in the literary societies.

Stringfellow Barr, '17, resigned in 1937 from the history faculty, and Scott Buchanan from the philosophy faculty, to join President Robert M. Hutchins's University of Chicago.

"Winkie" Barr, a former Rhodes Scholar who had been a member of the university teaching staff since 1924, was one of the most brilliant lecturers in the institution. He soon left Chicago to become president of St. John's College, Annapolis, Md. The curriculum there would be based on one hundred of the "best books of ancient and modern thought." Barr took Buchanan to Annapolis as dean.

When Prof. Arthur Fickenscher retired in 1941, he was accorded the almost unheard-of accolade of a front-page editorial in *College Topics*. He had served for two decades as the first professor of music in the McIntire School of Fine Arts. A graduate of the Royal Conservatory in Munich, Germany, he was the composer of numerous musical works and the inventor of an instrument called a Polytone. Many of his songs were performed in this and other countries, said *Topics*, which added that he was a pioneer in tonal effects whose stature might become much greater in time.

The university scene underwent a change in 1935 when the jangling orange and blue street cars that had functioned since just after the turn of the century were replaced by red and gray buses. The cars, which ran up Main Street and along University Avenue and Rugby Road to the C&O Railroad and back again, were operated by four motormen who had been performing this rite for from twenty-three to thirty-two years each. They were Bay S. Maupin, otherwise known as "Pegasus on Wheels," C. M. Childress, and F. F. and W. B. Birckhead. Three of them expressed dismay at the prospect of shifting from the helm of a trolley car to the wheel of a bus, but all accepted the invitation of the Virginia Public Service Company to pilot the new conveyances. Students, faculty, and other members of the community were pleased that this familiar quartet would continue to perform their transportational functions. The fare on the buses, as on the street cars, was 5 cents.

The familiar orange and blue cars disappeared, but another landmark remained. This was "Tim," the "Professor of Bumology," who had been hanging around the university premises in one capacity or another for some three decades. Born in Belfast, Ireland, of pauper parents who came to the United

States in 1872 when he was three years old, Tim went to sea at age eighteen and then joined the U.S. Navy. He arrived at the university about 1907 and for a time was landscape gardener for Dr. and Mrs. John Staige Davis. He married, and he and his wife had four children. When his wife died Tim decided to "retire and become Professor of Bumology." With his gray beard and his panhandled second-hand clothes, he hung around the Corner for many years. He seemed to subsist entirely on the coins he could wheedle out of students or others; they also treated him to an occasional beer.

Tim was "on the lam" from the police at frequent intervals on charges of vagrancy. Since the annexation of 1939 left the university Grounds outside the jurisdiction of Charlottesville's minions of the law, Tim would leap over the wall on University Avenue to university property when he saw one of the cops approaching, and thumb his nose from that safe haven. Occasionally the police would creep up on him when he was sunning himself on the Corner steps and haul him off to durance vile. Once he was seen walking down the street "with the seat of his pants missing," and Captain Mac, the resident lawman, sought to take him into custody; but Captain Mac had a bad leg and Tim outran him.

Tim died in 1943 of pneumonia. The students took up a collection and contributed a spray that covered the casket inscribed "From the U. Va. Student Body." They also contributed toward the cost of his tombstone. He was buried in Oakwood Cemetery. Apparently Tim's real name was Frederick Morris.

Much more important than Tim as a university institution was Beta, the black and white mongrel dog who served as mascot for the teams and was regarded as nothing less than a member of the student body. Called Beta because the Beta Theta Pi fraternity bought his license at least once, the philosophical canine attended many university functions, barged in on the professors' lectures and sat down, to applause, and otherwise made himself at home. So many stories were told of him that it was often impossible to know which ones to believe. But he was hailed at the university as the nation's "No. 1 college dog," was mentioned on a nationwide radio program, and photographed for *Look* magazine. Beta's "list of social activities included university dances, fraternity parties and Cavalier brawls," said *College Topics*. And Gil Faatz, whose excellent column was a feature of that paper, wrote: "They used to paint football scores all over him in the good old days when there were some scores that we didn't want hidden. . . . Also, the Virginia Players used to advertise by hanging signs on him— and he loved it."

But in the spring of 1939 Beta was hit by an automobile and his back was broken. He had to be chloroformed. The funeral procession from the Beta House to the University Cemetery was a long one, with an estimated one thousand students in line. Riley Scott, a visiting journalist and poet, composed verses in Beta's memory that were read over radio station WCHV at the start of the funeral procession, and Dean Ivey Lewis delivered the tribute at the grave, situated just outside the cemetery wall and near the main entrance. "There are many one-man dogs," Dean Lewis said, "and many one-family dogs, but Beta was a whole university's dog." A handsome stone marker was placed at the grave during the 1940 Finals. On it was an etching of the deceased, with the following inscription: "In Memory of 'Beta,' Beloved Friend and Mascot of the Students at the University of Virginia. Died April 6, 1939."

A notable visitor to the university at this period was John J. Moran, '02, who, forty years earlier, had voluntarily contracted yellow fever in Cuba as part of the successful effort of Dr. Walter Reed, another alumnus, to eradicate the dread disease. Yellow fever had taken tens of thousands of lives and was one of the world's most terrible scourges. Moran was told that he would be paid $500 for risking his life in the experiment, but he agreed to let the infected mosquitoes bite him only on condition that he receive no money. On his visit to the university in 1940 he was guest of honor at a dinner given by the medical staff. In 1901, following his recovery from the yellow fever he had deliberately contracted in Cuba, he entered the university's Medical School, from which Dr. Reed had been graduated in 1869. However, Moran lost heavily in the stock market and had to withdraw. On his visit in 1940 he promised to bequeath to the Alderman Library the gold medal struck off by Congress commemorating the "conquest of yellow fever," engraved with his name and a record of his heroism. Moran's widow sent the medal to the library following his death in 1951.

Hitler's invasion of Poland on Sept. 1, 1939, was the ominous signal that a general European war was virtually inevitable and that the United States was likely to be drawn in. There had been no large student antiwar rallies at the university since the middle 1930s, but certain organizations on the Grounds continued to agitate against our involvement. Chief among these was the American Student Union (ASU), a combination of the National Students' League and the Student League for Democracy. *College Topics* attacked the ASU two months after war broke out in Europe as a group of "chronic malcontents." It mentioned that one of the organization's members, in a letter to the paper, "openly laughed at some of the treasured traditions of the university." The paper said ASU "represents hardly more than 1 percent of the student body." In a letter to *Topics* a student wrote that "ASU is not a Communist organization," but "it is obvious . . . that the Communists and their 'fellow-travelers' form a very vocal part of the Union."

David Carliner, chosen editor of the *Virginia Spectator* for the 1940–41 session, was arrested in the summer of 1940 for distributing pacifist literature in Charlottesville without a permit and fined $5. He gave a false name when arrested and failed to appear in Police Court at the proper time, and for this "contempt" was fined $20 and given ten days in jail. On an appeal to the Corporation Court, the contempt charge was dismissed and the $5 fine was remitted, but the conviction was allowed to stand.

The university's Administrative Council ruled that Carliner's encounter with the police and his giving a false name made him ineligible to return to the Law School for his third and final year. He passed the bar examination, nevertheless, opened a law office in Washington, became successful, represented such liberal organizations as the American Civil Liberties Union, and was a guest lecturer on several occasions in the 1970s at the University of Virginia Law School, from which he had been dismissed years before.

Registration under Selective Service was carried forward at the university in the autumn of 1940, with Charles H. Kauff-

42. *The Corner in 1946.*

mann in the role of supervisor. Each student was directed to carry his registration certificate at all times. *College Topics* said editorially: "Our station is at the university, by order of the commander-in-chief of the Army and Navy. We must stay here and do the very best job we can. . . . The congress of the United States has decided that university students can best serve the national interest by remaining at their posts in lecture room and laboratory. . . . We are given a chance to become better trained to lead our country in times of peace, or, if need be, in times of war."

A Naval Officers' Reserve Training Corps was organized, and the 107 students who were accepted were issued uniforms and equipment. Classes were held on Mondays, Wednesdays, and Fridays.

The "Minute Men of 1940," a student organization, sought to stimulate discussion of the nation's needs and to bolster support of the Selective Service Act. Organized before the session opened, the Minute Men kept in touch with similar organizations they helped to form in other colleges and universities.

Thirty-one members of the university faculty volunteered to speak and lead discussions in all parts of Virginia on the topic "Democracy: What does it mean, what has it meant, and what obligations does it impose?"

The Department of Engineering set up a Committee on Defense Cooperation under the chairmanship of Associate Prof. Thomas H. Evans. As a result, the department was giving instruction from Tidewater to beyond the Blue Ridge in aerodynamics, materials testing and inspection, production supervision, engineering drawing, principles of radio, time and motion studies, testing of chemicals, and engineering in chemical manufacture. Nearly four hundred men and women were enrolled, and the cost was underwritten by Congress. Business and industrial leaders throughout the state were advised that the instruction was available.

This entire program was separate from the regular extension courses given by the department under the direction of Prof. Arthur F. MacConochie. Many men with important positions in industries essential to national defense were attending the classes. MacConochie also was coordinating methods of producing high-explosive shells. The trade magazine *Steel* collected a series of his articles into a small volume and published it for the information of American shell manufacturers.

President Newcomb counseled the students on Founder's Day in the spring of 1941: "In spite of the clear statement made by President Roosevelt as commander-in-chief of the armed forces, it seems difficult for youth to realize the fact that they are rendering the most useful service to the health and safety of the nation, and at the same time making the best preparation for their peacetime occupation, by going steadily forward with their education until they may be needed for another kind of service." Many young men were leaving the colleges and universities to volunteer for the army, navy, and marines, despite the exhortations of those in authority. In another category, forty-one students who received degrees at the university Finals in June were sworn in as reserve officers within less than an hour after graduation. Ground was being broken for construction of the naval ROTC building on the edge of Monroe Hill between Minor Hall and Dawson's Row. Enrollment in the naval ROTC was expected to double at the upcoming session. Extracurricular aviation training was well under way, and the university's research laboratories in physics and chemistry were busily engaged in special investigations of importance to the armed forces.

And then, like a thunderclap, came Pearl Harbor. Near hysteria swept the Grounds. President Newcomb appealed once more to the students to remain in school and await the call of the government, but there was no holding large numbers of them. Like many other Americans, they were infuriated by the Japanese attack and determined to enlist. Peacetime activities and attitudes were at an end, and the nation braced itself for the grim task ahead.

FOUR

The University
and World War II

THE JAPANESE ATTACK on Pearl Harbor caused an instant revolution in the climate of opinion on the campuses of America. A few faculty members and students at the university were already involved on the side of the Allies, but the great majority there and throughout the United States had been strongly determined not to be drawn in. They had been sympathetic to Great Britain and France, while remaining resolutely opposed to "fighting Europe's battles." But when the Japanese left our Pacific fleet a ravaged ruin with their sneak attack, a "staggering" change, as *College Topics* put it, occurred at once. "College students—long criticised for their peacetime isolationist leanings—have immediately united and are ready for the personal sacrifices war will demand," said the paper.

The first university alumnus to die was 2d Lt. Harry H. Gaver, U.S. Marines, who was killed in the Pearl Harbor bombing and strafing. He had been graduated with a B.S. degree in 1939, after serving as captain of the tennis team and head cheerleader. More than three hundred other Virginia men would give their lives in the conflict.

Maximum participation by all university students and personnel in the war bond drives was urged by President Newcomb, who was the first to buy a bond.

All but three departments had been operating on a twelve-month basis during 1941. The Law School offered an extra term of classes in he summer of that year, and about a dozen students expected to complete work for their degrees in March. The Medical and Engineering schools were drawing up plans for continuous operations. Arrangements for accelerated study were again in effect for the summer of 1942. It was announced in May that students in all departments would be completing degree programs in June, September, December, and March.

Carefully protected research in various laboratories had been carried on since late 1941. From Christmas Eve of that year through New Year's these operations were guarded around the clock by armed members of the Virginia Protective Force, later changed to men in less conspicuous civilian attire. Such researches and experiments would continue, on an expanded scale, throughout the conflict.

The Naval ROTC, established two sessions previously, seemed to be the nearest approach to the ROTC and SATC of World War I. The university was cooperating with the navy in a long-range program of student training designed to turn out men who would be ready to take positions as junior officers on ships and planes as they came from the shipyard ways and the factory assembly lines.

Bombing raids by the Germans on or near the East Coast were felt by the authorities in Washington to be a possibility. Airplane spotters were accordingly stationed on Lewis Mountain, just west of the university, with each spotter doing a three-hour stint. If a strange plane was sighted, pursuit planes would be sent up by the Army Air Force. By Feb. 11, a total of forty-four students had volunteered, but thirty-five more were needed. Special difficulty was experienced in getting volunteers for the hours from midnight to 6 A.M.

The university, in collaboration with the city of Charlottesville and the county of Albemarle, was preparing for possible service as a hospital evacuation center for Washington, Baltimore, or Norfolk. Faculty and students were sharing quietly in civilian defense preparations.

College Topics warned that it was important to obey all directives of the civil defense wardens. "Turn out all lights when you leave your rooms at any time," it counseled. "Familiarize yourself with the instructions that will be given you in regard to procedure in blacking out and taking general protective measures." Charles H. Kauffmann headed the University Civil

Defense Organization. Under him were air raid wardens, auxiliary fire wardens, and special police wardens.

Programs of physical training were announced by Capt. Norton Pritchett. The Department of Physical Education prepared a series of "'V' Tests" by which students could judge their physical fitness. Included were sit-ups, pull-ups, floor dips, the quarter-mile run, the one hundred-yard swim, wall scaling, and so on. A more intensive program called for body building, handball, boxing, squash, fencing, acrobatics, and basketball. Large numbers of undergraduates enrolled.

All students between seventeen and twenty-six years of age were called to meet in Cabell Hall in April 1942, at which time they were told by President Newcomb how they could complete their officer training in the army, navy, or marine corps while finishing their college courses. Every able-bodied student in the university would be in some branch of the armed services within six months, it was stated.

Shortly after classes began the following fall, President Newcomb announced that there would be compulsory physical training for all students in the college and the School of Education, with plans to be worked out later for the other departments.

A volunteer unit, usually known as the Dawn Patrol but sometimes called the Dusk Patrol, had 400 men enrolled. "The boys really worked at it," said the *Alumni News*, "even unto drilling at 7 o'clock in the morning." Close-order drill, manual of arms, the marine marching manual, military and naval discipline, and traditions and customs of the armed forces were included.

Enrollment in the Engineering, Science, and Management Program, begun two years previously by Engineering Prof. Thomas H. Evans, was increasing rapidly. The number taking the courses in twelve centers throughout the state had reached approximately two thousand by early 1943.

A School of Military Government was established at the university in 1942, with Prof. Hardy C. Dillard, a West Point graduate, granted a leave of absence from the Law School to join the staff with the rank of major. The school was under the supervision of Maj. Gen. Allen W. Gullion, with Brig. Gen. C. W. Wickersham as commandant. Purpose of the school was to train high ranking army officers for future assignments in

43. *Virginia's eastern intercollegiate championship boxing team of 1948, with six individual champions. Left to right: Allen Hollingsworth, 125-pound champ; Grover Masterson, 130-pound champ; the Marigliotta brothers—Jimmy, Basil, and Joe, 135, 145, and 155-pound champions, respectively; Bolling Izard, 165; Ralph Shoaf, 175-pound champion; and Lapsley Hamblin, heavyweight; with Coach Al York. Portrait in background is of the late coach Johnny LaRowe in his wheelchair.*

military government and liaison work. An enrollment of about sixty was expected at the outset. By early 1944 six classes, totaling 750 men, had been graduated. The school "has attracted attention throughout the world," said the *Alumni News*, "and its 'alumni' are administering governmental affairs in hundreds of communities in numerous nations now conquered." Seven foreign countries had sent officers to the school. Brig. Gen. E. R. Warner McCabe, 1900, became commandant in 1944.

Objectives for which the war was being fought were strikingly portrayed by Randall Thompson, head of the Division of Music, in his composition *A Testament of Freedom*, first rendered on Jefferson's 200th birthday in 1943. Thompson was asked to compose a symphony or a tone poem celebrating Jefferson and his ideas. He accepted and happened to run into Prof. Bernard Mayo, who was in the process of reading proof on his book *Jefferson Himself*. These proofs were just what Thompson needed. He went to the University Chapel and worked steadily, soon turning out all four movements. The premiere was given in Cabell Hall on Apr. 13 and received a standing ovation. *A Testament of Freedom* has since been performed all over the United States and in many countries. While on the university faculty Thompson also received the Elizabeth Sprague Coolidge Award for distinguished services to chamber music. Soon thereafter he accepted a call to Princeton.

The university had operated a hospital unit overseas in World War I, but it seemed at first that this would not be possible in World War II. Dean Harvey Jordan declined an invitation in 1940 from the U.S. surgeon general to organize such a unit. He and others felt that since the university's medical faculty was one of the smallest in the country, its members could not be spared without devastating effects upon the school. But those who made this decision reckoned without Dr. Staige D. Blackford, professor of internal medicine. He was determined to organize a hospital unit, and he finally convinced Dean Jordan that it could be done without irreparable damage to the Medical School. So an evacuation unit was organized, with emphasis on surgical cases, in contrast to the general hospital operated by the university in 1917–18. Dr. Blackford became chief of medicine and had overall supervision. Dr. E. Cato Drash, associate professor of surgery, was chief of surgery and recruited the surgical personnel. Recruitment of nurses was under Miss Ruth Beery, who had been an instructor and assistant superintendent of nursing in the university's School of Nursing. She remained chief of nurses for the unit throughout the war.

The 8th Evacuation Hospital sailed in November 1942 to back up the North African invasion and landed at Casablanca. After service in North Africa, it moved to Italy in September 1943, suffering a disaster en route when the ship carrying all its equipment was sunk. The unit somehow scrounged more equipment. For the rest of the war the 8th Evac was in Italy. It moved northward with the American forces, living and operating in tents, much of the time in cold, snow, sleet, rain, and mud. Despite these handicaps and ordeals, it cared for over 48,000 cases in the hospital and another 45,000 in the outpatient departments. High commendation came from Lt. Gen. Mark W. Clark and other army brass, and the unit was awarded the Fifth Army Plaque and Clasp and the Meritorious Service Unit Plaque. The complete story is told in *The 8th Evac*, a highly readable and authoritative account by Dr. Byrd S. Leavell, professor of internal medicine at the university, who was with the unit throughout and was its chief of medicine from April to September 1945. Dr. Leavell's delightfully graphic diary is a highlight of the volume.

Students at the university did not forget those who were serving in the 8th Evac. They bought 20,000 cigarettes in the spring of 1943 and sent them to the unit. And the university's Medical School and hospital, with their reduced staffs, made the best of difficult circumstances. Dr. C. S. Lentz, administrator of the hospital, wrote concerning his problems for the session of 1943–44: "I have been administrator of a university hospital constantly since January 1, 1922, and I can truthfully say that even in the darkest days of the depression I have not had to face the problems, many of them insoluble, nor have I had nearly the amount of work and worry that I have had in the past year."

An increased burden also fell on the School of Physics. Prof. L. G. Hoxton reported that the school was able to handle the added load because of the "efforts, competence and scientific standing of Drs. Beams and Snoddy." He added that "in addition to being in responsible charge of one of the war contracts, Dr. Snoddy has been co-director with Dr. Beams of the largest and most important contract we have. Without him that contract would have had to be abandoned."

Dean F. D. G. Ribble of the Law School was called to the Department of State in Washington. Prof. William H. White, Jr., served as acting dean in his absence. Blind Prof. T. Munford Boyd traveled alone by train each week to Washington for three days' service on the War Production Board's legal staff and taught the other three days in the Law School.

The Extension Division was providing special war-related courses in cooperation with the University of Wisconsin. Most of the home study courses offered by a selected list of colleges and universities were included. Studies in some twenty-one fields were scheduled for persons in various parts of the state who wished to concentrate on subjects having a direct bearing on the military duties to which they might be assigned or which they might wish to follow after the war. Courses in English, economics, history, psychology, and sociology were among those offered.

On another facet of the home front, the steel rails that had carried the now defunct street cars to and from the university and out to Fry's Spring were dug up and turned over to the country's war machine for use as scrap for the manufacture of weapons. Before the war many steel rails and other varieties of scrap metal had been bought in the United States by the Japanese.

The Naval ROTC moved from Thornton Hall to Maury Hall, the newest building on the Grounds, where courses were offered in such subjects as naval training and navigation, seamanship, electricity, ordnance and gunnery, engineering, naval history, administration, regulations and leadership, communications, aviation, military and international law, and infantry drill. The Raven Society and Omicron Delta Kappa offered an award to the company amassing most points in drill, communications, and rifle and pistol matches. The instructional staff was composed of naval officers, with Capt. E. M. Williams commanding. Members of the university faculty provided courses in science and the liberal arts.

In January 1943 the U.S. Naval Flight Preparatory School

44. Fleet Adm. William M. (Bull) Halsey, 1900, one of the heroes of the Pacific in World War II.

was added to the other units functioning at the university. "The dorms now become barracks," said the *Alumni News*,

and the counselors naval officers. Where 400 students once lived, 600 blue jackets will be quartered. Old Commons will be their mess hall. These boys will come in relays of 200 each month for a course of 12 weeks. . . . Classes will be held from 7:30 to 4:30, with an hour out for lunch and an appropriate time for physical conditioning. . . . The faculty will be provided by the university. . . . Discipline and routine matters will be handled by naval officers. The curriculum, formulated by the Navy Department, includes the following courses: principles of flight, aerology, aircraft, engines, mathematics, physics, navigation, communication.

The naval program at the university underwent various modifications during the war. It became the V-12 program in early 1943, replacing the preflight school and incorporating the NROTC training program. At least 10 percent of the trainees assigned to V-12 had seen active service.

But the navy was not the only branch of the armed services represented at the university. The U.S. Army Pre-Meteorology School was established there in February 1943, attended by 200 cadets of the Army Air Force. As with the naval units, academic instruction was provided by the university faculty, with Prof. Gordon T. Whyburn as executive head. Many officers handled administrative routine and military indoctrination. Mathematics, physics, geography, history, political science, and English were taught. Purpose of the school was to provide basic instruction for the study of meteorology. The students were housed in the old Albemarle Hotel on Main Street, and in the mornings they marched to the university singing. They were mainly good students, but the end of the war prevented them from actually pursuing the study of meteorology.

All these various military and naval units located at the university during the war kept the institution alive and functioning when so many of the regularly enrolled students had left college to enlist. Much of the cost of instruction, as well as of food and housing, was paid by the federal government. President Newcomb and the faculty remained firmly in control as teachers and researchers, and as referees over army-navy rivalries.

Athletics at Virginia from 1942 to 1945 were necessarily on an abnormal basis. The fact that a number of star athletes from other institutions were enrolled in the naval units at the university, and were eligible to play for Virginia, made it possible to carry on a fairly comprehensive program. The navy emphasized competitive athletics as a part of its intensive training, whereas the army made no provision for such activity. Eight intercollegiate sports, including football, functioned at the university to a greater or lesser degree from 1942 to 1945. Long trips were out of the question, and nearby service teams often were played. Among these were Woodrow Wilson Hospital, Fort Belvoir, North Carolina Pre-Flight, and Cherry Point Marines. Intramurals were continued during the war but on a reduced scale.

The 480-yard shuttle hurdle race at the Penn Relays was won in 1943 with comparative ease by the Virginia team—Captain Thomas H. Todd, Bud Capers, Bill Mohler, and Bart Todd. Captain Todd added other important laurels at that and other meets. He retained his indoor I.C. 4-A hurdle crown—then went on to carry off the outdoor 120-yard high hurdle I.C. 4-A title and thus became the first Virginia track man to win both indoor and outdoor I.C. 4-A championships. He also won the Southern Conference 70-yard high hurdle crown and the 120-yard high hurdle outdoor race at the Millrose Games in New York.

The Honor System was subjected to special strains during the war years owning to the large number of matriculates from other parts of the country who had come to the university as members of military or naval units. Many were unfamiliar with the workings of the honor code.

The centennial of the Honor System's founding had been observed May 16, 1942. A rather elaborate program had been planned, but the outbreak of the war caused it to be drastically revised. Virginius Dabney, '21, a member of the Honor Committee in 1919–20, was the speaker at ceremonies in Cabell Hall. All former members of the committee were invited, and a good many came. A dinner was held at the Monticello Hotel.

Two years later an uproar arose over whether "false musters" in the Naval Training Unit and the NROTC Battalion were violations of the Honor System. The Honor Committee had ruled during the previous session that false musters did not constitute violations, but in June 1944 an open letter to *College Topics* signed by thirty-nine prominent students requested a reversal of this ruling. "A lie, with whatever it may be concerned, is a violation of the code," said the letter. This communication got prompt results, for the Honor Committee of 1944 took the position that the committee of the previous year had erred and that false musters could not be exempted. *Topics* published an extra carrying the committee's pronouncement, "creating fully as much excitement as the Allied invasion of France, which was announced the same morning," Henry Wilson, the paper's editor, wrote. A mass meeting of students in Cabell Hall was called for the following day by President Newcomb at the request of the Honor Committee. Many naval trainees in attendance asked that they be allowed to hold a referendum on whether they should accept the Honor System in its entirety, including the ruling against false musters, or be excluded completely from it. The vote was taken, and it was overwhelmingly in favor of remaining under the system. A significant result was the decision by student leaders to provide a more thorough orientation thereafter for incoming first-year men with respect to the honor code. More than three hundred entered in July and were divided into small groups for the purpose. No further crises in the operation of the code arose during the war, although the number of violations increased, albeit not in connection with false musters. In 1944 *Topics* began announcing expulsions under the Honor System on the front page, giving the offense but not the name of the offender. Between Feb. 1 and Sept. 1, 1944, there were thirteen such announcements, with cheating on tests or examinations the offense in twelve and stealing in the other. Four of these dismissals took place within three weeks in the late summer of 1944, and *Topics* editorialized on "the almost unprecedented record." It attributed the situation largely "to the influx of many transfer students."

Another aspect of the problem was addressed by *Topics* the following year, when it expressed the view that there were not enough counselors in the dormitories. Before the use of the dorms as naval barracks, the student counselor system "was far from satisfactory, even with twice the number of counselors recommended," said the paper. "The counselors simply did not have time to do justice to the job." "For instilling the Virginia Honor System in students from the beginning, there can be no substitute for personal associations," *Topics* declared, and it went on to say that the system, from its inception, "has depended for its continuous existence upon orientation programs and the imparting of its spirit to new men by their associations with older students."

The *Alumni News* reported in 1944 that in the preceding fourteen years the great majority of students expelled under the Honor System were from the Northeast. During that period three students from "the former Confederate states" south of Virginia were shipped, as compared with seventy-one from New York and New Jersey. The ten Southern states had 2,914 registrations during the period in question, whereas New York and New Jersey had 6,393. "We want more boys from the South, and a higher proportion of good ones from the North," said the *Alumni News*. "We don't draw from the Southern states as we used to." C. Alphonso Smith, Jr., a former chairman of the Honor Committee, wrote a letter to the Richmond *Times-Dispatch* in 1936 in which he said he had studied all Honor Committee cases for the preceding sixteen years, and that in the preceding ten years twenty-six Virginians had been expelled under the Honor System as against sixty from New York and New Jersey.

The rigors of wartime did not adversely affect the sartorial elegance of the dancing Cavaliers, for at Openings in the fall of 1942 white ties and tails were still being worn. However, by January the gasoline shortage caused forty-five girls to walk to Madison Hall for a University Center dance. They met their dates there. Mrs. A. E. Walker, the longtime hostess at such affairs, expressed herself as pleased and said she anticipated revival of the Gay Nineties custom of carrying dancing slippers in slipper bags, to be put on upon arrival. Midwinters were held as usual in the gym, but proceeds went to navy relief, and a less expensive orchestra than was normally employed played for the dancing.

The university coeds confounded the male contingent by giving what was termed "one of the most successful dances that Madison Hall has ever witnessed." It was primarily for the naval preflight students, but many other undergraduates attended, along with a group of Charlottesville girls. A fourth-year man was quoted as saying, "This has perhaps been the best Madison Hall dance that I have yet seen."

Not all coeds were appeased, however, by the favorable reception given their gala affair. In a letter to *Topics* one of them wrote denouncing the university's "snobs" in the following harsh terms: "For years and years I have heard of the glorious tradition of a 'gentleman' at the University of Virginia. This is no gentleman I have found here. This is a narrow-minded, backward and utterly detestable egoist! This is assuredly a *snob*—in its worst and most warped form."

A lounge and soda fountain called the Dry Dock was opened in the Madison Hall basement in 1943 and was pronounced a howling success. It was said to be the first thing remotely describable as a student union that the university had ever had. The installation was leased from the University Center by W. B. Gibson, manager of the University Bookstore, who also managed the Dry Dock. Cold drinks and sandwiches were available, and there were a nickelodeon and pinball machines. *Topics* commented enthusiastically that it could be a gathering place for all students, and added: "The new lounge makes another step in the many projects which the University Center has sponsored this year. We speak of the excellent dances, the organization of the Cavalier Ladies, and a great part in the orientation of the first-year men, among others."

Mrs. A. E. Walker was observing the twenty-fifth anniversary of her service as hostess at Madison Hall, in which capacity she had made a lasting contribution to the well-being of the students. "It was a brand new idea to have a woman at Madison Hall," said the *Alumni News*. She "started right in as though not scared at all with her tea dances. . . . She has poured tea for generations of students . . . and makes them like it. But Mrs. Walker does vastly more than pour tea. It is a bit of a mystery what she does, but she has been doing it to Virginia students for twenty-five years. . . . She's the Queen of Madison Hall. Parson Powell started calling her the queen."

Two student hangouts that had almost become landmarks at or near the Corner disappeared during the war years. The Cavalier was torn down to make way for expansion of Jameson's Bookstore, to include a soda fountain, sporting goods, and other commodities. Johnson's emporium on the crest of

45. *Dumas Malone, author of the definitive life of Thomas Jefferson.*

the rise beyond the C&O bridge went out of existence. The Cavalier had been a beer-hoister's haven, but Jameson's was unable to provide lager. "No beer at the Corner!" was the anguished cry. Johnson's had not been a beer tavern but a place for midnight snacks, "a malt and soda with your girl," said the *Alumni News*. In years past "the boys dropped in at Johnson's after seeing the Flora Dora Girls at Levy's Opera House. Perhaps they took their best calic [date] there for a hot chocolate after a chilly ride in a fashionable rig from Irving's Livery Stable. They continued to resort to Johnson's with the coming of Rudolph Valentino, prohibition and two cars in every garage."

Grief over these two closings was partly assuaged by news that the Virginian was to open at the Corner, after a period during which it had ceased to function. The Virginian, a student watering place, had been a companion establishment to the Cavalier, and its reemergence was hailed with fervent hosannahs. Advertised as "Ye Olde Wahoo Heaven," it was under the management of the Gianakos brothers. Nick Gianakos, a star on the university's football team a short time before, had made a stunning catch of a pass from Bill Dudley in the 1941 Yale game—lost to the Elis, 21–19.

Sports columns in *College Topics* from the pens of its two sports editors were appearing in the fall of 1942. One who wrote under the heading "Sideline Slants" was a young man named Frank L. Hereford, Jr., and the other, whose column was called "How about It?," was Henry Howell. The former would be president of the university thirty-two years later, and the latter would run unsuccessfully three times for governor of Virginia.

Automobiles for first-year men were banned in 1942 in the college, engineering, and education departments, with exceptions for physical disability. Governor Darden suggested that autos be prohibited to all students. Three months later *College Topics*, edited by Gordon L. Crenshaw, recommended that all autos be banned to students for the duration. The Board of Visitors put this regulation into effect in July 1943, with a few exceptions for hardship cases.

Two prominent alumni, Louis Johnson, '12, and Edward R. Stettinius, '24, had leading roles just before and during World War II.

Johnson, former national commander of the American Legion, was appointed in 1937 as assistant secretary of war. He worked intensively on getting U.S. industry to a state of maximum readiness should the country be plunged into armed conflict. As director of the War Department's Industrial Mobilization Plan, he earmarked 10,000 civilian plants for war production and said that "all are eager to cooperate." Johnson resigned when Henry L. Stimson succeeded Harry W. Woodring as secretary of war. He was then named chairman of an advisory commission to assist our war effort in India.

Edward R. Stettinius, '24, chairman of the board of the United States Steel Corporation, was appointed in 1939 head of the new War Resources Board. John Lee Pratt, '05, was named a member of the board. By 1941 Stettinius had been elevated to the directorship of the Division of Priorities in the Office of Production Management. Later in the same year he was named to succeed Harry Hopkins as head of the important lend-lease program, under which this country supplied its allies with huge quantities of weapons and matériel. Walter Lippmann, the famous columnist, wrote concerning his service in that post: "Mr. Stettinius has done as much and perhaps more than any man in Washington to show how to set up an agency and how to conduct it without bureaucratic feuds and without obscurity and confusion." By 1943 Stettinius was under secretary of state, and when Cordell Hull resigned in late 1944 as secretary of state, Stettinius was appointed to succeed him. In that capacity he accompanied ailing President Roosevelt to the Yalta Conference where Roosevelt met with Joseph Stalin and Winston Churchill. Stettinius also headed the American delegation to the conference at San Francisco in 1945 at which the United Nations was got into operation. When President Harry S. Truman took office, he appointed James F. Byrnes to head the State Department and named Stettinius permanent American representative to the United Nations General Assembly.

When news that Japan had surrendered hit the Grounds in August 1945, there was wild jubilation. "The Corner was jammed with everybody yelling and waving and waiting to see what everybody else was going to do," Bill Lyle wrote in *College Topics*. "There was a near-riot in the Virginian which required one of the local gendarmes to dispel. Cars piled high with 18 or 20 students and girls and bristling with the dear old Confederate flags, roared up and down the main drag all evening. Blasting horns, banging fireworks, barking dogs, ear-splitting yells. . . . Vinegar Hill and the 'downtown' section of Charlottesville defied accurate description."

But despite the exultation, bulletins continued to come in from Europe and the Pacific concerning the missing and the dead. These appeared for months in the *Alumni News*, which during the war had carried thousands of items concerning the men in the service, their experiences, heroism, and decorations. It also published many photographs of alumni on the far-flung battle lines of the world.

By the fall of 1945, 1,000 naval students had been trained at the university, 213 army men in the specialized training program, 2,820 in the School of Military Government, and 200 in the army's Pre-Meteorology School. At the same time it was announced that the university's navy unit would get a $110,000 armory for its continued use in peacetime. Work had already begun on the structure, which would be located eighty feet south of Maury Hall. The following year plans were announced for a naval ordnance research laboratory near the McCormick Observatory, with physics Professors Beams and Snoddy to be in charge of the experimental work. The laboratory was built at a cost of approximately $125,000, and the navy furnished it with $250,000 worth of equipment, as well as ample funds for operation.

Part of the research on the atomic bomb that devastated Hiroshima and Nagasaki was done at the university. Jesse Beams's ultracentrifuge, operated on the same principle as the cream separator, played a significant role in separating the uranium known as U-235 from U-238 and U-234. Dr. Beams had been a member of the original five-man committee appointed to study uranium fission under the National Research Council. After the university's physicists concluded their wartime work on uranium in the Rouss Laboratory, they turned their attention to the development of guided missiles and were equally successful. Distinguished service certificates were awarded by the navy for this latter activity to Prof. L. G. Hoxton, head of the School of Physics, Professors Beams and

46. *Ivey F. Lewis, dean of the university and the college,*
1934–53.

Snoddy, and two able younger scientists, Frank L. Hereford, Jr., and Dexter Whitehead.

The alumni had two Medal of Honor winners. Gen. Alexander Archer Vandegrift, '08, commander of the U.S. Marines on Guadalcanal in one of the most desperate engagements of the war in the Pacific, was decorated by President Roosevelt in 1943 for his leadership in that heroic and successful action. General Vandegrift had already been awarded the Navy Cross. He was the first full general to command the marine corps and was decorated by Lord Halifax with the Most Honorable Order of the Bath.

The other Medal of Honor winner was navy Lt. Arthur Murray Preston, '38, a law graduate of the university who was practicing in Washington, D.C., when the war broke out. He joined the navy and on being commissioned was sent to the Pacific. In September 1944 Preston volunteered to command two PT boats into the mined harbor of Wasile Bay, Morotai Island, to a point less than two hundred yards from a well-guarded Japanese dock and supply area. He was attempting to rescue a pilot who had been shot down and had parachuted into the bay. Preston and his men were under fire for two and a half hours, and he was given the medal for "conspicuous gallantry and intrepidity at the risk of his life." He also was awarded the Navy Cross and promoted to lieutenant commander.

The Medal of Freedom was awarded to two alumni for conspicuous service during the war. Charles Wertenbaker, '25, author and journalist, chief of the Paris Bureau of *Time* magazine, was given the medal in Paris in late 1947 for "especially meritorious actions" while a correspondent in Europe, 1944–45. Marc Peter, Jr., '23, received the same accolade at the Pentagon for his work in London from 1942 to 1944, where he created novel and highly effective methods of bombing urban areas that "contributed materially to the success of the air war against Germany and Japan."

With the end of hostilities in the late summer of 1945, the university faced a series of problems. It had to do a fast turnaround to take account of the new situation. A greatly accelerated program of studies for the session of 1945–46 had to be arranged in order that normal, unaccelerated programs could be put into effect in September 1946. Three semesters were crowded into the next 12 months. Housing for returning veterans or veterans entering for the first time had to be provided, and first-year men living in fraternity houses were moved to the dormitories.

Although the war was over, 160 V-5 trainees were enrolled in the university on November 1, 1945. These naval aviation cadets matriculated in college courses for three terms, after which they were transferred to bases for continued preflight training. At the university they occupied quarters in the dorms vacated by graduating V-12 and NROTC men. For years after the war the university continued to enroll units of the NROTC, and these were joined later by Army and Air Force ROTC. Photographs of the various units appeared in *Corks and Curls* over a ten-year period.

Demobilization of the men in the armed forces proceeded steadily during the winter and spring, and by September 1946 the veterans were pouring back into the colleges and universities. Enrollment at the University of Virginia was 40 percent ahead of the largest previous figure, that of 1939–40. A total of 4,204 had been registered by early fall.

Absent from the registration procedure for the first time since 1919 was Miss Virginia Moran. She had been associated with the university since 1899, having first become affiliated with the institution as an employee in the bursar's office. Upon the retirement of Howard Winston as registrar in 1919, Miss Moran became assistant to his successor, Mrs. Anna Tuttle Heck. When Mrs. Heck died in 1922, Miss Moran was appointed registrar and remained in that position until her retirement in 1946.

Two-thirds of the students registering at the university in the fall of that year were returned veterans. These relatively mature men were regarded by the faculty as a superior group, more serious about their studies, and willing to work six days a week. Again, Episcopalians were more numerous than members of any other religious denomination, followed by Methodists, Presbyterians, Baptists, Roman Catholics, and Jews, in that order.

Housing for many of the men who were flooding in was unavailable at the university or in Charlottesville. About five hundred of these veterans could be accommodated in the

Woodrow Wilson Army Hospital near Staunton, whence they commuted to the university by bus, thirty-five miles each way. Lectures also were given at Woodrow Wilson by some faculty members.

At Woodrow Wilson the students were able to use the excellent facilities of the former Officers' Club. The bar was available for snacks, and the sports areas were used with the help of equipment supplied by the university. All university students left Woodrow Wilson by the end of 1946, since accommodations of one sort or another had been found at or near the university.

Construction was beginning on a "veterans' village" at Copeley Hill, adjoining the university grounds just north of the intersection of Routes 250 and 29. A total of 320 married couples and 500 single students were to be cared for in apartment units and trailers.

The Student Senate had ceased operations in the spring of 1942 because of war conditions. Three years later the Student Council arose in its stead and elections were held. Again in the fall of that year, 1945, there were Student Council elections. The council's function was to investigate matters pertaining to the well-being of the undergraduates and to discuss with the administration means by which grievances might be adjusted.

The first football rally in the fall of 1945 was announced by *College Topics* with great fanfare. "Football rally processions of past years used to start from the Cavalier (now deceased), and end up on the Lawn," said the paper. "Tim (now deceased) used to lead them with his torch and his four-legged pal Beta (now deceased). We haven't got the Cavalier, Tim or Beta, but we can promise a roaring good time. Bring your dates."

The rally was a "flop," according to *Topics*, and so was the cheering at the game with the Coast Guard, won by Virginia, 39–0. "Feeble, disinterested yells," at this and other gridiron contests were blasted by the journal, which declared that "any little down-country high school could show more spirit at one football game than we at the U. Va. have displayed all season."

Festivities on Homecoming weekend November 9–10 were convincing evidence that things were indeed getting back to normal. There were two dances, a football game, and a dozen fraternity parties. Such jollity was not appreciated by under-

graduates scornfully termed *meatballs* by their more cantankerous fellows. A meatball was defined in the *Spectator* as "a
socially maladjusted individual usually found in the library
general reading room on Saturday night; one who considers
a weekend 'a good time to catch up.'"

Discussion continued over whether one should speak to students one didn't know. Fontaine C. Armistead, '42, one of the
ablest students, had made a speech on tradition some years
before in which he defended the custom of speaking only to
acquaintances. It was reprinted a number of times and was
generally well received, but one phrase drew criticism. "Instead of grinning and gushing indiscriminately," said Armistead, "the Virginia student speaks only to people he knows,
and thus enjoys a more sincere relationship than if he spoke
to all." The words "grinning and gushing" were regarded by
some as inappropriate, although widespread agreement was
expressed with Armistead's general thesis.

Lucy Lou Floyd of Waynesboro, a graduate student in the
School of Education and associate editor of both *College Topics*
and the *Spectator*, was one of those who felt that the overall
attitude of reserve was desirable. On the other hand, Prof. T.
Braxton Woody conducted a forum under the auspices of the
University Christian Association at which the consensus was
that students should *not* consider it "sticking your neck out" to
speak to those with whom one was not personally acquainted.
There was criticism of the long-established custom of not
greeting strangers.

Lucy Floyd was one of the few women during this era to win
a place on the editorial staff of a university publication. In
1948 Mildred Callis served on the staff of *Corks and Curls*,
while Margaret Potts achieved a similar place on the *Spectator*.

College Topics came in for an overhaul in the spring of 1946.
Ed Myers and Chris Cramer, editors in chief, announced that
they had "cleaned house" because of the "low caliber" of the
paper. It had recently been "little more than a political football," they said, and "men have gained important posts
through their friends and fraternity affiliations rather than
through skill and service." The editors declared that "a new
Topics is emerging; it has already enlisted the help of the Student Council and the administration, but it is sadly lacking in
personnel."

The *Spectator* was named by the Student Council in 1948 "the official magazine of the student body." This publication had combined the year before with another journal, *Crust*, under the name of *Spectator and Crust*, sponsored by the Jefferson Society. *Crust* was dropped from the title a few months later.

The ban against operation of automobiles by other than first-year students had been removed in 1945, and first-year men were allowed to have cars the following session. As a result, the weekend exodus was resumed. The *Spectator* observed that during Founder's Day ceremonies in April "nine-tenths of the students either perform a little sleep-catching or embark on the traditional week-end."

Nor did the greater maturity of the postwar generation of students alter their aversion to literature, in the view of two members of the university's teaching staff. English Professors Joseph L. Vaughan and E. C. McClintock contributed an article to the *News Letter* of the College English Association in which they wrote: "Real progress can be made in the teaching of required literature courses at the undergraduate level only if the fact is squarely faced that a large majority of students do not like literature."

The recently adopted alphabetical grading system was objectionable, in the unanimous view of the Student Council. It requested a return to numerical grading on the ground that the alphabetical system "is non-illuminating and too indeterminate."

Appointment of James H. Newman, dean of men at the University of Alabama, to the newly created office of dean of men at the University of Virginia was announced. He took office in February 1946 and assumed general supervision over student activities, thus "relieving Dean Ivey Lewis, dean of the university, of many of the details of student life which he had been administering." Lewis was named dean of the college. George O. Ferguson, who had been in charge of admissions for many years, was appointed dean of admissions and registrar. In the lastnamed post he succeeded Miss Virginia Moran, who had retired after 24 years.

Edward R. Stettinius, a member of the university's Board of Visitors, was elected rector of the university in 1946, succeed-

47. *Rowland Egger, dean of the faculty, 1962–63.*

48. *Prof. Weldon Cooper, director of the Institute of Government and editor of the University of Virginia* News *Letter.*

ing R. Gray Williams, who had died shortly before. Stettinius had been extremely prominent and popular during his student days at the university, but he had been a decidedly mediocre student and had not graduated. When he became chairman of United States Steel and then head of Lend-Lease and secretary of state, he was given honorary degrees by the following universities and colleges: Oxford, California, Columbia, Colgate, American, New York, Rutgers, Lafayette, Union, and Elmira.

As rector, silver-haired, deep-voiced "Ed" Stettinius was extremely active in the affairs of the university. He knew that he had a health problem and that he should not subject himself to undue strain. Yet during and after the war he did not spare himself. In fact his zeal for the university was such that, as rector, he injected himself into matters that were really beyond his proper sphere. By the spring of 1949 he had exerted himself to such an extent that he had a heart attack and had to resign. That fall he died, aged forty-nine. He was one of the most illustrious of all the university's alumni and the author of two books having to do with his public service—*Lend-Lease, Weapon for Victory* (1944) and *Roosevelt and the Russians*, edited by Walter Johnson, which appeared almost simultaneously with his death.

The high quality of the student body immediately after the war, with a heavy injection of veterans, was remarked upon in later years by Prof. B. F. D. Runk. "Back in those days," he said, faculty and students "went to school for long periods and didn't think anything of it. The GI's flooded us and we had full classes; we would teach from Monday morning through Saturday afternoon. The students were desirous of getting back into academic work, many working toward graduate school. I have often remarked that we did better teaching than we do today with our reduced teaching loads, with our leisurely Monday through Friday schedule."

Growth of the Alderman Library collections, following the library's dedication in 1938, had been extraordinary. In the first ten years the number of books "made available for use" rose from 303,502 to 484,826. This was better than the normal growth of book collections, but it paled beside the astronomical leap forward of the manuscript collection—from about five hundred thousand to over three million documents in the decade. Among the more important manuscript acquisitions were the Cocke and Bruce family papers, manuscripts of the "Edgehill" Randolphs, the Carter Glass papers, and the Fred O. Seibel collection of newspaper cartoons. A significant addition to the book collection was an assemblage of material on Charles Darwin exceeding anything in the world except Darwin's own collection in England. Presented by an anonymous donor, it is rich in source materials on the history of science and includes virtually all of the first editions and variant issues of Darwin's works. There are also important letters, essays, and photographs, as well as first and other editions of writings on the subject of evolution by such Darwin contemporaries as Herbert Spencer, Thomas Huxley, and Sir Joseph Hooker.

In view of the University of Virginia's high rank in the field of science, it was fitting that the Darwin collection should come to Alderman Library. In volume 6 of *American Men of Science*, eleven university faculty members were "starred," a greater number than any other southern university could show, one more than Yale had and one fewer than Harvard. The eleven starred Virginia professors were Jesse W. Beams, Arthur F. Benton, Francis P. Dunnington, Harvey E. Jordan, William A. Kepner, Ivey F. Lewis, Edward J. McShane, Samuel A. Mitchell, Carl E. Speidel, Lyndon F. Small, and Gordon T. Whyburn. It should be noted, however, that when Virginia was ranked on the basis of the number of faculty members elected to the National Academy of Sciences, it made a much less impressive showing. The university had only four members, highest in the South except Texas, but was in a five-way tie with Michigan, Minnesota, Iowa, and Indiana for seventeenth place nationally. Harvard had fifty-one members of the academy, California thirty-four, and Yale eighteen.

The Law School inaugurated a course of graduate study in 1945–46 leading to the degrees of S.J.D. and LL.M. It involved the acceptance of each graduate student by one member of the faculty, who worked closely with him. The student was required to take certain seminar courses. For the doctor's degree a dissertation was necessary, and two years would normally be needed to complete it. For the master's degree a thesis equivalent in quality and quantity to a *Law Review* article was prescribed. There were two graduate students in 1945–46.

Dean Ribble stated that the high standing of the university's Law School—and it was generally conceded to be among the top dozen in this country—was due "more than any single factor" to its *Law Review*. The great majority of students in the school were from outside Virginia, giving it a cosmopolitan outlook and contributing to its excellent national ranking. In 1946–47 there were 410 non-Virginian students to 237 from Virginia, and at the two succeeding sessions the figures were 496 to 264 and 346 to 194. Returning veterans accounted for the large enrollment in the years immediately after the war, but when they were graduated, the total fell. Then the Korean War broke out, and there was a still sharper drop. The figures for 1951–52 were 226 non-Virginians and 147 Virginians.

Enrollment in the postwar years was falling in several directions, and the number taking Latin and Greek was low. In 1947–48 only fifty-five were taking Latin and thirteen Greek. For the two succeeding sessions the figures were thirty-eight and eighteen and forty-three and twenty-one.

The name of the School of Germanic Languages was changed to the School of Germanic Languages and Russian in order to call attention to the fact that courses in Russian were being offered by Prof. Matthew Volm. This instruction had been available since 1943, but the fact had not been made sufficiently clear in the university catalogue, and enrollment, in consequence, had not been up to expectations. It climbed when the availability of the courses was emphasized.

An Institute of Foreign Service and International Affairs was established in 1945, with two new degrees offered to matriculates. The idea for such an institute was suggested in 1943 by Branch Spalding, '24, who had become editor of the *Alumni News* the previous year. Spalding proposed that "an outstanding school of international studies" be established at the university and that the first step be the raising of $35,000 to provide the nucleus of its book collection, which would be a memorial to alumni lost in the war. The money was raised and the idea caught on. It was given added impetus by the support of Secretary of State Stettinius, who expressed the belief that there was great need for a school devoted to training diplomats and foreign service personnel. The newly established institute opened July 2, 1945. Liberal arts education, with emphasis on foreign languages, was the basis for the specialized study to be concentrated in the third and fourth years of the course leading to the B.A. in international affairs, while for the M.A. particular attention was given to more advanced courses. These were in the areas of Latin-American affairs, international and maritime law, the British Empire, international organization and economics, diplomatic practice, and related matters.

A few months after the institute opened, Jesse H. Jones, a wealthy Texan who was a great admirer of Woodrow Wilson, agreed to give $20,000 a year over a period of fifteen years for faculty salaries and lecture fees toward establishment of a Woodrow Wilson School of International Affairs. Jones said that Wilson "sacrificed his life for world peace," and he wanted to make this $300,000 contribution in his honor. Wilson had been a law student at the university from 1879 to 1881. President Newcomb said that the school would be an integral part of the Institute of Foreign Service and International Affairs. Prof. Hardy C. Dillard was appointed head of the Wilson school, but he was wanted by the War Department to assist in the reorganization of the Army War College, and Prof. Robert K. Gooch was named acting head. During the war Gooch had been a special adviser to President Roosevelt on problems of Western Europe, working through the Office of Strategic Services.

Librarian Harry Clemons said in 1949 that the international studies library begun during the war was "a very live collection indeed," and he quoted Professor Fernbach of the Woodrow Wilson School as saying that "every class in foreign affairs constantly uses these materials, and they have been vital to the development of graduate studies in the Woodrow Wilson School." A plaque explaining that the volumes are a memorial to missing and dead alumni of World War II was placed in the Browsing Room of Alderman Library.

The Bureau of Public Administration "has regained a position in the mainstream of the administrative life of the state not appreciably inferior to that which it enjoyed in the prewar years, 1936–42," Prof. Rowland Egger, its director, reported. The program of research and service in county government became well established in 1945, Egger said, and the bureau had reentered the municipal field, which had been its principal concern in earlier years. It had recently assumed primary responsibility for the research work of the Richmond Charter Commission and was engaged in a survey of the revenue system of Norfolk. A program in county government was being carried on in collaboration with the League of Virginia Counties, and close relations were being maintained once more with the League of Virginia Municipalities. The bureau, furthermore, was serving as the secretariat of the Virginia chapter of the American Society for Public Administration and the Virginia Social Science Association.

The Bureau of Population and Economic Research, headed by Prof. Lorin A. Thompson, was established at the university in 1944 as a combination of the Bureau of Industrial Research and the Population Study of the Virginia State Planning Board, both of which had been inaugurated four years before. Files and information of the agency, as well as its staff, were available to all interested parties and agencies in Virginia. The bureau dealt with the industrial development of the state and addressed the problems of manufacturing, marketing and distribution, employment, agriculture, mining, family income, and related matters. "From time to time the bureau will make special area studies which will appraise the prospects for future economic development," Thompson said.

More than one thousand contestants, a record, took part in the annual Virginia High School League state championship contests at the university in the spring of 1947, Extension Director George B. Zehmer reported. The league, formerly known as the Virginia High School Literary and Athletic League, had achieved an unprecedented high school membership, with 350 of the 391 Virginia schools enrolled in 1946–47, far more than in any previous year. The contests were in dramatics, public speaking, publications, tennis, track, and field. Regional clinics for coaches and sponsors in these areas of activity, as well as in football and basketball, were attended by over four hundred and fifty persons. Richard R. Fletcher, executive secretary of the league for the preceding two years, "has now the confidence and enthusiastic cooperation of the high school officials," Zehmer reported. "Through the Virginia High School League, the university has the most numerous, effective and lasting contacts with the high school officials and pupils," he went on. "No other activity brings as many high school officials and pupils to the university every year." Professor Zehmer was given a leave of absence in

49. Dr. Vincent W. Archer of the medical faculty.

1946–47 to aid in organizing the University Center in Richmond, of which the university was a member, after which he resumed directorship of the Extension Division.

A highly constructive activity of the division was publication of the New Dominion Series by Jess and Jean Ogden. Begun in 1941, the leaflet appeared eighteen times a year, and the Ogdens told there of efforts in local communities to improve the level of living. In Lexington, for example, a health survey of school children uncovered "an alarming number of children with defects," and led to remedial action. Other numbers in the series described the maintenance in Charlottesville of a nursery to care for children of working mothers, a processing plant for tomatoes in Buckingham that added to farmers' cash income, and so on. Sociology classes and theological seminaries were using the series, and it was the basis for community studies in several states. A fieldworker in the U.S. Office of Education wrote: "We hope that you will be able to keep on preparing and distributing these leaflets indefinitely. I don't know any material that compares with this in value for helping people see the possibilities in community organization."

The Summer Quarter was placed on a new schedule of a single eight-week term in 1947, instead of two six-week terms, as in previous years. Prof. Lewis M. Hammond, '28, acting dean of the summer session, explained that the new arrangement would permit attendance of many teachers and school administrators with early and late summer workshop and conference commitments. The normal schedule would consist of two classes daily six days a week.

Hospital Administrator C. S. Lentz, who had had such severe wartime problems, declared that he was having others. In his annual report for 1945–46, he said concerning the hospital's executive committee (no names mentioned): "After a desultory period which has lasted during the war and during which time they have in general had little time for committee business, certain members have now determined that they are full-blown hospital administrators, and are attempting to prove this in a very obnoxious way. . . . Several members go off half crocket [*sic*] without ever investigating the matter under their consideration. . . . Something must be done . . . to take care of their attempted high-handed methods." Whether anything was "done" did not appear in subsequent reports.

Dr. Lentz also complained that he not had a raise in salary during his fifteen years with the hospital, and that he was the only employee connected with the Medical School whose compensation had not been increased during that time.

The School of Nursing was given complete accreditation in 1948. It had been included since 1941 in the list of nationally accredited schools, but the war had prevented it from fulfilling certain requirements. In 1949 it was placed among the top 25 percent in the country by the National Commission for the Improvement of Nursing Service, the criterion being its basic programs in nursing. In 1951 the B.S. degree was instituted, and three years later all programs were consolidated in a Department of Nursing.

Prof. John H. Yoe, internationally known chemist, was in the Pacific during the spring and summer of 1946 as head of a committee of U.S. and foreign scientists to observe the atom bomb tests near the island of Bikini. He had worked from 1940 to 1945 as a section member and investigator for the National Defense Research Committee, after which he was made an official investigator for the Chemical Warfare Service. In 1943 Dr. Yoe received the Charles Herty Award "for outstanding work in the field of chemistry in the South." He was the author of numerous books and several score scientific papers and was in demand as a lecturer all over the United States.

Another member of the university faculty was honored when Prof. Edward J. McShane was given one of the highest accolades that can come to a mathematician—an invitation to deliver the twenty-fifth in the series of Colloqium Lectures before the American Mathematical Society's annual convention. This was in recognition of his work on the calculus of variations which he had developed since joining the university faculty in 1935.

Remarkable demand from various parts of the country was being expressed for the lectures of Prof. David McCord Wright. A typical year for Wright was 1947–48, when he taught for six weeks in the summer at the University of California at Berkeley and the other six weeks at the same university in Los Angeles. In December he gave a seminar before members of the Yale economics and law faculties and a seminar at Harvard the same weekend. Later in the month he spoke at the annual meeting of the American Economics Association. A series of lectures in March at the University of Buffalo was followed somewhat later by service as visiting professor at Harvard for the summer.

"He was brilliant, also eccentric, and he had a low boiling point and high temper," said Prof. Tipton R. Snavely, head of the university's Economics Department. "He didn't hesitate to go over my head to speak his complaints to the dean or the president or anybody else. He was in President Newcomb's office one day . . . on a committee, and they were having a meeting. He suddenly disagreed and grew angry, walked out and slammed the door of the president's office. In 10 minutes or so he came back and apologized to the group. That was typical of David Wright."

Dr. Fletcher D. Woodward, '19, head of otolaryngology in the Medical School during these years, had a distinguished career in that speciality as physician, lecturer, teacher, and administrator. He introduced new techniques and took part in many state and national medical programs. Among the positions he held were president of the American Laryngological, Rhinological and Otological Society, chairman of the sections in these specialties for both the Southern Medical Association and the American Medical Association, and member of the American Board of Otolaryngology. On a different level, Dr. Woodward was nationally known for his efforts in the area of automobile safety, where he was a pioneer. His obituary in the Richmond *News Leader* in 1969 said that "a number of ideas he advanced years ago are now standard features of the modern automobile, such as safety belts and shoulder harnesses, a collapsible steering column, padded dashboards, elimination of projecting knobs and antiglare windshields." He was awarded the *Medical Tribune*'s automobile safety award in 1962 for "life-saving achievement in the service of health."

Prof. Joseph L. Vaughan of the Engineering School's English faculty was getting numerous offers from other institutions, Dean W. S. Rodman stated in recommending him for promotion to full professor. "Other institutions have recognized his abilities and are continually trying to induce him to sever his connections here," said the dean. He remained at the university and was promoted to full professor. Vaughan was

50. *Henry H. Cumming, Olympic track star and university faculty member who died of polio in Italy during World War II.*

lent by the university to the nearby Institute of Textile Technology, which he served as president from 1951 to 1953.

A coveted fellowship in physics was awarded Frank L. Hereford, Jr., who had received his B.A. at the university in 1943. This was the National Research Predoctoral Fellowship, awarded by the National Research Council. Hereford had done war work following graduation and was given the Certificate of Merit by the Office of Scientific Research and Development. He returned to the university for the session of 1946–47 to resume his studies, looking toward the Ph.D. degree.

The University of Virginia Alumni Fund, launched some years before World War II, broke all records in 1945, with $85,690 collected, more than double the total for the preceding year. Branch Spalding, who had succeeded Eugene E. Wager as director of the fund, resigned in the fall of 1945 as fund director and editor of the *Alumni News* to join the English faculty at Episcopal High School. Another record for collections was set in 1947, when over $105,000 came in from the alumni.

In that same year some twelve hundred old grads came back to a whopping Victory Reunion, June 20–22. Nearly all classes since 1882 were represented, the Big Tent was jammed to more than capacity, and the beer flowed freely. A huge crowd attended the barbecue at the pits below the old university golf course. The Alumni Ball took place that evening in the gymnasium, while stags continued to celebrate in the Big Tent. On Sunday a memorial service to the alumni who died in the war was held in the University Chapel. The Seven Society unveiled a memorial near the gymnasium to the nine members of the society who gave their lives. That afternoon in Cabell Hall tributes were paid to President Newcomb, who was retiring. Additional details concerning these tributes and Newcomb's retirement appear at the end of this chapter.

The Alumni Association took over all concessions on the Grounds, effective July 1, 1946, pursuant to action of the Board of Visitors. Stands operated in Monroe Hall, Clark Hall, Thornton Hall, Madison Hall, and the dormitories came under the association's jurisdiction, while concessions at all athletic contests likewise were assigned to that organization.

Proceeds went to various university causes in need of funds, such as scholarships, honor loans, the *Virginia Law Review*, the Engineering School's library, and so on. Much disappointment was expressed at the Dry Dock, established in the Madison Hall basement in 1943, since the profits from its operations were said to be needed to finance student recreation.

Several important faculty deaths occurred during and just after the war.

Prof. George B. Eager, '10, member of the law faculty for more than three decades, died in 1942 at age fifty-four after a period of failing health. He conducted his classes until a week before his death. Professor Eager was the author of numerous papers in the law reviews. In his college days at the university he was on the track and tennis teams and was several times singles champion of Kentucky. He had a part in establishing boxing as a major sport at Virginia.

Francis P. Dunnington, '72, professor of analytical and industrial chemistry, died in 1944 after being in retirement for about a quarter of a century. Recognized as one of the foremost analytical chemists of his time, he was awarded the Charles Herty Medal in 1935. It was given him not only for his service to chemistry in the South but "especially for his splendid record as a teacher of chemists who have attained renown." Trained under the famous John W. Mallet until Mallet retired in 1908, Professor Dunnington was thoughtful in his concern for his students. One of them, Dr. Charles L. Reese, '84, for many years chemical director for E. I. DuPont de Nemours, related that when Dunnington noted in class that he was ailing, the professor took him to his home, where he and Mrs. Dunnington nursed him back to health. Professor Dunnington was an elder in the Presbyterian church and a dedicated temperance advocate. This last was the subject of a few sly jokes, since "Old Dunny" had a conspicuously red nose, probably induced by his practice of identifying chemicals by sniffing the vials.

Dr. William A. Lambeth, who took his M.D. from the university in 1892 and his Ph.D. in 1901, died in 1944. Born in North Carolina, he attended the Harvard School of Physical Training after graduating from the University of Virginia Medical School. He then graduated from Harvard and returned to the university, where he took his Ph.D. Loaded with these academic honors, Dr. Lambeth joined the university's medical faculty and became head of the Department of Physical Education and superintendent of buildings and grounds. He is remembered especially for his leadership in the field of intercollegiate athletics and his insistence on high standards of eligibility and conduct. Termed "the father of athletics at the University of Virginia," he was associated for many years in this work with Prof. Albert Lefevre. Lambeth also was known for his longtime interest in Italian history and civilization. He was twice decorated by the Italian government for promoting understanding between Italy and the United States, and he furnished the Italian room in the Romance Pavilion on East Lawn.

The death of President Franklin D. Roosevelt in April 1945 was noted by *College Topics* with a rare "extra." FDR was the only president most of the students could remember clearly, as he had been in the White House for a dozen years. His death occurred on the eve of a university dance weekend, and the Friday and Saturday night dances were canceled. *Topics* expressed the hope that "as dates roll into Charlottesville from all corners of the country, they will understand."

A wartime casualty involving a faculty member occurred when Col. Henry H. Cumming, Jr., died in Italy from polio. He was assistant professor of political science at the university before entering the war. In his student days he had been captain of the track team and an Olympic sprinter at the 1928 games. At the time of his fatal seizure in 1945 he was assistant chief of staff G-2 at Peninsula Base Headquarters in Italy.

The university community was shocked on the last day of 1946 by the sudden death of Prof. Walter S. Rodman, dean of the School of Engineering since 1933. He made a report on faculty salaries and promotions in 1929 which Prof. William H. Echols termed "one of the finest pieces of work I have ever seen, and one of the greatest contributions to the progress of the university since the time of Thomas Jefferson." It paved the way for substantial salary increases at the session of 1930–31. Dean Rodman was secretary of the university's chapter of Phi Beta Kappa for nearly a quarter of a century. During his years as dean of engineering the school experienced unprecedented growth both in enrollment and equipment. He served for more than thirty years as critic of manuscripts on electrical engineering for the New York publisher McGraw-Hill.

Richard Heath Dabney, '81, who had retired in 1938 after forty-nine years on the faculty, died in 1947, aged eighty-seven. He had been dean of the university's first Graduate School for almost a quarter of a century and a one-man history department for a longer period. Thomas J. Wertenbaker, '10, who took his Ph.D. under Dabney and then joined the Princeton faculty, where he was serving when elected president of the American Historical Association, wrote: "With the passing of Richard Heath Dabney the last link was broken with the faculty of the nineties. The students of half a century ago, while they mourned the loss of others of the inspiring group at whose feet they sat—Frank Smith, Jack Mallet, Charles Kent, Milton Humphreys, etc.—consoled themselves with the thought, Mr. Dabney still lives, to greet us when we visit the university. . . . How often have we heard the remark, 'It was Heath Dabney who gave me my lifelong interest in history.' Mr. Dabney not only opened new intellectual vistas to his students, he had a profound influence in shaping their characters."

Dr. Samuel A. Mitchell, internationally recognized astronomer, retired in 1945 as professor of astronomy and director of the McCormick Observatory after thirty-four years in those posts. As professor emeritus he continued his research. In 1949 he was awarded the Watson Gold Medal of the National Academy of Sciences, awarded only ten times since its establishment in 1887, and only four times to an American. Dr. Mitchell's longtime associate, Dr. Harold L. Alden, succeeded him as head of the department and director of the observatory.

Prof. William A. Kepner, '08, one of the most interesting lecturers on the faculty, retired in 1946 as professor of biology. Physically he was of small stature, but his mental capacity was wide-ranging. It was at the request of Clarence Darrow, the famous defense counsel for John T. Scopes at his trial for violating the Tennessee antievolution law, that Dr. Kepner testified in Scopes's behalf. Following his retirement, Kepner was honored at a reception given by his former students and colleagues. Students from distant points were there, and several spoke. A volume edited by his faculty associate Prof. Bruce D. Reynolds, '20, was presented. It contained research papers by some of the outstanding research biologists who had studied under Kepner. He was the author of *Animals Looking into the Future* (1925) and of more than sixty research papers and other articles in leading scientific and educational journals.

Another longtime university figure retired in 1947 when Elmer I. Carruthers relinquished the post of bursar, which he had held since 1912. He had succeeded I. K. Moran in the position, after serving as a bank teller for several years. Carruthers had organized the university's first course in accounting in 1918 when the U.S. Army required such training for some of its soldiers. He received the Algernon Sydney Sullivan Award and was elected by the Students to Omicron Delta Kappa. Ill health forced his retirement, and he died in 1951.

Vincent Shea, '35, was appointed bursar and would be a leading influence in university affairs from that time forward. A specialist in public administration and finance, he got his M.S. at the university and then took graduate courses in public administration at the University of Chicago and Stanford. On his return to Charlottesville he became research assistant to the Virginia Commission on County Government under Prof. George W. Spicer, its chairman. Subsequently he joined the Bureau of Public Administration and became its acting director during the absence of Rowland Egger. Shea also served for two years as field director of studies in reorganization of state financial agencies and as financial consultant to the Richmond Charter Commission. He was elected president of the National Association of Business Officers.

John L. Newcomb announced in 1946 that he would resign as president of the university on his sixty-fifth birthday, December 18. Thomas B. Gay, '06, was named chairman of a Board of Visitors committee to seek a successor. High tributes were paid to Newcomb at the 1947 Finals. Rector Stettinius spoke and presented him with a silver box on behalf of the visitors. Robert B. Tunstall, '02, pointed out that under Newcomb, despite depression and war, "in plant, in appropriations and in equipment the strength and power of the university have approximately doubled." He added that the new library is "the greatest single step toward realizing the aspirations of a cen-

51. F. D. G. Ribble, dean of the Law School, 1939–63.

tury." The faculty was virtually twice as large as when he took office and twice as many Ph.D.'s had been graduated as in the entire previous history of the institution. Two years later President Newcomb's bust by Charles Rudy was placed in the entrance hall of Alderman Library alongside that of Alderman. The ceremonies were simple, in accordance with Newcomb's wish. Dean F. D. G. Ribble of the Law School presented the bust and President Colgate Darden accepted it.

After his retirement there were expressions of high praise from various faculty members for the manner in which he discharged his duties in extremely difficult times. But Stringfellow Barr entered a strong dissent: "Newk was a nice guy, but he hadn't the slightest idea what it was all about. I was devoted to him, but I thought it was a kind of awful choice." On the other hand, Prof. Robert K. Gooch said that "on the whole, I think he was the best president we ever had." Randall Thompson declared: "I never worked under a president who was more benign, more understanding, fairer, more patient, more considerate of my rights. . . . He has been a kind of yardstick for me at other places where I have taught." Professor Thompson's opinion is shared by many of those who served on the faculty during Newcomb's presidency.

FIVE

Colgate Darden
and the Students

COLGATE W. DARDEN, JR., chancellor of the College of William and Mary, former governor of Virginia, onetime member of the U.S. Congress and of the Virginia House of Delegates, was elected president of the University of Virginia in the spring of 1947. From the outset he had been the odds-on favorite for the position. Prominent alumni backed him, and the Alumni Association's board of managers urged his election unanimously. But the faculty and students were far from enthusiastic. Many professors viewed him askance because as a politician he had not come up the academic escalator, while the students feared that he planned to abolish fraternities and otherwise put the screws on the undergraduates. Yet both groups swallowed hard and their spokesmen promptly expressed themselves favorably, even enthusiastically concerning the new president. A faculty assembly, representing all departments, adopted resolutions without a single dissent voicing "complete confidence in Mr. Darden and pledging him full support and cooperation." This was an effort to counteract some of the extreme positions being taken, such as threatened resignations. *College Topics* hailed the new president without reservations.

As governor, Darden had manifested a great concern for the improvement of education in the state at all levels. He was anxious to increase the percentage of public school pupils matriculating at Charlottesville. What alarmed many of the undergraduates at Virginia was his recommendation as governor to the William and Mary Board of Visitors that students there be forbidden to live in fraternity or sorority houses, a recommendation that was adopted. His reasoning was that fraternities and sororities were "undemocratic" and placed a financial burden on parents. University of Virginia students somehow got the idea that Darden, a member of Phi Gamma Delta, planned not only to seek a similar regulation affecting them but also that he wanted to abolish fraternities entirely. Repeated denials that he wished to liquidate the university's Greek letter organizations failed to convince them. He did say that he thought stricter discipline was essential to the fraternities' proper functioning, but he added that the discipline should be in the hands of the students.

As a result of all the discussion aroused by Governor Darden's position on the issue, the university's Board of Visitors in 1942 had appointed a ten-man committee, headed by Judge A. D. Barksdale, '15, to examine the fraternity situation at the institution and make recommendations. This group, which included representatives of the faculty and alumni, as well as fraternity and nonfraternity men, reported unanimously in early 1943 against forbidding the students to live in the houses. After a careful investigation, the committee concluded that such a prohibition would entail heavy financial problems for both the fraternities and the university. The thirty-three fraternities had 610 rooms where students could stay, at less cost than in the dorms and much less than in the boarding houses, its report declared. Additional rooming facilities would have to be found elsewhere or built, if students were forbidden to live in the quarters of the Greek letter organizations. The committee said, further, that grades of the fraternity men were slightly higher, overall, than those of the nonfraternity men (a temporary phenomenon). It stated, too, that living in the houses was beneficial "in the formation of character, discipline and studious habits," although there had been "too frequent instances of conduct . . . that did not reflect credit on the fraternities." The committee strongly urged that the state provide funds for "a modern, well-equipped student union or student center where facilities will be available to all students for social gatherings and entertainment." This would take care of the complaint that nonfraternity men had no such facilities.

With the election of Colgate Darden as president of the university four years later, discussion around the Grounds of his views concerning fraternities was intensified. He had told the General Assembly while governor that he did "not object to the fraternities themselves" but to "conditions at the university to which fraternity houses have made more than a modest contribution." He added that "fraternity house life at the university is entirely too free and easy" and that "if the students are unwilling to institute reasonable rules and regulations, especially for supervision over mixed parties, then the university administration must do so." By the time he took over as president in 1947, the students had published page after page in *Corks and Curls* showing carousals in the fraternity houses, with girls and boys waving whiskey bottles, girls sitting in boys' laps, some in a semicomatose state, and a student or two lying prone on the floor. The fact that similar photos graced the annuals at various other institutions of higher learning did not lessen President Darden's conviction that the time had come to institute stricter rules at Virginia.

Many students appeared at his inauguration on Oct. 1, 1947, wearing black neckties, signalizing their concern over what they took to be his plans. The principal speaker was Sir Alfred Zimmern, emeritus professor of international relations at Oxford, where Darden had studied for a year under a Carnegie fellowship in the early 1920s. Gov. William M. Tuck also spoke. Representatives of many universities and learned societies in this country and overseas were present, along with thousands of visitors.

In his inaugural address the University of Virginia's new president offered the suggestion that "we should give careful consideration to the establishment of colleges giving two years of sound work to both men and women," adding that "this has been done with great success by the College of William and Mary in both Norfolk and Richmond, and the experiment has enabled many to secure the training they desire at a cost within their means." President Darden also urged "a carefully prepared program of adult education," on the theory that "the day will come when adult education will eclipse in effectiveness anything ever done with children."

A ban against first-year men and women joining fraternities or sororities had been instituted by the Board of Visitors be-

fore the inauguration, effective at the session of 1947–48. It
had been announced the previous spring that such a prohibition was part of President Darden's plan for the university.

The visitors also decreed that the incoming group of first-
year men be organized into a class, of which they were to remain members during their four years in the college. Each
succeeding new class was to be similarly organized. This edict
of the board was either withdrawn or ignored. Little more was
heard of it.

The Richmond *Times-Dispatch* had published an editorial ap-
proving the rule against first-year men joining fraternities, on
the ground that the rule "should automatically eliminate the
young wastrels from outside the state who now manage to
spend a year or two at Virginia, for they probably will not wish
to come at all." It also called these plutocratic undergraduates
"the Buick and bankroll set." The foregoing references caused
near tantrums among the Cavaliers, and the editor of the
Times-Dispatch—the author of the present volume—was denounced for a decade or more in student publications as a
"constant critic," "perennial critic," and "active critic" of the
institution.

Although a graduate of the university who had grown up
there, and the son, grandson, great-grandson, and great-
great-grandson of graduates, he was excoriated as knowing
little or nothing about its history and traditions and was depicted as on the lookout for opportunities to publicize it adversely. The sole basis for this prolonged brouhaha was the
"wastrel" editorial, plus condemnation by the paper of some
of the more outrageously undisciplined performances of the
students—at the university, in Philadelphia hotels, and elsewhere.

George O. Ferguson, dean of admissions and registrar, issued a statement following the appearance of the above
quoted *Times-Dispatch* editorial, intended to show that in 1947
there were no "wastrels" in the university. He conceded that
there were plenty of them in the 1920s, but contended that
when a couple of hundred were dropped in 1928 and new
requirements adopted, the problem was solved. It wasn't, although the postwar group of students was perhaps the best in
modern times at the university. Consulted in the 1970s concerning Ferguson's statement, Colgate Darden expressed ad-

52. Jesse W. Beams, internationally famous physicist.

miration for the dean but said there was a problem in 1947 with a group of well-heeled loafers who should not have been in the institution, a fact confirmed later by Edgar Shannon. Darden was successful in eliminating many of them by instituting stricter requirements. But the ban on first-year men joining fraternities was abandoned after a trial of several years, and a rule against rushing during the first semester was substituted. The fraternity members were unhappy about that too.

Darden criticized fraternities in his report to the Board of Visitors for 1948–49, saying that "the university has suffered too often in the past from the activities of a group of fraternities and societies dedicated primarily and sometimes exclusively to the outward and visible signs of social distinction." He added that these organizations "have failed signally as organizations to share the legitimate interests of a university community, nor have they furnished the leadership which might be expected of them."

Fraternities at Virginia "have been subject to less control by the administration than at any other university in the nation," *College Topics* declared in 1947. The paper trotted out all over again the argument that the new rules covering the houses ran counter to Jeffersonian principles. "To withdraw recognition of the rights and respect accorded the university students' ability to act as gentlemen is to deny that the University of Virginia, throughout its unique history, has been a successful institution," said *Topics*. "We who have grown to love the university for what it was cannot take it lying down." No mention here of the fact that in 1825–26 Thomas Jefferson counted on the young men to "act as gentlemen" but that those scions of the Virginia aristocracy behaved like hoodlums, and the "uniform and early rising laws" were enacted as a result (see chapter 1). Those laws, of course, were far more stringent than anything even conceived of by Colgate Darden or any other modern president of the university.

Or consider the provisions of the "Laws of the University of Virginia" enacted in 1897. Under those regulations, as Staige D. Blackford, Jr., later a Rhodes Scholar, pointed out in 1951, "students could be meted out minor punishments for such iniquitous actions as 'non-attendance on classes, inattention to the exercises prescribed, misbehavior or inattention in classes.'"

Furthermore, "it was a major offense for a student to show 'perseverance in habits of expense [and] . . . all meetings of students in the public rooms of the university are prohibited, unless the written consent of the chairman of the faculty is first obtained.'" Blackford observed that in view of these and other restrictions, "one might believe that the university could have been more famous in tradition as the citadel of administrative despotism, rather than as the shrine of student liberty." He went on to say that "the students here in the great traditional past enjoyed about as much liberty as a modern kindergarten child." Yet most of the undergraduates in the mid-twentieth century continued over the years to proclaim that the university in the past had been a uniquely free institution. When any sort of mild restrictions were placed on them covering the use of automobiles, chaperones in fraternity houses, public drinking, or what-not, they bellowed that the sacred Jeffersonian traditions were being undermined and Virginia was being turned into "just another prep school."

The Interfraternity Council (IFC) offered a set of rules governing women in the fraternities, but they were rejected by the visitors, who proposed the following: No women in the houses on Monday through Friday before 3 P.M. or after 8 P.M.; none on Saturday or Sunday before 11 A.M. or after 8 P.M., except that on Saturday night women were to be permitted until 1 A.M. if chaperones approved by the dean of students were present. Women were to be entertained in living and recreation rooms only, and officers of each fraternity were to be held responsible for enforcement. Alumni almost everywhere were overwhelmingly favorable to these new rules.

The IFC asked for and got a hearing before the visitors. It requested certain minor modifications, namely extension of the curfew for an hour after the university dances and exclusion of mothers, wives, sisters, and domestic servants from the restrictive provisions affecting the visits of women to the fraternity houses. These requests were granted.

Pursuant to President Darden's plan to impose greater and greater responsibility on the students for maintaining discipline in the university, he and Dean Newman arranged for the Student Council to assume complete jurisdiction over all such matters. This was the result of months of conferences between the administration and the council. Darden stated that council decisions would be overruled only in case of a miscarriage of justice or upon the discovery of new facts that justified a reversal.

Conduct of students at football games had left something to be desired and was placed in 1948 under a student committee of thirty which, in turn, was responsible to the Student Council. The committee members were readily identifiable by arm bands. A similar committee had functioned the previous year, but it reported to the administration rather than to the Student Council. An undergraduate judged by the committee to be guilty of public drunkenness at one of the games was put under "strict probation" until the end of the semester. This meant that he was prohibited from participating in any extracurricular activities or functions sponsored by the university and from taking part in athletic contests or attending dances or concerts.

Several students were disciplined by the Student Council in the spring of 1949 for misconduct. One was suspended for the rest of the semester, seven were put on strict probation until June 1950, and others were given lesser penalties.

On another front, the Interfraternity Council fined a fraternity and closed its house to all social activities for sixty days. These penalties were imposed for violations of rules laid down by the Board of Visitors governing chaperonage of parties in the house. The IFC acted under authority delegated to it by the Student Council. President Darden said that the council was operating "under the broadest grant of power given to students by any educational institution in the United States." He expressed gratification over the action of the IFC in the above mentioned case.

The roughest penalty imposed by the Student Council during this period was its recommendation for expulsion of an undergraduate who violated the strict probation under which he had been put by the council earlier in the year, by going to several parties. He was expelled. *Corks and Curls* said shortly thereafter that President Darden had never reversed the council in any of its decisions, though at times he had disagreed.

Easter Week 1950 was "notable for its decorum and general good behavior," Chester Goolrick wrote as editor of the *Alumni News*. This was especially true, he said, of the quadrangle parties, "though they were attended by literally thousands of people." These affairs took place in the quadrangle on Rugby Road surrounded on three sides by the Kappa Sigma, Delta Tau Delta, and Chi Phi fraternity houses. A major reason for the good behavior, he said, was "an open letter signed by 12 presidents of student organizations . . . calling on each student to be 'conscious of his own behavior at all times.'" The signers went on to say that "it is time to revive the respected ideal of the Virginia Gentleman . . . proud of his university and of his responsibility to it." The year before at the quadrangle party "an estimated 2,000 students and dates passed in and out," in the words of the *Virginia Spectator*. An annual feature of these parties was the fracas known as the Kappa Sig's Halitosis Brawl.

Only 20 percent of the students were members of the twenty-four fraternities still on the Grounds during the session of 1948–49, according to the *Alumni News*. A number of the Greek letter organizations had faded out since the early 1940s. Enrollment in the university broke all records in 1948–49, with more than five thousand students, of whom over three thousand were financing their education by means of the G.I. Bill.

Behavior of university men in Philadelphia following football games with the University of Pennsylvania in 1947 and 1948 received highly unfavorable nationwide publicity. While the conduct of some was bad enough, certain accounts contained serious exaggerations. The events in the Pennsylvania city followed by a few weeks some misbehavior by university students at the Hotel Roanoke in Roanoke after the VPI game.

Sensational newspaper accounts of the happenings in Philadelphia misled the Student Council at the university into issuing a somewhat more vehement statement than the facts warranted. It spoke of "wanton destruction . . . in the hotels and in the city of Philadelphia generally after Saturday's game [lost by Virginia, 19 to 7]," and went on to detail damage to three hotels. "Action will be taken in this matter," the council declared. However, the Philadelphia *Inquirer* interviewed several hotel men a few days later and said that while there were undoubted incidents, the overall behavior was not so bad as had been painted. Yet it was reprehensible; President Darden spoke of the "very severe damage," and he added: "The only thing that stood in the way of decisive action was the lack of reliable facts." Neither the Pennsylvania authorities nor the Student Council could identify any of the guilty parties, so nobody was punished.

When Virginia defeated Penn two years later, 26 to 14, there was further disorder in Philadelphia hotels, but once again the episodes seem to have been painted in too lurid colors. The president of the Hotel Association of Philadelphia issued a statement saying that "we never saw anything like what happened here," and he added that no more reservations would be accepted from University of Virginia students. They had come to the game "steamed up on whiskey and waving Confederate flags," he added. The manager of the Adelphi Hotel where the principal celebration took place said the brawl was broken up at midnight by police, and that "chairs, glasses, everything you can think of were thrown out of the windows." But the University of Pennsylvania student newspaper quoted the manager of the Benjamin Franklin Hotel a few days later as terming the hotel association's pronouncement "unfortunate" and "ridiculous." He said he would be glad to accept University of Virginia students at his hotel at any time.

President Darden and three members of the Student Council went to Philadelphia for a conference. When it was concluded, they issued a statement that "property damage to hotels was not as great as we have been led to believe" (figured overall at $1,150), but that "we were shocked by some of the conduct that had taken place . . . in public rooms." They emphasized that every effort would be made "to see that hotels were paid for any damage traceable to university students." Unfortunately, "no names of those guilty of these misdeeds were secured," most of the misbehavior having occurred in public rooms. Total damage to all hotels was put at less than $800 in the final reckoning some months later. In the fall of 1950 Virginia played Penn again, but there were no complaints of student misconduct.

Virginia undergraduates were wont to treat their fraternity houses at times approximately as roughly as they did the Philadelphia hostelries, especially during weekend parties. Time and again Greek letter organizations would collect

53. *J. Malcolm Luck, director of alumni activities, 1930–55.*

$20,000 to $30,000 from alumni members for doing the place over, only to see it virtually wrecked by the next series of parties.

Prof. T. Braxton Woody, the first chairman of the university's Housing Committee, said concerning the fraternities: "One of our major problems was to inspect these horrible places. . . . Just beyond belief, nobody can imagine human beings ever lived in such places. We would tell them 'this must be cleaned, this must be done,' and we would come back a little later, nothing done at all. . . . Or a boy would work like a dog, get the place cleaned up, maybe he would get an alumnus interested. They would spend thousands of dollars sanding the floors, cleaning it up, renovating. Then a year or two later . . . all that money gone down the drain."

Student Adviser B. F. D. Runk, who would become dean of the university in 1959, was critical of the fraternities during the 1950s since, in his view, "they were not doing their job." A fraternity man himself who believed in the Greek letter societies, he felt that "they were not fulfilling the function they had here"—were not giving proper leadership to the university, although "all of the student leaders were fraternity men." They had let their houses run down, "were just beating the houses all to pieces." However, he praised the Student Council for the record it made during these years.

As governor, Colgate Darden had projected plans for a Student Activities Building at the university, with the idea of making conditions for students more comfortable and economical and providing social facilities for all, especially nonfraternity men. He estimated that about $3,000,000 would be needed for construction of an adequate student center with dining hall, lounges, reading rooms, offices for student publications and other organizations, and so on. This would give the university "equipment that virtually every great university in the nation except Virginia already has," said the *Alumni News*. But while that publication was strongly in favor of the plan, most fraternity men after the war were grimly opposed. This represented a complete reversal from a few years before, when nearly everybody—faculty, students, and alumni—seemed to want a Student Activities Building. One exception on the faculty was history Prof. Thomas Cary Johnson, who addressed the Richmond alumni on "Darden's First Year," and accused the president of "ruining the university." When Darden heard about it, he called in Johnson to learn more about his speech. The latter repeated that he was ruining the university by "making it a catch-all for everybody who wants to go to college in the state." "That's what it's supposed to be," the president replied. "Neither of us convinced the other," Johnson said later in describing the incident. Cary Johnson, who spoke of himself as "a reactionary," was one of the wittiest lecturers in the university.

Many fraternity men apparently feared that the Student Union would undermine their prestige and their domination of university affairs. However, it was in fact necessary not only for the nonfraternity men, who were without adequate recreational and dining opportunities, but for everybody.

The University Center, revolving about Madison Hall and established around 1940, had been christened the Student Union in 1948, looking toward the ultimate construction of an adequate Student Union building. The union was active in offering various types of cultural and recreational activities, with the indefatigable Mrs. A. E. Walker presiding over all. However, Madison Hall, with its limited size and facilities, could not possibly provide everything that was required by the steadily growing student body.

In 1952 the General Assembly appropriated $400,000 as a sort of down payment on the much-debated Student Union. A total of $2,750,000 finally was made available by the legislature. Fraternity men had been lobbying against it, writing Gov. William M. Tuck and members of the General Assembly that it would be a waste of money. Some contended that the sum would be much better spent for higher faculty salaries or for a field house. A three-man committee of the Student Council recommended against the project, "since present plans do not provide facilities that would be attractive to students." The building was jeeringly referred to on many occasions as "the ping pong palace." The *Virginia Spectator* published an editorial evidencing a discovery of horrendous bugaboos under the bed: "We stand on the threshold of 'State U-ism,' that haven of the dungaree doll, the second-rate professor, the pigmy-brained student, and the monolithic 'campus,'" said this organ of student opinion. "The title of 'Virginia gentleman' will no longer command respect, but will become a rather ludicrous misnomer." Another writer in the *Spectator* remarked sarcastically: "Thriftily priced at only three million dollars, the structure [the Student Union] will be unobtrusive, and probably not much larger than the combined new dormitories and the Alderman Library." To all of these fatuities President Darden replied, "I am not going to change my position." His influence with the General Assembly far outweighed that of the opposition.

The Student Union was built, of course, and named for former President Newcomb. This led to the derisive student appellation of "Mamma Newk," applied to the Union by students who were using it regularly but had fought it bitterly. The most important and necessary structure on the Grounds since the erection of Alderman Library, Newcomb Hall had to be enlarged in subsequent years, so essential was it to the well-being of all the students, fraternity and nonfraternity alike. The same type of undergraduate who had fought its erection in previous years now denounced the president for delay in carrying out its enlargement. Much credit for its almost immediate acceptance and success has been accorded Donald M. McKay, formerly director of housing, who was placed in charge.

There were other causes of friction with Darden during the mid-1950s, in addition to Newcomb Hall. Rules as to student housing set off renewed lamentations that Jeffersonian liberties were being undermined.

And there was the "sex scandal" on East Lawn in the spring of 1954, involving a dozen students and a girl. The event occurred Apr. 4, but did not become known to the public until May 19, when the *Cavalier Daily* unveiled most of the facts. The student newspaper, edited by Frank M. Slayton, expressed approval of the dismissal of some students and the suspension of others. This set off a great uproar, and many undergraduates wrote to the paper expressing strong disapproval of its stand and of the penalties meted out. There was especially bitter criticism of the Board of Visitors and of Richard R. Fletcher, director of student affairs, who had recommended the penalties. Three of the men were suspended be-

54. *Tipton R. Snavely, professor of economics.*

cause they failed to put a halt to actions of the others. These suspensions were shortened.

All this, combined with the new housing regulations, the building of Newcomb Hall, the perennial fear that fraternities would be abolished, and other grievances, real or imagined, caused the Student Council to call a mass meeting in Cabell Hall. The council claimed, among other things, that its powers had been "usurped" by "Dick" Fletcher in the "sex scandal" matter, and requested that Fletcher's office be eliminated. The Board of Visitors refused to grant the request.

In all this hullaballoo it is probable that the students did have a genuine grievance or two against the university administration. Some of those who led in mobilizing sentiment against President Darden and his associates were young men of intelligence and integrity. For example, Stuart Valentine, president of the college, said he had attended numerous conferences with Darden, but "when asked direct questions, the president has dodged them completely. . . . Many times he has been asked whether the administration is going to do away with fraternities. His indefinite answer has always been that as long as fraternities keep up their standards, he has no complaints. The question is, whose standards—his or what the students consider good standards." It would seem that if the president had been a bit more categorical in his denials, he could have saved himself a good many headaches. Stuart Harris, a former member of the Student Council, said the council had been bypassed and overruled on various occasions. Also that a fraternity had been warned against playing softball on Sunday "miles from the university." Just what was involved in these episodes was not made plain. It may be that the boys were not given a "fair shake."

Colgate Darden would have been the first to admit that he was not infallible, and he could well have made some serious mistakes in his relations with the students. If he had not done so over a period of a dozen years in office, it would have been little short of miraculous.

There were occasional cross-burnings near the president's house on Carr's Hill, evidencing student wrath over this or that administration policy. President Darden put a notice in the paper saying that it didn't matter to him how many crosses were burned, but please to stop leaning them against the fine old oak trees since it was harmful to the trees and they were valuable. There were no more cross-burnings.

When the Board of Visitors met in the early fall of 1954 and heard the complaints of a student committee, it voted unanimously to support President Darden and rejected totally the contention that he was trying to turn the university into another "state-U" or to drive out the fraternities. It commended Beta Theta Pi for employing a mature and experienced hostess who would be present at all parties to which young women were invited and recommended that the other fraternities follow suit.

Out of the ferment and controversy generated by the foregoing events there came agreement on a far-reaching change in the system of student government. President Darden and the Student Council put together a plan for a nine-member student Judiciary Committee which would try all cases of student misconduct referred to it by the council and impose penalties. Honor code violations would remain under the Honor Committee. Cases to be handled by the Judiciary Committee would be those dealt with during the preceding five years by the Student Council. At the same time, the latter organization's powers were broadened, and it would act as an advisory body to the president of the university. The office of director of student affairs would be retained and its occupant would forward to the Student Council any cases that he felt should involve disciplinary action. The Judiciary Committee had no jurisdiction over the coeds since they had their own form of government, the Women Students' Association. President Darden expressed himself as greatly encouraged by these developments, and the *Cavalier Daily* was ecstatic, saying: "Here we have an unbelievable amount of freedom, and that freedom has been broadened by the establishment of this new student government." The plan was ratified overwhelmingly by the students in a referendum. Five years later Dean Raymond C. Bice wrote: "The student government, with its separate judiciary function, has evolved from cooperative efforts between students and administrators to make the University of Virginia students envied by their counterparts in colleges throughout the world."

A committee of seven administrators and professors, with Prof. George W. Spicer as chairman, was named in 1954 to study the fraternity situation and make recommendations. Its report, made known the following spring, contained significant proposals. Preparation and publication of a general policy for fraternities was one of them. Another was appointment by President Darden of a nine-man committee, which would include three IFC representatives, this committee to be responsible for the organization and regulation of fraternity affairs. Also, each chapter would be required to secure the services of a hostess approved by the university, "who shall be present at all social events." However, fraternities on the official list would be permitted to "entertain a limited number of women guests in their fraternity houses during specified periods without the presence of a hostess or chaperone." Appointment of food service and housing service advisory committees was urged, as well as strengthening of the system of resident fraternity advisors, especially with respect to finances. Hazing in connection with initiations should be prohibited, and no initiation activities should take place outside the house. Scholarship performance of each chapter should be closely watched, and suggestions for improvement made by the 3-3-3 committee, when this seemed indicated. An immediate study of rushing policies was urged. These recommendations were approved by President Darden.

Fraternity rushing rules were overhauled for the umpteenth time, pursuant to the report. Major objectives were to reduce the amount of time and money expended in rushing prospective "goats." Road trips with goats to nearby women's colleges were banned. The time for rushing, about the same as before, was limited to the period between Thanksgiving and the Christmas holidays, the first two weeks of the second semester, and the third week of that semester (formal rush week).

The Delta Kappa Epsilon fraternity was caught paddling initiates in broad daylight in the field in front of the Deke house. This was in violation of the rules, so penalties were imposed. But since various other fraternities had been doing the same thing without being detected, some of the penalties were removed. The Dekes, it was pointed out, were at least not trying to conceal what they were doing.

The "Cross Fraternity Scholarship Award" was established by Mrs. Virginia Cross of Philadelphia, mother of Richard S.

Cross, '22. An engraved trophy or plaque would go to the fraternity with the highest scholastic average for the previous season.

As noted in an earlier chapter, students were predicting in the 1920s that if the university's enrollment went beyond two thousand, the Honor System would be endangered if not destroyed. These premonitions were unduly alarmist, for the system held up well for decades after many more than two thousand students were enrolled. By the 1950s, however, there were signs that the honor spirit was being subjected to unwonted strains. A substantial percentage of the students in that era had had no previous experience with the workings of an Honor System such as had functioned at Virginia for more than a century.

In the middle 1950s a "long line of thefts in the dressing room" at the gymnasium was mentioned in the *Cavalier Daily*. Some said it was the work of outsiders, but the paper spoke of "a general feeling that the real culprits were closer to home." Charges that students were misrepresenting their ages at the ABC stores to get liquor also were disturbing. And something called "synthetic sickness" was causing concern. Students were excusing themselves for class absences under circumstances deemed suspicious—"one of the few shams in an otherwise sincere university," as the *Cavalier Daily* expressed it. On top of all this, the student Bad Check Committee was "facing a definite crisis from a mounting number of unredeemable bad checks passed by university students." It appeared that "almost $250 worth of these 'back-handed larcenies'" had accumulated. The Bad Check Committee announced that a student failing to rectify a "rubber" check within two weeks of notification by that agency must appear before the Honor Committee.

On the favorable side, the number of dismissals under the Honor System had dropped sharply, as compared with the years immediately following World War II, when enrollment had zoomed to more than five thousand.

In addition, excellent results were being reported from the Ivey F. Lewis Honor Loan System, under which students who could get funds nowhere else could borrow small sums, usually under $25, and sign a pledge to repay the money "as soon as I reasonably can." During the session of 1952–53, for example, a total of $8,735 was loaned and $9,260 was repaid from previous years. Of the amount made available to students the preceding year, $700 was unpaid, but it was expected that all, or nearly all, of this sum would be forthcoming. Some time previously, a man borrowed $100, and when two years went by without repayment, the loss was about to be written off when a check for $150 arrived from him. No interest was charged on these loans, but he felt that he should include it anyway. It was evidence of the fact that the honor spirit remained alive and well among the vast majority of students at the University of Virginia.

Differences between the older and younger generations as to what constituted obscenity were apparent with publication of the "Paunch" issue of the *Spectator*, intended as a parody on the British magazine *Punch*. Many students were infuriated when President Darden appointed a faculty committee to report on the issue, and the *Cavalier Daily* said that statements made by him concerning the matter "made us wonder at the soundness of mind of the president." It apologized later for this remarkable assertion, but continued to maintain, along with several leading student organizations, that there was nothing objectionable in the magazine. The consensus among students, with few exceptions, seemed to be that the "Paunch" issue was one of the best ever. Yet the faculty committee, headed by Dean of Women Roberta H. Gwathmey, found unanimously that the issue was a "discredit" to the university, and the entire Board of Visitors expressed the same view. President Darden referred to the issue's "coarseness and vulgarity which are utterly out of keeping with the innate good taste which has distinguished the University of Virginia." The Board of Visitors voted to ban the *Spectator* permanently because of what was deemed its unsavory record over the past few years. A new publication, *Harlequin*, promptly appeared as its successor but was panned by the *Cavalier Daily*, which accused it of purloining most if its material from old issues of the *Spectator*. It soon faded out and was heard of no more.

Problems surrounding student automobiles were frequently of concern to the administration. First-year men had been forbidden since before the war to have cars, but the ban had been

55. *Col. Staige Davis Blackford, M.D., professor of internal medicine and organizer of the university's 8th Evacuation Unit in World War II. From a portrait by Irene Higgins.*

enforced only halfheartedly. Strict enforcement was decreed by President Newcomb in the fall of 1946, pursuant to action by the Board of Visitors, but the edict was withdrawn soon afterward, following a student protest. It appeared that the ban worked a hardship on many of the newly enrolled war veterans who couldn't get living quarters near the Grounds. The visitors revived the ban against cars for first-year men, effective with the session of 1950–51. Transfer students and those entering professional or graduate departments were exempt from the prohibition, as were the physically handicapped.

Things were fairly quiet on the motor vehicle front until the fall of 1958, when parking and traffic problems and the proliferation of student cars to a total of over three thousand out of four thousand six hundred enrolled caused new regulations to be announced. The effect of these rules was that only fourth-year men could have cars, beginning with the 1960–61 session, and no student on probation could have one. The Student Council voted to fight the regulations and to support the petition of first-year men for driving privileges. A few weeks later a riot broke out, with about fifteen hundred students participating. After the youths had surged around the Grounds and along Main Street, some sixty police dispersed them with tear gas. Three were arrested. Professor "Dee" Runk, in charge of enforcing the car rules, was hanged in effigy. Shortly thereafter about one thousand students filled Cabell Hall, protesting the regulations as to cars and other rules deemed objectionable. President Darden announced that "it is not my purpose to consider grievances formulated by a segment of the student body fresh from hanging Mr. Runk in effigy." The students apologized, but they were determined to obtain concessions from the administration. The young men got a hearing before the Board of Visitors, and the rules were substantially modified, following conferences between the students and President Darden. Hereafter the use of a car would be tied to grades made by the student. First-year men could operate automobiles at Midwinters and Easters if they made the required grade, but at no other time. Undergraduates who were on probation or had had a warning of any kind could not operate a motor vehicle.

The turmoil over the car regulations caused a certain

amount of tension between professors and students. In order to lessen this feeling and promote understanding, the Student Council initiated a series of bimonthly coffee hours, when faculty and students would hold five simultaneous sessions in the dormitories between 7 and 9 P.M. on designated evenings. The first of these were largely attended and were pronounced highly successful.

The drinking problem remained to the fore in the postwar years. Whether there was more drinking at Virginia than elsewhere has always been debatable, but it was more public there in the period following the war. "Exhibition drinking," that is, consuming grain alcohol drinks from mason jars or highballs from glasses on University Avenue, at concerts in Cabell Hall, or on the Lawn, made its appearance. The phrase "exhibition drinking" had not been heard before 1946. In that year the Interfraternity Council and the Student Council forbade such drinking for a coming "big weekend," and "filled mason jars" were banned both at dances in Memorial Gymnasium and at concerts. The Student Council said the rules would be enforced.

The students seemed to go out of their way to give the university a reputation for excessive tippling. *Corks and Curls*, in particular, with its photographs of riotous parties in fraternity houses and exaggerated descriptions of drinking bouts helped to create this image. The myth was put forward that wassail was even more widespread and unrestrained at the university under prohibition and in the years that followed than in the 1950s. An article on "The Playboy Era" in the *University of Virginia Magazine* in 1966 speaks of the prohibition years as "these wild prohibition days," "this wild era" and "wild soirées." The fact is that whereas there was wholesale violation of the dry laws, the carryings-on were by no means as uninhibited and wild as those of later decades at the university. For one thing, with liquor illegal, drinking could not be nearly so open as it subsequently became, and for another, during much of the prohibition era girls could not even enter the front door of a fraternity house, much less behave in the manner depicted in innumerable photographs placed before the public in the 1940s and later by the university annual.

Realizing in 1948 that the university was getting a bad

name, Joseph C. Carter, Jr., president of the Interfraternity Council and later of the Student Union, wrote a guest editorial for *College Topics* in which he said: "It seems that excessive publicity is given, generally, to the drinking at the university. We, as students, are in part responsible for such reputation as we have. But definite allusions, such as 'Purple Passion affairs,' should be cut to the minimum, in order to counteract the public conviction that this is an institution of alcoholism. We know that it is not true, and it behooves us not to bray forth continually of our capacities for consumption." *Topics* followed with an editorial suggesting that "students here quit bragging about Virginia's rather dubious distinction for drink." The Student Council announced a crackdown on exhibition drinking in connection with the dance concert at Openings in the fall of 1951 and said that "the necessary disciplinary action will be taken if this request is not carried out." A year later the council said it would not tolerate any excessive drinking "at football games, girls' schools and public assemblies." *College Topics* issued a blast against those who were bringing the university into disrepute with their swinish conduct. "Why can't students of normal mentality see reckless drinking as something that does immeasurable harm to the university?" asked the *Cavalier Daily*. "Why do men who are not insane seek to convince the public that they belong in Staunton [at the Western State Hospital]? How can a person with some astuteness behave as a complete ass?" Yet arguments against exhibition drinking were met with the contention that President Darden and others who urged that it stop were asking the students to be hypocritical and drink, but not to drink in public. And when the Richmond newspapers, especially the *Times-Dispatch*, chronicled outrageous doings at the university or commented adversely upon them, the papers were denounced in the *Cavalier Daily* as "that bright yellow journalistic combination" and the editor of the *Times-Dispatch* as an exemplar of "yellow dog journalism."

Most of the university carousing went on during big party weekends when girls came for the dances and other festivities from all points of the compass. These weekends were given enormous prominence in the *Cavalier Daily*, which published the name of every girl and her date, covering many columns,

56. Buzzy Wilkinson, all-American basketball player, 1955.

and heralded the oncoming events with such across-the-page headlines as "Weekend to Feature Bacchus, Bands, Babes" and "Buddy, Bottles, Babes, Boogie Form Phalanx of Festivity." The vast majority of students seemed to look forward to these weekends with great eagerness, despite the gargantuan hangovers that often resulted. But two prominent student leaders, Curt Bazemore and Alfred McCormack, Jr., said that they found these affairs to be nothing less than frightful bores. Bazemore wrote: "After four years of them we feel as if we were sitting in on the worst movie ever made for the fourth straight time. How people can honestly say they have a good time amid such screaming, shouting scenes of madness . . . is beyond us." McCormack wrote, under the heading "University Party—Phooey," that "one phase of university life we can do without are big parties and big weekends such as those given on Openings, Midwinters and Easters."

No account of the extracurricular diversions of university students would be complete without mention of Carroll's Tea Room, a small, one-story, two-room frame building at the corner of Barracks Road and Route 29. It was owned, beginning in 1941, by Carroll Walton, but he sold out later. The place retained the name Carroll's in the 1940s and 1950s, however, but during much of that time a current joke had it that there was "no Carroll, no tea, and no room." Oceans of beer flowed through Carroll's, but tea was not even kept in stock. It claimed to sell more beer than any other emporium in Virginia, and reportedly served as many as five thousand customers in a day. An advertisement in 1954 said: "Did you know we served one million people last year? Ten at a time— all were satisfied." The congestion was fierce, for the two rooms were only twenty by thirty feet, and hundreds of students patronized the place every night. Some imbibed too freely, of course, but with the undergraduates' usual penchant for exaggerating the extent of inebriation in former days, a student writer in 1973 said that "wild pandemonium and drunken vigils took place nightly in Carroll's." It was indeed a place where friends met for a seidel or two of lager in an atmosphere of jollity and good fellowship, and some of them got drunk. Carroll's moved in 1957 a mile and a half to the north on Route 29, corner of Rio Road and was never the same again.

Housing for students in the years immediately following World War II was a serious problem, since enrollment skyrocketed with the return of men from the service. The problem was complicated by the fact that many of the veterans were newly married, and a considerable number had small children. The university accordingly bought 120 acres in 1945 from the Massie property, lying along the west side of Route 29 across from Lambeth Field and just north of the C&O Railroad tracks. This was Copeley Hill. A hundred expansible trailers were installed in 1946, and these were followed by eighteen one-story frame buildings containing seventy-six apartments. Then fifty-six more apartments, some with two stories, were added, plus thirty faculty apartments and fourteen two-story barracks buildings for single students. There was also an area for privately owned house-trailers. A census in 1950 showed 1,366 persons living on Copeley Hill, including 260 children and 450 single students. "Because the stork is a frequent visitor, no count of the children can be accurate for more than a few hours," said the *Alumni News*. A mayor and council of eleven were elected twice yearly, and represented the group when the university administration was considering matters affecting the area. Wives, babies, and dogs were important members of the community, and a general feeling of cordiality and good relations prevailed. Residents pitched in to build a playground, and a woman's club provided bridge games and other recreation for the ladies.

All was serene until acrimony arose between the group that had babies and the one that had dogs. As President Darden relates it in his *Conversations With Guy Friddell*, "The parents wanted their children to play out in the yard and the street, and they did not want the dogs running loose . . . and knocking their children over. The dog-people wanted the parents to build fences around their property to keep the dogs out. . . . One night in a discussion of the dogs-children issue, a councilman jumped right over on another councilman and pulled his shirt off. . . . I made up my mind that something had to be done." Richard Poff, the future longtime member of Congress from Roanoke and then a justice of the Virginia Supreme Court, was a law student at the time and mayor of Copeley Hill. Darden sent for him, and said: "I'm tired of listening to mothers hollering at me about children and the dogs. . . . Take

it over and I'll back you up, but I want some peace and quiet."
That did it. "I never had another peep out of Copeley Hill.
Poff organized it perfectly."

The hill continued for some time to be used for student and
faculty housing. In 1960, for example, it had 250 family units
with a population of around eight hundred. All this construction, which was never intended to be anything but temporary,
was pulled down subsequently to make way for more substantial buildings.

In another area of the Grounds, the denizens of East and
West Lawn were unhappy in 1948 over the lack of adequate
bathing and shaving facilities. The East Lawn dwellers had
only one shower room with two showers and two wash basins
for about fifty men. "The razor-nicked faces of East Lawn
residents are being raised in an appeal for additional mirrors
and bowls," said the *Cavalier Daily*. The West Lawners, who
had been similarly dissatisfied, were rejoicing over installation
of a more adequate hot water system. "No more standing in
line to use the one hot water faucet," they said. Despite the
relatively primitive facilities on the Lawn and Ranges, these
quarters have for several decades been the most coveted
rooms in the university. In 1949 it was announced that
whereas for a good many years only Virginians had been
deemed eligible to inhabit these precincts, they would now be
thrown open to student leaders, irrespective of geographical
origin. In the summer of 1956 all student quarters on the
Lawn were rehabilitated under the supervision of Prof. Frederick Nichols, the fireplaces and doorways restored to their
original 1825 condition, and the rooms equipped with appropriate furniture to replace the battered and nondescript items
that had graced those chambers. Concern was expressed,
however, over "the exclusion of the single rooms . . . one of
the most popular aspects of Lawn life." The demand for
rooms on the Lawn and Ranges has long exceeded the supply.

New vitality came to the Lawn after World War II with the
reactivation of the West Lawn Chowder and Marching Society,
an ancient association of congenial spirits inhabiting the west
side of the Lawn. The society had been founded more than
half a century before but had become extinct "due to lack of
interest and chowder." In 1953 the organization changed its
name to the Lawn Chowder and Marching Society, thus mak-

ing eligible any dweller on either side of the lovely stretch of green extending from the Rotunda to Cabell Hall, provided he was "a great guy and a good friend." Officers were elected, and the head marcher and chowder consumer rejoiced in the sobriquet of "The Purple Shadow." All and sundry were assured that the organization was "under no circumstances a scholarship or a drinking club, but an honorary society." Another manifesto spoke somewhat confusingly of an "Operation Barrel," but lest this be misconstrued it was explained that what the society is seeking is to "determine how much fun a 'barrel of monkeys' really is." Photographs of the group in *Corks and Curls* show the members dressed in all varieties of nondescript and outlandish costumes.

When not garbed for such special high jinks, Virginia men, at least those belonging to fraternities, tended to dress very much alike in the postwar 1940s and 1950s. In the words of the *Spectator*, the typical fraternity man "wears what amounts to a uniform, and unless he conforms to it, is ostracized by his friends and cast into outer darkness. . . . First, he wears an unpressed and sagging tweed coat . . . worn with the bottom button buttoned . . . a black string tie which, by virtue of much age and wear, has stretched to about twice its original length." Slacks accompanied the tweed jacket, and white buckskin shoes were often worn, sometimes with white socks. The *Cavalier Daily* had a special lament: the tradition that first-year men were supposed to wear hats went out, "but fast," after World War II.

Normal routine at the university and all other educational institutions was disrupted in 1950 by the outbreak of the Korean War. Young men in college or about to matriculate were once more uncertain as to what the future held. Enrollment at the university in the fall of that year was 4,168, a drop of 548 compared with the total for twelve months before. This was due, in part, to the calling up of reserves for the Korean conflict and also to a decline in the number of students enrolled under the GI Bill, since many of them had completed their collegiate schooling. President Darden urged all matriculates at the university to remain there until called. He stated that "the best way for students to serve their country is to maintain the highest possible level of scholarship until they are directed to serve in other ways," and he added: "It was found during World War II that one of the most serious weaknesses of the military organization was the scarcity of college-trained personnel." Defense Secretary George C. Marshall stressed the importance of students' enrolling in reserve units and remaining in college to complete their education and their military training "as a patriotic duty." He described the ROTC as "a fundamental element in all Department of Defense planning."

Unification of the armed forces at the university became a reality when the Department of Defense authorized the establishment there of an Air Force Reserve Officers' Training Corps. Reserve officer units of the army and navy were already on the Grounds. In addition, students were training in the summers at Quantico in the platoon leaders' class for marine corps officers.

The Navy Officer Training Corps had been functioning at the university since 1941, and the army transportation corps since World War II, while the Army Signal Corps established a unit at the university in 1951. Students in these various units who completed the required courses for the baccalaureate degree qualified for commissions as second lieutenants or ensigns. Twenty-five to fifty students would go to Richmond every week for preinduction physical examinations and would then return to Charlottesville. Many Virginia men served in Korea; twenty-nine lost their lives.

By 1954 peacetime routine had returned, and the *Cavalier Daily* was protesting "ungentlemanly conduct" by altogether too many students. "We have more people wearing repp ties than we have gentlemen," said the editor. "Those men who 'boo' and 'hiss' in class, at movies and athletic events behave as anything but gentlemen. . . . We have on occasion witnessed the flagrant disregard of respect in class when members have felt it necessary to 'boo' the instructor." Accompanying this comment was a letter from James N. Pendleton, "an off-and-on resident of Charlottesville, with a wide acquaintance among the faculty and students," who wrote: "A number of university students have succeeded in making the term 'Virginia gentleman' a complete and utter travesty . . . ill-bred adolescents who, unable to hold their liquor, make asses of themselves at so many of the sporting events . . . [and] in the local movie houses." Not only so, but by 1958 the *Cavalier Daily* said standards of dress were deteriorating shockingly: "As each spring day moves by, the dress of a large number of students becomes more appalling and outrageous. . . . T-shirts, soiled sport shirts, dirty khakis and sockless feet can all be seen at some time during a walk through the Grounds. . . . Warm weather does not excuse such poor taste."

In the area of college politics, the University Party, controlled by the fraternities, had long been dominant. The rival Cavalier Party had been successful only once since the war, in 1951. Lambda Pi and Skull & Keys, two societies in the college, were both affiliated with the University Party, which had become so powerful that it was decided to end this arrangement and place each society at the head of a party. For decades before World War II such an arrangement had been in force, with Lambda Pi heading one group and Skull & Keys the other. During the war the navy's V-12 was so important and influential that the two organizations felt it necessary to combine in order to form an opposition bloc. In 1953 they decided to separate again, and in the spring of that year the two parties that they sponsored nominated slates. Each fraternity was given votes in choosing the nominees, as were the residence houses and the old dorms. Students not coming under any of these headings were granted at-large representation in the voting. The system seemed an improvement, and somewhat more interest in the elections was created. The Engineering School, with Theta Tau and Trigon as rival organizations, was operating under a similar plan.

But even with the new and better-balanced arrangement, there was too much indifference in the college among the rank and file. A small segment of the student body was involved in many forms of extracurricular activity but, as William L. Tazewell, editor of the *Cavalier Daily*, expressed it, the rest of the students "attend classes occasionally, the flicks frequently, and have a 'great time' on weekends." Two years later dismay was still being voiced over the indifference of the average student to university politics and all other types of politics, national and international, as well as to "cultural and educational events, famines, hurricanes—everything with the possible exception of the World Series." As Staige D. Blackford, Jr., phrased it a few years before, "A man who might bring up the question of world affairs at a 'bull-session' is usually about as welcome as a descendant of Thaddeus Stevens at a Daughters of the Confederacy convention." Yet the political parties at the university during this era at least had platforms, involving such questions as the Honor System, dormitory living, proctors, class cutting, parking, establishment of a student bookstore, and so on. These platforms were given lavish publicity in the student newspaper. Back in the 1920s there were no platforms; two slates of candidates were nominated, but nobody on either of them had a word to say concerning issues, if any.

And while the great majority of undergraduates in the 1940s and 1950s also were oblivious to significant events on the Grounds and uninterested in political or cultural movements for the advancement of the university, the opposite was true of the small group of student leaders. The extent and diversity of their involvement in university affairs was highly impressive. They served on a great variety of extracurricular organizations and committees, such as the Student Council, Judiciary Committee, Stadium Committee, Bad Check Committee, Honor Committee, Student Union, Interfraternity Council, as dorm counselors, editors of publications or officers of the Jefferson Society, on debating teams, in the Glee Club or dramatics, and on athletic teams, both intercollegiate and intramural. The extraordinary extent of their involvement made one wonder occasionally when they found time for their studies. Yet these leaders were often excellent students.

The dorm counselors were hailed as "unsung heroes . . . better-than-average students who take time from their own activities to lend a helping hand to first-year men." They were willing to be interrupted while studying and even to be awakened in the middle of the night by distraught students, the student newspaper said.

As a special inducement to newly arrived matriculates to "hit the books" instead of the road to Sweet Briar or Hollins, a chapter of Phi Eta Sigma for high-ranking freshmen scholars was installed after World War II. An average grade of at least 90 was required for membership. In 1951, 29 first-year men out of 603 were initiated, the following year 35 of 523, and the year after that 52 of 564.

57. Captain Norton Pritchett, director of athletics, 1935–51.

The university administration was in favor of adopting the class system, Josh Darden, president of the Student Council, informed that body in 1958. He said such a system, a subject of discussion for many years, was regarded as promoting "togetherness" and as enabling first-year men to adjust more readily to college life. Also, it was seen as stimulating alumni activity. He himself favored the class system, as did the *Cavalier Daily*. But the Student Council ended by defeating the plan, 8 to 5. A few weeks later the editor of the paper overheard two first-year men discussing the question. "What do you think of the class system?" one asked. "Not much," was the reply. "Hell, nobody goes to class around here anyway."

University of Virginia debating teams were making a good record in the postwar years. In the various tournaments they won more than 60 percent of their contests. Among those in which they took part were the Atlantic Coast Conference debates at Chapel Hill, the New York University tournament, the Temple University novice tournament, and others. In 1956 the record was superlative. The university team was undefeated in its presentation of the National College Topic for that year, "Resolved, that the U.S. should discontinue direct economic aid to foreign countries." Five Virginia students also won the National Contest in Public Discussion of the Speech Association of America, without leaving Charlottesville. It was done with a tape recording and was a twenty-five minute exploration of how best to carry out the U.S. Supreme Court's decision for racial integration in the public schools. Top debaters were elected to the national honorary debate society, Delta Sigma Rho. Much credit for the good showing of the university's debaters during these years was given to Dr. J. Jeffery Auer, coauthor of a textbook in the field, and Robert C. Jeffrey, director of debate.

Students in the McIntire undergraduate School of Commerce tied in 1958 with those from two other institutions for the highest score in the United States in a nationwide contest participated in by 6,000 students from some fifty colleges and universities. These tests were devised to evaluate qualifications for business careers, especially those having some relationship to accounting. University of Virginia entrants in these contests had rated above the national average for some years.

Art and architecture students revived the Beaux Arts Ball in 1952 after it had been abandoned for nearly a quarter of a century. The annual event had been allowed to lapse during the depression. More than four hundred costumed dancers whirled about in the revived version of the ball, which took place in the Art Museum.

Attendance at the regular dances in the Memorial Gymnasium at Openings, Midwinters, and Easters was falling sharply in the 1950s. Warnings were issued that the quality of the music at these affairs would deteriorate unless there was improved patronage. Fraternity parties were more and more to the fore on big weekends. The Elis and Tilkas were combining during this period to sponsor a dance each year away from the university Grounds. In 1958, for example, it was held at the Villa Riviera, on Route 250 east of Charlottesville.

While these two organizations had their critics, especially during the 1960s, they also had their defenders. The critics charged that Eli Banana and Tilka were concerned only with sponsoring dances and having a good time and were not interested in any sort of activity designed to improve the university or the community. Defenders conceded that the two ribbon societies were not endowed with a social conscience and indeed were not panting to save mankind, but argued that they had a useful role to play. Dean B. F. D. Runk, for example, said he regarded the ribbon and ring societies as "part of the hierarchy"; they were "looked upon with dignity and respect . . . and on the whole did a great deal of good for the university . . . a part of the tradition."

An organization which did not fall into the abovementioned category but which undoubtedly did much constructive work for the university was the ultrasecret Seven Society. Its insignia, consisting of a large 7, plus alpha, omega, and what appears to be the symbol of infinity, is seen all over the Grounds, often in the most unexpected places. Founded just after the turn of the century, it moves in such secrecy as to baffle those who would penetrate its mystery. Funds for many important causes have been contributed by the society, whose members become known only after their deaths. A typical episode—at commencement exercises in the late 1940s—was described in the *University of Virginia Magazine*: "The speaker was concluding his address when suddenly a small explosion was heard just above the proscenium arch, and a piece of paper fell to the floor . . . a check made out to the Bursar for $17,777.77. Directions attached stipulated that the money was to be used as a loan fund in honor of Dr. John L. Newcomb, the retiring president of the university." New electronic chimes were provided by the Sevens for the University Chapel in 1957, at a cost of $9,777.77. The Sevens also donated the handsome silver mace carried at the head of all academic processions. When "Jim" McConnell of the Lafayette Escadrille was shot down over the battlelines in France during World War I, "a mysterious floral Seven appeared before his tomb—three thousand miles from Charlottesville," wrote Henry Noble Taylor, one of the most brilliant young journalists of his time, who would himself be killed some years later in a crossfire in the Congo. And in 1920, when the $423 traveling fund of the Virginia baseball team was stolen from the team's manager in a Washington hotel, the manager found $423 in an envelope under his pillow, on his return to the university. With the money was a small card bearing the "7" insignia.

The name *College Topics* had been considered for some years to be provincial and inappropriate for a university publication, and in the spring of 1948 a student poll was held to test sentiment concerning a change. Of those taking part, 62 percent favored a new name, and the preferred designation was the *Cavalier Daily*. It was adopted in May of that year. By 1950 circulation of the paper had risen to 5,000.

Two publications of the Law School were receiving wide acclaim, in addition to the *Virginia Law Review*, which had enjoyed a national reputation from its inception. One was the *Virginia Law Weekly*, adjudged year after year the best newspaper published by students at any American law school. The other was the *Reading Guide*. In a resolution passed by the Alumni Library Committee of the Law School, this publication was praised highly, and the committee added: "Outstanding lawyers and judges from various parts of the country volunteered the information that this book review had really become their reading guide."

A widely repeated canard concerning the graduation of Franklin D. Roosevelt, Jr., from the Law School in 1940 and Prof. Armistead M. Dobie's appointment to a federal judge-

*58. Tom Scott, the university's first
two-sport all-American—in football,
1952, and lacrosse, 1953.*

ship was finally laid to rest in 1954. Fulton Lewis, Jr., a university alumnus who conducted a nationally broadcast radical right-wing radio program, stated over the air that young Roosevelt's grades were so low that his father had to agree to make Professor Dobie a federal judge and deliver the address at Finals in order for young Roosevelt to graduate. Officials of the Law School wrote Lewis immediately that "Roosevelt's grades are available at the registrar's office and are far better than Lewis assumed." It also was pointed out that Dobie had been named to the federal bench approximately one year before the younger Roosevelt graduated. About the only accurate statement had been that President Roosevelt did make the Commencement address in 1940—at which time he took occasion to denounce Mussolini of Italy for plunging his dagger into the back of his neighbor, France. Fulton Lewis made a complete retraction and apology, as requested by the Law School. He said he had heard the story from many directions and had received letters on the subject from prominent lawyers.

Robert F. Kennedy, who would later serve as Attorney General in the cabinet of his brother, President John F. Kennedy, was a 1951 law graduate. He was president of the Student Legal Forum and brought to the university as speakers many prominent Washington figures, including Thurmond Arnold, Arthur Krock, William O. Douglas, Ralph Bunche, James M. Landis, and Joseph McCarthy. He was complimented on the quality of his programs.

Edward M. (Ted) Kennedy, brother of "Bobby" and "Jack" also was a Law School graduate (1959). Some alumni and others objected strongly to his admission, since he had been suspended at Harvard for cheating. The rationale for allowing him to enter seems to have been that since he had been readmitted to Harvard, had successfully completed the course there, and had been certified by Harvard's dean as a student and graduate "in good standing," there was no valid basis for refusing him admission to Virginia. Like his brother, he was president of the Legal Forum there. He won the moot court competition, although his professors said he was only an average student.

The academic deans decided a few years later, in the early 1960s, that there would be no further admission of students who had been disciplined in other colleges for lying, cheating, or stealing.

The *Virginia Business Review*, said to be the first publication of its kind issued by an undergraduate School of Business, appeared at the university in 1958, sponsored by the McIntire School. The *Review* was issued in the spring and fall and was widely distributed to businessmen, corporations, and educators in the eastern United States. Each number was underwritten by one or two Virginia industries or businesses.

The university had "the only Speech *and* Drama graduate program in the Atlantic Coast states between Florida and New York," according to Professor Jeffery Auer, chairman of the Department of Speech and Drama. The Virginia Players, in addition to their regular series of five public dramatic productions, scheduled an annual Shakespearean play. High school students from throughout central Virginia were invited to a special performance; in each of several years during the 1950s about seven hundred of these students saw such plays as *Othello* and *Romeo and Juliet*. Other shows of a different type were presented during this period by the Punch and Julep Club, founded in 1953 and giving one performance annually.

The Glee Club was providing musical entertainment at the university and for alumni chapters in various cities. It offered "serious choral literature" as well as lighter numbers. Frequent concerts with nearby women's colleges provided opportunities for music with both male and female voices.

The university marching and concert band had come in for much adverse criticism over the years, but now an organization had been put together that evoked high praise. "Around this school," said the *Cavalier Daily*, "there has always been a lot of criticism of almost everything. Dissatisfaction with the status quo has almost become a standard characteristic of the standard 'Virginia gentleman.' . . . It is now time to commend and congratulate the university band for a surprising recovery and a fine showing at last Saturday's athletic endeavor." President Darden had set up a faculty committee in the spring of 1959, and a $12,000 appropriation had been obtained for uniforms, instruments, and facilities. Director Sidney P. Hodkinson of the music faculty was in charge, and much favorable comment was heard. But a few years later there were renewed laments and criticisms, and the football cocaptains were meeting with the band to try to solve the shortcomings. Membership in the band had shrunk to twenty-five.

A Rifle and Pistol Club was formed to promote target shooting and hold rifle and pistol competitions. The club also sent teams to compete in National Rifle Association matches.

Opening of the radio station WUVA, owned and operated by students, was a feature of the year 1947, and it soon became well established. From a modest beginning it gradually expanded its programming and coverage. The "Cavalier Magazine of the Air" was used as a nucleus at first, Martin Hiden was the manager, and music was the principal offering, plus student forums, group discussions, and newscasts from United Press. Athletic events that were not being broadcast by anyone else were covered. WUVA claimed to have "the widest coverage of any station of its type." Revenue was obtained from advertising. By 1952 it was on the air daily from "Yawn Patrol" at 7 A.M. to 1 A.M. Four years later it began to devote itself mainly to popular music. In 1962 it affiliated with the Columbia Broadcasting System, broadcasting CBS programs and five newscasts daily.

Another radio station, WTJU, began broadcasting on the Grounds in 1956. It was organized as an extension of the Speech and Drama Department under the direction of George P. Wilson and has always been a nonprofit and noncommercial FM station, owned by the university's rector and visitors and supported by student fees and contributions. Only classical music was played at first, but the station later broadcast a much greater variety of music. Both WTJU and WUVA serve as training grounds for careers in radio.

Religious life at the university during the years following World War II was well organized and included a diversified series of programs under the leadership of the Reverend Oscar B. Woolridge, Jr., secretary of the YMCA. On the agenda were regular services at the chapel, student and faculty meetings for discussion of contemporary religious problems, interfaith conferences, and the annual University Preaching Series, during which classes were suspended. (The shade of Thomas Jefferson must have shuddered at this class suspension!) The annual Richards Foundation Lectures on Religion were given by a noted scholar or churchman. Other such lectures were presented each Sunday evening in Madison Hall by members of the faculty.

Programs and services were sponsored by the Interfaith Council, composed of two representatives of each denomination or faith, to promote greater understanding and cooperation among Protestants, Catholics, and Jews. Voluntary services, conducted by students, and with a faculty member or Charlottesville pastor as speaker, were being held on Sunday and Wednesday afternoons in the chapel. The Sunday services included musical programs by visiting choirs from colleges and prep schools around the state. Closer relations between faculty and students were promoted by a series of student meetings in the homes of professors. Such subjects as "Christianity and Communism" and "What Constitutes the Educated Man?" were discussed.

Student groups sponsored by local churches were cooperating with the "Y." They included the Canterbury Club, Episcopal; Wesley Foundation, Methodist; Westminster Club, Presbyterian; Baptist Students Union; Unitarian Student Club; Newman Club for Catholics; and Hillel Foundation for Jews.

Students guided underprivileged Charlottesville youths in an athletic and recreational program, under the auspices of the Belmont Boys Club and sponsorship of the "Y."

The YMCA also sponsored frequent recreational programs for students at Madison Hall, including dances and buffet suppers. These were said to be especially popular during university dance weekends.

When the "Y" celebrated its centennial in 1958, there was a yearlong program of lectures and other events. Eminent religious leaders from Oxford, Harvard, and elsewhere participated. Daniel L. Gibbs, Jr., director of the "Y," arranged the program, in cooperation with a faculty committee headed by Prof. Hardy C. Dillard. Woodrow Wilson had been the speaker in 1905 when Madison Hall was dedicated.

The Newman Club, headquarters of the Roman Catholic students, acquired a new home on Jefferson Park Avenue in 1958. A large building was purchased and converted. The Baptist Student Union obtained a new home the following year, also on Jefferson Park Avenue, replacing the organization's headquarters adjoining the University Baptist Church. Weekly Saturday night suppers were scheduled, and study hall, recreation, and counseling for students also were on the program.

A University of Virginia athlete who had an international impact after World War II was Harold M. Burrows, Jr., of Charlottesville. He was tennis captain for three years and winner of the Virginia state men's singles in each of those years. Known as "Prince Hal" for his attractive personality and fine court manners, he also was a star in intramural athletics. Following graduation he began playing the national and international tennis circuit. Burrows defeated thirty-three members of Davis Cup teams from various countries in matches all over the world, including Drobny of Czechoslovakia, at that time the number one player in Europe. In his best year he ranked eleventh in the United States. As a doubles player, teamed with Straight Clark, he won many matches against internationally ranked players, notably Lew Hoad and Ken Rosewall, whom Burrows and Clark prevented from winning the "grand slam." Hoad and Rosewall had taken the Australian, French, and Wimbledon titles, but they lost to Burrows and Clark in the national grass-court doubles finals at Brookline, Mass. The American team ranked number three in the United States. Burrows was a Davis Cup Squad member in 1954.

Tennis was one of the most successful of all sports at Virginia, thanks to such stars as Hal Burrows and Alphonso Smith, and to Carl ("Red") Rohmann, who coached the Cavalier teams for twenty-eight years. The team usually won the great majority of its matches, but the university did not provide tennis scholarships and was at a serious disadvantage in competing with institutions that offered them. Red Rohmann said that "the best team we ever had was when Shelton Horsley was captain in 1950."

Boxing was resumed full blast in 1946, and the Cavaliers won five of six dual matches, losing to Wisconsin, the national champions, 4-½ to 3-½. Virginia was runner-up to Army in the Eastern Intercollegiates. A gratifying accolade came to the Cavaliers in 1947. They were barely defeated by Syracuse at the university, but "the ovations given Syracuse before and after the bouts were . . . the finest reception ever given a visiting team," R. D. Simmons, head coach of Syracuse, wrote. "The sportsmanship shown by everyone was of the finest order."

*59. Mrs. A. E. Walker, hostess at the
Student Union for 35 years and
friend and counselor to countless students.*

The following year Virginia won the Eastern Intercollegiates for the first time, six individual championships going to
the orange and blue. The six winners were the three Mira-
gliotta brothers, Jimmy, Basil, and Joe; Grover Masterson,
Ralph Shoaf, and Allen Hollingsworth.

Lacrosse, wrestling, and soccer were recognized as major
sports during these years.

An editorial on athletics entitled "Failure to Educate" appeared in the *Alumni News* for November 1948 and caused
much discussion. The author was Marvin B. Perry, Jr., '40,
managing editor of the paper, later a dean at Virginia and
president of Goucher College. He said, in part:

What kind of education are our colleges giving, consciously or not,
which produces alumni who will contribute hundreds of thousands
of dollars for winning athletic teams when their colleges stand desperately in need of funds for better libraries, for research in conquest of disease or the development of industrial processes, for
scholarships for men of outstanding minds and limited means, for
adequate salaries for teachers and scholars? . . . It is a condition
which American college alumni must consider soberly. There can be
little compromise, and if we are indeed educated men there can be
but one answer.

Praise from alumni in letters to the *Alumni News* was almost
unanimous, although many who disagreed evidently didn't
trouble to write. A notable dissenter who did so was Harrison
Mann, '31. He wrote that "considering the editorial in a vac-
uum, possibly it is theoretically correct, but I submit that the
alumni who did something about the problem facing the university in the thirties were not dealing with a theory but with
a fact." Mann went on to say that "an 'interest' in the football
team increased alumni interest generally and brought more
alumni back to the university, and in time created a better understanding of its problems. . . . The common recognition
among the alumni who supported the 'scholarship' program
that football was not an end in itself conspired to turn the
energies of these same men into other fields of alumni endeavor. . . . It was largely this self-same group of alumni who
were responsible for the annual alumni-giving drive which has
done so much for every phase of the university's life."

Football at Virginia after the war was in a stronger than normal position, thanks to a stellar group of athletes from all over

the country brought in by the naval units and to Coaches Murray and Guepe. Murray left in 1945 but the team continued winning under Guepe.

The most sensational victory of all occurred in 1947 when Harvard was trounced 47–0 at Scott Stadium, the worst defeat sustained by the crimson since 1884. It was the first trip any Harvard football team had made into the South, and this was supposedly the best eleven they had fielded in fifteen years. The famous columnist Red Smith wrote in his New York *Herald Tribune* sports column that Harvard's defeat was "the most terrific triumph for the cornpone aristocracy since the first Bull Run." He added that "last year they beat Princeton [20–6] . . . the first time they'd ever scored against the Tigers, too." The Harvard game was notable also for the fact that Chester Pierce, a black, was in the Harvard lineup. No Virginia team had ever played against a black before, and it had hardly ever happened in the South. Careful preparations were made at the university for this precedent-shattering event, and it was stressed to the students that the entire country would be watching. All went smoothly; Pierce was applauded as he left the lineup. "I have never seen a better-conducted crowd at a football game," President Darden said. Harvard coach Dick Harlow declared that Virginia "played as clean football as any team I have seen in a long time." Members of that eleven, which lost only to North Carolina and Tulane during the season, included Grover Jones, John Papit, George Grimes, Bruce Bailey, George Neff, Joe Kirkland, Billy Pennell, Lockwood Frizzell, Joe McCary, Bob Weir, John Thomas, and Ray Brown. Several of these would star in the future, and fullback Papit would be chosen a first-team all-American by NEA in 1949. He was the first college back to gain over one thousand yards in each of three seasons. Papit joined the Washington Redskins in 1950 and two years later was traded to the Green Bay Packers.

Art Guepe had seven winning seasons at Virginia before leaving in 1953 to become head coach at Vanderbilt. On his teams were two other all-Americans in addition to Papit. One was Joe Palumbo, captain and guard on the 1951 team, chosen by Associated Press and NEA to the first eleven, and Tom Scott, defensive end, a first-string Associated Press selection in 1952. Scott went to the Philadelphia Eagles and finished his career with the New York Giants as an all-pro linebacker. As a lacrosse player at Virginia, Scott was also given honorable mention for all-American.

The University Senate ruled in 1951 that although many of Virginia's rivals were playing first-year men on their varsity teams, the university could not do so. This ruling was reaffirmed the following year.

The University of Virginia had made it clear by 1949 that it had no intention of abiding by the so-called sanity code of the National Collegiate Athletic Association (NCAA). This code had been devised, it was said, in order to avoid excessive commercialism. It provided that athletes could receive pay only if they performed work in jobs around the institution. The university refused to create phony jobs in order to meet this provision, and declared frankly that it was giving athletic scholarships. The Student Aid Foundation had just been organized for the purpose, with Robert V. Hatcher, '23, as president. In refusing to abide by the sanity code the university was risking expulsion from the NCAA. However, that body not only decided against penalizing Virginia; it dropped the sanity code.

The university received a shattering blow in 1951 when Capt. Norton Pritchett, age fifty-seven, director of athletics since 1935, died of a heart attack. He had done much to improve the athletic situation at Virginia, both intercollegiate and intramural. Admired by all, Captain Pritchett had been a strong and consistent influence for clean competition and aboveboard standards. Chauncey Durden, sports editor of the Richmond *Times-Dispatch*, termed him "gentleman and sportsman," and said that whereas Pritchett had great hopes for the sanity code when it was introduced, "his brilliant speech [at the 1949 meeting of the NCAA] sealed the doom" of the code. When Captain Pritchett died, Durden wrote: "Poised, handsome and intellectual, 'Cap' was an imposing figure when he faced an audience. His voice was of finest timbre and his diction was perfect. His sincerity was overwhelming. There was a man." President Darden said, "His youthful enthusiasm, his unimpeachable integrity, and his deep love for everything connected with the university, won for him the admiration and affection of all with whom he worked." His portrait was presented to the Athletic Department in 1955.

60. *Fredson T. Bowers, professor of English and dean of the faculty of Arts and Sciences.*

61. *Ralph W. Cherry, dean of the School of Education, 1956–68.*

Another setback was sustained when Robert (Pic) Fuller, head coach of lacrosse, assistant football coach, and sometime wrestling coach, left in 1953 to enter private business. He "virtually fathered lacrosse as a major sport and coached the Cavaliers to three winning seasons and a share of the national championship in 1952" with Rensselaer Polytechnic, said the *Cavalier Daily*. First-team all-Americans at Virginia from 1948 to 1954 were Bobby Proutt, Billy Hooper (twice), Gordon Jones, Tom Compton, and Jimmy Grieves. Pic Fuller was so highly regarded that the Raven Society gave him a farewell dinner at which he was presented with a silver cocktail shaker and tray.

A monumental hullaballoo erupted in 1951 when the Gooch Report on athletics was issued. Prof. Robert K. Gooch, a Rhodes Scholar and onetime star athlete, was chairman of a faculty committee appointed to make recommendations concerning the university's athletic policy. The other members were Professors Arthur Kyle Davis, Jr., also a Rhodes Scholar, and Jesse Beams, the internationally famous physicist.

The committee recommended that all athletic scholarships be eliminated and that the faculty be given back control of athletics. It expressed a preference for abandonment of intercollegiate football at Virginia, rather than continue prevailing policies. The report declared that the university had surrendered "to 'big time' athletics," and referred to "various reprehensible aspects of the present situation . . . abuses resulting from athletic scholarships, athletic activities of student aid foundations and the like . . . institutional payment for the academic coaching of athletes, pressure—especially on younger instructors—for grades or continuance in the course . . . the withdrawal of athletes at the end of the season, and so on." The committee's definition of "reprehensible" apparently differed from that of the *Cavalier Daily*, which said that "nowhere does the report intimate that there is any malpractice involved in the administration of Virginia's athletic program." The faculty of the College of Arts and Sciences endorsed the Gooch Report's recommendations overwhelmingly, but the faculties of the other schools rejected the report "after trying to revise it," the *Cavalier Daily* said.

Many alumni were furious. The *Alumni News* referred to their "outraged shrieks," and the Board of Managers of the alumni association declared unanimously in formal resolutions that the report "was conceived, formulated and presented in an unreasonable, unfair and misleading manner." It "smelled of high treason," in the view of many, the *News* declared. Irate alumni were asking two questions: "What has the faculty to say about the source of any student's means as long as he passes his work, and . . . who in heaven's name chose such a miserable time to bring forth anything that could be construed as criticism of the university's athletic program?" Virginia was having a series of highly successful football seasons. There had been recent scandals at other institutions, and the Gooch Report's criticisms and conclusions were seen as implying that there might be similar irregularities at Charlottesville. Professors Gooch, Davis, and Beams, whose motives were above reproach, were abused and attacked by some alumni and their integrity was impugned.

President Darden pointed out that no university or state funds were being used for the athletic scholarships and that of eighty-one students who earned football letters from 1945 to 1948, no fewer than fifty-two received academic degrees, or 64.2 percent, as against 67.3 percent for the college as a whole. And while the athletic scholarships being given were larger than any offered for academic achievement, they covered only room, board, tuition, and books, the *News* pointed out. It also mentioned that athletic aid would be withdrawn if the grantee failed to advance toward a degree and that revenue from successful football teams helped pay for other intercollegiate sports and for intramurals. "To give up football, which means so much to student, teacher and alumnus alike, is unthinkable," said the *News*.

Another furor arose when President Darden announced in November 1951 that although Virginia had won eight games that fall and lost only one, the team would not be permitted to accept a "bowl bid," if one were received. There were howls from many alumni over this, but Charles R. Fenwick, a former football star at Virginia and supporter of athletic scholarships, said that Darden was right. Bowls are "totally unnecessary and make no contribution to the soundness of the game," said Fenwick. He also urged elimination of spring practice.

The *Cavalier Daily* pointed out early in 1952 that the recommendations of the much-denounced Gooch Report were similar to those of the American Council on Education. It added that "there are some athletes here that dress and act more like gorillas than gentlemen." The paper drew solace from the fact that "requirements established for the rewarding of scholarships next year show that steps are being taken to remedy this situation." This was apparently the only tangible result that flowed from the Gooch Report.

Virginia's seven winning football seasons under Coach Art Guepe were suddenly terminated when Guepe accepted an offer to be head coach at Vanderbilt. The university entered immediately into a staggering series of almost unbroken defeats.

The Atlantic Coast Conference (ACC) had just been formed, and there was hot debate as to whether the university should join. President Darden and Rector Barron F. Black opposed the move, while Athletic Director Gus Tebell backed it strongly. A poll of students returned a majority in favor of joining. When the Board of Visitors met, Darden and Black expressed opposition, as did a considerable percentage of alumni. Opponents argued that some of the members of the ACC had few if any standards of eligibility and that Virginia would end up in the cellar. But the board voted 6 to 4 to accept the invitation to join, thus terminating seventeen years during which the university was not a member of any conference. Doubts as to the wisdom of the move were soon heightened by a series of disastrous football seasons, and *Corks and Curls* said, "We find ourselves against a number of colleges believing in 'big time' athletics in every respect. Perhaps we are over our heads."

Further grief came to the student body with the passing of Seal, the much beloved canine mascot of Virginia teams. Seal was a cross-eyed black mongrel mutt who attended all games and many other university functions and distinguished himself particularly in 1949 at the Virginia-Penn football game in Philadelphia. Seal was about ten years old when he succumbed in late 1953 to a combination of ailments. He was buried with ceremonies and tributes accorded few citizens of the university community. The "V" Club was in charge of arrangements and the Athletic Department paid for the casket and gravediggers. Some two thousand persons turned out for the procession from the University Hospital, where Seal died, to the grave just outside the University Cemetery. The cortege was led by the University Band playing the *Dead March*; a giant-sized portrait of the deceased was carried by admirers, an elegant hearse bore the remains, and it was followed by a black Cadillac containing "student dignitaries." The flag in front of the Rotunda was at half-mast as the procession passed. Pall-bearers at the cemetery were leading student athletes. Seven handsome wreaths from that number of organizations, including Eli, Tilka, and Z, decorated the grave. Dr. Charles J. Frankel, varsity team doctor, delivered the funeral oration.

Seal had made himself more or less immortal by showing his contempt for the opposition in no uncertain terms during the half at the Pennsylvania football game in 1949. As described by Jack Hunter, editor of the *Cavalier Daily*: "Slowly he walked from midfield to the Quaker side. Indifferently he inspected their cheerleading appurtenances. Eighty thousand people watched with bated breath. Coolly, insolently Seal lifted a leg—the rest is history." One of the Pennsylvania cheerleader's megaphones had been copiously irrigated, to raucous applause from the Cavalier contingent in the stands. Seal was known from time to time thereafter as *Caninus Megaphonus Pennsylvanus*.

Dr. Frankel's brief funeral oration was built around this piquant episode. "I can see Seal now," he declared, "leading the celestial parade with golden hydrants and gilded megaphones at his disposal. . . . I know of no other individual at the university, or animal, who could attract as many mourners to his funeral. Of course, none of us has ever had the same opportunity with a megaphone." Taps was sounded and the program ended with "The Good Old Song." Seal's grave was next to Beta's near the cemetery entrance; it was later marked with a headstone similar to Beta's, bearing Seal's likeness, and with lines that spoke of him as "Mascot and Friend of the Students of the University."

There was never another dog around the Grounds with an appeal comparable to that of Seal or his charismatic predecessor, Beta. A nondescript hound named Nasty, or Nasty N. Dog, seemed a possible successor. But Nasty was hit by a beer truck and killed after only two years as the "official barker and mascot." He never really caught on.

This was a dismal era for Virginia football, but there were

some bright spots. Mel Roach was a fine quarterback as well as a good basketball player and a particular star in baseball. As a second baseman he had offers from several big league teams, and he signed with the Milwaukee Braves. Gus Tebell called Roach "the finest all-around athlete I've seen in my 23 years here." Joe Hicks, a hard-hitting Virginia outfielder, signed with the Chicago White Sox and played for ten years in the major leagues.

Other outstanding football stars were fullback Jim Bakhtiar, chosen by *Look* magazine in 1957 on its first-string all-American team, after he had led the ACC in rushing, and tackle Henry Jordan. Jordan would later be a mainstay of the championship Green Bay Packers and one of the top professional football players in the country. At the university he was also heavyweight wrestling champion of the ACC, winning thirty-seven dual and tournament matches during his college career and losing only one dual and three tournament matches. He was runner-up for the NCAA heavyweight championship.

In basketball Buzzy Wilkinson was all-American in 1955. He set university records in points scored, best scoring average, most field goals, and most free throws scored. He also holds the university record for best single season average, with 32.1 points, tops in the U.S., and 30.1 the preceding year. No University of Virginia player before or since has approached these figures. Yet in 1954 Virginia finished seventh in the ACC and in 1955 sixth. Wilkinson's jersey was retired; Bill Dudley was the only other university athlete who had received this honor. It would be accorded Barry Parkhill, the all-American basketball player, in later years.

The year 1954 was marked by a special event: Mary Slaughter, daughter of Edward R. (Butch) Slaughter, the admired coach of several sports at Virginia over the years, was awarded a varsity letter in tennis, the first woman in the history of the institution to be so honored. She won the Women's Eastern Intercollegiate title.

And in 1957 Mebane (Meb) Turner, captain and star of the university's wrestling team, went on to win the 174-pound Amateur Athletic Union (AAU) championship. He was invited to travel with the national AAU team on a summer tour of Japan. Turner was later president of the University of Baltimore.

62. *Colgate Darden, president of the university, 1947–59, and his wife, Constance.*

Pop Lannigan, whose Virginia basketball teams won 290 games and lost only 90, was elected posthumously to the College Basketball Hall of Fame.

Archie Hahn, who succeeded Lannigan as track coach, died in 1955 after a year of ill health. Hahn had produced some stellar track and field men and Virginia recordholders. He came to Virginia from Princeton and was track coach for twenty-two years. As a student at the University of Michigan he performed the astonishing feat of winning the 60, the 100, and the 200 meters at the Olympic Games at St. Louis in 1904.

There was a flurry of discussion at this time as to the advisability of returning to cardinal red and silver gray as the university's colors. Orange and blue had been adopted in the late nineteenth century, in part because red and gray dyes were said to be unsatisfactory. But now this situation had changed for the better, it was argued, and a few students and alumni were sentimentally drawn to the symbolism of the earlier colors, representing the Confederate uniform stained with blood. Nothing came of it.

Football went from disaster to disaster. Ned McDonald, who had succeeded Art Guepe as coach, resigned, and Ben S. Martin of the U.S. Naval Academy's coaching staff took his place. Martin gave up after two years. As an example of what he had to contend with, Virginia lost the opening game in 1959 to William and Mary 37–0, and the next nine games, nearly all of them by equally lopsided scores. Joseph W. Dunn, Jr., an alumnus, wrote that the William and Mary game was "the most miserable exhibition of half-hearted, I-don't-give-a-damn attitude ever put on by a college as large as the university." Martin was succeeded by Richard Voris, line coach at the U.S. Military Academy. He left after two years. Virginia football had hit an all-time low. Only one game out of ten had been won in 1958, and all ten were lost in 1959 and again in 1960. In other words, the Cavaliers lost twenty-eight straight—close to a national record.

There was far better performance in the somewhat exotic game of polo. Launched in 1953 by a small group of interested students, polo at Virginia soon was ranked with the best in the nation. Part of Brook Hill Farm, owned by Prof. E. J. Oglesby of the Engineering School, was rented by the polo enthusiasts, and funds were raised from various sources.

Among the contributors were playboy Porfiro Rubirosa and Dominican dictator Rafael Trujillo, each of whom gave $500. Don Hannah, a fourth-year student and the leader in getting polo started at Virginia, was the first captain of the team and a nationally ranked player. Other outstanding captains were Malarkey Wall and Dick Riemenschneider, the last-named rated in 1957 the number one player in the United States. Virginia's rivalry with Yale was a particular feature, and the Cavaliers defeated the Elis twice in succession during these years. They also downed Cornell, another national power in polo. Virginia came close to winning the national championship in 1957. The Cavaliers defeated Cornell but lost to Yale 10–9 in the finals. Some two thousand spectators often turned out during Easters at Brook Hill Farm to see the matches.

The University of Virginia and Washington and Lee lacrosse teams combined in the summer of 1959 for a tour of Australia. The Virginia team had toured England five years previously, winning eight games and losing one. Eugene F. (Gene) Corrigan, athletic director at Washington and Lee, arranged the Australian tour before coming to Virginia as lacrosse and soccer coach. The young men from both institutions were lavishly entertained "down under," and much good will was displayed. There were toasts at banquets and an exchange of gifts. The Virginia and W&L players seemed to be on friendly terms throughout, despite hot rivalry at home. Student newspapers at the two universities were careful to make only sportsmanlike references to one another's athletic teams, but they not infrequently took digs at each other in areas having to do with academics or social behavior. For example, when the internationally famous British historian Arnold Toynbee delivered a series of lectures at W&L, the *Cavalier Daily* asked sneeringly why on earth Toynbee had accepted this invitation from "the academy across the mountains," given its "comparative educational insignificance." And *Ring Tum Phi* at the Lexington institution was not averse to making pointed remarks concerning the supposed alcoholic consumption of the average Wahoo.

Intramurals at Virginia took a great leap forward in 1957 when Butch Slaughter was placed in charge. Under his able and imaginative leadership this branch of sport came to occupy an increasingly important role in the university's affairs.

The long-anticipated campaign for a field house at the university was launched in 1959 under the auspices of the alumni association. At a dinner in Newcomb Hall $500,000 was announced as the immediate goal, with Lawrence Lewis, Jr., president of the association, and W. Wright Harrison, president of the People's National Bank of Charlottesville, as co-chairmen of the drive. Memorial Gymnasium had been outgrown years before, and an adequate intercollegiate athletic center was, by common consent, the greatest single athletic need of the university. The site had been chosen on Copeley Hill, directly across Emmet Street from Lambeth Field.

SIX

Significant
Progress under Darden

Far from being a handicap, Colgate Darden's service as governor was a great asset to him in his university presidency. Some felt that a politician without experience in academe would not have the know-how and background to be a successful educational executive, but matters turned out decidedly otherwise. As governor, Darden had been able to obtain long-deferred aid for the university through larger state appropriations and also to learn much concerning the institution's needs and goals. In addition, he had solidified his friendships in the legislature, so that when he took over the presidency of the university, he was successful in obtaining funds to cover essential improvements.

In fact, the finesse that he exhibited in dealing with the lawmakers left experienced observers shaking their heads in admiration. Carter Lowance, confidential brain truster to half a dozen governors, was awe-struck. He said concerning Darden's modus operandi: "When he became president of the University of Virginia, he became the only head of a state institution in my memory who was able to submerge dollar figures of his budget in such philosophical rhetoric as to emerge with near unanimous legislative approval without his ever having mentioned the sum total of his requests."

President Darden was anxious to increase the number of high school graduates attending the university, and many of his plans and programs were directed toward that end. The statistics were discouraging. Of 352 accredited high schools in the commonwealth, only 54 sent students to the university during the session of 1950–51. Richmond's two high schools for whites, Thomas Jefferson and John Marshall, sent only 38 graduates to Virginia during the three years ended in 1950 out of 750 to 800 who went to college from those schools. The great majority were attending VPI, VMI, and William and Mary.

An orientation period was instituted at the opening of the 1948–49 session for the benefit of the first-year men. It lasted for four days, and the new students were given a number of tests preliminary to their enrollment, were told about the university and its student activities, and became acquainted with one another. Dean James H. Newman organized the affair; it was felt to have been a success and worthy of continuance.

Separation of the College into Upper and Lower Divisions was announced during the same session. As explained by Dean Ivey Lewis, "The plan involves closer supervision of the younger and less experienced students, more encouragement to good academic performance, and increasing freedom for those students who demonstrate their ability to do good work at the college level." He added that "normally a student will be enrolled in the lower Division for his first two sessions and earn advancement to the Upper Division by successful completion of the program of studies advised by the Lower Division." As soon as the new dormitories could be completed they would be used by the new students, and would be units of the Lower Division.

The university now was operating on a two-semester basis for the nine-month session instead of the previous three terms. The summer session was accordingly revised, and instead of two terms of thirty class days each, it became a single eight-week session of forty-eight class days. For the session of 1948–49, summer enrollment was 1,862 as compared with 1,598 for the year before. This substantial increase contrasted with the decline in enrollment being experienced in nearly all the large summer schools in the United States.

Faculty salaries were being raised during these years. There was marked improvement in the late 1940s, and then a substantial increase was announced in 1955, to be financed, in

63. Roberta Hollingsworth Gwathmey, dean of women, 1934–67.

part, by higher student tuition. The Medical School did not share in this latest advance since salary adjustments had been made there the year before.

Enrollment in the university, which had been falling for several sessions, was taking an upward turn in 1954 and was just under three thousand six hundred when classes closed for the Christmas recess. It had gone beyond five thousand immediately after World War II. Distinctly better work was being done by entering students. Credit for this improved showing was being given, in part, to the president's plan for supervision of the first-year men in the new residence houses.

Since 1952 out-of-state students applying for admission had been required, with a few exceptions, to take college board examinations, and this requirement was extended in 1957 to Virginia applicants. The University of Virginia thus became the first state university in the country to rule that all persons seeking admission must take the college boards.

In order to bring persons of distinction or promise to the university for scholarly research, the Alumni Board of Trustees of the Endowment Fund established the Thomas Jefferson Fellowships. The sum of $15,000 was made available for the session of 1953–54, and the plan was to make a similar amount available each year. Grants would average about $3,000 annually, but might go as high as $5,000 for research in literature, the arts, or the sciences in materials available at the university.

A number of important shifts in administrative positions took place in the mid-1950s.

Vincent Shea, bursar and administrative assistant to the president as well as secretary to the Board of Visitors, was elevated to the new post of comptroller, created by the board. Shea became a key figure in the university's affairs, with great behind-the-scenes influence over many aspects of the institution's life. In fact it would probably be fair to say that for a few decades nobody in the institution except the president was as quietly potent as he. Admirably trained, with a fine business mind, his influence was decidedly salutary.

Francis L. Berkeley, Jr., university archivist and library curator, was persuaded by President Darden in 1953 to take over the secretaryship of the Board of Visitors, succeeding Vincent

Shea. A recognized authority in the archival field, Berkeley had been with the library for a decade and a half, interrupted by war service, and had performed valiantly, touring the state for years rounding up manuscripts for the Alderman archives. He demurred when approached by Darden, for he realized that the profferred post was a demanding one, and he wanted to remain where he was. He had returned the previous year from ten months in England and Scotland under a Fulbright grant, during which he had uncovered valuable material having to do with Virginia's colonial past. It was his desire to do some writing in that field. However, in response to the president's urging, he consented to accept the secretaryship of the Board of Visitors. It was the beginning of some two decades of service rendered by Frank Berkeley to the university in areas largely divorced from his archival specialty. First he was secretary to the visitors, and when Edgar Shannon was elected president, succeeding Colgate Darden, Shannon prevailed on Berkeley to become his executive assistant, and Weldon Cooper was chosen secretary of the board and administrative assistant to the president.

George O. Ferguson, Jr., retired in 1951 as dean of college admissions after a quarter of a century in that position. He served as acting dean of the college following the retirement of Ivey F. Lewis in 1953 and then was appointed dean—the second time that he had held the position. In addition, Dean Ferguson had been registrar since 1946, and for thirty-five years had taught educational psychology. He was for many years faculty representative on the Athletic Council and helped to organize the Southern Conference when its membership ranged from Virginia to Louisiana.

With Ferguson's relinquishment of control over admissions, a new arrangement was made, with a five-member faculty committee and a director of admissions. Richard R. Fletcher was named to the latter post, but a year later was appointed director of student affairs, in which position he became a storm center, as noted in the previous chapter. He resigned in 1954 to become general secretary of the Sigma Nu Greek letter fraternity. Fletcher was tendered a farewell dinner by sixty residence hall counselors who presented him with an engraved silver tray in appreciation of his "19 years of unselfish service to the University of Virginia." When "Dick" Fletcher joined the university staff he was director of first-year athletics and head coach of football, basketball, and baseball.

As successor to Fletcher, Raymond C. Bice, assistant professor of psychology and a superlative lecturer, was appointed director of admissions for the college. In order to facilitate his work and provide prompt information concerning the admissions picture, "Ray" Bice performed the amazing feat of inventing a computer from parts taken from pinball machines confiscated by the Danville police. A decade would pass before digital computers would be placed on the market, which meant that he had to put together miscellaneous parts from pinball machines with little to go on except his own ingenuity. Yet the thing worked, and Bice was able to furnish information almost instantly concerning the various categories of applicants and their status. He decided in 1958 not to "make admissions a career" and was named assistant dean of the College, later associate dean. At the same time he was an Association dean, with responsibility for some four hundred students. Just what an "association" was is explained later in this chapter.

B. F. D. Runk, associate professor of biology, was named Student Adviser in 1955, in which capacity he took over the principal duties exercised by Dick Fletcher. The latter's responsibility for working with student residence house and hall counselors was assigned to Donald M. McKay, director of housing. Runk was instructed to work with the fraternities in putting into effect new regulations governing them. The following year he was named registrar of the university, and in 1959 was appointed dean of the university, with powers not exercised by any dean since the retirement of Ivey Lewis. He said he would continue to teach some of his courses; his ability as a teacher and lecturer was exceptional. In his new post he had supervision over student government, exercised by President Darden for the preceding decade. "Dee" Runk had an excellent relationship with the students; he was the recipient of the first IMP Award, given by the IMP Society "to a faculty member who had been outstanding in promoting student-faculty relations and perpetuating the traditions of the university." Subsequently he received the National Service Award of Omicron Delta Kappa, presented in the United States only once every three years. Edward W. Lautenschlager, '56, an instructor in the Department of Biology, was named registrar, succeeding Runk.

Weldon Cooper became director of the Bureau of Public Administration, succeeding Rowland Egger, who was in such demand, both in this country and overseas, that he was on leave a large part of the time. For the 1956–57 session, when Cooper was made head of the bureau, Egger was chairman of both the university's Woodrow Wilson Department of Foreign Affairs and the Department of Political Science. During the previous year he had been on leave as Near East representative of the Ford Foundation, with headquarters in Beirut, Lebanon. Weldon Cooper had been associate director of the bureau for some years, and, beginning in 1950, served for fourteen months as executive assistant to Governor John S. Battle. Upon the retirement of Professor Wilson Gee in 1959, Cooper would take over the editorship of the *University of Virginia News Letter*, of which more anon.

William L. Duren, Jr., chairman of the Department of Mathematics at Tulane University, became dean of the College of Arts and Sciences in 1955, succeeding George O. Ferguson, Jr. Dean Duren was a nationally known mathematician who had succeeded the university's Professor McShane as president of the Mathematical Society of America. Duren was given a leave of absence to finish a college textbook in math; he had been named chairman of a committee of the mathematical society to produce this book. During his absence Prof. Robert K. Gooch served as dean.

Joseph L. Vaughan, '26, professor of English in the School of Engineering and a superlative teacher, was appointed provost, a newly created position, by President Darden. In that capacity he would serve as an administrative assistant to the president and would act for the president whenever the latter might be absent from the university. He would also study longtime requirements of the educational program of the university, building and space needs, and assist on budgetary matters affecting operation and maintenance. Professor Vaughan was relieved of many of these duties a few years later and given supervision over the Clinch Valley and University (George Mason) Colleges with the title of chancellor. But his first love, his real forte, was teaching. He returned to that, and the office of provost was discontinued for the remainder of the Darden administration.

Lewis M. Hammond, professor of philosophy, was appointed dean of the Graduate School of Arts and Sciences, succeeding James Southall Wilson, who retired in 1951. He was a University of Virginia Ph.D. who had been assistant to the president of St. John's College, 1942–45, and assistant dean of the university's summer session for several years. He had also been president of the Society for Philosophy and Psychology and of the Episcopal Guild of Scholars and a member of the editorial board of the *Anglican Theological Review*. After serving as graduate dean from 1951 to 1960, he would hold the chairmanship of the Department of Philosophy for six years.

Dean Hammond reported in 1954 that the Graduate School consisted of approximately 315 students working toward the M.A., M.S., and Ph.D. degrees. A notable event of the session then ending was the opening of the redecorated and comfortably furnished room at 59 West Range, designated as the Graduate Students' Center. It contained writing materials, books, magazines, and facilities for making coffee and tea. Most important, the center provided a convenient meeting place for graduate students where they could become acquainted and exchange ideas. By 1959 the number of these students had risen to about four hundred, with around one hundred degrees awarded annually. At that time, there was an "overwhelming demand for Ph.D.'s in response to increased enrollments and greater need for college teachers," the dean reported.

There were nine schools in the university—College of Arts and Sciences, much the largest, with 160 faculty members and 1,600 students in 1959; Law, Medicine, Engineering, Education, Graduate Studies, Architecture, Graduate Business Administration, and Commerce.

The College of Arts and Sciences was divided into four "associations," under a system devised by Dean Duren, and another was added in anticipation of future growth. Each association was given its own dean and two resident advisers. The system was designed to provide closer relationships among the students and between them and the faculty. Each association included two of the residence houses, and upperclassmen who

64. Allan T. Gwathmey, professor of chemistry.

did not reside in the houses were arbitrarily assigned to one of the associations. Thus each association had about one-fourth of the college population. The purpose was to create in each association the atmosphere of a small liberal arts college. The philosophy was said to be one of an advisory service rather than paternalism. Writing in the *Alumni News*, Prof. Irby B. Cauthen, Jr., declared that "the system has provided a closer supervision over the academic and extracurricular affairs of the college students, and has inculcated a growing awareness in students of the importance of proceeding satisfactorily to the college degree." He went on to say that "a student must maintain an average close to a 'C' to be permitted to remain in the college after his first year."

Faculty pay was rising, but sabbatical leaves for faculty members, whereby professors would be able after, say, seven years, to take a full year off with half pay or half a year with full pay, had never been possible at Virginia. Colgate Darden said in his inaugural address that this was one of the university's principal needs, but he was unable to put such a system into effect. Not until the sesquicentennial in 1969 would it be possible to institute a series of faculty leaves roughly equivalent to the sabbatical system.

Stringfellow Barr returned to the faculty in 1951, for two sessions as visiting professor of political science. He gave a course on the origin and development of American political institutions and was anxious to establish at the university something along the lines of his Great Books seminar at St. John's College, where he had been president. After "Winkie" Barr's departure, Associate Dean Marcus B. Mallett built on the foundations Barr had laid and developed what was known as Lower Division Seminar 1–2, which was nondepartmental and was designed to enrich the curriculum. From this course and the one that preceded it, various undergraduate honors programs were developed, growing out of the pioneering done by Prof. Robert K. Gooch back in the 1930s.

In a penetrating examination of the university as an educational institution, published in 1956, Robert B. Eggleston, editor of the *Cavalier Daily*, praised the honors program. Under it, he said, "one may spend the third and fourth years pursuing a course of study independently of the normal system." The student "conducts research under faculty guidance, attends classes as he wishes, and holds discussions with his advisor." He receives no grades, but has "a chance to discuss ideas," and he "must pass a much more rigid comprehensive examination than the other students." Eggleston believed the honors program "affords the best means of education open to an undergraduate at the university."

He was pessimistic with respect to certain aspects of the overall situation. "It is so easy to go through four years here without ever being required to put forth one iota of thought," he declared. "Our student body has a mental capacity higher than its anti-intellectual attitude would indicate."

Several efforts at course evaluation were made from 1954 to 1958 by student committees, with faculty cooperation. Results from the first two were unsatisfactory, mainly because too few students were willing to fill out the questionnaires. Some professors were apprehensive at first, thinking that the evaluation was a malicious plot on the part of dissatisfied students. It was explained, however, that the purpose was to be helpful to both professors and undergraduates. Another attempt was made in 1955, and the response was more representative. The results were published at great length in the *Cavalier Daily*. However, that publication concluded that the operation was "of little benefit, except to air student complaints of certain professors." In 1958 another evaluation, on a different basis, was attempted. This time Dean Duren and the Student Council sent questionnaires to selected students in each department. Questions had to do with the importance of lectures and textbooks, the value of outside reading, and the usefulness of discussion. Results were reviewed by the Student Council, the *Cavalier Daily*, and the dean's office.

Members of the liberal arts faculty were holding seminars during the middle fifties "to enhance the value of the baccalaureate degrees by providing intensive work in the liberal arts tradition." In 1957–58 for example, eleven faculty members were conducting seminars for three hours each week, with from seven to fourteen students in each section. There was no field of concentration or area of honors work or grade program. Professors taking part received no extra compensation.

A sore point with the students in another part of the curriculum was the requirement that first- and second-year men take physical education classes. After they had entered fervent and long-continued protests over a period of years, it was announced that those entering in the fall of 1955 would have to take only one year of "phys ed." And there would be no more classes at what the boys termed "the insane hour of 8 A.M." As far back as the early 1930s there had been lamentations over the required physical education course. The *Cavalier Daily* joined in 1952 in attacking it, and John Weatherly, writing in the paper, called the course "an absolute farce and a mockery." The Jefferson Society recommended its complete elimination. All this failed to produce the desired result, but reduction of the course to one year and abolition of the 8 o'clock "outrage" were gratefully received.

Needy but able students were being assisted financially by duPont scholarships. Made available in the middle 1950s, twenty-five regional scholarships were awarded annually, with one going to the winner in each of the 10 congressional districts and 15 to top-ranking Virginians without regard to geography. The amount of the stipend ranged from $2,000 to $3,400 for the four years.

The largesse from Philip du Pont that made the foregoing possible had been forthcoming back in the 1920s, but other smaller donations had come to the university in more recent years. John Lee Pratt, '05, contributed $125,000 in 1949 for research of "trace elements" by the Department of Chemistry under Prof. John H. Yoe. Dr. Yoe had been doing studies in the field for two decades and had published a two-volume treatise on the subject entitled *Photometric Chemical Analysis*. Mr. Pratt provided $500,000 anonymously for the Department of Physics in 1952, the money to be expended under Prof. Jesse Beams. Part of the money was to be used the following session for fellowships in graduate and postdoctoral work, while other funds would supplement faculty salaries, provide special equipment, and bring promising students to Virginia. "Some of the fellowships will be as attractive as any offered in the United States," said Beams, who termed the gift "magnificent." Pratt also gave $500,000 anonymously to the Department of Chemistry and another $500,000 to the Department of Biology. In 1958–59 the National Science Foun-

65. *Thomas P. Abernethy, professor of history.*

dation renewed the $250,000 grant it had made available the year before to enable selected high and preparatory school teachers of science and mathematics to study for a full session of special advanced courses at the university. The importance of scientific study and research was stressed still more after Soviet Russia created a worldwide sensation by putting up its first sputnik in 1957.

Establishment of a Graduate School of Business Administration at the university was suggested in the summer of 1946 by Prof. Tipton R. Snavely. Pointing out that there was no separate graduate business school in the South, he said in a written report that the University of Virginia was the logical place for one. The following October, Rector Edward R. Stettinius urged in his convocation address that the university establish a school of this type. In January 1947 Professor Snavely devoted seven pages of his annual report on the Department of Economics and the McIntire School of Commerce to a detailed proposal for implementing the plan.

President Darden was skeptical at first because of the cost, but he soon became enthusiastic and extremely active in pushing the proposal. A committee, headed by Homer L. Ferguson, president of the Newport News Shipbuilding and Dry Dock Company, was appointed, with the objective of raising an adequate endowment and persuading the General Assembly to appropriate funds. This committee was succeeded, upon the formation of the school, by a Sponsoring Committee headed by Henry E. McWane, '16, president of the Lynchburg Foundry Company and member of the Board of Visitors. It evolved into the University of Virginia Graduate School Sponsors, Inc., with McWane still as chairman and J. Harvie Wilkinson Jr., '27, prominent Richmond banker, vice-chairman. Both McWane and Wilkinson were deeply involved and extremely effective in promoting the project. President Darden spoke in its behalf in all parts of the state.

One of the major arguments for the school was that its location at a southern university would tend to encourage graduates to remain in the South, and, more specifically, in Virginia. Hundreds were going to Harvard, the University of Pennsylvania's Wharton School, and elsewhere and making their careers in the North or West, all of which tended to drain the South of many of its most promising business and industrial leaders. As Wilkinson put it, "No region can remain vigorous and suffer continued drain of its mental topsoil and its centers of ferment and creativity."

Business organizations throughout Virginia were favorably impressed by the plan, and a drive for funds was launched. It went slowly at first, but after several years a total of $1,250,000 was raised, and the state legislature matched the amount. The General Assembly also made an annual appropriation of $50,000.

In the spring of 1954 it was announced that Charles C. Abbott, a magna cum laude Ph.D. of Harvard and Converse Professor of Banking and Finance in the Harvard Graduate School of Business Administration, would be the first dean of the Virginia school.

"Charlie" Abbott, who had written widely on business and financial problems and was frequently voted the favorite professor of the Harvard students, was almost ideally fitted for the position at Charlottesville. As a student at Harvard he had edited the *Lampoon* and composed the class poem. Endowed with a keen wit, he described himself as "a carpetbagger," but his birth in Kansas and his schooling in the North were no hindrance to his success in Virginia. An admiring writer for the *Alumni News* said he was "the only dean at the university who keeps ready access to Beechnut chewing tobacco."

Dean Abbott arrived Sept. 1, 1954. Discussing it later, he said, "I think Mr. Darden wanted the school to open September 15, but I said I wanted a year to open, and we opened in 1955 with 38 students." After considerable conversation with Darden and "asking questions which Darden didn't understand, he [Darden] said 'Well, why don't you do what you damn well please; everybody does here, anyway.' That's all the instruction I ever had."

The school opened in Monroe Hall, with two faculty members besides Abbott planning the curriculum and preparing for the session of 1954–55. One was John D. Forbes, professor of business history, who "arrived in an elderly yellow Rolls Royce from Wabash College, Indiana," where he had taught since 1946. Forbes had done graduate work in economic history at Harvard, got his Ph.D. there, and held other degrees from the University of California and Stanford. The other member of the planning and teaching staff was Forrest J. Hyde, a 1915 law graduate of the University of Virginia who had served on its law faculty for several years and then entered practice in New York City, where he was associated with important business and financial interests. The rest of the faculty included Almand R. Coleman, Lee R. Johnston, Everard W. Meade, Maurice Davier, and Forrest E. Keller, with A. W. Zelomek as visiting lecturer. It was a two-year course, leading to the degree of Master of Business Administration (M.B.A.). Harvard's case system was used. Ability to communicate by the spoken and the written word was stressed, since it was felt that businessmen are deficient in these areas.

A "loyal friend of the university" created a Student Loan Fund, enabling talented students without means to attend the school. This anonymous "friend" who came forward frequently over the years to aid various university causes was almost certainly Colgate Darden. His identity was seldom made public, but time and again his generosity (or that of his wife, who also remained behind the scenes) helped to pull the university over a financial hump or to provide funds that could be used in imaginative ways to further the progress of the institution. In recognition of his wholehearted support as president of the university and as a continuing benefactor, the school was named for Mr. Darden in 1973. In the present instance this "loyal friend" offered a substantial sum to the sponsors of the graduate school on condition that they match it. They did, and $100,000 or more became available for the Student Loan Fund. Incidentally, Colgate Darden never accepted any salary from the university.

Describing the curriculum of the graduate school in broad terms, Dean Abbott said:

The school accents the case method of study where students meet actual problems and situations similar to those which will confront them in their work in future years. These problems are discussed by the students who seek to formulate their own questions and solutions, and the instructor, acting in the role of a discussion leader instead of a lecturer in most cases.

In the first year the school offers an intensified curriculum which concentrates on the several basic aspects of business endeavor. This provides the fundamental groundwork necessary to all businessmen, and enables the students to judge more readily for themselves which fields draw their particular interest.

The second year allows the student to select for himself one of several areas of concentration while also providing opportunities in the creative field of individual research work.

The prototypical student in the school has had two or more years of managerial or other significant work experience. While today admission standards are much tighter, attrition still ranges between 10 and 15 percent. About 40 percent of the students are married when they enter the school and 60 percent by the time they graduate. Virginia-born students enrolled have averaged around 43 percent of the total enrollment, those from the rest of the South 16 percent and from elsewhere 41 percent, according to *The First Twenty Years: The Darden School at Virginia*, edited by C. Stewart Sheppard.

A program leading to the degree of Doctor of Business Administration (D.B.A.) was instituted in 1965. The program is intended to train students for professional careers in teaching and research in business management. The degree may theoretically be earned in three years, but the demands of dissertation research are likely to extend the time to four years or more.

The faculty has expanded steadily from the early days, when there were nine members until now faculty and lecturers number about forty. As described by *Corks and Curls*: "Both the business and the academic worlds are well represented. Professional competence in engineering, history, psychology, law, economics, speech and public service are included in the group, as well as skills in the characteristically [*sic*] business fields of accounting, finance, marketing and production." The most significant single factor in the school's effectiveness "may be its small enrollment [about three hundred] and low faculty-student ratio," Professor Forbes has written. Eventual enrollment was projected at 480, to be achieved without sacrificing the intimacy of faculty-student relationships that characterized the school's early years.

A new headquarters building was felt to be essential, and the General Assembly was urged to appropriate the necessary funds. It made $3,200,000 available for a building to be erected on the Duke property northwest of University Hall.

President Edgar Shannon, like President Darden, favored the project, as did Dean Abbott and virtually the entire faculty of the school. Ground was broken in 1973, with completion scheduled for 1975.

An important feature of the Darden School is the Tayloe Murphy Institute, which began functioning in 1967 as a research affiliate. Named for the late W. Tayloe Murphy, an ardent supporter of the school, much-admired member of the General Assembly, and longtime friend of Colgate Darden, it received a million-dollar endowment from an "anonymous donor" whose identity was not difficult to guess. The gift was conditioned on $600,000 additional being raised; it was. The Institute now includes the former Bureau of Population and Economic Research, which was consolidated with it in 1972. Prof. Charles O. Meiburg of the Darden School faculty was made executive director. Dr. Lorin A. Thompson, for many years head of the Bureau of Population and Economic Research, had left in 1966 to become chancellor and then first president of George Mason College. The Tayloe Murphy Institute monitors the business progress and climate of Virginia and the nation and issues statements and statistics from time to time putting the business situation in perspective.

Another important activity of the Darden School is carried on by the Center for the Study of Applied Ethics. This grew out of the action of Mrs. Signe Olsson in establishing a chair in 1966 in memory of her husband, Elis Olsson. She had the following objectives, according to the Board of Visitors: "The donor has in mind the enormous importance of integrity in human affairs, and seeks through this gift to stimulate general public interest in and understanding of the ethical implications that necessarily adhere to the exercise of authority in both public and private life." Prof. Frederick E. Nolting, Jr., was named to the Olsson chair. Major conferences on ethics in business were held in 1973 and 1974, and several publications were issued.

When Charles C. Abbott retired as dean in 1972, he was succeeded by C. Stewart Sheppard, who had joined the faculty in 1961, after serving as dean of the Graduate School of Business and Public Administration at Cornell University. Dean Sheppard is a native of Wales, an M.B.A. of New York Univer-

66. Llewellyn G. Hoxton, professor of physics.

sity, and a Ph.D. of Columbia University. Soon after his arrival in Charlottesville he established the Institute of Chartered Financial Analysts, a professional organization located in the university's William Faulkner House. It tests and certifies financial analysts throughout the United States and Canada, and since it enjoys worldwide recognition and acceptance, membership is eagerly sought.

The Darden Graduate School of Business Administration has a high reputation throughout the United States. Certainly one of the premier graduate schools of business in the South, it is competitive with the best of its type in this country. A survey by Columbia University in 1974 placed it among the top eleven such schools in the United States. It has been disappointing, however, in that fewer of its graduates remain in the state and region than had been hoped for by the school's founders. For example, about 150 companies sent representatives in 1974 to recruit that year's 133 M.B.A. recipients. Of these, 48 percent accepted positions in the Northeast (half of them in New York City), 26 percent in the South (only 12 percent in Virginia), 11 percent in the Middle West, with the remaining 15 percent going to the Far West or to foreign countries. There is evidence also that Virginia employers, for some unknown reason, are less zealous in seeking these graduates than employers from other areas.

"The Darden School is a net exporter of M.B.A. talent from Virginia to the rest of the world," Prof. John L. Snook, Jr., has written. "Of nearly 400 M.B.A.'s whose domicile was Virginia during their student days, more than 200 have moved to other states, while fewer than 100 'foreigners' have been attracted to Virginia. . . . We may have to develop strategies to make Virginia business and industry more attractive to future M.B.A. classes."

The Darden School has over two million dollars in endowment, plus $500,000 in liquid assets. Sydney F. Small of Roanoke left it $500,000 in 1973 for a series of fellowships. Sustaining annual income from the sponsors totals over three hundred thousand dollars. Endowed chairs in honor of Dean Abbott and Professor Snavely were established in 1972, and resources for other faculty chairs were being solicited. As generous as the Sponsors' financial support had been over the years, continuing assistance would be needed if the excellence and diversity of the school's programs were to grow.

Steadily improving its performance and turning out extremely well-trained graduates year after year, the Darden School soon came to be recognized as among the foremost graduate schools of business administration in this country.

On another level of instruction in business and economics, an important development took place in 1952–53, when the McIntire School of Commerce was given status as a separate school, with its own faculty and dean. The James Wilson School of Economics remained as a department of the College of Arts and Sciences. Professor Snavely had been chairman of both departments since 1923.

After Professors Rutledge Vining and Lorin A. Thompson served briefly as successive deans of the independent McIntire School, Frank S. Kaulback, Jr., associate professor of accounting, was named so the position. As head of the school, he directed a two-year course of study leading to the B.S. degree in economics, and in 1972 a master's degree in accounting was added. Dean Kaulback was a consultant to bankers' associations and other corporations and was active in national organizations operating in the business education field. He interviewed each degree candidate personally, advising him or her as to academic, vocational, or placement problems.

The Department of Economics offers the M.A. and Ph.D. degrees. Economics had been taught at the university since the institution opened in 1825, so that it was one of the first universities in this country to give instruction in that discipline. The James Wilson Department was found by the American Economics Association to rank "eleventh among 42 leading American universities in the number of doctoral dissertations which were in progress . . . 1941–50." And in 1956 a magazine article "listed Virginia as among the 'Big 15' in respect to graduate work and research in economics." The philosophy of the university's economics faculty might be described as middle of the road. It is decidedly less liberal than the faculties of most American universities.

The economics faculty was strengthened in the mid-1950s by the addition of an able young professor named James R.

Schlesinger. He remained for seven years and later served in Washington as chairman of the Atomic Energy Commission, director of the Central Intelligence Agency, secretary of defense, and secretary of energy.

The Thomas Jefferson Center for Studies in Political Economy was organized at the university in 1957, with Prof. James M. Buchanan, chairman of the Department of Economics, as director. The impetus for the establishment of this interdepartmental agency came largely from the economics faculty. Its aim was to bring together economists, philosophers, political scientists, historians, and scholars in related fields. Prof. G. Warren Nutter, who was heading a special study of the Soviet economy, on which he was a recognized authority, was associate director of the center, and Prof. Leland B. Yeager, also of the economics faculty, was executive secretary. Financial support for the operation was provided by foundations. It was announced that the center would bring to the university each year a distinguished visiting scholar, would sponsor individual lectures or seminar discussions by invited guests, grant fellowships to graduate students and postdoctoral candidates, and act as a clearing house through which independent research projects by permanent members of the university faculty were administered.

President Darden had been in office only a few months when the long-forgotten controversy between the Medical School and the Medical College of Virginia in Richmond surfaced once more. Financial deficits of the two institutions disturbed Gov. William M. Tuck, who suggested, in the interest of efficiency and economy, that a "partial merger" might be desirable. The question was referred to Dr. Alan Gregg of the Rockefeller Institute, who left no doubt as to his position by recommending strongly against this. Dr. Gregg found medical education to be "ideally situated" in such an environment as that provided by the university, and he added that "the long future of medical education in the State of Virginia lies in the development of the Medical School at Charlottesville."

This ended any discussion of a partial merger between the two institutions, but it did not resolve President Darden's concern over what he termed the university hospital's "huge op-

67. *Gordon T. Whyburn, professor of mathematics.*

erating deficit." Darden pointed to the hospital's $900,000 shortfall for 1952, of which $300,000 was a loan from the state the previous year and $600,000 the current year's deficit. He termed this the most critical problem facing the university and appealed, with only a limited degree of success, to the city of Charlottesville and the surrounding counties to help in meeting this heavy cost, caused, in large measure, by the health needs of their indigent citizens. Dr. Richard J. Ackart became director of the hospital in 1951, succeeding Dr. Carlisle S. Lentz, who was given the post of consultant after twenty years as superintendent and additional years as medical director.

The Medical School also obtained the services of a new dean of medicine at about this time—Dr. Vernon W. Lippard, who came to the university in 1949 from Louisiana State, where he was medical dean. A highly regarded Yale graduate, he remained at Charlottesville four years and then accepted the deanship of the Yale Medical School. Dr. Lippard was succeeded at Virginia by Dr. Thomas H. Hunter, a cum laude M.D. of Harvard, who had taken part of his medical education at Cambridge University, England. At the time of his appointment as Virginia's dean of medicine he was associate dean of the Washington University Medical School, St. Louis. Dr. Hunter was widely known for his studies of bacterial infection of the heart, usually associated with rheumatic heart disease.

Dr. William H. Muller, Jr., one of the nation's leading heart surgeons, was named head of surgery in 1954. A native of South Carolina and graduate of the Duke Medical School, he was acting chairman of the division of general surgery at the University of California Medical Center, Los Angeles, at the time of his appointment as successor to Dr. Edwin P. Lehman, who retired after a successful career. Various members of the university's medical faculty were involved in many constructive activities beyond the boundaries of the institution, but Dr. Muller surpassed then all. For example, during the 1957–58 session, taken at random, he delivered ten addresses, from Chicago to Galveston, took part in seven discussions of papers in several different areas of the country, and had thirteen publications with four more "to be published." Dr. Muller also had five research projects in process or completed, while serving on eighteen committees and on the American Board of Thoracic Surgery.

A cobalt unit for cancer therapy superior to anything of the kind in Virginia at the time was obtained in 1956, thanks to a campaign for funds led by Mrs. Henry B. Mulholland, with the assistance of the dean's office. This was a cobalt-60 tele-therapy unit, and as more money was raised than expected, "a 1,000-curie source" was obtained, Dr. Vincent W. Archer, chairman of radiology, stated.

Dr. Henry B. Mulholland arrived at age sixty-five in 1958 and hence was retired as assistant dean of the Medical School, while continuing to teach. "Hank" Mulholland, widely liked and admired, had been extremely active in a number of dif-ferent directions—as a member of the House of Delegates of the American Medical Association and various committees of the AMA, as well as of the American Diabetes Association, not to mention several committees of the Medical Society of Vir-ginia and the State Department of Health. He was the major influence in launching the Virginia Council on Health and Medical Care, which won national recognition for its place-ment of hundreds of doctors and dentists in rural areas sorely in need of their services. For these conspicuous achievements an endowed chair was named for him in the Medical School, the first chair in the university to be named for an incumbent professor.

Dr. Mulholland was succeeded as assistant dean by Dr. Byrd S. Leavell, an able and dedicated member of the medical fac-ulty since 1939 and professor of internal medicine since 1945. Dr. Leavell was known for his clinical research and his writings on functions of the liver, on leukemia, pernicious anemia, sickle cell anemia, and other blood disorders. He was chief of the division of hematology from 1946 to 1971, chairman of the department of internal medicine from 1966 to 1968, and author of over fifty scientific papers and several books and monographs. Dr. Leavell was coauthor with Dr. Oscar Tho-rup, '46, of a textbook, *Fundamentals of Clinical Hematology*, which has gone through several printings.

Dr. Charles J. Frankel, associate professor of orthopedic surgery, in charge of the athletic teams, took a law degree in 1957. He had been teaching law in the Medical School for three years and medicine in the Law School for two years, and planned to continue both types of instruction. Dr. Frankel wrote many articles on the treatment of athletic injuries.

The Medical Center's School of Nursing was established in 1956, and replaced the old Department of Nursing. This reorganization set the school apart as a degree-granting body, coordinate with the Schools of Medicine, Engineering, and Law, and was the culmination of studies and proposals made over the preceding decade. Under the new arrangement the nursing students became more active participants in the affairs of the university community. For example, they placed themselves under the university's Honor System and incorporated their yearbook into *Corks and Curls*. Dr. Margaret G. Tyson was appointed dean, with responsibility to the director of the Medical Center. A leader at this time in nursing affairs at the university was Roy C. Beazley, who had served over a period of thirty-six years as nursing superintendent, acting department cochairman, director of nursing service, and faculty member. She became the university's first woman professor emeritus. The basic professional degree program was established in 1950. Under its terms the applicant spent two years at an approved institution, then gained practical training at the university and completed the course for a Bachelor of Science degree in nursing, and obtained a license as a registered nurse. Another year of study was required for the M.A. degree in nursing. For a time the school also continued to offer a three-year program leading to a nursing diploma.

There were serious suggestions that the entire medical complex, including the hospital, be moved to the North Grounds and rebuilt from the ground up. The group of buildings located near the Corner since the turn of the century had been enlarged from time to time, but it had been impossible to plan the expansion properly, under such circumstances. The argument was made that economy and efficiency would be enhanced if a well-planned and well-integrated facility could be constructed de novo. However, so huge a construction project would have entailed expenditures beyond the university's capacity, and President Darden was strongly opposed. It was decided to keep the medical complex where it had always been.

The Law School would not move to the North Grounds for some two decades, but already, in 1950, it was tending to drift away from the other schools at the university. Its students were concentrating on their legal studies and on the Law

School's extracurricular activities. The contrast was noted by Dean F. D. G. Ribble during the session of 1948–49: "I can remember, from my own student days, a substantial number of law students who looked on the study of law as very definitely a part-time pursuit. The life of the fraternity house, of the athletic field, or the social organizations and university politics received a very great share of their interest and time. Such is not now the case." He said that there had developed "a more complete concentration on the law," with extracurricular activities consisting of work connected with the *Virginia Law Review*, the *Reading Guide*, the *Virginia Law Weekly*, the Legal Forum, the Student Legal Research Group, the Law Student Council, and the Law Clubs. The dean expressed the view that these activities "develop in the law student a capacity for leadership, a capacity for meeting problems, for seeing their implications and for reaching solutions."

The Law School during the 1950s was a mixture of Virginians and other southerners plus a remarkably high percentage of Ivy League graduates. Dean Ribble said that "not counting the home state, this Law School probably has the highest percentage of Southern students of any school in the nation." As for the Ivy League, Harvard, Yale, and Princeton graduates made up, on the average, more than one-third of the total enrollment.

Former World Court Justice John Bassett Moore, class of 1880, presented 5,000 volumes on international law to the Law School Library in 1946. He had previously given the library 2,500 volumes in the same field. Moore was professor of international law and diplomacy at Columbia University from 1891 to 1924. He died in 1947, and two years later his bust was placed in Mural Hall at the Law School, the gift of his daughter, Mrs. de Raisnes Storey.

William Jett Lauck, one of the nation's leading labor economists, gave 5,000 volumes to the law library in 1948. Lauck had served with the Immigration Commission, the War Labor Board for World War I, the National Recovery Administration (NRA), and the railway arbitration commissions.

The 100,000th volume was presented to the library in 1953 at special ceremonies, with U.S. Supreme Court Justice Stanley Reed, '08, making the presentation. The library had become the largest law library in the South.

Miss Eleanor Gibson's work as associate director of placement for the Law School was praised "in the highest terms" by Dean Ribble. William H. White, Jr., was director of placement, but the greater part of the work was done by Miss Gibson. "It would be hard to overestimate the importance of an effective placement office on the morale of the Law School and our relationships with the alumni," said the dean. The placement office helps graduates seeking assistance and alumni seeking jobs or change of jobs.

Dean Ribble spoke of the significance of the Judge Advocate General's School's locating at the university. It is "a national service of importance to this university," said he. "Our school gains prestige through being the location of the legal center of the Army of the United States." He quoted General Dahlquist, commanding general of the army within the U.S., as saying that the J.A.G. School "gained prestige and stature by its association with a law school of the first rank."

Edward Watts Saunders, '17, was named dean of engineering in 1947 as successor to the late Dean Rodman. Saunders, president of his graduating class in engineering at the university and member of the State Board of Engineering Examiners since 1929, led in revising the undergraduate curriculum, developing the Master of Engineering degree, and expanding the research and service activities of the department. The M.E. degree required four graduate courses and residence for at least one session. There were a comprehensive examination and a thesis based on original research. Half of the required research time could be completed in industrial or governmental centers.

The department had offered extension courses since 1929 in the state's industrial areas. These courses, initiated by Prof. Arthur F. MacConochie, provided strong support for the first new graduate degrees. Enrollment had grown to the point where in 1948 about seven hundred persons had matriculated in thirty-six classes.

Organization of an alumni association of the Engineering Department was an important event of these years.

Also, the university joined with the Virginia Highway Department to establish the Virginia Council of Highway Investigation and Research. Under its auspices the first Interna-

*68. James Southall Wilson, professor of English and dean of the
Graduate School of Arts and Sciences, 1937–1951.*

tional Skid Prevention Conference was held at the university in 1958. European countries were devoting much more attention than the United States to problems of skidding by motor vehicles. Papers were delivered at the five-day conference by speakers from Great Britain, West Germany, Holland, and Spain.

Students at the university were able to take advantage of the research opportunities afforded by the Oak Ridge Institute of Nuclear Physics at Oak Ridge, Tenn., operated under a contract with the Atomic Energy Commission. Virginia was one of fourteen southern universities affiliated with the institute, and physics Professors Jesse Beams and Leland Snoddy were members of its council.

Saunders resigned as dean in 1950 because of ill health, and Charles Henderson was named to the deanship. He too had been president of his engineering class when he graduated at the university in 1920. By the end of Henderson's five years as dean, graduate programs had been instituted in chemical, civil, electrical, and mechanical engineering, and degrees were offered for the first time in aeronautical engineering and engineering physics. The School of Engineering (in 1952 the terms "department" and "school" were interchanged throughout the university) had grown to such an extent that it had a larger enrollment than either law or medicine. At about this time Christopher G. Memminger made a bequest of $300,000 for chemical engineering.

Charles Henderson reached the mandatory retirement age for deans in 1955 and resumed full-time teaching for six more years. He was succeeded by Lawrence R. Quarles, '35, who led the school for the next eighteen years until his retirement in 1973. A Charlottesville native and University of Virginia Ph.D., he had worked for several years with Westinghouse, specializing in electronics; he also had spent two years with the Oak Ridge Institute.

Dean Quarles developed a three-pronged nuclear energy program of teaching, research, and aid to industry and other agencies. He named a Nuclear Energy Advisory Committee to work with industrial, agricultural, and other concerned organizations and interests. A new degree—Master of Nuclear Engineering—was introduced, and the School of Engineering collaborated with the Department of Physics in offering the degree of Doctor of Science in Engineering Physics. A Doctor of Science in Chemical Engineering, the school's first doctoral degree, was initiated. Advanced extension courses in nuclear engineering were offered throughout the state.

Construction of a million-watt swimming-pool-type nuclear reactor was one of the university's significant building projects of the time. The reactor was used by many departments and schools of the university. Chiefly because he supervised its construction and served as the U.S. State Department's consultant to the Philippine Government on nuclear reaction, a chair in the School of Engineering and Applied Science (the new name of the department, reflecting the changed emphasis) was established in honor of Lawrence Quarles. This was one of only three such chairs that have been named for incumbent professors in the university.

Quarles's efforts to revise undergraduate curricula led to the first major changes since the end of World War I. They involved increased time for mathematics, science, humanities, and social sciences, and an expanded faculty.

The School of Medicine was using nuclear energy in two important ways, treatment by means of nuclear energy products, or radiation, and analysis by the use of these same tools.

The Department of Education underwent a transformation for the better during the Darden years. President Darden was determined to strengthen the operation, and on the retirement of Dean Manahan he brought in Lindley J. Stiles as dean. Previous emphasis on methodology was sharply reduced, and attention was focused to a much greater degree on subject matter—that is, every teacher was required to study the subject to be taught, rather than methods of teaching. Dean Stiles said in 1955 that entrance requirements had been raised to provide that "a B average or better" was required for entrance, as well as "adequate scores on Scholastic Aptitude Tests or achievement tests, and personal qualifications, including promise as a prospective teacher." It was possible to major in physical education, and thirteen football players were enrolled in the School of Education at that time, according to a letter in the student newspaper.

For the first time the school was offering graduate courses leading to the Master of Education and Doctor of Education degrees. The M.A. and Ph.D. in education would still be offered under the supervision of the Department of Graduate Studies. Dean Stiles regarded the training of graduate students as the principal function of the school.

The School of Education was now functioning as a separate professional department, "enjoying a status similar to that accorded the Departments of Engineering, Law and Medicine," the dean reported. "Students in the Department of Education are privileged to participate in the general student affairs of the university through elected representatives on the Student Council, the Honor Committee and the Women's Student Association." The School of Health and Physical Education and the intramural program were placed under the department.

The McGuffey Reading Clinic, headed by Prof. Ullin W. Leavell, was established by him in 1946 and developed in the succeeding years into an important agency for the improvement of reading ability for persons of almost all ages. Leavell was a pioneer in this field. In the late 1950s he directed an annual reading clinic with hundreds of participants from all over Virginia and beyond.

The phone in Leavell's office rang one afternoon, and he answered. It was a call from Ohio, and the operator said, "Is Mr. McGuffey there?" "No," said Leavell, "he is not here." "Do you know where he is?" said the operator. "Well," said he, "I think he is in one of two places." "When will Mr. McGuffey be in?" asked the somewhat impatient operator. "Mr. McGuffey died in 1873," was the answer. "God rest his bones!" said the operator, "Who's in charge now?"

During the five years of Dean Stiles's incumbency total enrollment in the Department of Education tripled, while graduate enrollment, including part-time extension courses, increased tenfold. The number of degrees awarded jumped astronomically. Establishment of the Division of Education Research was a feature of these years. It would serve the research and evaluation needs of educational agencies throughout the commonwealth. Prof. Francis G. Lankford, Jr., relinquished his post as director of the Division of Teacher Placements to serve as director of the new division. Dean Stiles did much to modernize and improve the Department of Education. In 1953 he accepted the deanship of education at the University of Wisconsin. Stiles was somewhat tactless at times, and he antagonized some of the administrators and professors in other departments, but his record was a constructive one.

Dr. Ralph W. Cherry was the next dean of education. He came from the University of Texas and took over the deanship in 1956, remaining in the post until 1968, after which he taught for six more years. He directed the summer session from 1956 to 1974. It was the opinion of influential members of the Arts and Sciences faculty that Dean Cherry raised the stature of the School of Education markedly within the university.

He aided the school's faculty in establishing annual conferences in subject matter areas, such as English, social studies, science, and mathematics. Still more significant was the fact that during his regime the school received accreditation by the National Council for Accreditation and Teacher Education, while the Division of Field Services was established under his leadership. The latter served as a formal channel for association with the state schools and educational agencies. The size of the faculty was more than doubled, and the number of matriculates rose to a record high of 300 full-time and 500 part-time graduate students. Those who commented on Dean Cherry's personal characteristics stressed his integrity, personal warmth, and human understanding.

Prof. Orland E. White relinquished the directorship of the School of Biology's Blandy Experiment Farm in Clarke County in 1955, after holding the position since 1927. White was curator of plant breeding at the Brooklyn Botanic Garden when he took over as professor of agricultural biology and director of the farm, with a view to making the latter a center for research in genetics. It was, as he put it, "a neglected piece of land with some dilapidated buildings, no modern improvements of any kind, a 20-year-old apple orchard of about 65 acres and more kinds of weeds that I had ever seen in my life." When he stepped down twenty-eight years later he turned over "a scientific institution with a laboratory and dormitory setup worth $100,000 or more, a good working library, much-improved farm buildings, a two-compartment greenhouse, and 130 acres of experimental plots, lawns, and arboretum landscaped and scientifically arranged with over five thousand species of woody plants, farm land in good condition, a herd of around 150 head of high grade Hereford cattle, a drove of hogs, up-to-date farm machinery, and a worldwide reputation and contacts." More than one hundred technical papers had been published by the staff and the students, more than forty graduate students had obtained high degrees, mainly Ph.D.'s, through their investigations and experiments at the farm. Foreign students had come from Germany, China, India, Ireland, and Canada. Orland White was succeeded on July 1, 1955, by W. Ralph Singleton, Miller Professor of Biology. White died in 1972.

The other institution affiliated with the Miller School of Biology and Agriculture is the Mountain Lake Biological Station in Giles County—described in some detail in chapter 3. During the twenty-five years the station had been in operation more than twenty-five courses in biology had been offered. Approximately seventy-five biologists from colleges and universities in this and other countries attended. Prof. Bruce D. Reynolds was in charge and had occupied that position during much of the time since the station was established.

Another university activity situated at considerable distance from Charlottesville was the Seward Forest in Brunswick County, an affiliate of the School of Forestry. It consisted of 3,600 acres bequeathed to the university in 1932 by Dr. W. M. Seward, '86, of Triplett. Active development of the area was begun in 1935 under the direction of Prof. Alfred Akerman. The Seward Forest was operated as a teaching facility for various methods of reproducing, caring for, and harvesting timber, and as a center for research. By the mid-1950s it had from ten to sixteen full-time employees, including several university students who gained practical experience in this way. Lectures in the school were occasionally supplemented by fieldwork in Brunswick County, but since the forest is 140 miles from Charlottesville, frequent field trips were impossible. Courses were on an undergraduate level.

The Division of Art and Architecture of the McIntire School of Fine Arts was expanding its curriculum in the late 1940s and preparing to require a five-year course as a prerequisite to the B.S. degree in architecture. The School of Architecture had been fully accredited since 1944, when the national accrediting board was established, but the board stipulated that the school would have to offer a five-year course in order to retain its accreditation. Prof. Edmund S.

69. *Henry Jordan, star university tackle and heavyweight wrestling champion of the Atlantic Coast Conference, 1957, shown in the uniform of the Green Bay Packers.*

Campbell, head of the division, stated in 1948 that provision was being made for every degree applicant to spend a year in the college and then four years taking the professional course. The division also was adding courses in painting, drawing, and design. In each of the two preceding years there had been over four hundred applicants to the division for only thirty-two places.

The university community was shocked in 1950 when Professor Campbell died suddenly in Washington while attending a meeting of the American Institute of Architects. He was sixty-five, and had come to Charlottesville in 1937 as head of the Division of Art and Architecture. Campbell had served as consulting architect for various projects around the Grounds and was recognized as a leading critic of design. He was also one of the nation's foremost watercolor artists, with examples of his work in many national exhibitions. Professor Campbell had been a member of the Virginia State Fine Arts Commission and of the State Examining Board of Architects.

He was succeeded by Thomas K. Fitz Patrick, who came to the university from Iowa State College. Fitz Patrick was appointed to head the university's School of Architecture, which was separated from the College of Arts and Sciences and established as a separate professional school under the name of McIntire School of Architecture. Its origins went back to 1919, when Prof. Fiske Kimball became chairman of the newly established McIntire School of Fine Arts.

Classes in architectural history, as well as art history, were held in the Bayly Museum, an innovation introduced by William B. O'Neal, professor in the School of Architecture and museum curator. New degrees in architectural history and city and regional planning were offered in 1958–59. Enrollment in the school at that time was slightly in excess of one hundred.

Charles W. Smith, who had served temporarily as acting head of the University of Virginia Press, was named chairman of the Division of Art in the College of Arts and Sciences. A famous Virginia-born artist and university alumnus, with exhibits in this country and Europe, he would be awarded a Certificate of Honor by Yale University "in recognition of his achievement as an artist and his distinguished contribution to the culture of his time." Smith had worked in oils, wood engraving, typography, lithography, and block printing, and he had experimented successfully in the design of wallpaper and textiles. His "block painting" process was revolutionary. William B. O'Neal, chairman of the university's Division of Architectural History, placed him "in a rank seldom achieved by an American artist." He retired as department chairman in 1963.

The Department of Music had made steady progress since the 1940s, when Randall Thompson began moving it forward. Further advance was achieved under Stephen Tuttle, and in more recent years much credit is accorded Ernest C. Mead, Jr., for the department's accomplishments. Mead returned from a year at Harvard and eventually became head of the department. The department had direction of the Glee Club, band, orchestra and brass ensemble, and the teaching staff devoted much time to each of these operations.

Ernest Mead had been a pupil of John Powell, for many years a devoted alumnus. Powell received what seems to have been a unique tribute when Gov. John S. Battle proclaimed Nov. 5, 1951, to be "John Powell Day."

Powell and Mead were enthusiastic supporters of the Virginia Music Festival, which came to an end in 1950, after functioning for four years and bringing musicians and music lovers to the university from all over the state. Scott Stadium was the scene of some of the major events, but the weather was so uncertain that Col. Francis P. Miller, festival association president, announced reluctantly that the affair could not be continued. Miller added that the festival did not have an adequately broad base of support.

The Institute of Public Affairs was revived in 1950 after having been suspended for eight years on account of World War II. George B. Zehmer, director of the Extension Division and dean of the summer session, was its director. Part of its nineteenth session, in 1952, was broadcast around the world in eleven languages. The Institute's two-week program overlapped the latter part of the eight-week summer session of the university.

George Zehmer, who had headed the Extension Division since 1925, retired from that position in 1958 but continued to teach in the School of Education. He had relinquished the deanship of the summer session in 1951, after nearly a decade and a half in the post, and was succeeded by Dean Lindley

Stiles. The Extension Division was expanding so rapidly that Zehmer wished to give it his undivided attention. Enrollment in 1925–26 had been only 370, distributed among twenty-six communities, whereas in 1955–56 there were nearly seven thousand persons enrolled from eight-six communities.

Upon his retirement as dean of the division, Zehmer was succeeded by Chemistry Prof. James W. Cole, Jr., whose new title was dean of the School of General Studies. Cole, a Ph.D. of the university, organized and directed the Academic Year Institute for Teachers of Science and Mathematics and planned to continue this work, financed by the National Science Foundation. He was chemical consultant to the U.S. Air Force and the Air Research Development Council. Zehmer died in 1961, and in that year the name of the school was changed to School of Continuing Education. A building on an eighteen-acre tract adjoining the university Grounds, formerly used by the Red Cross, was purchased. The structure was renamed Zehmer Hall.

The Bureau of Population and Economic Research was engaged in a five-pronged program of activity. Lorin A. Thompson, the director, reported in 1952 that it was functioning in the following areas:

(1) Editing and completion of a cooperative study on the measurement of county income, carried on with the cooperation of the universities of North Carolina, Georgia, Alabama, Mississippi, Tennessee, Kentucky, and the TVA; (2) detailed studies of the impact of industrial changes in rural counties which have been carried on in cooperation with the Virginia Department of Highways and the U.S. Bureau of Public Roads; (3) fundamental studies of the character of economic growth and commodity flows between and among areas; (4) preparation of interpretative reports analyzing the effects of population shifts and industrial development on the economy of the state; (5) studies prepared at the request of state departments and local committees on the impact of population and economic changes on selected administrative problems of the state and localities.

The growing body of research being compiled by the bureau was "finding its way into the instructional materials of the staff members of the schools of economics, business administration and sociology," Thompson reported.

The Bureau of Public Administration was observing its twentieth anniversary, and Rowland Egger, the director, re-

70. *C. Waller Barrett, donor to the university of the greatest collection of American literature in existence.*

ported that "especially since the war, the bureau has remained essentially a service agency providing consultant and technical advisory services, with research, training and education, and clearing house activities in a distinctly subsidiary role." The bureau was preparing a textbook on Virginia government, to be published by Crowell.

The question of whether one of the former state teachers' colleges should be made coordinate with the university had been to the fore during the gubernatorial administration of Colgate Darden. He recommended the appointment of a commission to study the advisability of designating Mary Washington at Fredericksburg as the university's women's college. The commission was appointed, and it approved the plan. Mary Washington became coordinate with the university in 1944. It had been founded in 1908 as the Fredericksburg State Normal and Industrial School, later became Fredericksburg State Teachers' College, and in 1935 Mary Washington, in honor of George Washington's mother. In 1944 it was no longer an institution for training teachers, since for the session of 1943–44 fewer than one percent of the students registered for teacher training.

Affiliation of Mary Washington with the university was deemed by those who shuddered at the thought of coeducation at Charlottesville to be a legal and proper solution of the coed problem. Daughters of Virginia taxpayers were now provided with adequate educational facilities at a state-supported institution—so the argument ran. Faculty and students at Mary Washington were enthusiastic over their new affiliation. President Newcomb, under the law, was designated chancellor of Mary Washington, and its chief administrative officers, with Morgan L. Combs, president of Mary Washington, as chief local administrative officer. The two institutions were placed under the university's Board of Visitors, which was enlarged by four members. Committees from the two faculties were named to work out details of the relationship. Dr. George O. Ferguson, dean of the College at the university, was chairman of the university's committee, and Dr. Edward Alvey, Jr., dean of the College at Mary Washington, headed that institution's committee.

The necessary arrangements and planning were completed. Within a few years it was possible to work out cooperative relationships between the two institutions whereby courses in nursing, elementary and graduate education, and medical technology could be offered, with both the university and the college participating.

All went smoothly until the session of 1953–54 when serious problems arose at Mary Washington. The trouble began when the eighty student waitresses in the dining hall were directed to wear caps and uniforms. This was bitterly resented, on the ground that the directive "demeaned the position of waitress to a servile role," as Dean Alvey expresses it in his history of Mary Washington. Hostility had been mounting among the students toward the administration, and the directive as to uniforms brought matters to a head. Dean of Women Isabelle Gonon resigned and there was considerable turmoil. President Combs was given an opportunity to be heard at a special meeting of the Board of Visitors in December 1953, and the board met again the following month. The outcome of all this was that there was a "rearrangement" of President Combs's responsibilities, and "supreme administrative authority" for Mary Washington was vested in Colgate Darden, chancellor of the institution. Combs retained the title of president but was relieved of all jurisdiction over "faculty relations, student relations, curriculum, internal budget and control." His authority extended only to "construction and development, solicitation of funds and related matters." Combs wrote the board that the arrangement "has my full approval and the implementation of it will have my full cooperation." Darden announced that Dean Alvey and Edgar Woodward, bursar, would divide administrative duties at the college and would be responsible to him. Alvey was placed in charge of faculty relations and curriculum, with Woodward handling the business side.

Morgan Combs became increasingly dissatisfied with this arrangement and more and more suspicious. In December 1954 he charged that five members of the college faculty and staff were engaged in a conspiracy against him and that when he signed the letter almost a year before agreeing to cooperate with the new arrangement, he did so "under duress." At about this time a document termed "scurrilous" by the Board of Visitors and entitled "The Whole Story at Mary Washington College" was widely distributed. No one knew who wrote it, but Combs was aware that it was being circulated. The visitors expressed "resentment of the completely false charges" and announced that "continued retention of Dr. Combs in any active capacity at Mary Washington would be against the best interests of the college." It removed him from office, effective April 9, 1955.

Morgan Combs was obviously not well; he was found to be suffering from leukemia. He entered a hospital in July and died in October, aged sixty-four. It was a sad end for a career that had been useful to Virginia education. President Darden expressed deep distress, saying that he had known for some time that Combs was gravely ill. The latter's career as president of Mary Washington had spanned twenty-six years, and during that time the institution has grown from a small teachers' college to a well-regarded liberal arts college for women. Enrollment had trebled, and whereas only four faculty members had the Ph.D. when Combs became president in 1929, nearly half of the almost one hundred teachers had the doctorate when he died. The handsome and greatly enlarged campus was much admired, the physical facilities had been expanded substantially, and the standards raised. When the new science hall was completed in 1959, it was named for Morgan Combs.

After a careful search, the Board of Visitors elected Dr. Grellet C. Simpson, dean and professor of English at Randolph-Macon College, Ashland, as chancellor of Mary Washington. A native of Norfolk, he was a B.A. of Randolph-Macon and an M.A. and Ph.D. of the University of Virginia. The college made excellent progress under his leadership, and he remained in office until his retirement in 1974. During President Simpson's eighteen-year administration, admission standards and degree requirements were raised, teaching loads were reduced and faculty salaries improved, and the physical plant was upgraded. The granting to the college in 1971 of a chapter of Phi Beta Kappa was convincing evidence of the progress that had been made.

Doubts concerning the value to Mary Washington of its affiliation with the university began to arise as the years passed.

These were accentuated in 1965 when Dr. John Dale Russell issued his report as chairman of the Higher Education Study Commission surveying the colleges and universities of the commonwealth. The report said that "Mary Washington College enjoys few advantages from its relationship with the University of Virginia, and there are some disadvantages"; and it went on:

Students at Mary Washington are treated the same as those from any other college in the country on applications for transfer to the university at Charlottesville. The benefits of the relatively large endowment funds of the university are not available for the support of the program at Mary Washington College. The college has no privilege of naming its alumnae for positions on the university Board of Visitors. There is suspicion in some quarters that the main interest of the university in maintaining Mary Washington College as a branch with enrollment limited to women students is to prevent pressure for a coeducational program in undergraduate arts and sciences at Charlottesville. Nevertheless . . . the establishment of the college on its own basis with its own Board of Visitors is not a matter of urgent importance.

However, the report went on to say that "Mary Washington will not achieve its potential as a distinguished institution until it has its own Board of Visitors and can enjoy equal status with the other state-controlled institutions of higher education in Virginia."

The advisability of terminating the relationship between Mary Washington and the university became obvious in 1970, when women were admitted to the university on the same basis as men. A coordinate college for women at Fredericksburg no longer had any reason for existence. Hence legislation was passed at the 1972 session of the General Assembly bringing the affiliation to an end. At the same time, admission of men to Mary Washington was authorized.

Foundations for two-year colleges in southwest Virginia and northern Virginia, affiliated with the university, had been laid by the Extension Division.

In the mountainous southwest numerous extension centers had been opened. There was no college or university in that extreme southwestern tip of the state. President Darden, Dean Zehmer, and Dean Stiles made a special trip to the ex-

tension center at Clinch Valley, Wise County, where enrollment was close to three hundred, with both daytime and
nighttime classes going full tilt. They were greatly impressed.
Soon thereafter leaders from that section of Virginia urged
that a two-year community college be established at Clinch
Valley by the university, and the university administration decided to open such a college on an experimental basis for the
session of 1954–55. It was an immediate success, despite numerous handicaps. President and Mrs. Darden bought about
one hundred acres of land, two lakes, and other property for
the campus. The first building was named for George Zehmer. A major influence in the development of the institution
was exerted by a remarkable man, Joseph C. Smiddy, son of
a coal miner who rose to become chancellor of the college
and guitar-playing leader of the Reedy Creek Boys bluegrass
quartet.

The Clinch Valley curriculum was divided into two parts,
the terminal program and the transfer program. The former
consisted of largely vocational and technical courses, while the
latter was modeled on the first two years of work in the College of Arts and Sciences at the University. Those who successfully completed the transfer course could shift to a four-
year institution of higher learning.

So much eagerness was demonstrated by the students and
so much cooperation by the surrounding area, that the General Assembly appropriated $110,000 for operations at its
1956 session and $500,000 for an academic building. It was
clear that Clinch Valley College was there to stay.

By the 1958–59 session the framework of the new academic
building had been erected, and the Seven Society announced
that it would provide a bust of Thomas Jefferson. Six houses
and a four-unit apartment house for faculty members had
been completed, and plans were being drawn for a gymna-
sium-auditorium. Prof. Archer Jones, who had received his
doctorate at the university in June 1958 took over as the first
dean of Clinch Valley.

Somewhat similar things were happening in northern Virginia, where the population was far more dense, and a large
percentage of the citizenry were connected with the federal
government in Washington. A great need for extension
courses was evident. An extension center was established

71. James Bakhtiar, all-American fullback, 1957.

there in 1948, and in 1956 the university's Board of Visitors authorized the setting up of a two-year coeducational branch college, which opened the following year in temporary quarters at Bailey's Crossroads, under the directorship of J. N. G. Finley, postwar dean of counseling at the university. It was called University College. In 1959 the City of Fairfax purchased 150 acres for a permanent branch campus, and donated it to the university. The institution was named for George Mason, the revolutionary statesman, and given the status of a community college.

Extension Division classes were being conducted by hundreds of study groups in practically every city and town in the state, with particular concentration in northern Virginia and the Hampton Roads area. In the latter region such highly technical subjects as the aerodynamics of supersonic flight, naval architecture, and advanced electronics were being taught. Some regular members of the university faculty were giving these courses, as with those elsewhere, but teachers from virtually all the colleges and universities in Virginia were participating in the far-flung activities of the Extension Division.

Accolades to President Darden and members of the university faculty came from many directions during these years. Darden was given highly important responsibilities of national if not international significance. In 1954 he spoke at Santiago, Chile, at the Congress of Latin American Universities, representing the Association of American Universities. The following year he was named a delegate to the United Nations. He spent about two months at the U.N. and returned to the university on several weekends when university business was pressing. In 1957 he left on a fifty-two-day world tour as a member of President Eisenhower's special committee on foreign aid. Some twenty-two thousand miles were covered and a score of countries in Europe and Asia were visited. When the group returned to Washington, they were in session at the old War and State Department Building across the street from the White House, and one member said, "Come on, let's walk over and give the President our report." "Oh no," said John L. Lewis, czar of the United Mine Workers who was a member of the committee. "We've got to go up in style. You phone and get a White House car." So a chauffeured Cadillac was summoned and the delegation drove to the main entrance, a distance of one block. All of which seemed highly absurd to Colgate Darden. . . . Two years thereafter he served as chairman of a commission to examine southern education. It issued a notable report, *Within Our Reach*, in which the point was made that the South must be judged on the same basis as the rest of the United States, with no more alibis for the region based on lower living standards or other differentials.

Teachers at the university also were honored in many ways—by European, Asian, and South American institutions or governments, as well as by some of the most prestigious universities and agencies in the United States.

Tributes to Prof. Joseph M. Carrière of the Department of Romance Languages were paid repeatedly by the French government. He was made an officer of the Academy, a knight of the Legion of Honor, was twice awarded the Prize of the French Language, elected a member of the *Centre Catholique Intellectuel Français*, and awarded an honorary degree by Canada's Laval University. Professor Carrière was chosen president of the American Association of Teachers of French and the American Association of Teachers and was elected twice to the presidency of the American Folklore Society.

Prof. Rowland Egger's awards and distinctions were so numerous as to be almost bewildering. A partial list would include financial and administrative adviser to the Bolivian government and administrative adviser to the prime minister of Pakistan, vice-president of the United Nations Administrative Tribunal, representative of the Ford Foundation in Lebanon, administrative consultant to the U.S. Departments of State, Treasury, Commerce, and Agriculture, and U.S. government representative at several meetings of the Pan American Congress. Dr. Egger was decorated by the governments of Bolivia, Belgium, and Lebanon. He was the first American to receive the British Royal Institute of Public Administration's Haldane Prize.

Prof. Oron J. Hale of the History Department was on a two-year leave of absence in 1950–52, serving as U.S. deputy land commissioner and then commissioner of Bavaria. Appointed by John J. McCloy, German high commissioner, as deputy to George N. Shuster, he succeeded Shuster when the latter returned to the presidency of Hunter College, New York. "Pat"

Hale was a recognized authority on modern Germany, the author of highly praised books and articles on that country's twentieth century history and politics.

Prof. Allan T. Gwathmey, '36, of the Chemistry Department received the Southern Chemist Award for 1952, a gold medal given at the southeastern regional meeting of the American Chemical Society. It was for his notable work with metal crystals, his leadership in establishing the Virginia Institute for Scientific Research in Richmond, which he served as president and board chairman, and "for distinguished service to the profession of chemistry in the Southern states." "Pete" Gwathmey also won the Jefferson Research Prize of the Virginia Academy of Science, of which he was elected president. The research award of the Oak Ridge Institute of Nuclear Studies likewise went to him, and he lectured to several professional groups in Europe on his work with crystals.

Recognition as one of the foremost bibliographers in this country and Europe came to Prof. Fredson T. Bowers of the English Department. He received a Fulbright grant to work on the bibliographical aspects of various Restoration plays and was in demand as a speaker in England, where he addressed the Student Book Collectors' Club in Oxford and the Bibliographical Societies in Oxford and London. His invitation to address the London Society was a most exceptional honor. Six years later, in 1958, Professor Bowers served as Sanders Lecturer in Bibliography at Trinity College, Cambridge, the first American to be invited to occupy this, the oldest bibliographical lectureship in England. The following year he was at Oxford for two months as James R. Lytell reader in bibliography. He also lectured at various leading American universities. Mrs. Bowers is Nancy Hale, the nationally known short story writer, novelist, and biographer, winner of numerous important literary awards.

The Butler Medal was awarded by Columbia University in 1952 to Prof. Albert G. A. Balz, '09, longtime chairman of the Philosophy Department. The medal goes annually to the Columbia graduate who has shown the most competence in the fields of philosophy or educational theory. Balz, a Columbia Ph.D., published *Cartesian Studies* in 1951 and *Descartes and the Modern Mind* in 1952.

72. *William S. Weedon, University Professor of Philosophy.*

73. *Joseph C. Smiddy, chancellor of Clinch Valley College.*

Mathematics Professors Gordon T. Whyburn and Edward J. McShane were winning so many honors that it was difficult to keep up with them. Whyburn was elected president of the American Mathematical Society and McShane was chosen almost simultaneously as president of the Mathematical Association of America. Several years later McShane was named to the presidency of the society. Whyburn was also vice-president and chairman of the American Association for the Advancement of Science and served as managing editor of the *Journal* of the American Mathematical Society. Both men represented the United States at the International Mathematics Conference at Amsterdam in 1954. McShane also was a delegate to the International Mathematical Union at The Hague.

Dr. G. Slaughter Fitz-Hugh, chairman of the Department of Otolaryngology in the Medical School, was elected president of the American Laryngological Association and the Virginia Society of Ophthalmology and Otolaryngology, as well as chairman of the Section of Otolaryngology of the Southern Medical Association. He received the Certificate of Merit of the American Academy of Ophthalmology and Otolaryngology and the Robley Dunglison Award of the university's Medical School.

Law Prof. Hardy C. Dillard, '27, was addressing prestigious groups in this country and abroad. A partial list of his appointments and engagements during the middle 1950s would include: member of the executive committee, American Society of International Law and of the editorial board of the *American Journal of International Law*; civilian consultant to the Army War College and lecturer there and at the Armed Forces Staff College; delegate to important conferences at Stanford University and Arden House, New York; lecturer at The Hague on "Some Aspects of War and Diplomacy," the lectures published in the *Recueil des Cours* of the *Académie de Droit International*.

Another member of the law faculty, Prof. Charles S. Gregory, was the recipient of honors that were international in scope. At the invitation of the Australian universities' law schools he spoke before seven of them in all parts of the country, under the auspices of the Carnegie Foundation. He also gave a series of public lectures in Australia on torts and labor relations. In addition, Gregory was appointed by Attorney General Herbert Brownell, Jr., to a committee for the study of the antitrust laws.

Prof. Jesse W. Beams was winning awards of great prestige for his invention of the ultracentrifuge. This device was not only significant in the development of the atom bomb, but it also contributed to the solution of biological and medical problems involving viruses, hormones, and enzymes. Solutions were brought nearer by virtue of the fact that it was possible with Dr. Beams's extraordinary device to spin tiny spheres at one million revolutions per second. The American Physical Society, of which he was elected president a few years later, awarded him the John Scott Medal and a check for $1,000. The Lewis Prize of the American Philosophical Society went to Dr. Beams for his address to the society on the ultracentrifuge. He was also the recipient of the University of Virginia's first annual Thomas Jefferson Award. This award was made possible by a gift from Robert E. McConnell of The Plains, who provided for a grant of $500 each year to the member of the faculty who has contributed "by personal influence, teaching and scholarship toward inspiring those high ideals for the advancement of which Mr. Jefferson founded the university."

Edward C. Stevenson, '31, professor of physics, was one of forty or more leading civilian scientists and industrialists who were serving on the Army Scientific Advisory Panel, established to advise the secretary of the army and army chief of staff on the development of a more effective and economical fighting force. Professor Stevenson was on the Harvard faculty for eight years before World War II and later was transferred to Los Alamos, N.M., where he helped to develop the firing mechanism for the atomic bomb.

The Fisher Award, highest award of the American Chemical Society in the field of analytical chemistry, with a check for $1,000, went to Prof. John H. Yoe in 1957. Dr. Yoé also was chosen chairman of the society's Division of Analytical Chemistry. In addition he was named as one of eleven U.S. delegates selected by the National Academy of Sciences and the National Research Council to represent the Academy Research Council at the Fifteenth International Congress of Pure and

Applied Chemistry at Lisbon. Yoe also attended a meeting of the International Commission on Analytical Reactions in the same Portuguese city.

Prof. Frank A. Geldard of the Department of Psychology was on leave for the session of 1956–57, serving as scientific liaison officer for the U.S. Office of Naval Research, with headquarters in London. He had served during the previous year as president of the Division of Experimental Psychology of the American Psychological Association and was elected to the Committee on Awards of that association and to the council of the American Association for the Advancement of Science.

A remarkable series of honors came to Dr. Vincent W. Archer, '23, chairman of the Department of Radiology in the Medical School for well over a quarter of a century. He was chosen in 1958 to head the American College of Radiology, with over five thousand members. Three years later he was awarded the College Gold Medal, the organization's highest honor. Dr. Archer had been a member of the American Medical Association's House of Delegates for many years. He also was credited with a greater degree of responsibility than any other individual for the Virginia General Assembly's $5,900,-000 appropriation in 1955 for the multistory addition to the university's Medical Center. Dr. Archer had received the first award of the Southern Medical Association in 1949 and in the same year the American Roentgen Ray Association's silver medal.

Lecture engagements in all parts of India were filled in 1958–59 by Prof. Edward Younger of the History Department under a Fulbright lectureship at the University of Allahabad, where he taught U.S. history and government. He would return for another lecture engagement in India three summers later and in 1960–61 would be on leave to the U.S. Naval War College as Ernest J. King Professor of Maritime and Diplomatic History.

Prof. Frank L. Hereford, Jr., accepted an invitation to spend a year as Fulbright scholar at Birmingham University, England, doing research with their multibillion-volt ion accelerator. He was cowinner, with S. Berko, of the J. Shelton Horsley Research Award of the Virginia Academy of Science.

Dean Thomas K. Fitz Patrick of the School of Architecture was elected president of the National Architectural Accrediting Board, of which he had been secretary for some years. He was past president of the Association of Collegiate Schools of Architecture and in 1957 was elected to the College of Fellows of the American Institute of Architects.

Studies of the Soviet Union's economic growth by Prof. G. Warren Nutter of the Economics Department had attracted "worldwide attention," according to Prof. James M. Buchanan, chairman of the department. Nutter had been engaged in this inquiry for four years, and the results had been "widely acclaimed."

The foregoing list of distinctions, citations, lectureships, and other accolades accorded University of Virginia professors during these years is by no means complete. It is, however, representative of the wide range of important recognition received by the institution's administrators and teachers.

Gregory Swanson, a black graduate of the Howard University Law School who had been practicing law for two years, applied for permission to take graduate courses in the University of Virginia Law School for the session 1950–51. Attorney General J. Lindsay Almond informed the university's Board of Visitors that "refusal to admit Swanson cannot be successfully defended in court." The board, nevertheless, rejected Swanson's application on the ground that acceptance would be a violation of Virginia law. Swanson appealed, and the U.S. Circuit Court of Appeals ordered him admitted, an outcome said on good authority to have been in full accord with President Darden's wishes. He entered the Law School in the fall of 1950. The black was well received, according to various opinions, but he remained in school only a few months and dropped out in July 1951. In Darden's view he did so because he was not sufficiently well prepared for graduate work. Swanson said that the university students did not care about racial equality or the welfare of the country, according to Bryan Kay's "History of Desegregation at the University of Virginia: 1950–1969."

Actually, Swanson had not been the first Negro enrolled at the institution. The decision of the court in the Swanson case validated the entry of other black graduate students, and Walter N. Ridley, with baccalaureate and master's degrees from Howard University, applied in January 1950 in order to complete his doctorate in the philosophy of education. Three years later the degree was awarded by the School of Education, and Ridley became the first black to earn a doctorate at a major white southern university.

In 1958 a tense situation arose in the Charlottesville public schools, two of which had been closed under the state's "massive resistance" policy, and student leaders at the university cautioned matriculates arriving in September to "refrain from any actions that may tend to aggravate the problem." They seem to have heeded this advice.

The coed question was a lively one during this period, and the prevailing view among the male students continued to be that such ladies as were already there had to be tolerated, but no more were wanted.

True, Elinor Mickey was nominated in 1949 by the Student Party for a place on the Student Council, an unprecedented thing. She was from the Department of Education and active with the Virginia Players. Miss Mickey agreed to run, but the *Cavalier Daily* demurred. It pointed out that the women students had their own governing association and that the Student Council "is concerned with the activities of male students." The council "would be embarrassed, we submit, by the presence of a coed member," said the editor. Miss Mickey withdrew from the race.

At the same time, the newspaper expressed sincere regret that Lucy Stockwell was resigning from the University News Service. "Her news releases, which are carried by the *CD* almost every day of publication without a by-line are a boon to harried city editors and . . . a boon to the paper and its readers," said the publication.

In another area the coeds had installed a branch of the Lychnos Society at the university. It recognized women students who were foremost in scholarship and leadership. Lychnos was not unlike the Raven Society.

"There are women everywhere—in my classes, all over the Grounds and generally in the hair of myself and of most of

74. Vincent Shea, vice-president for business and finance.

the friends I have made since I arrived here," Brockett Muir, Jr., a first-year man, wrote in a letter to the student newspaper. "Do not think I am a woman hater. I love them—in their place. But a woman's place is not in a gentleman's university. . . . I want to send my sons here, but not if the place has become infested with women."

Cavalier withers were being wrung by the spectacle of Virginia coeds returning in shorts from playing tennis. "All of the women's colleges in Virginia require a young lady to wear a raincoat at the very least when she is wearing shorts," the editor of the *Cavalier Daily* admonished. "And here at the university, where all the men attire themselves as befits a gentleman, even that little bit is not being done." The paper suggested that coeds should always "wear stockings and heels to classes, which (we are naturally and excusably a bit shaky on our facts at this point) seems to be the female equivalent of coats and ties."

Yet by the close margin of 1,237 to 1,064, coeds were given the right to vote in student elections. The decision had previously been made that they were ineligible for seats on the Student Council since they had their own governmental apparatus.

Tantrums erupted in the sanctum of the *Cavalier Daily* when an announcement was made asking "all students, male and female, interested in cheerleading . . . to attend the practice today." "After years of futile struggle," wailed the editor, "we have finally become at least tolerant of the female race in the classroom. . . . But must we face the unpleasant prospect of hearing their titters and giggles in front of us at every football game?"

A strong dissent from the bleating of these misogynists was sounded in verse by Jack Cole, who boldly proclaimed:

I've been a student here for not too long a time;
More than some, but less than some, and now I feel that I'm
To a fair degree accustomed to the sights and smells and sounds.
I know that "frat" is frowned upon, and campus means the
    Grounds.
I try to frown when someone mentions that ping-pong enormity
And just like everybody else I reek with non-conformity
Until about a month ago I seemed to fit in fine,
But now I'm having trouble with this attitude of mine.

There has lately been some mention of a move to this vicinity
On the part of certain schools which overflow with femininity.
A mere whispering of this has got some students most perplexed
But I think I might enjoy it—do you think I'm oversexed?
There've been letters to the editor a-voicing mournful wail
At the thought that in our little nest we soon might find some quail.
There've been some screams of anguish raised against our friends
    with tossing curls,
And I've tried to scream along in tune, but Dammit, I like girls!

This amusing dissent seemed all the more noteworthy in view of the vast preponderance of student sentiment in the opposite direction.

In another area of student opinion it was even more obvious than before that Jews were accepted without prejudice by the great majority at Virginia. William L. Shapero was elected president of both the Law School and the Class of 1951, and was a member of Tilka, IMP, and the Thirteen Society. A few years later Tom Hofheimer was vice-president of the Student Council, treasurer of Skull & Keys, and a member of the Ravens, Omicron Delta Kappa, and the Thirteen Society. About a decade after that, Tony Markel was an Eli, Z, and Thirteen, as well as vice-president of the College and a member of the IFC governing board. Other examples might be mentioned.

It was during these years that C. Waller Barrett, '20, was donating his monumental collection of books, manuscripts, and letters by American authors to Alderman Library. Authoritatively described as the most valuable assemblage of materials on American literature in existence, it includes some forty thousand books and three hundred thousand manuscripts valued at tens of millions of dollars. Having built a fortune in shipping, Mr. Barrett retired early and devoted his ability and energy to putting together this amazing collection, representing well over one thousand novelists, essayists, short story writers, historians, poets, and dramatists extending from the American Revolution to the present. Numerous rare manuscripts and letters, as well as first editions, many inscribed by the authors, have been brought together. Nearly five hundred of the writers were considered by Mr. Barrett to be of such importance that he collected them in depth, that is, everything

in printed form, as well as manuscripts and letters by or related to them.

The breadth of the collection may be partially glimpsed
from the fact that seven New England writers are so fully represented that "no research on these authors can safely be undertaken without consulting the material in the Barrett library," Herbert Cahoon, curator of manuscripts in New York
City's Pierpont Morgan Library, has stated. The seven are
Hawthorne, Longfellow, Holmes, Thoreau, Emerson, Whit-
tier, and James Russell Lowell.

The finest collection in existence of works by Edgar Allan
Poe was an early presentation by Waller Barrett. It was given
in honor of James Southall Wilson, whose letter to Barrett in
the early 1940s turned his attention as a collector to Alderman
Library. Included were Poe's rare first published work (1827)
as well as *El Aaraaf, Tamerlane and Minor Poems* (1829), both,
unfortunately, stolen from the library in 1974 and never re-
covered.

Other southern writers, such as William Gilmore Simms,
Paul Hamilton Hayne, Henry Timrod, Sidney Lanier, Joel
Chandler Harris, and O. Henry are covered in depth. Important modern authors, such as Willa Cather, Steinbeck, Hem-
ingway, Dreiser, Mencken, and Vachel Lindsay are well represented.

The Barrett Library, consulted by scholars from all over the
world, is handsomely housed in a paneled room adjoining that
of the McGregor Library, also in an appropriate room of its
own.

When the Barrett collection was formally dedicated, many
who attended the ceremonies adjourned to the Farmington
Country Club. Two university students were discussing the
gift, and one was overheard by Barrett to remark: "This university needs a football team, and what do we get—a goddam
liberry!" Nobody laughed any more heartily at this abysmal
gaffe than Waller Barrett.

The Alderman Library archival resources had been sharply
upgraded by the intensive work of Francis L. Berkeley, Jr., in
the years immediately after World War II. He had been appointed university archivist succeeding able Lester J. Cappon,
who resigned to accept a position with the Institute of Early
American History and Culture in Williamsburg. Berkeley was

"an ideal successor" to Cappon, in the opinion of Librarian Harry Clemons, and he spent the next five or six years "prowling through Virginia," as he put it, in search of manuscripts. It was high time that a dedicated effort of this sort was made to counteract, as far as possible, the massive roundup of Virginia materials carried away in the 1920s and 1930s by J. G. de Roulhac Hamilton and others, who carted them off to North Carolina and elsewhere. In a few years Alderman Library had so many manuscripts that it had difficulty making room for them, and it was obvious that the building would have to be enlarged. For his part in achieving this result and for his other services to scholarship, Frank Berkeley received high praise. Walter Muir Whitehill, an international authority in the field, wrote more than a decade later in his book *Independent Historical Societies*: "Few men are as widely beloved as he for their unobtrusive and disinterested service to learning. Berkeley continues not only to guide the manuscript division [of Alderman] but to play a vital role in the affairs of the Virginia Historical Society, of the project for microfilming Virginia materials overseas, and of most scholarly enterprises that concern Virginia history."

Harry Clemons retired as librarian in 1950 after a highly productive career during which he made an immeasurable contribution to the library in many directions, "while," as one of his associates expressed it, "subtly arranging matters so that somebody else got the credit." When Clemons became librarian in 1927 the book collection totaled 151,333 volumes and when he retired twenty-three years later the figure was 1,592,333. But the bare figures tell little of the "development of the personality, spirit and service of a great institution," as the *Alumni News* put it. Mr. Clemons's retirement was in large degree nominal, since he embarked at once on a three-pronged program which included a history of the library, an appraisal of its books and other collections, and preparation of a list of materials it needed.

Harry Clemons's successor was Jack Dalton, '35, who had been on the library staff since 1936 as reference and associate librarian. He was in the office for six years, at the end of which time he resigned to accept appointment as director of the international relations office of the American Library Association. An innovation of his incumbency was to open the library stacks to undergraduates. Dalton enjoyed "high esteem in the ranks of his colleagues throughout the world," John Cook Wyllie, '29, who succeeded him as librarian, wrote following his departure.

John Wyllie had been curator of rare books and of the McGregor Library when chosen librarian at Alderman. Described as one of the two ablest professional bibliophiles in the United States, he had a remarkably diversified career. After a year in the early 1930s spent touring Europe and visiting libraries, binderies, and booksellers, he was named curator of the Virginia manuscript collection. When Alderman Library opened he was appointed director of the rare books and manuscripts division. Before the United States entered World War II, Wyllie joined the American Field Service and drove ambulances for the British in the Middle East. Then he served as an officer in the U.S. Air Force, had hair-raising experiences in the China-Burma-India theater, and was decorated by the American, British, and Chinese governments. After his return to the university he received the Raven and Algernon Sydney Sullivan Awards. Wyllie reorganized the University of Virginia Press in 1948 and took a leading role in establishing the Albemarle County Historical Society and the University of Virginia Bibliographical Society. His indefatigability is seen in the fact that he sometimes worked all night at the library and was found asleep in his chair in the morning.

Wyllie appointed Francis Berkeley and Louise Savage associate librarians in 1958, and Berkeley resigned as secretary to the Board of Visitors. He was succeeded in the latter post by Weldon Cooper, professor of political science and director of the Bureau of Public Administration, which changed its name in 1964 to the Institute of Government. "Frank" Berkeley continued as curator of the library's millions of historical and literary manuscripts. As chief of acquisitions, Miss Savage, who had been with the library since 1930, continued to schedule the flow of some 40,000 or more books added to the collections each year.

The family of the late John Stewart Bryan gave the library valuable letters covering the period 1770–1887. The Randolph, Tucker, and Bland families, among others, were represented, and the collection included 150 letters from John Randolph of Roanoke, 200 from St. George Tucker of Wil-

75. Dr. Henry B. Mulholland of the medical faculty.

liamsburg, and numerous others from Theoderick Bland, Judge Henry St. George Tucker, Nathaniel Beverley Tucker, William Wirt, and Francis Walker Gilmer.

Valuable collections on optics were acquired through the good offices of two alumni, James P. C. Southall, of the Columbia University faculty, and Lincoln M. Polan, of the Zenith Optical Company. Southall was instrumental in securing the collection on optics of Adolph and Henry C. Lomb of New York State, and upon his retirement he presented his own fine collection on physics, a considerable part of which dealt with optics. Polan paid a portion of the cost of cataloguing the Lomb collection and solicited contributions from other optical companies toward a fund to expand the university's optics collection.

The *Virginia Quarterly Review* celebrated its twenty-fifth anniversary in 1950 amid tributes from various directions, and with a contributors' list over the years that sounded like an international who's-who of literary luminaries. Every short story published in the magazine the following year was selected for republication or honorable mention in one of the best-stories-of-the-year collections. The autumn issue had three nonfiction articles chosen among the country's "ten best" by a Council of Librarians. The *VQR* had three more articles among the "ten best" in its 1953 winter issue. Five years later the magazine received a remarkable tribute in the *Times* of London. Oliver Edwards stated in the newspaper's "Talking of Books" column that the *Virginia Quarterly* "provides as stimulating a harvest of reading as one can find anywhere." Charlotte Kohler was editor during this period and would remain so for nearly three decades, making a distinguished record. She succeeded Prof. Archibald B. Shepperson in 1946; he had returned from the service and resumed the editorship for one year. Miss Kohler had been acting editor during the war. A $125,000 bequest from Emily Clark Balch provided $1,500 a year for literary prizes to be awarded annually by the quarterly. Part of her legacy also went toward increases in salaries of English faculty members, and part made possible the appointment of writers in residence.

The first such writer was Nobel Prize winner William Faulkner. He came with Mrs. Faulkner during the second term of the 1956–57 session, visited with English classes, and answered questions concerning his books and writing in general. He also consulted with faculty and students and gave several public readings. Faulkner accepted an invitation to return as writer in residence for the second term the following session. He had been a frequent visitor to the university, since his daughter Jill was married to Paul D. Summers, Jr., a student in the Law School.

Katherine Anne Porter, author of novels and short stories, was the next writer in residence. She came in the fall of 1958 for one semester.

Dumas Malone, on a sabbatical from Columbia University, came back to Charlottesville for the session of 1958–59 as visiting professor of history. He conducted a seminar on the Jeffersonian period and worked on his monumental biography of Thomas Jefferson. Malone retired at that time from Columbia and remained at the University of Virginia as Thomas Jefferson Memorial Foundation Professor of History, a chair established especially for him. He subsequently became professor emeritus and biographer in residence, with grants from various national foundations to aid him in his work.

Serving with Malone at the university was Merrill Peterson, also an internationally recognized authority on the master of Monticello. Peterson, who succeeded Malone as Thomas Jefferson Memorial Foundation Professor, was the author of *Jefferson's Image in the American Mind*, awarded the Bancroft Prize, *Thomas Jefferson and the New Nation*, and other highly regarded works. He and Malone were two of the three leading authorities in the world on the career of the university's founder.

The University of Virginia Press—at that time, as it is now, a printing establishment but not a publishing house—was winning acclaim for the quality of its product. It moved in 1950 from the Corner into its new building between Scott Stadium and Thornton Hall. Managed from 1935 to 1950 by John S. Peters, an alumnus, the press had its origins as far back as 1829, when it was founded to publish the *Virginia Literary Museum*. Operations were fragmentary and primitive for many years. In 1912 President Alderman approved the purchase of a multigraph, which was set up in the southwest wing of the Rotunda in what was then the bursar's office. The press printed examinations and tests, hospital forms, circulars, and letterheads under the direction of Virginia E. Moran, an assistant in the bursar's office, until she left in 1919 to become assistant registrar. It functioned under the general supervision of the bursar until Peters came. Much better equipment was obtained at that time and the press turned out a series of books in collaboration with the McGregor Library and another for the Bibliographical Society, after the society's founding in the late forties. The first volume issued under the sole imprint of the University Press was a new edition of Charles Smith's *The University of Virginia—Thirty-Two Woodcuts*. Soon thereafter a new edition of *Memoirs of a Monticello Slave*, the recollections of Isaac Jefferson, was produced. Peters had left to accept a position at the University of Georgia, and Charles E. Moran, Jr., '36, recently proprietor of the Shamrock Press in Charlottesville, succeeded him. Under his direction the press continued to win awards for the quality of its work. In 1957, for example, two of its half-dozen books were chosen among the twenty-five best for the year in design and format, in competition with seventeen other publishers and printers. At that time the plant was printing the *Cavalier Daily*, university catalogues, and the *University News Letter*, as well as news letters for the Departments of Law and Medicine, hospital forms, and miscellaneous materials. President Darden had said early in his administration that establishment of "an endowed University Press" was one of his major objectives, but he was never able to bring this about. It remained for his successor in office, Edgar Shannon, to find the money and set in operation the University Press of Virginia. Important steps toward this objective were taken during the incumbency of Charles E. Moran, Jr.

Unprecedented expansion and improvement in the university's physical plant was carried out under President Darden. By the opening of the session of 1950–51 the following major undertakings had been completed or were under way:

Residence houses for men on the old golf links, ten units to accommodate 1,244 students, $3,000,000. They were named for Professors Charles Bonnycastle and John Patten Emmet, from the original faculty, and Professors Richard Heath Dabney, William H. Echols, Charles Hancock, Charles W. Kent,

76. B. F. D. Runk, dean of the university, 1959–68.

Albert Lefevre, John Calvin Metcalf, James M. Page, and Milton W. Humphreys, from more recent times.

Annex behind Cabell Hall, five stories and basement, U-shaped, accommodating all departments of the College of Arts and Sciences except the natural sciences, business administration, music, and art, $1,800,000.

Student Union Building (Newcomb Hall), three stories behind Peabody Hall, a center for all student activities, $1,800,-000.

Chemical engineering wing for Thornton Hall, $250,000.

Hospital wing to provide more space for care and feeding of patients, $370,000.

Cancer research wing of Medical School, three stories with upper floor devoted to neurosurgery, $250,000.

Women's dormitory near Alumni Hall, corner of Routes 250 and 29, $465,000.

Heat and power lines and plant, $1,000,000.

In addition, President Darden took a special interest in the beautification of the Grounds. He appointed a Restoration Committee, headed by Prof. Allan T. Gwathmey, and initiated a ten-year program. Many trees on the Lawn were in bad condition, and these were replaced. With the cooperation of the Garden Club of Virginia a plan to restore Thomas Jefferson's gardens between the Lawn and Ranges was launched. Mrs. Herbert McK. Smith of Staunton, a leader in the Garden Club and member of the university's Board of Visitors, was a key figure here. Proceeds from Garden Week over a number of years were devoted to the project, and the Maverick Plan, engraved by Peter Maverick for Jefferson in the 1820s, was followed. Restoration of the West Gardens was completed during Darden's term, but the East Gardens were not finished until he had retired from the presidency. Throughout his incumbency he spent much time touring the Grounds with Sylvester O'Grince, buildings and grounds director. From one hundred to two hundred trees, on the Lawn and elsewhere, were replaced. A shade-tree replacement nursery was opened on Copeley Hill, and a program of planting flowering trees to supplement shade trees was got under way. Darden sent to the Norfolk Botanical Gardens for azaleas, some of which were planted between Cabell Hall and its annex. An azalea and camellia nursery was opened in the picnic area across from the new dormitories. A small garden was planted at the Engineering School.

As part of Darden's plan for reducing the cost of attending the university, a cafeteria accommodating 600 students was opened on Emmet Street between the new residence houses and the university's academic buildings. "Good chow at a reasonable price," in the words of one student, was offered. The price was $190 per semester for all meals. Accommodations in the new dormitories were $135 for the session, and it was calculated that a student who took his meals at the cafeteria and lived in these dormitories would save something like $200 on the session.

A landmark was liquidated when the gymnasium's reflecting pool was filled in. Completed in 1923, the pool had been used for skating in winter and by youthful and overoptimistic fishermen in summer. But it filled gradually with mud, became an eyesore and was dubbed "the little Okefenokee." The area it had occupied became an intramural playing field.

A new organ for the University Chapel was dedicated in memory of Robert Osborne Price, '88, the gift of his widow. Mrs. Price came from California for the occasion. Bishop Henry St. George Tucker, '95, retired presiding bishop of the Episcopal Church, conducted the ceremonies, and Prof. Vernon McCasland, chairman of the Department of Religion, made the presentation on behalf of the donor.

Pavilions II, III, and VI on the Lawn were being restored in the mid-1950s, under the direction of Prof. Frederick D. Nichols, to make them as nearly as possible exactly as they were in Jefferson's day. All were to be occupied by professors. With the completion of the Cabell Hall annex the Department of Romance Languages moved there, and Pavilion VI, the Romance Pavilion, became available as a residence. Each of the ten pavilions had been enlarged at one time or another. These additions were not being given the strict restoration treatment that was accorded the original structures, but modern conveniences were installed in some of them.

A new $1,500,000 home for the Department of Physics on McCormick Road across from Thornton Hall was ready for the session of 1954–55. Together with the latter structure, it formed the nucleus of what was envisaged as the university's center for pure and applied science. The U.S. Army was using the university as its principal center for giving atomic scientists advanced training in nuclear physics.

Excavation was begun for a new dormitory costing approximately three hundred thousand dollars and located on the hillside back of Clark Hall, home of the Law School. The building was to be leased for five years to the Judge Advocate General's School for the use of officers staffing it or studying in it. The school's military men were attending classes in Clark Hall, where they had their own study hall and access to the Law School's excellent library. About one thousand two hundred officers were passing through the school each year.

Two famous rooming houses were in the news. Fire destroyed the third floor of Miss Betty Booker's fashionable rooming house, corner of University Avenue and Madison Lane, and damaged the first and second floors. Mrs. E. M. Page closed her boarding and rooming house, a landmark in the community for nearly sixty years. Mrs. Page sold the big brick building, and it was torn down to make way for a parking lot. Generations of students had lived there or taken their meals at her table. It was long the most socially acceptable dining facility on the Grounds.

When Newcomb Hall was opened in 1958, many wondered how there could have been so much student opposition. Kendrick Dure, president of the Student Union, remarked that he had heard numerous students say "I don't know how we've gotten along without it."

The new facility contained two cafeterias serving one thousand eight hundred students three times a day; lounges, meeting rooms, music rooms, and a large, handsome lounge that could be converted into a ball room, an auditorium, a motion picture theater, or a banquet hall for from five hundred to six hundred persons. The structure was six stories in all, including space for meat and food storage in the basement, air conditioning and heating operations, several dark rooms, and eight bowling alleys. There were billiard and pool tables, table tennis, game rooms for chess, checkers, and bridge. In addition, the offices of the Honor Committee, Judiciary Committee, and other student organizations and publications were in the building. Grass, shrubs, and trees were planted on the surrounding area.

Thornton Hall, built originally for not more than three hundred students, was being enlarged once more, at a cost of $761,000. This addition was to accommodate aeronautical and mechanical engineering students. Total enrollment had risen to 887 by 1959 with the largest group in electrical engineering, aeronautical and mechanical tying for second place, civil engineering next, and chemical last.

In order to attract instructors and assistant professors who would aid in caring for increased enrollment throughout the university, twelve small family housing units were being built on the Piedmont, or Maury, estate on Route 29 south of Charlottesville near the Albemarle County line. Six or eight more such houses were planned.

The new University Hospital, costing $6,700,000, was completed in 1960, after several years of construction. It provided beds for 419 patients, giving the hospital an overall total of 620 beds, all fireproofed and air conditioned. Of the total cost, the commonwealth appropriated nearly $5,900,000, with the rest coming from Hill-Burton and other federal funds.

Guiding and supervising the growth of the university's physical plant since 1931 was Frank E. Hartman, '11, who directed the planning and construction of a score or more of buildings over nearly three decades and the enlargement or renovation of many others, all at a total cost in excess of fifteen million dollars. Hartman succeeded Charles H. Chandler, '15, as director of buildings and grounds, a title changed by President Darden to "director of new construction." "As long as he had supervision of the university grounds, he gave constant care to their improvement and beautification," said the *Alumni News*. Frank Hartman died in 1959.

An ambitious program to raise $7,800,000 for university development was launched in 1947, with Fleet Adm. William F. Halsey, 1900, as chairman. Admiral Halsey, one of the heroes of the war in the Pacific, stated that part of the money would be used to acquire a new Alumni Hall to honor the alumni who served in the armed forces in World War II. The drive was launched in the spring of 1947 and continued for three years. At the end of that time only $1,431,000 had been raised. Various explanations were offered. Among them were unexpected postwar conditions that kept taxes high, the fact that various other institutions were carrying on similar fund-raising efforts, and the argument that the financial needs of a state institution should be met by the state. Only 18 percent of the alumni contributed, and not a single gift was obtained from any endowed foundation. In view of this disappointing outcome, a permanent fund-raising group called "Mr. Jefferson's Sponsors" was set up with Knox Turnbull, '41, a prominent Charlottesville insurance man, as president.

Despite the failure of the postwar drive for funds, money was secured to complete the remodeling and expansion of Alumni Hall as a memorial to alumni who died in the war. A loan for completion of the work was made from the University of Virginia Endowment Fund. It was expected that $80,000 could be raised in the annual alumni fund drive to pay off the debt on the building. Nearly one thousand alumni were on hand for the opening at the 1950 finals.

Other vitally important financial assistance had been made available from the university's Endowment Fund when it provided half the cost of acquiring Copeley Hill for the erection of housing for veterans returning from the war. The fund also made possible the acquisition of the property at the southwest corner of highways 250 and 29 on which a dormitory for women was erected. Another service was the purchase for Alderman Library of the notable book collection of Edward L. Stone of Roanoke, illustrating the history of the printing art.

A gratifying development in the area of alumni affairs was the selection of the *Alumni News* in 1949 as the best alumni publication in the United States and Canada with circulation between 4,000 and 6,999. Marvin B. Perry, Jr., was the editor.

A brick wall enclosing the yard on the side of Alumni Hall was contributed in 1955 by Mr. and Mrs. Colgate Darden in tribute to J. Malcolm Luck for his twenty-five years as director of alumni affairs. It bears a tablet expressing "grateful appreciation of the years of faithful service which Mac Luck has given the Alumni Association . . . . and as a token of devotion and respect for him." Edwin B. Meade, '20, president of the Alumni Association, announced that $6,150 had been raised from 927 alumni as a gift to Luck, and a check in that amount was presented to him. Three years later, at age sixty-five, Luck retired and was the guest of honor at a largely attended din-

77. *Mary Slaughter, first woman to win a varsity "V," 1954,
and women's eastern intercollegiate tennis champion that same
year.*

ner. President Darden was the speaker, and the retiring alumni secretary was presented with a Cadillac automobile, $5,000 in cash, a handsome silver tray, a portrait, and other gifts. Responding, Luck thanked Darden for his unfailing cooperation and his willingness to speak at countless alumni meetings. He added that President Alderman also had been quite cooperative, but that while President Newcomb's attitude was friendly, his position, in effect, was "let the alumni run the Alumni Association and leave the running of the university to me."

Gilbert J. Sullivan, '48, assistant to Luck for a decade, was chosen to succeed him. A native of Fredericksburg, "Gilly" Sullivan received his B.S. in commerce at age nineteen, was a varsity quarterback in football, and member of O.D.K., Tilka, Z, the Raven Society, and Sigma Alpha Epsilon social fraternity. He had been named to the assistantship when Jere Hanson, the incumbent, was drowned. During his ten years in the post, Sullivan served as secretary to the Student Aid Foundation, member of the Colonnade Club's board of directors, and commanding officer of Company K, 116th Infantry, Virginia National Guard, the Monticello Guard.

Clay E. Delauney, '35, became director of the Alumni Fund in 1957, succeeding George B. Eager III, who resigned to accept a position with Colonial Williamsburg. Delauney had been on the staff of the National Association of Manufacturers for the preceding nine years.

Lewis D. Crenshaw, first full-time secretary of the Alumni Association, died in 1947 in New York City. A boulder in his memory was placed behind Alumni Hall in 1965 by the Class of 1914. The tablet says it was "in gratitude for his services in peace and war to his fellow alumni."

Many leading members of the faculty died during President Darden's incumbency.

French Prof. Richard H. Wilson passed on in 1948. There was probably never a faculty member like him, at the University of Virginia or anywhere else. As his colleague Prof. T. Braxton Woody expressed it: "He lived in a house down on Park Street. He would receive no one, no one was allowed inside his house. He cut himself off completely from the life of the university. He would come to his classes . . . leave to go home. He never went to a faculty meeting, he never was on a committee, he never did anything. He didn't have a secretary, he didn't have a typewriter, he didn't even write letters. It's just unbelievable that a man could be head of a department (Romance Languages), and do absolutely nothing as chairman." And that isn't all. "He had an elaborate contempt for what is now called scholarship, and he did not want any of his men to do any research. . . . No professor in the department ever published anything. . . . He was immensely popular, very, very eccentric. . . . His classes were enormous."

Professor Woody's account of oral examinations for the doctorate, held by Professor Wilson in the Salle Lafayette of the Romance Pavilion is equally memorable. The room had no light, no heat, and no air conditioning. "We would hold these things at night," said Woody. " 'Dickie' Wilson was a great showman; all the professors and candidates had to have on evening clothes. You would come in a tuxedo by candlelight, and you would have a silver pitcher and glass of water, and that was all. I will never forget one night that it was so blistering hot up there that we all nearly died. That was the night that Fillmore Norfleet and Roberta Hollingsworth Gwathmey got their Ph.D.'s."

A remarkable number of nationally eminent teachers of Romance languages were trained under Wilson. For years he taught all the French, Italian, and Spanish in the university, but was best known as a teacher of French. He wrote novels under several pseudonyms, two of which were successful, as well as numerous short stories.

Another loss was the death in 1949 of Prof. Garrard Glenn of the Law Faculty. Called preeminently "a lawyer's lawyer," he was much admired by his students and by the legal profession. He wrote highly acclaimed books on creditors' rights, fraudulent conveyances, liquidation, and mortgages. Prof. Armistead M. Dobie said of him that "as a teacher, Glenn had a few equals in the annals of American legal education. . . . A profound master of every subject he taught, he spoke as one having authority, yet the soundness of his scholarship was matched by his genuine humility and his enduring kindliness."

Almost simultaneously with the death of Garrard Glenn came that of Walter A. Montgomery, professor of Latin and a pupil at Johns Hopkins of the great Basil Gildersleeve. He had been on the faculty since 1929. Prof. John C. Metcalf wrote that he was "a man of wide and varied culture, versed in foreign languages and literatures, as well as in the classics. . . He knew his Shakespeare as well as his Plautus and Terence." Metcalf referred also to Montgomery's "ready wit, his infallible sense of humor, his clever repartee, his tolerance, and his genuine interest in life and letters."

A few months later the university community was shocked by the death of Dr. Staige D. Blackford, professor of the practice of medicine. Only fifty years of age, Dr. Blackford was at the height of his career when coronary thrombosis struck. He had reorganized the hospital's Outpatient Department and served as chairman of the Committee on Postgraduate Medical Education, both of which responsibilities he had discharged with unusual ability. In addition he was the first chairman of the hospital's clinical staff and first editor of the *Medical Alumni Bulletin*. Dr. Blackford had been a popular and admired leader since his days at Episcopal High School. At Virginia he had been captain of the football team and president of the class of 1925. The Raven Award was his in 1942. He enlisted as an ambulance driver in World War I, although under age for military service, and organized the 8th Evacuation Hospital in World War II, was decorated in both wars, and ended his career in the second with the rank of colonel. There was universal sorrow at the untimely death of this exceptionally talented and dedicated student of medicine and teacher of youth.

Only a week after Dr. Blackford's death the Medical School suffered another serious loss with the death of Dr. Robert V. Funsten, professor of orthopedic surgery, who succumbed to a heart attack at age fifty-six. He had been on the faculty since 1932 and had served as president of the Virginia Orthopedic Surgeons. Dr. Funsten wrote many scientific reports and developed numerous devices used extensively in the cure of orthopedic patients. His textbook on orthopedic nursing was regarded by many as the best in the field.

Another death in the summer of 1949 was that of Professor W. Harrison Faulkner, head of the Department of Germanic Languages and a member of the faculty since 1902, the year he got his Ph.D. at the university. He had retired four years previously, recognized as one of the superior teachers in the institution.

John Calvin Metcalf, one of the admired and beloved patriarchs of the university community, died in the same year, 1949. Dean of the Graduate School and professor of English, chairman of the faculty Library Committee, and longtime adviser to the *Virginia Quarterly Review*, Metcalf touched the life of the institution at many points. He had retired in 1940 and been honored with a volume of essays to which nineteen members of the faculty contributed. Raven and Algernon Sydney Sullivan Awards came to him. Metcalf's lectures, notably those on Shakespeare, were arresting and his manner ingratiating. The author of a number of books, including histories of English and American literature, he was an authority in both fields. In 1950 a memorial fund was established in his honor, to be used for the purchase of books for Alderman Library.

William Patton Graham, member of the faculty for a third of a century as professor of Romance languages, died on the last day of 1949. Professor Graham had studied at the University of Grenoble and was an authority on Maupassant, whose short stories he edited. He had retired in 1945 on reaching age seventy.

One of the most promising and popular of the younger faculty members was taken in 1950 when Peters Rushton died at age thirty-four. In his short life he had won a secure place in the esteem and affection of his colleagues on the faculty and the students in his English classes. A graduate of Princeton and Harvard, he studied for a year at Cambridge University. President Darden appointed "Pete" Rushton assistant dean of the college and of students, and Rushton was instrumental in founding the McGregor Room Seminars in contemporary prose and poetry, a series of lectures by distinguished critics and writers. It developed after his death that he had paid all expenses for carrying the lectures through their first year. The Peters Rushton Seminars were established in his memory as a sequel to the McGregor Room Seminars.

Dr. Dudley C. Smith, '16, nationally known authority in dermatology and syphilology, died suddenly in 1950 when on a professional visit to Washington. He was chairman of the School of Medicine's Department of Dermatology and Syphilology, which he founded in 1924. At the time of his death he was chairman of the American Medical Association's section having to do with these specialties. For the previous seventeen years "D. C." Smith had been a consultant to the U.S. Public Health Service.

Another loss to the School of Medicine occurred with the death, at age fifty-three, of Dr. George McLean Lawson, professor of preventive medicine and public health. He served as secretary of the medical faculty and chairman of the Medical Planning Committee that prepared for the extensive building program of the 1950s.

Dr. Lawrence T. Royster, '97, founder of the university's Department of Pediatrics, died at about this time. He served on the State Board of Health and was the author of various works on pediatrics.

A particularly distressing loss was that of fifty-two-year-old physics Professor Leland B. Snoddy, '29—another notable teacher taken at a comparatively early age. As the *Alumni News* expressed it, his death "not only depleted the ranks of outstanding scientists, but brought to countless associates, students and others an acute sense of personal loss, the loss of a great teacher and friend." Professor Snoddy had done significant work on experiments during World War II with the atom bomb and on atomic and guided missiles for the Navy Bureau of Ordnance.

And as if this catalogue of calamities were not sufficient, young English Prof. Dan S. Norton died at age forty-three. He had made a secure place for himself on the faculty and in the community. As Prof. Archibald Shepperson put it, the loss was "as serious as the university faculty and students could well sustain. . . Few, if any, have contributed as much to the advancement and enrichment of the best purposes of the university as he did during the 10 short years he spent here." Dan Norton had been first chairman of an organization founded in 1947 called the Friends of the University. The idea was suggested by Martin Hiden, a student, but Norton took hold and made it a reality. The organization's purpose was to bring to the university superior programs in the arts, literature, music, and drama. Within a few months 600 members had been enrolled from students, faculty, and community, and a score of

78. Edgar and Eleanor Shannon at the time of his election to the presidency of the university in 1959.

programs were presented at the ensuing session. The Friends became a fixture. Dan Norton's death and that of Peters Rushton removed two of the ablest members of the English faculty when they were on the threshold of what promised to be brilliant careers.

One of the veteran members of the faculty was lost when Gardner L. Carter, professor of chemistry since 1918, died. He retired in 1952 for reasons of health and died a year later. Of diminutive stature, he enlivened his lectures with stories that were regarded as somewhat pungent. Professor Carter was the author of several laboratory texts in chemistry.

Robert H. Webb, '06, professor of Greek for more than forty years, died. Described by President Darden as "one of the great humanists of the academic world," he had retired only a short time before and was busying himself with a translation of a play by Aristophanes. Enrollment in his classes was small, since fewer and fewer students were taking Greek, but Professor Webb was highly regarded as a teacher of the language and literature of ancient Hellas. He was also instrumental in organizing the music festivals of the Charlottesville Evening Concert Group. Following his death, a fund was collected with which to buy books for Alderman Library bearing a special bookplate in his memory.

Prof. Armistead C. Gordon, Jr., died suddenly in his middle fifties. A veteran of both world wars, he had served on the English faculty for three decades and was described by President Darden as a "keen and mordant teacher of American literature." Gordon had taken his B.A. at the College of William and Mary and his M.A. and Ph.D. at the University of Virginia. He was the author of *Virginian Writers of Fugitive Verse* and contributed well-written book reviews to leading media and many articles to the *Dictionary of American Biography*.

A memorial plaque was unveiled in 1954 to Charles H. Kauffmann, longtime director of placement and military affairs at the university, who had died a few months before. The plaque described him as "devoted leader, wise counselor and patriotic soldier." On the eve of World War II, the *Cavalier Daily* paid high tribute to Kauffmann, saying that the university had become "a happier place for thousands of students" because of the work done by him and his staff.

The death of John Lloyd Newcomb in 1954 cast a pall over the community. As president of the university succeeding Edwin A. Alderman, he made a highly creditable record in the face of handicaps caused by depression and war. Without brilliant intellectual talents or spectacular personal qualities, and not widely known when he took over the presidency, he carried the university forward by dint of great administrative ability, intimate knowledge of the institution's affairs, and complete dedication. Acquisition of Alderman Library was the most important single achievement of his administration. Additional improvements in the physical plant were mentioned in chapters 3 and 4, along with the inauguration of the honors program and other scholarly advances. Enrollment jumped from about two thousand five hundred to over four thousand and the faculty was doubled, while the number of Ph.D.'s granted was vastly increased. Research was emphasized and the professional schools strengthened. The final years of Newcomb's incumbency were shadowed by the death of his wife. As one of his longtime colleagues expressed it, "Until the cares of the world pressed too heavily upon him, his merry wit and lively humor made him a favorite among his circle of friends." Following his retirement from the presidency, his executive talents were put to excellent use by President Darden, who persuaded him to supervise the university's massive building program from an office on the Lawn. It was a particular satisfaction to Newcomb to preside over the erection of the six-story addition behind Cabell Hall, a concept he had originated. As dean of engineering and simultaneously the man who kept the university running under Alderman, as the president who carried the institution forward in difficult times, and then as the able coadjutor of President Darden, John Lloyd Newcomb left the University of Virginia deeply in his debt.

Dr. Stephen H. Watts, one of the foremost surgeons in the university's history, was memorialized in exercises at the end of 1954. Dr. Watts had died the preceding year and left $500,000 to the Medical School, from which he had retired long before. Dean Thomas H. Hunter said at the ceremonies that the legacy had made it possible to establish a chair of surgery in Dr. Watts's name, with Dr. William H. Muller, Jr., as the first incumbent. A portrait of Dr. Watts was presented to the Medical School. President Darden said Watts had begun making gifts to the school before World War I, "including a priceless collection of rare books on the history of medicine."

Prof. George T. Starnes, a recognized authority in the field of labor economics, died in 1955 after serving on the faculty for thirty years. He "made outstanding contributions to his chosen field of labor economics through his teaching and writing, as well as by his extensive work in the mediation and settlement of labor disputes," Professor Snavely wrote after his death. Both labor and management sought eagerly for Starnes's assistance in settling such disputes, Snavely declared, so great was their confidence in his "fairness and justice."

The death of economics Professor Duncan Clark Hyde from a heart attack brought special grief to his students, with whom he had a close rapport. Born in Canada and a Harvard Ph.D. who had taught for six years in Japan, Professor Hyde joined the university faculty in 1929. His dress and mannerisms, as a result of his sojourn in the Far East, were such that one of the students inquired of the department head, "Where did you all find Dr. Hyde?" But this feeling was short-lived, and he demonstrated such genuine concern for those in his classes that when he died, graduate students majoring under him asked the privilege of serving as his pallbearers. A scholarship was established as a memorial. Hyde had served as president of the Southern Economic Association.

Prof. Bruce D. Reynolds, '20, chairman of the Department of Biology, was another heart attack victim. He died at age sixty-three after thirty-three years on the faculty. A Johns Hopkins University Ph.D., he was the first director of the Mountain Lake Biological Station. A Biology Department spokesman was quoted as saying that Professor Reynolds was proud of having had more students complete requirements for advanced degrees than any other member of the department faculty. Graduate students and friends announced plans for a living memorial.

Another loss in the late 1950s occurred with the death of political science Prof. James Hart, '19, a member of the teaching staff since 1936. He had been president of the Southern Political Science Association and held important elective offices and chairmanships in the American Political Science Association. Professor Hart was an authority on the American presidency and administrative law.

Prof. Llewellyn G. Hoxton retired as head of the Department of Physics in 1948, aged seventy, after serving in that capacity since 1916. A Johns Hopkins Ph.D., he succeeded Francis H. Smith as the university's only professor of physics for a decade, at the end of which time he got assistance from Professors Carroll H. Sparrow and Frederick L. Brown. Professor Hoxton was a stimulating teacher with a sense of humor. On one occasion he put an examination on the board and announced that he would be in his office if anyone wished to ask him anything. "Are any of those questions optional?" a student inquired, as he gazed anxiously at the blackboard. "Hell yes, they're all optional," the professor replied, "Take them or leave them." Under him the department was built into one of the university's strongest, as it was he who brought in Jesse Beams and Leland Snoddy. Professor Hoxton's zeal was such that for years after his retirement, when he was well into his eighties, he continued to go daily to the physics laboratory, working on research projects in which he was interested. He died in 1966, aged eighty-eight.

Prof. John L. Manahan, first dean of the School of Education, a post he had held for twenty-nine years, retired from that office in 1949 and resumed full-time teaching. A graduate of Harvard, Manahan came to the university in 1916 as a full professor and four years later organized the School of Education. There were 17 students when Manahan became dean and 253 when he relinquished the position. He retired from teaching in 1957 and was tendered a dinner, a gold watch, and a bound volume of letters. Professor Manahan served for sixteen years as secretary-treasurer of the Virginia Association of Colleges and then was elected its president.

One of the major figures in the university's life, James Southall Wilson, retired in 1951 as graduate dean and also from active teaching. Stimulating lecturer and widely-recognized scholar, he was the first editor of the *Virginia Quarterly Review,* for the success of which he deserved a large share of the credit. Dean Wilson left a lasting impress on the university in various directions. Following his retirement he was visiting professor of English at various institutions, including Davidson College and Louisiana State University, and he continued as a lecturer for several summers at the Breadloaf School in Vermont. A volume of English studies in his honor was presented by his university associates, and Prof. Armistead C. Gordon, Jr., wrote perceptively in the foreword of his "measured but unstudied eloquence, made alive by apt illustration, circling humor, and a sense of the dramatic." An anonymous alumnus endowed a James Southall Wilson graduate fellowship. Professor Wilson died in 1963. Six years later the new arts and sciences classroom building was named for him.

Two veteran members of the School of Education faculty, Prof. William R. Smithey and Miss Louise Oates, retired in 1953. Dean Stiles commented on the former's contribution: "Dr. Smithey completed 33 years in the service of the university, establishing an enviable record of leadership in the field of secondary education." Smithey had served as secretary of the State Board of Education before joining the university faculty in 1919 and was subsequently elected president of the Southern Association of Colleges and Secondary Schools. He founded the Virginia High School Conference, which met each summer to give secondary school teachers an opportunity to discuss their problems. Concerning the service of Miss Oates, Dean Stiles wrote: "Professor Louise Oates established the Cabaniss Memorial School for Nursing Education, and served as its only head for 24 years. . . . The task of improving the preparation of nurses engaged in teaching, supervising and administering in Virginia presented throughout her entire professional career almost insurmountable problems. Upon the background of her efforts the future of nursing education in the University of Virginia will be developed."

British-born Prof. Sydney W. Britton retired from the medical faculty in 1952, after twenty-four years' service as professor of physiology. He and Mrs. Britton sailed for Nigeria where he would serve as Fulbright professor in the University of West Africa, doing research in the field of the endocrine glands, especially the adrenal glands of native Africans and giant apes. Professor Britton was widely recognized for important discoveries having to do with the adrenal cortex.

The Law School suffered a loss with the resignation of Prof. John Ritchie III, '17, to accept the deanship of the Washing-

79. Law Prof. Mortimer M. Caplin as U.S. commissioner of internal revenue.

ton University School of Law in St. Louis. Ritchie had been a member of the University of Virginia law faculty since 1937 and was assistant dean from 1942 to 1948.

Dean Ivey F. Lewis, an administrator and teacher who had been at the center of things at the university for decades, retired in 1953. He joined the faculty in 1915, and two years later, at age thirty-five, trounced Robert W. Bingham, Jr.—a student who had won the tennis singles championship of the university the previous year—in three straight sets with the loss of only four games. Then in the finals of the tournament he walloped F. R. Smith, a student who had been intercollegiate champion of New England, in three straight sets with the loss of only five games. That was on the eve of World War I, when professors played in the university tournaments. Ivey Lewis gave up tennis almost immediately thereafter, but he was a formidable performer as long as he was competing.

In 1934 he succeeded Dean James M. Page as dean of the university, and at the time of his retirement was dean of the university and the college. As James Southall Wilson wrote of Lewis: "His office . . . was administered by the dean and his faithful secretary, Miss Mary Proffitt, with simplicity, sympathy and dignity. Throughout the years the students of the college have come into closer relationship with Dean Lewis and Miss Proffitt than with any other officials of the university, and many of them have expressed their respect and affection, lasting often long after their college days." Ivey Lewis served as president of the American Society of Naturalists, the Botanical Society of America, and the American Biological Society— remarkable evidence of his national stature in the world of science. A botanical garden and arboretum were planted in his honor between McCormick Road and Scott Stadium, the gift of former students and friends, who also provided a portrait of him by Irene Higgins. Dean Lewis lived until 1964 and died, aged eighty-one, at the university.

E. A. Kincaid, a member of the faculty since 1922, who also served as vice-president of the Federal Reserve Bank of Richmond, retired in 1954. A University of California Ph.D., Kincaid was professor of commerce and business administration. His advice as a consultant was sought by the state of Virginia and the city of Richmond, among others. An unusually stimulating lecturer, he contributed to trade journals and financial publications. Upon his retirement, Kincaid was tendered a dinner by admirers. He died four years later.

A recognized authority on the literature and civilization of Spain and Latin America, James C. Bardin, professor of Romance languages, also retired in 1954 and was the guest of honor at a dinner. Bardin edited several texts in Spanish and did much research on the drama in the American colonial possessions of Spain and Portugal. He gave the university's first courses in Latin American civilization and history. Possessed of marked literary ability, Bardin was student editor of the *University of Virginia Magazine* in 1908–9 and won all three of the gold medals offered by the magazine for poetry, short stories, and essays. He contributed prose and poetry in later years to a variety of publications in this country and Latin America.

Harry Rogers Pratt, a leading figure for three decades in music and the drama at the university, retired in 1954. He had acted with the Ben Greet Players and other companies before joining the faculty in 1923 as assistant professor of music. Enrollment rose, in time, to over three hundred students, and he developed the Glee Club into an organization of ninety voices, which gave concerts throughout Virginia and in New York City. A skilled organist, Pratt played at many university functions. At the invitation of President Alderman he organized a School of Dramatic Art as part of the McIntire School of Fine Arts. Pratt offered the first courses at the university in playwriting and production and directed the performance of original one-act plays by students. Luther Greene, later the husband of the famous Judith Anderson, was Pratt's first assistant director. Mrs. Pratt was Agnes Rothery, author of well-known works. Some years after her death Harry Pratt lost his life in a fire at their home on Rothery Road.

Another professor who retired during these years was Franz K. Mohr, who had taught German since 1926. He wrote widely in that language, in both poetry and prose. Mohr was a native of Silesia, had studied in Vienna, and then graduated from the University of Chicago.

Tipton R. Snavely, '17, a major figure for many years in economics instruction and research on both the graduate and undergraduate levels and in the founding of the Graduate School of Business Administration, retired as chairman of the

Department of Economics in 1956 after thirty-three years in the position. He continued teaching until 1961. Professor Snavely had been adviser to many state and federal agencies, was president of the Southern Economic Association, and author of a history of the Economics Department and a life of George Tucker, chairman of the university's first faculty and authority on finance. The Department of Economics under Snavely produced no fewer than seventy-three Ph.D.s, and forty to forty-five of those dissertations were supervised personally by him, more than were directed by any other faculty member in the university down to that time, with the exception of history Prof. Edward Younger. Snavely was honored by fifty former students and colleagues at a special breakfast during the annual meeting of the Southern Economic Association in Atlanta, where he was presented with a collection of letters from all the students who had taken the Ph.D. under his supervision. Establishment of the Snavely Scholarship Fund, underwritten by his former pupils to provide scholarships for economics students, was announced at the breakfast.

Dr. David C. Wilson, '19, first chairman of the School of Medicine's Department of Neurology and Psychiatry, which he headed for twenty-one years, retired from the position in 1956. Dr. Wilson's portrait was presented to the School of Medicine in 1959 at a dinner and lecture in his honor. Following his retirement as department chairman he continued his teaching and also served as director of the Division of Alcoholic Studies and Rehabilitation.

Dean at one time or another of the College of Arts and Sciences and of Admissions, as well as Registrar, and teacher of psychology for thirty-seven years, George O. Ferguson retired in 1956. In addition to the foregoing he had a leading role in guiding the university's athletic affairs immediately after it joined the Southern Conference. Ferguson had been a member of the faculty since 1919, after receiving his Ph.D. from Columbia University. He died in 1960.

Chapin Jones, professor of forestry, who had taught conservation and forestry-related courses since 1915, was another who resigned in 1956. He was Virginia's first state forester and founder of the state forest service. The first state nursery and state forest also were created under his supervision. Chapin Jones was a Master of Forestry of Yale University.

*80. Political science Prof. Robert K. Gooch holding the silver
mace that he carried in official university processions.*

Prof. Albert G. A. Balz, '09, noted authority on the philosophy of Descartes and head of the Department of Philosophy since the death of Albert Lefevre, retired as chairman in 1957 but continued to teach. The Balz Philosophy Fund was established in tribute to him. He and Professor Manahan of the School of Education were the first two faculty members to be chosen professors emeriti. An emeritus professor may continue to work with his former students on theses or dissertations, serve on university committees, speak and vote in faculty meetings, and participate in academic functions. Balz was the author of several books and numerous articles. He had been a full professor since 1920, and for six years was chairman of the Charlottesville School Board. An expert flower gardener, he was also an enthusiastic fisherman. Professor Balz died only a few months after his retirement from the chairmanship.

Joseph K. Roberts retired in 1959 after a third of a century on the geology faculty. A Johns Hopkins Ph.D., he came to the university from Vanderbilt in 1926 as a full professor. The author of several books on geology, he was active in Sigma Xi, the honorary science fraternity, serving as president of the university chapter for one year, treasurer for ten years, and secretary for fifteen.

Retirement of Prof. Wilson Gee in 1959 brought to an end a career that had real significance, especially in its impact on graduate work and research at the university. Publication of books by members of the faculty was greatly stimulated through grants from the Institute for Research in the Social Sciences, which Gee headed from its inception. He had been brought to the university by President Alderman with a view to providing at Charlottesville something of a counterweight to the University of North Carolina's Howard W. Odum. The latter's Institute for Research in Social Science and *Journal of Social Forces* were pioneering efforts that brought much prestige to Chapel Hill. Gee never achieved fame comparable to Odum's, but his influence at Virginia was a salutary one. Scores of books and hundreds of articles were sponsored or stimulated by the university's institute. Gee was never fully accepted by the University of Virginia faculty, although some of those who criticized him behind his back did not hesitate to apply for and get grants from his institute. There were mixed reports from his students. Some, especially undergraduates, regarded his courses as dull and said he passed practically everybody, whereas others, notably graduate students, were almost lyrical in praise of what the *Cavalier Daily* termed "his understanding, his sincerity, his genuine goodness." As the time approached for Gee's retirement, he learned that it was proposed to abolish his Department of Rural Social Economics and merge it with the Department of Economics or the Department of Sociology, perhaps both. He objected strongly, but to no avail. Upon his retirement, the department was eliminated and its functions absorbed. A committee of his former students established the Wilson Gee Library in Social Science as part of Alderman Library's collections. Wilson Gee died suddenly in 1961, aged seventy-two, at Urbana, Ill., as he was preparing to teach a course at the University of Illinois.

The year 1953 marked the retirement from the university staff of two women who were themselves almost institutions— Miss Mary Proffitt and Mrs. A. E. Walker.

Miss Proffitt had served as secretary to Dean Page and Dean Lewis since 1912, but she was much more than a secretary. Her role was almost that of an alter ego for the dean, since she was privileged to make decisions far beyond the role of the average secretary. Not good looking, in the usual sense, and without anything remotely resembling what is termed "sex appeal," Mary Proffitt had a down-to-earth personality and a wealth of common sense that gave her remarkable influence over the students. Miss Proffitt's portrait was presented at retirement ceremonies on the Lawn along with a likeness of the also retiring Dean Lewis. Both, it turned out later, were members of the Seven Society.

Mrs. A. E. Walker, a widow, had been the beloved and indefatigable hostess at the Student Union for thirty-five years when she terminated her active career. The university "has lost one of its most cheerful faces," the *Cavalier Daily* commented. "She will be sorely missed." It pointed out that Mrs. Walker "opened her home to students on countless occasions and aided almost every university organization from dance societies to publications." Known as "the Queen," Mrs. Walker was on such close terms with the boys that she often sat in on meetings of the Student Union and even presided over some of them. She arranged and chaperoned hundreds of dances.

Her base of operations was always Madison Hall, headquarters of the Student Union until the construction of Newcomb Hall. When a social and recreational center for first-year men was opened on McCormick Road in 1950, "there was only one thing to call it, 'Queen's Club,'" said the *Alumni News*. There the Queen helped to carry out President Darden's program for aiding entering students to become adjusted to university life. The Seven Society presented Mrs. Walker with a silver platter after her retirement. She died in 1965.

Another admired woman in the university community was Mrs. Theodore Schultz, Rotunda hostess for more than a decade, who retired in 1958. She organized the University Guide Service, which grew to thirty members, and conducted tours of the university grounds. Mrs. Schultz, an experienced hostess who had represented Virginia at the Canadian National Exposition, wrote the pamphlet *A Brief Guide to the Lawn and Ranges*. A dinner in Newcomb Hall was given her by the Student Guide Service when she retired. Mrs. Edwin Betts, widow of Professor Betts, succeeded Mrs. Schultz as Rotunda hostess. Mrs. Betts, who had been associated with the university for nearly a third of a century, designed a complex pictorial map of Albemarle County that was sold for many years in bookstores.

The impending resignation of Colgate Darden as president of the university was rumored from time to time in the middle fifties. Questioned in 1956, he said he might give up the post in a year or two, but not until some of his plans had matured more fully.

During this period an amusing episode occurred at Finals. President Darden's son Pierre got two engineering degrees that year, and when he went up for his second, his father extended his hand in congratulation, as he did with all the other graduates. What happened next is best told by Colgate Darden in his *Conversations with Guy Friddell*: "Pierre turned loose in the palm of my hand an electrical device that spun around and gave me a shock that lifted me straight up in the air about half a foot. I never was more provoked in my life. I came within an ace of just giving him one awful kick in the rump. . . . It was like being hit by lightning. I reckon the spectators thought I'd lost my mind . . . that the long hot afternoon had finally gotten to me, that I had lost control and was jumping up and down on the platform. In a second it was all over and he was gone."

Pierre Darden was lost at sea in 1959, to the intense grief of his parents. An experienced sailor, he nevertheless ventured into the Atlantic in the late fall, in a small sailboat, en route to the Caribbean. He and his companion were never seen again.

Colgate Darden announced in 1958 that he would retire as president whenever the visitors chose his successor. Rector Frank Talbott, Jr., appointed a committee from the board to deal with the problem, and a committee from the faculty was appointed, on his recommendation, to have a significant and continuing part in the selection process. Darden was scrupulously careful to ease the transition in every possible way and to give his successor, whoever he might be, complete cooperation. His thoughtful willingness to confide in the faculty Senate concerning his intentions did much to allay hostility toward him among some members of that group. Rector Talbott was emphatic in saying that there must be no more leaks such as occurred in the early 1930s after the death of President Alderman, and one prospective successor after another was rumored in the press—correctly as it later turned out—to have declined the position.

The Board of Visitors passed resolutions of highest praise for Darden's achievements in the presidency. Mentioning additions to the physical plant totaling over twenty million dollars, the resolutions went on to cite reorganization of the College of Arts and Sciences, establishment of the Graduate School of Business Administration, a steady improvement in student standards and admissions, the unremitting effort to raise the scale of faculty compensation—it was doubled—and the notable expansion of Alderman Library's holdings and their greater use by students and faculty. The "loving attention" of the president to the "ancient beauty of the Grounds" also was mentioned, as well as his "generosity and kindliness to those who have worked with him" and "the inspiration of intellectual leadership, initiative and research on the part of the faculty." A special tribute was paid to Mr. Darden's "wife Constance, whose warm, vital, attractive personality has effectively aided her husband's effort." Mrs. Darden received the

Algernon Sydney Sullivan Award at the 1959 Finals as a person in the community with "such characteristics of heart, mind and conduct as evince a spirit of love and helpfulness to other men and women."

Whereas faculty and students had been decidedly skeptical, even hostile, in 1947 when Darden was chosen president of the university, they had done a 180-degree turn by the time of his retirement a dozen years later. *Corks and Curls* and the *Cavalier Daily* united in lauding his administration unreservedly; the faculty gave him the Thomas Jefferson Award, and the students presented him with the first Raven Award they had granted to anyone since he became president; the Class of 1959's gift was $1,000 for the purchase of books in his name for Alderman Library, especially works on history and political science. Members of the American Association of University Professors (AAUP) on the faculty, about one-fourth of the whole, adopted unanimous resolutions praising him for his "scrupulous adherence to the principles of academic freedom . . . and above all for the sense of security which the academic community has derived from the knowledge that the president . . . understands that a university can fulfill its function only if its members are free to pursue the truth without fear or favor." The AAUP members said they were "expressing the sentiments of the entire faculty." A fountain commemorating the presidency of Colgate Darden was placed on the east side of the Rotunda in 1960 "by the professors and staff of the university."

Important matters not mentioned specifically in the AAUP resolutions were the increase in the university's endowment from just over $12,000,000 to $40,000,000, and the quadrupling of the annual appropriation by the General Assembly to the institution. On an entirely different level there is the astonishing fact that it was not until the Darden years that rest rooms were installed at Scott Stadium, dedicated in 1931.

Although Darden announced cancelation of his subscription to the New York *Times* in 1957 because he felt material it had published concerning the university's position on segregation was "negative," the paper praised him highly the following year. Comparing him to Thomas Jefferson, it declared that the had "widened and deepened the appeal" of the uni-

81. English Prof. Peter Taylor, who has been called "the American Chekhov."

versity and had stressed the thought that the liberal arts are "the fountain of our culture."

There were a few adverse criticisms of President Darden, even near the end of his term. "He tried to run the university out of his vest pocket," in the oft-quoted words of a prominent professor. This observation appears to have had some validity. Darden was loath to employ adequate staff for his office, since he felt that the funds were needed elsewhere. Consequently he did too many routine things. Over his opposition, the Board of Visitors directed him to appoint a provost, and he did so.

An outside firm made a survey of the Darden Administration and concluded that he did not offer the faculty sufficient "leadership." His comment, years later, was, "I never thought that the business of the president was to lead the faculty around like a nurse leading a pack of children." He saw his function as "to set the ground for independent scholars to carry on their work. . . . I never thought of myself as the 'boss' of the university." A few faculty members remained unenthusiastic concerning the manner in which he conducted the institution's affairs.

Darden had special problems by virtue of the fact that whereas he took over the presidency with an inflated postwar enrollment of around five thousand, this soon fell drastically to around three thousand four hundred. When he relinquished the office, the number of students was moving up sharply. It would accelerate as a result of the "baby boom" that followed the war.

During the dozen years of his presidency, Darden managed to bring about an increase in the number and percentage of Virginia public school graduates attending the university, but not to the extent that he had hoped. His prime objective as president was to achieve a substantially larger number of public school matriculates and thus to make the university the "capstone" of the educational system that Jefferson envisaged. He conceded in later years that his success in this regard was only "modest."

While public school graduates in Virginia continued to go elsewhere in large numbers, a trend had been set in motion by President Darden, who did much to make the university more attractive to them. Furthermore, the consensus was that he advanced the institution in many other directions, intellectually, physically, and financially. The University of Virginia was regaining the prestigious position in the educational world that it had held much earlier. The foundations had been laid for the remarkable progress that was to be made under the administration of Colgate Darden's successor, Edgar F. Shannon, Jr.

SEVEN

Shannon Carries
the Institution Forward

THE FOURTH PRESIDENT of the University of Virginia, Edgar F. Shannon, Jr., was a forty-year-old professor of English who had been a Rhodes Scholar at Oxford and had taken his Ph.D. there as a specialist on the works of Alfred, Lord Tennyson. At Washington and Lee University he had made straight-A grades in all subjects for his four undergraduate years, with the exception of one B in Latin. A veteran of bloody battles in the Pacific in World War II, Shannon went down with the U.S.S. *Quincy* in the desperate engagement off Savo Island and was in the water for several hours before he was finally rescued. His principal administrative experience was gained in the navy as assistant operations officer and task group fighter director.

Shannon had been on the university faculty for three years and had just been promoted to full professor when he was elected president. He came to Virginia from Harvard, where he was head tutor in the English department, "a sort of chairman for the undergraduates," as he put it.

When the committee in search of a president for the University of Virginia called on Henry Wriston, the noted former president of Brown University, in the hope of getting advice, he gave them some. "The only thing I have to say, gentlemen," declared Wriston, "is take a good look at his legs. If he happens to have any brains, it's convenient, but not at all necessary. Legs are the important thing." Wriston then proceeded to outline the strenuous duties of a typical university president, with all the foolish demands that are made upon him. "After dinner in the evening you generally go out and dedicate some damn garage," he said. And, he added: "For God's sake don't look for a distinguished man. The day you make him president of the University of Virginia he will be just as distinguished as he can be. . . . Look for quality. . . . That's ahead of everything."

Edgar Shannon was not well known, even to the faculty of the university when he was chosen president. The selection, made in full cooperation with the committee from the faculty senate, headed by William S. Weedon, was kept completely secret until it was announced on Feb. 28, 1959. Rector Frank Talbott, Jr., presented Shannon to a faculty group without mentioning his name, and one professor present was quoted as remarking to a colleague, "This is all very fine, but who the hell is he?"

Mrs. Shannon, the former Eleanor Bosworth of Memphis, Tenn., had married Edgar three years before, after resigning as dean of women at Southwestern College, Memphis. She was a magna cum laude graduate of Sweet Briar, with an M.A. in history from Cornell. Personally charming and good looking, she was admirably qualified for her new and demanding duties.

Outgoing President Darden was altogether cooperative with his successor and helpful in many ways in smoothing the latter's path. The two men complemented each other, and their administrations were rightly described as a continuum.

The new president was inaugurated Oct. 6. It was a beautiful autumn day, and the ceremonies were held in bright sunshine on the Lawn, with Rector Talbott presiding. Geoffrey Reginald Gilchrist Mure, warden of Merton College, where Shannon had studied as a Rhodes Scholar, was the principal speaker. "Everybody in the college knew him, respected him and liked him," Mure declared in referring to Shannon. "He liked us and even, I think, respected some of us. He threw himself into every strange British activity. He played village cricket. He now and again played Rugby football." Gov. J. Lindsay Almond also welcomed the new president. Responding, Shannon reaffirmed the "Jeffersonian tenet that the University of Virginia be not only an exceptional state and regional university but also a great national university."

The university's new head got off to a rousing start with the faculty by announcing that Governor Almond had approved salary increases, effective for the session of 1959–60. Full professors would receive an additional $1,000, associates $800, assistants $600, and instructors $250.

Shannon had taken office at a propitious time for advancing the university in all directions. "There was a thrust of interest in education," he said, and the Federal government was beginning to make large sums available through the National Science Foundation and the National Institutes of Health. These things coincided with the rapid rise in the population, which brought an increase in the number of applicants to the university. Higher entrance requirements could be instituted without slowing the university's growth. These stiffer requirements had an impact throughout the institution, especially in the Schools of Engineering and Education, since before that time an applicant rejected by the College could apply to either of those schools. The larger enrollment also was significant in making possible the building of a stronger faculty, for distinguished professors could be obtained much more rapidly as a result. This, in turn, attracted promising younger teachers, and "the whole thing snowballed" as Shannon expressed it.

Another factor carrying the university forward was state legislation enacted during the Darden regime, and at Darden's instigation, which provided that it is the policy of the commonwealth to encourage state institutions to develop endowments from private funds. This enabled the university to build a substantial endowment and to use it, along with other private and federal resources, to give the institution its "margin of excellence," Shannon declared. Then, somewhat later, Gov. Albertis Harrison was instrumental in having the commonwealth establish the Eminent Scholars Fund with state money, to be matched by the various institutions. "That made it possible for us to compete nationally with salaries for any faculty member that we really tried to get," Shannon said. An anonymous gift of $2,000,000 launched the fund at the university, and it has been substantially increased. All this resulted subsequently in putting the University of Virginia among the top twenty institutions belonging to the American Association of University Professors, with respect to median faculty compensation. The only other state universities in the top twenty were California, Michigan, and Iowa.

At the first Finals held during Shannon's presidency (June 1960) tablets in memory of the 321 Virginia men who died in World War II and the 29 who died in the Korean War were unveiled on the north portico of the Rotunda. Rear Adm. Lamont Pugh, ret., '23, former chief of the navy's Bureau of Medicine, delivered the address. The World War II plaque was presented by the classes of 1943 and 1948, while that for the Korean War was the gift of the Seven Society.

"Reading days," in effect at numerous other institutions, were introduced at Virginia in 1960 at the suggestion of the *Cavalier Daily*. Dean William L. Duren of the College stated that May 27 and 28 would be set aside as a two-day review period before final examinations, during which attendance in class would not be required, but the professors would be available for consultation. The plan was temporarily abandoned until the 1962–63 session, when reading days were reinstituted before exams in January and May. In 1969–70 each department was authorized to grant up to five days for this purpose.

The Echols Scholar program, named in honor of the late Prof. William H. Echols, was launched at the 1960–61 session and has been a pronounced success. Under this program top-flight high school and preparatory school graduates are given much more freedom in choosing their courses and much less supervision than run-of-the-mine students. When the plan was gotten under way, thirty-five students entered, twenty-seven of them from Virginia. They lived in Echols House, one of the newer residence units, and were excused from first semester classes in math and English, while courses not generally open to first-year men were made available to them. Echols Scholars were selected not only for their high academic standing but also on the basis of "intellectual, cultural and community interests other than those solely related to academic work." There was a certain amount of jealous jeering at this privileged group when they first entered the university, and "Reserved for Echols Scholars" was painted on sidewalks. This attitude was apparently short-lived. By 1963–64 there were almost twice as many of these superior students as three years before. In 1970–71 it was announced that most of the eighty students who entered that year achieved combined college aptitude test scores of at least 1,400 and were in the top 5 percent of their high school graduating classes. These exceptional students had to meet fewer and fewer requirements under the evolving rules, and there was an increased emphasis on individual learning and initiative. They were encouraged to spend a semester or session away from the university, since "a high degree of restlessness" was prevalent among them in that era of widespread campus turmoil. Echols Scholars were not "mere" intellectuals and bookworms, the *Alumni News* pointed out. "An Echols Scholar is president of the Student Council," it declared, "another is an editor of the *Cavalier Daily*, still others helped found and now administer the Experimental University, which offers nonacademic courses to the community. They work at the student radio stations, play in the orchestra and participate in intramurals."

Pres. John F. Kennedy appointed three university alumni to important positions. He named his brother Robert, '51, attorney general of the United States; law Professor Mortimer F. Caplin, '40, commissioner of internal revenue; and David K. E. Bruce, '20, ambassador to the Court of St. James's. The assassination of President Kennedy in 1963 caused postponement until Thanksgiving Day of the university's football game with Maryland, scheduled for Nov. 23, the day after the murder. President Kennedy had promised to deliver the Founder's Day address at the university in 1964.

When U.S. Sen. and presidential candidate Robert F. Kennedy was assassinated in 1968, Dean Hardy C. Dillard of the Law School delivered a memorial tribute at the request of President Shannon. He announced that the graduating class in the Law School had, through voluntary subscriptions, funded the Robert F. Kennedy Memorial Scholarship, with preference to be given to members of minority groups when the awards were made. In 1959 Kennedy had established in the Law School the F. D. G. Ribble Scholarship Fund, under which a yearly scholarship would be granted.

Mortimer Caplin, the newly appointed commissioner of the revenue, had been editor of the *Law Review* in his student days, a star on championship boxing teams, as well as president of the Virginia Players and one of their most talented actors. Upon graduation he was given the Southern Society Award as the student who had contributed most to university life. After practicing law in New York as a tax expert, he returned to the university as a member of the law faculty.

David Bruce, one of the ablest diplomats of modern times, was the only American ever to serve as U.S. ambassador to London, Paris, and Berlin. His record in all three posts was exceptional.

Appointment of Marvin B. Perry, Jr., as dean of admissions, "a new position of vital significance to the university's future development," was announced by President Shannon in 1960. Perry was a university B.A. and a Harvard M.A. and Ph.D. who had taught English at Virginia for four years and then served in the Washington and Lee English Department for nine years. He would remain as dean at the university until 1967, when he accepted the presidency of Goucher College. Admission requirements for all the university's colleges were placed under him and were sharply upgraded.

Paul Saunier, Jr., was appointed in 1960 as assistant to the president for university relations and development. He was a University of Richmond graduate who had served in Washington for nearly a decade as secretary to Rep. J. Vaughan Gary of the Richmond congressional district. Saunier was given responsibility for all activities of the university affecting relations with the public and for coordination of the development program.

Dean William L. Duren, Jr., of the College resigned that post, after serving since 1955, to devote his full time to teaching mathematics, and Irby B. Cauthen, Jr., who had been assistant and associate dean, was named to succeed him. Dean Cauthen was an able teacher of English as well as the author of well-regarded works on English and American literature. In addition to higher admission standards, said he, the student body had come to accept the stiffer requirements covering probation and suspension, put into effect two years previously, although "there had been some initial bewilderment, shock and disbelief." Dean Cauthen added that the number graduating after four years in college had jumped from 59.5 percent in June 1959 to 75 percent four years later. He also noted that 83 percent of those expecting to graduate in June

1964 planned to go on to graduate or professional schools, 18 percent more than in 1960. By the fall of 1963 almost three-fourths of the first-year students came from the top quarter of their high school classes, and they also ranked well in extracurricular activities, with numerous class presidents, captains of athletic teams, and editors of school publications. Scholastic Aptitude Test (SAT) scores rose markedly over those of the preceding year, with average verbal scores of 606 and math of 646. A record number of Guggenheim, Fulbright, and Woodrow Wilson fellowships were awarded to students and faculty. The honors program, launched in the 1930s, was more firmly established than ever and more widely incorporated into the curricula of the various departments of the College.

A munificent gift of over $3,500,000 came to the university in the early 1960s in the will of Robert Coleman Taylor, a Law School graduate and prominent New York attorney. The funds were unrestricted and were devoted principally to professorships, but also to faculty disability insurance and honor scholarships.

The position of dean of the Faculty of Arts and Sciences was created in 1962, with the occupant of that position responsible to the president of the university for all matters affecting the faculty, with special emphasis on faculty procurement. The office of dean of the College, previously concerned with administering faculty affairs, as well as advising undergraduates, was reoriented to concentrate, with the assistance of associate deans, on programs involving undergraduate students and the significant changes in the curriculum that were to follow. Deans of the Faculty, beginning in 1962, were: Rowland Egger, 1962–63; Robert J. Harris, 1963–68; Fredson T. Bowers, 1968–69; David A. Shannon, 1969–71; Robert D. Cross, 1972–73; and Edwin E. Floyd, 1974–. More will be said later concerning several of these men.

The university ranked first in 1962 among public institutions in this country in the book value of its endowment in proportion to enrollment, according to a survey by the American Association of University Professors. Only a dozen institutions in the United States rated higher in the AAUP tabulation with respect to endowment, compensation of faculty, and related aspects of fiscal strength. There were 545 faculty members at the university, ranging from full professors to lec-

82. *World Court Justice Hardy C. Dillard, former dean of the Law School, in his judicial robes.*

turers, some part-time. A bill was introduced in the Virginia General Assembly to limit out-of-state students to 25 percent in all state-supported institutions of higher learning. Governor Harrison opposed it, and the measure was defeated. President Shannon said the following year that the university would seek to maintain a top enrollment of 10,000.

Shannon spoke in 1961 of the need in Virginia for a system of community colleges, and the suggestion was well received in various quarters, including the sanctums of several Virginia newspaper editors. He proposed that first-year and sophomore courses be taught at a number of locations, with this instruction expanded into a system of community colleges, as needed. Several years later the General Assembly established a system of nearly two dozen community colleges.

Two-year branch colleges of the university opened—Patrick Henry College at Martinsville in 1962 and Eastern Shore at Wallop's Island in 1964. George Mason and Clinch Valley were already in operation as two-year university branches and would be upgraded to four-year institutions. All these colleges, except Clinch Valley, which now had 780 students, would ultimately be separated from the university. George Mason, with 3,100, became independent in 1972, and the other two were absorbed into the statewide community college system when it was established.

The university was becoming more and more distinguished as a center of scientific research. There was increased emphasis on science in virtually all U.S. institutions as a result of Soviet Russia's putting a sputnik in space.

John Wesley Mitchell, a fellow of the Royal Society in London and internationally known for his studies of large metal crystals, joined the university faculty in 1960. Mitchell was born in New Zealand and had worked at the University of Bristol, England, with Spanish-born Professor Nicolas Cabrera, who was already on the University of Virginia faculty, and was also internationally celebrated. They pursued their researches together in the physics laboratory at Virginia and were hoping to find ways to strengthen structural materials.

The prestige of the university in the field of science was already great, thanks to the presence on the faculty of such men as John H. Yoe, Allan T. Gwathmey, and Randolph T.

Major, all in chemistry; Ralph Singleton in biology; Gordon T. Whyburn and Edward J. McShane in mathematics; and Jesse H. Binford, W. Dexter Whitehead, and Frank L. Hereford, Jr., in physics.

Frank Hereford, although only in his late thirties, was already known in Europe as a nuclear physicist and was in demand as a speaker both in this country and overseas. Named in 1962 to head the Physics Department at the university, he was chosen by the magazine *Industrial Development and the Manufacturer's Record* as one of three men to represent the South's "new leadership." The magazine said that his advanced training, international outlook, professional dedication, and sense of responsibility in serving the public led to his selection. Hereford had hardly settled in his position as department head when he was also appointed dean of the Graduate School of Arts and Sciences as successor to Dean Geldard. After four years as graduate dean he was named provost by President Shannon, in which position he would be the principal academic officer after the president. The office was a new one, and not identical with that occupied previously by Joseph L. Vaughan. All academic deans, as well as the chancellors of the Medical School and the community colleges, were to report to Hereford. In the year he was appointed provost Frank Hereford received the Thomas Jefferson Award, the highest award made to any faculty member.

The university's eminence in nuclear physics was the major factor in the institution's obtaining a $705,000 grant from the National Science Foundation for the acquisition of a 6,000,-000-volt Van de Graaf nuclear accelerator and a new nuclear physics laboratory. Part of the amount was to be matched by university funds. The physics lab would house not only the accelerator but a 75,000,000-volt synchroton given the university by General Electric. With this up-to-date equipment the university would have research facilities in nuclear structure physics comparable to the best anywhere.

The Physics Department received a bequest of $360,000 in 1970 from William Jackson Humphreys, '89, and the fund was used to support graduate fellowships. Humphreys had been chief physicist of the U.S. Weather Bureau and professor of meteorological physics at George Washington University.

For the overall development of science at the university the

National Science Foundation made a grant of $3,780,000 in 1965. This grant was one of six made to that number of institutions, and was given to centers of learning that were deemed to be on the brink of "recognized excellence in research and education in the sciences." When a distinguished group of university presidents and scientists made a two-day site visit in order to determine whether the grant should be approved by the National Science Foundation, a member of the visiting team inquired as to whether all this emphasis on research and graduate study would result in undergraduates being short-changed and instructed by none but junior members of the faculty or teaching assistants. When it was pointed out that two sections of first-year college physics were being shared that year by Jesse Beams, a member of the National Academy of Sciences, and John W. Mitchell, a Fellow of the Royal Society, there were no more questions along that line.

Establishment in that year of the Center for Advanced Studies, with Prof. W. Dexter Whitehead as director, was the outgrowth of the foregoing recognition and the liberal grant that accompanied it. Subsequent alumni contributions of $3,500,000 for faculty made it possible to include the humanities and social sciences in the center and to attract distinguished scholars in those fields as well. The salary level was comparable to that in the country's foremost institutions. Whitehead was successful in obtaining nearly $2,000,000 more from the National Science Foundation in 1969.

And, thanks to another grant from the foundation, the university acquired the only high-voltage electron microscope in operation at any American university. Custom-built by the Radio Corporation of America, the 500,000-volt microscope allowed scientists to scrutinize minute defects in the crystalline structure of alloys, the protein formations in human cells, and viruses floating in space. It was operated in the School of Engineering and Applied Science.

About thirty scientists, astronomers, and other specialists were moved to Charlottesville in 1965 from the National Radio Astronomy Observatory (NRAO) at Green Bank, W.Va. They would make use of the astronomy apparatus and facilities there, and those of the other sciences and disciplines at the university. Most of the work of collecting data and studying the universe through radio telescopes would continue at

83. Dr. Thomas H. Hunter, vice-president for medical affairs.

Green Bank, 115 miles west of Charlottesville. A $660,000 building was erected near the university on Mt. Jefferson, formerly Observatory Mountain, for the use of NRAO staff there. The university's Department of Astronomy was undergoing an extraordinary degree of expansion under the chairmanship of Laurence W. Fredrick. It had moved from the basement of Cabell Hall to Gilmer Hall, part of the growing science complex, and whereas at the former location it had one faculty member and one graduate student, eleven more faculty and staff were added by 1967, with twenty-six graduate students and nine undergraduate astronomy majors. An important part of this expansion was the new facility on Fan Mountain, some nineteen miles south of Charlottesville. Its thirty-two-inch reflector telescope, with sophisticated supplemental equipment designed to study the spectra of stars, added greatly to the department's potential. All this, combined with the NRAO staff and facilities, constituted what was said to be one of the largest groups of astronomers in the world. A 40-inch astronometric telescope was soon added at Fan Mountain, thanks to the National Science Foundation and other agencies. The twenty-six-inch refractor telescope, given to the university in the 1880s by Leander McCormick, was still in use. With that relatively primitive instrument, the university had collected 69,000 parallax plates, believed to be the world's largest collection. They show where the stars were fifty years ago and where they are now; stars do move, as viewed from the earth, it was explained. Such information is important in developing a system of space navigation.

Another significant gain for the university in the scientific field occurred in 1962, when the navy's Project Squid was transferred from Princeton University to Charlottesville. This was the navy's major long-range research program in aircraft, missile, and space propulsion.

By 1960 the School of Engineering was modifying its curricula and research to include post–World War II changes in science and mathematics. A new curriculum introduced engineering sciences and increased time for the humanities and social sciences, replacing the last vestiges of shop and field training. A core of studies common to all engineering programs was developed to include instruction in computer techniques. The Division of English became the Division of Humanities, charged with providing essential aspects of the humanities in the curriculum by teaching and advising students on elective choices in the arts and sciences.

The growth of research was closely related to the increasing graduate enrollment. The research laboratories for the engineering sciences actively sought and managed research support from government and industry. In addition to programs of study previously offered, new graduate curricula in materials science and biomedical engineering were introduced. These programs typified the increased attention to advanced science and to expansion of engineering interests into new areas of public concern.

Lawrence R. Quarles retired as dean in 1973. He had presided over a period of growth in enrollment and a qualitative change in program comparable to that under William M. Thornton (1875–1925) and Walter S. Rodman (1933–40).

"Changes in the university's approach to engineering education have reflected a profound national revolution," T. Graham Hereford and O. Allan Gianniny, Jr., have written in their *Short History of Engineering and Applied Science at the University of Virginia*. "Stimulated by the need for modern analytic-science–based technology developed in World War II, engineering education was reoriented toward an analytic methodology-based activity. The effect was to make engineering education more like other scientific studies. . . . This revolution was accomplished in the incredibly short time of a decade or less in the nation, and it had been largely accomplished at the University of Virginia in 1973 when [Dean] Quarles retired."

John E. Gibson was named dean and Commonwealth Prof. of Electrical Engineering in 1973. He was a Yale Ph.D. in electrical engineering and former dean at Oakland University, Rochester, Mich. Dean Gibson's first year suggested new priorities for the school, with strong efforts to integrate the knowledge and skills of engineering with the concerns of public policy and to admit a significant number of women and minorities. The faculty numbered approximately 130 at that time, the undergraduates 868 and the graduate students 316.

The Law School experienced significant changes and improvements in the 1960s. F. D. G. Ribble reached the age of retirement as dean in 1963 and was succeeded in that position by Hardy C. Dillard. Ribble continued as James Madison Prof. of Law and Dillard as James Monroe Prof. of Law. A direct descendant of John Marshall, Ribble had served for twenty-four years as head of the school, during which time it had been strengthened in many ways. He was honored at an alumni dinner as part of Law Day activities. Dillard, a member of the faculty since 1927 and a retired colonel in the army reserve, was experienced as a lawyer, consultant, administrator, scholar, author, international lecturer, and teacher.

The Law School was collaborating with the Schools of Foreign Affairs and Political Science in offering a new course in "transnational law." Two world-famous authorities in the field had been added to the university faculty—Percy E. Corbett, who had held important posts at Princeton, Yale, and Oxford and had been dean of the McGill University Law School, and Quincy Wright, who was internationally known and had come to Charlottesville from the University of Chicago. Teaching, research, and publication were on the agenda of the course in "transnational law." With the acquisition of two such scholars as Wright and Corbett, the university was said to have "the best international law team in the United States."

The Law School's programs in 1965 were expanded and invigorated by gifts, bequests, and trusts totaling over two million dollars, about 85 per cent of it from outside the state. Included were a trust established by Lammot duPont Copeland of Wilmington, Del.; bequests by Tazewell Taylor, Jr., of Norfolk and Joseph M. Hartfield of New York; and grants from the Henry L. and Grace Doherty Charitable Foundation of New York. The funds were used for financial assistance to students and special programs for enrichment of the curriculum, for research grants, and to augment some faculty salaries.

The degrees of Doctor of Juridical Science and Master of Law being offered by the Law School were bringing students from all over the globe. Eighteen legal scholars from the universities of Cairo, Freiburg, Ghent, Cambridge, Sydney, and Seoul, not to mention Harvard, Yale, and Northwestern, were enrolled for the session of 1967–68. Most of them planned to teach law or enter government service, and all were outstanding in their fields. More and more applicants were seeking to enter these courses each year.

Dillard retired from the deanship in 1968 after a productive career in that post and continued to teach. In 1970 he was named to the International Court of Justice at The Hague. No other University of Virginia alumnus except John Bassett Moore had ever been elevated to the World Court, as it was commonly called. The Hardy Cross Dillard professorship of law was established in Dillard's honor at the Law School.

His successor as dean was Monrad G. Paulsen, professor and legal scholar at Columbia University Law School. Paulsen was an internationally recognized authority on criminal law and law as it relates to children. He had lectured throughout this country and in Europe. His wife, Dr. Elsa Paulsen, joined the medical faculty as associate professor of pediatrics. Daniel J. Meador, dean of the University of Alabama Law School, succeeded Dillard on the Virginia faculty. Chief Justice Roger J. Traynor of the California Supreme Court retired from that post to teach at the University of Virginia Law School for the second semester of the 1970–71 session. Three years later the school received a bequest of $2,000,000 from Roy C. Moyston, '13, who had had a highly successful legal and business career in Texas and Maryland.

President Shannon announced a reorganization of the Medical School staff in 1964 in the interests of administrative efficiency. Dean of Medicine Thomas H. Hunter was appointed chancellor for medical affairs, and Dr. Kenneth R. Crispell was named to succeed him as dean. John M. Stacey, director of the University Hospital, was appointed director of the Medical Center.

Grants from the National Institutes of Health and the National Science Foundation totaling around three million dollars were received in 1966. They were to extend over a period of years and were designed to strengthen programs in the basic medical sciences and aid in establishment of a general clinical research unit. Three years later the U.S. Department of Health, Education, and Welfare provided nearly two million dollars more for improving selected clinical departments. Then in 1970 the National Institutes of Health awarded the school $2,700,000 to enable it to turn out more physicans. This also made it possible for the university to provide broadened educational experiences for medical students in a community setting, define admission criteria for potential medical students from lower socioeconomic groups, and emphasize training in family medicine.

The entering class jumped from 82 to 96 in September of that year, and the new federal grant would enable the school to admit 114 to the first-year medical class in 1971 and 120 in 1972. All this would be made possible by completion of the new $9,100,000 medical education building then under construction.

Community hospitals in Roanoke, Lynchburg, and Winchester were to be used in a "second faculty" concept. Certain members of the medical staffs of those hospitals were named as full-time faculty of the university Medical School and would engage in teaching duties there. Medical students at Charlottesville were permitted to obtain part of their clinical training in these community hospitals. As for the program in family medicine referred to above, it was planned to increase the faculty for the purpose, and approximately two hundred families would be a part of the program.

Another innovation revolved about an eight-week summer course involving up to thirty white and black applicants to the Medical School who were disadvantaged but had promising personal characteristics and were highly motivated. Drawn mainly from colleges in Virginia and southern Appalachia, these young men and women were given an opportunity to demonstrate in the summer course, which was tuition free and included a $400 living allowance, that they were Medical School material.

Thirteen departments in the Medical Center were devoting almost one-third of their floor space to research and treatment in the fight on cancer. An interdisciplinary center for the attack on this disease was contemplated, and the National Cancer Institute made $150,000 available for planning. The investigation was completed after eighteen months of study on a nationwide basis, and a report was made. The new cancer center would be molded around the Division of Cancer Studies, under the direction of Dr. Robert M. McLeod.

84. Charlotte Kohler, editor of the
Virginia Quarterly Review,
1946–75.

Dr. Thomas H. Hunter, who had been appointed vice-president for health sciences some years previously, retired from administrative duties and Dean of Medicine Kenneth R. Crispell was named to succeed him. The deanship was filled with the appointment of Dr. William R. Drucker, chairman of the Department of Surgery at the University of Toronto since 1966. An M.D. of Johns Hopkins and a Markle Scholar, Dr. Drucker chose the University of Virginia over various other institutions that were seeking his services.

A new medical curriculum introduced in the summer of 1973 made it possible to complete medical school in three years instead of four. A group of twenty-five students entered the school in July, with a view to pursuing the more intensified schedule of work, which included eight-week summer sessions.

The Medical School was the recipient of a $4,000,000 bequest from Mrs. Roy C. Moyston, whose husband had left $2,000,000 to the Law School. The Medical School had as its scholar in residence for 1973–74 Dr. Robert Q. Marston, former director of the National Institutes of Health, a native Virginian who would become president of the University of Florida.

A controversial division of the Medical School was its well-endowed Division of Parapsychology within the Department of Psychiatry, with Dr. Ian Stevenson as chairman. With him in the division in 1974 were Professors J. Gaither Pratt and Rex G. Stanford. Such phenomena as reincarnation, extrasensory perception, and psychokinesis were studied. Some in responsible positions in the university were by no means convinced of the value of these inquiries. The division was set up under a bequest of $1,000,000 from Chester F. Carlson, with the specific proviso that the money was to be used for the work of Dr. Stevenson in parapsychology. After much discussion and debate, the Board of Visitors decided to accept the funds. The division gave no courses and was concerned solely with research. Dr. Stevenson traveled to various areas of the world collecting data on reincarnation and has written a number of books on the subject. Pratt was on the research staff of the parapsychology laboratory at Duke University before coming to Charlottesville. Stevenson, Carlson Professor of Psychiatry in the Medical School, held one of only four endowed chairs in parapsychology in the world.

Zula Mae Baber, later Mrs. Raymond C. Bice, succeeded Dean Margaret G. Tyson as acting dean of nursing following Tyson's nine years of exceptional service. Dean Bice also made a notable record, and following her death a memorial lecture-ship was established in her honor. She was succeeded by Dean Rose Marie Chioni, under whom the School of Nursing was further upgraded. The three-year diploma program was phased out in 1968, and in 1972 the master's degree was of-fered in pediatric and psychiatric nursing. McLeod Hall and Fenwick Auditorium were opened in the latter year, and a new student housing facility went into operation soon thereafter on Brandon Avenue. The nursing program now covered four years plus a summer semester and included two years of lib-eral arts. Regular hospital bedside duties were eliminated, but clinical training included bedside care. The school conducted courses in several Virginia cities. Undergraduate enrollment in 1974 was in excess of four hundred.

Frank A. Geldard was appointed dean of the Graduate School in 1960, succeeding Lewis M. Hammond, who resigned and went on a two-year leave to serve as educational attaché in Bonn, West Germany. He had served as dean for a decade. Geldard, head of the North Atlantic Treaty Organization's ad-visory committee on defense psychology, had just presided at Paris over NATO's first defense psychology symposium. Gel-dard had been chairman of the university's Department of Psychology since 1946 and a member of the faculty since 1928. He was for three years chairman of the National Re-search Council's committee on military psychology and was the author of books and numerous scientific papers in the field. He resigned in 1962 as Graduate School dean to join the faculty of Princeton University and was succeeded by Frank L. Hereford, Jr. During Hereford's four years in office the num-ber of graduate degrees expanded in both quantity and quality. When he was named provost, Edward Younger was appointed to the deanship.

Younger had been chairman of the History Department for the preceding four years. That department had expanded greatly under his chairmanship, with the number of faculty and graduate students increasing markedly. His most valuable service was his direction of scores of Ph.D. dissertations in the field of Virginia history since 1865. As a result, he was said to have "done more than any living man to increase our knowledge of the history of Virginia since the Civil War." Between 1949 and 1974 Edward Younger personally directed fifty-six Ph.D. dissertations, more than any member of the university faculty had ever done, and the great majority dealt with the state's postbellum period, concerning which there had been a great dearth of information. He was the author of *John A. Kasson: Diplomacy and Politics from Lincoln to McKinley*, which won the university's Phi Beta Kappa Prize, and the editor of *Inside the Confederate Government: The Diary of Robert Garlick Hill Kean*, which was a Civil War Book Club selection. In 1974 Younger was elected an honorary member of the Virginia Historical Society and appointed Alumni Professor of History.

Dexter Whitehead, who succeeded Younger as graduate dean, reported in 1970 that the Graduate School was continuing to produce more and more degree recipients and that quality continued to mount. He stated that registration in the Graduate School had nearly tripled in the decade 1960–70 (1,212 as compared with 426), with a corresponding jump in the number of degrees granted. As director since 1965 of the highly successful Center for Advanced Studies, Whitehead had been a key factor in bringing to the university a large number of eminent scholars for teaching, study, and research.

Leading institutions from coast to coast were losing some of their most distinguished faculty members to the University of Virginia. For example, Prof. Norman A. Graebner of the University of Illinois was induced to come to Virginia as the first professor in the humanities brought in by the Center for Advanced Studies. Nationally known as a "superstar" who packed 500 students into his Illinois classroom to hear his lectures on American history or American diplomacy, Graebner was greatly admired by faculty and students alike. The students demonstrated when they found he was leaving for Virginia, and university administrators at Urbana were indignant that one of their most brilliant lecturers and seminar conductors had been lured away. Similar concern was expressed by students and faculty at the University of Pennsylvania when

Henry J. Abraham left for the University of Virginia, to occupy an endowed chair as professor of government and foreign affairs. A refugee from Nazi Germany, Henry Abraham
was decorated in World War II for his service in General Eisenhower's headquarters military intelligence unit. He joined
the University of Pennsylvania faculty after the war and made
a great reputation as a scholar and lecturer. In his final year
there he was chairman of the faculty Senate. Various other
high-ranking teachers were attracted to Charlottesville by the
excellent salaries and topflight library and laboratory facilities
and the beautiful grounds. More than fifty faculty and visiting
professors were brought to the university during the first decade of this program, greatly enhancing the quality of instruction and of life.

Similarly, an endowed chair in architecture brings to the
School of Architecture each year a world-famous architect,
who, as Thomas Jefferson Foundation Professor of Architecture, is given a medal and a $5,000 prize. Funds for the above
accolades for the noted recipient are provided by the foundation, which also underwrites ten annual scholarships at
$1,000 each for graduate students in the school. And there is
a "spirit of camaraderie" among the students of architecture.
Prof. Frederick D. Nichols has said that this spirit is such that
"it is difficult to get them to take electives in the College or to
attend lectures around the Grounds."

The Department of Art in the College of Arts and Sciences
acquired the services of internationally famous Prof. Frederick Hartt, chairman of the Art Department at the University
of Pennsylvania, who left that institution to become chairman
of the department at Virginia, succeeding Charles Smith, who
had retired. Regarded as one of the world's foremost art historians, Hartt had been sent by the U.S. Government to Flor-
ence, Italy, following the devastating floods there in the
middle sixties, to assess the damage and organize assistance.
He has been decorated twice by the Italian government.

The School of Education raised its entrance requirements
in 1962–63 to require that every entrant complete at least two
years of acceptable college work, or the equivalent, with fifty-
four hours of course work. This was to include a minimum of
twelve semester hours in the humanities, the social sciences,
and the natural sciences, with three hours in health and physi-

cal education. However, except for the twelve-year period between the sessions of 1950–51 and 1962–63, students had always been required to complete two years in the College in order to enter the School of Education.

The school was strengthened in 1965 when Prof. Francis G. Lankford, Jr., returned to the faculty as head of the Office of Institutional Analysis, after ten years as president of Longwood College. Commonwealth Prof. of Education and the author of textbooks in mathematics, Lankford also had served in 1962–63 as educational adviser to the Ford Foundation in Pakistan. He retired in 1972. Another admired member of the staff was Prof. William H. Seawell, chairman of the Department of Administration and supervisor of the School of Education.

Frederick E. Cyphert of the Ohio State faculty was named to the deanship in 1968 as successor to Dean Cherry and remained in the position until 1974. Cyphert resigned in that year to return to Ohio State, and Richard M. Brandt, who had served as a department chairman in the school, was appointed to succeed him. During Dean Cyphert's six years the faculty doubled to about one hundred members, and the dean was successful in obtaining significant grants. The Evaluation Research Center and Child Development Center were established, and Malcolm Provus and Donald Medley, said to be among the nation's top two or three scholars in evaluation and research, were added to the staff. The School of Education moved in 1973 into its modern new building, Ruffner Hall, on Emmet Street, planning for which had been under way for a dozen years. The faculty of the College of Arts and Sciences voted in 1970 to give no further degree credit in the College for physical education courses in the School of Education. A Department of Physical Education, separate from the College but under its dean, was established, and the course carried credit toward a degree.

Bruce W. Nelson, a University of Illinois Ph.D., came to Charlottesville in 1973 from the University of South Carolina as dean of the School of Continuing Education and assistant provost for continuing education. He succeeded André C. de Porry, who retired the previous year.

The Institute of Government got a new director in 1973 when Weldon Cooper retired from that position, and Clifton

85. *The heifer that was mysteriously transported to the Rotunda roof in May 1965 and died after being brought down.*

McCleskey of the University of Texas faculty succeeded him. Cooper, who continued to teach, was elected to the newly established Robert K. Gooch professorship. Praise came to him from many directions for his service with the institute and the *News Letter*, and he received a special citation from Gov. Linwood Holton. In the same year the institute was the recipient of a scholarship and a fellowship. Morton L. Wallerstein, '11, and Mrs. Wallerstein established the scholarship. Wallerstein had served as executive secretary of the Virginia Municipal League from 1921 to 1941 and had helped to found the institute. The Board of Visitors established a graduate fellowship in the name of Harold I. Baumes, who succeeded Morton Wallerstein with the Municipal League and who had just retired.

Special study centers for Latin-America and South Asia were established in 1965 and 1969, respectively. The former was one of only five undergraduate "language and area centers for Latin America" in this country. It was supported by funds granted under the National Defense Education Act, and students could obtain a B.A. degree with a major in Latin-American studies. Participating students would take courses in Spanish, Spanish-American literature, and Portuguese, with related courses in economics, geography, government, foreign affairs, history, sociology, and anthropology. Charles E. Reid, associate professor of Spanish, was chairman of the committee in charge of the program. The South Asian studies center was under the direction of John T. Roberts, assistant professor of Hindi and Sanskrit, and it would coordinate courses bearing on the area in the fields of government, foreign affairs, sociology, anthropology, history, general linguistics, religious studies, education, economics, and architecture. Degrees would not be granted by the center but by the various departments cooperating with it. An interdepartmental major in South Asian studies was available to undergraduates. The center planned to sponsor lectures and other cultural events.

In that era of nonconformity on college campuses the university's Student Council initiated a survey in 1967 of student attitudes toward the curriculum and the faculty. Five evaluation forms were sent to each undergraduate in the College of Arts and Sciences, with questions as to the courses and the professors and incisive queries as to the latter's performance. T. Jackson Lears, Jere R. Abrams, Stuart Pape and Ken Barry were supervising editors for the survey, and among their conclusions were the following: "Our investigation . . . uncovered a malaise which requires much more than cursory attention. There is evidence here to justify a radically new approach to the university's function as an institution, and more specifically to the undergraduate program." They called for "a more dynamic institution than now exists."

Adoption of a new curriculum for the College, pursuant to a careful study by a seventeen-member committee of deans, professors, and students, appointed in 1968, was a notable event. It would seem to have been an at least partial response to student criticism. Prof. Lewis M. Hammond was chairman of the committee. The new program of study replaced the long-established curriculum that "was set up after Noah landed," as Dean Cauthen expressed it. Much greater flexibility in the choice of courses by undergraduates was a salient feature, as was abandonment, at the discretion of the professor, of the rigid "no cuts" rule and of a comprehensive examination on the eve of graduation, if deemed desirable by the instructor. The plan with respect to class cuts replaced one adopted when enrollment was far smaller, and keeping track of wayward youths was consequently far easier. There had been almost endless grousing by students over the strict monitoring of class attendance. As for "comprehensives," it was pointed out that they had been held almost simultaneously with final examinations, and that many of the questions were identical.

Dean Cauthen noted that the students were now better prepared and more mature than formerly, and he felt that they had earned the greater flexibility offered by the new curriculum. In addition, he said: "The faculty provided all sorts of other opportunities for independent work, for work in seminars, possibilities for going into new and different majors, taking courses on pass/fail options, and expanding the number of courses that can be taken outside the College. Our students are ready for this kind of program. . . . This new curriculum has been the most far-reaching academic change and the most obvious example of our deepening commitment to the main tradition of this university. And it seems to be working out

well." The committee on the curriculum recommended abandonment of degree credit for Reserve Officers' Training
Corps courses offered by the army, navy, and air force at the
university. This was a period when the ROTC and all military
training were unpopular because of the Vietnam War, and
there were demonstrations against the ROTC in various parts
of the country. The committee's recommendation as to degree
credits was followed for a brief period, but a few months later
it was reversed by the Arts and Sciences faculty. One factor
could have been that the students voted 4,141 to 2,985 in favor of giving credit for the courses. About 780 were enrolled.
Another factor was the virtual certainty that the naval ROTC
would leave the university if credits were denied, and the
probability or possibility that the army and air force would do
likewise.

There was acute intellectual ferment on the campuses of
America in the late sixties and early seventies, and a question-
ing of ideas and attitudes previously regarded as immutable.
Evidences of this were soon seen at the University of Virginia.
An early sign was the organization in the spring of 1968 of the
University Forum, under the leadership of Peter Schenkkan,
an able student, later a Rhodes Scholar. "Some university-con-
nected gripe on your mind?" Schenkkan asked in a letter to
the student newspaper. "Causes, coeducation, counseling, culture? . . . Would you like to tell somebody besides your room-
mate about it?" The forum, with both faculty and students
involved, would give the two groups a chance to know each
other and work together for common objectives. The *Cavalier
Daily* pronounced it "by far the most promising and encouraging venture we have seen undertaken here in some time."
The forum was organized in May at a meeting in Maury Hall.
By the following fall an Experimental University had been set
up as part of a nationwide movement to supplement or replace existing degree programs. The prevailing curriculum
offered "no challenge" and there was no motivation to do
more than learn by rote, said the dissenting students at the
university. They wanted, among other things, an opportunity
for "give and take" with the professors. Leading figures in the
administration were sympathetic and several faculty members
agreed to conduct seminars. Elimination of "unsatisfactory"
courses and substitution of others was an objective of the par-

86. Dr. Kenneth R. Crispell, vice-president for health sciences, 1971–.

ticipating students. Proposed subjects for courses included "civil disobedience," "the generation gap," "Vietnam," "development of pop music," "educational TV," and "history of the mass media." It was proposed to "supplement, not supplant," the existing educational system, and it was hoped that credit would be given for the projected courses. Dean of Student Affairs D. Alan Williams was quoted as expressing "direct sympathy" with the concept but as warning that too much shouldn't be expected from it and that no "politically-oriented group" should be allowed to get control. About four hundred students registered for the thirty-one courses—considered an excellent beginning. By the second semester the emphasis had been changed, and sample courses were "foreign policy and morality," "bartending," "McLuhan and the media," and "introduction to general witching" (for women only). In the Experimental University, it was explained, there are no "teachers," "leaders," or "students"—only "participants." By the second semester of the session, 1969–70, the curriculum and method of operation had undergone further changes. It should be noted, however, that the Experimental University was purely informal, that it was set up by students and a few faculty members, and that it enjoyed no sanction or approval by the faculty, administration, or Board of Visitors. During the session of 1972–73 the program was in full swing, and over four hundred students were still registered. The experimental institution had "switched from academics to a more diverse curriculum," with such courses as "men's liberation," "balloon-making," "bee-keeping," "harmonica," "massage," "auto mechanics," "bridge," and "photography." Group leaders offered their services without charge, and the one-dollar registration fee was devoted largely to publishing the catalogue and providing class facilities.

First-year men were by no means immune from the currents sweeping over the campuses of the country, and twenty-six liberal arts seminars were offered at the session of 1969–70. Most of the seminars had more applicants than could be accommodated, with over four hundred registrants by early September. The seminars were held in the afternoons or evenings, with no extra compensation going to the professors in charge. Associate Dean of the College Marcus Mallett was director of the program, and degree credit was offered to those making satisfactory grades. By far the most popular seminars dealt with the following: "races, ghettos, and revolutions," "radicalism in politics," "the study of the future processes of social, economic, and political change," "the nature and meaning of revolution," "psychiatry, morality, and the law," "law and civil disobedience," "nonsense: its meaning and effect," and "sports: their role in the culture of man." A glaring light on the social and political climate of the era is shed by the eager interest of college freshmen in such subjects as these.

On a more conventional level the School of Continuing Education was offering adults throughout the commonwealth opportunities to continue their schooling in a great variety of fields. More than fifteen hundred graduate and undergraduate classes were available in 120 localities. Both credit and noncredit courses were available on the undergraduate level in liberal arts, commerce, engineering, technology, and education, and on the graduate level in engineering and education. Classes were held mostly at night. In addition, the school sponsored conferences, institutes, and short courses at the university for business and professional groups and also made available audiovisual services, including films and tapes, for use by discussion groups. Furthermore, the school helped to develop courses for the new FBI Academy at Quantico. In doing so the university cooperated in creating a national program of higher education for law-enforcement personnel throughout the United States. Some two thousand state, city, and county officials experienced in the criminal justice system were selected to attend the academy annually, taking courses in the behavioral sciences, law, management, communication, and forensic science. The academy opened in 1972. André C. de Porry had become dean of the university's School of General Studies in 1968, succeeding James W. Cole, Jr., who relinquished the post after serving for a decade, in order to return to full-time teaching. De Porry edited the book *For the Commonwealth: Extension and Continuing Education by the University of Virginia, 1912–1973.*

Soviet Russia's pioneer sputnik caused the universities of America to place so much emphasis on scientific advancement that other disciplines were having difficulty obtaining sufficient funds. It was gratifying, therefore, that $1,000,000 was given to the University of Virginia in 1969 to finance up to a dozen professorships in the fine arts and the humanities. The donor was the William R. Kenan, Jr., Charitable Trust. Kenan, a North Carolina native, began his career as a schoolteacher in Radford, Va., and then became one of the nation's most prominent industrialists and a great benefactor of the University of North Carolina. Income from his gift to the University of Virginia was matched by the state's Eminent Scholars Fund.

Additional emphasis was placed on the humanities at the Old Dominion Humanities Institute for Teachers, held at the university for four weeks each summer from 1966 through 1971. H. I. Willett and Lucien D. Adams, city school superintendents in Richmond, were successive chairmen of the Advisory Board. A carefully selected group of about sixty high and preparatory school teachers from all parts of the state attended these institutes, at which prominent university faculty members lectured. Professors Joseph L. Vaughan, T. Graham Hereford, and O. Allan Gianniny, Jr., were leaders in organizing and operating the institute, which was pronounced a notable success by many teachers who attended. Unfortunately, the program had to be terminated after the 1971 session for lack of funds.

Thirty-nine university professors received grants in 1968, totaling about $65,000, for study in the humanities and the social sciences during the summer, both in the United States and abroad. This represented a substantial increase over the amount available the preceding year and evidenced the growing emphasis on these disciplines.

A Federal Executive Institute for high-level government executives was formally opened in 1968 at the former Thomas Jefferson Inn, which, with its eight surrounding acres, had been leased for the purpose. Important officials in the federal establishment and other specialists were to lecture, along with university professors, during the series of eight-week courses, with a maximum of sixty persons enrolled for each.

A center for training historical and literary editors was established the following year, with George H. Reese, former assistant director of research at Colonial Williamsburg, in charge. Instruction for graduate students in English and history would be emphasized, and opportunities given for post-doctoral training and practical laboratory work in documentary editing. Reese, who held three degrees from the university, was appointed professor of humanistic sources and associate editor of *The Papers of George Washington*, to be published by the newly established University Press of Virginia. After World War II Reese spent six years in the foreign service. He subsequently headed the publications division of the Virginia State Library and was agent for the Virginia Committee on Colonial Records. In the latter capacity he spent eight years in England and France finding, abstracting, and filming millions of manuscripts relating to colonial Virginia.

Professorships in the Department of Economics and the School of Commerce were established about 1970 by groups interested in honoring persons eminent in the political and business worlds. The Virginia Bankers Association raised half of a $250,000 fund, with the other half contributed by bankers throughout the United States, for professorships in the Department of Economics in honor of U.S. Senators Carter Glass and A. Willis Robertson of Virginia. The first incumbent of the Robertson chair was Herbert Stein, former chairman of President Nixon's Council of Economic Advisers. Stein stated shortly before his appointment that Milton Friedman and the University of Chicago's conservative school of economics had been influential in shaping the courses in economics at Virginia and other institutions. Stein was a graduate of Chicago.

Some $2,500,000 was given to the university by Burkett Miller, a law school graduate, for the establishment of a conservative center for the study of public affairs, especially the presidency, with an equal amount to be bequeathed after his death. Miller took several years to decide whether to make the gift, since he feared that the center would fall into the hands of the radicals who were so active in the late sixties and early seventies. Finally he became convinced that the university could be trusted in the matter, and half of the money was made available. Plans were got under way in 1974 for the establishment of the White Burkett Miller Center of Public Affairs the following year. Prof. Frederick E. Nolting, Jr., was selected to be the center's first director.

Slightly over 62 percent of the Faculty of Arts and Sciences were tenured during the session of 1973–74—that is, they were assured of their positions until the age of retirement unless they engaged in some extremely serious misbehavior. The remaining 38 percent had three-year appointments which they were allowed to renew for another three years, after which a decision would be made by the administration as to whether they would be accorded permanent tenure. The faculty voted by a large majority to extend this six-year period by one year, if the candidate, the department chairman, and the dean of the faculty so desired. The question was raised whether it was wise to have as much as 62 percent of the faculty tenured. Some expressed the view that 50 to 60 percent was a more desirable figure.

The university's facilities were being used during the summer months by business, professional, educational, and governmental groups. Taking one such summer at random, we find the Graduate School of Business Administration holding a six-week management course with forty registrants from many states and the following groups meeting for from one to three days: national convention of Sigma Phi fraternity, School of Consumer Banking, Virginia Bankers' School, Nursing Home Institute, Realtors' Institute, Virginia Association of Insurance Agents, Steelworkers' Labor Institute, Virginia Credit Management Institute, Local Government Officials Conference, Virginia Association of Assessing Officers, Class Room Teachers' Conference, State School Superintendents' Conference, and Virginia Press Association News Seminars.

Prof. Robert K. Gooch relinquished the post of grand marshal of all academic functions in 1964 upon his retirement from active teaching. He had served for thirty-two years, having succeeded Armistead M. Dobie when Dobie was appointed dean of the Law School. Dobie had been grand marshal since "sometime after 1907." Dean B. F. D. Runk succeeded Gooch as marshal. Both men carried a handsome silver mace at the head of academic processions; the mace was presented to the university in 1961 by the Seven Society. It was made by Patek Philippe of Geneva, Switzerland, and bears a number of engraved university scenes and emblems. The university seal, pictures of the Rotunda, the serpentine walls, a colonnaded walkway on the Lawn, and the statues of Thomas Jefferson and James McConnell all appear on the artistically designed symbol of authority.

87. *William L. Duren, Jr., dean of the College, 1955–62, and University Professor of Mathematics.*

A number of significant administrative changes occurred in the 1960s. Robert J. Harris, chairman of the Vanderbilt University Department of Political Science, came to the university in 1963 as dean of the faculty of arts and sciences. A Princeton Ph.D., author of books in the governmental field, and former president of the Southern Political Science Association and editor of the *Journal of Politics*, he served as dean at Virginia for five years and then occupied the James Hart professorship of government. Upon his retirement as dean, he was succeeded by Prof. Fredson T. Bowers, who served for one year. Then David A. Shannon, chairman of the Rutgers University History Department, a lecturer in both Europe and the Orient, author of numerous historical works, and a University of Wisconsin Ph.D., succeeded to the position. Shannon occupied the deanship for two years and then was named vice-president and provost. Ernest H. Ern, assistant dean of the College of Arts and Sciences, was appointed dean of admissions in 1967, succeeding Marvin B. Perry, Jr., who left the university. A Ph.D. in geology from Lehigh University, Ern received two National Science Foundation grants in the preceding four years. D. Alan Williams, assistant provost since 1966, was named dean of student affairs two years later. B. F. D. Runk had resigned as dean of the university, and that office was discontinued. He remained as Samuel Miller Professor of Experimental Agriculture and Forestry. A Ph.D. of Northwestern University and professor of history, Williams would be responsible for student government and discipline, dormitory and student counseling, student health, and placement of financial aid. He also had supervision over foreign students, intramural athletics, and the University Union. The transition from Runk to Williams took place as turmoil in this and other student bodies throughout the nation was mounting steadily. The *Cavalier Daily* commented that "as chief disciplinarian and chief administration official in charge of student affairs" Dean Runk "has fulfilled his duties in these areas strictly but fairly.... His contributions to the university ... are invaluable." Raymond C. Bice was named assistant to President Shannon and secretary to the board of Visitors. In the latter capacity he succeeded Weldon Cooper, who remained as head of the Institute of Government. William A. Hobbs, '34, resigned from the Board of Visitors to fill a new position as head of the Department of Development and Public Affairs. He had been president of the M. A. Hanna Co. of Cleveland, Ohio, and senior vice-president of Clark, Dodge and Co., a New York investment banking firm. He would assist the university comptroller in assessing the institution's financial requirements.

A significant restructuring of administrative positions took place in 1970 when five vice-presidents were appointed by President Shannon. It was the first time that the university had had any vice-presidents. Four of the appointees were already there, and a fifth was brought in. The president explained that the basic functions of his principal deputies would continue, but as vice-presidents they would have "primary administrative responsibility and authority over the major divisions . . . that they administer." The five were: Provost Frank L. Hereford, Jr., appointed vice-president and provost; Comptroller Vincent Shea, vice-president for business and finance; Chancellor for Medical Affairs Thomas H. Hunter, vice-president for medical affairs; Dean of Student Affairs D. Alan Williams, vice-president for student affairs; and Edwin M. Crawford, who was serving as director of the Office of Institutional Research for the National Association of State Universities and Land Grant Colleges, vice-president for public affairs. William A. Hobbs, director of development and public affairs, had resigned several months before to accept the presidency of an investment firm. Crawford would be responsible for university-wide development, including all fund raising, and relations with local, state, and federal governments and alumni organizations.

The following year Dr. Kenneth R. Crispell, dean of the School of Medicine for the preceding six years, was named vice-president for health sciences, succeeding Dr. Thomas H. Hunter, who was returning to full-time teaching and research. As dean, Dr. Crispell had led the drive for increased production of health care personnel at the university, including a substantially larger enrollment in the Medical School. He was largely instrumental in securing the funding for the $9,100,-000 medical education building, which would make possible still higher enrollment.

Frank L. Hereford, Jr., resigned as vice-president and provost in 1971 to go back to teaching and research, and Dean

David Shannon was named to succeed him. Shannon also was made chairman of the Committee on the Future of the University, a post held by Hereford.

Robert T. Canevari, '64, assistant dean of students, was chosen dean, succeeding D. Alan Williams. Richard L. Godine, '53, a Charlottesville business executive, was appointed director of university development by Vice-President Crawford. Godine died about a year later, and Ward Sims, a '65 law graduate, was named to succeed him.

In the same year Robert D. Cross, until recently president of Swarthmore College, who also had been president of Hunter College and history chairman at Columbia, came to the university as dean of the faculty of arts and sciences. He succeeded W. Dexter Whitehead, who relinquished the post but continued as graduate dean. Cross would be chief adviser to the vice-president and provost on courses of study in graduate and undergraduate arts and sciences. He was typical of distinguished academicians who were being brought to the university during these years.

The first appointment of a student to the Board of Visitors occurred in 1970, when twenty-five-year-old J. Harvie Wilkinson III, an honor graduate of Yale and member of the second-year law class at Virginia, was named to the board by Gov. Linwood Holton. Wilkinson had written a widely praised book on U.S. Sen. Harry F. Byrd and his political organization and would soon join the law faculty, where he would be recognized as one of its ablest young members. His father, J. Harvie Wilkinson, Jr., retired from the board to make way for him.

Dean of Admissions Ernest H. Ern was appointed vice-president for student affairs in 1973, succeeding D. Alan Williams, who relinquished the position to return to teaching. Ern was to retain supervision over admissions, under a shift of authority, with direct control as dean vested in George B. Matthews, who had been serving as assistant dean of the School of Engineering and Applied Science. Matthews, a Princeton Ph.D., joined the faculty in 1960.

Edwin E. Floyd, former head of the Department of Mathematics, was appointed dean of the faculty of arts and sciences in 1974, succeeding Robert D. Cross, who resigned to return to the classroom. Dean Floyd had been a member of the faculty since 1949, and his work as a mathematician had been praised in the highest terms. Students protested that they had not been sufficiently consulted in connection with his selection as dean. Their opinions had been sought concerning several previous appointments, and they seemed to think that no one should be named to the administrative staff without prior ascertainment of their views.

William Faulkner, whose appointment as writer in residence during the fifties was mentioned in the previous chapter, continued as lecturer and consultant at the university until his death at Oxford, Miss., in 1962. The Nobel Prize winner, who divided his time between Charlottesville and Oxford, gave prestige to the institution's expanding sources and studies in American literature. Faulkner's observations on "Virginia snobs" caused something of a sensation. He liked the state, he said, "because Virginians are all snobs, and I like snobs. A snob has to spend so much time being a snob that he has little left to meddle with you, and it's very pleasant here."

There were mixed reports on Faulkner's performance as lecturer and consultant. *Corks and Curls* said after his death that he "gave freely of his greatness to this university which had so special a place in his affections." It went on to declare that he "met dozens of classes and other university and town groups, reading from his works and answering all manner of questions . . . held conferences with students and participated in the life of the university from classroom to athletic field." But an unnamed professor was quoted as saying: "A few times a year he meets with students reading his work, but often sheds little light on it. When asked about the meaning of some deeply significant passage, he is likely to say, 'Oh, it's just an old Mississippi folk tale, livened up by imagination,' or 'I was just trying to say something about the human condition.' Legend has it that when a puzzled student told him he had read 'Absalom, Absalom!' three times and still didn't understand it, Faulkner told him, 'Read it a fourth time.'" Faulkner left his manuscripts, books, and other materials to Alderman Library—described by President Shannon as "the most extensive [collection] in existence on the work of a single author."

Other writers in residence during the sixties and early seventies included Stephen Spender, English poet and critic; Richard Murphy, young Irish poet; John Dos Passos, novelist and historian, who left numerous manuscripts to the library, greatly supplemented after his death by Mrs. Dos Passos, to constitute one of the most complete collections anywhere for a single writer; Shelby Foote, American Civil War historian; and George Garrett, American novelist.

Former Ambassador Charles F. Baldwin became the university's first diplomat in residence in 1965. He had served as U.S. ambassador to Malaysia and in other diplomatic posts in many areas of the world. Baldwin did not teach a specific course but lectured in the Woodrow Wilson Department of Government and Foreign Affairs. The idea was to "expose the students to his practical experience." An eminent scholar in residence was Sir Robert Menzies, former prime minister of Australia, who spent four months at the university in 1966–67, lecturing in the Law School and the Woodrow Wilson Department. His wit was widely commented upon, and he and his charming wife, Dame Pattie, were extremely popular. Sir Robert was succeeded as scholar in residence by Sir John Wheeler-Bennett, the internationally known British historian to whom reference was made in chapter 3. He had lectured at the university periodically since the late thirties. Another distinguished visiting scholar was Lewis Mumford, historian and educator, who was on the Grounds in 1972 as Thomas Jefferson Memorial Foundation medalist and Foundation Professor of Architecture. He conducted a seminar in the School of Architecture on "The City in History." Pedro Beltran, former Peruvian prime minister, came for a few months as scholar in residence and lectured in the Graduate School of Business Administration. Beltran was publisher of Peru's largest newspaper as well as former ambassador to the United States.

The remarkable progress made by the university in its "pursuit of excellence," to employ one of Edgar Shannon's favorite phrases, is graphically illustrated in the number of the institution's endowed chairs. As already noted, establishment of the Center for Advanced Studies and the state's Eminent Scholars Fund had made possible the bringing to Charlottesville of prominent scholars from some of the nation's most prestigious universities to occupy these chairs. By 1974 the number of chairs was in excess of one hundred.

88. *Edward R. (Butch) Slaughter, coach in several varsity sports and director of intramural athletics, 1957–73.*

The degree to which excellence had been achieved also was evidenced in the number of important awards and other accolades won by faculty members during these years.

The highest award of the American Institute of Electrical Engineers was conferred on Engineering Dean Lawrence R. Quarles. He was made a fellow of the institute for his "contributions to engineering education and nuclear engineering."

Prof. Quincy Wright was chosen in 1961 by the American Council of Learned Societies as one of ten professors in this country to receive prizes of $10,000 for distinguished accomplishment in humanistic scholarship. He had been president of the American Association of University Professors, the International Political Science Association, and the American Political Science Association, was the author of important books, and had lectured in many parts of the world.

Various honors came to Dr. William H. Muller, Jr., chairman of the Department of Surgery. He was elected president of the Society of University Surgeons and later was chosen president, in the same year, of both the American Surgical Association and the Southern Surgical Association. Dr. Muller was named by Duke University as one of the five most distinguished medical graduates in the institution's history.

Prof. Joseph L. Vaughan, teacher of English in the School of Engineering and Applied Science, was one of only three active professors in the university for whom an endowed chair was established. He also was given the Alumni Association's Distinguished Professor Award in 1971. "It is common knowledge in the Colonnade Club, Alumni Hall, and around the Grounds that Joe Vaughan is one of the all-time great teachers," said an article in the *Alumni News*. "Somehow he has managed to convince some very hard-boiled students of science and business that there are horizons worth noticing beyond their slide-rules and statistics." Among Professor Vaughan's recreational diversions are painting and playing the violin.

The sixth annual Distinguished Service Award of the Mathematical Association of America went to Prof. William L. Duren, Jr., a former president of the association. He had been a delegate to various international gatherings and was the recipient of other honors, including appointment as University Professor in 1963–64. In that capacity he was considered a member of the faculty as a whole, and not attached to any single school or department.

Thomas P. Abernethy, Alumni Professor of History emeritus, was given the Award of Merit of the American Association of State and Local History for "writing state history with insight and distinction, furnishing a model for scholarly writing of localized history." Four of Abernethy's books were in the permanent library at the White House.

Frank S. Kaulback, Jr., dean of the McIntire School of Commerce, was chosen president of the 12,000-member American Accounting Association. He was also a member of the executive committee of the American Association of Collegiate Schools of Business, and for a number of years was a consultant to the comptroller general of the United States.

Prof. Jesse W. Beams added to the many honors that he had received previously when he was awarded the National Science Medal in 1968 for his contributions to the technology of the ultracentrifuge—one of twelve men who received this medal from the president of the United States. Five years later he was accorded a citation by the Atomic Energy Commission for his contributions to the nuclear energy program.

The Commander's Cross of the Order of Merit of the German Federal Republic was conferred on Prof. Oron J. Hale in 1969 for his service as deputy commissioner and commissioner for Bavaria more than a decade and a half before. Hale was a former chairman of the university's History Department and director of the Institute of Public Affairs. His *Germany and the Diplomatic Revolution* won the George Louis Beers Prize of the American Historical Association. Professor Hale received the Thomas Jefferson Award at Founder's Day in 1969. He retired in 1972.

Two members of the university faculty were named to high positions by President Nixon. Prof. Edwin S. Cohen, '36, professor of law since 1963, was appointed assistant secretary of the treasury for tax affairs. A nationally known tax lawyer who had practiced in New York City before joining the faculty, he was a member of Nixon's task force for tax reform during the 1968 presidential campaign. Prof. G. Warren Nutter, chairman of the Department of Economics and director of the Thomas Jefferson Center for Studies in Political Economy, was appointed assistant secretary of defense to represent the Department of Defense on the National Security Council. Nutter was considered an authority on the Soviet economy. In 1973 he was appointed an adjunct scholar at the American Enterprise Institute for Public Policy Research.

Two university faculty members were awarded the golden Grand Prix by France's minister of Housing and Equipment at the Festival of Building and Humanism at Cannes. They were Miss Merete Mattern, visiting professor of planning, and Mario I. Sama, assistant professor of planning in the School of Architecture. More than five hundred proposals from twenty-eight countries were submitted, and the university's winning entry was a projection of a theoretical community for the Fort Lincoln area of northeast Washington, D.C.

The university's English Department became one of the most distinguished in the nation during these years, and members of the faculty were winning awards right and left, both for teaching and for the writing of important books. "There's a kind of electricity in the community," said Douglas Day, one of the award winners, "something that encourages writing." He termed the department "better than excellent; it's superb." Day won the National Book Award for 1974 with his biography of Malcolm Lowry. He had taken three degrees at the university, including the Ph.D., and joined the faculty in 1962.

Principal credit for building up the department to so high a degree of distinction should go to Prof. Fredson T. Bowers, the noted bibliographer, who headed the department for a number of years. Also deserving praise for bringing several noted writers and teachers to the English faculty is Peter Taylor, a master of the short story, sometimes termed "the American Chekhov." A native of Tennessee, Taylor came to the university in 1967 from Harvard and was named Commonwealth Prof. of English. A New York *Times* reviewer described him as "one of the greatest writers America has ever produced," while a *New Republic* critic termed his work "old-style, Southern fried realism." He has contributed short stories to the *New Yorker* for many years. Taylor was elected in 1974 to the American Academy of Arts and Sciences. He has won the National Academy Award for fiction. His wife, Eleanor Ross Taylor, is an accomplished poet and has taught poetry writing.

English Prof. Francis R. Hart was chosen in 1969 by the Danforth Foundation to receive the $10,000 E. Harris Harbison Award as one of ten outstanding teachers in the United States. Hart was the author of various highly regarded books in the field of nineteenth-century British fiction and biography. In 1972 English Prof. Verdel A. Kolve, a specialist in medieval literature, won this same award. And Jacob C. Levenson, Edgar Allan Poe Professor, won it just before joining the English faculty. This gave the department three Harbison Award winners, the only English faculty in the country which could make that boast.

Longtime member of the English faculty Atcheson L. Hench, a recognized authority on the language, contributed to various dictionaries, including the *Dictionary of American English*, *Standard College Dictionary*, and *World Book Encyclopedia Dictionary*, as well as to the journal *American Speech*. He retired in 1962 and died in 1974.

Prof. Arthur Kyle Davis's *Matthew Arnold's Letters* received the university's Phi Beta Kappa Prize, and his three books on Virginia ballads were given the University of Chicago's Folklore Prize. Davis, a veteran English professor, had worked for forty years collecting more than three thousand songs and variants for the Virginia Folklore Society. His views on university affairs were often unconventional. As coauthor of the Gooch Report on athletics he urged abolition of all athletic scholarships, and he advocated elimination of Greek letter fraternities. Davis was also one of the early advocates of the admission of women to the university on the same basis as men. He retired in 1968 and died four years later.

A new award for professors deemed to have rendered special services to the university community beyond their academic or staff assignments was given by the Z Society in 1972 to law Prof. Charles Whitebread. In the two succeeding years it went to Kenneth G. Elzinga and Dante L. Germino, professors, respectively, of economics and history. These awards were presented at the annual dinner given by the Z Society to first-year students who had contributed significantly to the university in such areas as student government, sports, publications, or counseling. The society's 1971 Organization Award went to the university Glee Club for its excellent concerts, its album *The Sun Dial*, and its successful European tour. The services of U.S. Circuit Judge Albert V. Bryan, '21, who had just retired as rector of the university, were recognized when the Z Society established an intramural high point trophy in his honor in 1964. The society has been giving awards annually since 1953 to the student in each of about a dozen schools or departments who makes the highest grade for the session.

A father and son, Dr. Byrd S. Leavell of the medical faculty and Byrd S. Leavell, Jr., a third-year student in the College, received two of the university's highest awards in 1972. Dr. Leavell won the Distinguished Professor Award of the Alumni Association, his son the "Pete" Gray Award of the Arthur P. Gray IV Foundation, established in honor of "Pete" Gray, a much admired university student who lost his life in Vietnam.

Seven professors were cited in 1973 by a national committee of college and university officials for their exceptional service, achievements, and leadership in education. They were history Prof. Willie Lee Rose, College Dean Irby B. Cauthen, Jr., engineering Dean Lawrence R. Quarles, education Professors Richard M. Brandt and Richard A. Meade, architecture Prof. James A. D. Cox, and physics Prof. Robert V. Coleman.

An addition to the women's dormitory was named Roberta Hollingsworth Gwathmey House in honor of Roberta H. Gwathmey, dean of women from 1935 to 1967.

EIGHT

The Passing
of the Old University

THE DECADE OF the sixties and the early years of the seventies witnessed significant changes in the size and makeup of the university's student body, and this, in turn, brought drastic revision of some time-honored attitudes, traditions, and customs. The enrollment of hundreds of blacks and thousands of women in the seventies could not fail to bring far-reaching breaks with the past. The Honor System was affected in important ways, and this will be given detailed attention in chapter 10. But the institution's faculty, academic standards, and intellectual level were sharply upgraded, and the students manifested a greatly augmented concern for the less fortunate elements of society. The university's élitist image as a sort of academic pleasure dome where partying and drinking had been regarded—erroneously—by segments of the public as almost the sole interest of the undergraduates underwent considerable modification.

In the years immediately following World War II the prevailing student attitude was "complete opposition to any change whatever," Dean Raymond C. Bice wrote in the *University of Virginia Magazine* for April 1961. Also, a popular divertissement of the boys was shooting·out the lights on the Grounds with rifle fire as soon as they were installed, with the result that "concertgoers found it necessary to carry flashlights when attending events in Cabell Hall," Dean Bice recalled. And John A. Carter, Jr., '53, a brilliant student at the university and later a leading member of the Wake Forest faculty, wrote from that campus: "Should the whole continent of Europe be destroyed tomorrow by nuclear power, it would not surprise me to read letters to the *Cavalier Daily* which discussed the effect of that catastrophe upon the parking problem and rushing regulations."

Despite such attitudes and the cantankerous behavior of the postwar generation of university students, they "continued to behave as gentlemen," Dean Bice wrote. "Generations of faculty members have observed that University of Virginia students are a joy to teach because of the consistently courteous and cooperative attitude. On the other hand . . . the post-war student seemed satisfied with a 'C' grade, and the 'never-stick-your-neck-out' attitude was prevalent."

The "turning point for the University of Virginia student body" came during the middle and late fifties, Bice wrote. It was then that the students "began placing emphasis on excellence, rather than the previous emphasis on being permitted unlimited freedom." A general tightening up of academic standards brought no serious complaints from the undergraduates. Also, there was "an immense increase in interest in the affairs of the university, the nation, and the world."

The Honors Program, begun in 1937, had developed remarkably in the ensuing decades. It was "unique" and "the bravest program, the most thorough-going of any in the nation," David C. Yalden-Thompson, the professor in charge, and a graduate of both Oxford and Cambridge, said in 1962. The program called for rigorous study, a weekly conference with the faculty tutor, auditing of lectures thought desirable by the tutor, in addition to those regularly attended, preparation of papers and often of a thesis in the final year, extensive reading both during the session and the summers, and final honors examinations. The average number of students taking the course was six until after World War II, when the number increased gradually. There were twenty-five in 1957 and thirty-five two years later, seventeen of whom were candidates for degrees with honors.

As for student customs, one of long standing had undergone considerable modification, Prof. Robert K. Gooch said in an address at the 1965 Finals. This was the practice of not speaking to another individual to whom one had not been introduced. And the custom of donning coats and ties was

*89. Edward Younger, professor of history and dean of the
Graduate School of Arts and Sciences, 1966–69.*

gradually fading out, until in 1969–70 and especially in 1970–71 the wearing of these habiliments stopped. Many students also wore no socks. When pictures were taken for the annual, a number of the boys were inclined to dress up, but under ordinary circumstances coats and ties were seldom seen.

Prof. Jesse Beams noticed a young man outside his office window who was so frightfully dirty and unkempt that he sent his secretary to tell him that whereas "we no longer expect students to wear coats and ties, we can't have them going around looking as though they had just crawled from under a freight car." He urged the youth to take a bath, put on a shirt and shoes, and shape up. When the secretary returned from delivering the directive, she said, "Do you know who that is?" "No, who is it?" asked Beams. "That's your new assistant professor of physics from Berkeley." At about this time Dean of the Faculty Fredson T. Bowers admonished the professors concerning their dress. "This is certainly no order," said his memorandum, "but it is a strong suggestion that persons who meet their classes in less formal dress than many of their students have very little idea of good manners or of the proper dignity that ought to accompany this profession." A senior faculty member remarked that he and several of his friends had stopped going to faculty meetings because so many of the younger members were attending in their bare feet. Such capricious behavior by a minority of professors was a temporary phenomenon.

A fundamental difference between the university of this era and that of four or five decades earlier was the lack of participation in campus affairs by students in the professional schools and members of the principal athletic teams. Before World War II, class officers, editors of publications, and members of ribbon societies and other social organizations were often students in the law or medical schools, prominent athletes, or both. But in later years this was no longer true, at least not to anything like the same extent. The embryo lawyers and doctors were kept so busy with their studies in that highly competitive age that they had little time for anything else. Besides, the lawyers were separated geographically in their new home on the North Grounds. As for the athletes, notably the football and basketball players, they underwent such intensive training for so much of the year that they too were no longer able to participate in other extracurricular activities.

However, some students, almost all of them in the College, were more involved in university affairs than ever before. In 1967, for example, they had asked for and obtained membership on many committees that formerly were composed entirely of faculty and administration representatives. These included the committees on fraternities, housing, the calendar, university catalogues, awards, student activities and fees, registration, and the sesquicentennial.

Stricter discipline was imposed on the students when B. F. D. Runk took over as dean of the university in 1959. Upon him devolved the duty of enforcing the new rules, and there were not many dull moments for him during the ensuing years. Inevitably he was the target of brickbats from students who resented all efforts to control their misbehavior. In the words of *Corks and Curls,* "It is Mr. Runk who is called to the station at two in the morning to bail a student out, and it is he who presents the students' complaints to the Board of Visitors. He is in the ticklish position of trying to be friend and disciplinarian at the same time." The dimensions of Dean Runk's problem also may be glimpsed in the statement of Prof. T. Braxton Woody concerning the "tradition of freedom" at the university: "Those who cherish this tradition believe in the inalienable right of every student to do as he pleases, to live where he pleases, to take whatever courses he likes, to cut classes, to drive a car and park it anywhere, to get drunk, to get a real education, not merely to earn a diploma by passing a fixed number of courses."

There was a frightful uproar, for example, when rules were promulgated that forbade students from bringing whiskey bottles, buckets of ice, sixpacks of beer and similar drinkables, and their auxiliaries to the stadium at football games. This regulation was intended to achieve compliance with the state law that banned consumption of alcoholic beverages in public. But the student reaction was predictable: "Virginia is becoming just another prep school," "One more evidence of state-Uism," and similar observations. "Get thee to a nunnery!" was the admonition of one student to the dean. All this brought various students to Runk's defense, one of whom wrote: "I, for one, am fed up with his role as scapegoat. The number of people who make him a scapegoat, thereby betraying their naiveté and stupidity, is astonishing." The student added that the problem was not Dean Runk but the university's skyrocketing enrollment.

Two student riots in early November 1961 brought the university much unfavorable publicity and resulted in a ruling by President Shannon, concurred in unanimously by the Student Council, that any student participating in a riot would be suspended and that presence at a riot constituted participation. About four hundred students took part in both disorders, along fraternity row on Rugby Road. The first was said to have been triggered by a reduction in the Thanksgiving holiday, although the reduction had been announced a year previously. Several nights later there was a more serious riot when parties ended in the fraternity houses on Openings weekend. Twenty-one persons were arrested, only six of them students. This latter disturbance was blamed by the authorities primarily on outsiders who had come to the fraternities' "open parties." It was announced that no more open parties would be held.

University Chief of Police Rea Houchens sounded an encouraging note two years later when asked if the behavior of the students had improved during his thirteen years as chief. He said it certainly had. "Back in 1950," said Houchens, "we had a bad bunch of GI's here. Now they [the students] are much less rowdy."

The drug problem was growing more menacing in the late sixties, at Virginia and on campuses throughout the land. Dean Runk issued a warning against the use of "hallucinogenic drugs, particularly marijuana and LSD," saying that their possession or use by students "is considered an indication that they are not constructively interested in academic work in this university community, and may be given an immediate opportunity to withdraw or be suspended." This warning was repeated by D. Alan Williams when he succeeded Runk in 1968. Later, in commenting on his retirement from the deanship, Runk said concerning the demonstrations and other disorders that were mounting near the end of the decade, "I don't think I could have lived through the turmoil."

Smoking of marijuana, or grass, by the students was growing rapidly in 1966–67, according to one student publication,
and eight fraternities were said to have had "internal problems with marijuana" during the session. An unnamed seller
of the drug was quoted as estimating that "at least one thousand students" were smoking it, many regularly and others
occasionally. He said he was "sick" over the fact that "speed"
and heroin were also being used by some students. The prevailing view seemed to be, however, that drug use at the University of Virginia was below that at many other institutions.
But by 1971 state narcotics agent Carl Deavers said the heroin
problem had "grown immensely in the last year, not only at
the university level but at the high school level as well." Charlottesville was said to be the center of the drug traffic in central
Virginia, with the university grounds its "nucleus." Marijuana
was so much in evidence at concerts near the opening of the
1972–73 session that students were warned that the events
might be called off unless the smoking ceased. Several girls
left one concert for fear of getting high from the grass being
smoked around them.

The university community was shocked in the spring of
1973 when seven members of the Zeta Beta Tau fraternity
were arrested on "flagrant" drug charges. It was Zeta Beta
Tau's second offense, since it had been put on probation two
years before on similar grounds. The university, in conjunc-
tion with the fraternity's national headquarters, revoked recognition of the local chapter until 1976. This prevented ZBT
from conducting any kind of rush or participating in any interfraternity functions for three years. It changed its name to
"The Anchorage," and the spokesman said that although it
was not recognized as a social fraternity, it fully intended "to
campaign for and take in new members this year, just as will
all the fraternities."

A poll sponsored by the Student Council in 1973 indicated
that drug use at Virginia was below the national average.
Based on a 7 percent "representative sample," the returns
showed that 53.6 percent had used marijuana as against 67
percent in the nation; of those at Virginia almost 60 percent
said they used it only once a month or less. Use of hallucino-
gens (LSD, peyote, mescaline, etc.) was 17.4 percent as against
27 percent nationally, with 95 percent of those at the univer-

sity using these hard drugs no more than once a month. As for alcohol, 91.3 percent of the sample said they had drunk it compared with 98 percent nationally. About 88 percent declared that they had begun using it before they came to the university.

The fraternities were the source of many of Dean Runk's problems. He believed in them, provided they behaved themselves reasonably well and kept their houses in decent order, but their behavior and their living quarters often left much to be desired. Contrasting conditions in the houses in the 1920s and those prevailing some forty years later, Runk said that in the twenties the boys "liked to keep them up and liked them to look neat and orderly," and they were "entirely different from the hovels which are there today."

Fraternity houses were sometimes almost wrecked by the big weekend parties of the sixties and seventies. "It seems like some students get the idea that party weekends are occasions for the systematic demolition of furniture, walls, doors, etc.," the *Cavalier Daily* said in 1967. "The more frustrated members of the [student] community exercise their frustration by reducing windows and pianos to fragments." On the morning after parties the terrain in front of the houses, notably along Rugby Road and Madison Lane, was often littered with beer cans by the hundreds, whiskey bottles, and other debris. The student newspaper compared the university's fraternity houses to those at VPI, "the school you find so uncouth." It said those at VPI were "immaculate . . . the furniture like new, the walls clean, the stairs and doors in excellent shape and the party rooms veritable show places."

Early in the decade the dean put six fraternities on social probation for celebrations held in connection with Bid Sunday. Then Father William A. Stickle, Roman Catholic chaplain at the university, said it was "a sin for a Catholic to join a fraternity which follows morally objectionable practices." He provided no specifics, and contented himself with references to fraternity parties "or practices" and "immoral conversation." Lee Farris, a Catholic layman and Charlottesville schoolteacher, said in a letter to the *Cavalier Daily* that he considered Father Stickle "woefully misinformed . . . if he is convinced that serious sin of any kind takes place at the fraternity par-

90. *Charles C. Abbott, dean of the Graduate School of Business Administration, 1954–72.*

ties." The Interfraternity Council pointed out that "each fraternity must have a local adviser to both aid and guide it, and a university-approved chaperone to insure proper conduct at all social functions."

For each of the preceding ten years the scholastic average for fraternity men had been below that for all male students. This despite the rule that a pledge had to make a grade of at least 2.0 out of a possible 4.0 to be initiated. Also, any house with an overall average of less than 2.0 was put on social probation. The IMPs gave a trophy for the highest academic average achieved by a fraternity. At about this time Alderman Library sent emissaries into the fraternity houses, with no questions asked, looking for books that were missing from the library's shelves. They returned with seven truckloads.

The session of 1965–66 brought improved conditions in the Greek letter organizations. For the first time in a decade their overall scholastic average was better than that for the university's male population as a whole. As *Corks and Curls* expressed it, the fraternities were "attempting to help themselves through constructive action, constant evaluation and continual activity." Improved service to the community was stressed, as well as better scholastic performance. "New projects . . . were added to our standard Children's Rehabilitation Carnival, as all thirty-one houses gave their helping hands to Charlottesville through orphan parties at Christmas, work for the Recording for the Blind, collection drives for the Salvation Army, and contributions to the Rescue Squad," said the university annual. "The IFC aided the UGF throughout Charlottesville and also lent support to underprivileged children in 'big-brother' campaigns."

Yet the fraternity system was heading into an era when it would be under heavy attack and when its influence would reach its lowest ebb in the university's history. Leading fraternity men freely predicted during this period, when all aspects of "the establishment" were being assailed, that the Greek letter organizations might well be on the way out. Dean of Student Affairs D. Alan Williams said that while he did not foresee their "immediate demise," they would have to improve in order to survive.

Addressing a specific phase of the problem, the *University of Virginia Magazine* (November 1967), edited by Lawrence Siegel and Robert Aaronson, referred to "the yet almost completely unbroken agreement of non-integration between the Jewish and Christian fraternity houses. . . . The great enforcers of this . . . have been the fraternities themselves; undoubtedly the Jewish fraternities have been the most adamant supporters of the previous status quo, but the Christian houses have not been far behind. This year's rush has been officially declared open by the IFC. . . . We of the *UVM* hail the event."

Rules covering rushing were an almost constant subject of controversy. The period when rushing was to take place and the conditions that had to be observed were changing from time to time. Various fraternities were charged with violating the rules in an effort to gain an advantage over their rivals. "Dirty rush has never been more rampant," said the student newspaper in 1968, "and there is some evidence that the despicable practice of extracting rushees' invitations from their mailboxes has occurred again."

By the session of 1969–70, when the university and many other institutions of higher learning were in turmoil over the war in Vietnam, the fraternities were being sharply assailed in *Cavalier Daily* editorials. Robert B. Cullen, the editor, referred at the opening of the session to the fraternity system as "a slowly dying anachronism" and advised first-year men, "Don't rush, don't pledge." Yet Rod MacDonald, the paper's managing editor, took an adversary position in a signed reply. He suggested that the incoming student "weigh the real facts and meet the people himself before deciding whether to join." The student should not be "bullied into passivity by the ballyhoo of opposition," he declared.

At the 1970 Easters fraternities at the university embarked upon one of the most incredible forms of diversion in the annals of education. Students and their dates created artificial mudholes by hosing down areas in front of their fraternities and in Mad Bowl behind Madison Hall, and slithered around prone in the gunk. Large cans of grain alcohol mixed with fruit juice added zest to the occasion as the boys and girls got mud in their eyes, in their hair, down their necks, and all over their clothes. The affair was pronounced such a howling success that it became larger, noisier, and more frantic each succeeding year, with electronically amplified rock bands on Rugby Road providing an unbelievable din, passing motorists splattered with mud, and kindred spirits arriving from up and down the East Coast for what *Playboy* magazine described as "the best party in America." After this had gone on for three of four years, some ten thousand persons, many from distant parts, were estimated to be participating. The university's plumbing was being stopped up on a gigantic scale by students who repaired to their dormitories to remove the mud. Eight of the McCormick Road dormitories were turned into "mud torrents" in April 1972, an irate Dean Alan Williams declared. He pronounced it "the worst mess I've seen in my fifteen years here." Showers were plugged with mud, entire floors flooded and several dorm entrances "sealed with mud." On top of all else, the dorms had just undergone a major renovation. Students would be expected to clean the buildings and would be assessed for any needed repairs, Williams said. By 1974 it was becoming obvious that a halt would have to be called on these stupefying collegiate gambols.

By that year it was also obvious that fraternities were staging a comeback, not only at Virginia but in most institutions throughout the land. In 1973 the largest number of first-year pledges in the university's history, approximately 45 percent of the entering class, were signed by the various lodges. Fraternities were once more important in the university's undergraduate affairs.

A number of pranks, most of them involving the Rotunda, occurred during the Shannon years. The first was the flying of a Confederate flag from the roof of the building on Feb. 26, 1961—the one hundredth anniversary of the flying of a similar flag from the Rotunda dome on the eve of the Civil War. Seven students apparently clambered up after midnight, despite high winds, and flung the banner to the breeze, where passersby saw it next morning. The Rotunda dome was again in the spotlight on May 5, 1965, when persons on the Lawn noted a calf lying tied on the roof. Investigation showed that students had somehow gotten the animal up there in the middle of the night, after sawing through the latch designed to prevent such monkeyshines. The young Angus steer was given a tranquilizer and brought down. It died a few hours later from unknown causes. The episode got into the press, worldwide, and an avalanche of protesting letters arrived at the president's office from animal lovers. The students who were responsible doubtless were much grieved over the young steer's unexpected demise.

The Rotunda clock came in for some undergraduate attention in 1967 and again in 1971. In the former years, the countenance of Mickey Mouse suddenly shone forth from its face on the weekend of the University of North Carolina football game, and in the spring of 1971 Vice-President Spiro Agnew peered forth from the same spot. Nobody could ascertain who was responsible for these hazardous escapades.

What could have been a much more serious prank occurred on Saturday evening of the Easters weekend in 1968 when parties unknown toppled the statue of Thomas Jefferson from its pedestal in front of the Rotunda. It was found lying on its head in the grass. Fortunately, the bronze figure was not damaged. The halyards on the nearby flagpole also had been cut.

The fad for "streaking," that is, running about in public with few or no clothes on, swept the country's educational institutions in 1974, and the University of Virginia was no exception. Several male students were streaking about the Grounds on Feb. 20, despite the wintry atmosphere. One, clad only in a Batman's cape, sprinted across the Lawn, while another raced through Alderman Library wearing a motorcycle helmet and nothing else. Two days later dozens of streakers, including several coeds, appeared, especially in the McCormick Road dormitory area. A number of male students were arrested on Feb. 25 for displaying unwonted portions of their epidermis in public.

Homosexual students at the university began coming into the open in 1972. On May 12 of that year the *Cavalier Daily* devoted two pages to the subject and appeared not unsympathetic to this once-despised lifestyle. The Gay Student Union (GSU) had been formed shortly before, with some thirty members, and had adopted a written constitution "formalizing their commitment to the liberation of homosexuals at the university." "As many as 40 gays came to a GSU private party in the dorms last month," said one article. In the following fall the Student Union voted 12 to 9 in favor of allocating $45 to the Gay Student Union, but the Board of Visitors, on recommendation of President Shannon, vetoed the plan. The board held that "the GSU cultivates and advocates a style of sexual life," and "this is a private and personal matter which has no

relationship to the educational purposes of the university. . . .
The board has no power to authorize a disbursement of funds
unrelated to the purposes of the university." The *Cavalier Daily*
assailed Shannon and the board for their decision.

Although barriers to the enrollment of black students had
been breached in the middle fifties, only a few had matriculated a decade later. Wesley Harris entered the Engineering
School in 1960, and was graduated with honors in 1964. He
was the first black student to be given a room on the Lawn.
Harris endured many "venomous racial slurs" during his four
years, according to Bryan Kay's "History of Desegregation at
the University of Virginia: 1950–1969." The first black professor, Nathan Johnson, a former school superintendent in
southside Virginia, joined the School of Education faculty in
1967. In the middle and late sixties there was much agitation
among certain elements of the faculty and students for an end
to what was termed "racism" in the institution. Some three
hundred paraded down the Lawn in the rain in a "sympathy
for Selma" demonstration, exhibiting solidarity with the civil
rights leaders who were under heavy fire in Selma, Ala.

As the end of the decade neared and agitation of various
kinds swept the Grounds, the race question was much to the
force. The National Association for the Advancement of Colored People claimed that the university's Student Aid Foundation was discriminating against black athletes, but President
Shannon replied that "the established policy of the university
is not to discriminate against any persons by reason of their
race, color, religion or national origin." Difficulty was being
experienced in getting blacks of all kinds, whether athletes or
not. The first black athlete was enrolled from Lane High
School in Charlottesville for the session of 1967–68, but others were slow in coming. The university demanded high academic performance, and some blacks felt that there were few
opportunities for social diversion and contacts in and near
Charlottesville.

President Shannon resigned from the Farmington Country
Club because it did not admit blacks as members. Explaining
his action later, he said: "I felt we just couldn't possibly . . . be
in good faith if we were using that facility and reimbursing
people for those expenses." Comptroller Vincent Shea accord-

91. D. Alan Williams, *vice-president for student affairs, 1970–73.*

92. Lawrence R. Quarles, *dean of engineering and applied science, 1955–73.*

ingly sent each department head a written notice that university funds could not be used for entertainment at any segregated facility. Some alumni criticized the decision, but the Board of Visitors backed it as did the Student Council and students in other leadership positions. As early as 1966 the council, by a 10–4 vote, had declared off limits every local business that refused to serve anyone for racial reasons. The *Cavalier Daily* attacked the action, saying it was taken with seven council members absent and that the stand was "inconsistent with freedom of the individual and freedom of choice." But the following year the Student Council was threatening to request copies of the various fraternity constitutions with a view to determining whether they contained racially discriminatory clauses. In 1968 it voted unanimously that all university organizations should be prohibited from using segregated facilities. By then the council had one black member, elected by the student body.

The *Cavalier Daily*, edited by Charles C. Calhoun, a future Rhodes Scholar, was now a militant advocate of better attitudes toward the treatment of blacks, but it denied that the university was "racist." Richard B. Gwathmey, Jr., who succeeded Calhoun as editor, was still more militant. "The University of Virginia, wallowing in its whiteness, like a hippopotamus in the mud, took the first step toward lumbering out of that whiteness when it hired a black admissions officer last month," Gwathmey wrote in 1969. The paper demanded that any advertisements placed in its columns seeking housing for students' dates be accompanied by a signed agreement not to discriminate on racial grounds. Student Council passed a unanimous resolution urging university personnel to boycott barber and beauty shops that refused to accept black patrons. It also took a stand against racial discrimination in any student organization officially recognized by the council.

The university reacted to the murder of Martin Luther King, Jr., in early April 1968 by flying the Rotunda flag at half mast, taking part in the march to services in Zion Baptist Church, and holding services of its own in Cabell Hall on the "national day of mourning," with President Shannon and Dean Robert J. Harris as speakers. During King's funeral, classes at the university were made optional for both faculty and students.

Mrs. Elizabeth Johnson, a black on leave from the Virginia Union University faculty, was appointed full-time assistant dean of admissions, succeeding Fred T. Stokes, who had been serving only part-time. She would travel over the state talking with black high school seniors in the hope of doubling the university's Negro enrollment. Two blacks, John Thomas of Norfolk and George Taylor of Hampton, were appointed student assistant recruiters who would also travel in search of matriculates.

On Founder's Day 1969 the relatively small group of students who had been agitating for some time, albeit in orderly fashion, against what they termed "racism" at the university, staged a rally at the Rotunda. They urged those present to write their legislators in criticism of university practices. Having held their rally they moved to Cabell Hall for the Founder's Day ceremonies. On the program was a special humanitarian award of the Seven Society for promoting racial harmony in the community. The agitators against "racism" apparently assumed that the recipient would be "just another racist," and they stamped out of the hall as President Shannon rose to make known the name of the winner. They were left looking decidedly sheepish when they found later that the winner was the Reverend Henry B. Mitchell, the black rector of Charlottesville's mostly black Trinity Episcopal church.

As early as the session of 1966–67, President Shannon had issued a directive that where there was a black and a white applicant for a faculty or staff position and qualifications of the two were approximately equal, the black should be employed. Prof. William A. Elwood of the English Department, who was named subsequently an assistant to Shannon as coordinator for programs to further equal opportunity, said that in 1967–69 "there was quite a turnabout in student opinion here. . . . Students recognized the need to actively seek blacks and said so." In 1969 Shannon appointed a committee of both faculty and students, headed by William Rotch, to study the problem of increasing black enrollment and make recommendations. It reported in August of that year and urged appointment of a dean who would serve as coordinator of all activities relative to recruitment and retention of black students and faculty" and creation of "a new administrative position of significance responsible for generating and coordinating the development of a more broadly based student body." President Shannon "was able himself to administratively implement about 90 percent of the recommendations," said Vice-President and Provost David Shannon. He stressed the difficulties in getting qualified blacks for this and other university programs and pointed out that of all the Ph.D.'s in the United States, only 1.3 percent were black. "We have to pay them more than a white person with similar qualifications, simply because of the market," David Shannon said.

Two courses dealing with the history of the Negro in America were added to the curriculum at about this time, with Edgar Toppin of Virginia State as the instructor. Some seventy-five students showed up for the first lecture, but only eight or ten were black. An interdisciplinary course in Afro-American studies, to be conducted in part, by visiting black lecturers, was offered as the first portion of a new Afro-American studies program. Paul M. Gaston, associate professor of history, was the director. The student Committee on Fraternities passed a resolution affirming the university's stand against racial discrimination in the fraternity system. Among the 578 students pledged on Bid Sunday in October 1969, five were black. The Negroes had no fraternities of their own, but several of their fraternities and sororities would soon establish chapters at the university. These fraternities were "service oriented," they emphasized, and were not primarily social organizations. Their "major goal," they said, was "to serve the university and the surrounding community, aiding them through such projects as working for the March of Dimes, taking blood pressure readings, holding blood drives and sponsoring Boy Scout troops." These fraternities and sororities at the university had no chapter houses and were in need of a suitable place to hold meetings.

Summer programs to aid disadvantaged high school juniors and seniors in preparing for college were launched at the university in 1969. Also, there was a special institute for minority students who had graduated from college and wished to attend law school. High school students were given an opportunity in the summer, as part of the Upward Bound program, to learn more about college life and what might be expected of them and to undergird their academic performance. Would-be law students were given six weeks of intensive orientation designed to improve their analytical and verbal abilities and also aid them in deciding whether, after all, they wanted to attend law school. The institute was one of ten in the country held under the auspices of the Council on Legal Education.

Recruiting efforts at Virginia were paying off as total black enrollment in the fall of 1970 was 236, compared with 102 the year before, or almost 2.2 percent of the student body as against 1.3 percent. By the fall of 1971 the figure had been increased to 344. The university was praised by the National Association of State Universities and Land Grant Colleges for using black students as recruiters.

An important advance for the minority group came when James R. Roebuck, Jr., of Philadelphia, a black student in the Graduate School of Arts and Sciences, was elected president of the Student Council. Two years later Linda Howard, a black from Petersburg, was chosen president of the Law School. There were 31 Negroes in that school out of a total enrollment of 911.

Black Culture Week was being held annually, under the auspices of the University Union and Black Students for Freedom. There were exhibits, lectures, films, and discussions, all dealing with the general theme of black culture's influence in the United States. Many whites attended. Black History Week was held simultaneously. The Students for Freedom changed their name to the Black Students Alliance and provided a variety of services, including advising first-year black students on how to study and to cope with academic problems, acquainting undergraduates with members of the Charlottesville community, and providing dances, cookouts, and theater trips. The Muntu Fine Arts Guild, which began as the Muntu Drama Guild, and included a dance group, was organized. Black Voices of the University of Virginia, an organization of gospel singers, gave renditions in and near Charlottesville.

Despite the foregoing, there were vehement protestations from students of both races that there was no equality of treatment. Tom Collier, white president of the Student Council, declared in 1971 to a protest meeting on the Lawn that "we live with racism every day at this university." Willie Ivey of the Black Students Council read a list of grievances. He called a meeting of his organization in Newcomb Hall to discuss these problems and ousted two white students who sought to attend.

An Equal Opportunity Counseling Program was set up in the summer of 1973, with Paul Saunier, Jr., who had been named Equal Opportunity Administrator, and the Student Council cooperating. Larry Sabato, president of the Student Council, was a leader in establishing the program. By that fall four national black fraternities and one sorority had chapters on the Grounds, and the black enrollment had risen to over five hundred. Numerous members of that race had been added to the university faculty and staff.

The Student Council and *Cavalier Daily* began a crusade in 1974 intended to persuade members of the university community to resign from the Farmington Country Club, since it had no black members. "Our worst suspicions have been confirmed," said the student newspaper, edited by Tim Wheeler. "Farmington Country Club is a racist, all-white, discriminatory organization." It rapped university administrators who belonged to the club and praised President Shannon for resigning some years before. The paper published an entire page of interviews supporting its position. It called on Frank L. Hereford, Jr., who had just been elected president of the university as successor to Shannon, to resign from the club. He replied that he intended to remain as a member and to work within the organization for a change in admission policies. The *Cavalier Daily* praised the IMP Society, saying that "it has in some ways taken the lead," by electing to its membership "students who may have been left out of other groups, especially women and blacks."

Black students in 1974 were taking their places more and more as integral parts of the university scene. They were being elected to high office by the white students and chosen as members of the honor societies and ribbon societies, not to mention IMP and Z. A few were elected to the predominantly white fraternities, but many preferred to join their own organizations. In athletics they were making a significant contribution. All in all, despite openly expressed dissatisfaction by some black matriculates, integration was proceeding at the University of Virginia, and to a degree that would have been unthinkable a few decades earlier.

93. *Irby B. Cauthen, Jr., professor of English and dean of the College, 1962–.*

Women students in the middle sixties were limited principally to the graduate and professional schools, but they could enter certain undergraduate schools if they had had two years of college work elsewhere. Two were elected to the Student Council in 1966. More and more discussion was being heard concerning the desirability of admitting them to all schools on the same basis as men.

Attention at that time was focused primarily on requests from male students for permission to have their dates visit them in the dormitories, within certain specified hours. The Student Council voted unanimously in 1964 in favor or requesting permission for such visitations in the Alderman Road and Monroe Hill (graduate) dormitories. It was noted that few of the students in the Alderman Road dorms belonged to fraternities or had cars and that consequently they had only limited facilities for entertaining young ladies. Modest hours for visitations were suggested—Saturdays from 11 A.M. to 9 P.M. and Sundays from 11 A.M. to 7 P.M on Alderman Road, and 11 A.M. to midnight both days on Monroe Hill. Dean Runk turned down the request. "I am opposed to unsupervised visiting of females in male dormitories at any time," he said. "Likewise, I am opposed to males visiting in females' dormitories. I do not believe this is in accord with the sound educational philosophy and progress of the university." He added that he also did not think "the counselor system should be burdened with the problem of enforcement." Years before, in the Darden administration, a similar request had been turned down. In 1966 President Shannon rejected another request that girls be permitted to visit in the Alderman dorms. These rejections accorded with prevailing opinion at the time, although attitudes appeared to be shifting and in a few years would be completely reversed.

Mary E. Whitney, assistant to the dean of women at Northwestern University, was appointed dean of women at Virginia in 1967, succeeding the much admired Roberta H. Gwathmey, who retired after serving for a third of a century in that position. When women were admitted in 1970 on the same basis as men, the position of dean of women was abolished.

The male contingent, which some years before had deplored the spectacle of coeds appearing in shorts, now deplored their wearing slacks. "We find it quite appalling," said the *Cavalier Daily*, "that women students are beginning to wear slacks to classes. . . . Most girls look rotten in slacks; they (the pants, not the girls) reveal quite a bit which under a skirt or dress might best be left to the male imagination. . . . They hardly seem proper attire for young ladies attending classes. . . . Ladies, let the men wear the pants around here, please." A few months later the paper repeated what it had said many times before, that it looked "with horror" upon the prospect of a "large-scale female invasion, other than for the purposes of a party weekend, of these traditionally male Grounds."

During the season of 1967–68, it was decided by the Board of Visitors and the president that the boys could have girl visitors during specified weekend hours in the living areas of upperclassmen's dormitories and in rooms on the Lawn and Ranges. This decision was the result of a year-long study by a faculty-student committee. Student committees were appointed to supervise enforcement of the new regulations. The first visitation by girls in the dorms occurred on the football weekend of Sept. 29–Oct. 1, without untoward incidents. In the spring of 1969 the rules were liberalized again to allow first-year men to have girls visit in their rooms on Fridays, Saturdays, and Sundays at specified hours. Another novelty of that year was the appearance of female cheerleaders at football games.

Rules for visitations in the dormitories between members of the opposite sex were modified in a few years to allow this around the clock. One of the principal advocates of lowering the barriers was the Reverend Charles Perry, assistant rector of St. Paul's Episcopal Church, who said in a sermon in 1967: "If you wish to raise up men who will conduct themselves with honor, give them the privilege of entertaining women in their dorms. A community which limits assignations to automobiles, motels, and apartments is no more moral for it. If you wish to raise up men of honor, remind them that honoring a woman is far more important than honoring an exam pledge or the rules of a card game, and then let them have the freedom to exercise that honor." The foregoing strange reasoning may have had an impact on opinion in the university, although there was a nationwide trend at the time in favor of allowing male and female students to live together in university dormitories, and this would doubtless have happened at Virginia in any event. The newly adopted practices extended on a more informal basis to the fraternity houses, where girls had no hesitation about partying upstairs as well as down. The contrast between the rules and conventions of 1970 and 1920 could not have been more glaring.

Discussion of the desirability of admitting women to the College on an equal basis with men had reached such dimensions in 1967 that the Board of Visitors accepted President Shannon's recommendation that a study be made of the "need for admission of women to the College of Arts and Sciences." Shannon appointed a committee from the faculty, headed by Prof. T. Braxton Woody, to make the study. An important factor behind the scenes was realization that if the university didn't admit the ladies voluntarily, the courts in all likelihood would order it to do so. Such was the opinion of Rector Frank W. Rogers, a prominent Roanoke Lawyer, and others.

However, opposition to the move at the university had diminished steadily over the years. The committee circulated all faculty members of professorial rank, and those who replied were 15 to 1 in favor. Members of the leading student honor societies were about evenly divided. A letter to the forty thousand alumni brought only ninety-eight replies, of whom two-thirds were opposed. After an eighteen months' study, the seven-member Woody Committee recommended in favor of the ladies with only one dissent, that of History Prof. Julian Bishko. The final conclusions of the six other members were that the existing arrangement "unfairly discriminates against women. . . . The quality of academic life at Charlottesville would be strengthened by coeducation. . . . The social life of students of both sexes . . . would be improved, and coeducation would better prepare the students for the relationships of later years." The committee found that the University of Virginia was "the only state university in the nation which, by closing its main-campus college to women, forces them to attend a separate, autonomous college sixty-five miles away from the parent institution."

An aspect of the problem that gave the committee much concern was the effect admission of women might have on the Honor System. Its concern was especially acute, since the Honor Committee had concluded, after an investigation, that "coeducation will hurt the Honor System, and thus should not be recommended." The Honor Committee based this opinion to a large degree on the findings of William J. Bowers of Columbia University in his *Student Dishonesty and Its Control in College* (Bureau of Applied Social Research, Columbia University, 1964). Terming this work "generally recognized as the most comprehensive and authoritative . . . of its kind," the committee pointed to Bowers's conclusion that "an honor system at a coed school is slightly less than half as effective as an honor system at an all-male school." It conceded that its own correspondence with honor committee chairmen at thirty colleges and universities brought inconclusive results. Some thought coeducation would not harm the Honor System at Virginia, others thought just the opposite, and still others felt that it would have no effect.

Although the Woody Committee was disturbed by the conclusions of the Honor Committee, it believed that coeducation would not, in all likelihood, harm the Honor System. It was impressed by the fact that at Princeton, which has an excellent honor system extending to all academic matters, 85 percent of more than two thousand undergraduates responding to a questionnaire said they did not think the system would be affected by coeducation, while 7 percent felt that it would be strengthened. Spokesmen for the University of Virginia Honor Committee conceded that "they saw no detriment to the effectiveness of the Honor System in the present enrollment of some 1,000 women in the university."

The Woody Committee's report was made in November 1968, and the Board of Visitors directed President Shannon to prepare a plan for the gradual admission of women. As one evidence of changing opinion, the *Cavalier Daily* commented that the committee's conclusions "doubtless proved gratifying to most students (and faculty)." By the following fall the newspaper was strongly favoring the committee's recommendations.

But before the administration could put the plan even partially into effect, a suit was brought in federal court designed to force the immediate admission of women on a wholesale scale. This despite the fact that rooming facilities, toilet facilities, and many other accommodations could not be made available to that many female students within a few weeks or

months. Fortunately, the three-judge U.S. Circuit Court allowed two years for full compliance—much less than was felt
to be wise by the university authorities, but greatly preferable
to forced compliance at once, as the suit demanded. The administration agreed to admit 450 women to the College in
September 1970 and 550 more the following September, with
open admission thereafter.

The hundreds of girls who entered in 1970 seemed to want
to outdo the boys in the slovenliness of their dress. As was the
prevailing custom during that period throughout the United
States, both groups garbed themselves in patched, faded,
frayed blue jeans. The boys wore long, unkempt hair and
beat-up shoes. Both groups began dressing more neatly as the
years passed, but in 1970 the emphasis was on the sloppiest
conceivable attire.

Barriers to women in various honor societies and social organizations around the Grounds were not long in coming
down. The Ravens, IMPs, and Tilkas soon took them in, as
did the Air Force ROTC. The Jefferson Literary Society maintained its male chauvinist stance until 1972, when the threat
of a suit caused it to relent. Omicron Delta Kappa leadership
society began electing women in 1974. Eli Banana, the last
holdout of importance, had not admitted any by that year and
gave no evidence of planning to do so in the future. The privilege of living on the Lawn and Ranges was accorded to leading
women students in the early seventies.

With women admitted to the university on the same basis as
men, there was the problem of how to arrange for their housing in the dormitories. Some dormitories were set apart exclusively for women, some for men, and the remainder were
mixed. Where the two sexes were placed in the same building,
they were on different floors, and the women had a good deal
of control over who came and went. Sexual relations took
place in the dormitories between male and female students,
especially between those who were "going steady," but probably not to the extent that some imagined. Many of the girls
objected to promiscuity and did what they could to prevent it.
President Shannon felt that students should have the choice
of living in mixed dormitories or in those reserved for a single
sex, and he saw to it that they had the opportunity to choose.
Nationwide changes in mores concerning relations between

94. Joseph N. Bosserman, dean of architecture, 1966–.

the sexes had brought about a brand-new situation at Virginia and at nearly all other colleges and universities.

Applications from women for entrance to the university increased 150 percent in 1971 over those for the preceding year. About twenty-five hundred sought to enter the College compared with 970 the year before. Applications from out of state nearly trebled. The number of women who were full-time faculty members rose to 92 for the session of 1971–72, or nearly 10 percent of the whole. They were mainly in the College, Graduate School, Medical School, and School of Nursing. The number increased to 131 the following session and to 155 the session after that, or about one-eighth of the full-time faculty. There were then over one hundred women on the faculty full-time, in addition to 47 in the School of Nursing. A still greater increase in the part-time women faculty members was shown.

By 1972 it was being said that nearly everybody thought complete coeducation was a good thing. Malcolm Scully, '63, wrote after a visit of several days to the university: "In conversation with students and faculty members and administrators—old and new—I found no one who had serious doubts about the move to coeducation. They all agreed that women had improved the university's intellectual, cultural, and social atmosphere." The following year Frank Hereford said the admission of women was "a change that was very much for the better. . . . It really hasn't been as dramatic as many alumni who have been away a good many years may think." A disturbing aspect was the increase in rapes. There were twelve rapes or attempted rapes on or near the Grounds in 1972 as compared with seven the previous year. These events led the university to establish an escort system for women returning to their lodgings late at night. A more gratifying result of coeducation was seen in the fact that the male students were under less temptation to "roll" (to drive down the road) to nearby girls' colleges. These expeditions were not only distracting and time consuming but risky in that all too often the boys drank too much, and some were involved in fatal automobile crashes.

At the end of the two-year transition period, women constituted 39 percent of the entering class, and the College was 45 percent female. Two years after that, at the session of 1974–75 the first-year class of 2,317 was 42 percent female. Total enrollment in the university was 14,200, with two-thirds of the first-year class Virginians and 80 percent from the public schools.

Entry of women into the university on the same basis as men has been the most important development in the history of the institution since its early years. That, and acceptance of blacks, another event of the most far-reaching significance, has changed Mr. Jefferson's university so drastically that a graduate of, say, 1920 or even 1960 finds the university to be a greatly altered institution. Many of its basic virtues remain, but its outward manifestations are often in direct contrast to those of earlier days.

Among the areas in which the students of today have shown marked improvement is that of community service. The radical tendencies of the 1969–70 era have been transmuted into a remarkable solicitude for the disadvantaged. In direct contrast to the almost total lack of social concern on the part of earlier student generations, at Virginia and almost everywhere else, many of today's undergraduates are anxious to aid the underprivileged.

Between 1969 and 1973 more than one thousand students at the university were involved in projects of this type, under the sponsorship of what was then Madison Hall. They devoted several hours each week to this unselfish activity. Operation SCRUB was created in 1969 to aid victims of hurricane Camille, which devastated nearby Nelson County and adjacent regions. After the hurricane victims had been aided, the project was expanded in order to help meet local housing needs. Operation SCRUB received a citation from the National Center for Voluntary Action in Washington, which termed it the best project of its type in the United States.

The original Madison Hall, long the home of the YMCA, underwent a complete transformation when it was sold to the university in 1971, along with Mad Bowl, for $725,000. The charter of the university "Y" was revised to sever connection with the International YMCA. Madison Hall's usefulness, as the home of the Student Union, had declined steadily after the opening of Newcomb Hall, which provided facilities formerly available at Madison Hall and a great deal more. It was accordingly decided to redirect the "Y's" resources, so the Office of Volunteer Community Service was established, with headquarters in another Madison Hall on Lewis Mountain Road across from Memorial Gymnasium. This institution provided Operation SCRUB, Big Brother–Big Sister programs, tutoring, companionship therapy, medical services, consumer information and professional services, action line, and youth recreation. In recognition of its extraordinary contributions over the years, the Seven Society gave Madison Hall its Organization Award for 1971.

Then there was the role of an agency called the University Year for Action, launched in 1973, with offices in Peabody Hall, which offered participants an opportunity to obtain academic credit. On its agenda were programs dealing with mental health and retardation, community and children's education, counseling in cases referred to the police, and improvement of foster care and day care.

In addition to all this, university law students belonging to the Virginia Legislative Research Service worked on proposed legislation for members of the General Assembly, while classmates did legal and environmental research on ecological problems. Furthermore, about two hundred fifty students from the Graduate School of Business Administration and the Schools of Commerce and Law provided free assistance each year to area residents in preparing their tax returns. Students in Alpha Phi Omega, a national service fraternity for undergraduates, installed playground equipment at a rural Virginia school and built a riding ring for Holiday Trails, a unique camp for handicapped children. Some seventeen hundred students participated regularly in service activities through the Interfraternity Council and the fraternity houses. Twenty-two houses formed basketball teams of Charlottesville boys, ten to twelve years old, and set up a basketball league. Preparations were being made at the end of 1974 to transfer headquarters for student volunteers from Madison Hall to newly constructed Madison House at 170 Rugby Road, an independent nonprofit corporation supported by private and public funds. Madison House was not linked officially with the university but would draw nearly all of its volunteers from the university community.

The foregoing is only a partial list of the community and humanitarian activities in which University of Virginia students have engaged in recent years. It should be noted that these unselfish manifestations are by no means unique to the university. A Gallup Poll in 1974 found that approximately half of all college students had participated to some degree in volunteer social work, with about four hundred thousand on seventeen hundred campuses contributing their time on a regular basis.

A change in the traditional Finals exercises on the Lawn was instituted in 1962. The president conferred all degrees there, but graduates, except those in the College, went later to separate ceremonies for their respective schools and were given their diplomas. In past years graduates had sometimes waited for hours in the hot sun to get their sheepskins, whereas now the exercises were much briefer, and were described as "more dignified and meaningful." The Student Council evidently disagreed, since it had voted 16 to 1 in April not to change the format of the exercises. The Council was overruled.

The university's College Bowl team won five straight contests in 1963 over national television with that number of institutions and received a $9,000 scholarship, while each of the team members was given a $500 scholarship for graduate studies. Prof. T. Graham Hereford, the coach, was awarded $500 for postdoctoral work. Students announced that they would raise funds to supplement the $9,000 fund. Members of the winning team, the ninth from the entire country up to that time to remain undefeated in the College Bowl, were Michael Bennett, captain; Talmadge Wyatt, Jr.,; Richard Greer; and John Mortensen. Virginia defeated four of the five institutions by wide margins, namely, Oregon State, Ohio University, Drake University, and Washington State. It barely nosed out the University of Maine. Graham Hereford, who coached the team, was a University of Virginia Ph.D. who was associate professor of English in the School of Engineering and assistant to the dean of the school. Regarded as a dedicated and effective teacher of English, he also did an exceptional job with the College Bowl team.

University debaters were making excellent records during these years. The team tied for second place in competition with thirty other schools at the St. Joseph's College debate tournament at Philadelphia in 1961. Among teams they defeated were those from Dartmouth and Carnegie Tech. The following year debaters from the university won first place against thirteen schools in the Alleman Interstate Novice Debate Tournament at Louisville, and they also won the Atlantic Coast Conference Debate Tournament at Duke University. In 1963 the debaters from Charlottesville were victorious for the first time in sixteen years in the District VII eliminations for the National Debate Championship at Wilkes-Barre, Pa. The top record in the Ford Motor Co. Invitational at Oberlin, Ohio, in 1971 was made by Jim Poe and Greg Bittner of the university, in competition with eighty-eight of the ablest debaters on the East Coast. Other highly creditable records were made during these years by the university's representatives.

Considerable controversy arose in 1963 when the John Randolph Society at the university, a conservative student organization, invited Gus Hall, secretary of the Communist party U.S.A., and George Lincoln Rockwell, commander of the American Nazi party, to speak on the Grounds. President Shannon and the Board of Visitors agreed that the invitations were ill-advised but took the position that since they had been issued the programs should proceed, provided assurances were given that order and decorum would prevail. Both speakers addressed capacity audiences in Cabell Hall. A few catcalls and hisses were heard, but there was no disorder. The Board of Visitors admonished all student organizations "in the future to exercise an increased sense of responsibility toward the impact of their actions on the welfare of the University."

Martin Luther King, Jr., was heard by a large audience in Cabell Hall the following month, under auspices of the Virginia Society of Human Relations. He said the special objective at the time was to double Negro registration in the South, and added that integration was proceeding much too slowly. There was no disorder of any kind.

Coveted scholarships were being awarded to outstanding high school seniors both inside and outside the state. The University Regional and Honor Scholarships had been established in 1952 in tribute to Philip Francis duPont, whose $6,000,000 bequest in 1928 had approximately doubled by 1965

95. W. Dexter Whitehead, director of the Center for Advanced Studies, 1965–, and dean of the Graduate School of Arts and Sciences, 1969–.

and was providing about $240,000 annually in scholarship funds. In a more or less typical year, 1962, Regional Scholarships were awarded to twenty-one outstanding high school seniors, fifteen of them from Virginia. Another eighteen were granted Honor Scholarships, the next category of awards, while regular one-year scholarships went to twenty-eight promising high school seniors.

A still more coveted series of merit scholarships was established in 1963 by concerned alumni. Known as the University Honor Awards, they were offered annually to a select group of secondary school seniors. Counted among the thirty-five Honor Award holders, representing four classes enrolled in the 1966–67 session, were numerous Echols Scholars, staff members of the three major student publications, varsity lettermen, honorary society members, a number of participants in the university's counseling program, and past and present Honor Committee chairmen. The awards carried an annual stipend of $1,000 for Virginians and $1,500 for non-Virginians, without regard to financial need, and were renewable for each of a student's four years, provided the recipient maintained a dean's list average and participated in other phases of university life.

Since the cost of attending the university was said to be considerably higher than for most state universities, the need for scholarships was especially great. A survey by the student newspaper in 1968 found that the average undergraduate at the University of Virginia paid $1,704 per year for tuition, fees, room, and board, whereas the approximate cost at other state universities was $1,160. The survey at the university included the graduate and professional schools, whereas the paper did not know whether the figure for other state universities, compiled by the National Association of State Universities and Land Grant Colleges and Universities, included them.

Students in need of financial assistance could often find it through the Student Aid and Placement Service, with offices in Minor Hall. Directed since 1959 by Frank A. Williar, with Robert Canevari as his assistant, it provided scholarships, loans, and part-time employment. A counseling service also was part of the plan. Alumni in need of new positions found the service helpful.

Guidance of a different type was provided by the university's Counseling Center, directed by Earl Glosser, and established in 1967. Four full-time counseling psychologists and five half-time counseling interns were providing the service. Advice was furnished to students seeking to cope more effectively with themselves and their surroundings, Glosser explained. Once the student had achieved greater self-understanding, he or she was referred to the Aid and Placement Service for any additional guidance.

The number of students in the College who were on the dean's list had risen steadily, with the result that in 1972–73 the figure was over 50 percent. This was, in part, a reflection of higher and higher standards for entrance, but the rise was related to the fact that grading throughout the United States had become more lenient. Students at Virginia from the state's public schools were getting the best grades of any secondary school group, a survey for the period 1958–64 showed. Next came graduates of out-of-state public schools, with Virginia private schools coming in third and out-of-state private schools fourth.

Greater intellectual, cultural, and social exchange between faculty and students was the aim of the Serpentine Society, formed during the 1961–62 session by a group of upperclassmen who were members of St. Paul's Episcopal Church. It expanded rapidly, and professors and students of various religious backgrounds were brought in. The society met informally in the homes of faculty members for "social seminars"—pleasant evenings for animated discussions of current topics, usually led by a specialist in some particular field. Bedford Moore of the School of Engineering's English faculty was faculty adviser.

The Society of the Purple Shadows, a secret organization which, in the words of Marvin Garrette in the Richmond *Times-Dispatch*, "borrowed several of the Sevens' traditions," was formed in 1963. Like the Seven Society it had a page in *Corks and Curls*, but no list of members. There was no further information concerning it or its activities.

Another organization formed at about this time was the Society of the Cornish Game Hen. It recognized fraternity and nonfraternity men "who have given outstanding service but who," in the words of the *Cavalier Daily*, "have not been recognized by the other honorary societies because their participation was in lesser known or recognized organizations, such as the University Union or the Virginia Debaters."

The mysterious P.U.M.P.K.I.N. Society emerged during these years. About ten pumpkins were delivered annually to that number of recipients, both faculty and students. The basis for selecting those thus honored was not altogether clear. Sir John Wheeler-Bennett, one of the chosen, kept his pumpkin on his dining table "for several months, until it disintegrated to the point where visitors couldn't tell it from a squash."

Another altogether different organization was the Walter Reed Society, with thirty-two charter members and others added in subsequent years. Medical students and house staff officers were eligible, together with research fellows of the Medical School and the Graduate School of Arts and Sciences. A prize was awarded annually for the best paper in the field of medical research.

Returning students in good standing who had completed at least two full semesters with a cumulative grade average of 2.0 and were not receiving financial aid were allowed to have automobiles under rules approved in 1968. These privileges were extended to first-year men two years later on substantially the same conditions.

The Student Council inaugurated a bus system for students, faculty, and staff in the spring of 1971 in an effort to cope with traffic and parking problems. Busses were leased from a local firm on a trial basis. A survey the previous session had shown that there were 9,700 students, and only 5,831 parking spaces for 7,220 cars. The university attacked the problem in the fall of 1972 with a comprehensive bus service and a plan for pay parking. Visitors were required to park at metered spaces.

Campus politics was rather hectic at this period, reflecting the somewhat turbulent conditions prevailing at the university and throughout the country. A new party calling itself the Anarchists emerged in the 1968 College elections, announcing its intention to "put life in the Student Council." It elected its candidates with record-breaking pluralities and then disappeared. The Virginia Progressive party took its place at the next election, with some of the same candidates and supporters as the Anarchists, and they too were highly successful. The conservative Jefferson party emerged in the fall of 1969, and Skull & Keys and Sceptre (formerly Lambda Pi), which had been influential in College politics over the years, albeit with many ups and downs, voted themselves out of existence. In the spring of 1970 the Jefferson party swamped the opposition with a clean sweep of all offices.

The Student Council was being rapped in 1973 for "apathy and inaction," and "the failure of an alarming number of council members to work." Students, furthermore, were not attending council meetings and were unfamiliar with what the organization was doing.

The Council was galvanized into action when Larry Sabato of Norfolk was elected its president in 1973. An extraordinary number of programs were launched under his dynamic leadership, including a campaign before the General Assembly for a new undergraduate readers' library, testimony before the Housing Study Commission, expansion of the university's transit system, support for appointment of an ombudsman and off-grounds housing complaint service, publication of several booklets for students and for women's safety seminars, publicizing the equal opportunity counseling program, supporting new landlord-tenant legislation, improving alumni-student relations, and various other programs. Sabato was successful in achieving many of his objectives. President Shannon praised his "prodigious leadership." He was chosen a Rhodes Scholar.

Residents of the first-year dormitories were getting more constructive attention from older students. As the *Alumni News* expressed it in 1973: "This year there has been a variety of activities in the dorms not seen often before, ranging from seminars on human sexuality, which sound provocative, to bull sessions with the football coach, which don't. In between there have been both formal and informal undergraduate classes and orientations, both academic and social, lectures and mixers designed to give students more than just a feeling of living in a room in a building." The counselor system had its inception in 1950–51, when the new dormitories on Mc-Cormick Road opened; it developed in various directions in the intervening years.

Byrd S. Leavell, Jr., cochairman of the resident staff's first-year component in 1973 and winner of the Arthur P. "Pete" Gray IV Memorial Award the previous year, said that the objective was "to keep things happening in the dorms," and to offer "everybody a chance to become involved in something that interests them." A novel feature was the plan whereby coeds briefed the incoming first-year men on university traditions, an innovation that, in earlier days, could have brought older alumni to the verge of apoplexy. Resident advisers, who were either instructors or graduate students, also lived in the dorms with a view to aiding students with academic or other problems. The university administration credited the counselors and advisers with a major role in achieving a dramatic decline in the number of first-year dropouts.

Counseling in the upperclass dormitories was concerned primarily with academic orientation and career guidance. A program also was instituted for the 85 percent of the thousands of upperclass and graduate students who were living off-Grounds. They were mainly in houses and apartments, and seminars and social events were arranged for their benefit. Transfer students were given special attention, including a garden party during orientation week, when they could meet student leaders.

The rapidly mounting enrollment, well beyond expectations, was receiving much attention. An ultimate maximum of 18,000 students, double the figure for 1969, was seen by the administration as acceptable. Much of the increase already experienced was accounted for by the sharp reduction in the academic failure rate which, in turn, was tied to the steady rise in the qualifications of entering undergraduates.

But many of the students were greatly disturbed over the prospect of so rapid an increase in enrollment. As early as 1967 the *University of Virginia Magazine* expressed alarm lest the university become another "State-U" with a huge number of undergraduates and mediocre standards. It was concerned lest "the vital character of the university be lost." Four years later an enrollment of 18,000 by 1980 was officially envisaged. But ere long serious doubts began to arise in the administration, the Board of Visitors, and the Alumni Association's Board of Managers concerning the desirability of allowing enrollment to rise that high.

The students became greatly agitated. They pointed out that housing, classroom space, and parking were already critically inadequate, and in the fall of 1971 their opposition became louder and louder. On the night of Oct. 19 some twenty-five hundred marched through the Grounds in vehement disapproval, and five hundred spent the night on the Lawn, despite temperatures that dropped into the forties. They carried signs with such legends as "United We Stand Because We Can't Sit Down," "Help Stop Expansion, Eat a Student," and "Hell, No, We Won't Grow." Next day they staged a "study-in" at Alderman Library and an "eat-in" at Newcomb Hall, designed to show the inadequacy of facilities. The result of all this was that the Board of Visitors decided to limit enrollment to 16,500 for the foreseeable future.

Getting into the university was not easy. College board Scholastic Aptitude Test (SAT) scores for university entrants in 1974 were 592 verbal and 623 math for the College, 562 verbal and 659 math for engineering, and 608 verbal and 662 math for architecture.

The student body was much more cosmopolitan than that of most state universities. President Shannon was quoted as saying that "outside of the University of Colorado we have more out-of-state students than any other state university." The large number of Harvard, Yale, and Princeton graduates who attend the University of Virginia has been noted.

The university has always been among the top institutions in the country in the number of its students awarded Rhodes Scholarships to Oxford University, and far ahead of all other state institutions. Its total of thirty-five scholarship recipients through 1973 was the same as that for Stanford and was exceeded by only Harvard, Yale, Princeton, the U.S. Military Academy, and Dartmouth. The University of Washington is runner-up among state institutions with twenty-five, while the University of Mississippi is second in the South with twenty-one.

Use of university facilities for meetings of officially recognized religious groups was approved by President Shannon in 1973, provided there was no discrimination by race, creed, or sex. This was a reversal of a long-standing rule, adopted and maintained in deference to Thomas Jefferson's insistence upon complete separation of church and state. Shannon made his decision on the recommendation of the Calendar and Scheduling Committee, which felt that such meetings would not conflict with Jefferson's desires. Shannon had taken the opposite position in 1966.

The religious composition of the student body had undergone radical changes in the preceding decades. By 1973 and 1974 the percentage of Roman Catholics had grown to approximately double that of the second largest denomination on the Grounds. For generations the Episcopalians had led, but now the Roman Catholic percentage was nearly 22, or twice that of the Episcopalians, who were in a virtual tie with the Presbyterians, Methodists, and Baptists for second place. It was one more bit of evidence that the university had entered a new era.

NINE

The University
Rides the Storm

Turmoil and convulsion erupted across the campuses of America in the late sixties, and the University of Virginia was not immune. Many students were outraged over events in the Vietnam war and were determined to show their feelings by demonstrations and even violence. Small cadres of Marxist revolutionaries seized upon the situation to promote their goals. A few of these were operating in the shadow of the Rotunda.

Two busloads of University of Virginia students went to Washington in the fall of 1967 and joined in a march to the Pentagon by some seventy-five thousand others from throughout the nation who were protesting the war in Vietnam. There were arrests and clubbings on the Pentagon steps. A few days later the *Cavalier Daily* published five columns of letters, pro and con, concerning the war. One group of faculty members signed a statement terming the conflict "immoral and unjust," while another faculty group retorted that such demonstrations as had occurred in Washington "tend to prolong the war."

The *Virginia Weekly*, an ultraradical publication, began appearing at the university in 1967, and the Student Council made it a grant of $500. When the journal expired in 1972, the *Cavalier Daily* said its purpose had been "forging a revolutionary party capable of leading the working class to socialism."

Violence was escalating on campuses from coast to coast in

the spring of 1968, with Columbia University the focal point. Vandals wrecked the office of President Grayson Kirk, whereupon faculty members threatened to lie down to prevent police from clearing occupied buildings. Kirk ordered the police away. On other fronts U.S. Attorney General Ramsey Clark was temporizing with looters, arsonists, sitters-down in public thoroughfares, and other disrupters of the public business.

Aware that there was unrest at Charlottesville, President Shannon issued a sweeping statement on May 3, 1968, designed to prevent the spread of violence to the Grounds. It contained the following provisions:

(a) Notice of a demonstration must be filed with the Student Council office 96 hours in advance.

(b) Only organizations recognized by the Student Council may sponsor demonstrations on the university Grounds.

(c) Picketing is not permitted inside buildings.

(d) Outside picketing must not be carried on so as to interfere with entrance traffic or the normal flow of pedestrian and vehicular traffic.

(e) Precise boundaries and number of those picketing will be set by agreement among the Student Council, Department of Security, the organizations involved, and those in charge of any building specifically involved. . . .

Any student found guilty of participating in or inciting a riot or an unautorized or disorderly assembly is subject to suspension. . . .

The foregoing had been put together following a conference with student leaders. High praise was heaped on President Shannon for his forthright stand, which was cited as being in sharp contrast to the spineless surrender of some other educational executives.

A few days after this manifesto was issued the students elected two Anarchist candidates to the Student Council by unprecedented majorities. Walker Chandler and Charles Murdock wrote in a letter to the student newspaper on the eve of the election: "We are not running as a joke. We selected the title Anarchist because we intend to destroy the present style of student government. . . . Gentlemen, we are NOT kidding." Slogans for their campaign included: "What Has Order Gotten You?" and "Political Power Grows Out of the Barrel of a Gun—Chairman Mao." They said they hoped to bring about student strikes and sit-ins and to employ "skillful use of the threat of force, and force if necessary." Some students seem to have voted for these men as a sort of lark, but Chandler polled the biggest total in the history of Council elections down to that time, while Murdock was not far behind and well ahead of the third candidate. The following year the Anarchist party became the Progressive party, and Murdock ran for another term on the Council; he got an even bigger vote than Chandler had polled in 1968. The Progressives elected their entire slate, with one exception. The party, among other things, was definitely antifraternity and stood on a "liberal" platform.

Unrest and disorder on campuses throughout the land were intensified by the rioting that summer at the Democratic National Convention in Chicago. Some of the same persons who led the Chicago riots were active in the institutions of higher learning.

President Shannon held the first of a series of two-day retreats at Mountain Lake, Giles County, in September 1968 when selected Board of Visitors members, administrators, faculty, and students discussed various problems with a view to defusing rising resentments and getting to know one another better. These yearly meetings were held later at Graves Mountain Lodge, Madison County. Agitation among the students for more active and aggressive recruiting of black matriculates was a major topic at the first retreat. Another was implementation of a rule that second-year men would have to live in the dormitories. The latter issue aroused such antagonism that the Visitors, on Shannon's recommendation, rescinded the rule before the opposition could be fully organized. Editor Gwathmey of the *Cavalier Daily* wrote later that "after one meeting student members . . . were practically ready to go back home and riot. . . . Happily some of the meetings after the bitterest one were the most harmonious and productive. The participants found that they could get along after all."

Students for a Free Society, a "New Right" organization, was formed at the university as a counterweight to Students for a Democratic Society (SDS) and the Southern Student Organizing Committee (SSOC), both of which were active. The president of the conservative organization dedicated to "reform rather than revolution," was John Kwapisz, a second-year student in commerce and Russian-Communist studies. He also headed Young Americans for Freedom (YAF) at the university and the following year would debate with both faculty and student leaders in behalf of his firmly held views.

An eleven-point program drafted by the Student Coalition was announced at a rally on the Lawn in February. Something like one thousand students attended and heard speeches by Professors William A. Elwood and Willie Lee Rose, as well as Arthur (Bud) Ogle, a member of the Student Council and an ordained Presbyterian minister; the Reverend Howard Gordon and the Reverend David Ward, local clergymen; Robert Rosen, a fourth-year College student who edited *Rapier Magazine*; and others. The eleven-point program included higher wages for university employees, their affiliation with national labor unions with the right to strike, more black students, blacks on the Board of Visitors, a Black Studies Program, more aid for disadvantaged students, and a full-time black Assistant Dean of Admissions. President Shannon's reaction to the above proposals was regarded as unsatisfactory by the sponsors. A delegation of students went to Richmond to seek Governor Godwin's support but got no encouragement. He told them that as students their role was to get an education and not engage in social protest.

Rioting on the nation's campuses was intensified in the spring of 1969, when Harvard and Cornell were centers of agitation, and disorders of the year before erupted again at Columbia. Harvard deans were physically ejected from their offices by students, confidential papers were copied and made public, and administration buildings forcibly taken over. At Cornell about one hundred black students, many carrying rifles, shotguns, and belts of ammunition left Willard Straight Hall after the administration, apparently in order to avoid bloodshed, met demands the students made when they took over the building. At Columbia about two hundred students occupied Philosophy Hall, barricaded the doors, and trapped professors and other students inside. Various extreme demands were made.

The resignation of C. Stuart Wheatley, Jr., from the University of Virginia Board of Visitors was demanded by both SDS and SSOC because Wheatley, as a member of the General Assembly years before, had been a supporter of "massive resistance" against integration of the races. The organizations called for the appointment of a black in his place. In addition, they demanded the resignations of several board members, whom they termed "élitist." The calls for Wheatley's resignation were echoed by various other student leaders and organizations, who called his presence on the board "an affront to the black community." Wheatley finally convinced his critics that he had reversed his views on integration and the agitation subsided.

In the fall of 1969 President Shannon received legal advice that he felt made it necessary for him to modify his ruling of the year before with respect to student demonstrations. He was told that there was a considerable body of case law and court decisions necessitating this revision. On Sept. 4 he accordingly set forth the new requirements under which it was no longer necessary that organizations holding demonstrations be officially recognized by the Student Council, nor was it necessary for them to obtain permission four days in advance. Students were still forbidden to use university space in a manner that is "physically destructive [or] unlawful" and to "disrupt academic activities or any scheduled events." Students violating the rules would be "subject to standing university disciplinary procedures," including suspension, but due process was guaranteed.

The *Cavalier Daily*, which had a series of ultraliberal, if not radical, editorial executives during this period, had a new setup in September 1969 with a publisher and also an editor. Charles A. Hite III occupied the former position and Robert B. Cullen the latter. The new management lost no time in taking its far-out stance. "People leave because they find the university socially childish, politically repressive, or academically irrelevant and uninteresting," said the paper. Addressing the first-year men, it declared: "We welcome you to the University of Virginia, not with a call to seize the Rotunda (yet), but with an urgent exhortation that you will strive to be activists in the finest sense of the word, actively seeking to better yourselves and your university."

Extremely sour notes concerning the 1969 Mountain Lake retreat issued from the paper's sanctum, which apparently spoke for a small minority of those present at the conference. "The president's remarks reminded me of a father addressing his children or a nineteenth-century plantation owner addressing his slaves," wrote Publisher Hite. Shannon had told the "60-odd persons in the room that he had poured his heart and soul into the betterment of the university. . . . They believed him and applauded. We sat, arms folded, and tried to fight off the sense of hopelessness and frustration welling up inside." Hite added that students had "the ability and right to have a direct control in guiding their lives at the university. . . . This was the root of the distrust at the conference."

In an effort to obtain this much-discussed "student power," a group of undergraduates launched a movement the following week to "reform the University Senate" so as to include student members along with administration and faculty. Student Council approved the plan unanimously, and its president, "Bud" Ogle, was named chairman of a committee to work out the details. A senate with student representation had been set up at Columbia University following the riots there.

The faculty of the College of Arts and Sciences at the university voted to admit representatives of student publications and the two university radio stations to its meetings, but only as observers.

An electronic "bug," or eaves-dropping device, was found attached to the underside of the table in the room where the Board of Visitors was meeting in October 1969. It was not known how long the bug had been there. An investigation was launched, but the guilty party or parties were never discovered.

The so-called Vietnam Moratorium was observed nationally a few days later, Oct. 15. About three hundred students and others gathered the evening before in front of the first-year dormitories, and marched, carrying candles, to University Avenue and Rugby Road. President Shannon joined them at their request, and spoke briefly to them, saying: "I come to join with you in what I know is your desire and my desire for a peaceful resolution of this war. I understand your interest and your concern . . . to give consideration to all aspects of our foreign policy and the aspects of our responsibility and your concern as citizens of your country. And I do wish you well." He walked with them partway on their procession through the Grounds. As the marchers passed, some residents of the Alderman Road and Observatory Hill dorms chanted verses from "Dixie," yelled "Win the war!" and waved Confederate flags.

*96. Linda Howard, black president of the Law School,
1972–73, in conversation with another student.*

Talk of canceling classes for the moratorium had begun the previous month, and Chairman Kwapisz of Young Americans for Freedom announced that legal action to prevent it would be taken if such a move were tried. President Shannon announced early in October that classes would not be canceled.

"Many students exercised their right to stay away from class" on Oct. 15, the *Alumni News* said, "opting for formal and informal discussions of the war, for chapel services, or perhaps study."

The main event of the day was an address from the Rotunda steps at noon by Karl Hess, speech writer and campaign aid for Barry Goldwater in the 1964 presidential campaign. About one thousand persons heard Hess hail the moratorium as a "reassertion of our rights as citizens. . . . It tells Mr. Nixon much more than just the fact the war must end. We must become citizens again."

Ceremonies signalizing the climax of the university's year-long sesquicentennial observance—treated more fully in Chapter 11—took place the following week. When these were concluded, President Shannon accepted a prestigious award from the Danforth Foundation for two months at Oxford University. He had declined a similar offer the year before because of the pressure of events at Charlottesville. Those events left him very tired, according to Frank Berkeley, his executive assistant, and he needed a rest. However, Berkeley said further, in his oral deposition concerning these happenings, that "if he had been here at home, and had his ear to the ground better, I think a lot of things would have worked out better. . . . There were things building up at the university that he did not have his ear to the ground on." When Shannon returned he had to plunge into hearings before the General Assembly.

If he did lose touch, to some extent, with events at the university while he was in England—which he denies—he says he benefited greatly from the restful sojourn abroad. It enabled him, he declares, to stand the "continuous strain and virtually sleepless nights" which he endured during the demonstrations that erupted in May.

Another huge demonstration against the Vietnam war took place in Washington in mid-November, and some seventy-five university students attended. They gathered under a Virginia banner, took part in peaceable demonstrations at the Capitol, and marched to ceremonies at the Washington Monument. They were not involved in violence that broke out at the Department of Justice.

Meanwhile, at the university Rep. John Marsh of Virginia and Mayor G. A. Vogt of Charlottesville addressed a "Tell It to Hanoi" rally of over one hundred students called by Young Americans for Freedom at the Barracks Road Shopping Center. They stressed the need for telling Hanoi to begin serious negotiations looking toward an end for the war and demonstrating support for President Nixon in his efforts to "achieve a just and lasting peace in Southeast Asia."

Somewhat typical of the times was a letter to the *Cavalier Daily* from Jeremy Kahn, a fourth-year student, berating the paper for "prominent placing" of the Episcopal High–Woodberry football score. A small box on an inside page with "Episcopal High School 21, Woodberry Forest 0" was all that was published. Kahn commented, "It seems that the past represented by these exclusive schools is even more evil than that represented by today's bourbon drinkers."

Richard M. Kleindienst, deputy U.S. attorney general, appeared at the Legal Forum in December. The *Cavalier Daily* urged that he be given a courteous hearing, since "if his speech is disrupted, the effect will be to give the administration . . . evidence that it is the Left, and not the Right, which is intolerant and repressionist." He was interrupted repeatedly, and "outbreaks of verbal harrassment occurred frequently." Tom Gardner, a fourth-year College student, one of the principal agitators during this period, was a leader in these disruptive activities.

The left-wing Progressive party captured the four Student Council seats up for election. Judy Wellman, editor of the radical *Virginia Weekly*, was chosen by a big majority from the Graduate School of Arts and Sciences.

A strike was in progress at the General Electric plant in Waynesboro, and Tom Gardner exhorted students to aid the strikers. He solicited financial contributions. Thirty university students picketed the plant and distributed strike leaflets.

Corks and Curls for 1970, material for which was prepared during the 1969–70 session, was permeated throughout with extreme leftist doctrine, and the prominently featured article in the front of the volume was by "Bud" Ogle. Among other things, he said: "The promise is great. And administrators and 'student leaders' are frittering it away. *Our mentor Karl Marx* [italics supplied] once said: 'Until now philosophers have only sought to understand the world. The point, however, is to change it.' The point *is* to change it."

The foregoing is one more illustration of the fact that a group of extremists at Virginia had gotten control of important organs of student opinion and other agencies, as happened at a number of institutions. They worked while the average undergraduate slept. The surprising thing was that so many of the rank and file seemed to acquiesce in their plans, or at least not to oppose them. The students, as we have seen, voted these Marxists and other radicals into important offices on the Grounds. Undoubtedly some of this was due to a perverse desire on the part of college youths to oppose the Establishment "for kicks." And there is the further fact that the climate of opinion in most colleges and universities in those few years was much more leftist than at any time before or since. The Vietnam war was a prime factor in bringing about this condition.

In all this turmoil Rector Frank W. Rogers was spokesman for the conservatives on the Board of Visitors. He remained staunchly opposed to unwarranted concessions to the radical student agitators. He was also uninhibited in expressing himself. On the eve of his retirement as rector in February 1970, Rogers was quoted by the Associated Press as contrasting the current situation with that which prevailed eight years before when he went on the board. "Eight years ago you couldn't conceive of that terrible bunch of thugs that now make themselves so articulate" at the university, he declared. Rogers was referring to the handful of Marxist agitators on the Grounds. By contrast, some of the other leaders in the demonstrations were remarkably courteous.

J. Harvie Wilkinson III, the student member of the visitors, asked the Student Council for help "in making student opinions known to the board" and said he was "available to talk with any of you about matters concerning the university." Wilkinson added: "I might not agree with some of your views, but I think I could convey your ideas to the board, whether I agree with them or not." Several members of the council expressed satisfaction with his offer.

A peace fast, sponsored by the Vietnam Moratorium Committee, was held April 13–15 and was endorsed by a large number of presidents of undergraduate organizations and by student publications.

This relatively quiet situation became explosive when President Nixon announced the bombing of Cambodia. Soon thereafter four students at Kent State University were shot and killed, and nine wounded, by Ohio national guardsmen. These events aroused outrage on campuses from coast to coast and intensified unrest at Virginia and many other colleges and universities. Students everywhere in the United States had been tense and on edge since the preceding fall, when the draft lottery was instituted, with consequent termination of student deferments.

Students held a rally at the Rotunda on the night of May 4, the day after the Kent State killings, whence several hundred marched to Carr's Hill and read President Shannon a telegram they were sending to President Nixon. Shannon indicated that he shared their concern, but he refused to sign the telegram.

Some of the students marched thence to Maury Hall, headquarters of the naval ROTC, and tried to take it over. David Morris, president of the College, and Dave Bowman, vice-president, stood in front of the door for about fifteen minutes and refused to let them pass unless they agreed to be nonviolent. They agreed, and were admitted. President Shannon had had an injunction drafted in advance, to be ready for such an emergency, and this injunction, ordering evacuation of the building, was issued that night by Judge Lyttleton Waddell. It was delivered to Maury Hall by the police at about 4:30 A.M., and the students vacated the building without resistance.

About half of the group had gone back to Carr's Hill, arriving at around 3:30 A.M. They yelled "Strike!" and knocked on the door. President Shannon was not there, but Mrs. Shannon was. She came out and faced the crowd, told them that they would awaken the children, and insisted that they go away. They did.

A memorial service to the Kent State victims was held in Cabell Hall at about noon, on call of President Shannon and James Roebuck, black president of the Student Council. At the ceremonies Shannon expressed agreement with the students as to the Kent State shootings but stressed the necessity for nonviolence. He had been up all night, and when he spoke of his love for the university and the need to preserve its traditions, tears came into his eyes. The press reported that he was crying, which gave a distorted picture.

A strike committee, numbering about three hundred fifty students, was urging a "strike," or boycott, of classes. The term *strike*, as used by them, it is important to note, had no relationship to the sort of strike that takes place in industrial plants. The Student Council endorsed the plan unanimously and called on all students to stay away from classes. Twenty-nine of the thirty-three fraternities also endorsed the boycott; three of the remaining four had clauses in their constitutions that prevented their doing so. Over one hundred fifty faculty members supported the students' right to boycott. Some professors did not hold classes on May 6, although there had been no cancellation by the administration.

In an effort to calm the rising discontent, President Shannon and his advisers decided that it would be wise for the president to announce on that day that he had made arrangements with Senators Harry F. Byrd and William B. Spong to see and talk with students from the university the following Monday. He made the announcement to students gathered in front of Alderman Library. Professors Charles Whitebread and William Harbaugh, who had the confidence of the dissidents, were requested to follow Shannon's remarks with supportive statements. They did so. "Their appearance enabled the president to leave the rally," said Provost Frank Hereford. "We were genuinely concerned that there might be violence, particularly because of the large group of outsiders on the Grounds."

Weeks before these developments, radical student organizations at the university had invited William Kunstler and Jerry Rubin to speak in University Hall on May 6. Kunstler was defense attorney for the Chicago Seven, whose violence had disrupted the Democratic National Convention, and Rubin was one of the seven. Appearance of these men only two days after the Kent State shootings could not have happened at a worse time for the cause of law and order at Virginia. Their inflammatory remarks were like pouring gasoline on a smoldering fire. Kunstler, who had led the protests at Columbia, said: "We must now resist to the hilt. These fists have to be clenched, and they have to be in the air. When they're opened we hope it's in friendship, not around the trigger guard of a rifle. But if we're not listened to, or if the issue is forced, they may well open around trigger guards." "Yippie" Jerry Rubin then delivered a rambling, hour-long harangue, interlarded with innumerable obscenities, that turned off the audience. Many walked out while he was speaking.

After this program had been concluded a crowd estimated at two thousand, some of whom carried Viet Cong flags, assembled in front of the President's residence on Carr's Hill. Kunstler stood on a chair and all but told the shouting gathering to rush the building. He quoted Marie Antoinette's famous "Let 'em eat cake." President Shannon was conferring inside with university officials and student leaders. About thirty student marshals were lined up across the front of the house, determined to prevent any mob violence. After Kunstler finished speaking, nothing much was happening for several minutes. Somebody called out, "On to Maury Hall!" and the crowd melted away. In the group were a number of persons unknown to the university authorities who had come from elsewhere.

A couple of hundred of the demonstrators went to Maury Hall. After they had occupied it, a small fire broke out in a mattress in the basement, causing considerable smoke. This, coupled with a rumor that the police were coming, caused evacuation of the building.

Shannon had established various "command posts" and he moved from one to the other, "so as not to be a focal point," he said later. One of his temporary headquarters was in a room at the hospital where there were desks and telephones. A fantastic rumor got out that he was ill or having a nervous breakdown, and had entered the hospital for treatment.

An important asset for him in all this turmoil and confusion was the relationship he had with Jim Roebuck, the black president of the Student Council. "We didn't always agree," Shannon said, "but we had confidence in each other as human beings. . . . I felt that I could keep him advised of what I was thinking, what I was planning . . . and I sought his advice as much as possible. . . . Jim was concerned that the university not be damaged, and was absolutely trustworthy."

Students began interfering with traffic at the intersection of Route 250 and Emmet Street on the night of Thursday, May 7. The city police called for help from the state police, and there was a confrontation between students and law enforcement officers on Emmet Street below the Monroe Hill dormitories. When Dean Alan Williams announced on a bullhorn that the police were leaving and that the students should do likewise, they dispersed.

President Shannon, who had kept in touch by telephone with faculty and student leaders in the crowd and with the police, saw that there might be trouble the following night. "I made arrangements," he said, "for the State Police to be in the area Friday night in force, and to be responsible for security."

That night a large group of students congregated behind the stone wall on University Avenue in front of the Rotunda. Contrary to Shannon's wishes, Charlottesville Commonwealth's Attorney Jack Camblos arrived on the scene and invoked the Riot Act, with the result that state police charged the crowd and arrested sixty-seven persons, mostly students.

The precise circumstances surrounding these arrests are in dispute, which is probably typical of such situations when tensions run high. On the one hand, it is stated that police pursued students to the Lawn, entered some rooms, and arrested those who lived there. Also, in the University Avenue area student marshals who had volunteered their services in helping to maintain order on the Grounds were taken into custody, as well as such innocent bystanders as a senior employee of the university and a man delivering pizzas. There was a sense of outrage on the part of many professors and students, who felt that the police exceeded all proper bounds.

On the other hand, there are those who contend that the police did not behave irresponsibly, but were simply carrying out orders in pursuing students who had been warned repeatedly that they would be arrested if they did not disperse.

All those taken into custody were released immediately on bail, and the commonwealth's attorney later nol-prossed the charges.

With the Riot Act in effect, it was unlawful for as many as three people to congregate, and police cars were parked bumper to bumper along University Avenue and below Carr's Hill. President Shannon persuaded Captain Boone of the state police to withdraw his men from the central grounds in order to let scheduled university activities proceed on Saturday afternoon and evening. These included a political rally, baseball and lacrosse games, and a formal ball.

D. French Slaughter, Jr., president of the University of Virginia Alumni Association, sent a telegram on Saturday, May 9 to parents of all the undergraduates, urging them to "call your son or daughter expressing confidence in them to act thoughtfully and responsibly in this critical situation." The message said that students and outsiders were using the war in Southeast Asia "to demand that the university be closed down," and that "we feel this is no solution of the problem." Slaughter went on to say: "The administration is determined to do all it can to avoid violence, to keep the university operating while maintaining orderly and free discussion. Whether these objectives can be accomplished rests primarily with the student body." Many students resented the sending of the telegram and the student Council formally censured the Alumni Association for doing so.

President Shannon addressed students and faculty from the Rotunda steps on the afternoon of May 10. He had put his speech together hastily, with the aid of several persons, and it was poorly received, until near the end. At that point he attacked President Nixon's invasion of Cambodia, and said he would send a statement on the subject to Virginia's senators the next day. This brought loud cheers.

Copies of the message were left on the steps of Pavilion VIII on the Lawn so that anybody wishing to sign could do so. It expressed grave concern over "many evidences of anti-intellectualism and growing militarism in the national government" and went on to say:

The unspeakable tragedy at Kent State was received in terms that appeared challenging and callous. The promised disengagement in Southeast Asia has been agonizingly slow. The recent announcement of the invasion of Cambodia—a critical decision, vitally affecting the lives and futures of all our young men—was used to reflect personal and political credit upon the President. It has now become clear that the decision was reached without the advice and consent of either the Secretary of State or any committee of the Senate. . . . We therefore urge you to join your fellow senators in reasserting the authority of the Senate over the foreign policy of the United States, and the use of the armed forces in its support.

Nearly five thousand students and faculty signed the letter within twenty-four hours, and a delegation of students delivered the communication to the senators in Washington.

Explaining why he sent this message, Shannon said long afterward: "I was prepared to feel that the president shouldn't get into major public positions that have political implications, [but] that at this juncture it was really important and necessary to do so and appropriate to do so." He said his speech at the Rotunda, stating that the message would be available for signatures, "tended to turn things around. . . . This took the student pressure off me. . . . We were all together. It tended to pull the university together instead of having factions."

But if a substantial majority of the students and faculty were in accord with the president in this matter, many alumni were in violent disagreement. Gov. Linwood Hilton said, "I disagree with President Shannon's position." The recently chosen rector of the university, Joseph H. McConnell, '31, one of the leading business executives in the United States, president of Reynolds Metals and former president of Colgate-Pamolive-Peet and the National Broadcasting System, was an immediate dissenter. When he learned in Richmond of Shannon's speech, he called the president on the telephone to say that the speech should have been cleared with him in advance, and that he would never have agreed to its delivery.

Shannon said later that the principal thing that bothered him about his remarks at the Rotunda was the fact that somehow "the word 'frightening' got in there." He had referred to the "frightening fashion" in which students had shouted outside his home shortly before. The word *frightening* should have been *menacing*, he said, since "I wasn't frightened. . . . A lot of people thought I was scared to death." He was trying in his speech to explain "why the police had to come in." In Shannon's behalf, it should be said that anybody who, as a naval officer, had taken part in half a dozen of the most desperate

Pacific landings in World War II, and had gone down with the *Quincy* when she was sunk off Savo Island, would hardly have been "frightened" by a group of students.

Alumni Association President Slaughter wrote Shannon, apropos of the telegram to parents that the "overwhelming majority" of alumni "are opposed to any officials of the university taking a stand on political issues in a context which would indicate that this represents the views of the university in any way."

Shannon contended that the letter to Byrd and Spong "has been misunderstood and misinterpreted as criticism of President Nixon's decision to enter Cambodia," whereas "it referred to the '*announcement*' of the decision being 'used' for personal public relations purposes." However, this appears to be "a distinction without a difference," since Shannon himself said in the oral deposition he made years later that his Rotunda speech was "pretty critical of Mr. Nixon."

Thousands of letters from alumni poured in to Shannon's office, according to Frank Berkeley, his executive assistant. While many were extremely critical of the president, and some even demanded his resignation, more than 80 percent of those received in the first few months were favorable, Berkeley stated.

Elements of the press attacked the Shannon letter to the senators, and argued that there was a lack of punitive measures at Charlottesville against obstreperous students, in contrast to the arrest and jailing of more than one hundred students at VPI.

The comparison with VPI was not a fair one. The 108 VPI students who were arrested and jailed overnight had occupied Williams Hall and refused to leave when ordered out by the police. They did nearly $1,500 worth of damage to Williams Hall, and materials for making fire bombs were found there. Of those arrested, 101 were fined $50 and given a 30-day suspended jail sentence, while several others were fined $100 and made to serve five of the 30 days. The University of Virginia students had left Maury Hall promptly and peaceably when Judge Waddell's injunction was read to them. No arrests or fines were necessary.

While the disorders at the university were led by a relatively

IN MEMORY OF
"BETA"
BELOVED FRIEND
AND MASCOT OF
THE STUDENTS OF
THE UNIVERSITY OF
VIRGINIA
DIED APRIL 6, 1939

97, 98. Gravestones side by side near the entrance to the University Cemetery commemorate the devotion of the students to their two mascots "Beta" and "Seal."

TO PERPETUATE THE
MEMORY OF
SEAL
MASCOT AND FRIEND OF
THE STUDENTS OF THE
UNIVERSITY
DIED DEC. 11, 1953

small and tightly organized group of radicals, the extent to which the student body seemed to sympathize with some of their principal "demands" is surprising. On May 13 the students voted on ten issues raised by these agitators, including nine "demands." The Student Council had voted, 11 to 10, to submit the demands to the students in a referendum. Six of the demands were given overwhelming approval by the students. These included revocation of Judge Waddell's injunction; prohibiting university officers from carrying firearms and outside law enforcement officers from coming on the Grounds; and public support by President Shannon "for the right of university employees to strike and bargain collectively." By 6 to 1 the students approved a demand "that the university include women on an equal basis with men in both recruitment and admissions for all schools at the university"; and by over two to one that the university "publicly commit itself to a goal of 20 percent for the enrollment of black students and an allocation of $100,000 for black admissions programs." A demand that was rejected called for the abolition of the ROTC and defense-related research.

Gov. Holton said it was "time for the students to go back to class," and Senator Byrd criticized Shannon for a "lack of firmness." A minority of the university's administrators and professors agreed with Byrd. They believed that sterner measures should have been employed by the president.

In a public statement on May 13 President Shannon declared that "several hundred major universities" had been drastically affected by the events in Southeast Asia and at Kent State, and "most [of them] have been forced to suspend operations for varying periods of time, or to close." One that closed in early May for the rest of the session was Princeton. "The university [of Virginia] is still open," the president went on. "I am determined to keep it open. . . . All schools and departments are open. . . . No person has been injured on the university Grounds, and no serious damage to property has occurred. . . . The Students' Strike Committee has adhered to the university's provisions in the scheduling and location of the planned rallies. The responsible university committee temporarily suspended its rules for several impromptu gatherings that appeared reasonable under the circumstances. . . .

Disciplinary measures . . . are being initiated . . . and some persons (not all of them students) will be subject to prosecution." A former student, charged with attempted arson, was prosecuted, at Shannon's insistence.

The administration provided various options in the spring of 1970: A student and teacher could arrange any of the following for the undergraduate: (1) Complete work on time and take examination on the scheduled date; (2) accept the grade up to May 1 as the final grade; (3) take the exams during the following semester up to October 1; (4) substitute another requirement for the exam by June 1. The more active agitators left the university for Washington or worked in the community. Those wishing to leave without taking exams had to sign the following: "Because the dictates of my conscience do not allow me to continue academic work in this time of crisis, and because I feel that each person must actively contribute toward the solution of our pressing problems, I pledge my honor as a gentleman that I am actively working toward the goals of peace and the objectives of the Virginia Strike Committee."

While there was criticism of the foregoing arrangement, the fact remained that disruption at Charlottesville was much less than at numerous other institutions. No classes were canceled or suspended. As President Shannon expressed it: "Class attendance remained normal in many departments and schools, and returned to an essentially normal level by May 13 in all schools. A total of 1,974 students met the deadlines for their degree requirements and were graduated on schedule. . . . The work of student leaders and marshals was outstanding; our tradition of student self-government was strongly reasserted, and the rights of all were respected." At Finals President Shannon received a standing ovation from the graduating class.

It was a time of high tension, with Marxist agitators seeking to foment revolution, and under the circumstances, it was almost inevitable that mistakes would be made. The Board of Visitors placed its stamp of approval on Shannon's actions during the period. By an 11 to 4 vote it commended him for keeping the university in operation, maintaining its academic standards, preserving the right of free speech, and "avoiding the violence experienced elsewhere . . . despite individual differences of opinion as to methods used."

The session of 1970–71 witnessed a cooling of the revolutionary fires at Virginia. The National Student Association, with which the Student Council was affiliated, called for a general strike in February to protest the escalated bombing in Vietnam, but there was no strike at Charlottesville. About two weeks later Dr. Benjamin Spock addressed a student group at the university, and urged them to work for revolution. He said, however, that if they sought to achieve it now, they would be "reduced to grease spots." The following month the student newspaper stated that "this year [at the university] there were no demonstrations, only the most feeble protests against the war." The 1971 *Corks and Curls* continued to express a far-out leftwing viewpoint, but its tone was one of resignation, if not despair, since things were drifting back to the status quo ante.

There was a mild uproar a year later when U.S. Solicitor General E. N. Griswold spoke at the university. About eighty students walked out soon after he began and then returned to question him concerning the government's handling of the antiwar demonstrations. The question period was punctuated with "shouts and heated protests." Next day a few students picketed the Charlottesville draft board, and a score were arrested in Washington for taking part in civil disobedience disturbances. About a year after that, in the spring of 1972, the Student Council, in a telegram to President Nixon, unanimously protested the stepped up bombing of Vietnam, but this was far milder than the riots at Harvard, the University of Maryland, and elsewhere.

The fact was that most of the steam had gone out of the radical movement at the University of Virginia, which at one time threatened violent disruption of the institution. It was refreshing in the fall of 1973 to note the words of the *Cavalier Daily*, then under the direction of Tim Wheeler, editor in chief, and William B. Bardenwerper, editor. Commenting on the student attitudes of a short time before, the paper said: "Our frequent categorizations, blanket accusations and arrogant assessments were shallow, and the rut we had fallen into of thinking slogans rather than ideas only furthered [*sic*] to illustrate our fits of immaturity."

That about sums it up. Thanks largely to President Shannon's leadership, the radicals had been thwarted, the university had survived the crisis of 1969–70 better than many institutions, and Jeffersonian principles of academic freedom and freedom of speech had been kept inviolate.

TEN

The
Changing Honor System

THE UNIVERSITY'S FAR-FAMED Honor System has often been described as the institution's most priceless possession. Prof. Robert K. Gooch said in an address at Finals in 1965 that he regarded it as "the finest thing about the university." He added that "the great body of alumni are convinced that their association with the Honor System was the most important, the richest, the most permanently influential experience which they had during their search for truth as students at this institution."

Prof. George W. Spicer stated in the middle seventies: "I was here for 40 years. . . . As far as my own classes were concerned, as far as my own personal experience goes, there was only one occasion in which I had reason to believe a student had cheated." Prof. Arthur F. MacConochie said at about the same time, "In 39 years of teaching I had only one black sheep."

The Honor System at Virginia evolved over the years. When founded in 1842 it consisted of a pledge by the student that he had received no assistance on an examination. Later the pledge was amended to forbid the giving of assistance to another, but until the Civil War professors continued to keep a watchful eye on the boys during all written tests.

It was during the years following the Civil War that the university's Honor System, or Honor Spirit as some prefer to call it, is believed to have reached its finest flower. The institution was small and homogeneous, many of the students came from preparatory schools that had honor systems, and there was no further watching over them by the faculty during examinations. The Honor Spirit, as part of the code of the honorable gentleman, was probably more vitally alive during the closing decades of the nineteenth century than at any other time.

The spirit remained much the same during the early and middle years of the twentieth century. Enrollment was still relatively small, although several times as large as it had been in the late 1800s. Not until the period immediately following World War II did enrollment pass the five-thousand mark, and it soon fell to around three thousand five hundred upon the graduation of many returned servicemen who had flocked back to college. So the problems experienced by those who sought to preserve the Honor System were still readily manageable.

Rules of procedure for enforcing the system were first codified in 1909. They provided that anyone suspecting a breach should confront the suspect and "demand . . . an explanation of his conduct." (This, be it noted, is the exact opposite of talebearing, the allegation sometimes made against the system.) If the suspect's explanation was unsatisfactory, the accuser or accusers were to demand that he leave college. He had to do so at once or stand trial before the Honor Committee. In 1909 the committee consisted of the presidents of the five departments plus the vice-president of the department in which the alleged offense occurred. The accused and the accuser or accusers were allowed to have counsel from the student body. Votes of five of the six Honor Committee members were necessary for conviction, and from the verdict there was no appeal. A change was made in 1917 to provide that the participating vice-president should keep minutes of the proceedings. In the event of acquittal the minutes were to be destroyed.

"Honor cards" were introduced in 1932, with each first-year man signing a statement indicating his acceptance of the system. It was done at small group meetings where there was an opportunity for questions and a complete explanation.

Further changes came in 1934. It was recommended by the committee that minutes of trials be kept by a professional stenographer, if possible. A case resulting in a conviction could be opened only upon production of new evidence. It also was provided that all first-year men should hear an address at the opening of the session explaining the Honor System. Furthermore, members of the Honor Committee would meet the incoming students in small groups and discuss the system in detail. Explanation of the system appeared in early issues of university publications.

Some years later the president of each department appointed a "student adviser." These appointees consulted with the accused and accusers before a problem was brought before the Honor Committee, with a view to determining whether there was sufficient evidence to justify a trial. The committee felt that "by constant association with honor trials the advisers would be in a position to offer valuable assistance." After the dismissal of a student, the record of the proceedings could be opened to possible employers, to another college or university to which the offender might be applying, or to the armed services or the government, in the event that he was attempting to obtain a commission or an appointment. Or the record might be seen by his parents. As a regular practice the Honor Committee did what it could to aid any convicted student who sought to enter another institution or to obtain employment. Far from hounding the unfortunate after his dismissal, the committee and the university authorities were, and are, anxious to assist in his rehabilitation, and to give him a chance to rise above his difficulties and become a useful citizen.

It is important to note that the system at Virginia is entirely in the hands of the students and that there can be no appeal from their verdicts to the faculty, the administration, or the Board of Visitors. Many believe that therein lies the principal reason why the system has survived at the university while systems operated along different lines were failing at so many other institutions.

In earlier times students were expelled under the Honor System for a variety of offenses. Dean William M. Thornton writes in his *Genesis of the Honor System* (1904):

Men have been expelled under it for publishing in the University Magazine a stolen article and offering it in competition for a prize. They have been expelled for cheating at cards . . . or for evading payment of just debts by falsely claiming they had been robbed.

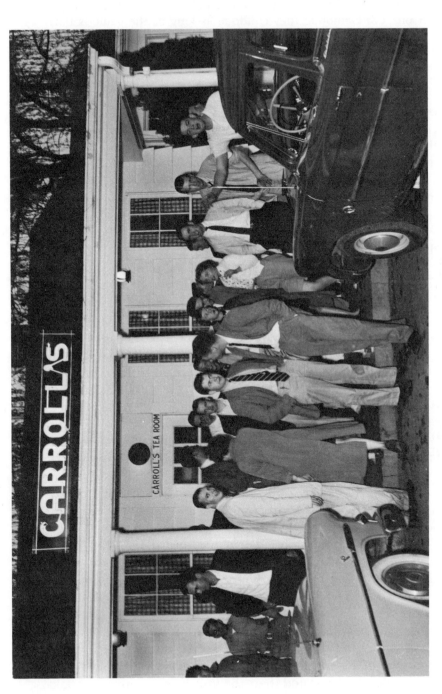

99. *Carroll's Tea Room, where tea was not to be had, favorite watering place of students for nearly two decades.*

They have been expelled for sexual crimes against younger students and for violent and insulting behavior to ladies or other defenseless persons. . . . Gambling they condone as long as the game is fairly played. Drinking they seem to consider one accomplishment of a gentleman, and drunkenness is simply the unfortunate error of an immature judgment.

Even in 1901 there were those who seemed to think it acceptable, under the Honor System, to answer "present" in class for their friends at roll call, when the friends were not on the premises. There appears to have been uncertainty at that time as to the scope of the system since *College Topics* said in 1905: "We are glad that it [the Honor System] does hold sway in the examination room, but why should it be limited to that sphere?. . . . Why should its spirit not pervade all college life? We believe that the present state of affairs can be remedied if the sentiment of the student body demands it."

Down the years the problem of just what offenses should be regarded as violations of the system has been debated, and in 1935 the written guidelines, later known as the "Blue Sheet," contained the following: "One of the greatest dangers to which an Honor System can be exposed . . . is that of being 'overloaded' with offenses. To avoid this, it is essential that the Honor System shall concern itself solely with those offenses which are classified as dishonorable by the public opinion of the student generation involved." At least as early as the second decade of the century the students appeared to focus on lying, cheating, and stealing as the three offenses that, by general agreement, could not be tolerated at the University of Virginia.

By 1955, however, doubts began to arise as to what constituted lying. Students were going to the ABC stores to obtain liquor and were giving false information concerning their ages. Honor Committee Chairman Howard Gill stated that such conduct constituted an honor offense, while others maintained that "lying to obtain liquor was a violation of state law but not of the code." The *Cavalier Daily* supported Gill, saying that "if a breach is allowed to become an accepted practice, the entire system will be placed in danger." Three years later the paper reiterated this opinion and added that multiple use at one meal of a contract cafeteria meal ticket was "clearly dishonorable." It also stated that "the improper removal of books from the various libraries of the university" is construable as an honor violation.

There were ominous indications that long-established views concerning the Honor System were changing, not only among the students but among numerous younger members of the faculty. A Raven Society committee for the College of Arts and Sciences reported in the spring of 1961 that almost half of the students interviewed favored grades of punishment for Honor System violations. Furthermore, said the report, "it is felt that many faculty members have neither a feeling for the spirit of the Honor System nor confidence that it works." The Raven committee went on to say that this "is particularly important in view of the fact that many of the first-year courses are taught by instructors new to the university." The foregoing situation was to a major degree an outgrowth of the university's rapidly increasing enrollment which brought in thousands of students who had never experienced an honor system before. This made the task of indoctrination at the opening of each session doubly difficult. The *Cavalier Daily*, echoing statements made since the 1920s, had declared in 1958 that "the Honor system can be preserved only if there is action on the part of the administration to limit the size of the university." Such action, as we have seen, came some years later.

It became customary, beginning in 1958, for the Honor Committee to send each member of the faculty just before final examinations, a memorandum warning against "subjecting students to unnecessary temptations." Among the practices warned against were take-home quizzes, giving the same quiz to more than one class section, and providing less than "ample room" between students seated during an exam, which "places the student in a delicate position."

The Honor Committee also issued a list of guidelines for examinations in 1965, which was repeated in several successive years, in order that students might "avoid circumstances which could be construed as suspicious": (1) Don't take books, notes, or unnecessary scratch paper into an examination room; (2) exams should be taken in the location designated by the professor; (3) while taking an exam, don't leave the room for too long a period; (4) don't stare around an exam room needlessly, for this could be interpreted as trying to copy another's answers; (5) once you are through the exam leave the immediate vicinity before you discuss the exam, because someone who is not through may overhear you.

Lack of understanding of the Honor System "on the part of many members of the student body, faculty, and university community," was mentioned by a former member of the Honor Committee as "the main problem." He also stressed that another weakness lay in "the fact that new members of the committee are not well-versed in the system."

Sharp disparagement of the system by students in the Law School became a special problem. The Law School had become "the 'hot box' of the university, with very severe criticism aimed at the Honor System," Scott Sykes, chairman-elect of the Honor Committee, wrote President Shannon in 1961. A committee from the Law School had just studied the system and had interviewed approximately 10 percent of the school's student body. Roughly 85 percent of those interviewed felt that "codification of the Honor System is necessary, if not imperative" because "the spirit of the Honor System here does not correspond to the ideals and morals of the world outside our doors." The report detected "a strong feeling that the Honor System is overextended" and cited the illegal purchase of liquor at ABC stores by students not twenty-one as "the most prevalent example," with "many gray areas that have grown up in recent years." Also, "A majority of the [law] students consider the lack of an appeal [from conviction] one of the greatest weaknesses." The report referred to "the failure of the orientation program" and asked the amazing and truly staggering question: "Since there is no honor in the world, why try to force an old outdated concept of integrity on students who are preparing to live in this modern world?"

The fact that any appreciable number of University of Virginia law students openly expressed this superlatively cynical view explains many of the problems experienced by the Honor System in those years. Furthermore, a visiting professor in the Law School dismissed the system as "a period piece reflecting the supercilious style of class consciousness."

There was much criticism of the system also in the Graduate School of Arts and Sciences. That school was growing rapidly, and it had a larger and larger contingent of students from institutions where honor systems were unknown. To a somewhat lesser degree this situation prevailed in the Schools of Medicine and Engineering.

The Honor Committee was expanded in 1961–62 from six to nine members, with the presidents of the Schools of Architecture and Commerce and the Graduate School of Business Administration added. Two years later the president of the School of Nursing became a member. A four-fifths vote was necessary to convict.

Although more and more persons were beginning to feel that the Honor System was being overextended, two Honor Committee chairmen in the middle sixties were firm in taking the opposite view. Chris Leventis, chairman for 1963–64, said concerning the question whether students on vacation are covered by the system, "We feel that if a student represents the University of Virginia, no matter where he is, he is bound by the Honor Committee." And George Morison, who succeeded Leventis, stated that in his view, the system "pertains to all phases of a student's life." Yet several older dormitory counselors were quoted as saying that they understood the system did not apply to any student on vacation.

Morison's Honor Committee recognized "no areas of 'gray' in the system." It also declared that "a student is considered a representative of the university no matter where he may be and no matter what the time of year. . . . A man could be held responsible for an act committed in the middle of the summer miles away from the university." While it was admirable to attempt to hold the line in this fashion, the question was whether it had become impossible.

One of those who felt that such broad interpretation of the system's jurisdiction was self-defeating was Prof. Hardy C. Dillard. "Although it may seem illogical to refrain from extending it to all the manifold affairs of life, it is yet wiser to limit it to academic matters, or, at least, to matters of honor which are focused on the academic community," he said.

Some years before, Dillard also had expressed the view that "after a half century of brooding" he had concluded that the Honor System would ultimately collapse if graduated penalties were introduced as a replacement for the single penalty of expulsion. Supporting this view in 1966, the *Cavalier Daily* said: "We must recognize that it would be unfair to the university community to readmit one who has already violated the trust of his peers. And the necessity with graduated penalties of the Honor Committee's deciding not only guilt or innocence, but also the degree of seriousness of the offense, would place too great a subjective strain on the fairness of committee members."

Hardy Dillard, a member of the Honor Committee in his student days, also enunciated the thesis that a "consensus of honor" should be the basis for decisions as to what was and was not properly included under the Honor System. In other words, those things that the students regarded as dishonorable should be so regarded by the Honor Committee. Relying to a considerable extent on this concept, the committee ruled in 1968–69 that thereafter its jurisdiction would not extend beyond the confines of Charlottesville and Albemarle County and that "lying for liquor" would not be within the system's purview. While it seems probable that the majority of students were in agreement with this decision, there was considerable doubt as to just what most Virginia students of that era could agree upon as to the precise metes and bounds of the Honor System. A large number of students objected to the committee's exclusion of "lying for liquor," and a petition protesting the ruling was signed by well over two thousand undergraduates. There were less strong objections to the geographical limitation. The committee's ruling with respect to misrepresentations at the ABC stores was "motivated largely if not predominantly by the probability that a first-year student dismissed for that offense could lodge a successful appeal in court against his dismissal for a non-University-related action," Shearer D. Bowman, '71, wrote in his history of the Honor System. This line of reasoning was not made public, he said, since the committee "was apparently afraid" to do so.

The time had come to reevaluate the system, in the opinion of Theodore S. Halaby, a Harvard graduate and third-year law student, who said he was "greatly impressed by the beneficial effect the system has had on the university community." Halaby objected to the single penalty and expressed the view that there should be "degrees of guilt," as in our legal system.

The approach to Honor Committee trials was becoming increasingly legalistic. A visiting law professor raised the possibility that "the total absence of any appeal from the Honor Committee's decision violates due process of law." Dean of Ad-

100. Students and their dates slither about in the mud as a favorite Easters diversion in 1974.

missions Marvin Perry had insisted that the Honor System and especially honor trials be kept "from a dry and spiritless legalistic system rather than a living expression of a spirit of honor," but the Honor Committee of 1967–68 thought otherwise. It initiated a movement "toward a more 'legalistic' Honor System," according to Bowman, "paralleling 'a clear trend' in contemporary legal opinion concerning educational institutions 'for the courts to hold a student's interest in pursuing his educational opportunities to be more than a privilege, and to recognize educational opportunity as an emerging right.'"

In two *Cavalier Daily* articles Carroll Ladt examined the workings of the Honor System as of 1968. After describing cheating on quizzes and examinations, and widespread skepticism, if not opposition, on the part of graduate students, law students, and some faculty, he concluded that more intensive orientation was essential to the system's preservation.

The Honor System was attacked in 1969 by the Radical Student Union, a pro-Marxist group. Joel Gardner, a fourth-year honor student in the College, said the organization "hit a new high in absurdity" with its assault. The RSU had said that we have finally come to see our "farcical" Honor System as one of the two greatest irrelevancies in the pursuit of knowledge, the other being the grading system. It added that the system generates an élitist feeling among university students, causing them to look down on their "common neighbors." Rather similar criticisms of the Honor System were being voiced by certain clergymen in the community.

The students voted in 1969 by 1,779 to 941 that the system should be altered to cover the university administration, faculty, coaches, and staff. The suggestion got nowhere. The persons concerned would have had to agree, and the Honor Committee would have had to be revamped.

A number of significant changes in the system were made in 1969 and 1970. First came the Honor Committee's decision to permit an appeal from a guilty verdict "upon a showing of good cause," as contrasted with its previous position that no appeal was possible except when substantial new evidence was produced. Another change permitted the accused in honor trials to retain the services of a local attorney. Such an attorney was allowed to sit in on trials, but not to act as "oral advocate."

And there was also the important announcement that the question of "intent" should be carefully weighed. In other words, even though the student committed a violation of the code, if he did not have "dishonorable intent," he could be adjudged not guilty. An example would be the commission of an offense by a person who was drunk and not fully aware of what he was doing.

Problems that plagued the Honor Committee during the sixties grew out of what some might term fine-spun distinctions. For example, a law professor explained: "A student accompanied by an eager and experienced companion of the opposite sex, not his wife, to a motel, is not breaching the Honor System when he signs the register with a false name; a student, whether so accompanied or not, who registers at a motel under a false name to bilk the proprietor of the rent, is." The foregoing was published several times as guidance for students.

The turmoil on college campuses in the late sixties and early seventies and the consequent weakening of traditional concepts and values had their impact at Virginia and elsewhere. This disorganization and disruption increased the problems of the university's Honor Committee.

Yet it is noteworthy that, despite this situation and greatly increased enrollment at Virginia, there were fewer dismissals annually under the Honor System from 1967–68 through 1970–71 than between 1960–61 and 1966–67. For the later period, the number expelled under the system each year ranged from three to ten, whereas for the earlier, dismissals ranged from eleven to twenty-one. Enrollment had more than doubled between 1960 and 1971, so that the falling off in expulsions is extraordinary. An interesting aspect of the dismissals over this period is that a larger and larger percentage were expelled for academic offenses, that is, cheating and plagiarism, and a smaller and smaller proportion for other offenses. This would seem to indicate that student opinion was leaning more and more away from regarding nonacademic offenses as honor violations worthy of permanent dismissal. One is also driven to the conclusion that since the number of expulsions dropped, despite much higher enrollment, the system was not working as effectively as formerly.

Student opinion was responsible in 1971 for a reversal by

the Honor Committee of a guilty verdict. A first-year student was ordered dismissed for stealing several drinks from an open vending machine. There was such a strong and immediate adverse reaction that the Honor Committee met again, reversed the verdict, and stated that "the current student generation does not consider this act so reprehensible as to warrant permanent dismissal." It was the first time that such a reversal had taken place. Justification was seen in the words of the Honor System's "Blue Sheet": "The Honor System shall concern itself solely with those offenses which are classified as dishonorable by the public opinion of the student generation involved." A few months later a straw poll of 1,100 students chosen at random by the Honor Committee resulted in a return of 750 ballots, and a 93 percent vote for maintenance of "an honor system." There was much less unanimity among the respondents as to what the system's precise metes and bounds should be. There was a 47 percent vote in favor of the single sanction, that is, dismissal for any conviction, as against 37 percent who favored graduated penalties.

The Seven Society, always a zealous supporter of the Honor System, provided the funds for publication of a special issue of the *Cavalier Daily* devoted entirely to the system. It appeared Mar. 13, 1972, and contained valuable analyses and discussions. Prof. T. Braxton Woody, who had delivered a much-admired address on the Honor System to the first-year students for a number of years, was presented with a special award by the Sevens for his contribution to the "continuing growth and vitality" of the system. But he soon stopped giving the address. "The Honor System was just not what it used to be, and I began to feel that I just could not give that same talk again," said Woody.

The Honor Committee voted 7 to 4 in 1972 not to introduce a two-penalty system. Such a system had been suggested by a group of law students, and the four committee members who voted in favor of it were all graduate students. Two weeks later a student poll returned a 68 percent vote in favor of retention of the single sanction, 3,717 for and 1,748 against. Gordon Peerman, who had just been elected president of the College, said he had consistently taken the position that if any changes came in the Honor System "they should come in scope instead of sanction." The Honor Committee voted unanimously the following year to retain the existing scope and sanction.

"Several thousand books were missing before the [check] system was enacted [at Alderman Library]", the *Cavalier Daily* said. "Many of the books were undoubtedly purloined. . . . We have a roughly analogous situation in the Newcomb Hall cafeteria . . . 'Thefts numbered in the hundreds per day,' [and protective measures had to be instituted]."

The dispersion of the student body, especially its upperclassmen, in housing far from the Grounds, was noted by Honor Committee Chairman Peerman as a major reason for the difficulties being experienced with the Honor System. He stressed the need for interpreting the system "both as something of value to the individual and to the university community" and stated that the increasing numbers of students who are not provided with adequate facilities are the crux of the problem. "You can't fabricate community," he said. "We're simply going to have to provide residential facilities for the students. It is impossible to maintain any kind of community for students who feel no more profound relationship to the university than that of simply attending classes."

Another aspect of this problem is seen in the removal of the Law School from Clark Hall to the North Grounds, where it has become more and more isolated and out of the main stream. Placing of the Graduate School of Business Administration on the North Grounds had a similar effect.

Not only so, but students in the Graduate Schools of Arts and Sciences, now numbering several thousand, were not indoctrinated in the principles of the Honor System as were the first-year undergraduates, Ben Ackerley, Honor Committee Chairman in 1964–65, told the Board of Visitors. "The expanding enrollment, especially in the graduate schools, is making it doubly difficult for the Honor Committee to orientate everyone," said Ackerley. "Effective orientation is still being maintained with first-year students through the dormitory complex, but no such control is available for graduate students."

Although incoming faculty members were under instructions from the president to attend the orientation session of the Honor Committee, difficulty was being experienced in getting them to obey this injunction. In 1974, for example, only about 25 out of 240 new faculty members went to the briefing. Those who did not were urged to respond to the committee's next invitation.

Gray areas of the Honor System were being handled increasingly by the student Judiciary Committee which, with the university's mounting enrollment, became much more active in the seventies. Five to ten trials were being held each semester. An example of a gray area would be misuse of student identification cards to obtain admittance to sports events. The committee was concerned with student misbehavior, much of it unrelated to the Honor System.

The trend toward greater legalization of Honor Committee trials, brought about by law students and such organizations as the American Civil Liberties Union, caused the committee to rule in 1973 that a written statement of accusation would be required in all cases. This was in order to "further insure due process," the committee explained. Such a written statement was no substitute for the original verbal confrontation and accusation, it was emphasized.

A film on the Honor System was provided by the Seven Society. It was paid for with a check for $47,777.77, buried seven inches from one of the goal posts at Scott Stadium and exhumed just before the University of North Carolina football game.

Testimony to the honorable conduct of students in repaying loans to the Seven Society and Ivey F. Lewis loan funds was given in 1974 by Dean of Students Robert T. Canevari, who was in charge of both operations. Neither fund requires any security for loans. The record of repayment in both cases was almost 100 per cent.

It is obvious that the University of Virginia's Honor System in 1974 was by no means identical with the system that functioned there for more than half of the twentieth century, not to mention the one that was in operation in the nineteenth century. The Honor Spirit that dominated a student body ranging in number from fewer than one thousand to some three thousand five hundred could hardly be unaffected by the stresses and strains induced by a skyrocketing enrollment several times as great. The more recent student body was not only much larger but much more heterogeneous, and for the first time included many women and blacks. Whereas in ear-

101. The Seven Society's mysterious symbol, visible only to passing airplane passengers, appeared suddenly in 1966 on the dome of newly completed University Hall.

lier days there was prevailing uniformity of background, with matriculates coming overwhelmingly from Virginia and other southern states, there was in the sixties and seventies far greater ethnic, geographic, and ideological diversity.

Like all human institutions, the university's Honor System evolved with the times. In the College the Honor Spirit burned brightest, for it was there that the first-year men were given orientation at the beginning of the session. In the graduate and professional schools, to which students came from all corners of the globe, it was relatively difficult to indoctrinate the newcomers. They were more mature, and those who had attended other colleges and universities which were without honor systems often had formed their own opinions on the subject before they arrived at Virginia.

Possible modification of the university's revered institution, such as the introduction of graduated penalties or a jury system for trials, were being considered, although such drastic modifications had been voted down more than once by the students. Restriction of the system to purely academic matters, such as cheating and plagiarism, also was being viewed as a possibility.

Older alumni deeply lamented the necessity for changing the system in any material respect, but modern trends dictated certain alterations already made, and others were conceivable for the future. In the oft-quoted words of Thomas Jefferson, "Laws and institutions must go hand in hand with the progress of the human mind." The University of Virginia which he founded has been unable to avoid the application of this principle in the evolution of its Honor System.

ELEVEN

Mr. Jefferson
Would Be Proud

Establishment of a university press, a long-sought objective at Charlottesville, became a reality in 1963. An oral agreement in the 1920s between President Edwin A. Alderman of the University of Virginia and President Frank P. Graham of the University of North Carolina had been an obstacle. Alderman was understood on good authority to have told Graham that a press would not be established at Virginia to compete with the one at Chapel Hill so long as Chapel Hill refrained from launching a magazine in competition with the *Virginia Quarterly Review*. This agreement held for several decades, but finally was allowed to lapse. The *Carolina Quarterly* appeared, and there was nothing to prevent establishment of a university press at Virginia.

The Virginia Historical Society in Richmond led in pushing the latter project. When there were delays, Samuel M. Bemiss, president of the society and a university alumnus, prodded the university into action. The result was that President Shannon, who was strongly in favor of the plan, was able to announce that the University Press of Virginia was ready for business. It would be the first university press in the nation to publish the scholarly output of all educational and other learned institutions within a state, and other such presses soon followed its example. Victor Reynolds, longtime head of the Cornell University Press, and former president of the Association of American University Presses, a man with a national reputation in the field, was the first director of the University Press of Virginia. The board of directors included four University of Virginia professors and three representatives of scholarly organizations. Operations were begun in cramped quarters in the Rotunda but moved in 1967 to a nine-room house on Sprigg Lane. The family of Samuel M. Bemiss, who had since died, made the move financially possible, and the organization functioned much more effectively in its commodious building—christened Bemiss House.

The press began publishing almost at once and more than met the publishing schedule originally laid out. After establishing it on a firm foundation, Victor Reynolds retired in 1969 and was tendered a dinner in the Rotunda. He was succeeded by his assistant, Walker Cowen, a native of Texas and Ph.D. of Harvard, where he was a Woodrow Wilson Fellow. Cowen had been with the press for three years and was a lecturer in the English Department. Under him the press has come to be recognized as one of the foremost university presses in the land, with management that has kept it in the black, in contrast to some others, and with a list of scholarly publications that is the envy of many.

The University Press of Virginia publishes and distributes books for no fewer than sixteen learned societies and groups outside the commonwealth, including such prestigious organizations as the Morgan Library, American Antiquarian Society, Winterthur Museum, Colonial Society of Massachusetts, and the Grolier Club. All this has made the University Press of Virginia the principal publisher and distributor for the learned societies of this country. Inside the state it has published works from a majority of Virginia's colleges and universities, as well as such notable organizations as Colonial Williamsburg, the Virginia Historical Society, and the Virginia Museum of Fine Arts. Its two major publishing projects are the multivolume *Papers of George Washington* and *Papers of James Madison*, the largest single publishing enterprise dealing with the papers of the Founding Fathers. It has also issued hundreds of books on a great variety of subjects. Assessing the significance of the press in the life of the university, President Shannon said: "It has immensely encouraged and stimulated the intellectual life and scholarly production of the faculty and graduate students, and has enhanced recognition of the university as a scholarly and cultural center. Another result has been its perceptible effect in drawing the university closer into relationships with sister institutions throughout the state."

Charlotte Kohler's retirement as editor of the *Virginia Quarterly Review* was arranged in 1974, to become effective the following year, the fiftieth anniversary of the magazine. She had served for nearly three decades in the position. Managing editor during World War II, she was appointed editor in 1946. The magazine received many tributes for its excellence during her editorship. A B.A. of Vassar College and M.A. and Ph.D. of the University of Virginia, Miss Kohler joined the university faculty in 1965 as associate professor of English and became a full professor in 1971.

Staige D. Blackford, Jr., editor of the *Cavalier Daily* in his student days and subsequently an editor at Louisiana State University Press, press secretary to Gov. Linwood Holton, and assistant to President Edgar F. Shannon, Jr., was named to succeed her.

New Literary History a publication that had an international impact, was founded at the university in 1969 as part of the sesquicentennial observance. Ralph Cohen, Kenan Professor of English, was the editor of this highly esoteric magazine, which attracted contributions from such writers as John Cage, Marshall McLuhan, Claude Lévi-Strauss, René Wellek, and Max Black. The journal "is designed as a forum for scholars rethinking such basic issues as the nature of literature in the lives of men," said Editor Cohen, and it was believed by many to be "altering the whole concept and theory of literary history in this country," said the *Alumni News*. *New Literary History* was the first American journal to publish an article written for it by a member of the Institute for World Literature. Issued three times a year, the magazine inquires into such matters as "what happens when a person reads, the concept of symbolism, form in nature, and the theme of a Mozart piano sonata." Cohen said in 1972 that there were 1,200 subscribers, considered good for so recondite a publication. He also was encouraged by the increasing intellectualism of his students. They were beginning to ask questions, he said, "not about rhyme schemes in a sonnet but basic questions about literary perception."

William H. Wranek, Jr., retired as director of the University News Service in 1961, after serving in that post since 1922 when he founded the service. Wranek also had been editor and managing editor of the *Alumni News* off and on for a good part of that time. He was, in addition, lecturer on journalism in the School of Education for seven years, and many of the journalists turned out at Virginia were trained under him, either in his course or on the student newspaper. He continued to serve the university as consultant and special writer after his retirement.

Bevin Alexander, Richmond newspaperman, was named to succeed him but with a new title, Director of Information Services. He remained for five years and resigned to accept another position. William H. Fishback, Jr., also a Richmond newspaperman, was appointed Director of Information Services in 1966. He was in fact editor of the *Alumni News*, although it was decided to list Director of Alumni Activities Gilbert J. Sullivan as editor, a position he had held previously. Sullivan had plenty to occupy his time directing the expanding Alumni Association, which he was doing successfully, while the editorship of the magazine was being ably handled by Fishback. A valuable service was rendered by Fishback during the student disorders of 1969–70 when he furnished the Virginia press with accurate information concerning happenings at the university, as a counterweight to the grossly biased material that was appearing in the *Cavalier Daily*. In 1973 "Bill" Fishback was promoted to the position of Director of University Relations, a new position. In that capacity he gave attention to community and state relations, and worked with the university's president and the vice-presidents on a variety of problems in the area of public affairs. He retained his responsibilities with the *Alumni News*.

A new student publication, *Plume and Sword*, appeared in 1960 and survived for eight years. Its contents, frequently critical of such agencies and organizations as the Student Council and the *Cavalier Daily*, consisted mainly of topical features, news and interviews, and some poetry and fiction. Its circulation was small. As for the *University of Virginia Magazine*, it was enjoying much greater acceptance from the student body in the 1960s. It frequently published authoritative ar-

102. Elizabeth Johnson, assistant dean of admissions, who helped in recruiting black students.

ticles by distinguished faculty members. For some reason it went out of existence in 1969 and was succeeded by a revived *Virginia Spectator*. The original publication of that name had been liquidated by President Darden because of its obscene content. In its new incarnation the *Spectator* "verbally assassinated" various prominent individuals, while nearly everybody else was "slightly slurred," according to an article by Fred Heblich. "But scattered among the dirty jokes and uncalled for insults is some legitimate literature and some clean humor," he added. Still another publication, *The Declaration*, a weekly newsmagazine, appeared in 1973. It was devoted to in-depth news, features, and sports and was a creditable enterprise. Like most student organs, it tended to be on the liberal side and endorsed Henry Howell for governor. The *Cavalier Daily*, for its part, got the highest award it had ever received from the Associated College Press in the spring of 1969—a "first-class honor" rating for the first semester of that year. It had been rated "first class" for several other semesters during the 1960s. The *Virginia Law Weekly* continued to win praise from the American Bar Association as the best student newspaper published by a law school with enrollment of between five hundred and one thousand. It was given this preeminent position in 1974 for the eighteenth consecutive year.

John C. Wyllie was named university director of libraries, and Ray W. Frantz, Jr., director of libraries at the University of Wyoming, was appointed to succeed him as university librarian. The community was shocked when Wyllie died suddenly in 1968, after less than a year in office. The Bibliographical Society of the university established in his memory the John Cook Wyllie Memorial Fund for the publication of books in the field of bibliography. Also, the Clinch Valley College Library was named for him. Frantz was appointed director of libraries.

Ray Frantz managed the university's library system well, but facilities were inadequate to cope with the steadily rising acquisitions and the mounting student enrollment. An addition to Alderman Library, costing about $1,500,000 was outgrown almost as soon as it was opened, and more space became essential.

Dr. Wilhelm Moll was brought from the University of Kentucky's Medical Center to take charge of the similar center at Virginia. He had a leading role in arrangements for a medical library in the projected Medical Education building. The old medical library had been badly overcrowded for years in a wing of the School of Medicine. In the middle sixties the medical library and the other library units at the university became a part of the teletype network (TWX), by which information could be obtained in a matter of minutes from libraries or business and governmental organizations in all parts of the United States.

The finest collection in existence of the works of Nathaniel Hawthorne and one of the finest on Robert Frost were two of the notable additions by C. Waller Barrett to his Barrett Collection at the library. A dinner was tendered him there on his seventieth birthday in 1971 with some seventy-five men of letters in attendance. Rare works were presented in his honor. Speakers at the dinner were President Shannon and Prof. Fredson T. Bowers. The following year Barrett was given Princeton University's Donald F. Hyde Award for "distinction in book collecting and service to the community of scholars." His collection was termed "unrivaled in quality and quantity."

A Tennyson collection, said to be the greatest remaining assemblage of Tennyson materials in private hands, was presented to the library by alumni and friends in honor of President Shannon, a leading Tennysonian scholar. Another valuable acquisition was a 10,000–volume collection of Chinese classics in the Chinese language, presented by the Ellen Bayard Weedon Foundation. Also, a rare collection of original cartoons and comic strips, ranging from Thomas Nast to Walt Disney and from H. T. Webster to Charles Addams, donated by Bernard M. Meeks of Arlington. And the extensive Walter Reed Yellow Fever Archive, assembled over three decades by Nobel Laureate Philip S. Hench was presented to the library by his widow. This archive was especially useful to Dr. William B. Bean, who is writing a biography of Reed. A different type of acquisition was a Gilbert Stuart portrait of George Washington, which had come down through the Rives family of Castle Hill, and was given to the library by Mrs. F. Bayard Rives and her son, George L. Rives. It was placed in the Mount Vernon Room at the library, a copy of Washington's library at Mount Vernon.

The 150th anniversary of the university's founding was observed in 1969 with a year-long celebration that brought renowned scholars to the Grounds from a number of countries. Its theme was expressed in Jefferson's famous phrase "The Illimitable Freedom of the Human Mind." The observance opened in January with a Charter Day dinner, was followed a few days later by a dinner in New York at the Hotel Pierre, under the auspices of the Newcomen Society, with President Shannon as the speaker; continued on through Founder's Day in April, and culminated in a three-day celebration Oct. 19–21. It was decided that the sesquicentennial observance should not be an occasion for self-congratulation but rather an opportunity to review the university's commitment to the fulfillment of Jefferson's ideals.

This was the era of nationwide campus agitation, and there were sour notes at Virginia from a small group of students, led by Robert Rosen, and calling themselves the Coalition. On Founder's Day they held a "counter-convocation" on the Rotunda steps, with perhaps one hundred persons in attendance. As the academic procession marched down the Lawn to Cabell Hall for the convocation, about a score of these students walked along carrying placards with such legends as "Thousands of Dollars for the Sesqui, But Not One Dollar for Integration" and "150 Years of Racism—What the Hell Have You Got to Celebrate?" These pickets, according to a statement by President Shannon years later, "were being partially instigated by the ministers over at St. Paul's, and they were making all their signs . . . in the basement of the church." A number of them walked out of the ceremonies at Cabell Hall. Before doing so they heckled the speaker, Esmond Wright, a university graduate in the class of 1940, member of the British Parliament and professor at the University of Glasgow. The *Cavalier Daily* termed the convocation "a monument to hypocrisy."

Except for these minor distractions, the sesquicentennial was a great success, with strong support from faculty, students, alumni, and the public at large. Such internationally known scholars and writers as Robert Lowell, Raymond Aron, Daniel Boorstin, and Philip Hauser appeared on various programs during the year, and a climactic event was the address in October by Philip Handler, president of the National Acad-

103. Barry Parkhill, all-American Basketball player, 1972.

emy of Sciences, who spoke on "The University in a World in Transition." Handler stated that Thomas Jefferson "would be pleased and proud to see . . . his university . . . giving to his state its leaders for a century and a half, spreading the Enlightenment, giving tone and character to Virginia and these United States." European institutions represented at the final ceremonies included the universities of Padua, Oxford, St. Andrews, Poitiers, Leyden, and Groningen, as well as scores of colleges and universities from all parts of the United States and many learned societies. A special feature of the celebration was the announcement of fifteen Sesquicentennial Professorships and the filling of these with the appointment of that number of distinguished men from the faculty. They were known as Sesquicentennial Associates of the Center for Advanced Studies and were freed of all teaching duties during the year while they pursued their researches, either at the university or elsewhere. These professorships were approximate equivalents of sabbaticals. Their number was substantially increased in subsequent years.

In thanking those who were chiefly responsible for arranging and carrying out the sesquicentennial program, President Shannon said: "Particular appreciation must be expressed to A. E. D. Howard, chairman of the committee who planned the celebration; to B. F. D. Runk, executive chairman for the sesquicentennial year, who directed all the activities with flair and enthusiasm; and to William A. Hobbs, alumnus, former member of the Board of Visitors, director of development and public affairs, who graciously carried the administrative responsibility for the entire undertaking."

The most dismal athletic record in the history of the university was being compiled in the late 1950s and early 1960s. To the loss of twenty-eight football games in a row was added the loss of nineteen basketball games in 1957, and three wins and twenty-two losses in 1961. The baseball tally for 1960 was equally devastating—two games won, fifteen lost, and two tied. Students gave little support to the teams, and there was much talk of pulling out of the Atlantic Coast Conference. Gus Tebell resigned as director of athletics, a post he had held since 1951. He had come to the university in 1931 and coached football, baseball, and basketball at one time or another. He was elected to the Basketball Hall of Fame in 1964.

Steve Sebo, head football coach at the University of Pennsylvania and then general manager of the Titans, later the Jets of the American Football League, was named to succeed Tebell. He filled this position until 1971, when Eugene F. (Gene) Corrigan, who had been director of sports information, was appointed director of university athletic programs, a new position, with overall charge of athletics. Sebo retained his title and was given various duties, including scheduling the games. His associate director was Evan J. (Bus) Male, a former football player for the Cavaliers and a wheelhorse in the athletic department for several decades. Male's chief responsibilities were attending to the finances and administering University Hall and the other athletic facilities.

Since the departure of Art Guepe as football coach, a series of successors in the job had been highly ineffective, but with the hiring in 1961 of William T. Elias, the George Washington University coach, there was a rift in the gloom. Elias began by telling the football squad, "Your first duty is to get an education, and your second duty is to play football"—refreshingly novel doctrine from a mentor of the gridiron. Eighty men came out for spring practice, a record. "Pep rallies" were held before several of the games, something that had happened hardly at all for years. William and Mary was defeated 21 to 6, and by the end of the season Virginia had won four and lost six, the best record since 1952. Elias was chosen ACC "coach of the year."

Yet despite these successes the students seemed largely indifferent during the games and "sat quiet-mouthed and placid, as though . . . attending some type of wake." The "V" Club was also criticized for lackadaisical behavior.

Gary Cuozzo, who quarterbacked the team at this time, was a Phi Beta Kappa and a Raven. He went from Virginia to the Baltimore Colts, where he was backup for the famous Johnny Unitas. When Unitas was injured in 1965, Cuozzo threw five touchdown passes against the Minnesota Vikings, more than Unitas had ever thrown, and the Colts won, 41 to 21.

The studied indifference of the student body came to an end with Virginia's 35–14 victory over Army in 1964. "Football frenzy captured the university. . . . What has happened to the traditional 'don't-give-a-damn' atmosphere which is supposed to prevail over Virginia?" the student newspaper asked. The Cavaliers won five and lost five that season, but despite the marked improvement remained in the ACC cellar.

The victory over Army was apparently responsible, in part, for the fact that Bill Elias was wooed away from the university by the U.S. Naval Academy. He left in January 1965 and was succeeded by his assistant, George Blackburn. Elias had recruited some genuine stars—Gary Cuozzo, Bob Davis, Don Parker, Tom Hodges, Ed Carrington, Jarvis, Stetter, and Kowalkowski—but the team seemed not to realize its full potential. Davis, Parker, Carrington, and Stetter were chosen as ACC all-stars in 1966, and Virginia ranked third in the conference. Quarterback Robert E. Davis, Jr., of Neptune, N.J., 6 feet 2 and 195 pounds, set a Virginia and ACC record for total offense, with 4,025 yards over a three-year period, compared to Bill Dudley's 3,469. Davis also had the highest total yardage in the conference for a single season, 1,688. He was chosen ACC athlete of the year and signed with the Houston Oilers.

Execrable taste was shown by some Virginia students before, during, and after the VPI game of 1966—which VPI won, 24 to 7. Adopting its usual sneering attitude toward the Blacksburg institution, the *Cavalier Daily* published an editorial entitled "Needed: Someone to Hate" a few days before the game. One sentence was, "Let's greet our guests with all the odium, execration, aversion and abomination in our twisted, venomous little minds." When the visiting team came on the field, it was loudly booed, as was the Highty-Tighty Marching Band. Two Virginia students ran back and forth through the band while it was maneuvering. The *Cavalier Daily*, apparently blissfully unaware of its own crude insults, sharply criticized the Virginia students the following week for their "blatant rudeness and ungentlemanly conduct." The newspaper received a barrage of denunciatory letters from university students who were embarrassed by its ill-bred comments. The Student Council wrote a letter of apology to the Highty-Tighty Band.

Virginia won four games and lost six in 1967, and then in 1968 it had its first winning season since 1952, with seven wins and three losses. Frank Quayle, the star back, was named ACC player of the year, the team averaged 32.8 points per game, and George Blackburn was named ACC coach of the year.

North Carolina State won the ACC championship, however. Offensive guard Chucker Hammer and offensive tackle Greg Shelly were all-Conference, while quarterback Gene Arnette and fullback Jeff Anderson were also outstanding. Quayle signed a contract with the Denver Broncos.

One reason why Virginia had so few seasons such as that of 1968 was that the institution's admissions standards were higher than those of the other universities in the Atlantic Coast Conference. Virginia led the ACC usually, but not always, in the number of its athletes with at least a B average in their studies. Prof. D. Alan Williams, faculty Chairman of athletics and president of the ACC, said in 1973 that the university "has the highest standards in the conference, and the ACC has the highest standards in the nation. We were the only school in the country last year to totally abide by the 1.6 grade projection." Virginia also may have been the only one that required a foreign language for entrance. A perfect example of the consequences of the university's higher standards is seen in the case of Don McCauley, who wanted to come to Virginia but was turned down because his grades were not high enough. He was promptly admitted at Chapel Hill, where he broke many records, was chosen ACC player of the year for two successive seasons, and was the nation's all-time leading rusher.

Coach George Blackburn laid down some curious rules for the Cavalier team in 1970, including "regular Sunday church attendance . . . avoid swearing and obscene words." The Student Council objected strenuously, and rightly, saying that the rules were "contrary to the spirit of personal dignity, religious freedom and amateur athletics." It also objected to the football players' having to live together for four years, unless they could present an acceptable excuse.

Coach Blackburn's contract was not renewed after the 1970 season, and he was succeeded by Don Lawrence, his assistant for four years. Lawrence remained in the post until 1973, when Ulmo (Sonny) Randle, '59, was chosen to replace him. Randle had starred at Virginia as the leading pass-receiver and kick-off returner in the ACC and had then gone to the pros. As end on the St. Louis Cardinals he was all-pro four times. He came to Charlottesville from East Carolina, where as coach he had been highly successful.

The arrival of Sonny Randle as coach of the Cavaliers opened a new era—temporarily. An intense, highly strung individual who demanded more complete dedication to the gridiron than had ever been demanded at the institution, Randle aroused great enthusiasm among football-minded alumni and misgivings in virtually all other quarters. Season ticket sales broke all records, but soon after the season opened various players left the squad. Randle put too much pressure on them, they said, and called on them to put football ahead of everything, including their classes. The latter allegation was denied by Randle, and he was supported by the President's Advisory Subcommittee, which concluded that the allegation was untrue. Yet nobody questioned that Randle was frantically emotional and almost on the verge of apoplexy during games—charging up and down the sidelines, often moving a few feet onto the field, waving his arms and growling at both officials and players. "There's a wild man over there," said one official. Randle's record for 1974 was four wins and seven losses, and while he expressed determination to do better the following year, there were serious misgivings as to whether his almost fanatical approach to football was what the University of Virginia needed.

Several players went to the pros. Harrison Davis, an end, was drafted in 1973 by the San Diego Chargers, and Paul Ryczek, a center, by the Atlanta Falcons. Kent Merritt, a speedy back who as a member of the track team tied Rector's long-standing 9.3 university record for the 100-yard dash, went to the New Orleans Saints as a wide receiver. The following year Dick Ambrose, all-ACC linebacker for two seasons, was drafted by the Cleveland Browns, and Ken Shelton, a record-setting pass receiver, signed with the Denver Broncos.

Behavior of some university students at games during the 1974 season was vigorously rapped. The North Carolina State marching band was showered with beer cans, ice cubes, and obscenities, the *Cavalier Daily* said. Conduct of certain students at the game the following Saturday was described by a writer to the paper as "barbaric."

The doings of Virginia undergraduates at basketball games over a period of years also were deplored, both at the university and outside. In 1965 a *Sports Illustrated* article called the University of Virginia's Memorial Gymnasium "one of the no-

104. Dr. Byrd S. Leavell and his son, Byrd Leavell, Jr., who won the Distinguished Professor Award of the Alumni Association and the "Pete" Gray Award, respectively, in 1972.

table snake pits" in the ACC. Students insisted, at many games, on throwing paper cups and other debris onto the floor and booing visiting players and officials. Similar lack of sportsmanship was shown when the games were moved to just-completed University Hall. "This is in sharp contrast to the excellent behavior of students of rival ACC schools on their home courts," said the *Cavalier Daily*. In 1973 Director of Athletic Programs Gene Corrigan wrote the paper protesting that "during the past several games 25 or 30 people have cast a black cloud over the university. . . . This not only gives the university the reputation of having the poorest crowds in the ACC, but it hurts our basketball team." By contrast, the Cavalier basketball players were praised for their continuing sportsmanlike behavior, despite a series of years in which they lost most of their games.

In 1971 Virginia had its first winning basketball season since 1954, with a record of 15 and 11. Coach Bill Gibson, who had been on the verge of being fired a few years before, was named ACC coach of the year. Barry Parkhill was the team's bright star. In 1972 the Cavaliers won 21 games and lost 7. Parkhill was ACC player of the year, Gibson coach of the year, and Parkhill was named a second all-American by the UPI. His jersey was retired. Scott McCandlish was a great rebounder, and others on this exceptional team were Frank DeWitt, Jim Hobgood, Tim Rash, and Chip Miller. Virginia ranked tenth nationally.

"Hoot" Gibson resigned as coach in 1974 to take a similar post at the University of Southern Florida and was highly praised at a farewell dinner. Shortly before, he had recruited such superior performers as Wally Walker, Gus Gerard, and Billy Langloh, who would play the following season for Terry Holland, Gibson's successor. Holland had made an exceptional record as coach at Davidson, and had played on that college's first nationally ranked basketball team.

In lacrosse the Cavaliers continued in the sixties and seventies to maintain their national ranking. As members of the National Lacrosse League they played against none but the top teams in the country and were regular contenders for the championship. As early as 1952 Virginia had a two-way tie for the national title, and then, after a three-way tie in 1970, won the NCAA championship in 1972. The Cavaliers also defeated a strong Oxford-Cambridge team in 1961. Virginia's first-team all-Americans between 1961 and 1974 were Henry Peterson, Hy Levasseur, Deeley Nice, Snowden Hoff (twice), Dick Peterson, Peter Coy, Jim Eustace, Doug Hilbert, Jim Potter, Pete Eldredge (twice), Tom Schildwachter, Tom Duquette, Bruce Mangels, Barry Robertson, and Boo Smith. Jay Connor was not only all-American twice in lacrosse but once in soccer, as well, while Mac Caputo won the same honor once in each sport.

Virginia's extraordinary record in lacrosse was due in no small measure to Gene Corrigan, coach from 1959 through 1967, himself an all-American at Duke. His reputation was such that he was offered the post of head lacrosse coach at Yale but turned it down. When Virginia won the lacrosse championship of the ACC in 1962, it was the first ACC title won by the university in any sport. Corrigan received the IMP award in 1967.

He was succeeded as lacrosse coach by Clayton Beardmore, all-American at Maryland, who remained for two years. Glenn Thiel, coach at Baltimore Community College, then took over.

In soccer Gene Corrigan was highly successful as coach from 1955 to 1967, during which time he had only two losing seasons. Paul Saylor was an all-American in 1960. ACC soccer championships were won in 1969 under Coach Gordon Burris and in 1970 under Jim Stephens.

The baseball team, coached by Jim West, won its first ACC championship in 1972. Its record was 9–4 against ACC teams and 20–9 overall. Standout players were Terry Dan, Steve Sroba, and Robin Marvin. A particular star of that era was Mike Cubbage, who went on to a successful career in the big leagues.

The Cavalier wrestlers were second in the ACC for each of the five years ended in 1973, and then in 1974 they dethroned Maryland, which had been invincible for twenty-one years. Wrestling at Virginia owed much to psychology Prof. Frank Finger, who coached the team for the seventeen years before 1963 and usually had a winning season. He was succeeded by Mebane Turner, one of the foremost grapplers in the university's history. Mike Caruso, who had just graduated from Lehigh, where he won three NCAA championships, followed Turner in 1967, but it was George Edwards whose team achieved the victory over Maryland.

The university's Law School provided two members of the 1963 U.S. Davis Cup tennis team for matches against Iran. They were Donald Dell and Gene Scott, who ranked seventh and eighth nationally and came to the Law School from Yale. C. Alphonso Smith, Jr., one of the foremost tennis players in University of Virginia history, was the nonplaying captain. The Americans made a clean sweep of the matches with the Iranians in Teheran.

The university's tennis facilities, provided by Lady Astor, had been outgrown, and in 1971 the Perry Foundation of Charlottesville donated the funds for eleven more courts near University Hall and at Bonnycastle Dell. Nevertheless by 1974 there were long waiting lines at all three complexes. The Perry Foundation also provided three new basketball courts in the "cage" at University Hall, these to be available to students when the varsity was not practicing in the building.

Outstanding facilities for track and field were completed on Copeley Hill near University Hall in 1970, replacing those abandoned on Lambeth Field. The complex was named for Pop Lannigan, the university's first track coach. Most of the required $200,000 was provided by the Athletic Department, with the rest coming from former members of the track team and the Alumni Fund. A baseball diamond also was constructed.

Scott Stadium, completed in 1931, was rehabilitated and upgraded in 1974. Over $360,000 was pledged by descendants of Frederic W. Scott the original donor, and an anonymous benefactor contributed $300,000 for the purchase and installation of astroturf. This last made possible much greater use of the stadium, especially for intramural sports and "phys. ed." classes.

With the coming of full-scale coeducation in 1970, women were increasingly active in athletics, on both intercollegiate and intramural levels. Barbara Kelly was appointed director of women's intercollegiate athletics at Virginia, and in 1974, for the first time, varsity women's tennis, basketball, and field hockey were played. These teams were eligible for university funding to cover equipment, travel, coaching, and publicity. Swimming and diving were to be added the following year. The first woman swimmer in the history of the ACC had been Mary Brundage, a third-year student at the university and member of the varsity swimming team in 1966. Women's teams had early success in varsity competition with other women in the seventies. The varsity field hockey team had a 9–4 record in 1974 and sent Kathy Devereaux and Cindy Hook to the Eastern Regional Tournament. The basketball team had a 10–5 record. In swimming, Ellen Feldman placed first in the 100-meter backstroke in the 1973 World University Games, and distance swimmer Susie Allen and backstroker Dottie Dilts competed in the National AAU championships the following year. Women constituted 40 percent of the 1,000 students taking "phys. ed." classes at that time and were extremely active in intramurals, where many of the games were coeducational. Men and women teamed together against similarly mixed competition, and found it exciting and enjoyable, according to the *Alumni News*. "This year," it said, "the hit of the season was inner-tube water polo, in which some 50 teams competed." Funds of the Student Aid Foundation were being used to finance women's sports, and it was anticipated that athletic scholarships would soon be awarded.

The Student Aid Foundation was launched in 1951 with a fund of $46,000; by 1965 the fund had risen to $115,000, and in 1974 was approaching $500,000. Grants in aid were given in the latter year to about 130 student athletes in football, basketball, golf, lacrosse, soccer, swimming, track, cross country, and wrestling. Baseball and tennis were not included.

The time had come when there were only female cheerleaders at varsity games, in glaring contrast to a decade before, when the male contingent was aghast at the mere thought of girls in that role. But while the males were not thoroughly acclimated to the presence of women in their classes and dorms, they concluded that cheers led by none but girls were a bit too much. In 1974 it was decided to divide the twenty cheerleaders equally between the sexes.

Intramurals at Virginia had expanded spectacularly under the able leadership of Edward R. (Butch) Slaughter, who retired in 1973 after forty-two years on the university's athletic staff and sixteen years in charge of intramurals. The latter program was said to be the best in the ACC, with many thousands of participants in a score of sports. Several tournaments in a number of different leagues were run each semester. As an example of the tremendous involvement, some twelve hundred students were taking part in 1972 in 185 basketball games in Memorial Gymnasium. Nonfraternity men and coeds made up a substantial percentage of the players in the various types of competition. In addition to directing this far-reaching program, Butch Slaughter, an all-American football player in his student days at Michigan, had coached football, baseball, and golf at Virginia and served as chairman of the Department of Physical Education. "He is probably a friend to more university students than any other man" said the *Alumni News*. Slaughter was given an award by the Seven Society for his devoted service to the university.

Another sports celebrity was honored when "Al" York was paid tribute for his leadership in boxing. Captain of the team when Virginia boxers were national powers, and coach thereafter for many years, York was given a watch by the Z Society at a dinner attended by over two hundred and fifty persons.

At varsity football and basketball games in the seventies a new and refreshing element was introduced by the antics of what was laughingly known as the Fighting Cavaliers Indoor/Outdoor Precision(?) Marching Pep Band and Chowder Society Revue. An outgrowth of the Pep Band that functioned spasmodically in the fifties and sixties, this zany outfit burlesqued the precision maneuvers of well-drilled bands at other institutions. Its clowning was deemed highly amusing and added a waggish note to the contests in Scott Stadium and University Hall.

The Alumni Association was growing steadily in memberships and contributions during the sixties and seventies. Gilly Sullivan had succeeded Mac Luck as director of alumni affairs in 1958, and a drive was launched during the 1958–59 session for life memberships at $200 each. This effort paid off handsomely, and a decade later Association President James L. Trinkle was able to announce that there were 6,116 life members (LM's), and the association's endowment had reached

105. *Avery Catlin, executive vice-president of the university,*
1974–.

$700,000, largely as a result of these memberships. Since many were buying them on the instalment plan, nearly five hundred thousand dollars more was to be collected. Life membership funds were placed in trust, and only the income was used. In that same year total membership in the association exceeded ten thousand for the first time, since there were more than four thousand regular members in addition to the LM's. "In recent years," said the *Alumni News*, "the figure for total alumni support has been in the area of $1,500,000." Circulation of the *News* was "rapidly approaching 20,000," and it was a remarkably good source concerning university happenings and trends.

There were so many different alumni organizations of one kind or another that the Office of University Development, established in 1970, had as one of its functions the coordination of their efforts. These agencies included the Law, Engineering, Graduate School of Business, and Student Aid Foundations, and the alumni associations of the schools of Law, Medicine, Graduate Business, Nursing, Education, and Architecture.

Funds received by the University of Virginia Alumni Association from dues contributed substantially to the association's activities. These included publication and distribution of the *Alumni News*, alumni chapter activities, homecomings and reunions, individual services to alumni, grants and loans to students and faculty members, and upkeep of Alumni Hall.

Officers from about thirty alumni chapters gathered at the university in the fall of 1963 for the first of a series of annual workshops designed to acquaint them with the progress of the university and the operations of the alumni association. After busy sessions on Friday afternoon and Saturday morning, they attended the Virginia–North Carolina football game, and then were guests at a dinner with two other alumni groups. President Shannon gave the address.

Three years later the association established two annual awards, one for outstanding teaching and the other recognizing exceptional student leadership, the awards to be made at the class day exercises each June. The faculty award carried with it a check for $500 and the student award $200. Both included life memberships in the association.

Also in 1966 the places where most university alumni live

were tabulated. Of the 37,058 alumni at that time, Virginia had 15,444, New York 2,729, Maryland 1,626, New Jersey 1,408, Pennsylvania 1,372, Florida 1,124, California 1,042, and North Carolina 984. Richmond was said to have "the largest concentration of university alumni in the world," with 2,072, followed by Charlottesville, with 1,951, and Norfolk with 1,023. Several years before, a faculty committee headed by Dean F. L. Geldard polled alumni for suggestions concerning the university. More than 40 percent of the replies urged continuation of the policy whereby a substantial percentage of out-of-state students attend the institution. It was held that there were distinct educational advantages in enabling the students from Virginia to have contacts with those from other states and that it enhanced the university's reputation as a national center of learning.

Contacts between students and faculty at the university were made closer and easier by a plan inaugurated in 1970. The alumni association made funds available to faculty members who wished to entertain students in their homes. Up to $35 was provided for each occasion, with a maximum of three such opportunities per professor.

By 1974 membership in the alumni association was just under fifteen thousand, a record, and contributions to the Alumni Fund totaled $583,035, another record. Alumni Fund Director Clay Delauney said that over the years about two-thirds of all contributions to the fund had come from outside Virginia, and much the same could be said of endowments. Under a succession of able presidents and with the competent work of Alumni Activities Director Sullivan the association was making gratifying progress.

The building program under Edgar Shannon was tremendous, although this was not anticipated when he took over the presidency. At the end of Colgate Darden's term, Darden remarked to Shannon: "Well, I've got the the buildings pretty well done now. Once you get the chemistry building, you can concentrate on the faculty." Shannon did concentrate on the faculty, with splendid results, but he also had to devote much attention to construction of additional physical equipment, made necessary by the unexpectedly rapid rise in enrollment and the accompanying expansion of the teaching staff.

The program for the decade 1960–70 was summarized as follows by Shannon:

New buildings were constructed for biology and psychology (Francis Walker Gilmer Hall); for chemistry; for arts and sciences (James Southall Wilson Hall); for mechanical engineering; for architecture (Edmund S. Campbell Hall); for fine arts (Fiske Kimball Library); for a nuclear reactor; for athletics (University Hall); and the dormitories (Alderman Road and Observatory houses). The university purchased the Old Ivy Inn [former home of U.S. Sen. Thomas S. Martin], with five satellite buildings on nineteen acres of land, and the 550-acre Birdwood Tract, the last large, undeveloped area anywhere near the university. Additions and renovations completed were the 1,000,000-volume stack addition to Alderman Library, the new ... hospital building in the Medical Center, the addition to [Alexander] Garrett Hall [formerly the Commons] to house record-keeping equipment for the registrar and bursar, the addition to Mary Munford woman's dormitory (Roberta Gwathmey Hall), and the addition to the nuclear reactor.

All this came to over fifty million dollars in state, federal, and private funds. By the time Edgar Shannon went out of office in 1974, the total would be more than double that amount.

The addition to Newcomb Hall in 1965 brought forth additional scathing comments from the students, despite the hall's indispensability, and its constant use by these same students. Termed an "environmental blunder" by a writer in the *University of Virginia Magazine*, and said to resemble a "dead elephant," the author declared that the addition made the hall look "like an even bigger dead elephant." He conceded that the addition provided "much needed space." Similar architectural criticisms had appeared in the *Cavalier Daily*, which also pronounced Newcomb Hall too expensive for what it provided.

Seven new dormitories on Alderman Road, estimated to cost three million dollars and housing more than eight hundred students, were built in the mid-1960s and were named for Professors Robley Dunglison, Edward H. Courtenay, and Socrates Maupin from the early faculty, and Thomas Fitzhugh, Francis P. Dunnington, William Minor Lile, and Albert H. Tuttle from the later.

106. The Big Tent was going strong in 1970 as a gathering place for returning alumni.

Morea, built in 1834 by Prof. John P. Emmet on what was later called Sprigg Lane, was purchased in 1960 through the generosity of Prof. and Mrs. William S. Weedon and the Alumni Board of Trustees and given to the university. It was renovated and furnished with antiques and then made available as a residence for visiting celebrities. The place was named Morea from the Latin word *morus*, meaning "mulberry tree." Emmet, the builder, planted mulberry trees there in the vain hope of introducing silkworm culture. The first VIPs to live there after the building's renovation were Prof. and Mrs. Arthur L. Goodhart. He was the only American to become master of a college at Oxford or Cambridge—University College, Oxford—and had recently retired as master there. Goodhart was visiting professor in the University of Virginia Law School for the second semester in 1965.

Acquisition in 1964 of a $1,000,000 Burroughs digital computer, replacing one that was much less sophisticated, was an important forward step. It was located in the basement of Gilmer Hall. At about the same time a $400,000 IBM computer was acquired for the university's administrative data processing center in Garrett Hall.

Working drawings were being prepared in 1965 for the new $5,100,000 chemistry building on McCormick Road, between Thornton Hall and Gilmer Hall, rounding out the group of scientific and technical schools in that area. It was expected to be ready in about two years, replacing the Cobb Chemical Laboratory built in 1920.

A new master site plan for the university was submitted that fall, the result of a three-year study by a university committee headed by Comptroller Vincent Shea, in collaboration with the Watertown, Mass., firm of Sasaki, Dawson, DeMay Associates, Inc. It called for five academic areas; liberal arts in and around Cabell Hall, science and engineering near Scott Stadium, fine arts on Carr's Hill, medicine at, and to the southeast of, the present center, and a graduate and professional area centering on the Law School in Clark Hall and the Graduate School of Business Administration in Monroe Hall. This blueprint was followed in subsequent years, with the exception that the Law School and Graduate School of Business were moved to the North Grounds. Wooded slopes of Mount Jefferson below the McCormick Observatory were reserved, under the plan, for special research facilities associated with the university's academic program. The nuclear reactor, physics acceleration building, radio-astronomy building, and research laboratories for the engineering sciences were already in place there. The University Center Area near Newcomb Hall would include the main library, administrative offices concerned with student affairs, dining halls, and student activity facilities. Intercollegiate athletics would be based on Scott Stadium and on Copeley Hill at and near University Hall, where new track, lacrosse, soccer, and baseball fields were to be provided. This would make Lambeth Field available for dormitory construction. Except for the abovementioned deviation with respect to the Law School and Graduate School of Business, the foregoing recommendations became a reality in the ensuing years.

University Hall—the auditorium, gymasium, and fieldhouse complex—was opened in 1965 with a concert by the Czech Philharmonic Orchestra. The long-sought structure was the result of seven years of hard work and planning. Shortly after the concert the first basketball game was played, against the University of Kentucky, with a capacity attendance of over nine thousand. Connected with the main building was "the cage," described as a "giant empty box used for indoor practice by the football, lacrosse, baseball and track teams." University Hall cost more than four million dollars, of which the alumni contributed $500,000, the General Assembly appropriated $2,367,692, and the rest was raised by revenue bonds. In 1970 additional facilities were made available. These included handball and squash courts and a six-lane, twenty-five-meter Olympic-size swimming pool.

The new fine arts center was a striking complex, situated on Carr's Hill and extending northward from the president's house. It comprised the School of Architecture and the department of drama. A new library, named for Fiske Kimball, first head of art and architecture at the university, served all departments. There was also a theater. An "exterior committee," composed of artists, architects, and scholars, mostly from Harvard and Columbia universities, had provided advisory help.

The home of the School of Architecture was said by Dean Joseph N. Bosserman of that school to be "the most significant building constructed at the university since Jefferson designed and built the original academical village, in terms of style, character, innovation, quality and almost any other good thing you choose." It was named for Edmund S. Campbell, head of the school from 1927 to 1950. Architects for the $3,300,000 structure were Rawlings and Wilson of Richmond, and it was designed by Pietro Belluschi and Kenneth DeMay of Sasaki, Dawson, DeMay Associates, Inc. Fayerweather Hall and the Bayly Museum, used for years by the school, were converted for use by the Department of Art.

The nearby $3,000,000 drama building on Carr's Hill was opened in 1974. It "makes a magnificent learning facility for students interested in acting, design and directing," David Weiss, chairman of the Drama Department, declared. The theater, seating 600 persons, is named for Sarah Gilder Culbreth, mother of Dr. David M. R. Culbreth, a medical graduate of the university in the class of 1877, who left $625,000 toward the cost of the ultramodern structure. Dr. Culbreth was the author of an interesting volume of reminiscences concerning his days at the university.

Restoration of the Rotunda to its original state, as conceived and carried out by Jefferson but with certain twentieth-century additions and modifications, had been a long-sought objective of Prof. Frederick D. Nichols of the School of Architecture. He initiated the project in the 1950s but had difficulty obtaining financing. A building committee with Francis L. Berkeley, Jr., as chairman and Nichols as consultant was formed in 1965 to work on the plan. A few years later a trust fund left by the late Dr. Cary D. Langhorne, a medical graduate in the class of '96, suddenly became available. The trust provided half of the cost of restoration on condition that this sum be matched. The matching amount was forthcoming from the U.S. Department of Housing and Urban Development, for an overall total from the two sources in excess of two million dollars. There was opposition by some faculty members and persons in the community since they regarded Stanford White's restoration after the 1895 fire, with its huge dome room extending to the roof, as superior to the Jeffersonian plan, which provided for two chambers, one on the ground floor and the other under the dome. But preponderant opinion favored Jefferson's original design, and work was begun in 1973 with a view to restoring the structure in accordance with his concept. It was anticipated that the project would be completed in time for Founder's Day 1976 and that the dedication would be a notable event of the nation's bicentennial observance. Ballou and Justice of Richmond, headed by alumnus Louis W. Ballou, a firm that had restored Jefferson's capitol in Richmond, were the architects, and R. E. Lee and Son of Charlottesville the building contractors.

While the importance of restoring the Rotunda would seem to be obvious, the extraordinary lack of information in some quarters concerning the building was a bit staggering. Two eighteen-year-old girls on a sight-seeing tour entered the university's version of the Roman Pantheon and inquired, "Where are the bedrooms?" On being informed that there weren't any, they asked cheerily, "This is Monticello, isn't it?"

The Rotunda had previously been listed in the National Register of Historic Places, and in 1971 the original Grounds as a whole were so listed. They were also included in the Virginia Landmarks Register.

The new $5,000,000 home of the Law School on the North Grounds opened in the fall of 1974, following its dedication the preceding spring. It made possible expansion of the school from an enrollment of 950 to 1,050. This figure was to be increased to 1,200 by the second phase of the construction program, to begin almost immediately, at a cost of $2,500,000 raised from private sources. It was expected that the Law Library would have 500,000 volumes upon completion of the second phase. Arthur J. Morris, '01, founder of the Morris Plan of consumer credit, gave $350,000 "to furnish the library" and then bequeathed $100,000 for a Morris Plan chair of consumer banking. The Law School, the $3,200,000 Graduate School of Business Administration, and the $5,000,000 Judge Advocate General's School were all going up simultaneously in the early seventies on the North Grounds.

The seven-story, $10,700,000 Harvey E. Jordan Medical Education building and the five-story, $2,400,000 Josephine McLeod School of Nursing building were both dedicated Nov. 10, 1972. Five basic science departments plus an animal research area were housed in the Jordan building, along with lecture halls, laboratory space, and student activity facilities. Closed circuit classroom TV and equipment for independent study, along with bedside demonstration of nursing techniques, were features of the nursing building. Both structures were important elements in the university's plans to increase its production of health care personnel.

Also highly significant in the foregoing program was the grant of over one million five hundred thousand dollars in federal funds toward construction of a new Health Sciences Library and Information Center. These funds were to be combined with General Assembly appropriations, plus contributions from alumni, friends, and foundations. More than eighty-six thousand medical texts and journals were to be housed in the library, which would be equipped with reading rooms, seminar and conference rooms, study cubicles, audiovisual facilities, and offices, plus stack capacity for 170,000 volumes. It would replace the libary built in 1929, planned for 6,600 volumes and a seating capacity of seventy-six. The new facility was to serve the current enrollment of over 750 medical and nursing students, as well as interns, residents, faculty, and visiting physicians. It too was expected to play a significant role in training more health personnel for the commonwealth and improving health care through continuing education and affiliated hospital programs.

With the removal of all athletic contests from Lambeth Field, plans were carried forward for the erection there of student apartments. Three of the twelve apartments in Phase One were ready for occupancy in September 1974, and the first 100 students moved in. All twelve apartments were completed a few months later, and 408 students were accommodated. Phase Two was expected to be ready in September 1975, with 840 students housed in the entire project. Restoration and renovation of the colonnade rimming the stadium was to begin shortly, thanks to a $75,000 alumni gift.

Plans were under way in 1974, with C. Waller Barrett as chairman, to seek $8,000,000 from various sources to construct a manuscripts and special collections library. It would house the invaluable materials cared for in Alderman Library—the Barrett, McGregor, and other collections and the millions of manuscripts—and would be placed on the site of the McIntire Theater. The latter facility had fallen into disuse as a place for ceremonies and concerts and was used as a parking lot. The McIntire site would be filled in to the level of surrounding buildings, under the plan.

See You at

THE BIG TENT

1947 Victory Reunion

107. Carl Zeisberg provided to returning alumni a multilingual exhortation for maximum attendance.

New dining facilities for students were made available in 1974 on McCormick Road, to provide breakfast and dinner for some fifteen hundred who had previously had all their meals at Newcomb Hall. Lunch was available to them at whichever of the two they preferred. At the same time, the Newcomb Hall grill had been remodeled and was open weekends and evenings, serving beer and delicatessen and short-order foods.

Extensive improvements on the Lawn were carried out in the late sixties and early seventies through the generosity of Mrs. Robert M. Jeffress, widow of a 1909 law graduate and prominent Richmond financier. The Lawn crosswalks were restored to their original herringbone pattern and brick splash courses laid along the colonnades, as protection for the white columns against the red mud of Albemarle. Brickwork around the statues of Washington and Jefferson was renovated, and the metal railings on the roofs of the buildings surrounding the Lawn were replaced with new white wooden railings of Jefferson's original Chinese Chippendale design. Mrs. Jeffress also contributed to the refurbishing of the Gwathmey Room at the Colonnade Club, a memorial to her brother, Allen T. Gwathmey, noted professor of chemistry and longtime secretary of the club.

Thomas P. Abernethy retired as professor of history in 1961, after thirty-one years on the faculty, during which time he was department chairman for a decade and director of the graduate history program for twenty-eight years. Eleven of his former students contributed to a Festschrift in his honor. Abernethy had supervised personally more than thirty doctoral dissertations and dozens of master's theses. He had taken his own doctorate at Harvard under the celebrated Frederick Jackson Turner, but following graduation he had written books that took issue sharply with Turner's much-quoted thesis that on the frontier "American character was constantly put to the test and remolded to be tough, resourceful and independent." Abernethy set forth a contrasting thesis in his *From Frontier to Plantation in Tennessee* (1932). He contended that the frontier produced "not democracy but arrant opportunism," and, in the words of his colleague D. Alan Williams, he argued that the frontier "fed the greed of the land-speculator politicians who promoted settlement and controlled government." Furthermore, "the voice of the people was negligible in the early years."

Charles Henderson, former dean of the School of Engineering and Applied Science, retired as professor in 1961. The Charles Henderson Professorship of Engineering was established in his honor.

The retirement of Robert K. Gooch in 1964 as professor of political science was the occasion for almost unprecedented tributes. In the words of the *Alumni News*: "Bob Gooch is one of the few persons at the university who, by general agreement, is praised by students, faculty and alumni as a 'master teacher, eminent scholar and beloved gentleman of Virginia.'" The *Cavalier Daily* termed him "the living symbol of the university," and the *University of Virginia Magazine* said he was "the students' professor" and "the Virginia man's Virginia man." For twenty-five years Gooch was the "inspiration, innovator and chairman" of the Honors Program. He had shocked the university community in 1931 with an attack on the institution's undergraduate program, which he compared to a "kindergarten or grammar school," a characterization that was a factor in bringing the Honors Program into being a few years later. Subsequently he provided the spark that led to establishment of the Liberal Arts Seminars. Bob Gooch was not only a star athlete in his student days but a Rhodes Scholar. He went on to get his Ph.D. at Oxford. His specialty was comparative government, and he wrote three books on French parliamentary government, one book on British, and another on American government. Gooch served for many years as chairman of the university's Department of Political Science and, for shorter periods, as chairman of the Woodrow Wilson Department of Foreign Affairs and the Institute of Public Affairs. He was president of the Southern Political Science Association and a member of the executive committee of the American Political Science Association and of the board of editors of the *American Political Science Review*; he was for many years an advisory editor of the *Virginia Quarterly Review*. The Robert Kent Gooch Scholarship Fund in the college was established in his honor by alumni, faculty, and friends, with the stipulation that the winner must have the approximate qualifications of a Rhodes Scholar. The Z Society provided an annual fund for the purchase of books for Alderman Library as a tribute to Professor Gooch. The Robert Kent Gooch chair of government was established following his retirement.

Chemistry Prof. John H. Yoe, an international figure in the scientific world, retired in 1963, after serving on the faculty since 1919. His many awards and distinctions have been mentioned in earlier chapters. The year following his retirement a pamphlet listing all of his publications was issued. There were no fewer than 412 books and articles, beginning in 1910. Two of his books were translated into Russian and several into French and Spanish.

Dr. Carl C. Speidel, professor of anatomy and a member of the medical faculty since 1920, retired in 1964. His nationally acclaimed discovery in 1931 of important secrets of nerve growth, which won for him the research prize of the American Association for the Advancement of Science, has been noted. He also won half a dozen other research prizes.

Dr. James E. Kindred, another veteran of the Medical School, also retired in 1964. On the faculty since 1923, Dr. Kindred was professor of anatomy for most of his career. He was twice winner of the President and Visitors Research Prize and coauthor with Dr. Harvey E. Jordan of a textbook on embryology that went through five editions.

Stanislaw Makielski retired in the same year as professor of architecture after serving since 1923. He received a citation in 1959 from the Association of Collegiate Schools of Architecture as "one of the great teachers of architecture." Professor Makielski served for a decade on the State Board of Architectural Examiners. The *Cavalier Daily* said he was "deeply admired and respected" by both students and faculty. He died in 1969.

Dr. Edwin W. Burton, a member of the medical faculty since 1930 and head of the Department of Ophthalmology for twenty-five years, retired from that post in 1965 but continued to teach. Twenty of his former students gave him a dinner at the Farmington Country Club and presented him with an inscribed silver tray and an album.

Thomas K. Fitz Patrick resigned as dean of the School of Architecture in 1966, after thirteen years in the position, to return to teaching. He was past president of the American

108. *The Clifton Waller Barrett Library.*

Collegiate Schools of Architecture, a member of the National Architectural Accrediting Board, and first chairman of the American Institute of Architect's Committee on Nuclear Facilities. During this deanship the curriculum was reorganized to establish three divisions: Architecture, under Prof. Frederick D. Nichols; architectural history, Prof. William B. O'Neal; and city planning, Prof. Paul S. Dulaney.

Assistant Dean Joseph N. Bosserman was named to succeed Fitz Patrick. A native of Harrisonburg, Va., and graduate of the University of Virginia and Princeton, Dean Bosserman had held Fulbright professorships in England and Germany and had also lectured in Spain and Scotland. He was a fellow of the Royal Society of Arts in England and served on the board of governors of the American Association of Architectural Bibliographers.

Chemistry Prof. Arthur F. Benton, a graduate of Princeton and California Institute of Technology and former chairman of the Chemistry Department at Virginia, retired in 1966. He served on the chemistry faculty for forty years.

Political science Prof. George W. Spicer retired in 1968 after a career in which he was especially active in promoting better county government. He was influential in drafting the Virginia legislature's act of 1932 establishing the county manager and county executive forms and was chosen chairman of the Virginia Commission on County Government in that year; a position he held until 1938. Professor Spicer also wrote several authoritative books in the field. In addition, he was active on behalf of civil rights, and in 1959 was consultant to the first U.S. Civil Rights Commission. Spicer served a term as president of the Southern Political Science Association.

Dr. Oscar Swineford, a member of the medical faculty for thirty-nine years and a specialist in allergy, retired in 1967. He was noted for his efforts to encourage the teaching of allergy in medical schools and was active as an author. The Oscar Swineford Allergy Fund was established in 1961 by former students. It made possible the holding of a yearly postgraduate conference on allergy at the Medical School.

Dr. Charles Bruce Morton II's significant surgical career came to an end with his retirement in 1970. He had brought to the Medical School a surgical technique different from that of the famous Halsted-trained Dr. Stephen Watts, and by his innovations "kept the surgical program from provincialism and inbreeding." Dr. Morton was the author of seventy papers, as well as a history of the Department of Surgery. He performed nearly 13,000 major operations during his career, and his earnings above salary contributed over $600,000 to the department.

Dr. E. C. Drash terminated his career as a thoracic surgeon in 1970, after forty years on the medical staff. He had been absent from 1942 to 1945 as chief surgeon of the university's World War II Eighth Evacuation Unit. During his years at the university Dr. Drash "developed associations with the various sanatoria for tuberculosis in the state," Bruce Morton says in his history of the surgical department, "and enjoyed phenomenal success in treating their patients."

Another leading member of the university faculty who retired in 1970 was the beloved T. Munford Boyd of the Law School. One of the first professors to win the Thomas Jefferson Award (1957), "Munny" Boyd was active in many phases of student life, despite the fact that he was totally blind. One of the university's foremost interpreters of the Honor System, his statements on the subject were memorable. The Algernon Sydney Sullivan Award was given him the year he retired for "excellence of character and service to humanity."

Several veteran members of the faculty retired in 1972:

Frederick T. Morse, professor of mechanical engineering, a member of the faculty since 1933.

William B. O'Neal, professor of architectural history, on the faculty since 1946.

Lorin A. Thompson, professor of business administration and president of George Mason University, member of the faculty since 1940.

Bernard A. Mayo, professor of history since 1940. As a student at the University of Maine in the early 1920s, "Bernie" Mayo was manager of a student orchestra that employed the subsequently famous Rudy Vallee to play the saxophone at $5 a night. "Rudy was a nice boy, but he never could sing well," said Mayo. While at Virginia, Professor Mayo wrote *Henry Clay: Spokesman of the New West* and *Myths and Men* and edited a collection of Jefferson's writings entitled *Jefferson Himself.*

Upon his retirement former students produced a volume of essays in his honor.

Professors who retired in 1974 included the following:

Dr. Andrew D. Hart, professor of internal medicine and former director of student health, after serving on the faculty since 1928.

Dr. John M. Nokes, professor of obstetrics and gynecology, on the faculty since 1931. He was a former president of the Virginia League for Planned Parenthood.

Francis L. Berkeley, Jr., curator of manuscripts and university archivist; in his latter years executive assistant to the president, a member of the faculty since 1938.

Richard H. Henneman, professor of psychology, on the faculty since 1947.

Edward C. Stevenson, professor of electrical engineering, a member of the faculty since 1950.

Edward J. McShane, Alumni Professor of Mathematics, member of the faculty for thirty-nine years. A three-day symposium in his honor was held by the Department of Mathematics, followed by a reception.

The departure of Prof. Neil Alford in 1974 to accept the deanship of the University of Georgia Law School was the cause of widespread regret. He was described by Tom Lankford in *The Declaration* as "one of the most outstanding teacher-scholars, who departs after 26 distinguished years"; he has "utterly charmed students . . . with his Southern drawl, his wide, friendly grin." Alford "collaborated with his mentor, John Ritchie, and with Richard Effland to produce what is the most widely used textbook on trusts and estates in the country." He also performed superbly for years as the university's attorney.

Dr. McLemore Birdsong, admired professor of pediatrics for thirty-four years, was preparing in 1974 to retire the following year. At various times president of the Medical Society of Virginia and the Virginia Pediatrics Association and chairman of the pediatrics section of the Southern Medical Association, "Mac" Birdsong was regarded as an exceptionally able teacher. He was the author of over thirty published works in the field of pediatrics.

Secretary to a succession of deans since 1926 and graduate programs assistant in the Graduate School of Arts and Sciences since 1965, Miss Elizabeth Purvis was honored by both the Seven Society and the Ravens for her conspicuous contribution. She began as secretary to Dean John C. Metcalf, then served Deans John L. Newcomb and Walter S. Rodman, and in 1938 became secretary to the Graduate School.

Prof. Oreste Rinetti, whose classes in Italian were said to be next to the largest in any American university, died suddenly in 1960. A native of Italy, he had taught Italian language and literature in his native land before coming to the United States in 1925 to join the Yale University faculty. He became a professor at the University of Virginia three years later. Professor Rinetti was made a *cavaliere* of the Crown of Italy by virtue of his great success in teaching Italian at the university.

The death of English Prof. Archibald Bolling Shepperson in 1962 brought tributes from the *Cavalier Daily* and others. The paper described him as "uniquely a gentleman" and added: "As a teacher, a writer, as editor of the *Virginia Quarterly Review*, as a member of the Raven Society, he rendered notable service to the university. But it is for his laudable personal virtues that we shall most remember him."

Prof. Allan T. Gwathmey died in 1963, aged fifty-nine, at the height of his career. In addition to accolades received by him in earlier years, he was voted the meritorious service award of the Virginia Academy of Science and the university's Thomas Jefferson Award. "Pete" Gwathmey's dedication to the cause of scientific progress and to the advancement of the university's scholarly standing was also recognized by his winning both the Raven and Algernon Sydney Sullivan Awards. The Allan Talbott Gwathmey Memorial Fund was established by colleagues and friends after his death to provide an annual scholarship for an outstanding graduate student doing research in the physical sciences.

Dr. Henry B. Mulholland died in 1967, five years after his retirement from the medical faculty, on which he had served for over forty years. He entered the private practice of medicine in Charlottesville following his retirement. The Thomas Jefferson Award went to him the year he retired, and in 1966 he was voted a mastership in the American College of Physicians, the organization's highest honor. The Seven Society, of which he was a member, contributed $777.77 toward the

Henry B. Mulholland Chair of Internal Medicine, established as a tribute to him.

A unique member of the medical community, Dr. Halstead S. Hedges, '92, died in 1968 a few days before his 102d birthday. Dr. Hedges, a pioneer ophthalmologist on the medical faculty, was honored at a reception on his 100th birthday, at which time a fund named for him was announced. His versatility was acclaimed by English Prof. Joseph L. Vaughan, who said: "Dr. Hedges is a man whose medical ability is matched only by his ability to outfish and outwalk all his residents, and who can calmly lean back and quote the first half of Book One of the *Odyssey* in the original just for the pleasure of hearing Homer's thundering lines."

Wilbur A. Nelson, who had served as chairman of the School of Geology and State Geologist from 1925 until his retirement in 1959, died ten years later. He had been a consultant for various governmental and business organizations. Nelson served as president of the Charlottesville Chamber of Commerce and helped to promote the establishment of the Shenandoah National Park and the Blue Ridge Parkway. In World War II he was director of priorities in the Office of Production Management and later organized and became director of the mining division of the War Production Board.

The passing in 1970 of F. D. G. Ribble, retired dean of the Law School, brought many tributes of admiration and affection. He was credited with major responsibility for a number of the school's advances, notably the establishment of the Law School Foundation in 1951–52. Member of the law faculty for forty-two years and dean for nearly a quarter of a century, Professor Ribble was not only a capable administrator but an editor and author of note. He edited the second edition of *Minor on Real Property* (1928) and wrote *State and National Power over Commerce* (1937), both of which were often cited in the courts. He received both the Thomas Jefferson and IMP Awards.

James S. Miller, Jr., professor of electrical engineering, a member of the faculty from 1920 until his retirement in 1969, died in 1972.

Dr. W. Gayle Crutchfield, professor of neurosurgery, a member of the faculty from 1941 to 1971, died the following year.

109. New home of the Law School.

The Medical Center sustained a loss in 1973 with the death at age fifty-five of John M. Stacey, its director for nearly a decade and previously director of the university hospital since 1953.

A nationally distinguished art historian and painter was lost by the untimely death in 1974 of Prof. William C. Seitz. Representatives of the Museum of Modern Art in New York and the National Gallery of Art in Washington attended his funeral. His monograph on Claude Monet (1960) was regarded as a masterpiece, and he soon came to be considered a major recorder and interpreter of the work of modern artists. Seitz was "literally irreplaceable," Prof. Frederick Hartt, Art Department chairman, declared.

Misses Betty Booker and Betty Cocke, two ladies who had kept much-patronized rooming houses on University Avenue for generations, passed away during these years.

Miss Booker, whose establishment was at the corner of Madison Lane, died in 1967 at the age of ninety-one. She had a notable career as a a lyric soprano in this country and Europe and made her debut at Covent Garden in 1911 with the Royal Opera at the coronation command performance of King George V and Queen Mary. Betty Booker sang in Cabell Hall on many occasions, usually for the benefit of St. Paul's Church. She gave up her operatic career to look after her mother and opened her rooming house at the university. Mrs. Booker had kept a close eye on her daughter during the latter's career on the stage. When Betty was in her late teens in her native Richmond, she was in a rehearsal for an opera with an Italian tenor from New York. As Miss Booker described the incident many years afterward, her mother was on the front row when the tenor complimented Betty and said, "And now, Miss Booker, this evening I give you one big kiss." "Oh no you don't!" exclaimed Betty's mother, as she rose indignantly in her seat.

Miss Betty Cocke, a great-granddaughter of John Hartwell Cocke of Bremo, one of Jefferson's coadjutors in founding the university, died in 1973 at age 100. Her sister, Louise, had died in 1969 at 101. They operated their rooming house next to St. Paul's Church for nearly seventy-five years, with Betty as the dominant figure. The *Alumni News* said after her death: "Aside from her captivating warmth, wit and sense of humor and matchless integrity, she had an uncommon ability to communicate with youth."

The University of Virginia was making rapid forward strides in the 1960s and 1970s as a center of academic excellence. State sales tax revenues and bond issues, growing out of reforms sponsored by Gov. Mills Godwin, helped markedly to strengthen departments and finance additional buildings and facilities. By 1970 the impact of both this increase in revenues and the remarkable achievement of the Center for Advanced Studies in bringing nationally known faculty to Virginia were evident in the university's improved educational ranking.

In 1970 the American Council on Education released the results of a survey of graduate programs in thirty-six disciplines in 130 institutions. Eighteen departments at the University of Virginia were rated above average or better, with four of these in the highest category. The four were English, ranked ninth in the country; history and math, twenty-third; and developmental biology, twenty-seventh. Six departments were rated "good," or in the second category of excellence, namely, astronomy, economics, physics, physiology, political science (government and foreign affairs), and zoology. Eight other departments were in the third category, or "more than adequate," namely, chemistry, chemical engineering, French, microbiology, molecular biology, pharmacology, philosophy, and psychology. The foregoing rankings were based on replies from some six thousand scholars and department chairmen throughout the country, and it was a far better showing than the university had made four years before in a similar survey. Yet in 1970 the University of North Carolina was given twelve departments in the highest category compared with only four for the University of Virginia. While the state of North Carolina was appropriating substantially more to its state university than the commonwealth of Virginia, it had a much smaller endowment, and persons informed as to the two institutions did not believe that there was so wide a disparity, if indeed there was any at all. Ian McNett, writing in *Change* magazine, said that the university at Charlottesville had "acquired a reputation as a first-rate academic institution according to all the traditional barometers of academic excellence." Loren Pope, College Placement Bureau Director in Washington, D.C., writing in *Newsday* praised the university's educational program and declared that among those institutions striving for individuality and diversity, "no private college does a better job than Virginia or Michigan."

Despite the foregoing favorable judgments, it appeared that the facts concerning the remarkable progress at Charlottesville had been slow in getting across to other sections of the United States. Many were judging the institution and its departments on the basis of impressions formed years before. About two decades are apparently required for word concerning the sort of progress made at the university to percolate to all areas of the nation's academic community.

Although there had been notable advances, the Carnegie Commission on Higher Education listed the state of Virginia in 1971 as one of twenty-one states that, in its view, were not providing sufficient support for institutions of higher learning. Fortunately the university's endowment of more than $100,000,000, as of 1974, helped to make up the deficiency.

The university had other assets, both tangible and intangible. Dean Joseph N. Bosserman said in 1968 that Charlottesville and "the intangible university atmosphere" were strong points in attracting faculty. He added that visiting professors "almost invariably go out of their way to comment on how polite and how bright the students are." He also cited the Honor System as a conspicuous asset, saying "a teacher knows that he doesn't have to go around spying on the students."

Four years later Vice-President and Provost David A. Shannon said he found that once prospective professors came to the university, "our chances of recruiting them are improved considerably. . . . They see it's an alive, dynamic institution" rather than "a sleepy coat and tie school."

The average compensation for all faculty at Virginia in 1973 was $21,369, higher than Princeton's $20,712, according to figures released by the American Association of University Professors. Harvard's average was $25,448, Stanford's $23,-784, Duke's $22,313, and Yale's $22,040. In average compensation for faculty, Virginia stood second only to Michigan among the twenty-three public universities belonging to the prestigious Association of American Universities. The *Alumni News* reported in 1968 that "in terms of fringe benefits we have as good a program as you can find at a state university."

More than twenty-five hundred students were receiving financial aid in 1970–71, totaling more than two million dollars. The average scholarship award was $884, the average amount paid on work-study programs $652, and the average loan $725.

Standards for admission were being raised steadily, and the number of applications also was rising rapidly. The institution's growing reputation for scholastic excellence was an important factor in the mounting number of applicants. Also, "the university is now one of the less expensive state-supported institutions in the commonwealth," Admissions Dean Ernest H. Ern declared in 1971. The preceding fall, entering college students averaged 590 on the verbal SAT test and 616 on math, more than 130 points above the national average. Applicants were being judged on the following basis: (1) the total academic record in secondary school and the school's evaluation of the candidate; (2) college entrance exams, board test scores; (3) extracurricular interests and activities. For the session of 1972–73 no fewer than 81 percent of the entering students ranked in the top 20 percent of their secondary school classes, a figure that had been rising steadily. Academic attrition amounted to less than 2 percent in the college annually, compared with 30 percent nationally. By 1974, 54 percent of the students in the college were on the dean's list. Furthermore, a much higher proportion of the entering class than ever before was graduating, and the number of graduates was mounting each year. For the session of 1973–74 the university awarded 3,741 degrees, including summer school, or 15.8 percent of all degrees granted by Virginia's state institutions. Included were 237 Ph.D.s, or 57.1 percent of those awarded in the commonwealth.

Forty-seven percent of the entering students came from out of state in 1959, but by 1973 this figure was down to 30 percent. While this was a substantial decline, it accorded with what appeared to be prevailing sentiment in Virginia. And it should be noted that the latter percentage was twice as high as that for the University of North Carolina and the University of Wisconsin, for example, where a 15 percent limit was fixed by state law. Every city and county in the Old Dominion was represented at Charlottesville in the 1973–74 enrollment, as well as every state in the union and forty-eight foreign countries. Black students numbered 463, and there were 4,524 women, about one-third of the total. The Schools of Law and Medicine "continued to be by far the most sought-after divisions of the university," President Shannon declared.

The first of the "chairs dinners" for holders of endowed name professorships and their spouses, was held in October 1973. They were an annual feature thereafter. More than one hundred of these chairs had been established at that time, seventy of which had been added since 1966.

Faculty-student relations were close, according to Frank Hereford, who said in 1974, "Certainly they are closer than they were when I was a student" in the 1940s. He added his "firm belief" that "the quality of student life is far better than it was when I studied here."

After struggling for many years to obtain adequate financing, Alderman Library emerged in 1973 in first place among Association of Southeastern Research Libraries, in both expenditures for books and total expenditures. It ranked among the top twenty-five university libraries in the United States. The next task was to obtain funds from private sources for an additional building to house its invaluable collection of rare books and manuscripts.

By 1974 the university's physical plant had been vastly expanded. The fifteen-year program under President Shannon totaled almost $115,000,000 in state tax funds, federal and foundation grants, private gifts and bequests, and revenue bonds.

Shannon told the Board of Visitors at its February 1973 meeting that he planned to resign as president in August of the following year. He would have been in office for a decade and a half, he said, and "I wish to pass on my duties to another while I am still enjoying them as I do." He added that his fifteen-year term of office was well beyond the average for college presidents, and that he wanted to spend more time with his wife and five daughters. Desirous of returning to his "first love . . . teaching and scholarship," he stated that he planned to continue his classes in the works of Tennyson, some of which he had taught throughout his presidency. He was elected Commonwealth Professor of English upon his retirement.

110. *Inside the Darden Graduate School of Business Administration.*

The senior class of 1973 presented him with two silver Jefferson cups "with thanks for a job well done." The Alumni Association gave him $1,000, to be spent on the Tennyson collection in Alderman Library, and said it was a token of his "demonstrable leadership in the university's rise to enviable distinction among the nation's institutions of higher learning." The Z Society announced an annual scholarship in his honor. Six years before, when the Thomas Jefferson Award went to him, the citation spoke of his "brilliant performance as president."

Since his election to head the university in 1959, Edgar Shannon had been chosen to high positions in the educational world. A partial list would include president of the Association of Virginia Colleges, of the Council of Southern Universities, the Council of Presidents of State Institutions of Higher Education, and president and chairman of the executive committee of the National Association of State Universities and Land Grant Colleges. He also served on the boards of the U.S. Naval and Air Force academies, as well as on countless committees.

It can readily be seen that much of Shannon's time was taken up with his duties in these various posts, not to mention the attention that had to be devoted to dealing with the General Assembly and with foundations and various other groups and agencies. A similar situation prevailed with most university presidents. In fact, one estimate was that these men and women spend as much as half of their time coping with such matters. Shannon expressed the view that this estimate was perhaps a bit too high but not greatly out of line.

Tribute to the remarkable progress made by the university between 1963 and 1973 was paid by Malcolm Scully, an alumnus who had served on the editorial staff of the *Chronicle of Higher Education* and was a contributing editor of the *Saturday Review*. He wrote: "If you have been associated with the world of higher education over the past five years . . . you have become aware that the University of Virginia has grown into a first-rate national university. You hear it at scholarly meetings when young Ph.D.s talk enviously of colleagues who have obtained positions at the university; you see it in the attention afforded the university in national magazines, you sense it in the general respect which the university receives in academic circles across the country. . . . Clearly the university is no longer simply the genteel, introverted place I left a decade ago."

Edgar Shannon had given the leadership that brought the university to this position among the nation's institutions of higher learning. He had achieved this despite the fact that he was not considered primarily an administrator; important members of the Board of Visitors did not feel that administration was his forte. Yet they were unanimous in acclaiming the striking advances made during his presidency and happy to accord to him the lion's share of the credit.

His wife, Eleanor, was regarded as having played an admirable role during his presidency. She received the Algernon Sydney Sullivan Award in 1972. The citation described her as "in the great tradition of the university president's wife . . . firm of belief, quick of mind, warm of heart," and spoke of "her many contributions . . . her many nameless acts of kindness, and of love to the university."

A committee headed by Rector Joseph H. McConnell chose Frank L. Hereford, Jr., as Edgar Shannon's successor in September 1973, one year before Shannon retired. Hereford's selection from a field of 159 nominees followed a seven-month search. He was Robert C. Taylor Professor of Physics at the time, as he had relinquished his position as vice-president and provost in 1971 to return to the classroom. With wide administrative experience in previous years as department head, graduate dean, provost, and vice-president, Frank Hereford was admirably equipped for his new task. Born fifty years before in Lake Charles, La., he was a B.A. and Ph.D. of the university. In his student days he was a member of Omicron Delta Kappa, Tilka, and Alpha Tau Omega social fraternity, as well as Raven and Phi Beta Kappa. Prof. Jesse Beams said Hereford was the ablest student he had ever taught. Personable and outgoing, with a quick and inventive mind, Frank Hereford appeared to be the man for the job. As provost he had had a significant role in attracting topflight faculty, and as chairman of the Committee on the Future of the University he had been involved with planning for the institution's development and the admission of women.

In addition to being an experienced administrator and an internationally known scholar, Hereford was fortunate in having married the former Ann Lane of Petersburg, who had studied at Swarthmore and Sweet Briar and was a B.S. of the university. Ann Hereford had just the right qualities for a university president's wife—lovely and charming, she knew how to entertain parents and alumni graciously, and at the same time was sufficiently knowledgeable to have a role in her husband's important decisions. The Herefords had two sons and two daughters.

Before taking office, Frank Hereford appointed Associate Engineering Dean Avery Catlin to the newly created position of executive vice-president of the university. Catlin was a B.A., M.A., and Ph.D. of Virginia who had been on the faculty since 1948. He was to coordinate all aspects of the university's academic and physical planning and serve as the institution's principal administrative officer for university development. He would function as acting president in the president's absence.

The new president was inaugurated on Oct. 9, 1974, a crisp and sunny autumn day. Several thousand persons were on the Lawn as the procession marched to Cabell Hall, led by Grand Marshal B. F. D. Runk, who had planned the program. Rector McConnell presided and the speakers were Gov. Mills Godwin and Frank Hereford. The latter spoke of the need to establish a "conscious perspective" in the relation between science and the humanities and proposed further study of the "intersections" between the two. He hoped that in this way mankind could attain "new understanding of the human situation, cultural unity through unity of understanding."

The university almost lost its new president in late December when he narrowly escaped drowning in the icy waters of Chesapeake Bay. He was on a duck hunt, and the small boat into which he, his son, and a friend were crowded, together with a dog, was swamped in choppy water and sank. The two boys managed to swim to a buoy, and the dog got to shore. But Frank Hereford's heavy clothing became waterlogged as he tried to swim, and he was barely able to stay afloat. Creek, the Labrador retriever, was alert to the emergency. He ran dripping to the lodge where they had been staying, rushed around barking and whining, jumped on his master's bed and lay there whimpering. The keeper of the lodge became alarmed, leaped into his boat, and headed for the duck blind

111. Frank and Ann Hereford accepting congratulations after his inauguration as president of the university in 1974.

in the darkness. En route he encountered the floundering and foundering Frank Hereford, who was barely managing to keep his head above water and would almost certainly have drowned had it not been for the warning given by his faithful dog.

The University of Virginia stood at the pinnacle of its prestige in modern times as Hereford settled into the presidency as successor to Shannon. Both men were hailed enthusiastically in the Virginia press. It was pointed out that the university's College of Arts and Sciences and its professional schools were widely admired, the faculty was of distinguished eminence, and the student body of unprecedented quality. Whereas in earlier times about a dozen Virginia counties were customarily unrepresented among the students at the university, such was no longer the case, for all the counties were now sending matriculates. And both blacks and whites, males and females, were enrolled in large numbers, testifying to the fact that the people of the commonwealth were the beneficiaries of the instruction being offered at Charlottesville. The public schools sent a much larger proportion of the student body than in former years. All this, it seems safe to say, would have gratified the university's founder, whose oft-expressed desire was to provide the widest possible system of education for those Virginians capable of profiting from it.

Truly, the center of learning that he founded had traveled far since that distant day in 1825 when some forty young men from southern plantations entered its portals. The Lawn and Ranges, the arcades and colonnades, were almost unchanged since the first contingent of students arrived and gazed upon the half-finished Rotunda. But the university's inner spirit and mission had been transformed. What some had called in modern times, with considerable exaggeration, "the country club of the South," had vanished. In its place had arisen a nationally ranked university, wide-ranging in its scholarship and untrammeled in its search for truth. If Mr. Jefferson could look down upon it today from his mountaintop, he would be proud.

Appendixes
Bibliography
Index

APPENDIX A

The Thomas Jefferson Award

Awarded to faculty members who contribute "by personal influence, teaching, and scholarship toward inspiring those high ideals for the advancement of which Mr. Jefferson founded the university."

1955	Jesse W. Beams	1965	Edgar F. Shannon, Jr.
1956	Harry Clemons	1966	Frank L. Hereford, Jr.
1957	T. Munford Boyd	1967	Hardy C. Dillard
1958	Colgate W. Darden, Jr.	1968	Gordon T. Whyburn
1959	Ivey F. Lewis	1969	Oron J. Hale
1960	Robert Kent Gooch	1970	Thomas H. Hunter
1961	Frederick D. G. Ribble	1971	Fredson T. Bowers
1962	Henry B. Mulholland	1972	Lawrence R. Quarles
1963	Allan T. Gwathmey	1973	B. F. D. Runk
1964	Dumas Malone	1974	Vincent Shea

APPENDIX B

Alumni Association Distinguished Professor Award

"To be conferred annually upon that member of the faculty who has, over a period of not less than ten years, excelled as a classroom teacher, shown unusual concern for students, and made significant contributions to the life of the university. . . . This award is primarily for the master teacher."

1966	Thaddeus Braxton Woody	1971	Joseph Lee Vaughan
1967	Raymond Curtis Bice, Jr.	1972	Dr. Byrd S. Leavell and John C. Coleman
1968	Charles Julian Bishko	1973	Mrs. Josephine Ludewig
1969	Charles Killian Woltz	1974	R. K. Ramanzani and Frederick D. Nichols
1970	Frank Whitney Finger		

APPENDIX C

Alumni Association Distinguished Student Award

"Made annually to that member of the student body who has won recognition in the academic community for leadership and for his concern in preserving the traditions of the university . . . [and] has won the admiration of the university for significant contributions in several areas of university life and has excelled in all of them."

1966	Russell McFarlane Lafferty	1970	Whittington W. Clement
1967	Howard Edgar Trent III	1971	David Lyttleton Morris
		1972	Thomas Richard Bagby
1968	Arthur Powell Gray IV	1973	James M. Rinaca
1969	Thomas Griffin Johnson, Jr.	1974	Larry J. Sabato

APPENDIX D

The IMP Award

To "a faculty member who has been outstanding in promoting student-faculty relations and perpetuating the traditions of the University of Virginia."

1953	B. F. D. Runk	1964	Irby B. Cauthen, Jr.
1954	T. Braxton Woody	1965	Edward R. Slaughter
1955	F. D. G. Ribble	1966	Thomas Graham
1956	Richard H. Henneman		Hereford
1957	Frank W. Finger	1967	Eugene F. Corrigan.
1958	Henry L. Kinnier	1968	Dr. James L. Camp III
1959	Louis Onesty	1969	Robert T. Canevari
1960	John C. Coleman	1970	Henry Conrad Warlick
1961	Raymond C. Bice, Jr.	1971	Norman A. Graebner
1962	No award	1972	William B. O'Neal
1963	James E. Kinard	1973	Ernest C. Mead, Jr.
		1974	William H. Harbaugh

APPENDIX E

Arthur P. Gray IV Memorial Scholarship

In memory of "Pete" Gray, a popular and greatly admired student who lost his life in Vietnam. Awarded to a student who excels in personal integrity, achievement, leadership, and humility, with emphasis on academics, extracurricular activities, and interest in athletic programs.

1971	Ross Augustus Howell Jr.	1973	Margaret Ann Brown
1972	Byrd S. Leavell Jr.	1974	Kenneth Bruce Botsford

APPENDIX F

The Z Society Award

Given annually to bear public witness to a member of the faculty or administration who has dedicated himself to his or her students, demonstrating a real concern for their academic and personal well-being.

1972	Charles H. Whitebread
1973	Kenneth G. Elzinga
1974	Dante L. Germino

APPENDIX G

The *Virginia Spectator* Award for Scholarship and Athletics

1938 L. Lang Dayton
1939 William B. Wright Jr.
1940 Robert Sheffey Preston, Jr.
1941 Phillip Edward Rothar
1942 William Reed Preston
Kenneth Charles Rathbun
1943 Richard Watkins Wiltshire
1947 Ward Hugh Speer
1948 Charles Warren (Chuck) Noe

1949 Ronald Joseph Richard
1950 William Herbert Morse
1951 Eugene Willard Schroeder
1952 William Walter Long, Jr.
1953 Stuart Horsley Harris, Jr.
1954 Evans Booker Brasfield
1955 Gessner Harrison Echols, Jr.
1956 Gordon Robins Trapnell
1957 James Mahlon Moyer

APPENDIX H

University Professors

Attached to the university as a whole, and not to any single school or department.

University Professor of Mathematics	William L. Duren, Jr.,
University Professor of Philosophy	William S. Weedon
University Professor of Applied Science	Doris Kuhlmann-Wilsdorf
University Professor of Architecture and Engineering	Lev Zetlin

APPENDIX I

Holders of Endowed Chairs

William W. Abbot	JAMES MADISON PROFESSOR OF HISTORY
Henry J. Abraham	HENRY L. AND GRACE DOHERTY CHARITABLE FOUNDATION PROFESSOR OF GOVERNMENT AND FOREIGN AFFAIRS
Dr. E. Meredith Alrich	CLAUDE A. JESSUP PROFESSOR OF SURGERY
Franklyn N. Arnhoff	JOHN EDWARD FOWLER PROFESSOR OF CLINICAL PSYCHOLOGY AND PSYCHIATRY
Thomas F. Bergin	WILLIAM MINOR LILE PROFESSOR OF LAW
Dr. Robert M. Berne	CHARLES SLAUGHTER PROFESSOR OF PHYSIOLOGY
Charles J. Bishko	COMMONWEALTH PROFESSOR OF HISTORY
Dietrich Bodenstein	LEWIS AND CLARK PROFESSOR OF BIOLOGY
Fredson T. Bowers	LINDEN KENT PROFESSOR OF ENGLISH LITERATURE
Theodore Caplow	COMMONWEALTH PROFESSOR OF SOCIOLOGY
Ralph W. Cherry	CURRY MEMORIAL PROFESSOR OF EDUCATION
Inis L. Claude, Jr.	EDWARD R. STETTINIUS, JR., PROFESSOR OF GOVERNMENT AND FOREIGN AFFAIRS
Edwin S. Cohen	JOSEPH M. HARTFIELD PROFESSOR OF LAW
Ralph Cohen	WILLIAM R. KENAN, JR., PROFESSOR OF ENGLISH

Almand R. Coleman	CHARLES C. ABBOTT PROFESSOR OF BUSINESS ADMINISTRATION
Weldon Cooper	ROBERT KENT GOOCH PROFESSOR OF GOVERNMENT
Dr. Kenneth R. Crispell	ALUMNI PROFESSOR OF INTERNAL MEDICINE
Lester G. Crocker	WILLIAM R. KENAN, JR., PROFESSOR OF FRENCH
Frederick R. Cyphert	CURRY MEMORIAL PROFESSOR OF EDUCATION
James E. Deese	COMMONWEALTH PROFESSOR OF PSYCHOLOGY
Dr. Milton T. Edgerton	ALUMNI PROFESSOR OF PLASTIC SURGERY
Irvin Ehrenpreis	COMMONWEALTH PROFESSOR OF ENGLISH
Edwin E. Floyd	ROBERT C. TAYLOR PROFESSOR OF MATHEMATICS
Mark G. Foster	WILLS JOHNSON PROFESSOR OF ELECTRICAL ENGINEERING
Laurence W. Fredrick	JOHN DOWNMAN HAMILTON PROFESSOR OF ASTRONOMY
John E. Gibson	COMMONWEALTH PROFESSOR OF ELECTRICAL ENGINEERING
Norman A. Graebner	EDWARD R. STETTINIUS, JR., PROFESSOR OF HISTORY
Robert J. Harris	JAMES HART PROFESSOR OF GOVERNMENT
Frederick Hartt	PAUL GOODLOE MCINTIRE PROFESSOR OF HISTORY OF ART
Julian N. Hartt	WILLIAM R. KENAN, JR., PROFESSOR OF RELIGIOUS STUDIES
Dr. David R. Hawkins	ALUMNI PROFESSOR OF PSYCHIATRY

Frank L. Hereford, Jr.	ROBERT C. TAYLOR PROFESSOR OF PHYSICS
E. Donald Hirsch	WILLIAM R. KENAN, JR., PROFESSOR OF ENGLISH
Dr. Edward W. Hook	HENRY B. MULHOLLAND PROFESSOR OF INTERNAL MEDICINE
Dr. Thomas H. Hunter	OWEN R. CHEATHAM PROFESSOR OF SCIENCES
Dr. John A. Jane	ALUMNI PROFESSOR OF NEUROSURGERY
Dr. Thomas R. Johns, II	ALUMNI PROFESSOR OF NEUROLOGY
Dr. Theodore E. Keats	ALUMNI PROFESSOR OF RADIOLOGY
Enno E. Kraehe	COMMONWEALTH PROFESSOR OF HISTORY
S. Morris Kupchan	JOHN M. MALLET PROFESSOR OF CHEMISTRY
Cecil Y. Lang	COMMONWEALTH PROFESSOR OF ENGLISH
Robert W. Langbaum	JAMES BRANCH CABELL PROFESSOR OF ENGLISH AND AMERICAN LITERATURE
Dr. Jan Langman	HARVEY E. JORDAN PROFESSOR OF ANATOMY
Dr. Joseph Larner	ALUMNI PROFESSOR OF PHARMACOLOGY
Gordon E. Latta	WILLIAM STANSFIELD CALCOTT PROFESSOR OF APPLIED MATHEMATICS AND COMPUTER SCIENCE
Shao Chuan Leng	HENRY L. AND GRACE DOHERTY CHARITABLE FOUNDATION PROFESSOR OF GOVERNMENT AND FOREIGN AFFAIRS
Jacob C. Levenson	EDGAR ALLAN POE PROFESSOR OF ENGLISH
David Levin	COMMONWEALTH PROFESSOR OF ENGLISH

John C. McCoid	ARMISTEAD M. DOBIE PROFESSOR OF LAW
Carl McFarland	HENRY L. AND GRACE DOHERTY CHARITABLE FOUNDATION PROFESSOR OF LAW
Roland N. McKean	COMMONWEALTH PROFESSOR OF ECONOMICS
Edward J. McShane	ALUMNI PROFESSOR OF MATHEMATICS
Daniel J. Meador	JAMES MONROE PROFESSOR OF LAW
John W. Mitchell	WILLIAM BARTON ROGERS PROFESSOR OF PHYSICS
Frederick C. Mosher	HENRY L. AND GRACE DOHERTY CHARITABLE FOUNDATION PROFESSOR OF GOVERNMENT AND FOREIGN AFFAIRS
Dr. William H. Muller, Jr.	STEPHEN H. WATTS PROFESSOR OF SURGERY
Frederick D. Nichols	CARY D. LANGHORNE PROFESSOR OF ARCHITECTURE
G. Warren Nutter	PAUL GOODLOE MCINTIRE PROFESSOR OF ECONOMICS
Monrad G. Paulsen	JOHN B. MINOR PROFESSOR OF LAW
Merrill D. Peterson	THOMAS JEFFERSON MEMORIAL FOUNDATION PROFESSOR OF HISTORY
Lawrence R. Quarles	LAWRENCE R. QUARLES PROFESSOR EMERITUS OF ENGINEERING AND APPLIED SCIENCE
Louis T. Rader	ALICE M. AND GUY A. WILSON PROFESSOR OF ELECTRICAL ENGINEERING
Rouhollah K. Ramzani	EDWARD R. STETTINIUS, JR., PROFESSOR OF GOVERNMENT AND FOREIGN AFFAIRS

B. F. D. Runk	SAMUEL MILLER PROFESSOR OF EXPERIMENTAL AGRICULTURE AND FORESTRY
Frank G. Ryder	WILLIAM R. KENAN, JR., PROFESSOR OF GERMAN
William C. Seitz	WILLIAM R. KENAN, JR., PROFESSOR OF THE HISTORY OF ART
Richard T. Selden	CARTER GLASS PROFESSOR OF ECONOMICS
C. Stewart Sheppard	TIPTON R. SNAVELY PROFESSOR OF BUSINESS ADMINISTRATION
Dr. David E. Smith	ALUMNI PROFESSOR OF PATHOLOGY
Walter H. Sokel	COMMONWEALTH PROFESSOR OF GERMAN
Richard E. Speidel	HENRY L. AND GRACE DOHERTY CHARITABLE FOUNDATION PROFESSOR OF LAW
Emerson G. Spies	JOSEPH M. HARTFIELD PROFESSOR OF LAW
Dr. Warren G. Stamp	ALUMNI PROFESSOR OF ORTHOPEDICS
Dr. Ian P. Stevenson	CARLSON PROFESSOR OF PSYCHIATRY
Peter H. Taylor	COMMONWEALTH PROFESSOR OF ENGLISH
Dr. W. Norman Thornton, Jr.	ROBERT C. TAYLOR PROFESSOR OF OBSTETRICS AND GYNECOLOGY
Vincent W. Uhl	UNION CAMP PROFESSOR OF CHEMICAL ENGINEERING
Joseph L. Vaughan	JOSEPH L. VAUGHAN PROFESSOR OF HUMANITIES
Walter J. Wadlington III	JAMES MADISON PROFESSOR OF LAW

Heinz G. F. Wilsdorf   WILLS JOHNSON PROFESSOR
                           OF MATERIALS SCIENCE

Charles K. Woltz   HENRY L. AND GRACE
                           DOHERTY CHARITABLE
                           FOUNDATION PROFESSOR OF
                           LAW

Leland B. Yeager   PAUL GOODLOE MCINTIRE
                           PROFESSOR OF ECONOMICS

APPENDIX J

Rhodes Scholars

1904	William A. Fleet	1929	Armistead L. Boothe
1905	Beverley D. Tucker, Jr.	1933	John Page Williams
1911	Francis F. Beirne	1933	Fenton Gentry
1914	J. V. Ray	1934	Herbert C. Pollock
1914	Robert K. Gooch	1935	William S. Mundy, Jr.
1916	George Wayne Anderson, Jr.	1936	Murat Willis Williams
		1936	Charles G. Bell
1917	Stringfellow Barr	1939	Luke Harvey Poe, Jr.
1919	Robert P. Hamilton, Jr.	1947	James B. Whitlatch
1919	Arthur Kyle Davis, Jr.	1951	John H. Funari
1920	Arthur Lee Kinsolving	1952	Staige D. Blackford, Jr.
1923	Eldridge H. Campbell	1957	George B. Thomas
1923	Benjamin M. Baker, Jr.	1962	John Joseph Kirby, Jr.
1924	Carter M. Braxton	1966	Donald H. Regan
1925	Coleman C. Walker	1969	Pieter M. Schenkkan
1926	Paul K. Hennessey	1969	Charles C. Calhoun
1926	Walter L. Brown	1970	William A. Wright
1928	C. L. Gleaves	1973	John M. Bowers

APPENDIX K

Rectors of the University of Virginia

Thomas Jefferson	1819–1826	W. C. N. Randolph	1890–1897
James Madison	1826–1834	Armistead C. Gordon	1897–1898
Joseph C. Cabell	1834–1836	Charles P. Jones	1898–1906
Chapman Johnson	1836–1845	Armistead C. Gordon	1906–1918
Joseph C. Cabell	1845–1856	R. Tate Irvine	1918–1920
Andrew Stevenson	1856–1857	John Stewart Bryan	1920–1922
Thomas J. Randolph	1857–1864	C. Harding Walker	1922–1930
T. L. Preston	1864–1865	Frederic W. Scott	1930–1939
Alexander Rives	1865–1866	Robert Gray Williams	1939–1946
B. Johnson Barbour	1866–1872	Edward R. Stettinius, Jr.	1946–1949
R. G. H. Kean	1872–1876	Barron Foster Black	1949–1956
Alexander H. H. Stuart	1876–1882	Frank Talbott, Jr.,	1956–1960
Wyatt M. Elliott	1882–1884	Albert Vickers Bryan	1960–1964
W. Roane Ruffin	1884–1886	Charles Rogers Fenwick	1964–1966
Alexander H. H. Stuart	1886–1887	Frank W. Rogers	1966–1970
John L. Marye	1887–1890	Joseph H. McConnell	1970–

APPENDIX L

Parents and Children on the Board of Visitors

Bryan, Joseph (father) 1898–1904
Bryan, John Stewart (son) 1918–1922

Duke, R. T. W. (father) 1853–1865
Duke, William Richard (son) 1920–1924

Gordon, Douglas H. (father) 1861–1864
Gordon, Basil B. (son) 1892–1896

Jefferson, Thomas (grandfather) 1824–1826
Randolph, Thomas Jefferson (father) 1829–1864
Randolph, Wilson Cary Nicholas (son) 1876–1898

Rogers, Frank Waters (father) 1962–1970
Holton, Virginia Harrison Rogers (daughter) 1974–

Shackelford, George Scott (father)1908–1912
Shackelford, Virginius Randolph (son) 1930–1932

Stuart, William Alexander (father) 1886–1890
Stuart, Henry Carter (son) 1902–1906

Wilkinson, James Harvie, Jr. (father) 1966–1970
Wilkinson, James Harvie, III (son) 1970–1973

Woods, John Rodes (father) 1865–1872
Woods, Micajah (son) 1872–1876

Bibliography

Abernethy, Thomas P. *Historical Sketch of the University of Virginia.* Richmond: Dietz Press, 1948.

The admission of Women to the College: Report of the President's Special Committee [The Woody Report], November 1968. University of Virginia Library.

Alderman, Edwin A. "Woodrow Wilson—Memorial Address." Dec. 15, 1924. 68th Cong., 2d sess. House Doc. no. 500.

Alvey, Edward, Jr. *History of Mary Washington College, 1908–1972.* Charlottesville: University Press of Virginia, 1974.

American Council on Education. *Report of Committee on Graduate Instruction.* Washington, D.C., April 1934.

Balz, Albert G. A. "Is Virginia Slipping Scholastically?" *University of Virginia Magazine,* October 1933.

Barr, Stringfellow. "Comments on a Social System." *Handbook of the University of Virginia, 1932–1933,* and several subsequent issues.

Barrett, Clifton Waller. "The Struggle to Create a University." *Virginia Quarterly Review,* Autumn 1973.

Barringer, Anna. "Pleasant It Is to Remember These Things." *Magazine of Albemarle County History,* vols. 24 and 27, 1965–66 and 1968–69.

Barringer, Paul B. *The Natural Bent.* Chapel Hill: University of North Carolina Press, 1949.

Bice, Raymond C. "Change at the University." *University of Virginia Magazine,* April 1961.

Boskey, Richard. "A Radical Tradition: Student Life at the University of Virginia, 1934–1935." Ms., University of Virginia Library.

Bowman, Shearer Davis. "The University of Virginia Honor System since September, 1955: A Critical Study." Senior thesis, Department of History, University of Virginia, 1971.

———. "Honor and Consensus in the 1960s: The University of Virginia Honor System." Graduate seminar paper, Department of History, University of California, Berkeley, 1975.

Bruce, Philip Alexander. *History of the University of Virginia, 1819–1919.* 5 vols. New York: Macmillan, 1922.

Bysshe, Algernon. "In Reply [to Balz, above]." *University of Virginia Magazine,* January 1934.

Carter, John Archer, Jr. "The Age of Anxiety." *University of Virginia Magazine,* October-November 1961.

Cartter, Allan M. *An Assessment of Quality in Graduate Education.* American Council on Education. Washington, D.C., 1966.

Catalogues, University of Virginia.

Cavalier, 1929–31 and 1936–37.

Cavalier Daily, 1948–75, inclusive.

———, Mar. 13, 1972, special Honor System issue.

Cantennial of the University of Virginia, 1919–1921—Proceedings of the Centennial Celebration, May 31 to June 3, 1921. New York: G. P. Putnam's Sons, 1922.

Clemons, Harry. *Notes on the Professors for Whom the University Halls and Residence Houses Are Named.* Charlottesville: University of Virginia Press, 1961.

———. *The University of Virginia Library, 1825–1950.* University of Virginia Press, 1954.

College Topics, 1911–48, inclusive.

Corks and Curls, 1888–1975, inclusive.

Culbreth, David M. R., M.D. *The University of Virginia: Memories of Her Student Life and Professors.* New York: Neale Publishing Co., 1908.

Dabney, Richard Heath. "University of Virginia." *Frank Leslie's Monthly,* August 1897.

Dabney, Virginius. "Richard Heath Dabney: A Memoir." *Magazine of Albemarle County History,* vols. 33 and 34, 1975 and 1976.

Darden, Colgate, W., Jr. *Conversations with Guy Friddell.* Charlottesville: University Press of Virginia, 1978.

Departmental Reports, University of Virginia, 1919–58, inclusive. University of Virginia Library.

de Porry, André C., ed. *For the Commonwealth: Extension and Continuing Education of the University of Virginia, 1912–1973.* Charlottesville: School of Continuing Education, 1974.

Eddins, Joe. *Around the Corner after World War I.* Charlottesville: Pub. by author, 1973.

Fitz-Hugh, G. Slaughter. "Otolaryngology: University of Virginia, 1896–1977." Ms., n.d., University of Virginia Library.

Goode, James M. "A Rowdy Beginning, an Unusual History: The Jefferson Society from 1825 to 1865." *University of Virginia Magazine,* December 1965.

Virginia, 1941–1945," Sam Kellams; "Social Consciousness of the Students at the University of Virginia during the Depression," unsigned; "Service and Sacrifice: Student Life at the University of Virginia, 1941–1945," Doug Good; "The Social Life of Students at the University of Virginia: The 1930s and 1940s," J. E. Sovocool, Jr.; "Social Life at the University of Virginia during the Thirties," Nancy Lewis; "Student Life in the Forties: A Compairson with Today," Jim Jenkins; "Anti-War Activity in the Late Sixties at the University of Virginia," Joe Dischinger.

———————

Transcripts of oral interviews with the following: Atcheson L. Hench, B. F. D. Runk, Thomas Cary Johnson, Dr. William B. Bean, T. Braxton Woody, Arthur F. MacConochie, Colgate W. Darden, Jr., Stringfellow Barr, Randall Thompson, Tipton R. Snavely, Zula Mae Baber Bice, James Constantine, Frederick Lyons Brown, Thomas M. Carruthers, Robert K. Gooch, George W. Spicer, Edgar F. Shannon, Jr., Francis L. Berkeley, Jr. All in the University of Virginia Library.

Hereford, T. Graham, and Gianniny, O. Allan, Jr. *Short History of Engineering and Applied Science at the University of Virginia.* Ms., University of Virginia Library, 1977.

The Honor System, Philosphy and Guidelines. Charlottesville: University of Virginia, 1976.

The Inauguration of Colgate Whitehead Darden, Jr., President of the University of Virginia. Charlottesville: 1947. University of Virginia Library.

The Inauguration of Edgar Finley Shannon, Jr., as President of the University of Virginia. Charlottesville: 1960. University of Virginia Library.

The Inauguration of Frank Loucks Hereford, Jr., as President of the University of Virginia. Charlottesville: 1975. University of Virginia Library.

Jones, Virgil Carrington. *Ranger Mosby.* Chapel Hill: University of North Carolina Press, 1944.

Kay, Bryan. "The History of Desegregation at the University of Virginia: 1950–1969." Senior thesis, Department of History, University of Virginia, 1979.

Leavell, Byrd S. "Distinguished Virginia Professor: Dr. William Cecil Dabney." *Virginia Medical Monthly*, November 1979.

Malone, Dumas. *Edwin A. Alderman: A Biography.* New York: Doubleday, 1940.

Matthews, Sarah S. *The University of Virginia Hospital (Its First Fifty Years).* Charlottesville, University of Virginia, n.d.

Moll, Wilhelm. "University of Virginia 'Firsts' in the History of Medical Education." *Virginia Medical Monthly*, March 1968.

Moore, John. "History of the Jefferson Society." N.p., Privately published, 1961.

Moore, John Hammond. *Albemarle, Jefferson's County, 1727–1976.* Charlottesville: University Press of Virginia, 1976.

Moran, Charles E., Jr., "The University of Virginia Press." *University Topics*, May 1956.

Morton, C. Bruce, II, M.D. *History of the Department of Surgery, School of Medicine, University of Virginia, 1824–1971.* Charlottesville, University of Virginia Medical Center. N.d.

O'Neal, William B. *The Rotunda.* Charlottesville: University of Virginia Press, 1960.

———, ed. *Pictorial History of the University of Virginia.* Charlottesville: University Press of Virginia, 1968.

———. "Account of Charles Smith's Career." Typescript, University of Virginia Library, n.d.

Patton, John S. "Henry Martin, 1826–1915." *University of Virginia Alumni Bulletin*, October 1915.

Index

Index

Abbott, Charles C., 341

Abell, Earl, 115, 116

Abernethy, Thomas P., 82, 463, 578

Abraham, Henry J., 443

Academic achievement, 302, 476, 501

Academic policy, 2, 468; class cuts, 447; class schedule, 19; course evaluation, 337; division plan, 328; examinations, 10, 31, 447; grading system, 252; honors program, 170, 336–37, 428, 468; independent study, 337, 425–26, 447; reading days, 425; seminars, 336, 401, 447, 448; terms, 328

"Academical village," 1

Academies, 31

Ackart, Richard J., 350

Administration, 120, 137, 140, 330–34; of Edwin Anderson Alderman, 44–60, 61–136; assistant to the president, 131–32, 427, 456; building and grounds, 395; bursar, 268; chairman of the faculty, 7, 34, 35, 42; comptroller, 330; of Colgate W. Darden, Jr., 271–421; deanships, 34, 35, 61, 67, 68, 106, 108, 175, 219–20, 252, 331–33, 410, 427, 428, 456, 458, 471, 472; executive vice-president, 596; of Frank L. Hereford, Jr., 595–96, 598; housing director, 332; of John Lloyd Newcomb, 137–229; offices, 456–59; pres-

ident, 42; provost, 333–34, 431, 456, 457; public relations and development, 427, 457; rector, 252, 254, 614; registrar, 105, 249, 252, 332–33; of Edgar F. Shannon, Jr., 422–66, 508–29; student affairs, 284, 286, 287, 332, 446–47, 458; vice-presidents, 457; *see also specific disciplines*

Admissions policy, 45, 78, 170, 172, 252, 330–32, 427, 456, 458, 505, 591

Agriculture, 28

Air Force Reserve Officers' Training Corps, 300

Akerman, Alfred, 360

Albemarle Academy, 2

Alcoholic beverages, 89, 90, 92–94, 96–97, 149–50, 152, 293–94, 296, 471

Alden, Harold L., 267

Alderman, Edwin Anderson, 42, 44–60, 61–136; awards, 63; biographical data, 42; on co-education, 68–69; death, 135–36; evaluation, 42, 44, 128–32, 134–36; illness with tuberculosis, 44, 62, 134–35; on medical college merger plan, 69–70, 72; on research, 79–80, 83

Alderman Library, 383–86, 388; acquisitions, 188–89; administration, 552–53; archives, 384–85; Barrett collection, 383–84, 553;

PHOTO CREDITS

Acme Newspictures: 38

Corks and Curls: 12 (1902), 20 (1920), 27 (1930), 30 (1919), 36 (1913)

Creative Media Group, Inc.: 37

Hardy C. Dillard: 82

Joseph C. Farber: endpapers

Byrd S. Leavell, *The 8th Evac.* (Richmond, Va.: Dietz Press, 1970): 55

Richmond *Times-Dispatch:* 35 (photo by Ralph Thompson), 101 (photo by Ed Roseberry)

Ed Roseberry: 99

University of Virginia Alumni Association: 15, 16, 29, 42, 53, 56, 69, 71 (photo by Ralph Thompson), 77 (photo by Ralph Thompson), 79 (photo by Cameraman, Inc.), 80, 104 (photo by Ralph Thompson), 106 (photo by Ralph Thompson), 107

University of Virginia *Alumni News:* 13, 17

University of Virginia Athletic Department: 103

University of Virginia Department of Graphics: 60, 105

University of Virginia Information Services: 83 (photo by Jon Goldin)

University of Virginia Law Library Archives: 24 (photo by Holsinger)

University of Library, Manuscripts Division: frontispiece, 1 (photo by Ralph Thompson), 2, 3, 4, 5 (portrait courtesty of Mrs. John C. Parker), 6, 7, 8, 9, 10, 11, 14, 18 (photo courtesy of Col. Paul Rockwell), 19 (photo by Underwood & Underwood), 21, 22 (photo by Ralph Thompson), 23, 25, 26, 28, 31, 32 (photo by Kaiden), 33, 34, 39 (Holsinger Collection), 40, 41 (photo by Dick Anderson), 43 (photo by Ralph Thompson), 44, 45, 46, 47, 48 (photo by Ralph Thompson), 49, 50 (photo by Ritchie Studio), 51 (photo by Ralph Thompson), 52, 54, 57, 58, 59, 61, 62 (photo by Ralph Thompson), 63, 64, 65 (photo by Ralph Thompson), 66, 67 (Holsinger Collection), 68, 70, 72, 73, 74, 75, 76, 78 (photo by Ralph Thompson), 81, 84, 85, 86, 87, 88, 89, 90, 91, 92, 93, 94, 95, 96, 97, 98, 100, 102, 108 (photo by Ed Roseberry), 109 (photo by Ed Roseberry), 110, 111